BASIC BUSINESS COMMUNICATION

BASIC BUSINESS COMMUNICATION

SECOND CANADIAN EDITION

▶ **Jan Bamford**
Northern Alberta Institute of Technology

▶ **Raymond V. Lesikar**
North Texas State University

▶ **John D. Petit, Jr.**
Austin Peay State University

▶ **Marie E. Flatley**
San Diego State University

Represented in Canada by:

McGraw-Hill Ryerson Limited

IRWIN

Chicago·Bogotá·Boston·Buenos Aires·Caracas
London·Madrid·Mexico City·Sydney·Toronto

McGraw-Hill
    A Division of the McGraw-Hill Companies

BASIC BUSINESS COMMUNICATION

This book is printed on recycled, acid-free paper containing 10% postconsumer waste.

1 2 3 4 5 6 7 8 9 0 QD/QD 9 0 9 8 7

ISBN 0-256-18212-4

Senior sponsoring editor: *Evelyn Veitch*
Project manager: *Jim Labeots*
Production supervisor: *Dina L. Genovese*
Designer: *Larry J. Cope*
Compositor: *Carlisle Communications, Ltd.*
Typeface: *10/12 Times Roman*
Printer: *Quebecor Printing Book Group/Dubuque*

Library of Congress Catalog Card number: 96-61194

http://www.mhcollege.com

For Blair
From Bob and Jan

Preface

THE RATIONALE

The information explosion is upon us. With it comes the demand for good communicators who can locate, use, and report information that is understandable and acceptable to the audience. The ability to communicate effectively is the common requirement of employers in all branches of business; the lack of that ability in job candidates is the common lament. The message is clear—effective communication is a key to success.

Basic Business Communication, now in its seventh U.S. edition and second Canadian edition, is a proven resource for students of business. It is a market leader not only as a clear textbook for students during their studies, but also as a reference book for graduates on the job.

THE GOAL

The constant feature of our society as we prepare for the 21st century is technological change. The field of business communication relies more and more on technology to put speed, accuracy, and flexibility within reach. *Basic Business Communication* challenges students to expand their awareness of the modern tools available to help them. But the skill and talent of the person behind the machine continues to be the key to success. Thus the primary goal of this text is to give students the skills they need to communicate clearly and concisely.

One theme woven throughout this book is attention to the human element in communication. Concepts such as you-viewpoint, audience analysis, listening skills, and awareness of nonverbal cues are taught and reinforced through practice.

THE CONTENT

- A concise presentation of communication theory.
- An analysis of communication styles appropriate for routine, bad news, and persuasive messages.
- Presentation guidelines for speeches and informal oral communication.

- In-depth coverage of the writing and presentation of reports including a description of special techniques for collaborative writing and team projects.
- A new chapter bringing together five essentials for effective communication: the skillful use of critical thinking, language, listening, nonverbal cues, and adaptation.
- New sections on the impact of technology including the Internet, voice mail, fax, electronic mail, and electronic meeting systems.
- Discussion of the trends in job search procedures.
- A self-administered diagnostic grammar test and an expanded grammar and punctuation review in the companion workbook.

THE METHOD

- The text is written in plain, everyday English—the kind the book instructs the students to use.
- All chapters begin with clearly worded learning objectives.
- Realistic introductory situations set the stage for each topic, providing context for the discussion and examples.
- Clear margin notes highlight topic development.
- Carefully selected examples with handwritten comments show how to apply the text instructions. Some contrasting bad examples clearly marked with the symbol shown in the margin also are included.
- Lists of research topics arranged by major business discipline allow instructors to assign reports in the student's area of specialization.
- A large selection of problems and cases give realistic business scenarios for assignments, while discussion questions and application exercises reinforce specific concepts.
- Practice Runs, integrated into the text, give students the opportunity to develop their expertise with basic skills before progressing to the more challenging end-of-chapter exercises.

THE SUPPORT

An extensive collection of support materials including an Instructor's Manual and a Student Workbook accompany this text. The Instructor's Manual includes:

Sample syllabi and grading systems

Summary teaching notes

Teaching suggestions

Discussion guides for the transparencies

Comments on end-of-chapter discussion questions and cases

Your McGraw-Hill Sales Representative will introduce you to additional resources and help you select the best combination of materials for your needs.

ACKNOWLEDGMENTS

Basic Business Communication has been used successfully for many years. This edition depends upon the work of all the previous contributors and, most especially, to the work of Dr. Raymond V. Lesikar. For the Canadian content, I must mention the many students who have participated in my classes and provided me with insights into the breadth, depth, and complexity of Canadian society. For helpful, timely and perceptive comments, my thanks goes to the reviewers of this manuscript:

Liesje de Burger, Durham College

M. Jeanette Bernardo, Fanshawe College

Ava Cross, Ryerson Polytechnic University

Karen Bishop, Lakehead University

Rudyard Spence, British Columbia Institute of Technology

Lloyd Rieber, St. Mary's University

For the cartoons, my laughter and thanks to Robert Doull. And finally, for support, encouragement, and inspiration in abundance, I thank my husband, Bob.

Jan Bamford

Contents

BASIC BUSINESS COMMUNICATION

INTRODUCTION AND BASIC WRITING SKILLS

Some Basic Introductory Words

CHAPTER OBJECTIVES

Upon completing this chapter, you will understand the role of communication in business. To achieve this goal, you should be able to

1 Explain the importance of communication to you and to business.

2 Describe the main forms of communication in the business organization.

3 Describe the formal and informal communication networks in the business organization.

4 Explain the process of communication among people.

5 Explain three basic truths about communication.

THE ROLE OF COMMUNICATION IN BUSINESS

Your work in business will involve communication—a lot of it—because communication is a major part and an essential part of the work of business.

• Communication is important to business.

The Importance of Communication Skills to You

Because communication is so important in business, all types of businesses want and need people with good communication skills. For evidence, consider these three sources. The Conference Board of Canada conducted a study in 1992 to discover what skills employers want from new employees.[1] The first skill group is communication, including speaking, listening, reading, and writing.[2] Gale Ruby, in her article on the role of written communication in accounting firms, agrees. Good communication wins clients, avoids costly misunderstandings, and saves time.[3] Representatives of Canada Employment Centres in Metropolitan Toronto released a report in January, 1996, called *Towards 2000: Occupational Trends*. Under "Changing Skill Levels", the report states the following:

• Good communicators are in demand in business because few people communicate well.

Surveys of businesses in the Toronto area have shown that the highest-priority sets of skills being sought by employers are the following: computer skills, communication skills and interpersonal skills.[4]

Despite the recognized importance of good communication, many graduates find their communication skills are challenged by the tasks given them at work. A former finance student telephoned her professor after the first day on the job to exclaim, "I had to cut a cheque for $136,000 and write a memo to accompany it. It wasn't as easy as I thought!" Gale Ruby points out, " . . . too many [accountants] realize the importance of good writing only when they sit down to compose a client letter and find they lack the skill to do so."[5] The communication shortcomings of employees and the importance of communication in business explain why you should work to improve your communication skills.

The simple fact is that whatever position you have in business, your performance will be judged largely by your ability to communicate. If you can clearly explain your ideas, summarize the steps in a procedure, or persuasively present your company's position, you are likely to find the doors to advancement easier to open. And the higher you advance, the more you will need your communication ability.[6] The evidence is clear: improving your communication skills improves your chances for success in business.

• By improving your communication ability, you improve your chances for success.

Why Business Needs to Communicate

To understand how important communication is to business, note how much communication business requires. Think of an example from your own work experience or that of someone you know—perhaps a part-time job in retail sales. Obviously as a salesclerk, your communication skills will assist you in every encounter with customers. They will also enhance your work experience as you relate to other employees in the store, learn about new stock from the manager, or receive training in store procedures. In other parts of the company, negotiations are made with suppliers and designers; market researchers

• Communication is vital to every part of business.

---

[1] Conference Board of Canada, National Business and Education Centre, *Employability Skills Profile: What Are Employers Looking For?* (Ottawa: Conference Board of Canada, 1992).

[2] For more information on employability skills, see Chapter 11, "Strategy in Job Search and Application."

[3] Gale Cohen Ruby, "Author! Author!: Why Your Firm May Be Paying a Heavy Price for Poor Writing," *CA Magazine* March 1993: 36–38.

[4] Canada Employment Centres, Metro Toronto Labour Market Analysis Group, *Towards 2000: Occupational Trends*. http://www.the-wire.com/hrdc/trend96.html (6 June 1996).

[5] Gale Cohen Ruby, "Author! Author!: Why Your Firm May Be Paying a Heavy Price for Poor Writing," *CA Magazine* March 1993: 36.

[6] Lyman K. Steil, L.L. Barker, and K.W. Watson, *Effective Listening: Key to Your Success* (Reading, MA: Addison-Wesley, 1983).

survey the public to determine their wants and needs; advertizers prepare campaigns to launch each season's line; contracts are written and signed; policies are detailed; and urgent matters are decided and communicated by telephone, fax, electronic mail, videoconference, or any number of other methods. Everywhere in the company employees receive and send information as they conduct their work.

Processing messages with computers, conducting interviews, answering letters, filling out forms, giving and receiving instructions, preparing training manuals and videos, sending fax messages, and leaving voice mail messages are all examples of communication at work.

All of this communicating is essential to the organized effort involved in business. Communication enables people to work together. It is the vehicle through which management performs basic functions. Managers direct through communication; coordinate through communication; and hire, plan, and control through communication. Through good communication they succeed.

Main Forms of Communication in Business

The overall communication activities of an organization fall into two broad categories: *operational* (including internal, external) and *personal.*

Operational Communication.   *Operational communication* is communication related to the work of the company. It is done to conduct the company's business and to achieve its goals. There are two types—*internal* and *external*—based on who is the intended receiver of the communication.

Internal Communication.   All the communication that occurs in conducting work within a business is classified as operational and *internal.* The employees communicate with each other to carry out the business's operating plan. By operating plan, we mean the procedure that the business has developed to do whatever it was formed to do, such as manufacture products, provide services, or sell goods.

Internal communication takes many forms. It includes the directions and instructions of supervisors, as well as conversations about work matters; reports and records that employees prepare concerning sales, production, inventories, finance, maintenance, and so on; and the memorandums and reports that employees write in carrying out their assignments. As technology advances, internal communication includes the use of voice mail, electronic mail, and computer networks. More information on the extent to which electronic technology has brought change to business communications is found in Chapter 18.

- Communication takes many forms.

- There are two main forms of communication in business.

- Operational communication is work-related.

- Internal communication occurs between people within a business.

External Communication.   The work-related communicating that a business does with people and groups outside the business is operational and *external* communication. This is the business's communication with the general public, its customers, suppliers, and service companies.

External communication includes the day-to-day interaction with the public by everyone involved with the company, whether president or receptionist, manager or shipping clerk. It includes sales communications—salespeople's "spiels," descriptive brochures, telephone callbacks, and follow-up service calls. It also includes advertizing— radio and television messages, newspaper and magazine advertizing, and point-of-purchase display material, to name a few. Also in the category of external communication is all that a business does to improve its public image, including its planned publicity, the courtesy of its employees, and the condition of its property. The importance of external communication with customers and potential customers is obvious.

In today's complex, fast-paced world, businesses must also communicate effectively with other businesses and government. Companies need each other in the production and distribution of goods and services. John Torella, the principal of Toronto-based John C. Williams Consultants, said at the Vision 1993 conference in Vancouver, "The line between packaged goods, institutions, manufacturers, developers and retailing is really blurred. We're all in the marketing and communications business."[7] Most businesses also need to communicate with government at several levels regarding by-laws, taxation, labour laws, safety practices, and many other topics. The success and survival of a company can depend on its success in using external communication.

- External communication occurs with people outside the business.

Personal Communication.   Not all the communication that takes place in a business is operational. Much of it is personal and without direct application to the business. *Personal communication* is the exchange of information and feelings between people whenever we come together. As social beings, we have a need to communicate. Much of our time with friends is spent in conversation. Even total strangers are likely to communicate when they are placed together, as on an airplane flight, in a waiting room, or at a ball game.

Such personal communication at the workplace is a part of the communication activity of any business. Although not central to the business's operation, personal communication can have a significant effect on the attitudes of the employees. For example, in a work situation where co-workers frequently have heated arguments or carry grudges, morale likely will be low. However, two people who talk about their interest in golf, their children, or jazz music may also be positive about working together. The employees' attitudes about each other affect their attitudes about their work.

In turn, the employees' attitudes toward each other and their work affect their performance. Certain tasks may be given a lower priority because of a personal conflict. Workers who do not get along on a personal level will find it more difficult to co-operate on a business level and productivity will be affected. However, a party atmosphere in a work situation is likely to have an equally bad effect on productivity. Somewhere between these extremes lies the ideal of a pleasant, productive workplace.

- Personal communication is not directly business-related.

- Personal communication affects employee attitudes.

- The nature and extent of personal communication permitted affects performance.

Communication Network of the Organization

Looking over all of a business's communication (operational and personal), we see an extremely complex network of information flow. We see an organization feeding on a continuous supply of information delivered in many forms and styles. We see hundreds, or even thousands, of individuals engaging in untold numbers of communication events throughout each workday. To understand this network better, we can identify two patterns. One is based on the direction of information flow—downward, upward, or horizontal. The second is based on the nature of the process—formal or informal.

- Information flow in a business forms a complex network.

---

[7]Bob Mackin, Jr., "Communications Key to Survival, Says Consultant," *Marketing* 17 May 1993: 11.

• The flow is mainly downward, but upward and horizontal communications are also important.

Traditionally, the flow of operational communication has been downward from the executives, to the managers, to the employees. However, most companies now recognize the need for more upward and horizontal communication to prevent costly errors and allow improvements based on input from all departments. Through programs such as Total Quality Management (TQM), those who are most closely involved with a process are challenged to make improvements and share their ideas with management and other departments. As companies grow larger, communication links between departments grow in importance. One writer calls these links "the glue that holds together the units of an organization."[8]

The Formal Network. Information flow in a modern business is a network like the veins and arteries in the body. Just as the body has blood vessels to carry blood, a business has major, well-established channels for information. These are the formal channels—the main lines of operational communication to move information upward, downward, or horizontally in the organization.

• The main (formal) flow of information follows established patterns and routes.

In general, the internal, formal network follows the lines of authority of the organization. However, formal, co-operative channels may be set up through standing committees and interdepartmental meetings. Special committees, quality circles, and focus groups are being used to extend the formal, internal channels.

For formal, external communication, certain people or departments are authorized to represent the company. Examples are the public relations department and the sales department. Through these channels flow the bulk of the communication that the business needs to operate. The challenge for modern business is to keep these formal channels responsive to changing needs.

• The informal network is dynamic, personal, and powerful.

The Informal Network. The informal network is a secondary network consisting primarily of personal communication, personal interpretation of current company policy and news, and gossip. It is a complex and rapidly changing network that cuts across the formal communication lines to link people on a personal level. It is comparable to the

[8]Michael Nisbet, "Write Right," *Canadian Banker* May-June 1991: 41.

small blood vessels and capillaries of the circulation system that develop and change as the body demands.

The complexity of this informal network, especially in larger organizations, cannot be overemphasized. Typically, it is not a single network but a complex relationship of smaller groups of people who have something in common. These groups change as individual circumstances change. The network is made even more complex by the fact that people may belong to more than one group and, therefore, have several links to the informal network.

* The informal network is highly complex and continually changing

Almost any common link can be the basis of an informal network. A group could begin with an in-house training program or a committee to plan a company party. These events give the employees contact with people they would not normally meet in the course of their regular duties. If when the event ends, the communication link continues, it is then an informal link, not a formal one. It is also possible that the basis of the informal network is not work-related. It could be a small group that lives in the same neighbourhood, has the same coffee break, or works out at the same fitness club. Add to this the impact of e-mail and the Internet, and the number of contacts in the informal network becomes astronomical.

Sometimes known as the *grapevine,* this network is far more effective than a first impression might suggest. Although it carries gossip, rumours, and idle talk, the grapevine also carries news and honest feelings that help people know one another better and form alliances that are positive for their work and their lives. Attention to the informal channel keeps everyone up to date on internal news.

* The grapevine carries news and feelings.

Secondly, in a large organization, the grapevine may carry business-related information much more quickly than the formal communication system. In the example illustrated in Figure 1–1, the employees are linked through formal channels; however, the employees in shipping are likely to hear of a new company policy first through the informal grapevine because of the cousin at head office. Its speed makes the informal network helpful to administrators as well. Rather than waiting for the slower, formal network, pro-active managers could connect with the grapevine by joining their staff for coffee to chat about an issue before making a decision.

* The grapevine may spread news faster than the formal network.

False rumours travel just as quickly as true information on the grapevine. Therefore, some caution needs to be exercised. Checking the facts with people at the source is sensible. Again, the wise manager listens to the grapevine to handle concerns before they become grievances and to correct false information that could cause damage.

* News from the grapevine needs to be considered carefully.

FIGURE 1–1   An Example of Formal and Informal Communication Networks

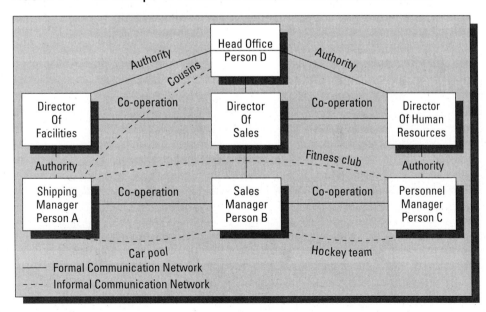

THE PROCESS OF HUMAN COMMUNICATION

- The communication process is often described in a standard pattern.

The standard pattern for understanding the communication process is as follows:

1. The sender has an idea and encodes it into a message of symbols such as words, pictures, and gestures.

2. The sender selects a channel and sends the message to the receiver.

3. The receiver receives the message and decodes the symbols into an idea.

4. The receiver considers the idea and prepares a response.

5. The receiver encodes the response into a feedback message to send on a chosen channel to the sender.

The Beginning: A Message Sent

- The process begins when Jennifer sends a message to Rajib.

To describe the communication process, we will use a situation involving two people named Jennifer and Rajib. Our description begins with Jennifer having an idea that she wants to communicate in a message to Rajib. Her message could be in any of a number of forms—gestures, facial expressions, drawings, or, more likely, written or spoken words. This process of turning an idea into a message involves the most complex workings of the mind. Her ability with language equips Jennifer with a variety of symbols (words) to express meaning. (See Figure 1–2.)

FIGURE 1–2   The Communication Process: Jennifer Communicates with Rajib

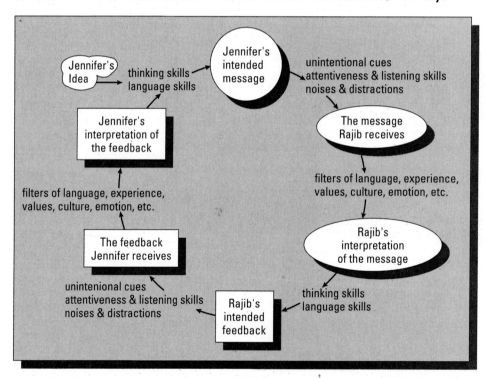

A message sent by Jennifer arrives in Rajib's "sensory world" (all Rajib's senses can detect from the surrounding reality). Rajib's senses pick up the message and also competing information from his sensory world. Jennifer's message is filtered through Rajib's unique mind and is given meaning. The meaning given may trigger a response, which Rajib's unique mind forms. Rajib sends the message to Jennifer. It enters her sensory world, and a second cycle begins, which echoes the first cycle.

Detection by the Senses

Jennifer's message then enters Rajib's sensory world. *Sensory world* means all that surrounds a person and can be detected by the senses (sight, hearing, smell, taste, and touch). Obviously, Rajib's sensory world contains more than Jennifer's message.

From his sensory world, Rajib's senses pick up stimuli (messages). We must note, however, that Rajib cannot receive *all* the messages around him. There are more signals than he can physically or psychologically handle. Just how much he can detect depends on a number of factors. One is the ability of his senses. As you know, not all eyes see equally well, and not all ears hear equally well. If Jennifer writes in very small letters, or speaks very softly, Rajib will not notice her message. Another factor is Rajib's mental alertness. There are times when he is keenly alert to all that his senses can detect, and there are times when he is in a daydream. In this case, if Jennifer's message does not include an attention-getting device, Rajib may miss it. Yet another limiting factor is Rajib's will. In varying degrees, the mind is able to tune in or tune out events in the sensory world. If Rajib is absorbed in a video game, he may not be willing to accept a message from another source. On the other hand, even in a noisy room full of people, the conversation of a single person can be the selected focus of attention.

As well as Jennifer's intended message, Rajib may receive other messages from her tone, facial expressions, and movements. From these cues, he will try to determine factors such as the urgency of her message and her feelings. His senses are also picking up other messages from the world around him that may support or interfere with Jennifer's message. The stimuli detected by the senses are relayed to the brain.

* The message enters Rajib's sensory world,

* where his senses may detect it.

* What Rajib's senses detect, they send to his brain,

The Filtering Process

In Rajib's mind, the messages go through a sifting or filtering process through which Rajib gives meaning to Jennifer's message. In other words, the message is filtered through the contents of Rajib's mind. Those contents include all his experience, knowledge, biases, emotions—in fact, all that makes Rajib the person he is. Because Rajib is unique, the meaning he gives to Jennifer's message may be unique as well.

No two people have precisely identical filters, for no two people have minds with precisely the same contents. Because people's filters differ, the meanings they give to comparable messages also differ. Thus, the meaning Rajib gives to Jennifer's message may not be the same as the one someone else would give it. More importantly, it may not be the meaning Jennifer intended. For example, assume that Jennifer used the word *liberal* in her message. Now assume that Jennifer and Rajib have had differing experiences with the word. To Jennifer the word is negative; for her it suggests a lack of order and values. To Rajib the word is positive; he sees creativity and generosity in it. Or perhaps Rajib immediately associates the word with a political philosophy and party. In either case, the meaning Rajib derives from the word would not be precisely the meaning Jennifer wanted to send. And so it could be with other words, depending upon the degree of commonality between their filters.

* where it goes through a filtering process.

* Because minds differ, message meanings differ.

Formation and Sending of the Response (Feedback)

At this point in the process, Jennifer should wait for some response from Rajib. When he gives his feedback, Rajib becomes a sender. He thinks out his idea and forms a message. That is, he converts meanings into symbols. Although he will most likely use the same channel as Jennifer did, he could choose spoken words, written words, gestures, movements, facial expressions, diagrams on paper, and so on.

* Rajib determines a meaning, forms a message, and sends a response.

The Cycle Repeated

If Rajib contributes a comment or question related to the topic, the conversation can continue. When Rajib sends his message to Jennifer, it enters Jennifer's sensory world. Her senses pick it up and send it through her nervous system to her brain. Through her

* Then the cycle is repeated.

unique mental filter, she assigns a meaning to Rajib's message. This filtered meaning may also bring about a response. If it does, Jennifer selects the symbols for her response, sends them to Rajib, and communication continues. Each time a message is received, there is opportunity for another exchange. New ideas can be introduced, arguments put forward, and rebuttals to those arguments presented.

The Role of Feedback in Effective Communication

In reality, communication is not always so successful or so polite. Many misunderstandings, interruptions, and interferences occur. It is relatively easy to spot the places in the process where problems could occur. A poorly conceived idea, an awkwardly shaped message, interference and noise during transmission, poor reception, and limited language abilities are examples of potential hazards in the communication path.

Constructive feedback is an essential step for achieving good results. Communication has been successful if the sender and the receiver both have understood the idea in the same way. They may not agree, but they have a common understanding of what the message contains. Feedback is the way to achieve this understanding. Paraphrasing (restating the speaker's ideas in different words), asking questions to clarify ideas, and summarizing the main points are examples of feedback that can help understanding.[9]

While feedback is part of the solution for communication problems, nonverbal cues can be a source of trouble in feedback itself. Just as a sender's message can be accompanied by nonverbal cues,[10] so can feedback. These cues may be deliberate and helpful. For example, a loud voice can be used to reinforce the words, and a gesture can indicate humour. However, sometimes, the nonverbal cues carry a message that conflicts with the words. A person who is checking the time while saying, "I'm glad to meet you, too," will not be convincing and may cause offense. Nonverbal cues may also send unintended messages. A slow response may be interpreted as lack of interest, when, in fact, the speaker only wants to consider the matter fully before responding. As you can see, complexities are involved throughout the process of communication.

Resulting Stress on Adaptation

Understanding the communication process can help you become a better communicator by alerting you to the weak links in the chain where the process could break down. At these points, the intended message could be distorted or lost. The process shows that communication is a unique event—that every mind is different from every other mind in many ways. Unless the words (or other symbols) used in a message have the same meanings in the minds of both the sender and the recipient, communication suffers. Communication scholars have tried to solve this problem by stressing the adaptation of messages to the minds of the recipients. By *adaptation* we mean the responsibility of the sender to fit the message to the recipients. By using words and other symbols tailored to the receiver, the sender carefully prepares a message that the recipient will understand intellectually and accept emotionally. Then the meaning understood by the recipient will be as close to the intended meaning of the sender as possible. As you will see, adaptation is the foundation for our review of communication principles in the pages ahead.

. . . .
THE COMMUNICATION PROCESS AND WRITTEN COMMUNICATION

Our description of the communication process illustrates face-to-face communication. Although there are some differences between oral and written communication, the process applies to both. Perhaps the most significant difference is that written communi-

---

[9]For more information on how to use these types of feedback, see the section on listening in Chapter 2, "The Essential Skills."

[10]Chapter 2 has more on nonverbal communication.

cation is more likely to be thought out carefully and logically. Because writing or typing a message takes longer than speaking it, writers have the opportunity to reconsider their ideas and their choice of words. They are wise to be careful because a written message is more permanent than a spoken one.

A second difference is the time between cycles. Often in face-to-face communication, cycles occur in rapid succession and are completed quickly. They may even be interrupted by a quick response before the full message is sent. In written communication, some delay occurs between the cycles. For reports and letters, feedback may take days, weeks, or months. The response to a fax, while relatively fast, will take several moments, at least. In addition, because they leave a permanent record, written communications may initiate communication cycles over extremely long periods of time as each new reader receives the message.

• (2) has longer cycles, and

A third difference is that written communication usually involves a limited number of cycles and oral communication usually involves many. In fact, some written communication cycles are very simple. Bulk advertizing is often sent and received. If the response is to throw the flyer in the garbage, this communication cycle is ended.

• (3) usually has fewer cycles.

SOME BASIC TRUTHS ABOUT COMMUNICATION

Analysis of the communication process brings out three underlying truths that will help us understand its complexity.

The Messages Sent Are Not Always the Messages Received

Because of interference, inattentiveness, or other barriers, the delivery of a message may be faulty. For example, sending an e-mail message does not guarantee its receipt by the intended reader. The message may be undeliverable, garbled *en route,* diverted to someone else, or successfully delivered. Interference along a channel was the basis for a cellular phone advertisement. On a competitor's poorer-quality telephone the wife heard, "I've left you for my secretary." If she had been using the advertizer's static-free telephone, she would have heard the real message. "I've left you a note for my secretary." Inattentiveness, unclear handwriting, and competing messages are some of the other reasons why we cannot assume the message sent is the message received.

• Messages may be changed in the process of sending and receiving.

Meaning Is in the Mind behind the Message

The mind of the sender holds an idea that must be encoded into a message. In this process, the full meaning is reduced into symbols that can be transmitted. The symbols

• Meaning is in the mind rather than in the symbols.

we use, especially words, are at best crude substitutes for the idea. Why do we use the word *dog* to describe a dog? Why did we choose those particular letters and sounds? Other languages use *chien, hund,* and *anjing.*[11] The symbols are assigned to ideas and meanings by common agreement, but they do not have meaning in themselves. The meaning is in the mind, not in the symbols of the message.

The Interpretation of Symbols Is Imperfect

- Symbols may be associated with several meanings.

Even if the message is received clearly and completely, and the receiver makes allowances for the limitations of symbols, some miscommunication can occur because of the interpretation given to symbols. Many words, gestures, and facial expressions can be understood in several ways. For example, the word *young* can mean under 10 years old to someone who is 20, or under 50 to someone who is 65. The Canadian Rockies, which are about 60 million years old, are also described as young! Looking at the word *run,* we can think of the action of running, colours that fade and run, a point in a baseball game, a flaw in a knitted garment, a string of events such as a run of good luck, or heavy financial trading such as a run on the bank or the stock market. These illustrations are not exceptions; they are the rule.

- Reality has more variations than symbols can conveniently transmit.

Moreover, symbols simply cannot account for the infinite variations of reality. For example, the verb *run* conveys only the most general part of the action; it ignores countless variations in speed, grace, and style. Sometimes the variations are so great that it is hard to define the similarities which place, for example, chairs in the category of *chair.* Think of recliners, rockers, pedestal chairs, "bean bag" chairs, folding chairs, straight-backed dining chairs, captain's chairs, and "kneeling" chairs for keyboarding. (See Figure 1–3.)

- Different filters lead to different understanding.

A third reason that differences in interpretation arise is that no two minds have identical storehouses of words, memories, values, or experiences. Especially in a multicultural society like Canada's, no two minds have the same filters. Since the meaning is in the mind, and minds are different, the interpretation of symbols into meanings changes from person to person. For example, for some people, the word *dog* brings to mind the picture of a family pet curled up with a child. For others, it is a working animal that sleeps outside in the barn. For still others, it is a wild, vicious animal that is unclean to touch.[12] Because of such differences, failures in communication are hard to avoid.

---

[11]These languages are French, German, and Indonesian, respectively.

[12]This interpretation was given by a student from Indonesia based on his culture and Islamic faith.

FIGURE 1–3   A Chair Is a Chair ... Or Is It?

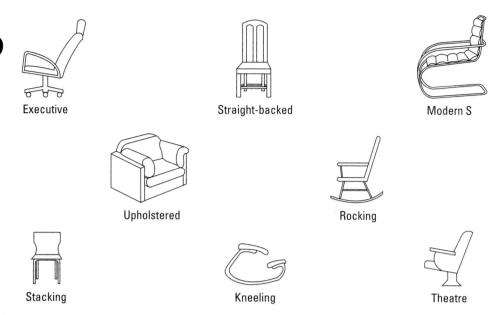

Executive   Straight-backed   Modern S

Upholstered   Rocking

Stacking   Kneeling   Theatre

In everyday situations, most people do a fairly good job of communicating. Still, miscommunication often occurs. The preceding comments bring to light the difficulties, complexities, and limitations of communication. People who assume that meanings intended are meanings received, who attach personal definitions to words, or who are not able to select words well are likely to experience difficulty. Those who recognize and appreciate the differences among people and the challenges of communicating are more likely to succeed in understanding others and, in turn, being understood.

• Even so, we communicate reasonably well.

. . . .
THE GOAL, PLAN, AND PHILOSOPHY OF THIS BOOK

The preceding discussion shows that communication is important to business, that it is performed in various and complex ways, and that it requires effort by the communicators to be accurate and precise. These observations suggest that communicating in business is not to be taken lightly. If you want to excel at communicating, you must develop your skills. Helping you do this is the goal of this book.

• The goal of this book is to help you improve your communication skills.

The Plan: Situations, Solutions, Summaries

To achieve this goal, the book introduces each major topic through a business communication situation that realistically places you in the business world. Each situation describes a possible communication problem. Then the following material instructs you on how to solve the problem. Opportunities for practice are included within the text under the heading, *A PRACTICE RUN*. Suggested answers for these questions are at the end of each chapter. For your study convenience, summaries of the text material appear in the margins and a general summary appears at the end of the chapters. Finally, questions, exercises, and short cases are provided for further discussion and practice.

• The book introduces topics by situations; then, it shows solutions. Summaries aid your study.

The Philosophy: Communicate to Understand and Be Understood

In presenting this subject matter, the book takes a practical, realistic approach. That is, it views business communication as having one primary goal—to communicate.

• Successful communication is the purpose of communicating.

• Some writers have other goals
(to impress, to entertain).
Business communication should
seek to communicate.

Although this statement may appear elementary, it has significant meaning. All too often other goals creep in. For example, communicators sometimes seek to impress—perhaps by using big words and involved sentences. Or they seek to entertain with a clever choice of words and gestures. Good business communicators rarely have these goals. They primarily seek to communicate. They use words and sentences that communicate clearly and quickly. If the message has any difficulty, the reason is that the subject matter is difficult. In no way should the words and the sentence structures add to the difficulty.

· ·

A SUMMARY OF LEARNING OUTCOMES FROM THIS CHAPTER

Communication is vital to business operations. Business needs and rewards people who can communicate. If you improve your communication skills, you increase your value to your employer.

One form of communication in a business organization is *operational*. All the communication that occurs within a business to carry out its operating plan is called *internal-operational communication*. Work-related communication with people and groups outside the business is *external-operational*.

The second form of communication in a business organization is *personal*. The communicating that does not relate to operations is called *personal communication*.

The flow of communication in a business is complex and changing. Information moves downward, upward, and horizontally. It travels along *formal* networks that usually follow the lines of authority in the organization. It also travels along an *informal* network, (sometimes called the *grapevine*), which is made up of small groups of people who have something in common. The common factor that links the group together may or may not be work-related.

The process of communication is as follows:

1. The sender has an idea and encodes it into a message of symbols, such as words, pictures, and gestures.

2. The sender selects a channel and sends the message to the receiver.

3. The receiver receives the message and decodes the symbols into an idea.

4. The receiver considers the idea and prepares a response.

5. The receiver encodes the response into a feedback message to send on a chosen channel to the sender.

6. The process continues, cycle after cycle, as needed or wanted.

Written communication differs from oral communication in that it is (1) more likely to involve preparation, (2) has longer cycles, and (3) usually has fewer cycles.

Three truths are evident about communication.

1. The message sent is not always the same as the message received because of interference, inattentiveness, or other barriers.

2. Meanings are in the mind and not limited to the symbols of the message.

3. The interpretation of communication symbols is imperfect because symbols may be associated with several meanings, because reality has more variations than symbols can conveniently transmit, and because people process ideas through their own unique filters.

QUESTIONS FOR DISCUSSION

1. Is the ability to communicate important to the job performance of a sales representative, a junior accountant, and a computer programmer? Explain the reasons for your answer.

2. List the types of external and internal communication that take place in an organization with which you are familiar (school, sport team, etc.).

3. Describe the network of communication in an organization or business with which you are familiar. Discuss and explain.

4. Make a list of the networks in which you are a member. Estimate how many people are "connected" through you in informal communication links (grapevines).

5. Describe what is in your sensory world at this moment. Contrast the parts that are usually in your awareness with the parts that are usually ignored or filtered out.

6. Using the model for the communication process as a base, explain why people reading the same message can disagree on its meaning.

7. Discuss some of the possible meanings that the following words could have for Canadians: Christmas, sovereignty, pro choice, Internet, Yom Kippur, pension fund, afternoon tea. Are some of these terms unfamiliar or insignificant to you? Increase your understanding and awareness by asking appropriate questions.

8. Give an example of a simple statement that could be misunderstood. Explain why. Then revise the statement for more precise understanding.

CASE 1–1

Paulina is in a job interview at Mercury Press, and the owner, Mr. Carlzon, has just offered her the position. She is very pleased and wants this job. The question of a split shift has been raised.

Mr. Carlzon: I'd like you to start on a split shift—8 to 11, and 2 to 5. Will that be a problem?

Paulina: Well, I know it may sound silly, but a split shift would work very well for me because I have a new puppy that needs attention every few hours. With a split shift, I could go home and look after the pup.

Mr. Carlzon: That's great. We'll get you settled in today so you can start on Monday at 8:00 A.M. You know, one of our senior employees brings Rex to work. That dog just sleeps under the desk and doesn't bother anyone.

What assumptions would Paulina be making if her next comment were

a) O.K. Then I'll bring my dog to work on Monday!

b) Really? What kind of a handicap does the lady who owns the dog have?

c) I don't think it's fair to give special privileges to some employees just because they're old.

CASE 1–2

Seeing Jason in the hallway reminds Maureen that she needs his report within the week. She says, "I want that report as soon as you can get it done," and hurries on to a meeting.

A little startled, Jason calls after her, "Sure. Uh, right away?" Maureen waves her hand as she disappears around the corner.

To himself, Jason says, "I guess processing that big order will have to wait so I can get the report to her today."

When Maureen learns of Jason's decision, she is angry. "I wanted that report *soon*, but not *immediately*. *Anyone* would know that an order takes precedence."

Refer to the stages in the communication model as you suggest what each person could have done to improve this exchange.

2

The Essential Skills

C H A P T E R   O B J E C T I V E S

Upon completing this chapter, you will understand five essential skills for successful communication: clear thinking, accurate listening, nonverbal support, correct language usage, and adaptation skills. To reach this goal, you should be able to

1 Apply the 6-C approach to clear thinking: clarify, collect, choose, combine, check, and conclude.

2 Develop proficiency in language skills by choosing words exactly, following the standard conventions of grammar, and using idiom correctly.

3 Understand the listening process and select the appropriate listening level for the situation.

4 Describe the role and importance of nonverbal communication in both oral and written communication.

5 Identify the receiver's circumstances and the key points that need to be adapted for that receiver.

AN INTRODUCTION TO THE BASICS

Before we look at specific tools and methods of communication, there are five basic skill areas to consider. *Thinking skills* are needed to plan and organize your message; *language skills* are needed to express accurately the idea you have thought out; *listening skills* are used to receive and interpret the intended meaning of the sender; *nonverbal skills* are needed to support the verbal message; and *adaptation skills* are used to visualize the receiver and adjust the message appropriately for the needs, interests, and circumstances of that receiver. While all of these essential skills will be applied throughout this book, they are discussed here as a foundation for your study of business communication.

CRITICAL THINKING SKILLS

What Is Critical Thinking?

There are many technical definitions of critical thinking. Most of them are too complicated for our purposes. We will consider *critical thinking* as thorough thinking based on knowledge and logic. Critical thinking is not negative thinking. Its purpose is not to find fault but to evaluate fairly. A critical thinker finds both the weaknesses and strengths in a statement, situation, or set of facts and then draws a reasonable conclusion that can be the basis for action.

* Critical thinking is thorough thinking.

When Should Critical Thinking Be Used?

Critical thinking is useful in many situations. As you study a textbook, read a newspaper, or listen to a speech, you can apply critical thinking to your benefit. You should use it almost anytime you are taking in information. For example, you should be using it when you watch advertisements on television. Based on your knowledge of life and logic, is it reasonable to believe that one detergent has an amazing, new ingredient to get mud and grass stains out of white socks while other detergents (even those made by the same company) do not? Or, that opening a pack of chewing gum will draw crowds of friends to you? Thorough thinking would lead you to hold those ideas in question.

* Use critical thinking when you receive information.

There are times when critical thinking is not appropriate. These times usually involve artistic and creative endeavours. When you go to an adventure movie, you should be willing to accept that the hero can transform into another shape or skillfully operate a helicopter, tank, snowmobile, and nuclear reactor! Another time to postpone critical thinking is the early stage in your writing process when you want to encourage the ideas to flow. Evaluating every word at this stage will shut down your ability to create. After the ideas have been drafted, you apply your critical thinking faculties to sift them.

* Creativity may require that you postpone evaluation.

There will be times when we must make a decision or form an opinion before we have all the factual information we would like. In such a case, we would use estimates, inferences, and value judgments to help us. That procedure is not in conflict with critical thinking, as long as we are open to re-evaluating our position when additional facts become available. A critical thinker would apply the new knowledge to the problem and, if warranted, change his or her decision.

* Be ready to review your ideas.

What Is the 6-C Approach to Critical Thinking?

To learn the skills of critical thinking, we will discuss them in the context of solving a problem. Each major step in the process begins with a *C* for easier recall: Clarify, Collect, Choose, Combine, Check, Conclude. We begin with working out what the problem is and what information is at hand to solve it.

* Use the 6-C approach to help your thinking process.

Clarify: State the Problem or Goal Clearly.

* CLARIFY the problem or purpose by investigating the situation and

Investigate. When presented with a difficulty, you sometimes need to begin by gathering basic information. Your goal at this stage is only to understand the problem well enough to state it clearly. This is not the time to try to solve it. If you are faced with a scheduling problem because some employees do not want to work on a particular day, you will want to investigate the reason. If there is an important event that day for those people, you can use that information to define the problem. If there are terms used that you do not understand, you will need to find definitions. Remember, your data gathering is aimed at defining the problem and stating it clearly, not solving it.

* applying your imagination to it.

Imagine. Some problems will require you to use your imagination as well. It may be needed to understand the problem from the other person's point of view. If you are trying to solve a customer relations problem, you will need to imagine what the customer is feeling. You may need to use your imagination to reach the root problem. If the supervisor says that people are spending too much time on the telephone, you will use a combination of investigation and imagination to discover if the problem is the amount of time on the telephone, the amount of time on personal calls on the telephone, or the amount of time on long-distance and the resulting costly bill.

* Write a clear purpose statement.

As soon as you can, state the goal in a sentence or two. This step may seem unnecessary because you understand the problem in your mind, but without a clear statement to refer to, most people end up chasing tangents. In the telephone example, if the problem is the long-distance bill, discussing local personal calls would be a tangent unrelated to the problem at hand.

In general, it is best to state the goal positively. For example, if the goal is "To cut spending on long-distance calls," prohibiting all long-distance calling would reduce the bill—and the profits! A more positive and practical approach would be "To maximize the benefit from every dollar spent on long-distance calls."[1]

* Collect information through research.

Collect: Gather and Process Information. Your research now begins in earnest as you gather evidence for the decision. You also apply good thinking here as you select likely sources for your investigation. An entire chapter (Chapter 19) is dedicated to the topic of research, so we will not cover the methodology here.

Choose: Select Evidence and Facts.

* Choose the evidence you need based on relevance,

Based on Relevance. Relevant facts for solving the telephone bill problem include historical information about the telephone bill over a period of time—perhaps a year to allow for seasonal changes in the business cycle; current information on rates and services of long-distance carriers; and information about the needs of telephone users in your company. A two-year old report comparing carriers will not be relevant. Low Sunday rates are of little value to most businesses. Comments about how cheap the telephone rates are in Arizona are also of limited relevance.

* quantity, and

Based on Sufficiency. Sufficiency means having enough information for a valid comparison. To ask only one carrier for current rates is inadequate. To ask several carriers for their North American rates may not be sufficient either if the company has extensive contacts in Europe or Asia. Asking for rates for fixed telephones may be insufficient also if many of your employees are on the road using cellular telephones or calling cards.

* quality.

Based on Acceptability. Acceptability points to the reliability of the information. You will need actual quotes or printed statements of these costs, not just the word of someone in the office across the street. You need the information within a time frame. If a carrier

---

[1]For more detailed information on the structure of purpose and problem statements, see the chapters on report writing, especially Chapter 12, "Basics of Report Writing."

is changing its rate structure next month and can give you only the existing rates now, their information is not acceptable. You will want to beware of information from biased sources. Groups or companies with a particular interest in only one side of an issue may not provide you with a balanced picture. At the time of writing, MCI and AT&T have a series of advertisements on television both claiming to have the best savings. Under certain circumstances, both claims are true. Neither can be taken at face value, however.

A PRACTICE RUN

Check the following statements for relevance and acceptability for the long-distance calling problem. Give your reasons for accepting or questioning these statements.

1. Carrier A's calling card didn't work when a friend of yours went to India last year. _____

_____

2. Carrier B has a very attractive brochure. _____

_____

3. Carrier C has the best fibre-optic links for static- free calls and rapid connections according to their sales representative.

_____

4. Carrier A has an additional family package for residential telephones. _____

_____

5. Carrier D promises to have a representative visit next week. _____

_____

Combine: Bring Related Ideas Together.   Once you have enough relevant, reliable data, you can begin to look for relationships and patterns. Sometimes the data itself suggests the answer. One path may be obviously better than the others. However, it is more often the case that each possibility has some merit. To make a decision, you will need to weigh the merits of each option, or generate new options.

• Combine ideas by sorting them

Make a Comparison or Show a Contrast.   To make a comparison, you must have some common factors to compare. If each carrier offers the same package of discounts and services, the comparison is simple (and unnecessary). If the offers differ, you decide which features are the most important and beneficial. For example, if one carrier offers excellent rates for calls from cellular phones but higher rates for calls from fixed phones, you need to know what percentage of calls in your company are made from each type of telephone. Then you can estimate the cost and compare it to another carrier's offer. As you examine the evidence, you will see more comparisons that can be made.

• into related or contrasting groups.

Build a New Idea or Pattern.   As you sift through the evidence, watch for patterns or combinations of ideas that might lead to a solution. Consider combining the strengths of several approaches into one new one. For example, would Carrier A consider a set rate for most months and a sliding scale discount for the two months when you have your highest volume of calls?

• Build new ideas from the old ones.

A PRACTICE RUN

Describe the steps you would follow to compare the features offered by these two carriers.

Carrier A offers a set discount (flat rate) for all long-distance calls billed to calling cards.

Carrier B offers a sliding discount based on volume for all long-distance calls.

_____

_____

_____

_____

Examine the problem from every angle just as you would if you were solving a puzzle. Could the timing of calls, especially fax messages, be improved? Is your voice-mail system easy to follow so that customers can leave complete messages to reduce the number of callbacks needed? Are accurate records kept so that calls are directed to the appropriate person without being transferred or put on hold? Perhaps a 1-800 number would help. Or could the company use e-mail more often?

Check: Test the Logic.

• Check carefully for inaccuracies,

Avoid Inaccuracies.   Check your sources, your facts, and your calculations. Be sure to quote your sources correctly. "We will not knowingly be undersold" is not the same as "We promise to offer the lowest prices."

• preconceptions, and

Avoid Preconceptions.   Check your assumption and ask questions until you are certain that you have the evidence to support your decisions and recommendations. Set aside your own preconceived ideas and listen or read carefully.

• faulty thought patterns that may have crept into your work.

Avoid Fallacies.   _Logical fallacies_ are statements or conclusions that at first glance appear reasonable but which, in fact, are based on faulty or illogical thought. Appendix B contains a selected list of some of the more common ones. Critical thinking requires that you avoid logical fallacies and check all your conclusions for sound evidence and reasoning.

• Conclude with a decision.

Conclude: Select the Best Way to Proceed.   The final step is to select the best solution. By now, it should be obvious to you; however, if it is not, you will return to the beginning to test your work. Can you restate the problem or break it into smaller parts? Can you gather more evidence to further clarify the situation? Have you thought of all the alternatives? Perhaps a brainstorming session would help you generate new ideas. Continue until you are comfortable with your conclusion, but always be ready to re-evaluate it if new evidence comes to light.

LANGUAGE SKILLS

The Role of Language Skills

• Communicating requires a knowledge of language.

From Chapter 1 we already know the importance of communication for a successful career in business. We also know the importance of symbols in the communication process. The sender uses symbols—usually words—to encode the meaning and idea into a message that can be sent to the receiver. Obviously, the better your knowledge of those symbols, the better your communication is likely to be.

A synonym is a word you use when you can't spell the word you first thought of.

Burt Bacharach

Vocabulary

Unfortunately, too many of us treat language carelessly. We use the first words that come to mind. We use words without knowing their meanings, or without being sure of their full meanings. The result is confusion for our receivers.

Select Words Precisely.   One strength of the English language is its richness in words with similar meanings (called synonyms). This feature allows variety in expression and accuracy in meaning. However, to take advantage of the exactness, colour, and emphasis available through careful word choice, you will need to study words to learn the fine variations in the meanings. For example, *weary, tired, listless, beat,* and *exhausted* all refer to the same thing. Yet in most minds, there are differences in the meanings of these words. In a formal message, *weary* would be more acceptable than *beat.* Similarly, *fired, dismissed, canned, separated,* and *discharged* refer to the same action but have different shades of meaning. So it is with each of these groups of words:

> • You should learn the shades of difference in the meanings of similar words.

Die, decease, pass on, croak, check out, expire, go to one's reward.

Money, funds, cash, dough, bread, finances.

Boy, youth, young man, lad, adolescent, juvenile.

Fight, brawl, melee, scrap, quarrel, fracas, battle royal.

Thin, slender, skinny, slight, wispy, lean, willowy, gaunt, spindly, lanky, wiry.

Ill, sick, under the weather, delicate, infirm, peaked, indisposed, out of sorts.

A PRACTICE RUN

List synonyms (words with similar meanings) for each of the following words. Discuss the shades of meaning as you see them with a classmate to compare your understanding of the differences.

a. Understand _____

b. Old _____

c. Tell _____

d. Inquire _____

e. Stop _____

Select Words Accurately.   Knowledge of language also enables you to use words accurately. For example, *fewer* and *less* mean the same to some people. But careful users select *fewer* to mean smaller numbers of items (fewer snowflakes, fewer dollars) and *less* to mean reduced value, degree, or quantity (less snow, less money). Because they sound alike, the words *its* and *it's* are used incorrectly by some people. But those who know language

> • You should learn the accurate meanings of other words.

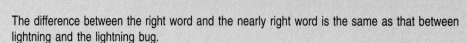
The difference between the right word and the nearly right word is the same as that between lightning and the lightning bug.

Mark Twain

know *its* is the possessive form of it (The dog ate its supper.), and *it's* means it is (It's too late to go now.). Similarly, careful writers use *continual* to mean a repeated but broken succession of events, and *continuous* to mean an unbroken succession. They write *farther* to express geographic distance and *further* to indicate more, or in addition in an abstract sense. They know that *learn* means to acquire knowledge and *teach* means to impart knowledge.

A PRACTICE RUN

Explain the differences in meaning for the word choices shown. Point out any words that cannot be used in the sentence.

1. The machine ran (continually) (continuously). _____

_____

2. His action (implies) (infers) that he accepts the criticism. _____

_____

3. Before buying anything, we (compare) (contrast) it with competing products. _____

_____

4. May I (loan) (borrow) your pen? _____

_____

5. This is an (effective) (efficient) plan. _____

_____

Grammar and Spelling

* The accepted standards of correctness help communication.

Although the language is changing, people in business are expected to know and follow the generally accepted standards of English. These standards have one basic purpose: to make the message as clear as possible so that the meaning will be shared successfully. The practical value of these standards is easily illustrated. In the following two sentences, the words are the same; only the punctuation differs. But what a difference the punctuation makes!

"The teacher," said the student, "is brilliant."
The teacher said, "The student is brilliant."

Here are two more sentences in which a small change in grammar makes a big difference in meaning.

> He looked at her cross.
> He looked at her crossly.

Established by centuries of use, the rules of grammar are based on custom and logical relationships. For example, the rules state that words must follow a definite sequence; altering the sequence changes the meaning. "A duck blind" means one thing while "a blind duck" means quite another.

• Clear writing requires that you follow the established rules of grammar.

Or, consider the rule concerning misplaced or dangling modifiers. Dangling modifiers confuse meaning by modifying the wrong words. On the surface this sentence may appear grammatically correct:

• Dangling modifiers confuse meaning.

> Believing that the price would drop, our purchasing agents were instructed not to buy.

However, the sentence would be correct only if the purchasing agents did the believing. In that case, knowing that the price would drop, they should also have known not to buy. Since the phrase "believing that the price would drop" cannot logically refer to the purchasing agents, it is described as dangling. The sentence is incorrect and the meaning is confused. The intended meaning was probably one of the following:

> Believing that the price would drop, we instructed our purchasing agents not to buy.
> Believing the price would drop, our purchasing agents decided not to buy.

Canadian business faces the additional challenge of defining current Canadian usage standards. Grammar and, more particularly, spelling are changing in Canada as the English language develops here. The influence of both British and American styles has been felt, but Canadian English is now recognized as a unique language form. *The Dictionary of Canadian English* was first published in 1967, and numerous dictionaries and style guides now exist for Canadian journalists, writers, and students.

• A unique challenge exists for Canadians.

Even so, the definition of "Canadian spelling" is under debate. For some words, Canadians have chosen to use the American spelling. Examples are *jail* for the British *gaol,* *curb* for *kerb,* and *reflection* for *reflexion.* In other cases, the British spelling remains. Canadians prefer *centre, cheque,* and *axe.* In still other cases, the preference varies from region to region, or from discipline to discipline. In general, newspapers and magazines follow the Canadian Press practice of using *-or* endings in words such as *color, labor,* and *behavior.* In other circles, *-our* is strongly preferred. However, the same groups may insist on *meter* rather than *metre.*

In this text, as with most Canadian publications, we have chosen a middle ground in response to current trends. We have preferred the *-our, -re* and *-ize* endings for words such as *behaviour, centre,* and *organize,* but have chosen *skillful* over *skilful,* and *skeptical* over *sceptical.* In your own writing, try to be consistent with like words. For example, do not mix *humor* with *colour,* or *metre* with *center,* or *realize* with *recognise.* Of course, if your instructor or the company who employs you has a style guide, follow that.

Idiom

As well as having a strong vocabulary and a sound grasp of the grammar, a proficient user of a language must master its idioms. By *idiom* we mean the way things are said in a language.

• Idiom is the way ideas are expressed in a language.

Much of our idiom has little rhyme or reason. For example, what is the logic in the word *up* in the sentence "Look up her name in the directory"? There really is none. This is just the wording we have developed to cover this meaning. Similarly, you "agree to" a proposal, but you "agree with" a person. Despite the seeming lack of logic, idioms must be used correctly if we want to be understood. Here

• There is little reason to some idioms, but violations offend and confuse the receiver.

are some illustrations of common errors in idiom. Be sure that you use the correct form.

FAULTY IDIOM	CORRECT IDIOM
Authority about	Authority on
Comply to	Comply with
Equally as bad	Equally bad
In accordance to	In accordance with
In search for	In search of
Listen at	Listen to
Seldom or ever	Seldom if ever
Superior than	Superior to

The goal here is not to list all the rules of correct usage, but rather to stress the importance of correct spelling, punctuation, and grammar to communicate clearly and to create a positive impression. Although some of the standards may appear arbitrary or unnecessary, they do reduce misunderstanding and make communication more precise. A self-analysis test, along with the corrections and explanations, is included in Appendix A at the end of this text. Use it to evaluate your skill in this area. As a final note, a handbook or workbook of grammar is an excellent investment.

A PRACTICE RUN

Correct any errors in idiom you find in these examples.

1. The purchasing officer has gone in search for a substitute product. _____

   _____

2. This letter is equally as bad. _____

   _____

3. She is an authority about mutual funds. _____

   _____

4. When the sale is over with, we will restock. _____

   _____

5. Our computer is different than theirs. _____

   _____

LISTENING SKILLS
The Role of Listening in Business

As our society moves faster, so does business. Information must be exchanged quickly because timely decisions mean thousands of dollars. While technology such as e-mail offers new ways to send and store messages, voice communication, in person or by telephone, radio or television, is still the common way to transfer information from one person to another. Speaking the message is one part of the process; listening to receive the message is another.

In a business, internal communication requires good listening skills for telephone and face-to-face conversations, voice-mail messages, briefings and meetings, instructional sessions, policy review sessions, and so on. In addition, it is important to listen to the informal grapevine, since, as we have seen, it plays a large role in the everyday functioning of a company. External communication requires listening for telephone and face-to-face conversations, interviews, luncheons, meetings, conferences, and speeches. Listening carefully to customers and clients is seen as good service. It is a fundamental of good customer relations and continuing customer satisfaction. With listening as a key element in all of these activities, it is not surprising to find a correlation between effective listening and productivity in the workplace.

• Effective listening and productivity go together.

A study on listening was designed to find the relationships between listening skills and level of employment. It found that good listeners were more likely to be promoted and that most of the supervisors had better listening skills than nonsupervisors. "What we can conclude from this study is that listening is related . . . to success at work. Better listeners held higher level positions and were promoted more often than those with less developed listening abilities. . . . It [listening] can enhance one's job performance, and perhaps promotion, raises, status, and power are more attainable for the better listener."[2]

• Research links listening with success at work.

Most business people spend over 50 percent of their work day listening. Those in management positions estimate their listening time to be higher yet.[3] Despite its importance, listening is an activity we seldom think about. As with walking and other basic skills, we began listening as children. Although we do a lot of listening, we may not listen well. Just as some people develop back pain because they walk improperly, so some people misunderstand or make mistakes because they do not listen effectively.

• Since most of us can expect to spend half of our working day listening, the importance of listening should not be overlooked.

Not all hearing is good listening. Because we hear so many voices, it may be understandable that we do not listen well 100 percent of the time. Moreover, there are occasions when effective listening means selective listening. In order to listen to what is important, we must filter out and not listen to the unimportant. At other times, effective listening means hearing what we might prefer not to hear. For example, effective listening may mean listening to people who have different viewpoints, strong opinions, or emotional reactions that we may find unsettling.

• Effective listening is a complex activity.

The Nature of Listening

Effective listening has four parts: hearing, concentrating, filtering, and remembering.

Hearing (receiving the message). Because our sense of hearing has limitations, we should do what we can to reduce interference so that the sound of the speaker's voice reaches us clearly. Perhaps we can eliminate noises by closing a door or turning off a radio. Sometimes we can move closer to the speaker or ask him or her to speak more slowly. The first basic step in listening must be the successful receiving of the sounds.

• Effective listening begins with hearing the message.

Concentrating (paying attention to the message). Concentrating requires physical and mental attending. *Physical attending* means arranging the physical surroundings to set the scene for the speaker and the listener. It helps the listener concentrate and demonstrates attention to the speaker. Steps for physical attending include facing the speaker and moving to a comfortable distance, usually about half a metre for face-to-face conversations. If seated, the listener could lean forward slightly. Eliminating from the setting such physical distractions as the sun's glare, a pile of work, an active computer screen, or a

• Concentrating requires physical and mental attending.

---

[2] Beverly Davenport Sypher, R. N. Bostrom, and J. H. Seiber, "Listening, Communication Abilities, and Success at Work," *The Journal of Business Communication* 26 (Fall 1989): 293–301.

[3] Lyman K. Steil, L. L. Barker, and K. W. Watson, *Effective Listening: Key to Your Success* (Reading, Mass.: Addison-Wesley, 1983).

ringing telephone helps the listener pay attention. And finally, making eye contact with the speaker prepares the listener to concentrate.

Mental attending is the willingness to concentrate and focus on the speaker. Because it is invisible, it is harder to measure and define. Steps for mental attending include a willing decision to select this message and not the competing ones that come from external or internal sources. Total concentration for more than a few moments is difficult since thoughts tend to wander. Finding reasons for concentrating, such as the importance of the topic or courtesy to the speaker, helps refocus thoughts on the subject of discussion. The effort required to control those errant thoughts means a good listener will be tired at the end of a conversation or speech.

• Filtering is the process of giving symbols meanings through the unique contents of each person's mind.

Filtering (making sense of the message).   From your study of the communication process in Chapter 1, you know that your mind serves as a filter through which you give meaning to incoming symbols and messages. This *filtering process* allows you to associate the symbols of the message with previously known information. Once you have assigned your meanings and sorted out the relationships, you should ask questions to be sure you have understood the message as it was intended.

• Remembering means to store the message in the mind so that it can be recalled later.

Remembering (storing the message).   *Remembering* what has been heard by storing the idea in the mind so that it can be recalled later is the final activity involved in listening. Usually, we retain only a little of what we have heard and only for a short time—perhaps a few minutes or hours. It is understandable that we forget some casual comments almost as we hear them. However, according to authorities, we also quickly forget most of the message in a speech or lecture. Although we listen and pay attention at the time, only a small amount of the information can be recalled after a few days unless we take specific steps to improve this result.[4]

Good listeners use memory aids such as organizing the points they have understood in some meaningful order. For example, they may rank the ideas by importance or order them in a time sequence. Using initial letters as memory aids often helps. It is easy to remember the major elements of marketing (place, product, price, promotion) because they all begin with *P.* Making notes during or immediately after the session also helps the memory because writing provides a review.

---

[4]Estimates vary, but most references suggest about a 25 percent retention rate. While this figure is often quoted, it is difficult to prove exactly. For our purposes, it is enough to know that the loss is significant and a cause for concern.

Active Listening

From the discussion of the nature of listening, it is clear that good listeners are not passive. Good listeners are actively involved in the communication process because they are trying to understand the complete message as the sender intended it. The listener's attitude should be, "What does this message I am hearing mean to you, the sender? When I understand your viewpoint, I can better articulate mine."

Use All the Clues.   Active listeners use their eyes to help them understand a message. A large percentage of the meaning of a message is carried by posture, distance, gesture, facial expression, and other visible cues. Therefore, all of these clues must be noted. Active listeners use their ears to hear more than words. They also hear the way words are spoken (*paralanguage*). They hear tone, speed, volume, and emphasis. (For more about paralanguage, see the discussion of nonverbal communication.) Active listeners gather all of the clues they can to understand the full meaning of the message.

- -

A PRACTICE RUN

Evaluate the supervisor's responses to these two employees who are handing in completed assignments. What did the supervisor miss in the employees' messages?

Situation # 1

Employee 1:   Here's that research report. Some pretty interesting results!

Supervisor: Ummm. Read this one, will you? And give me the highlights in a synopsis that I can take to the meeting this afternoon.

_____

_____

_____

Situation # 2

Employee 2:   I've finally finished this report!

Supervisor: OK. Just drop it there on the desk.

_____

_____

_____

- -

Use Door Openers, Encouragers, and Following Questions.   As well as watching for clues, active listeners can take the initiative and use door openers, encouragers, and following questions to get a more complete understanding of the sender's intended message.

Door openers are general questions to begin or change the direction of a conversation. They indicate an interest and a willingness to listen. Door openers include questions such as "How is your report going?", "Have you thought about where to spend your holidays?", and "Did you see the paper this morning?"

Encouragers are short phrases or nonverbal cues to show the continuing interest of the listener and to encourage the speaker to say more. Nods and smiles, and words such as "Oh, yes," "I see," and "Really?" tell the speaker that the listener is still attentive. Nonwords such as "Uhuh," "Hmmm," and "Ah" are also used. The point is to let the speaker know he or she should continue.

* Door openers are general questions to begin a conversation.

* Encouragers are short phrases or nonverbal cues to keep a conversation going.

Following questions also encourage further discussion, but they refer more directly to the topic of discussion. Clarifying questions may be following questions. Examples are "What did you do next?", "How did you finally get the report you needed?", and "Were you sure that she had the file?"

By using door openers, encouragers, and following questions, a listener will be actively involved in the process of receiving and understanding the full message.

Levels of Listening

Effective listening can be divided into three levels. The one you choose will depend upon the situation.

Content Listening for Information.   When the purpose of the communication is to exchange factual data, the appropriate level is *content listening*. To be sure that the pertinent facts are remembered, find the main idea and relate the supporting evidence to it. Look for similarities and differences between the new information and things you already know. Visualizing the content of the message can help, as in the example below when the purpose is to get directions. Asking clarifying questions and paraphrasing (restating what you have heard) ensures that you have understood the facts correctly and gives you an opportunity to review. In this example of asking directions, the exchange includes a question, an answer, clarifying questions and answers, and a final paraphrase.

> "How do I get from here to Northwood?"
> "It's not far. The easiest way is to continue in this direction for about eight more blocks and turn left at the East End Grocery. That's about 72nd Street. About three blocks will bring you to the parking entrance."
> "How big is the East End Grocery? Is there a major intersection before I get to it?"
> "Yes, there are lights at 70th Street and the grocery has a very large sign, so you won't miss the turn."
> "Great. So it's about eight blocks to the East End Grocery, then turn left and go north about three blocks to the parking gate. Thanks for your help."

Business applications for content listening are learning how to use new equipment, taking routine telephone messages, or following instructions.

Critical Listening for Evaluating Information.   There are times when we need to gather information and also test it. In these situations, *critical listening* is appropriate. (As with critical thinking, the word *critical* is used in the sense of measuring or evaluating, not in the colloquial sense of being negative.) A persuasive message is one that requires listeners to hear and evaluate the content. To accomplish this task, consider why the speaker is trying to persuade you. If the speaker is a sales representative who works on commission, you may want to investigate the product claims more closely than if the speaker is a friend who has successfully used the product for some time. Secondly, try to examine the speaker's qualifications and credibility. You might ask direct questions about the speaker's background, or you might listen for any clues the speaker gives. Your goal is to decide whether or not you can rely on this person as a source of information. Thirdly, while listening to the message, look for sound logic and evidence. You may want to challenge some statements. At least you will look for proof of claims made and for a correct interpretation without distortion. Sort out facts from opinions, and be sure that you have enough concrete information to evaluate the claims or justify the action suggested. Finally, when listening critically, take into account your own biases and preconceived ideas because you want your assessment to be objective.

Business applications for critical listening include purchasing and sales, new policy and procedure decisions, and planning meetings.

Empathic Listening for Understanding and Evaluating Facts and Feelings.   *Empathic listening,* sometimes called *reflective listening,* demands more effort from the listener. Empathic listening recognizes that the facts or information alone may not carry the full message because human beings are social and emotional. We hear the facts, but we understand the full message by listening for the feeling as well. If the message is expressed with emotion, a good listener will identify the emotion and assess its significance in the situation. A decision is made whether to address the content, the emotion, or both. If only the content is selected, the listener is using content listening as discussed earlier. However, it is wise to make a mental note of the emotion. If empathic listening is needed later in the conversation, remembering that emotion will help the listener understand the message.

If the listener decides to address the emotion, the usual pattern is to reflect or mirror the emotion in a statement such as "I can see that this has been worrying you" or "You're feeling angry because the delays may make you look bad." The empathic or reflective statement attempts to address the emotion so that the speaker can move on to the task of dealing with the facts of the situation in a logical way.

A statement such as "This stupid computer has messed up my files again" requires attention to the emotions of frustration, fear, or being overwhelmed. Once these emotions are addressed, the listener can find out more about what has happened and save the files, if possible. "I'm ready to kick this computer down the stairs" requires attention to the feeling and not the exact content. The speaker likely means he or she is frustrated by a problem, not that the computer is in danger of being destroyed. "Clear the building. There's a fire!" requires attention to the content first, regardless of the feeling. Although there is anxiety in the speaker's voice, a response such as "You're anxious because there is a fire danger" is not the appropriate one. However, hearing the anxiety should motivate the listener to respond by leaving the building promptly.

* Here are three examples.

Situations calling for empathic listening in business include determining how important a particular task is, how rigid a dress code policy is, how understanding a supervisor is about personal calls, time off, and so on.

A PRACTICE RUN

Describe other business situations for each level of listening.

Content listening would be appropriate if _____

_____

_____

Critical listening would be appropriate if _____

_____

Empathic listening would be appropriate if _____

_____

Improving your listening is largely a matter of mental conditioning—of concentrating on the activity of sensing. You have to want to improve it, for listening is a willful act. If you are like most of us, you are often tempted not to listen, or you just find it easier not to listen. Listening may be work.

* To improve your listening, you must want to improve it.

NONVERBAL SKILLS

The Powerful Role of Nonverbal Communication

Whether you are speaker, listener, writer, or reader, you will need to be aware of the impact of nonverbal communication. Usually, as in this example, nonverbal cues are used to supplement and reinforce the words of a message. A political speaker is promising

* Nonverbal cues reinforce or undermine a message.

funding for job-creation programs. By pointing at the audience while saying, "There will be jobs in towns like yours, and yours, and yours," the speaker reinforces the message, fitting the words and the gestures together. However, nonverbal cues that do not match the words will overpower them. Picture a jogger who, red in the face and gasping for air, says, "Sure, I can go another 20 laps." You dismiss the words as bravado almost immediately. Because nonverbal cues have a powerful place in the communication equation, we need to study them more closely.

Nature of Nonverbal Communication

- Nonverbal communication means all communication without words.

Nonverbal communication means all communication that occurs without words. For a speaker and listener, it includes general appearance, gestures, facial expression, tone of voice, volume, and voice quality. For a writer and reader, it includes the quality of the paper, the speed of the reply, the channel chosen, the apparent care with correctness, and so on. As you can see, the subject is a broad one.

Because there is so much variety in nonverbal communication, it is quite vague and imprecise. For instance, a frown on someone's forehead is sometimes interpreted to mean worry. In other situations, a frown could mean the person is deep in thought, is showing disapproval, or has a headache.

However, being vague or imprecise does not mean that nonverbal communication is weak. On the contrary, it is very powerful. Consider the number of meanings the phrase *Okay* can convey by simple changes in tone or emphasis. Try reading these variations: Okay? **OKAY!** Oookay. Hokay. While it is difficult to suggest the tone of voice through print, you will have some idea of the variations. As an aside, the different type styles (italics, bold, full capitalization) are nonverbal cues.

- Our culture influences our interpretation of nonverbal cues.

The number of possible meanings is multiplied even more when we consider the cross-cultural side of communication (Chapter 20). Our culture teaches us about body positions, movements, and various factors that affect human relationships, such as intimacy, space, and time. Thus, the meanings we give to nonverbal symbols will vary depending on our culture and our conditioning.

- Be sensitive to intended nonverbal meanings. Go beyond the obvious.

Because of the many possible meanings for nonverbal cues, you need to be sensitive to what others intend and to make some allowance for possible error in the meaning you receive. As a listener, you need to go beyond the obvious to discover what people intend with their nonverbal symbols. Perhaps one good way to grasp the significance of this suggestion is to look at the intended meanings you have for the nonverbal symbols you use. Think for a few moments about a smile on your face. When do you use it? What do you mean by it? Do you always mean the same thing? What could it look like to others? Could it be interpreted differently? Would someone from a different culture give a different meaning to it? If you are aware of the potential for multiple meanings in your own nonverbal symbols, you can appreciate the need for sensitivity and flexibility in interpreting those used by others.

Types of Nonverbal Communication

In Oral Communication.   We will examine body language, paralanguage, space, and time. These types are especially important to our discussion of speaking and listening.

Body Language.   Much of the information we send to others without using words is sent through the physical movements of our bodies. If we wave our arms and hands, stand at attention, slouch in a chair, frown, smile, stare into space, or wear formal clothing, we convey certain meanings. The face and eyes, gestures, posture, and physical appearance reflect the emotions in particular.

The face and eyes are by far the most important features of body language. For example, happiness, surprise, fear, anger, and sadness usually require definite facial expressions and eye patterns. The difference between a genuine smile and an imitation is in the eyes. Unless a smile begins with a change in the eyes, it is interpreted as insincere or forced. You should be aware that your true feelings may be showing in your eyes and face regardless of the words you are saying.

In addition, gestures are another way we send nonword messages. Through the movement of our arms, legs, hands, torsos, and heads, we can accent and reinforce our verbal messages. For example, observe the hand movements of another person while he or she is talking. Consider whether this person is natural or sporadic with such hand movements. Are the same gestures repeated over and over? As you observe these gestures, form a picture of the internal, emotional state of the person. Do the nonverbal cues fit the words and the way they are said? For example, the louder someone speaks, the more expansive the gestures usually are. If so, the message is clear and unified.

Another area of body language is physical appearance. It is suggested that in today's busy world, we make assessments based on appearance because we meet so many new people about whom we know nothing. A person's appearance makes an immediate impression and influences how a message is interpreted. Business dress carries with it the impression of confidence and authority before the person even begins to speak. The speaker's gestures, facial features, and posture will be perceived in relation to that first impression made by the appearance. Accordingly, you want to make sure that your appearance fits the situation and makes the impression you want.

Paralanguage.   *Paralanguage* is the way we say words—the tone and emphasis we use. Child care workers will use an exaggerated intonation range to make putting away toys sound like fun. The enthusiasm in their voices will persuade a child to participate in the activity, and, frequently, enjoy the task. Intonation is one of the elements of paralanguage.

Emphasis is another element. Consider the differences in meanings created by changing the emphasis in this sentence.

Sentence Example	Meaning
I bought the CD I love.	You didn't buy it; I did.
I *bought* the CD I love.	I didn't borrow it; I bought it.
I bought the CD *I* love.	It isn't your favourite; it's mine.
I bought the CD I *love.*	I don't just like it; I love it.

While English is not a tonal language, it does depend on intonation and tone of voice for clarity of meaning. Perhaps you have had the experience of being hurt or upset not by someone's words *per se,* but by the way the words were said. Paralanguage is at work when you suspect that "a joke" was not really intended as a joke but as a criticism. The speaker may even ask "What did I say? Can't you take a joke?" In truth, it was not a joke because a message is not carried in the words alone. It is not even primarily carried in the words, but rather through the accompanying nonverbal cues, including paralanguage.

* In oral communication, there are four common types of nonverbal communication: (1) body language, (2) paralanguage, (3) space, and (4) time.
* Our body language sends nonword messages.

* The face and eyes are the most important.

* Gestures send nonword messages.

* Physical appearance of the body—clothing, hair, jewellery, cosmetics, etc.—also communicates.

* Paralanguage is the way we say words.

* Paralanguage does change the meaning of a message.

The words "I'm not mad" said slowly, deliberately and almost on the same pitch will say to the listener that you are furious but determined to keep control. If said casually with a slight drop in intonation at the end, the listener is more likely to believe the basic meaning in the words. The speaker apparently is not upset.

Paralanguage is a powerful communicator of emotion. If the reaction of your listener is not at all what you expected, you would be wise to consider whether paralanguage is playing a role.

• Paralanguage is a powerful communicator of emotion.

Space.   Another type of nonverbal communication involves space. How we use space and how comfortable we feel in certain spaces tell much about us. Each of us has a space language crafted by our culture.

• Space is another type of nonverbal language.

Authorities tell us that North Americans create four different types of space—intimate (physical contact to about 0.5 metre); personal (0.5 to 1.5 metres); social (1.5 to 3.5 metres); and public (3.5 metres to range of seeing and hearing).[5] In each of these spaces, our communication behaviours differ and, therefore, convey different meanings. For example, consider the volume of your voice when someone is less than half a metre from you. How much eye contact do you have with that person? Now picture the person four metres away. The difference, caused by the distance involved, is obvious.

• Four types of space exist: (1) intimate; (2) personal, (3) social, and (4) public. Communication behaviour differs in each.

Our perception of appropriate (polite) distances for different circumstances is shaped by our cultural background. It is one of the least-exact, nonverbal cues but one that is felt strongly. For example, in the North American business scene, the person who stands too close tends to be seen negatively, perhaps as pushy or invasive. But the definition of "too close" is vague. It varies from person to person. Thus, you will need to be sensitive to the spaces of others—especially those from different cultures.

Time.   A fourth type of nonverbal communication involves time. There is a time language. That is, how we give meaning to time communicates to others. To illustrate, think about how you manage your daily schedule. Do you arrive early for most appointments or do you like to be just in time? Do you feel that 15 minutes after the scheduled start of a meeting is just in time because meetings seldom start when they are supposed to? How you respond to time communicates to others, and, of course, their attitudes about time communicate to you. In our time-conscious society, time seems to be an important part of the messages we send and receive. Time orientations are not always the same. Especially in the international arena, understanding another person's time language requires effort and adaptation.

• Time is a fourth type of nonverbal communication.

In Written Communication.   We have seen one type of nonverbal cue in written communication already. In the discussion of paralanguage, we tried to imitate tone of voice and emotion by using special effects. The use of type fonts and features such as italics and underlining can be used to add emphasis to written words. **Bold lettering** suggests **authority** and confidence; underlining reinforces a point and adds an emphatic note; and uppercase lettering imitates VOLUME and has the nickname SHOUTING.

Slightly more subtle are the meanings taken from nonverbal cues such as the quality and colour of the paper, the quality of the print, and the attractiveness of the page layout. If an invitation with hand-lettering on fine vellum paper arrives by special courier saying, "You are invited to the President's Luncheon," the message carries more prestige and importance than an e-mail note with the same message.

• The physical appearance of the document makes a lasting impression.

The importance of appearance is easily illustrated. Assume that you have a choice of reading either of two business reports on the same subject. One report has long paragraphs. Its pages appear solid with type. The second report has short paragraphs and thus provides frequent rest stops. At first glance, you can see the rest stops in the white spaces. Now, which would you choose? No doubt, you would prefer the report with short paragraphs. It is more inviting, and it appears less difficult. Perhaps the difference is largely psychological, but it is a very real difference.

• Most readers prefer to read short paragraphs.

[5]Edward T. Hall, *The Hidden Dimension* (New York: Anchor Books, 1990):114–129.

The appearance of a letter or a report plays a significant role in communicating the message. Sloppy work reflects unfavourably on the writer, the company, and the message itself. Attractively displayed messages reflect favourably and give an impression of competence and care. Moreover, their attractiveness tells readers, "You're important and deserving of a carefully prepared document." Chapter 21 concentrates on the physical presentation of letters and reports, but it is not too early to mention the effect of a document's appearance on the reader.

* The appearance of written documents affects the reader's response.

This principle of appearance carries over to the computer screen too. This principle has changed the nature of the Internet from full screens of text to short clips of information supported by colourful graphics and easy-to-use links to other web sites. We will see its impact again in Chapter 10 when we discuss the format for effective e-mail messages.

* Documents on a computer screen require the same attention to appearance.

Of course, there are the positive and negative impressions made by spelling, grammar, and punctuation. If the writer does not take enough care to spell correctly, the reader pauses to ask, "Will there be adequate attention to the details of my business with this company?"

* Spelling and grammar contribute to the nonverbal message.

ADAPTATION SKILLS

The Basic Need for Adaptation

People are not all the same. They do not all have the same cultural background. They do not all have the same amount of time, nor the same level of interest in a subject. As we saw earlier in the communication model, these differences between people can cause distortion in the intended message. To reduce the chances of misunderstanding, a sender uses adaptation. By *adaptation* we mean fitting the message to the specific receiver. Sometimes, it just involves being friendly and treating people in the way they like to be treated. Sometimes, it involves skillfully choosing words to make a desired impression on that particular receiver. To communicate clearly, you should know the receiver and adapt your message to fit that person's mind.

* For communication to be clear, it must be adapted to the receiver.

Adaptation Technique

The goal of adaptation is to communicate clearly by demonstrating an understanding of the receiver's point of view. Some of the skills required are the ability to visualize the receiver, to use the you-viewpoint, to use technical language appropriately, and to simplify or condense a complex topic when necessary.

* Demonstrate your understanding of your receiver's point of view.

Visualizing the Receiver.   Adapting your message begins with visualizing the receiver. That is, you form a mental picture by trying to answer some basic questions. How informed will the receiver be about the subject? What level of interest can be expected? Will the receiver have time to consider the message carefully or just to get the main points? What will the receiver be expecting? How familiar will the receiver be with technical terms and jargon? What feelings and opinions will already be in his or her mind? In short, you consider whatever you believe could have some effect on the receiver's understanding of your message.

* Adaptation begins with imagining what the receiver knows, feels, thinks.

Using the You-Viewpoint.   The you-viewpoint is an attitude in the sender's mind that places the receiver in the centre of things. The sender shows understanding for the receiver's point of view by deliberately choosing words that focus on the receiver. It is a client-centred approach to business that emphasizes the receiver (*you* and *your*) and de-emphasizes the sender (*I, we,* and *our*).

* Using the you-viewpoint means the sender decides to emphasize the receiver's interests.

You-viewpoint would explain credit terms from the client viewpoint by pointing out the benefits.

* These examples illustrate the use of the you-viewpoint.

"Your new charge account has been opened and is ready for you to use starting today. There are no credit charges if you pay your account before the 15th."

On the other hand, a we-viewpoint message could take this form.

"We are pleased to have your new account. We will charge interest on your outstanding balance unless you pay in full before or on the 15th."

Seeing these words, most readers would see a company concerned primarily with making money rather than customer service.

As a second example, a person presenting good news could say, "I am happy to report that I have your special order ready." Or they could begin with the you-viewpoint words "Your special order is ready to go." The message content is much the same, but the effect is different.

The third case is that of an advertizing copywriter who must describe the merits of a razor. Knowing the value of the you-viewpoint perhaps better than any other group, advertizers would never write: "We make Willet razors in three weights—light, medium, and heavy." An advertizer would place the reader at the centre and write about the product in reader-satisfaction language: "Your Willet razor will suit you to perfection. Just choose the weight that is right for your beard—light, medium, or heavy."

- You-viewpoint is an attitude of mind involving more than the use of *you* and *your*.

You-viewpoint involves more than using second person pronouns. *You* and *your* can appear prominently in sentences that emphasize the we-viewpoint, as in this example explaining terms of credit: "If you do not pay by the 15th, you must pay a penalty." The word *you* does not hide the true emphasis of "I want my money." You-viewpoint is an attitude of mind that is reflected in word choice.

. . . .

A PRACTICE RUN

Write you-viewpoint sentences to cover each of the situations described.

1. We will be pleased to deliver your order by the 12th. _____

_____

2. (From a memorandum to employees) We take pleasure in announcing that, effective today, the company will give a 20 percent discount on all purchases made by its employees. _____

_____

3. We make our file folders in three widths for your convenience. _____

_____

4. We are happy to report approval of your application for membership. _____

_____

5. Our long experience in the book business has enabled us to provide the best customer service possible. _____

_____

6. So that we can sell at discount prices, we do not permit returns of merchandise. _____

_____

7. You will want to buy from the enclosed catalogue. _____

_____

8. Madame Benoit's Canadian Pea Soup is hearty and delicious. _____

   _____

9. We can't give you the 2 percent discount because you didn't pay within 10 days. _____

   _____

10. We are pleased to inform you that we will permit you to attend classes on company time if the course relates to your
    work assignment and, therefore, benefits the company. _____

    _____

Using Technical Language.   A third point about adaptation technique concerns the use
of technical jargon. If you had to write a message to technicians, you would use the
theoretical and technical terms these people know well (as long as you also understand
these words fully!). The same topic discussed with labourers would include clear,
practical instructions that they could quickly turn into action. In both cases, you would
select words that are best for the intended receiver.

The following paragraphs from two company reports illustrate this basic principle of
adaptation. The writer of the first report visualized the readers as people who wanted a
general picture of company finances. Detailed figures could appear in accompanying financial
statements for reference. The text gives the overall picture in non-technical language.

Total sales for 1996 were approximately $117 million, which was slightly higher than
the year before. After deducting all expenses, there was a profit of $4.6 million, compared
with $2.8 million for 1995. Because of these increased profits, annual dividend payments
per share have increased from the 50 cents paid over the last 10 years to 75 cents this year.

The writer of the second report believed that the typical reader would be a stockbroker,
chartered accountant, financial analyst, or banker who would be familiar with financial
terms. These readers would need more specific information.

The corporation's investment in three unconsolidated subsidiaries (all in the development
stage) and in 50 percent–owned companies was $42.2 million on December 31, 1993,
and the excess of the investments in certain companies over net asset value at dates of acquisition was $1.76 million. The corporation's equity in the net assets as of December 31,
1996, was $41.8 million and in the results of operations for the years ended December
31, 1996 and 1995, was $1.35 million and $887,500. Dividend income was $750,000
and $388,000 for the years 1996 and 1995, respectively.

Which writer was right? Both, because each wrote for the intended audience. Avoiding
financial terminology, simplifying the format of the numbers, and giving the bottom line
figures made the first paragraph easier for the layperson to understand. Using exact
terminology, specific dates and figures, and significant background detail made the second
example credible to a financial expert. Both examples illustrate the technique of
adaptation. They use different approaches for different audiences, which is what you
should try to do.

Simplifying or Condensing a Message.   Assume you need to write for someone who
does not know much about your topic. Adapting to this receiver means writing simply.
You will have to select from your extensive knowledge the key points your reader will
need, and explain each point fully. You may need to include definitions of terms and give
examples to illustrate the main idea.

You also may need to condense your message if your receiver does not have the time
to study the details. A busy executive will want a brief outline and the conclusion and/or

• Often, you will need to simplify
your message.

A group of neighbours, including an author, a farmer, an optician, a cigar-maker, a tailor, an astronomer, and an electrician came over for a barbecue. "How is your business doing?" I asked. Which guest gave which reply?

"My business is looking up."

"Mine is going up in smoke."

"Mine is all write."

"Mine is just sew, sew."

"Mine is growing."

"Mine is light."

"Mine is looking better."

recommendation with supporting detail available for reference if needed. What about all those little points and clever illustrations you found so interesting? It may seem difficult to omit them or relegate them to an appendix, but, for the sake of clear communication, you should condense and select your material to suit your reader.

* If you write for one person in a group, you may miss the others.

Adapting to Multiple Receivers.   Adapting your message to one receiver or to a uniform group is not too difficult, but frequently your receivers are not a homogeneous group. Differences may be based in language, culture, religion, geographic region, experience, education, age, wealth, and so on. Official government policies such as bilingualism and multiculturalism recognize some of these differences. Faced with such diversity, how do you adapt so that the subgroups in your audience will understand and accept your message? One way is to look for common ground so that as many people as possible will feel comfortable. An insurance agent's year-end newsletter to clients could use a general form of greeting, such as "Best Wishes for the New Year." Similarly, public schools have adapted to their multicultural constituency by presenting Winter Concerts rather than Christmas Concerts. Winter is something all Canadian families experience in December, while Christmas is not.

As another example, consider the challenge of writing the instruction manual for a computer software package. Some of the purchasers will be experienced computer users, while others will be novices. Clearly, you have to consider the least experienced computer users or they will be lost; but in doing that, you risk boring the knowledgeable users. To adapt to this mixed group, write simply with adequate detail for beginners and provide short cuts for the more experienced users. These short cuts could be in the form of headings or summaries that guide the reader quickly, a short test with instructions to move to another section if the reader passes the test, or very precise indexing to allow the experienced user to select the section needed.

Each situation calls for sensitivity to the uniqueness of the audience. The perfect message, one that appears to address personally each member of a diverse group, is not possible. However, creativity in applying the principle of adaptation will go a long way toward achieving that goal of perfection.

A PRACTICE RUN

Explain how you would apply the basic principles of adaptation to each of the following writing assignments:

a. An editorial in a company newsletter. _____

_____

b. A memorandum to Joan Branch, supervisor of an assembly department, concerning a change in assembly operations.

_____

_____

c. A memo to a new clerk to accompany a brochure explaining pension benefits. _____

_____

d. A letter to company stockholders explaining measures taken to improve the company's financial position after a year-end loss.

_____

_____

Governing Role of Adaptation

The preceding discussion shows that adaptation is basic to communication. It is so basic that you will need to apply it to all the writing instructions in the pages ahead. For example, much of what will be said about writing technique will stress simplicity—using simple words, short sentences, and short paragraphs. You will need to think of simplicity in terms of adaptation. Specifically, you will need to keep in mind that what is simple for one person may not be simple for another and may be too simple for a third. Keep in mind the purpose of adaptation—to improve communication by fitting the message to the receiver—as you put into practice the principles in this text.

* Adaptation underlies all that will be said about writing. Apply it to the other writing instructions.

A SUMMARY OF LEARNING OUTCOMES FROM THIS CHAPTER

This chapter identifies five essential skill areas for effective communication, namely: critical thinking, language, listening, nonverbal cues, and adaptation.

Critical thinking is thorough thinking based on knowledge and logic. Following the 6-C approach is useful for critical thinking. The steps are as follows:

1. Clarify the problem and state it simply to keep your thoughts on track.

2. Collect all the information you need.

3. Choose the evidence that is most useful based on sufficiency, relevance, and acceptability, which means being sure there is enough data that is pertinent and reliable.

4. Combine ideas by sorting them into categories for comparison and contrast. Watch for emerging patterns and build new ideas for consideration.

5. Check your work for logical thought and accuracy of thought.

6. Conclude by making a decision.

Language skills play an important role in effective communication because words are the common symbols of communication. Developing a strong vocabulary is important for choosing those symbols precisely and correctly. Studying shades of difference in the meaning of words (*fight, brawl, fracas, donnybrook, battle royal*) that are similar but different, and learning standard grammar, spelling, and idiom avoids confusion and miscommunication.

Effective listening is a complex activity that can be improved with practice. Listening involves hearing (receiving the message), concentrating (paying attention to the message), filtering (making sense of the message), and remembering (storing the message for later use). To be successful, the listener must actively participate in the communication process by using all the clues including nonverbal cues and by using door openers, encouragers, and following questions to encourage the speaker.

Three levels of listening can be identified. Content listening is primarily concerned with accuracy of the factual message. Critical listening is used to understand the message accurately and evaluate it. Empathic or reflective listening, the most demanding level for the listener, requires the listener to understand the factual information as well as the emotional. The listener must decide how significant the emotion is to the full meaning of the message and respond appropriately.

Nonverbal cues can either reinforce or undermine the verbal message. If they conflict with the words of a message, most people will believe the nonverbal cues. Nonverbal cues vary widely in meaning. They are usually culturally defined.

Oral communication has four major types of nonverbal cues. They are body language, paralanguage, space, and time. Written communication also includes nonverbal cues in such elements as type fonts, layout, and spelling.

The skill of adapting your message to your receiver involves knowing and understanding who the receiver is. Using you-viewpoint, you construct your message to suit the receiver's interests, needs, and knowledge. The need to use technical language, to use simple language, or to condense a message is determined by the sender's analysis of the receiver.

QUESTIONS FOR DISCUSSION ▶ Critical Thinking

Picture the situation as you read the following description.

> "There was an accident near the parkade on campus. A van was just turning the corner and—crunch! Fortunately neither Professor Heron nor the student was hurt, but it took fifteen minutes to release the bicycle from the bumper. The student laughed it off, but Professor Heron was angry because the accident made him late for class."

Now read this more complete description.

> There was an accident near the parkade on campus. A van, driven by a student, was just turning the corner and—crunch!

Professor Heron had ridden into the van. His bike was caught in the rear bumper. Fortunately, neither person was hurt, but it took fifteen minutes to release the bicycle from the bumper. The student laughed it off, but Professor Heron was angry because the accident made him late for class.

What does this exercise reveal about your preconceptions? Discuss your reactions.

▶Language Skills

A fellow student says, "I've never been a good writer. But I have other places to put my study time. I'm a management major. I'll have secretaries to handle my writing for me." Give this student your best advice, including the reasoning behind it.

▶Listening Skills

1. "Effective listening is the key to productivity." Discuss.
2. "Conferences are OK because I don't have to do anything. I just sit and listen." Explain the error in this thinking.
3. What is the purpose of encouragers in the active listening process? Distinguish door openers from following questions.
4. Have someone read a list of 15 nouns. After you have listened to the list, write down (a) the last two items, (b) the first two items, and (c) as many as you can recall. Interpret your results.

▶Nonverbal Skills

1. "What's wrong with people? They always think I'm mad at them!" What nonverbal cues could be behind the miscommunication this person is experiencing?
2. In a small group, have someone say a simple sentence several different ways, varying the emphasis and tone. The others note the meaning they got from the sentence each time. Compare the results and discuss the power and accuracy of paralanguage.

▶Adaptation Skills

1. "Technical words are so precise. They say so much in so short a time. I think they should always be used to get the message across as fast as possible." When is this idea correct? When is it incorrect?
2. "You-viewpoint, client orientation, adaptation to the receiver. It sounds like a lot of work. Is it really worth it?" Answer this question using your own experience with being a customer.

CASE 2-1

Imagine that you are responsible for part of the programming on the Discovery Channel. You need an expert for tomorrow to explain a recent discovery in outer space. You have narrowed the choice to three candidates and now must select one for a live, on-air interview for the general science program. The goal of this program is to make science interesting and accessible for adults and teens. These are your possible experts.

1. Professor Bob Doull is an engineer and physicist from a well-known Canadian university. Prof. Doull conducts space research and teaches. He also writes for scientific journals. He is an advisor and resource person for the science centre and planetarium.

2. Dr. Peter Dimitrou is a world-renowned physicist and astronomer. Dr. Dimitrou has recently moved to Canada from Greece and has brought with him a lifetime of detailed research on two stars in a neighbouring solar system. He was hired by a research firm immediately because of his specialized knowledge and his reputation as a brilliant scientist.

3. Ms. Renata Dittrich is an amateur astronomer and lab technician from a major hospital. Ms. Dittrich comes highly recommended as someone who loves studying outer space. She feels her interest enhances her life and helps her in her lab. She often volunteers to speak to children's groups, community groups, and senior's groups about the stars and space.

You plan to telephone each one to ask for answers to some technical questions. What will you be looking for? What criteria will you use to make your decision? Organize your answer around critical thinking, language, listening, nonverbal, and adaptation skills.

CASE 2–2

You have been asked to write an article for the newsletter of your .... club about e-mail. If enough members have access to e-mail, your mailing costs will be greatly reduced. You know that the level of computer knowledge varies widely across your audience. Here are some of your first thoughts. Analyze them and make suggestions based on your knowledge of critical thinking, adaptation, and nonverbal cues.

To use ELECTRONIC MAIL (e-mail) you MUST have some communication software (Software is the name given to the set of instructions that tell a computer what to do.) added to your computer. (And of course you need a computer.) You MUST have a modem. Most computers now have modems built into them. Check your invoice or call your supplier to see if you have one. If not, you should purchase one that has a 28.8 baud rate. (The baud rate is the speed at which the modem can communicate.) Although a slower modem would be fine for e-mail, the faster speed is HIGHLY recommended because this modem will also let you link to bulletin boards and the WORLD WIDE WEB (if you also get the software for that). Once you have your modem and software, you will need to register with a company to get your e-mail address.

The more people who sign up, the better. We can then get in touch with you quickly and keep you up to date on events. We can also reduce our mailing costs and our office costs such as paper and duplicating.

ANSWERS TO PRACTICE RUNS

▶ Critical Thinking

Relevancy and Acceptability of Evidence

1. Acceptability: information is a year old; need information from the carrier. Relevance: does your company send representatives to India; are there plans to expand your business there?

2. Acceptability: good first impression is a good sign; is this careful attention typical of this carrier? Relevance: look for content behind the presentation.

3. Acceptability: ask for independent assessment; do other companies make the same claim; don't most carriers share the same physical system?

4. Relevance: the offer must meet the goal of maximizing value of long-distance charges for the business.

5. Acceptability: poor first impression—would service always be this slow; the information is needed now.

Comparing and Contrasting the Evidence

Suggested steps are: Find out if you can distinguish calling-card calls on the last year's bills; if so, calculate percentages for each month; calculate costs over an appropriate period (perhaps one year) using Carrier A and Carrier B for all types of long-distance calls; compare the results for A, B, and last year's bill.

▶ Language Skills

Vocabulary: Precision

Answers will vary. Here are some suggestions.

a. Understand: comprehend, see, get, know, realize, grasp

b. Old: ancient, aged, elderly, senior, antiquated, old-fashioned, archaic

c. Tell: state, aver, declare, say, relate, narrate, recount, describe, report

d. Inquire: ask, demand, request, question, query, probe

e. Stop: quit, cease, die, finish, end, halt, desist, terminate, discontinue

Vocabulary: Accuracy

1. *Continually* means frequently (on and off) over a period of time while *continuously* means without stopping.

2. *Implies* means suggests. *Infer* means to surmise or take a meaning from a situation. It cannot be used in this sentence.

3. *To compare* means to look for similarities and differences. *To contrast* means to look for differences.

4. *Loan* is a noun related to the verb *to lend. Borrow* is correct in this sentence.

5. An *effective* plan is one that achieves its goal. An *efficient* plan is one that works with a minimum of effort.

Vocabulary: Idiom

1. The purchasing officer has gone in search of a substitute product.

2. This letter is equally bad.

3. She is an authority on mutual funds.

4. When the sale is over, we will restock.

5. Our computer is different from theirs.

▶Listening

Active Listening

Situation # 1   The supervisor ignored the employee's excitement and interest in the report. No thanks was expressed. The response was totally centred on the supervisor's needs.

Situation # 2   The supervisor ignored the feelings and heard only the content of the message. The employee is either frustrated with problems encountered while writing the report, or exhilarated that it is complete. The supervisor minimizes the work done by the employee by the words said, by the words not said, and by the action of not personally taking the report.

Levels of Listening

Content listening would be appropriate if instructions are given, routine messages taken.
Critical listening would be appropriate if policies are being considered, new purchases are being made, procedures or schedules are being changed.
Empathic listening would be appropriate if someone is leaving under difficult circumstances, major changes are being made (for example, relocation of the company).

▶Adaptation Skills

You-Viewpoint

1. Your order will reach you by the 12th.

2. As an employee, you are entitled to a 20 percent discount on all purchases.

3. Your documents will easily fit into one of the three sizes of file folders we make.

4. Your application for membership has been approved.

5. What is the benefit you will receive because of our long experience in the book business? The finest customer service possible!

6. So that you can continue to enjoy these low discount prices, all purchases are final.

7. A catalogue is enclosed for your shopping convenience.

8. Can't you just taste Madame Benoit's hearty and delicious Canadian Pea Soup?

9. The 2 percent discount applies if you pay within 10 days. *or* You earn the 2 percent discount by paying within 10 days.

10. You may attend classes on company time for courses related to your work assignment.

Adaptation Technique

a. Picture the mixed audience. Use you-viewpoint to include all employees. Be positive.

b. Write clearly, breaking down the message into steps. Ask for input for problems she may see from her firsthand knowledge of the department. Offer support and assistance.

c. Use plain language. Include a few highlights from the brochure that apply to her now (perhaps vacation leave, but probably not seniority benefits) to encourage her to read it.

d. Remember the mixed audience. Keep the document positive, short, simple. Refer to more complete documents for those wanting more detail.

3

The Selection of Words

Upon completing this chapter, you will be able to select the most effective words for use in business communication. To reach this goal, you should be able to

1 Prefer words that are familiar and short.

2 Decide when it is suitable to use technical words.

3 Select words appropriately on the basis of their strength.

4 Use concrete words and the active voice, in most cases.

5 Decide when it is suitable to use the passive voice.

6 Use words that do not discriminate.

▶ to Choosing Words That Communicate

As a means of introducing yourself to business communication, imagine this situation. Doreen Lam is the owner and manager of a small franchise selling frozen yogurt, nutritious sandwiches, and drinks. She has a kiosk in a busy mall, and business is picking up. Last year, she broke even; this year, she hopes to see a modest profit.

A small community newspaper is sending a summer student to interview her for a feature article. She is anxious to take advantage of this free exposure and publicity, so she drafts a short piece about herself and her business. Here is the opening paragraph:

> Doreen Lam, proprietor of the Good 'n Nice kiosk situated in Westridge Mall, participated in her convocation from Georgian Business College two years ago. Believing herself to possess the essential qualities necessitated for success as an entrepreneur, she chose to gain entry into the business world by means of an enterprise of her own rather than being a cog in the machinery of big business. She procured this franchise operation with the facilitation of her acquaintances, kin, and financial institution. To the current time, this business venture has achieved a status of financial solvency, but has not yet generated a surplus of funds.

On reading this, she sees that she has fallen into the trap of using too many big words. Just as she learned in class, the result is stiff and cold—not at all the way she wants potential customers to see her. "It's time to get out the communication text and review the chapter on selecting words," she admits to herself. ■

SUGGESTIONS FOR SELECTING WORDS

A major part of adaptation is selecting the right words. These are the words that communicate best—that have correct and clear meanings *in the receiver's mind.* Selecting the right words depends on your ability to use language, your knowledge of the receiver, and your good judgment. Few hard-and-fast rules apply. As you review the following guidelines, remember that you must use them with good judgment. You must consider them in light of the need to adapt the message to your receiver or receivers.

* Selecting the right words is a part of adaptation.

As you will see, most of the suggestions support simplicity in communication. This approach is justified by three good reasons. The first reason to strive for simplicity is that the sender usually knows the subject of the message better than the receiver. The material is so well-known to the sender that the process by which it was learned may have been forgotten. It is a common mistake to assume "everybody knows that" and forget to explain some of the steps. If the sender does not work at keeping the message simple to suit the receiver's circumstances, communication will likely be difficult.

* These suggestions stress simplicity for three reasons: (1) the sender usually knows the subject better than the receiver;

Keeping our oral communication simple is easier than writing simply. Many of us tend to write at too difficult a level. Instead of being our normal, friendly selves when we write, we change character and become cold and stiff. We work to use big words and complex structures. Winston Churchill referred to this tendency when he remarked: "Little men use big words; big men use little words." We should follow the example of this big man and remember that the primary goal is to communicate, not impress. Wise people will see through the awkward big words and not be impressed anyway.

* (2) many people tend to write at a difficult level;

The third reason for simplicity is that experience supports it. A grade 10 level of writing is comfortable for most business people to understand in one reading. This is the level of most popular news magazines and television documentaries. You would do well to follow the advice and example of experts.

* (3) the results of experience support simplicity.

Prefer Short, Familiar Words

The foremost suggestion for word selection is to use short, familiar words. These are the everyday words that most of us use in conversation. For example, instead of using the longer, less familiar word *endeavour,* use *try.* Instead of using *terminate,* use *end.* Prefer

* Short, familiar words communicate.

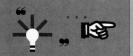

In "All the world's a stage" (a famous speech from Shakespeare's *As You Like It*), there are 212 words—150 of them (about 70 percent) are one-syllable words.

The Lord's Prayer has 66 words. Seventy-two percent have only one syllable.

In Abraham Lincoln's speech, "Gettysburg Address," 196 of the 268 words are of one syllable, which is 73 percent.

use to *utilize, begin* to *initiate, find out* to *ascertain,* and *stop* to *discontinue.* Because words that are familiar to some people may be unfamiliar to others, you will have to rely on your judgment and select words with care.

• Difficult words are not all bad. Use them when they fit your needs and are understood.

The suggestion to use familiar words does not rule out some use of more difficult words. You should use them when these two conditions are met: (1) the meanings of the difficult words fit your purpose best, and (2) you are sure your receiver understands them clearly. The mistake that many of us make is to overwork the more difficult words. We use them so much that they interfere with our communication, not only because the receiver has to work out the meanings of the difficult words, but also because they tend to be longer words that slow down the process of communication. Longer words simply take more time to read or hear. Some receivers will understand the longer words, but they will not likely enjoy wading through the volume of print. Even worse, they may not make the effort.

A PRACTICE RUN

Rewrite these sentences using short, familiar words.

Ms. Smith's idiosyncrasies supply adequate justification for terminating her employment. _____

_____

The decision was dependent on the assumption that an abundance of monetary funding was forthcoming. _____

_____

Definitive action was effected subsequent to the reporting date. _____

_____

This antiquated merchandising strategy is ineffectual in contemporary business operations. _____

_____

Use Technical Words with Caution

• All fields have specialized words.

Whether the field is mining, law enforcement, truck driving, or business, each occupation has its own set of technical words. Many fields, including business, have specialized dictionaries to interpret the terms. (See Chapter 19 for some examples of dictionaries and handbooks for business.) As you work in your chosen field, these specialized words will no longer seem strange to you, and you will use them freely with people in your area.

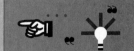
This is as it should be, for these words are useful. Frequently, one word will communicate a concept that would otherwise take dozens of words to describe.

A problem comes about, however, when you use technical terms with people outside your field. Because these are everyday words to you, you tend to forget that not everyone knows them. On occasion, people will have heard the term and have some idea about its meaning, but not a full understanding. If they incorrectly guess at the meaning, miscommunication results. Therefore, use specialized words only when your receivers know them, or you have taken time to explain them.

• But technical words may not communicate with outsiders. Use them with caution.

Examples are easy to find. *Annuity* has a clear meaning to someone in insurance. *An investment that guarantees an income for a period of time* would have more meaning to outsiders. Computer specialists know *LISP* and *C ++* to be popular programming languages, but these words are meaningless to most others. To a trucker, *bobtail* means a tractor cab without trailer. Nontruckers might think of a rabbit, a bird, or a horse groomed for competition in a show. Or they might pretend to know the meaning when they don't. Whatever your technical language, be careful not to use it when you write to people who do not understand it.

• Some examples are annuity, LISP, and bobtail. These words are well known to people in special fields, but not to most outsiders.

Probably the most troublesome specialized language for business is that of the legal profession. Terms common in legal documents, such as *thereto, whereas, per,* and *herein,*

• Legal language has worked its way into business writing.

Governments at all levels in Canada are writing and revising documents using the principles of plain language. The reason is easily seen in the following example.
In the original legal style:

Validity of by-law or resolution
A by-law or resolution passed by a council in the exercise of any of the powers conferred and in accordance with the Act, and in good faith, is not open to question, nor shall it be quashed, set aside or declared invalid, either wholly or partly, on account of the unreasonableness or supposed unreasonableness of its provisions or any of them.

The Municipal Government Act
Revised Statutes of Alberta 1980
Chapter M-26, section 108

In plain language:

Validity of bylaws
A bylaw is not to be declared wholly or partly invalid because it is or is thought to be unreasonable.

The Municipal Government Act
Alberta Municipal Statutes Review Committee
Second Discussion Draft 1990
Part 6, section 138

have too often worked their way into business communication. The result has been to add unnecessary words and cause confusion. Such words also have a dull and formal effect. For example, "the land adjacent thereto" can be written "the adjacent land" without loss in meaning. Where possible, replace legal language with plain words. The legal profession is working on using simplified language, so business should not persist in using the old, cumbersome terms.

Select Words with the Right Strength and Intensity

- Words have personalities. Select the stronger ones for effect.

In a way words are like people; they have personalities. Some words are strong and dynamic. Some are weak and dull. And some fall between these extremes. Good writers know these differences and use them to advantage. They use plain words to carry a message without adding emotional overtones. Then, they add strong words selectively to add emphasis and make a point stand out.

- To select words wisely, you should consider shades of difference in meanings.

Selecting words with just the right personalities requires that you learn language well—that you learn to distinguish shades of difference in the meanings of words. The dictionary definition of a word may not reflect the impact the word carries in current usage. As a language is used, words take on additional meanings because of the context in which they come to be used. For example, you should recognize that *tycoon* has overtones of meaning not found in *very successful business person. Boom* is a stronger word than *a period of economic prosperity,* and the word *mother* includes an emotional content not found in *female parent.*

- Sometimes, weaker words serve your purpose best.

You will not always want the strongest and most dynamic words. Sometimes, for good reason, you will want to soften a point and will, therefore, choose weaker words. Because the phrase *your bill* is strong, most companies prefer *your statement.* The same principle applies to *debt* and *obligation, die* and *pass on, spit* and *saliva,* and *fired* and *dismissed.*

In selecting the stronger words, you should keep in mind that the verb is the strongest part of speech. Verbs are action words, and action carries interest. Therefore, if your verb is weak, your entire sentence will lose impact. Note the increase in strength in the following examples.

• Verbs are the strongest words.

I had the responsibility for training new staff members.
I was responsible for training new staff members.
I trained new staff members.

She suggests you call Mr. Royle.
She encourages you to call Mr. Royle.
She insists you call Mr. Royle.

. . . .

A PRACTICE RUN

Rewrite these sentences making them stronger.

My duties included the organization of staff luncheons. _____

_____

I appreciated having Mr. Buchinsky for a coach. _____

_____

. . . .

Second in strength is the noun. Nouns are the main characters of the sentence. Because they also attract attention, you should choose them carefully. For strength, let the noun stand alone; to soften the impact, add adjectives and modifying phrases. Consider these examples.

• Nouns are second.

Strong Noun and Verb
Interest rates have plummeted.

Noun Softened by Modifiers (Note the imbalance with the strong verb.)
Lending rates for mortgages and personal, secured loans have plummeted.

Softened Noun and Softened Verb
Lending rates for mortgages and personal, secured loans have been reduced by 1 percent.

Adjectives and adverbs are weak words. They add length and distract from the key words, the nouns and the verbs. In addition, adjectives and adverbs require judgment because they carry subjective content like personal opinions and points of view. You should not try to eliminate adjectives and adverbs from your writing, but you should use them wisely.

• Adjectives and adverbs are weak words. Use them sparingly.

Prefer Concrete Words

Good business communication is marked by words that form a sharp, clear meaning in the mind. These are the concrete words that stand for things we can see, feel, taste, or smell. Included are such nouns as *chair, desk, calculator, road, automobile,* and *flowers.* Also included are words that stand for creatures and things: *Mike Tymchuk, Michelle LeBlanc, Mr. Dressup,* the *CN Tower,* and *Queen Street.*

• Concrete words are specific words.

The opposite of concrete is abstract. Abstract nouns, on the other hand, cover broad meanings—like concepts, values, and ideas. Their meanings are general, as in these examples: *administration, negotiation, wealth, inconsistency, loyalty, compatibility, conservation, discrimination, incompetence,* and *communication.* Note how difficult it is to visualize and define what these words represent.

• Abstract nouns have general meanings: administration, negotiation.

Concreteness also involves how we put words together. Exact or specific wordings are concrete; vague and general wordings are abstract. For example, take the case of a researcher who must report the odour of a newly developed cleaning agent. The

• Concreteness also means exactness: a 53 percent loss, within the hour.

researcher could use such general words as "It has an offensive odour." Now note how vividly concrete language communicates: "It has the odour of rotting fish." The second example is concrete because it recalls a specific odour from memory. Notice the difference in communication effect in these contrasting pairs:

ABSTRACT	CONCRETE
A significant loss	A $2,000 loss
Good attendance record	89 percent attendance record
A time-saving machine	Does the job in half the time
Light in weight	Less that 1 kilogram

A PRACTICE RUN

Make these ideas more concrete by making them more specific.

The majority _____

_____

In the near future _____

_____

Substantial amount _____

_____

Now, study the difference concreteness makes in the clarity of longer passages. Here is an example of abstract wording:

It is imperative that the firm practise extreme conservatism in operating expenditures during the next few years. The firm's past operating performance has been poor because many administrative assignments have been delegated to personnel who were ill-equipped to perform in these capacities. Some recent administrative changes stressing experience in operating economies have improved this condition.

Do we know how serious the problem is, who caused it, what steps have been taken to overcome it, what degree of improvement has been realized, or when the problem will be completely corrected? The answer in each case is no.

Written for concreteness, this message might read as follows:

We must cut operating expenses by at least $2 million during 1995–96. Our $1.35 million deficit for 1993–94 was caused by the inexperience of our former chief administrators. We have replaced them with Ms. Pharr and Mr. Kunz, who, respectively, have 13 and 17 years of successful experience in operations management. By 1997–98, we should be operating clear of the deficit.

By using specific figures, dates, and names, the problem and the solution have been clearly defined, and realistic expectations for the company's future have been laid out.

Prefer the Active Voice

* In the active voice, the subject does the action; in the passive voice, the subject receives the action.

In the active voice, the grammatical subject of the sentence does the action. In the passive voice, on the other hand, the subject receives the action. For example, the sentence "The auditor inspected the books" is in the active voice because the subject (the auditor) is doing the action of inspecting the books. In the passive voice, the sentence would read

"The books were inspected by the auditor." Now the subject is *the books,* and the subject receives the action.

These two sentences show the advantages of the active voice. Clearly, the active-voice sentence is stronger. The subject does the action, and the verb is short and clear. In the passive-voice sentence, the extra helping word *were* dulls the action. In addition, placing the doer of the action (*auditor*) in a prepositional phrase presents the information indirectly rather than directly. Note also that the active-voice sentence is shorter.

• The active voice is stronger and shorter.

You should prefer the active voice to the passive voice for three reasons. First, the active voice produces stronger, livelier communication by emphasizing the action. Next, it involves the receiver more by making ideas easier to visualize. Finally, the active voice usually saves words.

• Prefer the active voice to the passive voice.

For further proof of the advantages of the active over the passive voice, compare the following sentences:

PASSIVE	ACTIVE
The new process is believed to be superior by the investigators.	The investigators believe the new process is superior.
The office will be inspected by Mr. Hall.	Mr. Hall will inspect the office.
The results were reported in our July 9 letter.	We reported the results in our July 9 letter.
A complete reorganization of the administration was completed by the president.	The president completely reorganized the administration.

· ·

A PRACTICE RUN

Rewrite these sentences in the active voice.

This policy has been supported by our union. _____

_____

The policy was enforced by the committee. _____

_____

An increase of 30.1 percent was reported for hardware sales. _____

_____

· ·

As with the earlier guidelines for improving your writing, this point can be carried to an extreme. The suggestion that you prefer the active voice does not mean that you should never use the passive voice. The passive voice is correct, and it has a place. The problem is that many people overuse it, especially in report writing. Your business writing will be more interesting and will communicate better if you use the active voice more frequently than the passive voice.

• The passive voice has a place. It is not incorrect.

Your decision on whether to use the active or the passive voice is not simply a matter of choice. Sometimes the passive voice is needed, for example, when the identity of the doer of the action is unknown or unimportant to the message. The passive voice properly de-emphasizes the doer.

• Passive is better when the doer of the action is not important.

During the past year, the equipment has been sabotaged seven times.
Advertizing is often criticized for its effect on price.
Petroleum is refined in Alberta.

The passive voice is preferable in another situation. If the sender does not want to name the doer of the action, the passive voice is best. It also will avoid accusing someone of an action.

• It is also better when the sender prefers not to name or seem to accuse the performer.

The interviews were conducted on weekdays between noon and 6:00 P.M.
Two complaints have been made about you.

- when the doer of the action is unknown
- when the doer of the action is unimportant to the message
- when the writer prefers not to identify the doer of the action
- when the active voice would suggest an accusation
- when the rhythm or pacing of the message needs a change

The damage was caused by exposing the material to the sunlight.
The colour desired was not specified in your order.

- Use the passive voice to add clarity.

Finally, in some instances, the passive voice is preferable for reasons of style. It brings variety in sentence structure and a change in the pacing of a paragraph.

Avoid Overuse of Camouflaged Verbs

- Avoid camouflaged verbs. You camouflage a verb by changing it to a noun form and then adding action words.

An awkward construction that should be avoided is the camouflaged verb. When a verb is camouflaged, the verb describing the action in a sentence is changed into a noun. Then action words have to be added. For example, if you take the action word *recommend* and make it into a noun *recommendation,* you would have to say something like "make a recommendation" to show the action. If you change *consider* to *consideration,* you would have to add words again. Using these camouflaged verbs, your sentence might be: "I have made a recommendation that your request be given consideration by our customer service representative." The sentence is long, indirect, and passive. By avoiding the weak, camouflaged constructions, you have the stronger, clearer sentence, "I have recommended that our customer service representative consider your request."

Note the differences in overall effect in these contrasting sentences:

CAMOUFLAGED VERB	CLEAR VERB FORM
The *amortization* of the account *was done* by the staff.	The staff *amortized* the account.
Application of the mixture *was accomplished.*	They *applied* the mixture.
We must *bring about a reconciliation* of our differences.	We must *reconcile* our differences.
The *establishment* of a rehabilitation centre *has been accomplished* by the company.	The company *has established* a rehabilitation centre.

A PRACTICE RUN

Rewrite these sentences using clear verb forms.

Control of the water was not possible. _____

_____

The new policy involved the standardization of the procedures. _____

_____

From these illustrations, you can see that the suggestion on camouflaged verbs overlaps the two preceding suggestions. First, camouflaged verbs are abstract nouns. We suggested that you prefer concrete words over abstract words. Second, camouflaged verbs frequently require the passive voice. We suggested that you prefer the active voice. In summary, if you choose concrete words and prefer the active voice, your communication will be clearer and more powerful.

• Avoid camouflaged verbs by (1) writing concretely and (2) preferring the active voice.

SUGGESTIONS FOR NONDISCRIMINATORY WRITING

Although discriminatory words are not directly related to writing clarity, our review of word selection would not be complete without some mention of them. By *discriminatory words,* we mean words that do not treat all people equally and with respect. Words that identify a person or group by religion, race, gender, sexual orientation, or political preference are considered discriminatory. While such references may not be overtly derogatory in nature, they run contrary to acceptable views of correctness and respect. They have no place in business communication.

• Avoid words that discriminate.

Many discriminatory words are a part of the vocabularies we have acquired from our environments. We often use them in ignorance, not realizing how they affect others. We can eliminate discriminatory words from our vocabularies by examining them carefully and placing ourselves in the shoes of those to whom they refer. The following review of the major forms of discriminatory words should help you achieve this goal.

• Discriminatory words may be without bad intent, but they are still unacceptable.

Avoid Words that Stereotype People

Words that stereotype all members of a group are unfair, since members of any group vary widely. Thus, it is untrue to suggest that Canadians are cold and reserved, or that women are bad drivers. Unfair references are sometimes subtle and not intended, as in this example: "In a recent study of substance abuse, a sample of 100 teens from the inner city were questioned." Such words unfairly suggest that substance abuse is restricted to this group.

• Words depicting groups in a stereotyped way are unfair and untrue.

Also unfair are words suggesting that a minority member has struggled to achieve something that is taken for granted in the majority group. Although perhaps well intended, words of this kind carry subtle discriminatory messages. For example, a reference to an "intelligent blonde woman" suggests that she is an exception to the rule— that most blond women[1] are not intelligent, but here is one who is. So too, references to "a responsible teenager" and "an alert senior" are considered discriminatory.

• Words that present people as exceptions to stereotypes are also unfair.

Eliminating unfair references from your communication requires two basic steps. First, you must consciously treat all people equally. You should refer to minority membership only in those rare cases in which it is a vital part of the message to be communicated. Second, you must be sensitive to the effects of your words. Consider your word choices carefully and evaluate them from the viewpoints of others.

• Eliminate such references by treating all people equally and by being sensitive to the effects of your words.

Use Inclusive Language

Sexist words are words that discriminate on the basis of gender. Although this form of discrimination can be against men, the problem usually concerns discrimination against women because many words used in English were developed in a male-dominated society. In business communication, inclusive language is the currently accepted standard.

• Avoid using words that exclude a group on the basis of gender.

Avoid Masculine Pronouns When Referring to Both Sexes. Perhaps the most troublesome words are the masculine terms (*he, his, him*) when they are used to refer to both sexes, as in this example: "The typical university student eats *his* lunch at the

• Avoid using the masculine pronouns and adjectives (he, him, his) for both sexes.

---

[1]Note that correct usage also prefers *blond,* the base form of the adjective, rather than *blonde.* Even further, there is the question of the relevance and propriety of comments about personal appearance and gender in this context. *She is intelligent* or *She is an intelligent person* are better choices.

cafeteria." The use of *his,* suggesting that university students are male, can be seen as a slight against female students. Historically, of course, the word *his* as it is used here has been considered to include both sexes; but this usage is no longer appropriate for the Canadian business scene.

- Avoid the general use of masculine pronouns (1) by rewording the sentence;

You can avoid the general use of masculine pronouns in three ways. First, you can reword the sentence to eliminate the offending word. The illustration above could be reworded as follows: "The typical university student eats lunch at the cafeteria." Here are other examples of successfully reworded sentences:

Sexist
If a customer pays promptly, *he* is placed on our preferred list.
When an unauthorized employee enters the security area, *he* is subject to dismissal.

Inclusive
A customer who pays promptly is placed on our preferred list.
An unauthorized employee who enters the security area is subject to dismissal.

- (2) by making the reference plural;

A second way to avoid this gender slight is to use the plural form. Fortunately, the English language has plural adjectives and pronouns (*their, them, they*) that refer to both sexes. Using the plural in the examples given above, we have these inclusive revisions:

Inclusive
If customers pay promptly, *they* are placed on our preferred list.
When unauthorized employees enter the security areas, they are subject to dismissal.

· ·

A PRACTICE RUN

Rewrite these sentences in three ways using inclusive language.

A supervisor is not responsible for such losses if he is not negligent.

When a customer needs service, it is his right to ask for it.

Inclusive by Rewording the Sentence

_____

_____

_____

Inclusive by Making the Reference Plural

_____

_____

_____

Inclusive by Substituting Neutral Expressions

_____

_____

_____

· ·

A third way to avoid the general use of *he, his,* or *him* is to substitute a neutral expression (*he or she, one*) or to repeat the noun. The problem sentences revised in this way become:

• or (3) by substituting neutral expressions.

Inclusive
If a customer pays promptly, *he or she* is placed on our preferred list.
When an unauthorized employee enters the security area, *that employee* is subject to dismissal.

You should use such expressions with caution, however. Some people find them offensive feeling that phrases such as *he or she* draw attention to the issue of gender when it is not relevant to the topic. Moreover, neutral expressions tend to be awkward, particularly if they are used often. If you use them, pay attention to their effect on the flow of your words. Certainly, you should avoid sentences like this one: "To make an employee feel he or she is doing well by complimenting him or her insincerely confuses him or her later when he or she sees his or her co-workers promoted ahead of him or her."

• Neutral expressions can be awkward. Use them with caution.

Avoid Words Suggesting Gender-Specific Roles.   Many of our words are masculine even though they do not refer exclusively to men. Take *chairman,* for example. The person who conducts a meeting may be male or female, yet the word does not sound that way. More appropriate and less offensive substitutes are *chair, presiding officer, moderator,* and *chairperson.* Similarly, *salesman* suggests a man, but many women work in sales. *Salesclerk, sales associate,* or *sales representative* would be better. Although some words do not have simple substitutes—*personhole cover* would not serve as a replacement for *manhole cover*—some creative and careful thought will lead to success in finding an acceptably inclusive term. *Maintenance cover* stresses the function rather than the person and works well.

• Avoid words suggesting gender-specific roles.

Other inclusive language examples are as follows:

SEXIST	INCLUSIVE
Man-made	Manufactured, synthetic
Manpower	Personnel, workers
Businessman	Business executive, business person
Postman	Letter carrier, mail carrier
Policeman	Police officer, constable
Fireman	Fire fighter
Cameraman	Camera operator

Finally, the feminine form of words that refer to work roles is considered sexist. In this group are *lady lawyer, authoress, sculptress,* and *poetess.* Since gender is not significant to the quality of their work, women and men in these work roles should be referred to as *lawyers, authors, sculptors,* and *poets.*

Be Aware of Changing Norms

Stereotyping people by race, religion, cultural heritage, gender, age, physical attributes, or sexual orientation is not an acceptable practice in business. Society's norms are changing. In deciding which words to avoid and which to use, be responsive to this growing awareness. Remember that your goal should be to use words that are fair and that do not give reasonable cause for offence.

• Show respect for the concerns of all sectors in society.

The preceding suggestions for selecting words are the basic work tools you will need. Resolve to keep these basics in mind every time you write or speak. Consciously and conscientiously use them. The results will make you glad you did.

• The preceding suggestions are realistic ways to improve your writing. Use them.

A SUMMARY OF LEARNING OUTCOMES FROM THIS CHAPTER

To communicate clearly, you must adapt to your receiver by selecting familiar words. Usually these are short, everyday words (*old design* rather than *antiquated configuration*).

Use technical words with caution. Technical words are appropriate with technical people, but not with others.

Select words with the right strength and intensity. Develop a feeling for the personalities of words (*bear market* is stronger than *a generally declining market*).

Use concrete (specific) words (*77 percent* rather than *a majority*).

Prefer the active voice unless there is a reason to use the passive voice (*we reported the results* rather than *the results were reported*). The active voice is stronger, more vigorous, and more interesting, but the passive voice is correct and has a place.

Avoid overuse of camouflaged verbs—making a noun of the logical verb and then having to add a verb (prefer *appear* over *make an appearance*).

Avoid discriminatory words. Do not use words that suggest stereotyped roles for minorities, for such words are unfair and untrue. Use inclusive (nonsexist) language.

QUESTIONS FOR DISCUSSION

1. "Some short words are hard, and some long words are easy. So, the suggestion to prefer short words doesn't make sense." Discuss.
2. "Technical language typically consists of jargon; abbreviations; and long, hard words. It contributes to miscommunication and should be avoided in all business communication." Discuss.
3. Evaluate this comment: "Simplifying writing so that stupid readers can understand it is lame! Why not challenge readers? Why not give them new words to learn—expand their minds?"
4. Select a news article from a publication known for its sensational style rather than its objectivity. Discuss differences in word strength for words used in that article compared to those that might be used in a police report of the same event.
5. Define and illustrate active and passive voice. Explain when each should be used.
6. Discuss the following statement by Mrs. Eberhard. "It's such a bother to try to reword things to avoid the general *he, him, his.* Is it really necessary to change? It doesn't upset me, and I don't mean anything by it. I think other women will see that and let it pass."

APPLICATION EXERCISE

Instructions: Assume that your readers are at about the grade 10 reading level. Revise these sentences for easy communication to this audience.

1. A proportionate tax consumes a determinate apportionment of one's monetary flow.
2. Business has an inordinate influence on governmental operations.
3. Ms. Goldstein terminated Kevin's employment as a consequence of his ineffectual performance.
4. The preponderance of the business people we consulted envision signs of improvement from the current siege of economic stagnation.
5. Requisites for employment by this company have been enhanced.

Instructions: Revise these sentences to make them conform to the writing suggestions in this chapter.

Using Strong, Dynamic Words

6. I have an idea in mind of how we can enhance our savings.
7. Mr. Jordan possesses qualities that are characteristic of an autocratic executive.
8. Many people came into the store during the period of the promotion.
9. We are obligated to protect the well-being of the hired employees.
10. Companies promoting their products in the medium of the newspaper are advised to produce verbal messages in accord with the audience level of the general public.

Selecting Concrete Words

11. Improve and return this report to me quickly.
12. Our phone bills have been way too high recently.
13. If we don't receive the goods soon, we will cancel.
14 Some years ago, she made good money.
15. Damage from the fire was significant.

Limiting Use of Passive Voice

16. Our action is based on the assumption that the competition will be taken by surprise.
17. It is believed by the typical union member that his or her welfare is not considered to be important by management.
18. You were directed by your supervisor to complete this assignment by noon.
19. These reports are prepared by the salespeople every Friday.
20. Success of this project is the responsibility of the research department.

Avoiding Camouflaged Verbs

21. It was my duty to make an assessment of the damages.
22. Harold made a recommendation that we fire Mr. Schultz.
23. Acceptance of all orders must be made by the chef.
24. A committee performs the function of determining the award.
25. Verification of the amount is made daily by the auditor.

Avoiding Discriminatory Language

26. Our new sales manager, who used to be a priest, seems to care about the staff.
27. The typical postman rarely makes mistakes in delivering his mail.
28. Our tax lawyer, a Progressive Conservative, always advises us to contribute to a charity.
29. The committee consisted of a businessman, a lawyer, a lady doctor, and a retired teacher.
30. A good secretary screens all telephone calls for her boss and arranges his schedule.
31. An efficient salesman organizes his calls and manages his time.
32. Our company was represented by two sales associates and an engineer who spoke good English for a Chinese.
33. Three people applied for the job: a responsible-looking teenager, a man who walked with a limp, and a grey-haired lady in her 50s.
34. Parking spaces near the door are strictly for the use of the crippled.
35. He has modern ideas for someone of his generation.

CASE 3-1

"Who do you get for computers, Brent?"

"Jensen! I'm gonna fail for sure."

"Won't she give you some extra help?"

"Sure. But it doesn't make any difference. She doesn't speak English, you know. She speaks Computereze! I did really well last term, but I had Wong then. He made a lot of sense. I always seemed to know what he was talking about."

"Yeah, Wong is great. I get it when he teaches me, but Jensen's classes are tough. Can you transfer out?"

"It's my only hope."

Analyze the difficulty Brent is having with his teacher, Ms. Jensen.

Advise Ms. Jensen on how to make her classes more understandable by using the concepts you have learned in this chapter.

Advise Brent on the options he has (other than transferring to another class).

CASE 3-2

"I'm exhausted! With the staff cuts because of health care cutbacks, there just aren't enough of us to get everything done around here."

"Aren't mealtimes crazy? It sure would be nice if more people came in to help give meals to those who can't manage to feed themselves."

Overhearing this conversation between two nurses at an extended care facility made André angry at the system. He decided to prepare a letter to the editor of the city's major newspaper.

Health care cuts are disastrous for our hospitals and homes for the disabled. Nurses cannot give adequate care to the sufferers. Some patients don't even get fed! How can this travesty of justice go on? How can we all be party to such

abuse to the old and sick. These helpless people need the action of the community, and they need it now.

When Stacey saw the paragraph above, she urged, "André, I think you have to tone it down. You're just going to upset people—and some of them will be the people you want to help."

André agreed. Her arguments made sense, but now he had to decide how much he should change. After all, the issue was important. He was angry about it, and he wanted people to take action. "If my letter gets too gentle, it won't get any attention," he thought.

Who might be hurt by this letter? What words would you change? How can André get the attention he wants for the issue from this letter?

ANSWERS TO PRACTICE RUNS

▶ Prefer Familiar, Short Words

Long, Unfamiliar Words	*Short, Familiar Words*
Ms. Smith's idiosyncrasies supply adequate justification for terminating her employment.	Ms. Smith's peculiar ways justify firing her.
The decision was dependent on the assumption that an abundance of monetary funding was forthcoming.	The decision was based on the belief that there would be more money.
Definitive action was effected subsequent to the reporting date.	Final action was taken after the reporting date.
This antiquated merchandising strategy is ineffectual in contemporary business operations.	This old sales strategy will not work in today's business.

▶ Select Words with the Right Strength and Intensity

Weaker Verbs	*Stronger Verbs*
My duties included the organization of staff luncheons.	I organized staff luncheons.
I appreciated having Mr. Buchinsky for a coach.	I enjoyed having Mr. Buchinsky for a coach. *Or* I loved having Mr. Buchinsky for a coach.

▶ Prefer Concrete Words

Abstract	*Concrete*
The majority	Supply a number or percentage such as *62 percent*
In the near future	Supply a date such as *By Thursday noon*
Substantial amount	Supply the value such as *$3,529,000*

►Prefer the Active Voice

Passive Voice

This policy has been supported by our union.

The policy was enforced by the committee.

An increase of 30.1 percent was reported for hardware sales.

Active Voice

Our union supported this policy.

The committee enforced the policy.

Hardware sales increased 30.1 percent.

►Avoid Overuse of Camouflaged Verbs

Camouflaged Verb

Control of the water *was not possible.*

The new policy *involved the standardization of* the procedures

Clear Verb Form

They *could not control* the water.

The new policy *standardized* the procedures.

►Use Inclusive Language

Sexist

A supervisor is not responsible for such losses if he is not negligent.

When a customer needs service, it is his right to ask for it.

Inclusive by Rewording the Sentence

A supervisor who is not negligent is not responsible for such losses.

A customer who needs service has the right to ask for it.

Inclusive by Making the Reference Plural

Supervisors are not responsible for such losses if they are not negligent.

When customers need service, they have the right to ask for it.

Inclusive by Substituting Neutral Expressions

A supervisor is not responsible for such losses if she/he is not negligent.

When service is needed, one has the right to ask for it.

Construction of Clear Sentences and Paragraphs

4

Upon completing this chapter, you will be able to construct clear sentences and paragraphs by emphasizing short sentences and effective paragraph design. To reach this goal, you should be able to

1 Write sentences limiting the content and economizing on words.

2 Design sentences that give the right emphasis to content.

3 Employ unity and logic in writing effective sentences.

4 Compose short, unified paragraphs that communicate ideas clearly.

5 Use topic sentences and movement in writing good paragraphs.

▶ to Writing Sentences and Paragraphs That Communicate

Doreen has concluded that not all of her writing problems involve word choice. (See the Introductory Situation to Chapter 3.) True, the revision using more familiar words made an improvement. Still, she feels something else is wrong. Here is the first paragraph as she revised it.

Doreen Lam, owner of the Good 'n Nice kiosk in Westridge Mall, graduated from Georgian Business College two years ago. Believing herself to have the essential qualities needed for success as an entrepreneur, she chose to enter the business world through a business of her own rather than working for a large company. She bought this franchise with the help of her friends, family, and bank. So far, this business has broken even, but it has not yet made a profit.

Short words and correct grammar, she decides, are not enough. "These sentences are too complex to communicate clearly. Some of the paragraphs are very long and involve more than one major topic. It's time to look at the chapter on sentences and paragraphs," she tells herself. ■

FOUNDATION POINT OF ADAPTATION TO THE AUDIENCE

Choosing the right words is a building block of clear communication. Arranging those words into sentences builds a wall. Both the words and the sentences rest on the foundation of adaptation to the intended audience.

• Sentences should be adapted to readers.

In adapting sentences for business audiences, successful communicators have learned to use the simpler sentence structures that do not tax the mind of the receiver. They have realized that the task of the sender is to do as much of the work as possible. It is risky to assume that the receiver will be willing to expend extra effort to understand the message. Thus, some simplification is best. Keep this point in mind as you read the rest of this chapter.

• Some simplification is best for all readers.

Using computerized grammar checking programs will help you reach the goals of this chapter. They are useful aids for improving the structure and impact of your writing. These programs analyze your work and flag possible errors in grammar and style. (The grammar check program used on the manuscript of this chapter flagged all the sentences in the exercises and the bad examples!) Note that grammar checkers only make suggestions. Although these programs are becoming more sophisticated, they cannot yet analyze all the peculiarities of the English language. Moreover, they do not know your receiver. You must make the final decision about what is best.

• Computerized grammar checking programs will help.

EMPHASIS ON SHORT SENTENCES

Why Keep Sentences Short?

Writing simpler sentences usually means writing shorter sentences. As the number of words grows, so does the number of possible relationships between them. The sender's ideas can be lost in a tangle of twists, turns, and tangents that no longer lead to the goal. Overloading the receiver's mind with too much information at one time will cause confusion. Either the words will be blocked out, or they will be processed inadequately. Unless they are processed and stored properly, the words and the ideas they represent will be unavailable for later retrieval. The more words there are in a sentence, the greater the possibility for error both by the sender and the receiver.

• Short sentences communicate better.

- Clarity and brevity save time and money.

Mark Twain once said, "I didn't have time to write a short letter, so I wrote a long one instead."[1] It is a truthful description of the process. Short, clear messages take longer to create. Even so, they usually save time and money for businesses. Because the receiver understands the message quickly and correctly, the sender does not have to repeat it or correct misunderstandings.

- Short means about 16–18 words for middle-level readers.

The definition of a short, readable sentence is related to the reader's ability. For business, a middle-level is appropriate with 16 to 18 words per sentence on average. Sentences of this length are easily understood in one reading by most people.

- Sometimes longer sentences are justified.

This emphasis on short sentences does not mean that you should never use long sentences. You may use them occasionally, and you should—if you construct them clearly. Longer sentences are useful in subordinating information. The information needed to complete a thought sometimes requires a long sentence. What you should be concerned about is the average length of your sentences.

- The writer's purpose will affect sentence length.

The writer's purpose will affect the length of the sentences chosen. More difficult sentences are expected in certain types of writing. A technical research report, for example, can be expected to be harder to read if its purpose is to report complex, new findings to people who are already familiar with the basics. A promotional letter needs shorter, simpler sentences to accomplish its purpose of attracting new customers. A persuasive presentation could require longer sentences to explain points and shorter sentences to push for action.

The following sentence from an employee handbook illustrates the negative effect of long sentences when they are used inappropriately:

When an employee has changed from one job to another job, the new corresponding coverage will be effective as of the date the change occurs; however, if due to a physical disability or infirmity as a result of advanced age, an employee is changed from one job to another job and such change results in the employee's new job rate coming within a lower hourly job-rate bracket in the table, the employee may, at the discretion of the company, continue the amount of group term life insurance and the amount of accidental death and dismemberment insurance that the employee had prior to such change.

The chances that you got a clear message from this single sentence when you first read it are slim. The explanation for the communication difficulty is not in the words used; you probably know them all. They are familiar and simple. Neither is it in the ideas presented; they, too, are relatively simple. The obvious explanation is the length of the sentence. So many words and relationships are in the sentence that they cause confusion.

How to Keep Sentences Short

- Shorter sentences are achieved in two ways.

You can write short, simple sentences in two basic ways: (1) by limiting sentence content, and (2) by using words economically.

- Limiting content is one way to make short sentences.

Limit Sentence Content. Limiting sentence content is largely a matter of selecting thought units and making separate sentences of most of them. In the employee handbook example above, the idea that insurance coverage will be adjusted on the date the employee starts the new job needs its own sentence. The explanation of that standard procedure should not be combined with the exceptions. The advantage of limiting sentence content is evident from the following contrasting examples:

Long Sentences Are Hard to Understand

The first-semester class cards that are being distributed with this memorandum are to serve as a final check on the correctness of the registration of students and are to be used later

Short Sentences Are Easier to Understand

The first-semester class cards are being distributed with this memorandum. For now, these cards will serve as a final check on student registration. Later, they will be used for

---

[1]Source: Starling Technology. *Quote Search.* http://www.starlingtech.com/quotes/qsearch.cgi searching the USENET fortune file (24 August 1996).

> Write a wise saying and your name will live forever.
>
> *Anonymous*

as the midsemester grade cards, which are to be submitted prior to November 16.

Some authorities in personnel administration object to expanding normal salary ranges to include a trainee rate because they fear that, through oversight or prejudice, probationers may be kept at the minimum rate longer than is warranted, and because they fear that a trainee rate would encourage the increasing spread from the minimum to the maximum rate range.

midsemester grades, which are due before November 16.

Some authorities in personnel administration object to expanding the normal salary ranges to include a trainee rate for two reasons. First, they fear that, through oversight or prejudice, probationers may be kept at the minimum rate longer than is warranted. Second, they fear that a trainee rate would increase the spread between the minimum and the maximum rate range.

Without question, the long sentences in the examples are harder to understand, and the shorter versions are easier. In each case the difference is primarily in sentence length. The shorter sentences give more emphasis to content and better organization to the subject matter.

. . . .

A PRACTICE RUN

Rewrite this sentence in shorter, easier to understand sentences.

Regardless of their seniority or union affiliation, all employees who hope to be promoted are expected to continue their education either by enrolling in the special courses, which are scheduled to be offered by the company after working hours, or by taking approved correspondence courses selected from a list that may be seen in the training office.

_____

_____

_____

. . . .

Economize on Words.   A second technique for shortening sentences is to use words economically. Anything you write can be expressed in many ways, some shorter than others. The shorter wordings save the reader time because they are clearer and easier.

• Another way to shorten sentences is through word economy.

Substitute Shorter Expressions.   Some expressions can be replaced by shorter wording without loss of meaning. The savings achieved in this way add up. Usually the shorter ways are direct and communicate better. This sentence illustrates the point:

• Substitute shorter expressions.

The department budget *can be observed to be decreasing* each *new* year.

This sentence uses too many words to get to the point. A more direct and better sentence is this one:

The department budget decreases each year.

Here are more examples of sentences with suggested improvements:

Long:	Improved:
In the event that payment is not made by January, operations will cease.	*If* payment is not made by January, operations will cease.
The union is *involved in the task of reviewing* the seniority provision of the collective agreement.	The union *is reviewing* the seniority provision of the collective agreement.
It is essential that the income be used to retire the debt.	The income *must* be used to retire the debt.

. . . .

A PRACTICE RUN

Complete the following chart.

Long Phrase	Shorter Substitution
for the reason that	_____
in the near future	_____
in the neighbourhood of	_____
in view of the fact that	_____
with regard to, or with reference to	_____

Rewrite these sentences substituting shorter expressions where possible.

In spite of the fact that they received help, they failed to exceed the quota.

_____

The president is of the opinion that the tax was paid.

_____

During the time that she was employed by this company, Ms. Carr was absent once.

_____

Use your improved paragraph from the earlier practice run (Regardless of their seniority or union affiliation . . .) and make it shorter and clearer by economizing on words.

_____

_____

_____

_____

. . . .

* Avoid repetitions of ideas (redundancies).

Avoid Unnecessary Repetition. One special type of wordiness is *redundancy* or the repetition of ideas through different words that mean almost the same thing. Examples are *free gift, true fact,* and *past history.* Under special circumstances, such as in advertizing, redundancies can be used for emphasis. However, because redundancies add to sentence length and are illogical, they should be avoided. Note the redundancy in this sentence:

The provision of Section 5 provides for long-term disability benefits.

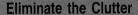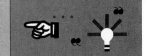

COMMUNICATION IN BRIEF

Eliminate the Clutter

Some suggestions for reducing unnecessarily long phrases.

Long Phrase	Shorter Substitution
along the lines of	like
at the present time	now
in accordance with	by
in the amount of	for
in very few cases	seldom
on the basis of	by
on the occasion of	on
with a view to	to

The duplication, of course, is in the meaning of *provides*. By definition, a *provision* provides. So the repetition serves no purpose. Two solutions are shown here.

> Section 5 provides for long-term disability benefits.
> The provision of Section 5 is long-term disability benefits.

One expression that is heard often is, "In my opinion, I think." Since the meaning of these words is "I think that I think," the following versions would be better choices.

> *Redundant:* In my opinion, I think the plan is sound.
> *Improved:* I think the plan is sound.
> *Improved:* In my opinion, the plan is sound.

Here are other examples of redundancies and ways to eliminate them:

Needless Repetition	**Repetition Eliminated**
Please endorse your name on the back of this cheque.	*Please endorse* this cheque on the back.
Todd Wilson is the *present incumbent.*	Todd Wilson is the *incumbent.*
We should *plan in advance for the future.*	We should *plan.*

. . . .

A PRACTICE RUN

Rewrite these sentences eliminating the repetition.

If you are not satisfied, return it back to us.

_____

The consensus of opinion is that the tax is unfair.

_____

Please repeat that over again.

_____
. . . .

- Eliminate extra meaningless words.

Eliminate Empty Words.   As well as using long expressions, we often use extra words. To write economically and make sentences stronger, eliminate the empty words that add nothing to the meaning. In the following example, the improved, shorter version keeps the full message of the longer version.

Long: *There are* four rules that should be observed.
Improved: Four rules should be observed.

Long: *In the period* between April and June, we detected the problem.
Improved: Between April and June, we detected the problem.

. . . .

A PRACTICE RUN

Rewrite the following sentences eliminating the empty words.

It will be noted that the records for the past years show a steady increase in special appropriations.

_____

In addition to these defects, numerous other defects mar the operating procedure.

_____

I am prepared to make a report to the effect that sales have increased.

_____

. . . .

. . . .

VARIETY IN SENTENCE STRUCTURE

- Overusing short sentences gives an annoying, choppy effect.

Clear, short sentences are the norm for business writing. However, a long succession of short, choppy sentences can give the impression of elementary writing. You do not want to suggest that you are visualizing your reader as a child. Using the employee handbook example again, this revision has too many sentences:

An employee is going to change jobs. His or her old insurance will end. The new job will include new insurance. We will adjust the coverage. The effective date will be the first day of the job.

- Use a variety of sentence types: simple, compound, complex.

To help you avoid the negative effects of too many long or too many short sentences, vary the length and structure of your sentences. Here are examples of three basic types:

Simple Sentence: (one subject and one predicate)
You will have insurance on your new job.

Compound Sentence: (two equal simple sentences together)
You will have insurance on your new job, and your old insurance will end.

Complex Sentence: (one or more subordinate clauses and a main clause)
Although your old insurance will end, you will have insurance on your new job, because we will reinstate it on your first day.

- Vary the word order with cumulative and periodic sentences.

Sentences can also be varied in word order. A cumulative (or loose) sentence has the main information at the beginning, followed by modifying phrases and clauses. In a periodic sentence, on the other hand, the main information is at the end of the sentence. This reversed placement makes periodic sentences tiring to read if too many are used in succession. Used with care, however, periodic sentences make a change and create interest. In business writing, the cumulative sentence is found more frequently.

Cumulative: You will have insurance on your first day, although your old coverage will lapse.

Periodic: On your first day, although your old coverage will lapse, you will have insurance.

A PRACTICE RUN

Identify the type (simple, compound or complex) and order (cumulative or periodic) for each sentence.

	Sentence Type	Sentence Order
Four rules should be observed.		
Because her performance was good enough, she qualified for a promotion.		
He performed very well on the test, and he received a promotion.		

Determining Emphasis in Sentence Design

The sentences you write should give the right emphasis to content. Any written business communication contains a number of items of information, not all of which are equally important. Some are very important, such as a conclusion in a report or the objective in a letter. Others are relatively unimportant. Your task as a writer is to form your sentences to reflect the importance of each item.

Sentence length affects emphasis. Short, simple sentences carry more emphasis than long, involved ones. They stand out and call attention to their subject and verb. (Remember, verbs and nouns are the strongest elements of a sentence.) Thus, short sentences give the reader a single message without the distraction of additional information.

Longer sentences give less emphasis to their content. Adjectives and adverbs weaken the impact of the main idea. When a sentence contains two or more ideas, the ideas share emphasis. How they share it depends on how the sentence is constructed.

To illustrate the varying emphasis you can give information, consider this example. You have two items of information to write. One is that the company lost money last year. The other is that its sales volume reached a record high. You could present the information in at least three ways. First, you could give both items equal emphasis by placing them in separate short sentences:

The company lost money last year. The sales volume reached a record high.

Second, you could present the two items in the same sentence with emphasis on the lost money:

The company lost money last year, although it enjoyed record sales.

Third, you could present the two items in one sentence with emphasis on the sales increase:

The company enjoyed record sales last year, although it lost money.

* You should give every item its due emphasis.

* Short sentences emphasize contents.

* Long sentences de-emphasize content.

A PRACTICE RUN

Rewrite these two ideas in one sentence, emphasizing the first idea.

He went to the bookstore.   He hadn't bought his textbook yet.

_____

Now emphasize the second idea.

_____

• Determining emphasis is a matter of good judgment.

This example is taken from the introductory situation. In Doreen's original draft (in Chapter 3), her opening sentence was full of long words and awkward phrases. When she simplified the language the sentence read,

Doreen Lam, owner of the Good 'n Nice kiosk in Westridge Mall, graduated from Georgian Business College two years ago.

After studying this chapter on sentences and paragraphs, she realized that she also wanted to change the emphasis. The newspaper article was being written because she operated her own business, not because she graduated from Georgian Business College. Therefore, her latest revision reads

Doreen Lam, a graduate of Georgian Business College, is the owner of the Good 'n Nice kiosk in Westridge Mall.

The following paragraphs further illustrate the importance of thinking logically to determine emphasis. In the first, each item of information gets the emphasis of a short sentence and none stands out. However, the items are not equally important and do not deserve equal emphasis. While reading the paragraph, decide which points should receive emphasis. Also notice the choppy effect that the succession of short sentences produces.

The proposed building was inspected on October 1. Mr. George Wills inspected the building. Mr. Wills is a vice president of the company. He found that the building has 600 square metres of floor space. He also found that it has 225 square metres of storage space. The new store must have a minimum of 500 square metres of floor space. It must have 200 square metres of storage space. Thus, the main building exceeds the space requirements for the new store. Therefore, Mr. Wills concluded that the main building is adequate for the company's needs. The storage space is also adequate.

These two points should stand out: (1) the building is large enough, and (2) storage space exceeds minimum requirements. In the next paragraph, some of the items are subordinated, but not logically. The really important information still does not receive the emphasis it deserves:

Mr. George Wills, who inspected the proposed building on October 1, is a vice president of the company. His inspection, which supports the conclusion that the building is large enough for the proposed store, uncovered these facts. The building has 600 square metres of floor space and 225 square metres of storage space, which is more than the minimum requirement of 500 and 200 square metres, respectively, of floor and storage space.

The following paragraph shows good emphasis of the important points. The short beginning sentence emphasizes the conclusion. The supporting facts that the building exceeds the minimum floor and storage space requirements receive main-clause emphasis. The less important facts, such as the reference to George Wills, are treated subordinately. Also, the most important facts are placed at the points of emphasis—the beginning and ending.

The proposed building is large enough for the new store. This conclusion was reached by Vice President George Wills after his October 1 inspection of the site. The building's 600 square metres of floor space exceed the minimum requirement for the new store by 100 square metres. The 225 square metres of storage space exceed the storage requirement by 25 square metres.

A PRACTICE RUN

Rewrite this paragraph to emphasize the approval of the 4 percent raise.

Jenny has a good knowledge of office procedures. She works hard. She has performed her job well. She is pleasant most of the time; however, she has a bad temper, which has led to personal problems with her team. I cannot recommend her for promotion. I approve a 4 percent raise for her.

_____

_____

_____

_____

Now write the paragraph to emphasize the refusal to promote her.

_____

_____

_____

_____

The preceding illustrations show how sentence construction can determine emphasis. The choice is yours. You can make items stand out; you can treat them equally; or you can de-emphasize them. Be sure that what you do is the result of thorough thinking and not simply a matter of chance or habit.

Giving the Sentences Unity

Good sentences have unity. For a sentence to have unity, all of its parts must combine to form one clear thought. In other words, all the words put into a sentence should have a good reason for being together.

* All parts of a sentence should concern one thought.

Violations of unity in sentence construction fall into three categories: (1) unrelated ideas, (2) excessive detail, and (3) illogical constructions.

* There are three causes of unity error.

Unrelated Ideas.   Placing unrelated ideas in a sentence is the most obvious violation of unity. Putting two or more ideas in a sentence is not grammatically wrong, but this practice offends logic unless the ideas have a reason for being together. They must combine to complete the single goal of the sentence.

* First, placing unrelated ideas in a sentence violates unity.

You can create unity in these sentences in three ways: (1) You can put each idea in a separate sentence. (2) You can make one idea subordinate to the other. (3) You can add words that show how the ideas are related. This sentence lacks unity:

* You can avoid this error by (1) putting unrelated ideas in separate sentences, (2) subordinating an idea, and (3) adding words that show relationship.

Mr. Jordan is our sales manager, and he has a degree in law.

There appears to be no reason for these facts to be combined in one sentence. A better arrangement would be to put each idea in a separate sentence:

Mr. Jordan is our sales manager. He has a law degree.

If these two ideas are related, they could be kept in one sentence. The relationship should be shown by subordinating one idea to the other. In this way the main clause provides the unity of the sentence.

Mr. Jordan, our sales manager, has a law degree.

Although Mr. Jordan has a law degree, he works as our sales manager.

The point of good writing is knowing when to stop.

Lucy Maud Montgomery
Anne's House of Dreams

Here is another example of a sentence with two ideas that seem unrelated.

Our production increased in January, and our machinery is wearing out.

One way of improving it is to make a separate sentence of each idea.

Our production increased in January. Our machinery is wearing out.

If the two ideas are related, the sentence should be revised to make the relationship clear.

Even though our machinery is wearing out, production increased in January.

A PRACTICE RUN

Rewrite the following ideas to show the relationship.

The bill has not been paid, and they placed another order.

_____

There is a serious problem, and we have to take action.

_____

Sales volume for the month has declined. We have not definitely determined the causes. We know that during this period, there was construction on the street adjacent to the store. The construction severely limited traffic flow. There were several resignations in the advertizing department, and promotion efforts dropped well below normal.

_____

_____

_____

* Excessive detail is another cause of lack of unity. Use a separate sentence.

Excessive Detail.   Putting too much detail into one sentence tends to hide the central thought. If the detail is important, you should put it in a separate sentence. This suggestion strengthens another given earlier in the chapter—the suggestion that you use short sentences. Obviously, short sentences cannot have much detail. Long sentences full of detail may lead to lack of unity, as illustrated in these contrasting examples:

Excessive Detail

We have attempted to trace the Ply-tec insulation you ordered from us October 1, and about which you inquired in your October 10 letter, but we have not yet been able to locate it, although we are sending you a rush shipment immediately.

Improved

We are sending you a rush shipment of Ply-tec insulation immediately. Following your October 10 inquiry, we placed a trace on your October 1 order. We expect to have the answer shortly.

Excessive Detail

In 1989, when I, a small-town girl from a middle-class family, began my studies at Northern Business College, which is widely recognized for its accounting program, I set my goal for a career with a major accounting firm.

Improved

A small-town girl from a middle-class family, I entered Northern Business College in 1989. I selected N.B.C. because of its widely recognized accounting program. From the beginning, my goal was a career with a major accounting firm.

. . . .

A PRACTICE RUN

Rewrite this paragraph eliminating the excessive detail for better unity.

Our Montreal offices, considered plush when they were built in the 1970s, but now, in the 1990s, being badly in need of renovation, have, as is the case with most offices that have not been maintained, been abandoned to the wrecker's ball.

_____

_____

_____

. . . .

Illogical Constructions. Illogical constructions are created by careless thinking. That they remain in a message is the result of incomplete editing or revision. By taking the time to consider your message carefully, you should be able to prevent illogical constructions in it.

Even though this first example contains two correct clauses for its two main thoughts, it violates the standard of unity.

First we cut prices, and then quality was reduced.

These two clauses cannot be used together, because one clause is in active voice (*we cut*), and the other is in passive voice (*quality was reduced*). To achieve unity make both clauses active, as in this corrected version:

First we cut prices, and then we reduced quality.

The mixed constructions of the following sentence do not make a clear and logical thought. The beginning clause belongs with a complex sentence, while the last part is the predicate of a simple sentence.

Because our salespeople are inexperienced caused us to miss our quota.

Revised for good logic and unity, the sentence might read:

Because our salespeople are inexperienced, we missed our quota. *or* The inexperience of our salespeople caused us to miss our quota.

* Illogical constructions can rob a sentence of unity.

* Active and passive voice in the same sentence can violate unity.

* So can mixed constructions.

. . . .

A PRACTICE RUN

Rewrite these sentences eliminating the illogical constructions to improve unity.

Knowing that she objected to the price was the reason we permitted her to return the goods.

_____

My education was completed in 1989, and then I began work as a sales representative for Xerox.

_____

. . . .

CARE IN PARAGRAPH DESIGN

• Paragraphing organizes and emphasizes the information.

Paragraphs show readers where a topic begins and ends, thus helping them to organize the information in their minds. Correct paragraphing creates a clearer explanation for the readers who usually have less knowledge of the subject than the writer. Paragraphs also help make ideas stand out. Therefore, designing paragraphs requires the ability to organize and connect information. It requires critical thinking skills, especially logic and imagination.

Giving Paragraphs Unity

• The contents of a paragraph should concern one topic or idea (unity).

Like sentences, paragraphs should have unity. When applied to paragraph structure, unity means building a paragraph around a single topic or idea. When you have finished a paragraph, you should be able to say, "Everything in this paragraph belongs together because every part concerns every other part."

A violation of unity is illustrated in the following paragraph from an application letter. As the goal of the paragraph is to summarize the applicant's coursework, all the sentences should pertain to coursework. By shifting to personal qualities, the third sentence violates paragraph unity. Taking this sentence out would correct the fault.

At university, I studied all the basic accounting courses as well as specialized courses in petroleum, and information systems. I also took specialized course work in the behavioural areas, with emphasis on human relations. *Realizing the value of human relations in business, I also actively participated in organizations such as a social fraternity, the YMCA, and our Men's Glee Club, which I particularly enjoyed.* I selected my elective course work to round out my general business education. Among my electives were courses in investments, advanced business report writing, financial policy, and forecasting. A glance at my résumé will show you the additional courses that round out my training.

A PRACTICE RUN

Identify the sentence that breaks the unity of this paragraph.

Databases are organized files of information. They can be as simple as an expense file with receipts and bills organized by month and type of expense. This type of file takes a lot of time to maintain, however, because it has so many pieces of paper. An example of a computerized database is the telephone directory.

Keeping Paragraphs Short

• Generally, paragraphs should be short.

As a rule, you should keep your paragraphs short. This suggestion overlaps the suggestion about unity. Short paragraphs are more likely to have unity, and paragraphs with unity are more likely to be short.

• Short paragraphs show organization better than long ones.

As noted earlier, paragraphs help the reader follow the writer's organization plan. Writing marked by short paragraphs identifies more of the details of that plan. In addition, such writing is inviting to the eye. As we saw in Chapter 2 when we discussed the nonverbal cues of written communication, people prefer to read writing with frequent paragraph breaks.

• About eight lines is a good average length.

How long a paragraph should be depends on its contents—on what must be included to achieve unity. An average length of eight lines for longer papers such as reports is recommended. Keep in mind that this suggestion is only an average. Some good paragraphs may be well over this length. On the other hand, one-line paragraphs are appropriate in memos to emphasize major points, and one line may be all that is needed to close a letter with goodwill.

• A good practice is to question paragraphs over 12 lines.

A good guideline to follow is to question the unity of all paragraphs 12 lines or longer. If after looking over such a paragraph, you conclude that it has unity, leave it as it is. If you find more than one topic, divide it to give each topic a separate paragraph.

Making Good Use of Topic Sentences

One good way of organizing paragraphs is to use topic sentences. The topic sentence expresses the main idea of a paragraph, and the remaining sentences build and support that idea. In a sense, the topic sentence serves as a headline for the paragraph, and all the other sentences supply the story. Not every paragraph must have a topic sentence. Some paragraphs, for example, introduce ideas, relate succeeding items, or present an assortment of facts that lead to no conclusion. The central thought of such paragraphs is difficult to put into a single sentence. Even so, you should use topic sentences whenever you can to define the unifying idea of each paragraph.

• Although not every good paragraph has a topic sentence, a topic sentence helps make a paragraph good.

How a topic sentence should fit into a paragraph depends primarily on the subject matter and the writer's plan. Some subject matter develops best if details are presented first, followed by a conclusion or a summary statement (the topic sentence). Other subject matter develops best if it is introduced by the conclusion or the summary statement. These two commonly used arrangements are discussed here.

• Placement of the topic sentence depends on the writer's plan.

Topic Sentence First.   The most common paragraph arrangement begins with the topic sentence and continues with the supporting material. As this arrangement fits most units of business information, you should find it useful.

• The topic sentence can come first.

To illustrate the writing of a paragraph in which the topic sentence comes first, take a paragraph reporting on economists' replies to a survey about business activity for the coming year. The facts to be presented are these: 13 percent of the economists expected an increase; 28 percent expected little or no change; 59 percent expected a downturn; 87 percent of those who expected a downturn thought it would come in the first quarter. The obvious conclusion—and the subject for the topic sentence—is that the majority expected a decline in the first quarter. Following this reasoning, we would develop a paragraph like this:

A majority of the economists consulted think that business activity will drop during the first quarter of next year. Of the 185 economists interviewed, only 13 percent looked for continued increases in business activity and 28 percent anticipated little or no change from the present high level. The remaining 59 percent looked for a recession. Of this group, nearly all (87 percent) believed that the downturn would occur during the first quarter of the year.

Topic Sentence at End.   The second most common paragraph arrangement places the topic sentence at the end, usually as a conclusion. Paragraphs of this type present the supporting details first to lead up to the conclusion. Such paragraphs often begin with what may appear to be a topic sentence; however, the final sentence covers the key point, as in this illustration:

• It can come last.

The significant role of inventories in the economic picture should not be overlooked. At present, inventories represent 3.8 months' supply. Their dollar value is the highest in history. If considered in relation to increased sales, however, they are not excessive. In fact, they are well within the range generally believed to be safe. *Thus, inventories are not likely to cause a downward swing in the economy.*

Leaving Out Unnecessary Details

Include in your paragraphs only the information needed. The chances are that you have more information than your readers need. Thus, a part of your communication task is to visualize your readers and adapt the content of your paragraph to their needs. You will include what they need you to tell them and omit what they do not need. If you follow this procedure, your paragraphs will be short, unified, and adapted for your readers.

• In writing paragraphs, leave out unnecessary information.

The following paragraph from a memorandum to maintenance workers presents excessive information.

In reviewing the personnel history form you filled out last week, I found an error that needs to be corrected. The section titled "work history" has three blank lines for information. The first is for dates employed; the second is for company name; the third is for type of work performed. On your form you wrote the company name across all three blanks. You did not indicate years employed or your duties. This information is important. It is reviewed by your supervisors every time you are considered for promotion or for a pay increase. Therefore, it must be completed. I request that you come by my office and complete this form at your earliest convenience.

The message says much more than necessary. The goal is to have the reader come to the office. Everything else is of little value until the employee is present to make the changes to the form. This revised memorandum is better:

Please come by my office before this Friday to correct some important details in the personnel form you filled out last week.

Giving Paragraphs Movement

* Each paragraph should move an additional step toward the goal.

Good writing has movement. Movement is the writing quality that takes the reader toward the goal in definite and logical steps, without side trips and backward shifts. The progress is steadily forward. The sentences move step by step to reach the paragraph goal, and the paragraphs move step by step to reach the overall goal.

Perhaps movement is best explained by example:

Three reasons justify moving from the Crowton site. First, the building rock in the area is questionable. Recent geologic explorations confirm that the Crowton deposits are nearly exhausted. Second, the distances from the Crowton site to major consumption areas make transportation costs unusually high. Obviously, transportation costs are reducing company profits. Third, the age of the machinery at the Crowton plant makes this an ideal time for relocation. The old equipment could be scrapped and more modern equipment purchased for the new site.

The flow of thought in this paragraph is orderly. The first sentence sets up the paragraph structure, and the parts of that structure follow smoothly and logically to the conclusion.

. . . .

A PRACTICE RUN

Rewrite this paragraph eliminating unnecessary detail and providing movement to show that this person is prepared to begin a career.

I majored in marketing at university and graduated in 1991. Among the marketing courses I took was Marketing Strategy. It was a very difficult course. The prof was great though. I also took promotions and marketing research. My best friends were made during our marketing research project because we had to work long hours together. These courses and my retail experience in Sports-wear and later in Cosmetics at Olympic Department Stores under Ms. Ross and Ms. Lesage have prepared me for a career in retailing.

_____

_____

_____

_____

. . . .

. . . .

A SUMMARY OF LEARNING OUTCOMES FROM THIS CHAPTER

In addition to choosing the right words, you should arrange those words into sentences that communicate clearly. This task involves adaptation. You adapt by writing sentences with your readers in mind. In general, you should use short sentences, averaging 16–18 words long for middle-level, adult readers.

You can make your sentences short in two ways: (1) by limiting content, and (2) by using words economically. Limiting content to keep sentences short means creating separate sentences for each of your thought units. Be careful not to use too many short sentences in succession, however, because they will make your writing choppy.

Using words economically involves looking for shorter ways of saying things. Here are some specific suggestions: (1) substitute shorter expressions, (2) avoid unnecessary repetition, and (3) eliminate empty words.

Give every item you communicate the emphasis it deserves. Use short sentences to emphasize points. Combine points into longer sentences to de-emphasize them. How you combine points (by equal treatment or by subordination) determines their emphasis.

Construct sentences to show that the parts belong together. You can achieve sentence unity by separating unrelated thoughts, by eliminating excessive detail, and by avoiding illogical constructions.

You should construct paragraphs that have unity—that is, that build around a single topic or idea. Such paragraphs are generally short. For that reason, it is wise to doublecheck paragraphs that are longer than 12 lines to be sure all the sentences are related. Using a topic sentence helps to ensure unity. A topic sentence usually occurs at the beginning of a paragraph, but other orders are used. Unified paragraphs do not include unessential details. Finally, unified paragraphs progress step by step toward the goal.

QUESTIONS FOR DISCUSSION

1. How are sentence length and sentence design related to adaptation?
2. What is the effect of sentence length on emphasis?
3. How can unity apply equally well to a sentence, to a paragraph, and to longer units of writing?
4. What are the principal causes of lack of unity in sentences?
5. "Although some people think differently, variety in sentence structure is just a matter of taste. As long as the ideas are in the sentence somewhere, I don't think it matters very much which comes first. Just because you have to wait until the end of the sentence for the main idea, you shouldn't want to stop reading. Having a series of periodic sentences wouldn't be a problem to me." Comment on this opinion and on the way it is expressed.
6. "Of course my paragraphs have topic sentences. They don't need much thought. I just repeat what the other sentences in the paragraph say." Discuss.

APPLICATION EXERCISE

Instructions: Break up the long sentences into shorter, more readable ones. Combine the short sentences into longer, less choppy ones.

1. Our Consumer Education Committee depends on information from Consumer and Corporate Affairs Canada to accomplish the committee's assigned duties of keeping informed of the qualities of all consumer goods and services, especially of their strengths and shortcomings, of gathering all pertinent information on dealers' sales practices, with emphasis on practices involving honest and reasonable fairness, and of publicizing any of the information collected that may be helpful in educating the consumer.

2. This is an elective procedure. It will not be covered by provincial health insurance. If you want the bill to be covered, you need to sign up for our private plan. The private plan costs $13 per month. The company will match that amount.

3. This course includes five short quizzes. Students may have an approved, excused absence from one quiz. Those students may take a special makeup examination that will be given during reading week, unless those students wish to use their average grade on the course as their grade for the missed quiz.

Instructions: Revise the following sentences for more economical wording.

4. In view of the fact that we financed the experiment, we were entitled to some profit.
5. Mr. Wong outlined his development plans on the occasion of his acceptance of the presidency.
6. I will talk to him with regard to the new policy.

7. There are many obligations that we must meet.
8. The chairperson is busy in the process of preparing a program.
9. In all probability, we are likely to suffer a loss this quarter.
10. The requirements for the job require a minimum of three years of experience.
11. The salespeople who were most successful received the best rewards.
12. The reader will note that this area ranks in the top 5 percent in per capita income.

Instructions: Rewrite the following paragraphs in two ways to show different placement of the topic sentence and variations in emphasis of contents. Note the differences in meaning in each of your paragraphs.

13. Last year our sales increased 7 percent in Nova Scotia and 9 percent in New Brunswick. Ontario had the highest increase, with 11 percent. Although all areas in the western region enjoyed increases, Alberta recorded only a 2 percent gain. Sales in BC increased 3 percent.

14. Our records show that Penn motors cost more than Oslo motors. The Penns have less breakdown time. They cost more to repair. I recommend that we buy Penn motors the next time we replace worn-out motors. The longer working life offsets Penn's cost disadvantage. So does its better record for breakdown.

15. Recently China ordered a large quantity of wheat from Canada. Likewise, Russia ordered a large quantity. Other countries continued to order heavily, resulting in a dramatic improvement in the outlook for wheat farming. Increased demand by Eastern European countries also contributed to the improved outlook.

CASE 4–1

The *Northern Torch* is your university newspaper, and you are its editor. Your team usually works very well together, but this week there's trouble. The news writers have criticized the book/movie reviewer's style, and she hasn't taken it well.

"Go stuff it. You just think you're so great. Well, you've got great, loud voices, but you don't have a clue about writing. I don't get top marks in English Lit by accident, you know."

The book and movie reviews are full of long, compound and complex sentences, with lots of adjectives and adverbs. The paragraphs are long, and many of the sentences are periodic—"to build interest and suspense," Anna-Lise says.

Aaron and Kristal insist on the importance of crisp, short sentences when reporting for a newspaper. They also believe in using familiar words and short paragraphs.

"What you write is just a snore, Anna-Lise. You've gotta grab student's attention with short, punchy sentences. And then, keep them glued to the paper with action!"

Before things get worse, you decide to step in to mediate this dispute. What can you say?

CASE 4–2

Work as a class or in small groups. Select a problem on your campus that you would like to see addressed, or choose a current political issue. Decide who would be the best person to speak to about the problem.

Using the information in Chapters 2–4, analyze this audience. Write a list of the characteristics that you would take into consideration when communicating with this audience.

Then, select the appropriate key words that you would need to use to present a solution. Define the terms that are unknown to you and any terms you want to use that may be unfamiliar to your audience.

What other elements of this communication effort should you plan to be sure that you will make a good impression on your audience and gain respect for your solution?

ANSWERS TO PRACTICE RUNS

►How to Keep Sentences Short

Limit the Content.

Long, Hard to Understand Sentence	Shorter, Easier to Understand Sentences
Regardless of their seniority or union affiliation, all employees who hope to be promoted are expected to continue their education either by enrolling in the special courses , which are scheduled to be offered by the company after working hours, or by taking approved correspondence courses selected from a list that may be seen in the training office.	Regardless of their seniority or union affiliation, all employees who hope to be promoted are expected to continue their education in either of two ways. (1) They may enrol in special courses to be offered by the company after working hours. (2) They may take approved correspondence courses selected from the list in the training office.

►Economize on Words

Substitute Shorter Expressions

Long Phrase	Shorter Substitution
for the reason that	because, since
in the near future	soon
in the neighbourhood of	about
in view of the fact that	since, because
with regard to, with reference to	about

Long:	Improved:
In spite of the fact that they received help, they failed to exceed the quota.	*Although* they received help, they failed to exceed the quota.
The president *is of the opinion that* the tax was paid.	The president *believes* the tax was paid.
During the time that she was employed by this company, Ms. Carr was absent once.	*While* she was employed by this company, Ms. Carr was absent once.

Use your improved paragraph from the earlier practice run (Regardless of their seniority or union affiliation . . .) and make it shorter and clearer by economizing on words.

First Improvement

Regardless of their seniority or union affiliation, all employees who hope to be promoted are expected to continue their education in either of two ways. (1) They may enrol in special courses to be offered by the company after working hours. (2) They may take approved correspondence courses selected from the list in the training office.

Second Improvement

Employees in all categories who want a promotion should continue their education in one of two ways. (1) They may enrol in special courses offered by the company after work. (2) They may take approved correspondence courses listed in the training office.

Avoid Unnecessary Repetition.

Repetition

If you are not satisfied, *return it back* to us.

The *consensus of opinion* is that the tax is unfair.

Please *repeat* that *over again*.

Repetition Eliminated

If you are not satisfied, *return it* to us.

The *consensus* is that the tax is unfair.

Please *repeat* that.

Eliminate Empty Words

Long:

It will be noted that the records for the past years show a steady increase in special appropriations.

In addition to these defects, numerous other defects mar the operating procedure.

I *am prepared to make a report to the effect that* sales increased.

Improved:

The records for past years show a steady increase in special appropriations.

Many other defects damage the operating procedure.

I will report that sales increased.

Variety in Sentence Structure

	Sentence Type	Sentence Order
Four rules should be observed.	simple	cumulative
Because his performance was good enough, he qualified for a promotion.	complex	periodic
He performed very well on the test, and he received a promotion.	compound	cumulative

. . . .

▶ Determining Emphasis in Sentence Design

He went to the bookstore.   He hadn't bought his textbook yet.

Emphasizing the First Idea.
He went to the bookstore because he hadn't bought his textbook yet.

Emphasizing the Second Idea.
Although he had gone to the bookstore, he hadn't bought his textbook yet.

Jenny has a good knowledge of office procedures. She works hard. She has performed her job well. She is pleasant most of the time; however, she has a bad temper, which has led to personal problems with her team. I cannot recommend her for promotion. I approve a 4 percent raise for her.

Emphasizing the 4 Percent Raise:
I approve a 4 percent raise for Jenny. She has a good knowledge of office procedures. She works hard, and she has performed her job well. She is pleasant most of the time, but I cannot recommend her for promotion because her temper has led to personal problems with her team.

Emphasizing the Refusal to Promote Her:
I cannot approve Jenny for promotion. Although she is pleasant most of the time, she has a bad temper. Her temper has led to problems with the work group. However, I will approve a 4 percent raise for her because she works hard and has performed well. She also has a good knowledge of office procedure.

▶ Giving the Sentences Unity

Unrelated Ideas

Unrelated	**Improved**
The bill has not been paid, and they placed another order.	Although the bill has not been paid, they placed another order.
There is a serious problem, and we have to take action.	We have to take action to solve a serious problem.
Sales volume for the month has declined, but we have not definitely determined the causes. We know that during this period there was construction on the street adjacent to the store, and this construction severely limited traffic flow. Also there were several resignations in the advertizing department, and promotion efforts dropped well below normal.	Sales volume for the month has declined. Although we have not definitely determined the causes, we know that during this period there was construction on the street adjacent to the store. Since this construction severely limited traffic flow, it may be partly to blame. Another factor may be lower than usual promotion efforts because of resignations in the advertizing department.

Excessive Detail

Excessive Detail	**Improved**
Our Montreal offices, considered plush when they were built in the 1970s, but now, in the 1990s, being badly in need of renovation, have, as is the case with most offices that have not been maintained, been abandoned to the wrecker's ball.	Our Montreal offices were considered plush when they were built in the 1970s. But they have not been maintained, so now they are badly in need of renovation. As is the case with most offices in this condition, ours have been abandoned to the wrecker's ball.

Illogical Construction

Illogical Construction	**Improved**
Knowing that she objected to the price was the reason we permitted her to return the goods.	Because we knew she objected to the price, we permitted her to return the goods.
My education was completed in 1989, and then I began work as a sales representative for Xerox.	I completed my education in 1989 and then began work as a sales representative for Xerox.

▶ Giving the Paragraphs Unity

Databases are organized files of information. They can be as simple as an expense file with receipts and bills organized by months and type of expense. This type of file takes a lot of time to maintain, however, because it has so many pieces of paper. An example of a computerized database is the telephone directory.

The sentence that breaks the unity is *This type of file takes a lot of time to maintain, however, because it has so many pieces of paper.*

▶ Giving the Paragraphs Movement

I majored in marketing at university and graduated in 1991. Among the marketing courses I took were marketing strategy that was very difficult. The prof was great though. I also took promotions and marketing research. My best friends were made during our marketing research project because we had to work long hours together. These courses and my retail experience in Sportswear and later in Cosmetics at Olympic Department Stores under Ms. Ross and Ms. Lesage have prepared me for a career in retailing.

With Movement to Show Qualifications

I graduated with a marketing major in 1995. Marketing strategy, promotions, and marketing research were important courses in my preparation for a career in retail. In addition, my training at Olympic Department Stores gave me the experience I needed.

5

Writing for Effect

Upon completing this chapter, you will be able to write business documents that emphasize key points and have a positive effect on human relations. To reach this goal, you should be able to

1 Discuss the rationale for using goodwill, a conversational tone, and a sincere approach.

2 Use a conversational style that avoids both stiff, formal language and clichés.

3 Use the you-viewpoint, positive language, and courtesy to foster goodwill.

4 Use four major techniques for emphasis in business writing.

5 Employ major transitional devices to write letters that flow smoothly (have coherence).

6 Follow the process of preparing, drafting, revising, and proofreading to create effective business messages.

▶ to Writing for Effect

Doreen is feeling better about her biographical sketch for the newspaper. (See the Introductory Situation to Chapter 4.) It took a lot of work, but she achieved her goal of writing a clear, short outline. She now wonders if the letters she dashes off so quickly should have a little more time spent on them. Perhaps they don't create the effect she wants.

She finds the letter she wrote two weeks ago to the property manager of Westridge Mall.

Dear Ms. Woitas:

In reply to your letter of April 12, this is to inform you that I do wish to continue my lease at this kiosk for my Good 'n Nice business.

However, I regret to report that a three-year term is unacceptable. It is much more reasonable to consider two years.

I'm very sorry that I can't agree to your suggestion for a longer term, but my business is just beginning to flourish, so I'm sure you'll understand my hesitation.

Yours sincerely,

Doreen Lam
Good 'n Nice

Reading this letter now does not make her feel happy. She sees in it a lack of confidence and positiveness. She is also unhappy at what she doesn't see in it. Her letter does very little to build a good relationship with someone who is important to her success.

"Maybe this explains why I haven't had a reply yet," she muses. ∎

• • • • • • • • • • • • • • •
NEED FOR EFFECT

As noted in the preceding chapters, clarity will be your major concern in most of your business writing. For internal communication—reports, memorandums, e-mail and voice mail messages, for example—your primary concern will be to give information clearly. Your efforts to deliver information quickly and accurately will be appreciated.

• Written communication within a business primarily requires clarity.

Building and communicating goodwill is a valuable business practice. Not only the information in a message but also the way it is said will determine public attitudes toward the company. People in business know that their success depends on what the customers think about the business.[1] What the customers think is influenced by what they have experienced in dealing with the business. What the customers have experienced is shared with others who will then decide whether to become customers.

• Use goodwill to create and maintain good customer relationships.

The success of messages depends upon even more than clarity and goodwill. Credibility and sincerity are also important. For example, to encourage someone to accept an unfavourable decision, you will need to be persuasive. Persuasion requires credibility to back it up. In sending congratulations or good news, you will need sincerity. Congratulations without sincerity is quickly identified as empty flattery. Credibility and sincerity will build a solid reputation for you and the company you represent.

• Use credibility and sincerity to build a good reputation.

As we have seen, the nonverbal cues surrounding the way in which information is presented will make a difference. Good quality paper and print, an attractive layout, and timeliness will give a positive impression. Positive, confident words add to that impression.

• Create a positive impression.

---

[1]Valerie Beckford. "Keep Customers for Life!" *Business Mart* Vol.2–6. http://www.eklipse.com/business-mart/frames/v2-6-3.html (11 June 1996). [Note: *Business Mart* is an on-line magazine available through the Business Mart Publications web site. Business Mart is based in Surrey, British Columbia.]

These are a few of the characteristics that you will want for your business messages. When these characteristics appear together, they create overlapping patterns that reinforce your good intentions toward the receiver. Goodwill in human relations will help you build networks of relationships to accomplish your business purposes.

CONVERSATIONAL STYLE

* Writing in conversational language has a favourable effect.

One writing technique that helps build goodwill is to use good conversational language. We mean language that is warm, natural, and polite. It is informal but not slang. Imagine relating an event to your grandparents. You speak warmly but not as casually as you talk to your friends. This pleasant and professional language in a letter leaves an impression that people like.

Resisting the Tendency to Be Formal

* We tend to be stiff and formal when writing.

Writing conversationally is not as easy as you might think, because most of us tend to write formally. The result can be a cold and unnatural style—one that doesn't produce the goodwill we want in business letters. The following examples illustrate this problem and how to correct it.

Stiff and Dull	Conversational
Reference is made to your May 7 letter, in which you describe the approved procedure for initiating a claim.	Please refer to your May 7th letter about how to file a claim.
Enclosed herewith is the brochure in which you expressed an interest.	Enclosed is the brochure you mentioned.

A PRACTICE RUN

Rewrite the following sentences in conversational tone.

I shall be most pleased to take advantage of your kind suggestion when and if prices decline.

_____

Please be advised that you should sign the enclosed form and return it before the 5th.

_____

Cutting Out Clichés

* Clichés are expressions used by habit every time a certain type of situation occurs.

Clichés are expressions used by habit every time a certain type of situation occurs. They are used automatically rather than because they fit the present situation well. How many times a day do you hear "Have a nice day!"? How many of those times do you believe the words are meant especially for you?

* They give the effect of routine treatment. It is better to use original words.

Because they are used routinely, clichés give the impression of routine treatment, which is not likely to impress readers favourably. Such treatment tells readers that the writer has no special concern for them—that the present case is being handled in the same way as others. In contrast, words specially selected for the situation are likely to impress. They show the writer's concern for and interest in the readers.

* You can avoid clichés by treating each situation as if it were unique.

You do not need to know all the clichés to stop using them. You only need to write as if this is the first time you have encountered the situation. Writing for the present case will help you avoid these overused phrases.

"THE EFFECT OF BAD WRITING
CAN BE REWARDING"
(THE DOG BOOK OF PROVERBS)

A REMINDER ABOUT YOU-VIEWPOINT

In Chapter 2 we discussed the importance of adaptation and the you-viewpoint in involving your receiver in the communication process. We mention it here because you-viewpoint also helps build goodwill and consideration into your writing. People usually appreciate the courtesy and attention to their interests seen in you-viewpoint writing. As a result, their attitude is positive toward the sender and then, hopefully, toward the purpose of the communication.

* The you-viewpoint creates goodwill.

ACCENT ON POSITIVE LANGUAGE

Whether or not your letter achieves its goal will often depend on the words you use. There are many ways of saying something, and each way conveys a different meaning.

* Each way of saying something has a unique meaning.

Effects of Words

Positive words are usually best for achieving your letter goals. This is not to say that negative words have no place in business writing. Such words are strong and give emphasis. You will sometimes want to use negative words, but you will need positive words more often. When your goal is to change someone's position, for example, positive words are most likely to do the job. They tend to put the reader in the right frame of mind, and they emphasize the pleasant aspects of the goal. They also create the goodwill atmosphere we seek in most letters.

* Positive words are usually best for achieving business goals, especially when persuasion and goodwill are needed.

Negative words tend to produce the opposite effect. They may stir up your reader's resistance to your goals and to you. They are likely to damage the goodwill businesses strive to earn. Thus, to reach your goals, you will need to remember the negative and positive impact of your words.

* Negative words stir up resistance and hurt goodwill.

You should generally be wary of strongly negative words. These words convey unhappy and unpleasant thoughts and usually detract from your goal. They include words of blame, such as *mistake, problem, error, damage, loss,* and *failure.* Also included are words that deny, such as *no, do not, refuse,* and *stop.* Finally, there are words whose sounds or meanings have unpleasant effects. Examples would differ from person to person, but many would agree on these: *itch, guts, scratch, grime, sloppy, sticky, bloody,*

* So beware of strongly negative words (*mistake, problem*), words that deny (*no, do not*), and ugly words (*itch, guts*).

Thank you for your letter. (opening sentence)
If I can be of any further assistance, please do not hesitate to call me. (closing sentence)
Thank you for your kind attention to this matter. (closing sentence)
This will acknowledge receipt of . . .
According to our records . . .
This is to advise you that . . .
It has been a pleasure to do business with you.
I look forward to seeing you again sometime.

nauseous. Run these words through your mind and think about the meanings and feelings they produce. You can see that they work against most of the goals of effective business communication.

Illustrations of Positive Word Choice

To illustrate, take the case of a company executive who had to deny a local civic group's request to use the company's main meeting facilities. The group could use a smaller conference room. The executive came up with this response.

I regret that you cannot use our club room for your meeting. The Ladies' Book Club asked for it a long time before you did. You could use our conference room, but it only seats 40.

I regret tries to show concern, but this phrase emphasizes the bad news. The decision is stated negatively (*you cannot use*). The second sentence contains a mild criticism by suggesting poor planning by this club in comparison with the Ladies' Book Club. Finally, notice how the good news of the message is handicapped by the limiting word *only*.

Had the executive searched for more positive ways of covering the same situation, he or she might have said:

Although the club room has already been reserved by the Ladies' Book Club, you could meet in our 40-seat conference room.

Not a single negative word appears in this version. Both approaches achieve the primary objective of denying a request, but their effects on the reader differ sharply. There is no question which approach does the better job of building and holding goodwill.

For a second illustration, take the case of a correspondent who must write a letter granting the claim of a woman for cosmetics damaged in transit. Granting the claim, of course, is the most positive ending that such a situation can have. Even though this customer has had an unhappy experience, she is receiving what she wants. However, the negative language of an unskilled writer can so vividly recall the unhappy moments that the happy solution is moved to the background. As this negative version of the message illustrates, the effect is to damage the reader's goodwill:

We received your claim in which you *say* that you received three *damaged* cases of Midnight Magic lotion. We assure you that we sincerely *regret* the *problems* this has caused you. Even though we feel in all sincerity that our shipping clerks have not been *negligent*, we will assume the *blame* and replace the *damaged* merchandise.

Obviously, this approach is not conducive to goodwill. The phrase "in which you say" implies some doubt about the legitimacy of the claim. The doubt is raised again in discussing the shipping department. The expression of regret reminds the reader of the event that caused the trouble while the negatives *blame* and *damage* strengthen that recollection. The claim is granted grudgingly. But why? If the claim is just, an adjustment should be given. If there is evidence the claim is false, it should be refused. The company only adds to its losses with this "negative yes" approach.

In the following version of the same message, the writer refers only to positive aspects of the situation—what can be done to settle the problem. The job is done without using a negative word, without discussing the troublesome situation, and without suggesting suspicions about the honesty of the claim. This approach is likely to maintain good business relations with the reader:

Three replacement cases of midnight Magic lotion are on their way to you by Mercury Freight. They should be on your sales floor by Saturday.

For additional illustrations, compare the differing results obtained from these contrasting versions (italics mark the negative words):

Negative	Positive
You *failed* to give us the fabric specifications of the chair you ordered.	So that you may have the one chair you want, please check your choice of fabric on the enclosed card.
We *cannot* deliver until Friday.	We can deliver on Friday.
You were *wrong* in your conclusion, for paragraph 3 of our agreement clearly states . . .	The conclusion based on reading paragraph 3 of our agreement is that . . .
We *regret* that we *overlooked* your coverage on this equipment and apologize for the *trouble* and *concern* it must have caused you.	You were quite right. You do have coverage on the equipment. Thank you for calling the matter to our attention.
We *regret* to inform you that we must *deny* your request for credit.	For the time being, we can serve you only on a cash basis.

A PRACTICE RUN

Rewrite these negative sentences in a more positive form.

Smoking is not permitted anywhere except in the lobby.

_____

Chock-O-Nuts do not have that gummy, runny coating that makes some candies stick together when they get hot.

_____

You should have known that the Peyton fryer cannot be submerged in water, for it is clearly explained in the instructions.

_____

COURTESY

A major contributor to goodwill in business letters is courtesy. By *courtesy* we mean treating people with respect and friendly concern. Courtesy in business letters leads to a better climate for solving problems and doing business.

* Courtesy is a major contributor to goodwill in business letters.

Developing courtesy in a letter involves a variety of specific techniques. First, it involves the three discussed before: writing in conversational language, employing the you-viewpoint, and choosing words for positive effect. It also involves other techniques.

• Courtesy involves the preceding goodwill techniques.

Singling Out Your Reader

• It also involves writing directly for the one reader.

One of the other techniques is to single out and write directly to your reader. Letters that appear routine have a cold, impersonal effect. On the other hand, letters that appear to be written for one reader tend to make the reader feel important and appreciated. Using the reader's name in the letter text is one good way. You can gain the reader's favour by occasionally making such references as "you are correct, Mr. Brock" or "as you know, Ms. O'Neill." As another example, a letter granting a professor permission to duplicate copyrighted material for a class could end with "We wish you the best of success in your class this semester." This specially adapted comment is better than one that fits any similar case: "If we can be of further assistance, please let us know."

• It is possible to use computers to accomplish this task.

Because a personal letter is costly to produce, most businesses use the capabilities of word processors and databases to personalize letters. By selecting from a bank of prewritten paragraphs and using the merge feature on a word processor, any business can make a routine letter more personal. Chapter 18, "Technology in Communication" will explain more about these possibilities.

Refraining from Lecturing

• The effect of courtesy is helped by not lecturing (preaching).

You can help give your letters a courteous tone by not lecturing. Except in the rare case in which the receiver looks up to the sender, a preaching tone hurts goodwill. Most people like to be treated as equals rather than being bossed or patronized. Thus, writing that suggests unequal writer–reader relations is likely to make the reader ask, "What right do they have to tell me what to do?"

• Lecturing may arise from efforts to persuade or involve the reader.

Lecturing may not be intended. It often occurs when the writer is trying to be convincing, as in this example: "You must take advantage of savings like this. The pennies will pile up. In time you will have dollars!" Strong persuasive statements such as "you need to," "you will want to," and "you will certainly agree that" suggest that the readers need to be told what to do or how to feel. In addition, obvious statements like "Rapid inventory turnover means better cash flow" seem to talk down to the receiver. And finally, there is the pattern of a question and its obvious answer: "Would you like to make a 38 percent profit? Of course you would!" Most people will resist such messages. Lecturing, whether intentional or unintentional, will hinder your efforts to achieve good relations with your reader.

Doing More than Is Expected

• Doing more than necessary builds goodwill.

One sure way to gain goodwill is to do a little bit more than you have to do for your reader. We are all aware of how helpful little extra acts are in other areas of our personal relationships. Too few of us, however, use them in our letters. Perhaps in the mistaken belief that we are being concise, we include only the barest essentials in our letters. The result is brusque, hurried treatment inconsistent with our efforts to be courteous and build goodwill.

The writer of a memo refusing a request for use of company equipment, for example, only needs to say no to accomplish the primary goal. A courteous writer who is conscious of goodwill would briefly explain the refusal, perhaps suggesting alternative steps that the reader might take. A supplier's brief extra sentence to wish a retailer good luck on a coming promotion is worth the effort. So are an insurance agent's words of congratulations to a policyholder who has earned some distinction. Likewise, a salesperson uses good judgment in an acknowledgment letter that includes tips about using the item purchased.

• Conciseness means word economy—not leaving out beneficial points.

To those who say that these suggestions are inconsistent with the need for conciseness, we must answer that the information we speak of is needed to build goodwill, which is one of the overall goals of effective communication. Conciseness concerns the number of words needed to say what you must say to accomplish all your goals. It never involves leaving out information vital to any of your objectives. On the other hand, nothing we have said should be interpreted to mean that any amount of information is justified. Say what you need to to achieve your goal and satisfy the receiver.

Avoiding Anger

Most angry comments do not provide needed information but merely serve to let the writer blow off steam. Such comments take many forms, such as sarcasm, insults, and exclamations. One might argue that angry words "tell it as it is"—that what they say is true. Even so, they convey much more than the literal meaning of the words. They show anger and lack tact. The effect of angry words is to make the reader angry. With both writer and reader upset, the two are not likely to get together on whatever the letter is about.

* Rarely is anger justified in letters. It destroys goodwill.

In instances where you must take a firm stand or demand a certain action, being assertive will be more useful than being angry. Being assertive means being direct and forceful while still being courteous and professional. When you are assertive, you are strong, definite, and calm. These behaviours are quite different from an angry tirade that makes you appear childish. Assertive behaviour is much more likely to achieve your objective.

* Being assertive is more effective than being angry.

Being Sincere

Courteous treatment is sincere treatment. The best way of ensuring sincerity in your letters is to believe in the techniques you use. If you honestly want to be courteous, if you believe that you-viewpoint treatment leads to harmonious relations, and if you think that tactful treatment that spares your reader's feelings is worth your time and effort, you are likely to apply these techniques sincerely. Your sincerity will show in your writing.

* Efforts to be courteous must be sincere.

There are two extremes you can avoid to help your writing have the quality of sincerity. They are overdoing the goodwill techniques, and overstating your case.

Overdoing the Goodwill Techniques. Goodwill techniques can be overdone. For example, in your efforts to write to this one person, you easily can use your reader's name too often. Overdoing the goodwill effort may be caused by lack of experience or too much zeal, but from the reader's viewpoint, the likely interpretation will be insincerity.

* The goodwill effort can be overdone.

Overstating the Case. The second area that you should check is overstating your case. Although some exaggerated statements are conventional in sales writing, even here they can leave a mark of insincerity. Such words cause us to question; we rarely believe them.

* Exaggerated statements are obviously insincere.

Many exaggerated statements involve the use of superlatives. Although frequently used, only rarely do they fit the reality being described. Words like *greatest, most amazing, finest, healthiest,* and *strongest* are seldom appropriate. Other strong words are *always, never, extraordinary, sensational, terrific,* and *revolutionary.* Remember, it is easy to see through most overstated claims, and your credibility is at stake.

* Superlatives (greatest, finest, strongest) often suggest exaggeration.

. . . .
THE ROLE OF EMPHASIS

As we saw in Chapter 4, messages contain a number of facts and ideas. Some are more important than others. A part of your job as a writer is to determine the importance of each item and to give each item the emphasis it deserves. It is time to consider the role and practice of emphasis in an entire message, such as a letter or memo.

* Every item communicated should get the proper emphasis.

To give each item in your message proper emphasis, you must use certain techniques. By far the most useful are these four: position, space, structure, and mechanical devices. The following paragraphs explain each.

* There are four basic emphasis techniques.

Position and Emphasis

• Position determines emphasis. Beginnings and endings carry emphasis.

The beginnings and endings of a writing unit carry more emphasis than the centre parts. We have seen this rule of emphasis in sentences and paragraphs in the last chapter. Your designing of paragraphs took into account the emphasis positions of the beginning and ending sentences. Now finally, in letters, memos, reports, or speeches, the beginning and the closing are the major emphasis positions. You must be especially mindful of what you put in these places. This principle is easy to visualize if you think of a parade. The parade marshall and local dignitaries lead off the parade and the big star, such as Santa Claus, is at the end.

In summary, use the beginning and ending positions for the points you want to stand out. Between these positions, place the points that you do not need to emphasize.

Space and Emphasis

• The more space a topic is given, the more emphasis the topic receives.

The second technique for giving emphasis to a topic is to give it more space. The more you say about something, the more emphasis you give it; and the less you say about something, the less emphasis you give it. If your letter devotes a full paragraph to one point and a brief sentence to another, the first point receives more emphasis. To produce the desired effect in your letter, you will need to say just enough about each item to give it the degree of emphasis that is appropriate.

• Emphasis and forcefulness are not the same.

A note of caution should be added here. Giving more space to a topic to demonstrate its importance works only up to a point. If the discussion goes on and on, the audience may stop paying attention all together. A short, strongly worded comment in a meeting often carries more force than long-winded discourse. The same is true in a letter, memo, or report. Belabouring a point shows its importance to the sender but robs it of force and impact.

Sentence Structure and Emphasis

• Sentence structure determines emphasis. Short, simple sentences emphasize content; long, involved ones do not.

As well as position and space, sentence structure plays a role in emphasis. As noted in Chapter 4, short, simple sentences call attention to their content; long, involved ones do not. If an idea is important, develop it fully and give it the space it needs. You can use a series of short sentences to make the key point stand out from the longer descriptive sentences. Then it will not have to compete with other information for the reader's attention. Combine the less important points into longer sentences, taking care that the relationships are logical. In your combination sentences, place the more important material in independent clauses and the less important information in subordinate structures.

Mechanical Devices and Emphasis

• Mechanical devices also give emphasis to content.

The most obvious emphasis technique is the use of mechanical devices. By *mechanical devices*, we mean any of the things that we can do physically to give the printed word emphasis. The most common devices are underlining, quotation marks, italics, boldface type, and solid capitals. Lines, arrows, and diagrams also can call attention to certain parts. So can colour, special fonts, and drawings. These obvious, nonverbal cues most frequently appear in persuasive sales letters.

. . . .
COHERENCE

• Messages should be coherent. The relationships of parts should be clear.

A message is more than a random collection of bits of information. A part of the message is in the relationships of the facts presented. Thus, to communicate successfully, you must make the relationships clear. This task is called giving coherence to your message.

The best thing you can do to give your message coherence is to arrange its information in a logical order—an order appropriate for the strategy of the particular case. So important is this matter to letter writing that it is the primary topic of discussion in following chapters. Thus, discussion of this vital part of coherence will be postponed until it can be given full treatment.

But logical organization by itself is usually not enough to create a coherent message. Various aids are needed to bridge or tie together the information presented. These aids are known as *transitional devices*. We will discuss the four major ones: tie-in sentences, repetition of key words, use of pronouns, and use of transitional words and phrases.

- Presenting information in logical order aids coherence.

Tie-In Sentences

By structuring your message so that one idea sets up the next, you can skillfully relate the ideas. That is, you can design the sentences to tie in two successive ideas. Notice in the following example how a job applicant tied together the first two sentences of the letter:

- Sentences can be designed to tie together succeeding thoughts.

As a result of increasing demand for precision instruments in the Humboldt area, won't you soon need another experienced and trained salesperson to call on your technical accounts there? With seven successful years of selling Morris instruments and a degree in civil engineering, I believe I have the qualifications to do this job.

Contrast the sentence above with the abrupt shift that this next sentence would make:

As a result of increasing demand for precision instruments in the Humboldt area, won't you soon need another experienced and trained salesperson to call on your technical accounts there? I am 32 years of age, married, and interested in exploring the possibilities of employment with you.

Planned Repetition of Key Words

By repeating key words from one sentence to the next, you can make smooth connections of successive ideas. The following sentences illustrate this transitional device. They come from a letter refusing a request to lecture at an advertizing clinic.

- Selective repetition of key words connects thoughts.

Your advertizing clinic is so well planned that it can provide a really *valuable* service to practitioners in the community. However, to be truly *valuable,* I think you will agree, all elements of the program must be given the *time* a thorough preparation requires. As my *time* for the coming weeks is heavily committed, someone else who has the time to do justice to your program will need to be found.

Use of Pronouns

Because pronouns must refer to words previously used, pronouns make good transitions between ideas. Use them from time to time in forming idea connections. Especially use the demonstrative pronouns (*this, that, these, those*) and their adjective forms, for these words clearly relate ideas. Be sure that each pronoun clearly refers to a noun. The following example illustrates linking through the use of demonstrative pronouns (in italics).

- Pronouns connect with the words they represent.

Ever since the introduction of our Mark V model 10 years ago, consumers have suggested only one possible improvement—automatic controls. During all *this* time, the efforts of Atkins research personnel have been concentrated on making *this* improvement. Now we proudly report that *these* efforts have been successful.

Transitional Words

In everyday conversation most of us explain our ideas by linking them with transitional words to show relationships in time, cause, direction, and so on. Unfortunately, when we write, most of us forget to use them enough. Be alert for places that need to be connected or related. Whenever sharp shifts or breaks in thought occur, consider using transitional words.

- Use transitional words in your writing.

- Transitional words tell the thought connection between following ideas.

Among the commonly used transitional words are *in addition, besides, in spite of, in contrast, however, likewise, thus, therefore, for example,* and *also.* A more extensive list appears in Chapter 12, where we review transition in report writing. That these words bridge thoughts is easy to see, for each one gives a clue to the nature of the connection between what has been said and what will be said next. *In addition,* for example, tells the reader that what is to be discussed next builds on what has been discussed. *However* clearly shows a contrast in ideas. *Likewise* tells that what has been said resembles what will be said.

A Word of Caution

- Do not use transitional words arbitrarily. Make them appear natural.

The preceding discussion does not suggest that you should use these transitional devices arbitrarily. Much of your subject matter will flow smoothly without them. When you use them, use them naturally so they blend in with your writing, and use them logically so they achieve their purpose of guiding the receiver. Otherwise, you will confuse the reader as in this exaggerated example of illogical, unnatural transitions.

Before then, I had given the speech. Moreover, the audience was very attentive. However, the projector didn't work in addition to the room being hot. Nevertheless, the time passed quickly.

A FOUR-STAGE APPROACH TO CREATING BUSINESS MESSAGES

The following chapters review the most common types of business situations. They analyze the problems involved in each situation and then recommend an organizational plan and a strategy for communication. These specific plans and strategies are derived from the following four-stage approach to planning business communication: Prepare, Draft, Revise and Edit, and Proofread.

Stage 1: Prepare

In the preparation stage, you need to do five things: (1) Get the Complete Picture. (2) Determine the Objective. (3) Determine the Receiver's Reaction. (4) Select the Plan. (5) Select the Channel.

- Get all the information you need.

Get the Complete Picture.   Your first step is to get all the information you will need. In a business situation, this means listening to the customer, consulting with other employees, getting past correspondence and records from the files—in fact, doing whatever is necessary to inform yourself fully of the situation. This research includes taking the time to visualize your receiver as discussed in Chapter 2. Without a complete picture, you may make costly mistakes.

- Determine your objective for the message.

Determine the Objective.   With all the background information in mind, you next determine your objective. Do you need to report information, acknowledge an order, ask for something, demand payment of a bill, reject an applicant, or what?

- Predict how the receiver will react.

Determine the Receiver's Reaction.   Next, you try to predict the likely reaction to the content of your message. Based on what you know about your receiver and your objective, will the reaction be positive, negative, or somewhere in between? Although you cannot be certain of how the receiver will react, your prediction will help you choose an appropriate strategy.

- Select the plan. The anticipated receiver reaction influences your plan.

Select the Plan.   The direct and indirect approaches are possible depending upon how positive you think your receiver will be toward your message. These are not hard and fast rules, but rather matters of judgment.

If you predict that the receiver's reaction will be positive or neutral, you will generally use a direct approach. That is, you will get to your objective right away. This plan, commonly called direct order, is easy to use. Fortunately, it is appropriate for most business communication. In positive or neutral situations, you usually have no need for opening explanations or introductory remarks. Instead, right at the beginning, you will make your request, answer the questions you have been asked, report your information, or state whatever your goal is for this message. Getting to the point quickly in routine matters is appreciated by people in business because they are busy. Your consideration of their time will begin to build goodwill right away. (The direct order is discussed and applied in Chapters 6 and 7.)

* Use direct order for favourable reactions.

If you predict a negative or skeptical reaction from your receiver, you should use an indirect approach. Indirect order is the opposite of direct order. In this plan you lay some groundwork before getting to the objective. As you will see, the indirect order typically requires more skillful use of strategy and word choice than the direct one does. (See the application of indirect order in Chapter 8.) If you expect resistance to your request, you should consider not only an indirect plan, but also a persuasive approach. (For a discussion of persuasive letters, see Chapter 9.)

* Use indirect order for unfavourable reactions.

At this point you may discover gaps that require you to return to an earlier step. For example, if you decide that the receiver's attitude will be skeptical, you may need to gather more facts to satisfy that skepticism. Or if you anticipate very favourable reactions, you may find that you can expand the objective of your message. The point is that communication is a process that can include cycles of revision.

* Planning is a process.

After you know the facts, your purpose, your receiver's probable reaction, and the plan to follow, you are ready to select the channel for communication.

Select the Channel. The channel is the physical path chosen to send a message. Channels can be divided into two broad categories—written and oral. Written channels include the traditional paper formats of letters, memos, and reports, as well as the newer computer networks, electronic meetings, and faxes. Oral channels transmit the message audibly. They include face-to-face conversations, meetings, telephone calls, audio or video teleconferencing, and recordings.

* Select the channel. The channel is the physical path used to send a message.

Each channel has strengths and weaknesses. No one channel is always the best. Consider the choices carefully. Your choice will depend on many factors. Here are a few:

* Each channel has strengths and weaknesses. Consider them carefully.

How many people need to receive this message?

How quickly should it reach the receivers?

How permanent a record of it is needed?

How detailed is the message?

How private or sensitive is the topic?

How expensive will this message be to send?

Stage 2: Draft

If you decide to write, you need to prepare a draft. Organize your key points in the direct or indirect order as required by the type of message you are writing. Use the techniques discussed in the preceding chapters—choosing words the reader understands, constructing sentences that present their contents clearly, and using words that create just the right effect.

* Draft the message, striving for clarity and the right effect.

A good place to begin is to jot down the main idea in a rough form, thinking of how to tailor it to your reader. If you find a blank computer screen or an empty piece of paper intimidating, begin at any point of the message that seems easy. Some people like to start by setting up the format and greeting; others like to dive into the paragraph that contains the key points and write the opening material later.

* Begin at any point.

Record ideas as they occur to you. It is important not to begin revising and editing too quickly. Criticism, even self-criticism, tends to slow down creative thought. Once you have a rough draft, then you can move sections, edit, and make revisions.

A PRACTICE RUN

Identify the factors that will influence the choice of channel for each of the following situations. Evaluate the channels chosen. If they are inappropriate, recommend better channels.

A voice mail message to advise a staff member that budget cuts place his or her job in jeopardy in three months.

_____

_____

_____

An expanded edition of the company newsletter to explain a proposed reorganization of departments. _____

_____

_____

A letter from a broker to obtain a client's permission to buy into a hot investment opportunity and to sell some stocks that are falling in value. _____

_____

_____

* Oral messages require planning too.

If you decide to use an oral channel, you should organize your thoughts in note form at least. In this way you can reduce the number of awkward silences, embarrassing mistakes, and annoying omissions. As with a written message, you follow the strategies for the type of message you are sending. Use the techniques of the previous chapters to help you find the right words and make the right impact. The plan is basically the same; only the method for transmitting the message is different.

Stage 3: Revise and Edit

* Next, revise and edit.

Whether you have chosen a written or an oral channel, as you revise your draft, ask yourself questions such as the following:

Will I accomplish my purpose?

Am I using you-viewpoint appropriately? Have I tried to anticipate my receiver's questions and needs?

Are my ideas clear? Where might misunderstandings occur?

Am I being concise while keeping the meaning precise?

Is the overall effect what I want to achieve? Have I built goodwill?

Make any changes that you think will improve your work. With written communication, you may use only a small fraction of your first draft in your final version, but you will have a better message. With oral communication, planning and revising is especially important because the message is received almost as soon as it is spoken. Then those words cannot be changed.

* If possible, ask for suggestions from others.

Input from others can also benefit the refinement of your message. As you may have experienced, it is difficult to find errors or weaknesses in your own work; yet others seem to find them easily. (Hint: If time permits, setting your work aside for 24 hours helps you see it in a new light.) Unfortunately, most of us are thin-skinned, and we tend to be defensive when criticisms are made. Practise receiving them with an open mind, evaluating them objectively, and using those that seem reasonable.

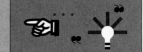

What is written without effort is in general read without pleasure.

Samuel Johnson

Stage 4: Proofread

After you have made all the revisions you think are needed, you have the final draft. Now for written communication, you become a proofreader, looking for errors in spelling, punctuation, or grammar. You perfect the format and layout so the final document represents your best standards in writing.

* Lastly, proofread for the final copy.

With oral communication, you may want to practise aloud. Stating aloud what you plan to say will help to clarify your message. You will also have a chance to check nonverbal cues, transitions, and, of course, grammar.

A SUMMARY OF LEARNING OUTCOMES FROM THIS CHAPTER

Clarity will be your major concern in business communication, but you will also want to convey goodwill.

Use a conversational style that is friendly and professional. Such a style requires that you resist the tendency to be formal. It also requires that you avoid clichés—words that are used routinely and without thought *(We are happy to report, if we can be of any further assistance)*.

You will need to emphasize the you-viewpoint and understand the negative and positive overtones of words. In general, select positive words to achieve your goal. Negative words have unpleasant overtones; positive words have pleasant ones *(We cannot deliver until Friday versus We can deliver on Friday)*.

You should be courteous in your letters. You can show courtesy by practising the goodwill techniques, by singling out your reader (writing for the one person), by not lecturing, by doing more than is expected of you, and by avoiding anger. In addition, you can show courtesy by being sincere. Being sincere is an attitude and a question of personal integrity that can be demonstrated by avoiding exaggeration and using goodwill techniques ethically.

Emphasis is another useful means of achieving effect. Every message contains a number of informational items, some deserving more emphasis than others. You should show differences in emphasis (1) by position (beginnings and endings receive prime emphasis); (2) by space (the greater the space devoted to a topic, the greater the emphasis); (3) by sentence structure (short sentences emphasize content more than longer ones); and (4) by mechanical means (colour, underlining, boldface, and so forth).

You should work to make your messages flow smoothly. You do this by presenting their information in logical order with one thought setting up the next. You show the relationships of thoughts by various transitional devices: tie-in sentences, word repetitions, pronouns, and transitional words.

In preparing a business message, a four-stage plan is useful. In stage one, you prepare. First, assemble all the information you need to get the complete picture. Then, determine the objective of the message. Next, predict the receiver's reaction and select the plan. If the likely reaction is positive, or even neutral, you should usually choose the direct order, which means getting to the objective right away. If the likely reaction is negative, you should usually choose the indirect order. Finally, you select the channel.

In stage two, you draft your message. In stage three, you revise and edit to produce your final draft. In stage four, you proofread to perfect your work.

QUESTIONS FOR DISCUSSION

1. Discuss this comment: "Building goodwill in letters requires extra effort. It takes extra time, and time costs money. We can't afford the luxury."

2. "Normal conversation is pretty laid back. Like, I'm sure I use slang and sentence fragments when I talk. Probably other grammar mistakes too. So what do you mean when you say my letters should sound conversational?" Answer this student's concern.

3. "If a company really wants to impress the readers of its letters, the letters should be formal and should be written in dignified language that displays knowledge." Discuss.

4. "I have some favourite ways of saying things that I like to use over and over. It makes my job a lot easier to have a few 'old reliables' around." Discuss.

5. Evaluate this comment: "It's hard to argue against courtesy, but, let's face it, business people don't want to appear soft. They want their letters to go straight to the point—without wasting words and without sugar coating."

6. "I use the words that communicate the message best. I don't care whether they are negative or positive." Discuss.

7. A writer wants to include a negative point in a letter but not to emphasize it. Use the four emphasis techniques to show how to de-emphasize the point.

8. Using illustrations other than those in the text, discuss and illustrate the four major transitional devices.

APPLICATION EXERCISE

Instruction: Rewrite these sentences in conversational style.

1. Attached, please find the receipt requested in your May 1st inquiry.

2. You are advised to endorse the above-mentioned proposal and return same to the undersigned.

3. This is to advise that all invoices shall be submitted in duplicate.

4. Permission is granted to delay remittance until the 12th.

5. We deem it a great pleasure to accept your kind offer to serve on the committee.

6. As per your request, please note that the report has been forwarded under separate cover.

Instructions: Underline all words that create a negative impression in these sentences. Then rewrite the sentences for positive effect.

7. If you will be patient, we will get the order to you when our supply is replenished.

8. We regret that we must call your attention to our policy prohibiting refunds. Only exchanges are allowed for merchandise bought at discount.

9. You cannot visit the plant except on Saturdays.

10. Tuff-Boy work clothing is not made from cloth that shrinks or fades.

11. One coat of stain is not enough to protect the wood in your deck.

12. We did not cancel your account.

13. No dogs without a leash are allowed in the park.

14. I regret the necessity of calling your attention to our letter of May 1.

15. Real Nanaimo Bars wouldn't have such a thin layer of chocolate on top.

16. Do not walk on the grass.

Instruction: From the letters in the rest of this text, or other business writing samples you may have, find examples of the following techniques of good writing.

17. Find examples of the four major emphasis techniques discussed in this chapter: position, space, sentence structure, and mechanical devices.

18. Find examples of these techniques for coherence: repetition of key words, use of pronouns, and transitional words.

19. Rewrite Doreen Lam's letter found in the "Introductory Situation" at the beginning of this chapter. Watch for ways to improve the positive tone, you-viewpoint, credibility, and conversational language. Make other corrections that you feel will help Doreen build a better working relationship with Ms. Woitas.

CASE 5-1

Amanda has been hired for the summer to work with students who volunteer at a seniors' residence. Part of her job is to train these volunteers on some important questions of safety and courtesy in dealing with the residents. Here is her list of things she thinks should be included in the training session.

- Don't be late. Call if you can't come.
- I'm Amanda, and I'm your boss for the summer.
- Speak clearly and slowly, speak up, and pronounce words carefully because, at their age, the residents cannot hear well.
- Introduce yourself every time. Old people are forgetful.

- You can't smoke anywhere in the building. The smoking lounges are for the residents only. The staff lounge is a no-smoking, smoke-free environment.
- Be polite.
- Don't forget to sign out if you are taking a resident for a walk because we need to know where you are and where the residents are in the unlikely event that there is a fire, emergency, or crisis while you are away.
- Squat down or bend over to talk to people in wheelchairs. Don't make them look up all the time.
- The wheelchair belongs to the resident. It's not a place to hang your sweater.

- Don't all go for breaks at the same time.
- Have fun and have a nice day, every day!

Using *all* the knowledge you have gained so far from this book, help Amanda to select, organize, and reword these ideas for her training session.

In this case there are opportunities to practise positive, conversational, and non-discriminatory language. You can help Amanda be more concise in some places. You can also demonstrate how she could build goodwill with the volunteers by being courteous and using you-viewpoint. Finally, to organize the ideas, use the techniques for emphasis, and use logical order and transitional devices to create coherence.

ANSWERS TO PRACTICE RUNS

▶ Resisting the Tendency to Be Formal

Stiff and Dull

I shall be most pleased to take advantage of your kind suggestion when and if prices decline.

Please be advised that you should sign the enclosed form and return before the 5th.

Conversational

I'll gladly follow your suggestion if the price falls.

Please sign this form and return it to me before the 5th

▶ Illustrations of Positive Word Choice

Negative

Smoking is *not* permitted anywhere except in the lobby.

Chock-O-Nuts do not have that *gummy*, *runny* coating that makes some candies *stick* together when they get hot.

You should have known that the Peyton fryer *cannot* be submerged in water, for it is clearly explained in the instructions.

Positive

Smoking is permitted in the lobby only.

The rich chocolate coating of Chock-O-Nuts stays crispy good throughout the summer months.

The instructions explain that the Peyton fryer should be cleaned carefully with a damp cloth.

▶ Select the Channel

1. A voice mail message to advise a staff member that budget cuts place his/her job in jeopardy in three months. *Concerns:* This is a sensitive issue that requires personal treatment, not a recorded message. Permanent documentation is also a concern because a lay-off or redundancy is a legal matter governed by contract. *Evaluation:* A voice mail message is a poor choice. A more appropriate channel would be a personal interview accompanied by a written document.

2. An expanded edition of the company newsletter to explain a proposed reorganization of department. *Concerns:* Everyone in the company must be reached with this message at about the same time. Individual telephone calls, for example, would not be appropriate. A full explanation is important. The grapevine will have carried news of this reorganization, with varying degrees of accuracy and completeness. A short memo would not address all the points fully. *Evaluation:* An expanded edition of the newsletter is an appropriate choice, assuming that further discussion is encouraged to answer questions and allay fears. Telephone numbers of those in charge, information sessions, or training seminars are possible ways of dealing with individual concerns.

3. A letter from a broker to obtain a client's permission to buy into a hot investment opportunity and to sell some stocks that are falling in value. *Concerns:* Speed and confidentiality are important. *Evaluation:* A letter is too slow. E-mail is not private enough. A personal telephone call, or a general voice mail message such as, "This is Richard Viswanathan with a message for Dorothy Wilkins. It is 9:00 A.M. on Friday, November 17th. It's important that we talk about your portfolio at your earliest convenience. Please call me before 3:00 P.M. (PST) at 1-800-222-3333."

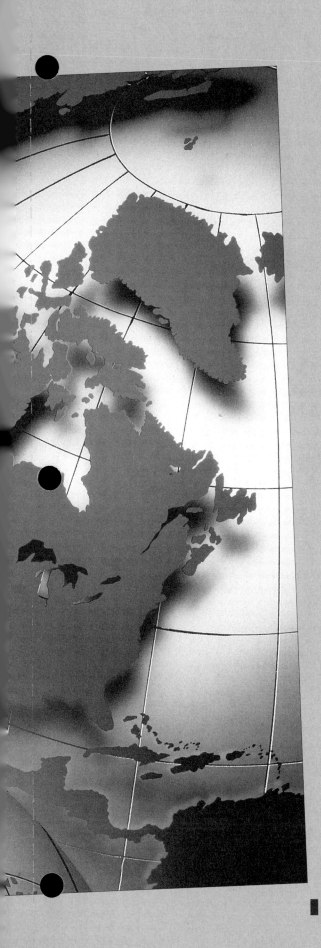

PART TWO

WRITING FOR BUSINESS: LETTERS, MEMORANDUMS, AND JOB SEARCH DOCUMENTS

Directness in Routine Inquiries

Upon completing this chapter, you will be able to employ directness effectively in initiating routine inquiries. To reach this goal, you should be able to

(1) Prepare routine requests for information or action that begin with the objective, include a clear explanation, and end with goodwill.

(2) Place orders that contain a clear authorization, a well-organized description of the items, the shipping and payment information, and a goodwill closing.

(3) Prepare claims that clearly state the expectations and present supporting facts in a firm but courteous manner.

(4) Make reference requests that gather useful data and respect the rights of the people involved.

A PROCEDURAL COMMENT

The next sections of this text will concentrate on written communication for three reasons. The first reason is simplicity. It is clearer to explain the communication strategies using only written forms as the model. The second reason is the growing use of written communication. Remember that written communication is more than letters and memos printed on paper. It also includes the electronic channels such as e-mail, electronic discussion groups, and electronic bulletin boards. Courier services, local area computer networks, and the Internet make written communication more convenient and popular than ever before. The third reason is most communication courses will require written assignments for purposes of evaluation.

This practical simplification does not mean that the strategies and techniques discussed in these chapters apply only to written communication. Wherever possible, examples, exercises, and assignments will include both written and oral channels.

Furthermore, the choice of written channels for teaching and explanation does not mean that a written approach is always the best. There are many occasions when other channels of communication are either more appropriate or absolutely required. To review the choice of channel, refer to "A Four-Stage Approach to Creating Business Messages" in Chapter 5.

DIRECT-ORDER REQUESTS

The first message type we will consider is the routine request. This letter is written when you want specific information that applies to your situation. While some of the answers you need may be in a general brochure, you make a request because you want more detailed information. In addition, the direct request is also used to ask for action that is routine and straightforward. Finally, this letter serves as an initial contact with your reader. It introduces you and your company, and opens a channel that you can use later if you decide to develop the contact. In other words, the routine request may be the beginning of a network or business relationship that will prove mutually beneficial.

- A routine request asks for specific information.

The exchange of information is a typical, daily occurrence for businesses. It is an opportunity to present products and services to interested contacts. Therefore, the routine request assumes a receptive reader and uses the direct-order plan.

- Because the request is routine and the reader is receptive, use the direct order plan.

The direct plan for making routine requests includes these points:

- Follow this general plan for direct-order requests.

- Begin directly with a request. When possible, make your opening sentence a question.

- Include necessary explanations wherever they are most appropriate and logical.

- If additional requests are involved, plan their presentation.

- End with goodwill words or future action suitable to the circumstances.

Beginning with the Objective

In a routine request letter, you place the request at the beginning, usually in the first sentence and usually in question form. A question beginning is clear and commands attention. The "It would be nice if you would tell me. . ." and "I would like to have. . ." types of sentences are not true questions. They do not ask—they merely suggest. The requests that stand out are those written in question form: "When will I be able to use my preferred customer discount?" "Does your computer network allow 75 users at the same time?"

- Begin with a request in question form.

If your inquiry involves just one question, you can achieve your primary objective with the first sentence. After any necessary explanation and a few words of closing, your letter is done. If you have several requests, however, you will need to consider their order. Select one or possibly two questions for the opening paragraph and place the others later in the letter.

The first question you ask should be the one that is the most important to your situation. If for example, you need a supplier who will deliver to your location within 48 hours of ordering, you begin by asking if that delivery schedule can be guaranteed. Regardless of the selection of goods available through this company, you cannot deal with them unless they can deliver on time. As another example, you may be looking for information about a specific piece of office equipment. Your first question would ask if the company sells and services this make and model. If they do not, your conversation need go no further than closing with a pleasant thank-you.

• Begin with the most important or most basic question.

Explaining Adequately

• Explain enough to enable the reader to answer.

Getting to the main point quickly does not mean omitting explanations. If your reader needs information to help in answering your questions, you must include it. Deciding what information the reader needs is an important step. If you do not explain enough or if you misjudge the reader's knowledge, you make the reader's task difficult. For example, answers to questions about a computer often depend on the specific needs or characteristics of the company that will use it. The best-informed computer expert cannot answer questions accurately without knowing the facts of the company concerned. Your goal is to be concise while still giving all the necessary details.

• Place the explanation anywhere it fits logically.

Where and how you include the necessary information depends on the nature of your letter. Usually, the best place for general explanatory material is following the opening question or questions. If it is brief, it may fit logically in the first paragraph, qualifying or justifying the letter. In letters that ask more than one question, you will sometimes need to include explanatory material either in its own paragraph or accompanying each question.

Presenting Additional Questions

• If there are several questions, make each stand out. Do this by (1) using the question form of sentence, (2) placing each question in a separate sentence, (3) structuring the questions in separate paragraphs, and/or (4) marking or numbering the questions.

As discussed earlier, if your inquiry involves just one question, you put it in the first paragraph. When you have several questions to ask, you put the most important or most basic one in the first paragraph. The additional questions are asked in a logical order in a later paragraph. To ensure the reply includes answers to all these questions, you make them stand out. By using one or more of the following presentation methods, you will give your receiver a convenient check for completeness.

First, you present your requests in question form. As we have seen, true questions stand out. Sentences that merely hint at a need do not attract much attention.

Second, you make each question a separate sentence. Combining two or more questions in a sentence de-emphasizes them and increases the likelihood that some of them will be overlooked.

Third, consider giving each question a separate paragraph. This practice is logical only when your explanation and other comments about each question justify a paragraph.

And finally, consider marking your questions with symbols such as the bullet (•) or by ranking them. To rank them you can use words (*first, second, third*), numbers (*1, 2, 3*), or letters (*a, b, c*).

Ending with Goodwill

• End with a pleasant comment.

Because it is natural in the North American business culture to end an exchange with a polite closing, you should end your letter with some appropriate, pleasant comment. Ending your letter at the final question is like turning your back on someone without saying goodbye. Such an abrupt ending would register negatively in your reader's mind and would defeat your goodwill efforts.

• When possible, customize the closing to the specific case.

Your letter will receive a more positive reception if you base your closing words on the case. Sweeping statements such as "A prompt reply will be appreciated" and "Thank you in advance for your assistance" suggest goodwill, but they do little to create a sense of personal attention because they are general and overused. Instead, use a closing that is

specific to the situation, such as this: "If you could get this registration data to me by Friday, I would appreciate it." A goodwill closing may be one that points to future action such as: "The remainder of your order will be shipped as soon as we receive your clarification."

We now will consider some specific types of direct-order requests, namely, Asking for Information, Asking for Action, Placing Orders, Asking about People, and Making Claims. While each type has special characteristics, they all use the basic direct-order plan.

. . . .
TYPES OF DIRECT-ORDER REQUESTS

INTRODUCTORY SITUATION

➤ to Letters Using the Direct Order in Asking for Information

The marketing key for Good 'n Nice is nutritious, fresh food, so Doreen is always looking for new developments and trends in healthy eating.

Recently she has heard of a low-fat, energy drink that can be served as a snack to prevent hunger pangs and between-meal nibbling. *Vitality* comes as a powder, she has learned. By varying the amount of water, *Vitality* can be made into a drink, a shake, or a topping.

Would *Vitality* be suitable for her customers? As Doreen considers the situation, she comes up with the following questions:

1. How easy is it to prepare? Does it require special equipment? Can it be made ahead?

2. What is the nutritional value of the product?

3. How long can it be kept on the shelf in powder form?

4. Who is the local supplier?

5. What flavours does it come in?

These are her questions. Now she needs to organize her thoughts into a letter requesting this information from the manufacturer. ▪

Asking for Information

• Letters asking for information are routine.

Letters that ask for information are among the most common because businesses frequently need information from their clients and other businesses. These routine requests for information appropriately use the direct-order plan. The following comments adapt the general plan to the request for information.

• Begin with (1) a specific question or (2) a general request for information.

Beginning with the Request.   Because your objective is to get answers to your questions, you begin with a direct question. You may use either of two types of question beginnings: (1) a specific request for an item of information wanted, or (2) a general request for information.

If Doreen decides that the nutritional value is the key factor in her decision about *Vitality*, she might begin with these words:

> Will you please send the nutritional information about *Vitality*, your new, powdered health drink?

Some business writers prefer the second type of beginning, believing it has a less startling effect. This approach starts with a general request for information. For Doreen's letter, this sentence would be possible:

> Will you help me determine if your new health food drink is suitable for my business? Please answer the following questions about *Vitality*.

This beginning is less direct than the first type because the specific questions must still be asked. However, it is useful because it can set up a numbered list of questions. Either type of question beginning is better than an explanation-first plan.

Your next paragraphs will include necessary explanations, additional questions, and a goodwill closing as described earlier in the general plan for direct-order requests.

• The following examples show poor and well-written inquiries.

Contrasting Inquiry Examples.   Bad and good techniques are illustrated in the following letters about *Vitality*, the health food drink for Doreen Lam's Good 'n Nice business.[1]

An Ineffective Inquiry Letter

The first example begins slowly. Some of the information is vague or unnecessary; other key facts are buried in long sentences. The second paragraph introduces the general type of information needed, but it contains no true questions. These are only hints of what Doreen wants to know. The objective of her letter does not appear until the third paragraph. Even then, the points do not stand out; they are vague and difficult to answer. The closing paragraph is a cliché. Doreen will not receive the information she needs from this ineffective letter. The likelihood is that she will get an advertisement, or perhaps another copy of the brochure she has seen already.

• First is the bad example. The reader will find this letter difficult to answer.

> I noticed some advertizing about your new health drink called *Vitality*. I understand that it comes in powdered form and can be mixed with varying amounts of water to form a topping, a shake, or a drink—a feature that is certainly preferable to the premixed beverages of some of your competitors.
>
> I wonder if your product would be suitable for my customers. I have a Good 'n Nice kiosk. I sell nutritious snacks such as frozen yogurt and fruit juices, as well as lunch sandwiches and salads, to customers for whom freshness and nutrition are very important.
>
> Please let me know more about your product—everything from cost, to shelf life, to flavours, to preparation instructions.
>
> Thanks and have a nice day!

---

[1]These examples include only the texts of the letters. The Case Illustrations that follow show complete letters along with handwritten comments pointing out highlights. These two illustration forms are used throughout the letter portion of this book.

The Direct and Effective Inquiry Letter. The second example begins directly by asking a question that sets up a list of specific questions for the manufacturer. Adequate explanation is included to help the reader answer the questions in the context of Doreen's business. The closing is courteous and positive to build goodwill.

• This direct and orderly letter is better.

Will you help me determine if your new health food drink is suitable for my business?

My Good 'n Nice franchise is established in a suburban mall kiosk. Most of my customers are health and wellness conscious. They appreciate the low-fat yogurt, fruit juices, and fresh sandwiches that I offer. However, the teenagers from the local high school just want good taste. I want to serve both groups.

Please answer the following questions about *Vitality*.

1. What are the nutritional ratings for *Vitality*?
2. What shelf-life does *Vitality* powder have?
3. Do you supply full instructions and recipes for its use?
4. What flavours are available?
5. Who is the local supplier?

If *Vitality* is accurately described in the advertisement I saw in *Total Health* magazine, I look forward to including it in my menu.

. . . .

A PRACTICE RUN

Use the following table to evaluate these requests for information about some land.

Letter 1

We have seen your advertisement for a 50-hectare tract on the St. Lawrence River in the June 1 *Globe & Mail*. In reply, we are writing you for additional information concerning this property.

We would be pleased to know about the depth of the river frontage; the quality of drainage, including high and low elevations; and the availability of public roads to the property.

If the information you supply is favourable to our needs, we will be pleased to inspect the property.

Hoping to hear from you soon.

Letter 2

Does the 50-hectare tract you advertized in the June 1 *Globe & Mail* have deep frontage on the St. Lawrence River? We are seeking such a site for a new plant, and it appears that your property could meet our needs.

How level is the land? Is there adequate drainage? In your reply, please send a written description of the terrain including minimum and maximum elevations.

Can the property be reached by an existing all-weather road? If so, what is the composition and condition of this access road?

As we must move quickly on the building project, may I have your reply within seven days? Then, if your answers indicate that the site meets our needs, we will want to inspect the property as soon as possible.

I hope that we can come to a mutually beneficial arrangement about this land.

Elements of the Direct-Order Request for Information	Letter 1	Letter 2
Opens with the request		
Uses a direct question		
Explains adequately		
Explanation is logically placed in the letter		
Additional requests have structure. That is, they		
1. are direct questions		
2. are in separate sentences		
3. have their own paragraphs with explanation		
4. have bullets or numbers		
The closing shows goodwill		
The closing is specific to the situation		

A letter is a deliberate, written conversation.

Gracian

Remember this: write only as you would speak; then your letter will be good.

Goethe

There is one golden rule to bear in mind always: that we should try to put ourselves in the position of our correspondent, to imagine his feelings as he writes his letters, and to gauge his reaction as he receives ours. If we put ourselves in the other man's shoes, we shall speedily detect how unconvincing our letters can seem, or how much we may be taking for granted.

Sir Ernest Gowers

Do not answer a letter in the midst of great anger.

Chinese Proverb

Don't cry whilst writing letters. The person receiving the letter is apt to take it as a reproach.

Mavis Gallant, A Fairly Good Time

And to describe the true definition of an Epistle or letter, it is nothing but an Oration written, conteining the mynd of the Orator, or wryter, thereby to give to him or them absent, the same that should be declared if they were present.

William Fulwood, The Enemie of Idlenesse, 1568
(earliest known book on letter writing in English)

FIGURE 6–1 Expected Reactions Influence Planning: *A Judgment Continuum*

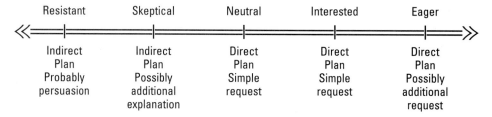

Asking for Action

When asking someone to do something for you, you again consider your reader's reaction. If in your judgment, your reader will not hesitate to comply, a direct-order request is appropriate. If you think your reader will be very enthusiastic about your request, you may consider increasing what you are asking for to benefit from that enthusiasm. For example, you might ask an enthusiastic reader not only to serve on a committee, but also to take a leadership role. Figure 6–1 illustrates the changes in approach based on the anticipated reactions to a request.

A direct request for action is similar in structure to the direct request for information except that it includes more explanation. Since what you are asking will require more effort from your reader, you explain your request in greater detail.

If the situation is complex, direct requests for action may even have one or two sentences of background information before the request is made. Since these are not

* Direct requests for action need clear explanations.

* A brief introduction may be necessary.

Good 'n Nice

Frozen Yogurt

173 Willow Bank Road, Mississauga, ON L4Y 4G6

April 10, 1997

Mr. Ronald Dryber, Secretary
Canadian Management Forum
c/o 148 Drummond Drive
Regina, SK   S4N 2B3

Dear Mr. Dryber:

The inquiry begins directly with a question.

Will you kindly send me some information about the
Canadian Management Forum?

I am the owner and operator of a small business. It
is my hope that your association will help me make
contacts and learn new skills to build my business.

The writer gives adequate background information to help the reader.

The questions are structured to prompt a complete reply.

Some specific questions I have are
* Are your conferences limited to CMF members?
* How do I become a member of CMF?
* Are there local chapters near me in the Toronto
  area?
* Do you publish a magazine or newsletter?

The questions are specific and organized logically.

The letter closes with polite and positive comments.

As you can see, I know very little about CMF. I
happened to notice a poster about one of your
conferences on the bulletin board at the college
where I take evening classes. I will look forward to
hearing more about the activities of the Canadian
Management Forum.

Sincerely,

Doreen Lam

Doreen Lam

persuasive letters, this introduction is very brief and the request follows immediately.[2] All other details or questions come later as is usual in a direct-order letter.

• Here is an example.

Requests for action include situations such as asking for an estimate to be done, inviting someone to speak at a luncheon, asking for credit, or requesting service. The following example is clear and direct. The objective is stated in the first sentence, enough supporting detail is given for clarity, and secondary questions are asked in an orderly way.

We would like your written estimate for carpeting throughout our offices before September 20th.

The area is approximately 200 square metres. We require a hard-wearing carpet for the hallways and reception areas and something slightly more luxurious for our executive offices. Your estimate should include removing and replacing the furniture, disposing of the old floor covering, and installing the new carpet and underlay.

Since it is important that disruptions during business hours be kept to a minimum, we prefer that the installation work be done on a weekend. Are there additional charges for this service?

Please have your estimator visit our offices during regular business hours and ask for either Kim Jubinville or David Shew. Your firm was highly recommended by one of our clients, so we look forward to the opportunity of dealing with you.

INTRODUCTORY SITUATION

▶ to Order Letters

Back at the Good 'n Nice kiosk, Doreen Lam has been challenged by a few situations recently. She would like to feel more confident about her abilities as owner and manager. She saw some book reviews in an article called "The 10 Most Valuable Books for Small Business Owners." These books would be useful in her personal library.

Unfortunately, her local bookstores do not have these specialized titles in stock. Since the article gives publisher names, prices, and necessary descriptions of the books, she has decided to order them directly from the publishers. A business directory in the library contains the publishers' addresses and fax numbers.

One of the orders will be sent to Business Books, Inc., the publisher of three of the books she wants. She is ready to order, but what is the best way to organize the request? What information should she include? The answers to these questions appear in the following discussion. ▪

Placing Orders

• A special type of request for action is the order.

An order asks for a specific type of action. Unless a company provides an order form, orders will be placed by telephone, fax, or letter. In any case, planning is important. Because telephone orders take place quickly, you need to organize all the relevant information ahead of time and be ready to give it as you are asked for it. Written orders need to be complete and accurate to avoid delays.

The direct method is best for organizing the details of an order. A few modifications to the basic plan are given here.

• Use this overview to plan an order letter.

• Rather than using a question, begin with a statement that you are placing an order. The reader needs clear authorization to proceed with the order.

• Explain what you want to purchase by systematically arranging the items with all the necessary identifying facts.

• Cover shipping instructions and manner of payment.

• End with a goodwill comment.

---

[2] Chapter 9 discusses persuasive letters. Some additional information applying persuasive techniques is found in the chapters on reports and oral presentations.

NOAA
The Northern Ontario Association for Accounting

P. O. Box 116, Sault Ste. Marie, ON P5R 2M6

August 6, 1996

Mr. W. Schilds
Schilds & Wiebe Associates
104 Newton Road
Bowmanville, ON   K2J 3B9

Dear Mr. Schilds:

The specific request is given in question form after a very brief statement that puts the request in context.

The Northern Ontario Association for Accounting is holding its biennial conference in Sudbury on June 9 - 12, 1997. Would you please accept this invitation to be our keynote speaker for the three morning sessions on Thursday, Friday, and Saturday?

Our theme, *Accounting to the Year 2020*, looks ahead to the need for growth and change in the field in response to the dynamic needs of Canadian business. Your expertise with computerized accounting makes you our first choice for theme speaker.

The writer gives further information to the reader and creates a positive rapport.

This additional explanation includes possible benefits to encourage compliance with the request.

Approximate attendance at the conference will be 125 people, all from the accounting field. The schedule calls for the large morning session, followed by workshops and seminars in the afternoon. If you wish, you would be welcome to attend the special events planned for each evening.

I would appreciate receiving your reply by August 24th. This promises to be an exciting conference, and I hope you are able to attend.

The closing is positive, personal, and friendly.

Yours sincerely,

Wendy Yao

(Miss) Wendy Yao
Secretary
1997 Conference Committee

Directly Authorizing the Order.   Because the order means business and profits to the reader, you should begin the order letter directly with a clear authorization to ship goods. Your first main words should say something like "Please send me." Any less direct wording falls short of the ideal. For example, beginnings such as "I am in need of" or "I would like to have" are not as clear and direct. If applicable, include your customer number or account number.

Specifically Covering the Details.   The remainder of your letter is an exercise in clear and orderly coverage of all the details your reader needs. Unless these facts are well organized, confusion and errors will result.

One way to arrange the details for quick and clear understanding is to use a table. Most word processors have a tables feature allowing you to arrange information simply in columns and rows. As a general pattern, begin with the quantity needed. Then give the stock or catalogue number and confirm it with a basic name and model. Then describe any special features such as colour or size. End with the unit price and the total price. Depending upon the situation, you may need to add other costs such as GST, PST, shipping, or import duties. The following table could be the detail you would put in the body of an order letter.

Quantity	Item Number	Description	Colour	Unit Price	Total
3 dozen	2411	Ball point pens, fine point	Black	12.00	36.00
5 reams	712912	Classic paper, 20 lb.	White	28.50	142.50
1	12271	Paper shredder		79.50	79.50
		SUBTOTAL			258.00
		Shipping & Handling			23.22
		GST			19.69
		TOTAL			**300.91**

Organizing information with tables makes it easier for both you and your reader. You will include all the information since the headings will prompt you for complete detail; your reader will be able to find the information to fill your order accurately.

In addition to listing the items required, you need to include instructions for shipping and payment. You may work this information into the beginning of the letter, following the authorization statement, or you may include it with your closing remarks.

• Cover the shipping and payment details.

• Close with pleasant words. If possible, tailor them to the situation.

Closing with a Friendly Comment.   You should end the order letter with an appropriate, friendly comment. As we mentioned earlier, you could include some of the shipping instructions here, especially if they are unusual. Your closing should be tailored to the situation as much as possible, as in this example:

This model has sold so well, that we have only three left in stock. We will appreciate your promptness in filling this order by December 6th.

A Clear, Well-Organized Example.   This sample letter begins with a direct authorization to ship goods. Then it lists all the details about the books wanted in an orderly fashion. In the closing, the remaining matter of additional charges is handled. The closing attempts to create goodwill.

Please send me the following books:

1 cop	*Basic Management* 2nd ed., 1996	Al Bevins	@ 86.95	86.95
1 cop	*Now You Own a Business* 1996	Monica Gruen	@ 91.95	91.95
2 cops	*Managing Your Team* 3rd ed., 1997	Hugh W. Bass	@ 55.95	111.90
			GST	20.36
			TOTAL	$311.16

* This well-written order letter is fast and efficient.

The enclosed cheque for $311.16 covers the cost of the books. Please send them by ground courier and bill me for the additional amount.

My order is based on the reviews in this month's *Business Administrator.* Since my local bookstores do not carry these titles, I appreciate your handling this small, special order.

A PRACTICE RUN

Critique this letter ordering the same books. Referring to the example above will help you.

Information I have indicates that your company is the publisher of three books I would like for my personal library. I would sincerely appreciate it if you would be so kind as to send them to me. They are as follows: *Basic Management,* price $86.95, by Al Bevins, 1 copy; *Now You Own a Business,* by Monica Gruen, price $91.95, 1996; and *Managing Your Team,* price $55.95, by Hugh W. Bass, 2 copies.

I have enclosed a cheque in the amount of $290.80. Just let me know any additional charges for shipping and tax.

_____

_____

_____

_____

_____

I N T R O D U C T O R Y   S I T U A T I O N

▶ to Claim Letters

Vitality has proven itself to be a popular addition to the menu at Doreen's Good 'n Nice kiosk. Her customers are particularly fond of the Wild Berry flavour.

Three days ago she ordered two Orange, four Strawberry, and eight Wild Berry containers of *Vitality* powder. She specified the one-kilogram size because it costs less than two of the 500-gram size. When her shipment arrived, Doreen noticed a problem. Although she received the correct flavours, the containers were all the 500-gram size rather than the one-kilogram size she had ordered. The invoice charged her for the larger size.

Before telephoning the supplier, Doreen took a moment to think. What did she want the *Vitality* supplier to do for her? Her first thought was to ship the order back and have it replaced. However, she might run out of *Vitality* before the replacements arrived. Besides, reshipping these bulky goods was a nuisance. No, she decided, a paper transaction would be preferable. Did she want the invoice adjusted to reflect the amount of product she had actually received? In that case, she would have to order again very soon and pay the higher price for the small containers. She finally decided she would like permission to use the 500-gram containers she had received. She wanted the balance of her order sent to her without any additional charges for the smaller containers or for shipping. Since the invoice correctly showed what she had ordered, she would pay it as soon as the full amount of the *Vitality* arrived. ■

This order letter was faxed to the supplier. Overnight courier delivery means next day service for this small business operator.

DONNY'S SOUVENIRS

June 23, 1996

Novco Supplies
Unit 6, 722 Islington Avenue
Rexdale,   ON   M9S 4V3

Attn: Order Department

The direct opening statement authorizes the order and the special delivery method.

Please use overnight courier to rush these novelty items to me from the Spring 1996 catalogue.

2 dozen	#1325	Blue Jays Baseball Caps @ $3.75	90.00
1 dozen	#1167	Montreal Expos Mugs @ $2.98	35.76
2 dozen	#2118	Montreal Expos T-shirts @ $7.98	191.52
2 dozen	#2119	Blue Jays T-shirts @ 7.98	191.52
			508.80

The details of the order are clearly stated in a simple table.

The method of payment is stated plainly.

These costs plus GST, PST, and shipping and handling should be charged to my account #106-72A.

With baseball season in full swing, I've been caught a bit short on these items. I appreciate your priority service that keeps me ahead of the game.

The positive and amusing closing encourages swift handling of the order.

Sincerely,

Don Mah

Don Mah
Donny's Souvenirs

1717 Sparks Street
Ottawa, ON K1P 5G8

Making Claims

Claims are made when something has gone wrong between a business and its customers. Goods have been damaged or lost; a product has failed to perform; or, service has been unsatisfactory. Typically, the customer realizes the problem first and calls it to the attention of the company for correction. Such a claim can be made in person, by telephone, or by fax or letter.

You may think that because a claim results from a negative situation, you should use the indirect approach. The indirect, persuasive approach should be considered if a claim needs special attention for some reason such as being made after the warranty period.[3] However, for normal situations, a claim is written in the direct order.

Using Directness for Routine Claims.   There are two reasons for using the direct order for routine claims. First, most business people want to please their customers. When they do not please, they want to make the adjustment necessary. That attitude makes them a receptive audience. Businesses prefer their customers to make a claim and receive an adjustment rather than to complain to others about the problem and cause further loss of business. Thus, when you make a legitimate claim, you do not need to persuade the reader or to soften the news. In other words, there is no good reason why you cannot begin with the claim as long as you give adequate explanation and support for it somewhere in the letter.

Second, directness lends strength to the claim. Beginning with the claim emphasizes it and shows the writer's confidence in reporting it. In fact, some readers would interpret indirectness in these circumstances as weakness. To show your confidence in the justice of your claim, you should use the approach that strengthens it.

This section discusses a plan for handling claims by adapting the direct order plan as follows:

- Begin directly. Identify the situation (invoice number, date, etc.) and state briefly what you want done.

- Present enough evidence to support your claim.

- Give additional detail about what you want done, and how. If appropriate, describe other acceptable courses of action.

- End pleasantly and yet firmly.

Identifying the Claim.   A claim letter concerns a particular transaction, item of merchandise, or service call. So that your reader quickly knows what your claim is about, you include the necessary identification information at the beginning in a subject line or in the first paragraph. You may need to include an invoice number, an order number or date, or the serial number of a product. Give whatever unique identifiers you have to pinpoint the subject of your claim.

You can begin with a subject line. A *subject line* is a mechanical device usually placed after the salutation (*Dear Mr. Zalasky:*) to identify the subject of the letter. Typically, the subject line begins with an identifying term, such as *Subject:, About:, Concerning:* or *Re:*. The words that follow are emphasized by underlining, italicizing, or capitalizing. Because a direct beginning is appropriate in a claim letter, the subject line (which actually begins the message) is direct. These examples illustrate good wording and content:

Subject: Replacement of damaged fire extinguishers.
Your invoice no. 1314C.

CONCERNING: CREDIT FOR BREAKAGE OF SEA MIST COLOGNE.
INVOICE NO. 31747, JULY 5, 1997.

Re: Further service on our Damson L3 refrigeration unit.
Work Order 7133 for the original repairs.

Margin notes:
- Claim letters are written to correct for damages.
- Routine claims use the direct order for two reasons: (1) the reader is likely to want to correct the error;
- (2) the direct order is strong.
- Routine claims should follow this plan.
- Identify the transaction involved early in the letter.
- You can begin with a subject line.

---

[3]Persuasive writing is discussed in Chapter 9.

State what you want done.

State what you want the reader to do. Perhaps you want your money returned, the merchandise replaced, or some repairs made. Explicitly making a reasonable request strengthens your case, for the reader has to clear the hurdle of justifying the refusal if he or she does not accept. Here are two examples.

Please credit my account for the damaged merchandise in my recent order.
Further repair is needed on our Damson L3 refrigeration unit. The latest service has not solved the problem.

If you have not used a subject line to identify your claim, your opening paragraph should include that information.

Please credit my account for the damaged merchandise in my recent order on your Invoice 31747, July 5, 1997.

Further repair is needed on our Damson L3 refrigeration unit. The latest service (November 28, 1996, Work Order 7133) has not solved the problem.

State the facts that support your claim.

Explaining the Facts.   A good claim letter is a combination of courtesy and firmness. You want the tone to say "I'm being reasonable in my claim, and I expect fair treatment. Resolving this situation could lead to continuing business." So, you give a summary of the facts that led to your claim in a straightforward manner, being as objective as you can. You will need to tell your reader just what went wrong, what evidence you have, and what the damage is. Careful documentation of the situation will speed your claim and maintain your credibility.

For added strength, you may explain the damage caused by the problem (inconvenience, lost sales, etc.).

In some instances, you may choose to do more than just state the problem. You may also choose to describe the effect of the problem on your business. A broken machine, for example, may have stopped an entire assembly line. Or damaged merchandise may have caused a decrease in sales or even the loss of a customer. A factual explanation of the consequences created by the problem strengthens your claim. The following sentences illustrate this technique:

With 8 of the 11 cartons of Sea Mist cologne broken, we could not continue with our advertising promotion.

When the freezer that we purchased from you last September suddenly quit working, we lost $312 of frozen foods.

Be careful to use words that do not show distrust or anger.

In presenting the facts of the case, you should choose your words carefully. Words that accuse or imply distrust may work against the claim. So may words of anger. Angry and accusing words tend to put the reader on the defensive and create resistance that will reduce your chances of getting a good settlement.

Add additional detail, if needed.

Giving Additional Detail.   Once you have clearly made your claim and given your evidence, you may need to add further detail. Examples would be how soon you need the replacement item, or which shipping company you will use to return the items.

You might wish to suggest alternative courses of action.

If you are uncertain about the best course of action, you may wish to present some alternatives. For example, if the damaged goods are bulky, you may not know whether it is better to ship them back to the manufacturer, or to dispose of them yourself. Which would your supplier prefer?

You can leave the decision to the reader.

When you know that your reader has a favourable adjustment reputation, you may wish to let the reader decide what to do. Most companies try hard to make fair adjustments. In fact, they often do more than is necessary and, on occasion, more than you would have asked them to do.

Your closing words should show your cordial attitude.

Overcoming Negativeness with a Pleasant Closing.   Your final pleasant words should remove all doubt about your cordial attitude. You might express appreciation for past good service, or restate your expectation of a satisfactory resolution and future business dealings with this company.

A Firm Yet Courteous Example.   This letter follows the plan suggested in the preceding paragraphs. A subject line quickly identifies the situation. The letter begins with a clear statement of the claim. Next, in a tone that shows firmness without anger, the letter tells what went wrong. Then it requests a specific remedy and asks what to do with the damaged goods. The ending uses subtle persuasion by implying confidence in the reader. The words used here leave no doubt about continued business dealings.

> Subject: *Replacement of damaged Fireboy extinguishers.*
>   *Your Invoice No. 715C.*
>
> Please send replacements for the 24 Fireboy extinguishers received today. Their corroded condition makes them unfit for use.
>
> Our receiving supervisor and the Red Arrow driver made note of the poor condition of the shipment at the time of delivery. Upon closer inspection, we found six of the extinguishers had leaked from the cap screws. As a result, the chrome finish on all the units has been badly damaged.
>
> We need to have the replacements by Monday because this is a matter of plant safety. We consider it urgent. Also, will you please send instructions for the disposal of the defective units?
>
> I am aware, of course, that situations like this can occur in spite of precautions. Your promptness in replacing the extinguishers will be appreciated.

* This letter closely follows text suggestions.

. . . .

A PRACTICE RUN

Doreen feels she is ready to make the telephone call to the supplier. (See the Introductory Situation to Claim Letters.) Read over her notes and add any other information you think she will need. (There are omissions.) Then role-play the telephone claim with a partner. The "supplier" should pretend to know nothing of the case in advance. Perhaps an alternate solution could be worked out.

Order date April 17, 1997   Invoice 971733

Flavours of *Vitality* received are as ordered, and my customers like the product.
Received wrong size containers, but need to use them.

Supplier should send the balance without additional charge.

_____

_____

_____

. . . .

I N T R O D U C T O R Y   S I T U A T I O N

▶ to Asking about People

Westridge Mall has decided to extend the hours of operation in November and December to accommodate the extra shoppers at that time of year. Doreen will need another part-time employee for Good 'n Nice to meet this demand. She needs someone who is responsible enough to work alone, someone who can handle the pressure of rush times and the monotony of slow times, and someone who is willing to work for minimum wage.

A few students have applied. Their references include Mrs. Andrew, the high school counsellor. Doreen decides to make an appointment with Mrs. Andrew to ask some questions about her applicants. She knows what she would like to ask, but she remembers that there are legal and moral considerations. What are they? This next section and Chapter 11, "Strategies in Job Search and Application," will provide some answers. ▪

In this letter about defective carpeting, the writer presents her claim directly, forcefully, and yet politely.

CHARLES
HOTEL

2-201 East 15th Street, North Vancouver, BC V7M 1S2   604-678-9080

September 17, 1997

Mr. Luther R. Ferguson, President
Rich's Carpet, Inc.
13171 Industrial Boulevard
Delta, BC   V4K 1G8

Dear Mr. Ferguson:

The subject line clearly identifies the transaction.

Subject: Replacement of our Kota-Tuff carpeting
         under warranty Invoice 3147, January 3, 1997

The Kota-Tuff carpeting you installed here last January has not lived up to its warranty. Please replace it with a more suitable carpeting.

The claim is made directly and confidently.

Additional details support the claim.

Although your written warranty says that the colour will "withstand the effects of sun and water," it has faded badly. The original forest green colour now is mottled with varying shades of green. The damage is especially noticeable next to the pool.

If you are unable to supply satisfactory replacement carpeting, a refund of the full purchase price, including installation, is acceptable.

An alternative solution is offered.

The cost to both parties is noted. Offering co-operation ends the letter positively.

Since the condition of the carpet is an embarrassment to the hotel and to the reputation of Rich's Carpet, I will co-operate with you in any way possible to have this problem corrected promptly.

Sincerely,

Joyce Gibbs

Joyce Gibbs
Manager

Asking about People

If you are an entrepreneur with plans to begin your own business after graduation, you will write personnel request letters to help you choose people to work with you. If you are at college to upgrade your business training, you may be returning to a job in which you are responsible for hiring. These letters will help you gather the information you need about the candidates. Even if it is some time before you need to write this type of letter, you will be the subject of such requests when you search for a job. Understanding these letters will help you choose your references who will have to answer requests for information about you.

As you will see from the following discussion, a letter asking for information about a person is a special form of routine inquiry. The personnel request follows the general pattern of direct order inquiry letters, but it involves a special requirement, which is why we review this letter type separately.

Respecting Human Rights.
Respecting the rights of the people involved is the special requirement. Protecting human rights in exchanging information about people is to seek truth and to act in good faith. Keep these points in mind when requesting personal information: (1) You should ask only for information that can be supported by factual data. (2) You should ask only for information you need for business purposes. (3) You should ask only when the person being considered has authorized the inquiry. (4) You should hold all information about people in confidence.

The Canadian Human Rights Commission publishes *A Guide to Screening and Selection in Employment,* which outlines the *Human Rights Act* and gives examples of appropriate and inappropriate questions. It states: "The *Canadian Human Rights Act* bans discrimination in federal jurisdiction on the grounds of race, colour, national or ethnic origin, sex, religion, age, marital status, family status, pardoned conviction or disability."[4] This guide is available in both official languages from Supply and Services Canada. Most provinces also have human rights offices and additional legislation covering their jurisdictions. A reference librarian can help you locate the additional regulations that apply to your area.

Adapting Question Content.
As in any routine inquiry, you should include any information that will help the reader answer the question. Usually the reader needs to know the nature, responsibilities, and requirements of the job the applicant wants.

Letters inquiring about job applicants vary because they are specific to that job and that applicant. For a sales job, for example, you might ask questions about the applicant's sales experience and demonstrated ability to meet and get along with people. For an accounting job, you probably would seek information about knowledge of the field, and experience working in teams. In all cases, you would ask for factual data and examples to support any conclusions drawn by the person providing the reference.

An Example Showing Care and Consideration.
This example gives evidence of good analysis of the job and the applicant. The letter begins directly with an opening question that serves as a topic sentence. The beginning also includes helpful explanation. Then the letter presents the specific questions. Each question stands out and is easy to answer. Worked in with each question is an explanation that will help the reader understand the position for which Shawn Hart is being considered. The closing is courteous and tailored to the case. Note also the concern for the rights of the people involved. Clearly, the inquiry is authorized, is for business purposes only, and will be treated confidentially.

> Will you help me evaluate Mr. Shawn Hart for the position of office manager? In authorizing this inquiry, Mr. Hart mentioned that he worked for you from 1993 to 1996. Your answers to the following questions will help me determine whether Mr. Hart is the right person for this job.

---

[4]Canada. Human Rights Commission, *A Guide to Screening and Selection in Employment* (Ottawa: Minister of Supply and Services Canada, 1985).

Marginal notes:
- Knowing how to ask for information about people is a practical skill.
- Letters asking for information about people are a special form of inquiry.
- Such letters need to protect the rights of people.
- Explaining the job requirements helps the reader.
- The questions asked should suit this person and this job.

Duffield Department Stores

1403 Hochelaga Street, Moose Jaw, Saskatchewan S6H 3K4

May 10, 1997

Ms. Ward-Meyer
Ward's Music
1113 Rosser Avenue
Brandon, MN   R7B 6L7

Dear Ms. Ward-Meyer:

The request is authorized.

Ms. Robin Tosto gave your name as an employment reference. Please answer the following questions to help us assess her application for a position as Sales Supervisor. She would supervise a staff of three full-time and eight part-time employees in our music department that has annual sales of approximately $500,000.

The job conditions are explained.

The questions are bulleted and separated to draw attention to them.

- In the three years that Ms.Tosto worked for you, how did she show her enthusiasm for the job and her interest in improving her skills?

- What particular strength did she demonstrate in interpersonal skills with her co-workers and her customers?

- In which area of a sales supervisor's duties do you feel she needs more training? Please explain your choice based on your experience supervising Ms.Tosto.
  Dealing with customer complaints
  Planning and managing time
  Motivating staff to excellence
  Giving constructive criticism

The questions ask for factual data and concrete examples from the applicant's behaviour.

Details are provided to ensure the response is timely. The choice of mail or fax is a convenience for the writer of the reference.

I am conducting the first series of interviews and hope to hire within three weeks. I would appreciate receiving your response on behalf of Ms. Tosto by Friday, May 25th. You may mail it to my attention at the address above or fax it to me at 1-306-692-3404.

Thank you for investing time in Ms. Tosto's future.

Sincerely,

Denise Lambert

Denise Lambert
Personnel Officer
Duffield Department Stores

Ours is a growing company. The person who manages our office will need to know good office procedures and how to adapt them to changing conditions. What is your evaluation of Mr. Hart's leadership ability, including human-relations skills, to run an office of 11? Please describe a situation in which Mr. Hart demonstrated this ability while employed at your firm.

Would you also comment on your observations of Mr. Hart when in a high-stress situation? With us, he would have to cope with a high-volume, pressure-filled operation. Does he have the skills and experience necessary for this role?

We will, of course, hold your answers in strict confidence. We appreciate whatever help you can give Mr. Hart and us.

A PRACTICE RUN

Here is another letter for your critical evaluation. It is not a good example of a personnel inquiry. List the errors and omissions in the space provided.

Mr. Shawn Hart has applied to us for employment and has given your name as a reference. He indicates that he worked under your supervision during the period 1993–96.

We would be most appreciative if you would give us your evaluation of Mr. Hart. We are especially interested in his ability to handle responsibility, knowledge of office procedures, and work habits.

Thanking you in advance for your assistance.

_____

_____

_____

_____

_____

A SUMMARY OF LEARNING OUTCOMES FROM THIS CHAPTER

This chapter considers certain types of routine letters that are normally written in the direct order. Routine inquiries appropriately begin with a request followed by enough explanation to enable the reader to answer accurately. If the inquiry involves more than one question, the questions are separated to make them stand out. Consider adding numbers or bullets. The letter ends with an appropriate, supportive comment.

The most common type of routine inquiry is the request for information. It begins with the one question to be asked, the most important of several questions to be asked, or a general question that sets up a list of questions.

A request for action also uses direct order. Because the reader is asked to do more than answer questions, more explanation is given to support the request.

Order letters are best written in the direct order. Begin them with a direct authorization to ship the goods. Then systematically identify the items you want (quantity, catalogue number, basic name, descriptive points, unit price, total price, etc.). In addition, include all other information vital to the sale (shipping instructions, method of payment, time requirement). End the letter with appropriate, friendly words that have been tailored to the circumstances.

Routine claims are made using the direct approach because, even though they carry bad news, the reader usually wants to correct the problem. Also, directness strengthens the claim. (For unusual claims, consider the indirect, persuasive approach.) Early in the routine claim letter, in a subject line or in an incidental comment, you identify the transaction involved. Then you make your claim stating what went wrong, perhaps with some interpretation of the effects. Give a clear review of the facts without showing anger. You may want to suggest an alternative remedy. As usual, your ending words should be cordial.

Inquiries about people require special care, as they concern the moral and legal rights of people. Thus, you should know the legal requirements of your province or territory. Ask for a factual assessment of the person's work experience and skills, and act in good faith.

ANSWERS TO PRACTICE RUNS

▶ Asking for Information

Elements of the Direct-Order Request for Information	Letter 1	Letter 2
Opens with the request		✔
Uses a direct question		✔
Explains adequately		✔
Explanation is logically placed in the letter		✔
Additional requests have structure, that is, they		✔
1. are direct questions		
2. are in separate sentences		✔
3. have their own paragraphs with explanation		✔
4. have bullets or numbers		
The closing shows goodwill	✔	✔
The closing is specific to the situation		✔

▶ Placing an Order

The letter begins indirectly. The first sentence is useless and merely delays the main message. This message comes in the second sentence, but it is more a suggestion than an authorization. The information on the books is not orderly, and the layout does not display it clearly. Neither the number of books wanted nor their prices stand out. One has to look for this information. The book titles are clear and will probably lead the reader to the right books, but edition numbers have been omitted. This information could be important. Payment details appear in the closing, but they are vague and incomplete. The letter's abrupt ending will produce little goodwill.

▶ Making a Claim

"Doreen" should have the amount of the invoice, and a list of the specific items missing. She would likely have a customer account number with this regular supplier. Her claim should begin directly. Leave the customer reactions to the product until later.

The "supplier" will have to use some imagination. Be sure to insist on knowing exactly what flavours and what amounts are missing. An alternate plan might be to guarantee delivery of the goods within 48 hours, i.e., soon enough that Doreen will not have to use the smaller, more expensive containers. Another might be to have her keep and use only what she needs immediately. She would pay only for that amount, return the rest for credit, and have new supplies in the correct size sent out.

▶ Asking about People

The opening to this letter is indirect. Although the explanation is needed, it does not deserve the emphasis that the beginning position gives it. There are several serious errors in the question paragraph. It does not explain the duties of the job or even mention what kind of position is being considered for Mr. Hart. The items of information wanted could be overlooked because they are not worded as questions, and they are not in separate sentences. Though appearing to be courteous, the closing words are empty and overused.

QUESTIONS FOR DISCUSSION

1. Why is the direct order appropriate in letters requesting action? When would you use the indirect order? Give examples.

2. "Explanations just take up space. If inquiry letters are brief, the reader can spend more time answering and less time reading." Where are the loopholes in this thinking?

3. "In writing inquiries about people, I don't ask specific questions. I want to know all I can, so I leave things wide open." Discuss the weakness of this approach.

4. "I don't need to be concerned with organizing the details because I always telephone my order. If they need to know something, they'll ask." Give reasons why this is not valid.

5. Discuss the relative directness of these beginnings of an order letter:

"Please send me the following items . . ."
"I would like to have the following . . ."
"I need the following items . . ."
"I would appreciate your sending me the following . . ."
"Can you send me the following items . . .?"

6. A claim means something has gone wrong. Usually negative topics need to be introduced and explained carefully. Why should claim letters be in direct order?

CASE 6–1

Armand and Shauna are in their final semester. That means that along with doing more papers, reports, and projects than ever before, they are also sending out résumés for jobs. Today they are discussing one of Armand's prospects.

Armand: "For this job, I want to get Mr. Sekora's recommendation. He'd be a good one. I have an appointment to see him tomorrow morning to ask him about it."
Shauna: "What are you going to say to him?"
Armand: "Well, I hadn't really thought. I guess I'll remind him about the class he taught me. And I'll say I hope it won't be too much trouble if I ask him a favour, and I'll understand if he can't do it. Maybe I should offer to take him for coffee while we talk."
Shauna: "Wait a minute. Do you think he'll need all this persuasion to give you a reference? If so, maybe he isn't the one you want to ask after all. You want someone who remembers you well and thinks you're good for the job, not someone whose arm you have to twist."
Armand: "Oh, he'll know me and give me a good reference, all right. Do you think I can be direct about asking him?"
Shauna: "Well, if he really is a good reference for you

to choose, he shouldn't mind being *asked*. He can still say no."
Armand: "OK. How about, 'Hi, Mr. Sekora. Will you write a reference letter for me? I can come by and pick it up on Thursday after my first accounting class.' "
Shauna: "Hmmm. Well, that's direct all right. But I had something more in between those two in mind."

To find the middle ground that Shauna refers to, consider these questions.

1. What category of direct request fits Armand's request to Mr. Sekora? (Asking for Information; Asking for Action; Placing Orders; Making Claims; Asking about People)
2. What category of direct request fits the employer's request to Mr. Sekora? (Asking for Information; Asking for Action; Placing Orders; Asking about People; Making Claims)
3. What elements were missing from Armand's very direct approach?

Now write some notes to help Armand effectively organize his request.

LETTER PROBLEMS

Refer to Chapter 21 for information on the layout and format for letters.

▶ Asking for Information

1. For the past four months, your firm, Fun and Games Travel, has enjoyed good success organizing group vacations. Now you are working on a seven-day ski vacation to Whistler Mountain.

You plan to fly groups of skiers to Vancouver and then take them to Whistler by chartered bus. Each group will arrive on a Sunday and will depart at noon the following Saturday. Thus, you will need six nights of accommodation for each group. You have the information you need about air transportation to Vancouver and bus transportation to Whistler Mountain. Now you must get information about the six nights of lodging, ski rentals, food, lift tickets, and so on.

The Silver Moon Lodge is one of several hotels you are considering for the three groups of 40 people you plan to organize. The trips will be between November 1

and December 15. (You may select specific dates.) The Lodge has 122 rooms, a restaurant, ski rental shop, and lounge. Their standard daily room rates for this period are single occupancy $110 and double occupancy $125, but you will want a group discount.

Breakfast at the Lodge and lunch on the slope are the individual's responsibility. Dinners, however, would be a group affair—preferably in a private dining room. You believe that this arrangement encourages camaraderie among group members and thus adds to their enjoyment of the trip. A sample menu would make it easier for you to evaluate food costs and gratuities.

The Silver Moon is "conveniently located just minutes away from the best ski slopes in Canada." (Source: Their brochure.) You need to know how skiers get from the hotel to the slopes. The possibilities you can think of are a hotel shuttle bus, your own charter bus, and skiing in and out. You also want to know about ski rentals and lift tickets, which, you assume, come with discounts for groups. There may be still other questions. Think about the possibilities carefully so that one inquiry letter will give you all the information you need. (For class purposes, you may specify any additional information that you need as long as it is consistent with the information given here.)

2. You are interested in going into business for yourself. For the past few weeks, you have been looking through the "Business Opportunities" section of your newspaper's classified ads in search of the right opportunity. Today's search produced the following interesting ad:

Pizza cafe, in Port Elizabeth. Independent (not a franchise). Successful for 29 years. Owner-founder retiring. $120,000 firm. Write P. O. Box 729, Port Elizabeth.

You are interested in this ad. Port Elizabeth would be a nice place to live, and you like the idea of an independent, established business. But before you take a long trip to look over the business, you want more information. Of course, you want information about operating records; in particular, you need gross sales and net income data. And you want this information for a period of recent years so that you can determine trends. Then there is the matter of financing. You would be able to cover about half of the $120,000 with cash, but you would need financing for the rest. Would the owner be willing to finance the remainder? If so, on what terms?

There may be other pertinent questions, perhaps questions about competitors and key personnel. Think the matter through. Then write the letter.

3. As the business manager for Dr. Cecil W. Hertenberger, you are responsible for making all arrangements for this investment adviser's lecture tours. Today you find that a scheduled lecture in Drummond cannot be held at the Golden Triangle Motel on the 21st of next month. The motel's meeting rooms were badly damaged by fire and will be closed for at least three months. You will have to make other arrangements.   One good possibility is the Wayside Inn, which is located on the major highway serving Drummond. Its location satisfies Dr. Hertenberger's preference to be away from the downtown traffic. Now you must write the Wayside manager to determine whether this motel can meet his other needs.

Specifically, Dr. Hertenberger needs a meeting room that will accommodate a maximum of 100 people who will pay to hear his very popular lecture on investment techniques. The room must be free from outside noise (no loud celebrations, dances, receptions, and such in nearby rooms). Preferably, it should have solid walls and not be part of a large room which has been partitioned by screens. Of course, it must be equipped with the standard lecture equipment—lectern, overhead projector, screen, and whiteboard. Because the people who attend the lecture are likely to come by car, the motel must have ample parking. You will also require two coffee breaks and a full-course noon meal. As you think through the problem, you may find a need for additional information. When you have completed your thinking, write the letter.

4. Play the role of a staff trainer for Beaverbrook Industries. You are impressed with a brochure you have received on the Niagara Executive Training program, which is held on the campus of the University of Niagara. So impressed are you that you are considering enrolling Beaverbrook executives in this program instead of running in-house programs. The Niagara literature names the companies that have sent executives to the program. You know one of the trainers of Mastodon Oil well enough to ask for an evaluation of Niagara's program.

Of the information you want, the most important is Mastodon's overall experience with the program from the point of view of the executives themselves and the company. What benefits justify the time and cost? You are also concerned about the level of instruction. You would enroll your middle managers because budget cuts have meant many changes for this group. Finally, you want Mastodon's evaluation of the program format—a three-week intensive course rather than one evening a week for six months. You can see possible benefits and drawbacks.

Prepare the questions to ask Dana Laing at Mastodon Oil about the Niagara Executive Training program.

5. Play the part of the office manager for the Browne-Ragsdale Insurance Agency. Your office badly needs a _____(your choice of office equipment). Today you read an advertisement on this product in a business journal. You liked what you read, but you need to know more. So you will write the manufacturer or telephone the local representative for this information.

For class purposes, you should prepare at least three questions and include explanations and background information about the needs of Browne-Ragsdale.

▶ Asking for Action

6. You are working on a STEP (Student Temporary Employment Program) grant for your instructor over the summer. Part of your job is to handle routine correspondence.

Your school teaches business communications to about 700 students a year. In order to make a textbook selection, the instructors need to have complimentary preview copies. They also need the instructors' manual and copies of any reviews that are available.

Write to Nicole Cowan, the representative for your area, requesting six copies of this text for preview. (Supply a local address for Ms. Cowan.)

7. You are on the social committee for your company, Presto Pasta. Each year, the company provides the food for a summer picnic for the entire staff. The social committee looks after entertainment.

This year you want to try something new. You think a small group of musicians from the local music conservatory would be a fine idea. There is a brass quartet called *Four Strong Winds* that plays classical, jazz, and contemporary music. You think this student group would be pleased to play because the opportunity will offer them experience and a small honorarium.

Write to *Four Strong Winds,* c/o Amy Tuckwell, 116 Maple Road, in your city. Supply other details you think they will need to know to reach a positive decision.

8. Some trees that the city planted in the road allowance have grown very tall and are now resting on the power lines. You are concerned that in a wind storm the weight of the trees could break the lines and create a hazard. You want action right away.

You are sure that the city will respond by sending a work crew, but before you call to report your concern, you organize your thoughts on paper.

Write out in full the key points you need to explain to the city clerk when you call. Supply any details that are necessary.

▶Placing Orders

9. After returning to your store, The Great Outdoors, from your annual trip to the regional trade fair, you look through some of the literature you picked up. You are especially interested in these items from the Damon Company brochure:

THE WOODSMAN. Men's winter jacket. Wind-stopping nylon shell is fleece-lined for amazing warmth without weight. Plus it's treated with Weatherguard to resist moisture and stains. Machine wash/dry. Choose from four rich colours: sand, burgundy, grey, and blue. Sizes: S(34–37), M(38–41), L(42–44), XL(46–48), XXL(50–52). $214.98 each, 5% discount on orders of 24 or more.

FRONTIER LEATHER BACKPACK. Modern version of the famous backpack of yesteryear. 100% durable leather. All-chrome hardware. Roomy cargo compartment plus three handy, expandable pockets. $67.45 each. Oversize model, $73.45 each. 5% discount on orders of 6 backpacks, regardless of size.

You will order two dozen of the coats in an assortment of sizes and colours (specify your choices based on what you think you can sell). And you will order six backpacks (four regular and two oversize). You will send a cheque with your order for the goods, PST (if applicable), and GST. You will pay shipping charges when the goods arrive.

10. As the owner of Gifts Unlimited, you are always looking for appropriate items for your exclusive gift shop. In today's issue of *The Specialty Shop Journal,* these items advertized by Northern Specialties, Inc., interest you:

HANDWOVEN PLACE MATS. Individually hand-woven in treadle looms. Made of 100% natural fibres and dyes. Authentic West Coast Designs. Offered in the following colour combinations: natural and teal with black; light grey and indigo blue with white; light grey and red with white. In sets of eight, $90 per set.

STERLING SILVER EARRINGS. Handcrafted by artisans in three designs: a dolphin, a totem pole, and a bell. Length about 6 cm. $39.50 per pair.

You will order these products by letter: one dozen place mat sets (four of each of the colour choices); eight pairs of earrings (two dolphins, two totem poles, and four bells). As the advertisement allows COD shipment, you will specify this manner of payment.

11. Catalogue shopping is growing in popularity because of its convenience and speed. From a suitable catalogue of your choice, select at least three items. Then prepare a written order to fax to the company. Make certain that you give all the information needed to complete the sale including shipping instructions and manner of payment.

▶Asking about People

12. You are a personnel assistant in the home office of Country Clubs which owns and operates four country clubs. The Bonaparte Country Club is its most recent acquisition. Your office must find a manager for it.

The Bonaparte Country Club has a membership of 750. As with most country clubs, its manager is in complete charge. Reporting to the manager are the persons responsible for the club's various activity and operational areas: golf pro, tennis pro, grounds manager, lounge manager, office manager, and foods manager. The ideal country club manager knows enough about the work of each of these people to judge their performance. In other words, the ideal manager knows every phase of club activities. The manager is solely responsible for ending each year with a profit.

In addition to running the country club profitably, the manager must maintain good personal relationships with the members. Each club has a Membership Committee to advise the manager who then makes the final decisions. The committee has control over membership affairs that do not affect financial operations. Truly, the job of club manager calls for an individual who is personable, gregarious, and prudent—a strong leader and an accomplished diplomat.

Among the applicants for the job is Mr. Thomas Martino. As shown by his résumé, Martino was in the Armed Forces for 28 years. During the last 15 years of his military service, he managed officers' clubs. This was good experience, of course, but it lacked the profit incentives that managing the Bonaparte would have. Martino has been the assistant manager of the Pompano Bay Country Club for almost two years.

You will write to Janic Kvanli, the manager of the Pompano Bay Country Club to ask all the questions that will enable you to evaluate Martino's suitability for the Bonaparte job.

13. You are part of a panel responsible for hiring a research assistant for Info-Search. The panel wants a young man or woman with thorough training and some experience in marketing and marketing research. Cathy Simonini seems to be just the person for the job if her references support her application.

As Cathy reported her record, she was an honours graduate of Stonehill University with a major in marketing. She has a thorough foundation in marketing research methodology, having taken all the undergraduate courses available in this area. She also has a strong background in computers and quantitative methods. How well she learned these subjects should have been reflected in her job performance. So you will write to her boss on the job she held after leaving school.

Cathy was a marketing research assistant at International Foods, manufacturer of a wide line of packaged cereals. Cathy noted on her résumé that she worked for International Foods for two years and that towards the end of her tenure she was in charge of two projects. She resigned because her husband was transferred to your city.

Your letter to Charlton Burkhalter, Director of Research (the person she listed as a reference), needs to discover Cathy's ability to conduct research independently and to take charge of small teams. Research has to be carefully planned and executed within strict deadlines. All the research done by your organization has to be written up, and Cathy would have to do some of this writing.

As you turn these requirements into questions, you may think of other information that you need.

▶Making Claims

14. The Candy Corner has built a reputation for fine quality sweets. That's why you were disturbed when a customer returned a box of Brubaker chocolates saying the nuts in them were rancid.

You have been selling Brubaker products since you opened your store, and they have always been good. "Perhaps the problem is limited to the one box," you hope. However, the unsold boxes you check are bad, and you must assume that the entire shipment is stale. A count shows that you have sold 29 boxes and in all likelihood have 29 dissatisfied customers.

Brubaker Sweets needs to know what has happened and what you want done. You want Brubaker to reimburse you for any returned boxes of the 29 already sold. And you want a credit note for 31 boxes you are removing from your shelves. You'll return those chocolates at Brubaker's expense, or you'll destroy them if Brubaker prefers. And finally, you want three dozen fresh boxes to restock your shelves.

15. The employees of Hi-Tech, Inc., were elated last week when they moved into their new office building. It was truly beautiful. The most beautiful feature of the building was the giant aquarium in the ground floor lobby. It was landscaped with aquatic plants, and it was teeming with colourful tropical fish—almost $2,500 worth. Its beauty was short-lived, however, for within a day many of the tropical fish were dead or dying.

The supplier, Cullum's Tropical Fish and Garden, has to correct the situation. When you could not reach Mr. Cullum by telephone, you decided to turn your notes into a letter to fax to him.

You want those dead and sick fish removed immediately! Moreover, before Hi-Tech spends any more money on replacing the fish, you want him to check the entire system. With some compensation, answers and guarantees in place, you might continue doing business with him.

16. You are the manager of the Athlete's Locker, a sporting goods store in your city. A few weeks ago you made what you considered to be a very good purchase of women's warm-up suits. Manufactured by B. B. Kennon, Inc., these garments impressed you at first sight. Their rich colours—turquoise, hot purple, and teal green—would quickly catch the eyes of your customers, you thought. And they did. Within a week you sold over half of the six dozen you ordered.

This morning one of your good customers came in with the warm-up suit she purchased. It was a mess. It had turned a murky brown, obviously a result of the colours running into one another. "I washed it just like the instructions on the collar said," she told you. You refunded her money.

A few hours later another woman returned her warm-up suit with virtually the same story. You think there will be still others. The product is clearly defective, and you must do something about the situation. You will tell the Kennon people what happened. You want replacements for all the warm-up suits, and you want them quickly. Furthermore, you feel that reimbursement for the two returned suits and for any others that might be returned is mandatory.

Although you are angry, as you write the letter, you remember that you have had a good relationship with Kennon over the years. There must be an explanation. Even so, you will be direct and firm because your business has suffered.

17. As a salesperson for Global Pharmaceutical, you must use your own car for work purposes. Global reimburses you for mileage related to your job. A few days ago, you traded in your old car for a current model (you name the brand and model). After driving the new car for a few miles, you noticed a sporadic jerking at speeds exceeding 60 kilometres per hour. You then returned the car to the dealer that sold it to you.

    After explaining the problem to the service manager, you left the car with him for repair. When you picked it up at the end of the day, he said, "Just had to make a few adjustments. That's not unusual with a new car. It was really no problem at all."

    As you drove home, you noticed the same jerking. The next morning you brought the car back to the service manager. At the end of the day you returned to pick the car up. "Couldn't find much wrong." the service manager told you. "We ran a diagnostic and adjusted the fuel injection. Runs perfect now." So you drove home again, and again you noticed the jerking. This time you went right back to the dealer. "I can't check it now," the service manager said. "It's too close to closing time. You'll have to make an appointment at the desk and bring it back tomorrow." You became irate and in not very diplomatic language said that you would get another opinion and take your complaint to the manufacturer.

On the way home you stopped at the shop of an independent mechanic, who happened to be a good friend. After checking out the car, your friend told you that the problem was in the automatic transmission. "It's an expensive job," he said. You decide to write a letter to tell the manufacturer about the problem with your car and the dealer. You'll ask the manufacturer to replace the car or have it repaired by a dealer other than the one that sold it to you.

18. Put yourself in the position of sales manager for the C. E. Greene Insurance Agency. Once each year, all the Greene salespeople (79 this year) attend a dinner and hear a motivational speaker. The part you like best is the presentation to the year's top five salespeople.

    This year, the awards are beautiful desk sets. The gold-plated base of each set is being inscribed with the salesperson's name (top line), "Greene's Top 5" (middle line), and the year (bottom line). You ordered the five awards from Trophy World at a cost of $144 each. They arrived today, and they are impressive, but the company name is spelled "Green" rather than "Greene." A check of your copy of the order shows that the error is Trophy World's.

    Replacements will have to be provided. With only one week before the dinner, the job would be rushed. You wonder if the quality would still be as high. You decide to handle the situation this way. You will present the awards as they are. After the dinner, you will take them back and have them returned to Trophy World. Trophy World will make the corrections and deliver the awards directly to the winners. Now you must work on a clear wording to explain your requirements to Trophy World.

Directness in Routine Responses

Upon completing this chapter, you will be able to answer routine business letters effectively. To reach this goal, you should be able to

1 Use the direct approach in favourably answering business requests for information or for action.

2 Compose favourable responses that include some bad news yet maintain a positive tone and foster goodwill.

3 Use acknowledgment letters to clarify orders, explain difficulties, and build goodwill.

4 Appreciate the challenge of being fair to all in reference letters.

5 Compose letters involving adjustment grants that will regain the customer's confidence.

6 Write letters that have long-term, goodwill goals.

▶ to Routine Response Letters

Doreen has been serving *Vitality* at Good 'n Nice for a few months now. As a regular user of this product, she has been included in a customer satisfaction survey.

Dear Ms. Lam:

Will you take a few moments to answer these questions to help us serve you better?
How would you rate *Vitality* compared to other similar products you have used? Please comment on the following features:
· ease of use
· variety of flavours
· quality of taste
· nutritional value
· cost
· service by our supplier
Any additional comment you wish to make will be welcomed. Thank you for helping us improve this product and our service to you.

Sincerely,
Mark Wikholm
Mark Wikholm
Customer Service

Doreen was so pleased with the product that she wrote back promptly. Her letter began:

Dear Mr. Wikholm:

Vitality is an excellent product that sells well, is easy to use, and generates a solid profit for my business . . . ▪

· · · · · · · · · · · · · · · · · ·

FAVOURABLE RESPONSES

When you write letters that give favourable answers to requests, your primary goal is to tell your readers what they want to know in a concise, clear style. Because their reactions to this goal will be positive, you should use the direct order. Sending a prompt reply and getting to the point are positive features that build goodwill. The indirect order would be inappropriate because it delays the answer unnecessarily by placing the main point near the end of the letter. Use the guidelines presented here for positive replies.

> • Anticipated favourable reader reaction justifies the direct plan.

- Begin with the good news. Give the answer or state that you are complying with the request.

- Identify the correspondence being answered (either incidentally or in a subject line).

- Continue with necessary details in an orderly arrangement.

- Handle any negative information carefully to avoid overemphasizing it.

- Consider including extra comments or actions to support goodwill.

- End with a friendly, adapted comment.

Beginning with the Good News

The most direct beginning is to start with the positive reply to the major request. In answering the letter about *Vitality* (see the Introductory Situation), Doreen gets off to a quick start.

> • Begin by favourably answering the major request.

Vitality is an excellent product that sells well, is easy to use, and generates a solid profit for my business.

* Or begin by saying that you are complying with the request.

An alternative possibility is to begin by stating that you are giving the readers what they want—that you are complying with their request. While less direct, it is a favourable beginning. Using this approach, Doreen would begin her letter with words such as these:

I am very pleased to give you some feedback about your excellent product, *Vitality.*

Identifying the Correspondence Being Answered

* You should identify the letter being answered.

* The subject line is a good way to identify the letter being answered.

It is important to identify the letter being answered by date and subject. This identification information is useful for filing purposes. It also helps the reader recall the situation.

A good way to identify the letter being answered is to use a subject line, a mechanical device discussed in Chapter 6. A useful subject line in a routine response would state the topic of the letter being answered, give a date reference to it, or a file number if available. If a subject line is used, it immediately follows the salutation and precedes the first paragraph. For Doreen's letter about *Vitality,* these subject lines would be appropriate:

Subject: Your April 3 questionnaire about *Vitality.*

Re: Your customer satisfaction survey for *Vitality.*

* Identification can be made in the first paragraph.

Another way of identifying the letter being answered is to refer to it at the beginning of your letter. While identification is necessary, it does not deserve strong emphasis. A subordinate clause or phrase is sufficient. If she chooses not to use a subject line, Doreen could continue

In answer to the first point in your recent customer satisfaction survey, I like the handy measuring scoop included in each package.

. . . .

A PRACTICE RUN   How would you rate these opening sentences to favourable response letters?

In response to your April 3 inquiry about our Chem-Treat paint, I want you to know that we appreciate your interest and will welcome your business.	
Strengths	*Weaknesses*
Yes, I am pleased to inform you that all our international flights do prohibit smoking.	
Strengths	*Weaknesses*
Your May 5th letter about your Rigo FAX391 (your file 97-116) has been received.	
Strengths	*Weaknesses*

. . . .

Logically Arranging the Answers

* If one answer is involved, give it directly and completely.

If you are answering just one question, you have little to do after handling that question in the opening paragraph. You answer it as completely as the situation requires by giving the requested information or agreeing to perform the requested action, and you give whatever explanation or other information is needed. Then you are ready to close the letter.

If, on the other hand, you are answering two or more questions, the body of your letter becomes a series of answers. As in all clear writing, you should work for a logical order. Answering the questions in the order your reader used is one possibility. Sometimes one question is fundamental to the others and answering it first is a good approach. Or if one question is more important than the others, a logical order would be to answer that important question first.

> • If more than one answer is involved, arrange the answers in a clear, logical order.

As discussed in Chapter 6, layout can help organize and emphasize the points of a letter. As a courtesy to your reader, make the answers stand out. For shorter answers, you may find it helpful to indent them in a series of points. They could be marked with bullets or numbers. If the answers are complex, each one should be in a separate paragraph. If your reader numbered the questions, number the answers correspondingly for easy reference.

> • Layout can support the logical order.

Skillfully Handling Any Negatives

When your response concerns some bad news along with the good news, handle the bad news with care. Bad news stands out, and unless you are careful, it is likely to receive more emphasis than it deserves. To restore the balance you sometimes need to subordinate the bad news and emphasize the good news. (Of course, if your letter has mainly bad news, you no longer have a favourable response. You should be considering the bad-news letter form discussed in Chapter 8.)

> • Emphasize favourable responses; subordinate unfavourable responses.

In giving proper emphasis to the good- and bad-news parts, you should recall the techniques of emphasis discussed in Chapter 5, especially *Position* and *Space*. That is, you should place the good news in positions of high emphasis—at paragraph beginnings and endings and at the beginning and ending of the letter as a whole. You should place the bad news in secondary positions. In addition, you should give less space to bad news and more space to good news.

> • Place favourable responses at beginnings and ends. Give them more space.

You also should select words and build sentences that communicate the effect you want. Generally, this means using pleasant words and avoiding unpleasant ones. Note that you are not glossing over the bad news. Because bad news stands out, these devices just keep it in perspective. Your overall goal should be to present the information in your response so that your readers get a true picture and just the right effect.

> • Use words skillfully to maintain the positive impression.

A PRACTICE RUN

Improve the wording in the following sentences. They carry the only bad news in an otherwise favourable response letter.

I cannot be a workshop leader at your four-day conference because I have a conflicting engagement on one of those afternoons. However, I can be the speaker on the mornings you requested. Although I can participate in the rest of the conference, I will be away on Saturday afternoon.

_____

_____

Except for your error in converting Australian dollars to Canadian dollars on page 3 of your expense report where you claim you spent $56.00 for business entertainment, your report is accepted.

_____

_____

_____

_____

Considering the Extras

- The little extra things you do for the reader will build goodwill.

For the best in goodwill effect, you should consider including extras with your answers. These are the things you say and do that are beyond the standard requirements. Examples are the inclusion of some additional information that may prove valuable, and a comment or question showing an interest in the reader's problem. Such extras frequently make the difference between success and failure in the goodwill effort.

Illustrations of how extras can be used to strengthen the goodwill effects of a letter are as broad as the imagination. A customer service representative replacing a damaged film with a new roll of film could include a coupon for developing and printing. A technical writer could clarify complicated answers with simple sketches. In Doreen's letter, additional information such as innovative uses of the product would be helpful. Such extras genuinely serve readers and promote goodwill.

Closing with a Cordial Comment

- End with friendly words adapted to the one case.

As in most routine business letter situations, you should end routine responses with friendly, cordial words that make clear your willing attitude. As much as is practical, adapt your words to the case. For example, Doreen might close her letter with these words:

I hope you can see how much I like *Vitality*. Please call me if you need more detail in any of my answers.

TYPES OF DIRECT-ORDER MESSAGES

Giving Information

- Replies giving information usually use the direct order.

A reply that contains information that was requested usually uses the direct-order approach. Even if some of the information is negative or not available, the requester will want the reply and, therefore, is considered to be receptive. If the reply refuses to give the information or contains mostly negative information, the indirect approach should be considered. (The indirect order for bad-news letters is discussed in Chapter 8.)

- Follow the general plan for favourable responses.

The letter giving positive news follows the general plan for favourable responses.

- It begins with the information and the identification of the original request.

- The letter continues until all the reader's questions have been answered.

- Negative information and extra information are handled as described in the previous sections on Favourable Responses.

- The closing is friendly and positive, of course.

A Sample Letter Giving Information. This sample letter responding favourably to a request for information uses a subject line to identify the inquiry. The letter begins directly, with the most favourable answer. Then it presents the other answers, giving each the emphasis and positive language it deserves. It subordinates the one slightly negative point (that two coats are needed for best coverage of dark surfaces) by position, amount of space, and structure. More positive information follows, showing another benefit of the extra coat—greater durability. The closing is goodwill talk, with some subtle selling strategy pointing to the successful use of the product.

• Here is a good example of a favourable response letter using the direct order.

Concerning: Your April 3 inquiry about Chem-Treat.

Chem-Treat is a high-quality paint that is guaranteed to prevent mildew. We know it works because we have tested it under all common conditions. In every case, it proved successful. We stand behind it with our money-back policy.

When you carefully follow the directions on each can, Chem-Treat paint is guaranteed safe. As the directions state, you should use any paint, including Chem-Treat, in a well-ventilated room—never in a closed, unvented area.

A four-litre can of Chem-Treat is usually enough for one-coat coverage of 50 square metres of previously painted surface. For the best results over a dark paint, you will need to apply two coats, allowing one four-litre can for every 30 square metres. These two coats will give you five years or more of beautiful protection.

We sincerely appreciate your interest in Chem-Treat, Ms. Motley. We know that you'll enjoy the long-lasting beauty of this durable paint.

Taking Action

Favourable responses to a request for action begin with a statement of the good news—that you will be the speaker, or that you will serve on the committee, or that you will write an article for the company newsletter. As in the general plan for favourable responses, you will identify the earlier correspondence. For the rest of the letter, follow these modifications of the general plan.

- If you have questions, place them in the second paragraph, arranging them logically as you did in request letters.

- Limitations or qualifications you may want to place on the agreement are handled as negative news. They should not overshadow your basic positive message.

- You may include additional offers of assistance, or you may simply close with a friendly comment or positive remark about the future.

The Case Illustrations give examples of this type of good-news letter.

Acknowledging Orders

Order acknowledgments are becoming less frequent for routine orders because of the costs. If a routine order can be filled immediately, an acknowledgment is not necessary. Receipt of the goods will satisfy the customer. In lieu of an acknowledgment, some companies assign a confirmation number to the transaction. Telephone orders are often handled this way. The number is the key to all the records about that order. If there is an error or a delay, the customer simply inquires about the order by giving the confirmation number. Again, in most cases, the prompt receipt of the goods satisfies the customer.

• Prompt delivery has changed the use of order acknowledgments.

However, individually written order acknowledgment letters are sometimes justified for new accounts, large orders, or special situations. For example, for a custom order that will take more time, an acknowledgment may be sent for two reasons: (1) to reassure the customer and build goodwill, and (2) to confirm details and act as an informal contract. Another situation that would justify an acknowledgment is an order that will be delivered in stages over a long period. The acknowledgment confirms the order and strengthens the relationship with the customer.

• Order acknowledgment letters are used for special circumstances.

RAVEN
Paper Products

100 Eagle Road, Cambridge, ON N3H 2Y2 (519)653-7919

August 7, 1997

Mme. Hélène Boisvert
Dominion Packaging & Supplies
PO Box/C.D. 6808
MONTREAL, PQ   H3C 5P4

Dear Mme. Boisvert:

A positive statement sets up the answers and identifies the original letter.

A part of the philosophy of Total Quality Management is the willingness to share experiences. I am happy to answer the questions from your August 3rd letter about our TQM program. TQM is an exciting venture for any company, and I'm sure you will see its benefits in your firm.

Executive Response: Yes, our executives had mixed feelings about the effectiveness of TQM at first. They feared a loss of authority and independence. After thorough training and a few very successful pilot projects, most of the antagonism subsided.

Every answer refers to a question in the original letter.

Each answer is marked by a heading.

Cost Effectiveness: In the long term, TQM will definitely save us money. After we reach our ideal staff size through normal attrition, we estimate the monthly saving will be about $8,800. More importantly, we have improved our processes to turn out a better product.

Employee Response: Changing our way of doing things created a temporary morale problem among our employees, even though we assured them that changes would be made only after consultation and input from all stakeholders. As they have seen us keeping that promise over the months, the morale is improving.

Each answer has its own paragraph.

Further Assistance: As I mentioned at the beginning, we are quite willing to share our experience with you. I am enclosing a list of our Quality Circle members. Please call any of them to arrange an interview.

The pleasant closing includes a sincere offer of further help.

I'm sure that after reviewing this information, you will have other questions. If an inspection of our company would help, you are welcome to visit us.

Sincerely,

David M. Erb

David M. Erb
Quality Manager

DME:gt

encl.

Seven Stoner Road, Ottawa, Ontario K1S 4W4

March 12, 1997
Darren Van Essen
Apt. 602-22 Athabasca Drive
Fort McMurray, AB   T9H 4H4

Dear Darren:

The main request is answered and the original correspondence is identified.

Enclosed is the complimentary copy of our latest annual report that you asked for in your February 27th letter.

Our customer service branch has recently prepared two brochures. One outlines our services, and the other describes our proposed expansion into Western Canada. A copy of each is enclosed because we think you will find them useful for your project.

Additional information is given to create goodwill.

The cordial closing is relevant to the reader's situation.

Good luck on this assignment and on your year's studies.

Sincerely,

J. W. Almas

(Mrs.) J. W. Almas
Customer Service

JA:aeb
encl.

c/o University of Niagara
611 University Avenue
Brockton, ON   L3G 2M6

November 21, 1997

Rebecca Korbut
Stonehill University
1767 Laurentian Drive
Marlborough, ON   N4P 1T1

Dear Rebecca:

The subject line identifies the topic.

Re: Joint Presentation for ABCC

Your suggestion about preparing a proposal for the Association of Business Communicators in Canada is appealing. I'll be glad to work with you on it.

The sender begins with the main point and the good news.

The writer confirms the good news by taking appropriate action.

I am enclosing an outline of my thoughts for my part of the presentation. I am assuming that the proposal must be only one page long. If more detail is allowed, I can fax you a fuller version. Does this seem to fit with what you had in mind?

If you have a copy of the latest edition of the Business Writer's Journal, there is an interesting article on the topic of adaptation and you-viewpoint that offers some further insight into the technique. It would be a useful reference for our presentation, I think.

Co-operation and goodwill are demonstrated with this additional information.

The positive closing maintains the tone of the letter.

I look forward to your feedback. I'm confident we can work well together to present an excellent paper to the delegates.

Sincerely,

Simone Cody
Simone Cody

SC:ab

encl

These letters use the direct plan, of course. They begin by acknowledging the order and giving its status. The remainder of the letter may express appreciation, or it may reassure the customer of the wise choice of product. The goodwill closing often looks ahead to continuing service.

Skillfully composed acknowledgment letters can do more than acknowledge orders, though this task remains their primary goal. These letters also can build goodwill. Through a warm, personal tone, they can make the reader want to continue doing business with a company that cares.

• Acknowledgment letters build goodwill.

Tact in Handling Delayed Shipments. One issue that may need special handling is a delay in filling the order. The order may not have included all the information needed, or some items may be out of stock. A note about a back order on the invoice may be all that is required. However, a short letter or telephone call may be more appropriate.

• Minor difficulties with the order should be handled according to the situation.

In the case of a vague order, you should ask for the information you need without appearing to accuse the customer of being careless or ignorant. To illustrate, you gain nothing by saying, "Your order is being held because you failed to state the colours you want." But you gain goodwill by writing, "So that your order can be completed, please check your choice of colours on the enclosed card." This tactful sentence handles the matter positively and makes the reply easy to give.

• In vague orders, request the needed information positively.

Similarly, you can handle back-order information diplomatically by emphasizing the positive part of the message. Instead of writing, "If our new stock arrives on time, we may be able to ship the Crescent Farms individual cheeses to you on the 9th at the earliest," you can write, "We will rush the Crescent Farms individual cheeses to you as soon as we receive our new stock which is due May 9." If the back-order period is long, you may choose to give your customer a way out of the transaction. A phrase such as "unless we hear from you by that time" following the back-order handling should take care of this matter. Remember that negative news is only a minor part of this letter. Most of the order has gone smoothly. If you have more bad news to give, you should consider the indirect order for your letter. See the following chapter for a more complete discussion of how to handle such negative news.

• Emphasize the expected delivery of back ordered items.

An Example of an Order Acknowledgment. The letter begins directly, telling Mr. Chapman that he is getting what he wants. The remainder of the letter welcomes the dealer and reinforces the business decision by promoting the products and the company. Notice the good use of you-viewpoint and positive language. The letter closes with a note of appreciation and reassurance.

Your selection of Protect-O paints and supplies should reach you by Wednesday, for the shipment left today by Blue Darter Express. As you requested, we are enclosing our invoice for $1,743.30, including PST and GST.

As this is your first order from us, I welcome you to the Protect-O circle of dealers. Our representative, Ms. Cindy Wooley, will call from time to time to offer whatever help she can. She is a highly competent technical adviser on paint and painting.

As a dealer for Protect-O products, you are supported by efficient service from the home plant. In addition, you can depend on this company to develop the best possible products—like our new Chem-Treat line of paints. As you will see from the enclosed brochure, Chem-Treat is a breakthrough in mildew protection.

We appreciate your order, Mr. Chapman. We are dedicated to helping you build a dealership that will be successful for many, many years.

• This letter acknowledges the order and builds good customer relations.

Giving References

Letters of reference are challenging to write because they place the writer between the hiring company and the candidate. While the overall objective of finding the right job for the right person is shared by everyone involved, each party has special concerns and points of view.

In Canada, provincial and federal human rights legislation has affected the information on job applications that may be reported. As noted in Chapter 6, reports about an applicant's age, race, religion, sex, marital status, and family status are generally

• Abide by legal requirements regarding the information that may be reported.

This letter concerns an order that cannot be filled exactly as requested. Some items are being sent, but one must be placed on back order, and one is on approval because the customer did not give specific information. The negative points are handled skillfully.

K-C SUPPLY

1701 Kingston Road
Scarborough, Ontario M6P 3B9
PHONE: (416) 485-5885
FAX: (416) 483-2905

October 7, 1998

Mr. Terry Fletcher
Fletcher Machine Works
4772 Worth Road
Windsor, ON   N6H 2M2

Dear Mr. Fletcher:

The best news is in the first paragraph.

By noon tomorrow, your three new Baskin motors and one Dawson 110 compressor should reach your Meadowbrook shops. As you requested, I marked them for your west side loading dock and sent them by Warren Express.

For the handcart you ordered, I am sending our heavy-duty Model M on approval. I believe its extra weight load will suit your needs best; however, I am faxing a description of our lighter model along with this letter for your consideration. An exchange is possible if you wish.

Since the order was unclear, the writer makes a reasonable decision and offers an alternative.

The bad news is stated positively.

Your three-dozen 317 T-clamps should reach you by the 13th. As you may know, these very popular clamps have been in short supply for some time now, but I have been promised a limited order by the 11th. Three dozen have been reserved for rush shipment to you.

As always, we appreciate your business. We will continue to serve you with quality industrial equipment and personalized service.

The closing is positive and forward-looking.

Sincerely,

Shannon E. Kurrus

Shannon E. Kurrus
K-C Supply

SEK:bim

prohibited. So are reports about an applicant's criminal record, citizenship, organization memberships, and mental and physical handicaps. Exceptions may be made in the rare cases in which such information is clearly related to the job.

The Justification for the Direct-Order Plan.   A letter of reference is organized in the direct order. The justification for the direct order is that the reference will be favourably received by the reader who requested it. The letter follows the general pattern for favourable responses with, as we will see, special attention to fairness.

• Personnel recommendations use the direct order because they satisfy the reader's need for information about someone.

The Challenge of Fair Reporting.   As a fair-minded writer, you want any reference letters you write to convey an accurate picture. Presenting your information too positively would be unfair to your reader. Presenting your information too negatively would be unfair to the applicant. Your task is to convey just the right picture through your words, remembering that negative points stand out unless handled carefully. To illustrate, take a report on an employee who, in spite of a personal problem, has a good work record. If you mention the personal problem in a position of emphasis or write too much about it, you make this one concern stand out. It will overshadow the more important fact that this person does good work.

• Letters of reference should be fair to all.

Nothing we have said means that you should hide shortcomings or communicate misleading information. Before you agree to write a reference, you should point out that you intend to communicate an accurate picture. If your subject has a poor work record and knows that you will report this fact, he or she may want to ask someone else for the reference.

• The goal is to report precisely and truthfully.

Granting a Claim

When you can grant an adjustment, the situation is a positive one for your customer. By compensating for an error, you are doing what your customer asked. A letter written in the direct order, giving that good news first, is appropriate. The special concern with granting a claim is to rebuild goodwill by careful handling of the negative event and by taking extra efforts to demonstrate good faith.

• Good news in adjustments justifies directness.

Regaining Lost Confidence.   Even though your basic objective is a good-news one, the adjustment situation is not entirely positive. If you place yourself in your reader's situation, you will understand why. As the reader sees it, something bad has happened—goods have been damaged, equipment has failed to work, or deadlines have been passed. The reader could be experiencing ill feelings toward your company and toward your products or services.

• Overcoming negative impressions takes a special effort.

Granting the claim is likely to take care of any ill feelings that your reader may have about the particular incident. But just correcting the error may not be enough to regain the reader's lost confidence in your products or services. Your larger goal is to improve the long-term relations between this customer and your company.

• Just correcting the error does not overcome the reader's negative impressions.

As a first step, you should select words that add to the positiveness of your answer. You may, for example, present your decision in terms of customer satisfaction, as in this beginning sentence:

The enclosed cheque for $87.99 is our way of showing you that your satisfaction is important to us.

Secondly, throughout your letter, you should avoid using words that recall the situation you are correcting. Since your goal is to change your reader's mental picture of your company and your product from negative to positive, your emphasis is better placed on positive things, such as what you are doing to correct the wrong. If you need to talk about the problem be brief, use positive language, and surround the negative topic with good news.

• Avoid negative references to the problem. Emphasize correcting the wrong, not the wrong itself.

Also to be avoided are the apologies that have become routine in such letters. Even though well intended, the "We sincerely regret the inconvenience caused you . . ." type of

Apex

Apex Manufacturing

5079 Sahali Trail
Kamloops, BC V4E 2T6

May 16, 1997

Ms. H. Brooking
Red Arrow Transport
106 Grandview Way
Kelowna, BC   V1X 7W7

Dear Ms. Brooking:

The subject line identifies the correspondence.

Subject: Your May 10 inquiry about George Adams.

Mr. Adams was our assistant shipping clerk from March 1987 to August 1992. During that time, he steadily improved in usefulness to our company. We wanted to keep him with us, but with economic conditions as they were, it became apparent that we could not offer him a promotion. Since leaving us, he has worked as head shipping clerk at Mountaintop Industries.

The relationship of the writer to the candidate is defined and the key points about work habits are made.

The responsibilities and achievements of the candidate are explained.

While working with us as first assistant, he substituted at the head clerk's desk. He became familiar with problems of rate scales and routing. His main assignment, however, was to supervise the car and truck loadings. By making a careful study of this work, he reduced our shipping damages noticeably within the last year. This job also placed him in direct charge of the labour force, which varied from six to ten workers.

We always found Mr. Adams honest, resourceful, and dependable. I highly recommend him to you.

The closing summarizes and concludes the reference.

Sincerely,

Eric McKinnon

Eric McKinnon
Supervisor

EMcK:rd

comment emphasizes the negative happenings and is read with skepticism. In most instances, your efforts to correct the problem speak louder than words and show adequate concern for your reader's interest. If you sincerely feel that you must apologize, you may do so, but recognize that you risk the negative effect of an apology.

Thirdly, if something can be done to correct a bad procedure or a product defect, you should do it. Then you should tell your reader what has been done as a result of this experience. Be certain that this explanation is positive. Assuring the reader that the staff member who made the mistake has been fired is negative and inappropriate. That a refresher training course is being given is positive and offers the likelihood of better service for the customer in the future.

> * Work to regain lost confidence by explaining or telling of corrective action.

Furthermore, the positive explanation sounds less like an excuse. You want the reader to understand, not feel sorry for you. "Our staff were very overworked because our computer was down, and there weren't enough people to run the manual system" is negative and sounds like an excuse. The reader will ask, "Why didn't you call in more help?" or "Why don't you have a better backup system for your computer?" Instead,

A PRACTICE RUN

Suggest improvements for these sentences to help restore the reader's confidence in the product and company.

We hope that the enclosed voucher for a free oil change makes up for the trouble you experienced.

_____

_____

Since our employees are trained to handle all chemicals carefully, we are at a loss to explain how the marks on your floor occurred. We certainly don't have many situations like this.

_____

_____

We aren't going to sell the XYZ model sprayer anymore because it sometimes clogs and leads to complaints like yours.

_____

_____

explain how you corrected the situation. "We had a busy hour or two until extra help arrived, but we were back on track by noon. Since then, we have been working to streamline the manual system. Now you should have speedy service whenever you call."

• End the letter with a pleasant and positive comment.

Positiveness in the Closing.   Your choice of subject matter for the closing will vary. It could be a forward look to happy relations, a comment about a product improvement, or the mention of a coming promotional event. Certainly, you should not say anything that recalls the original, negative situation.

Contrasting Examples of an Adjustment.   The techniques previously discussed are illustrated by the following adjustment letters. The first, with its indirect order and grudging tone, is ineffective. The directness and positiveness of the second clearly make it the better letter.

A Slow and Negative Treatment.   The ineffective letter begins with an obvious comment about receiving the claim. It recalls vividly what went wrong and then painfully explains what happened using negative words such as *fault* and *failure*. As a result, the good news is delayed for an additional paragraph. Finally, after two delaying paragraphs, the letter gets to the good news. The instructions for returning the original shipment are vague and unhelpful. Though well intended, the apologetic closing leaves the reader with yet another reminder of the trouble.

• This poorly written letter is needlessly slow and negative.

We have received your May 1 claim reporting that our shipment of Fireboy extinguishers arrived in badly damaged condition. We regret the inconvenience caused and understand your unhappiness.

Following our standard practice, we investigated the situation thoroughly. Apparently, the fault was in our failure to check the seals carefully. As a result, the fluid escaped in transit, damaging the exteriors of the fire extinguishers. We have taken corrective measures to assure that future shipments will be more carefully checked.

I am pleased to report that we are sending a replacement order. It will be shipped today by Red Arrow Transport and should reach you sometime Saturday. You can send back the damaged Fireboys by truck for reimbursement.

Again, we regret all the trouble you experienced.

The Direct and Positive Treatment.   The better letter uses a subject line to identify the transaction. The opening words tell the reader what she most wants to hear in a positive way that adds to the good news of the message. After handling the second essential matter of disposing of the damaged merchandise, the letter then reviews what happened. Using a you-viewpoint that focuses on the reader and keeping a positive tone, the letter clearly explains the cause of the problem and the solution. The letter closes with positive resale talk far removed from the problem.

• This well-written letter is direct and positive.

RE: YOUR MAY 1 REPORT ON INVOICE 1348.

Two dozen new and thoroughly tested Fireboy extinguishers should reach your plant Saturday afternoon. They were shipped early today by Red Arrow Transport. When the new Fireboys are delivered, the driver will collect the original group. We will pay all transportation charges.

As your satisfaction with our service is important to us, we have thoroughly checked all the Fireboys in stock. In the past, we assumed that all of them were inspected for tight seals at the factory. We learned, thanks to you, that we must systematically check each one. We now have added this routine to our normal handling procedure.

Fireboy extinguishers are a wise product choice because they have practically revolutionized the extinguisher field. Their compact size and efficiency have made them the most popular industrial fire extinguishers we carry. We are confident that they will be an asset to your plant's safety program.

Building Goodwill

• Some occasions permit an entire message dedicated to creating goodwill.

In each communication we have discussed so far, we have tried to create goodwill as well as accomplish a specific goal. In some circumstances, a direct-approach letter can be written that has as its only purpose the building of goodwill. The sender is not so

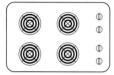

Consort Appliances   (204) 949–4720
5317 Davenport Avenue   **Winnipeg, Manitoba**   **R2Y 1K6**

December 9, 1998

Mr. Harvey P. McShane
3913 Martin Road
Flin Flon, MN R8A 0N4

Dear Mr. McShane:

The opening gives the good news that the claim is granted.

The attached cheque for $406.58 is reimbursement for the returned cappuccino maker plus GST and postage costs.

Because we want to provide our customers with the best service we can, we thoroughly tested the unit. A small plastic ring was not sealing properly. Such unexpected happenings can occur even with an excellent brand-name product such as this one. Without that seal, the necessary pressure for foaming the milk could not be maintained. This fluctuation triggered a safety shut-off device to protect you from the possibility of injury from the escaping steam.

The thoroughness in handling this claim is described to regain the confidence of this customer.

The closing emphasizes the safety and quality of products and looks forward to future business with this customer.

This type of safety protection is typical of the quality products we carry. You can depend on Consort's commitment to fine products and excellent service.

Sincerely,

John McNicoll

John McNicoll
Consumer Relations

JMcN:sg
Attachment

November 04, 1995

Ms. J. Wilson & Mr. R. Edwards
2123 -Willow Rd.
Edmonton, AB
T1T-3T3

Dear Jan & Bob:

Just a note to let you know...after many years of helping other people make the right kind of moves, it's now my turn. RE/MAX Real Estate has invited me to join their "Central" office, offering me the opportunity to move towards real independence. I'll explain...

The RE/MAX system works like a medical clinic or law office. Professionals functioning as independent practitioners, sharing facilities and resources, pooling their knowledge for your benefit when the need arises. Only seasoned Realtors can become RE/MAX "Sales Associates", demonstrating the abilities required to meet the challenge that I find both exciting and desirable. Best of all, my association with RE/MAX can be of benefit to you as well.

As an independent practitioner, I'm free to be creative and innovative in order to market your property successfully. Since I am not limited in my advertising budget, you can be sure I will go that extra mile to get you the best price in the shortest possible time.

As well, I'm not working alone, I have the support of a full time Assistant and the International RE/MAX Organization, with over 28,000 Sales Associates across North America, possessing sophisticated marketing tools and a referral system that is World Wide in scope.

I feel I have taken..."A Step Above The Crowd".

Jan & Bob, I look forward to serving your real estate needs with greater proficiency in the future. Please feel free to drop in or give me a call if you or your friends require my services.

Sincerely,

Sarah Blanche Urquhart

RE/MAX® **real estate**
central branch
2nd floor, 10814 - 106 avenue
edmonton, alberta t5h 4e1
tel: (403) 426-4461 fax: (403) 426-5700

[2]Used with permission of Sarah Blanche Urquhart and RE/MAX real estate.

concerned with promoting a product, answering a question, or requesting an action. Instead, the goal is to maintain contact with the receiver and build goodwill for long-term rather than short-term benefit.

As an example, a goodwill letter of congratulations could be sent on the occasion of a wedding, a promotion, a birth, or a retirement. A goodwill letter of condolence could be sent at a time of bereavement. The writer will not realize any immediate benefit such as a sale. The purpose is to create long-term benefits that might someday lead to a referral or repeat business.

To be successful, goodwill letters should be

- short and to the point. The focus is on the one circumstance that has prompted the message.

- you-centred. The focus is on the receiver.

- personal and sincere. The feelings expressed are genuine.

- timely. The effect is lost if the message arrives long after the event has taken place.

The following note was written by a veterinarian to a client who had recently had a family pet put to sleep. The note was hand-written on a card by the veterinarian himself and posted to the client within a day or two.

Just a note to express my condolences and sympathy following the passing of Penny. She was a good friend to you all for many years. I know you will really miss her. She went peacefully and will no longer suffer.

Once again, my sympathy and that of our staff.[1]

A second example appears in the case illustration.

Events of passage or change are examples.

Goodwill letters are direct, short, and sincere.

This example is a note of condolence.

. . . .

A SUMMARY OF LEARNING OUTCOMES FROM THIS CHAPTER

When responding favourably to letters requesting information or action, you should begin directly with the good news. If your response contains only one answer, begin with it. If it contains more than one answer, begin with a major one or with a general statement indicating that you are answering the questions. Early in the response, perhaps in a subject line, you should identify the letter being answered. Your answers (if more than one) should be arranged logically. The layout of your letter should enhance the content by, for example, making the points stand out. If your message contains both good and bad news, you should give each the emphasis it deserves. This approach may involve subordinating the negative. To build goodwill, consider adding extra information or helpful suggestions. End your letter with appropriate cordiality.

Order acknowledgments are another form of favourable response. They are written to build a good relationship with a new or major customer, to clarify an order, and to handle minor problems with an order. You should begin such a letter directly, telling about the status of the goods ordered. If there are negative points to discuss, you should handle them carefully. You may be able to include some selling or reselling as well as an expression of appreciation. End the letter on a goodwill note with an appropriate friendly comment.

Although personnel evaluations may contain both negative and positive information, you should handle them directly. After all, you are complying with the reader's request. You have two logical choices for beginning such a letter. You can begin with an answer to one of the questions asked—preferably an answer deserving the emphasis that the opening position gives it. Or you can begin with a statement that you are complying with the request. Somewhere early in the letter, perhaps in a subject line, you should refer to the letter being answered. Your presentation of the information

---

[1]Used by permission of Dr. Craig W. Wilkinson, Terra Losa Animal Clinic, Edmonton, AB.

requested should flow in a logical order, with each item of information standing out. You can number the answers, especially if the questions you are answering were also numbered. You must report fairly and truthfully, stressing the facts and avoiding the opinions. After giving each item the emphasis it deserves, end the letter with a sentence or two of appropriate, friendly comment.

A letter granting an adjustment is another type of a positive response deserving the direct order. The significant difference is that it concerns a very negative situation in which something has gone wrong. You are correcting the wrong, but you also must overcome the negative image in the reader's mind. You can do this by first telling the reader the good news—what you are doing to correct the matter. In the opening words and throughout, emphasize the positive and avoid negative words such as *trouble, damage,* and *broken.* Then try to regain the reader's lost confidence, perhaps with explanations or with assurances of corrective measures taken. End the letter with a goodwill comment; use words that do not recall what went wrong.

A goodwill letter has the objective of building goodwill and keeping in touch with the receiver. These short, timely, and sincere letters are written with special attention to you-viewpoint.

ANSWERS TO PRACTICE RUNS

▶ Favourable Responses: Opening Sentences

In response to your April 3 inquiry about our Chem-Treat paint, I want you to know that we appreciate your interest and will welcome your business.	
Strengths Identifies the letter being answered by date and subject.	*Weaknesses* Does not give the good news. A request for business before answering the questions is out of place.
Yes, I am pleased to inform you that all our international flights do prohibit smoking.	
Strengths Answers one of the questions asked.	*Weaknesses* Quite wordy (I am pleased to inform you that). Negative wording. An improvement would be "our international flights are smoke free." Does not identify the letter being answered. A subject line could be used.
Your May 5th letter about your Rigo FAX391 (your file 97-116) has been received.	
Strengths Identifies the letter being answered by date, topic, and file number.	*Weaknesses* Delays the good news. Not to the point. Gives obvious information—there would be no reply if the request had not been received. Wastes the emphatic opening position.

▶ Favourable Responses: Handling Negative Information

The first example gives the negative news twice—once at the beginning and again at the end. Both of these are positions of emphasis. The good news is subordinated.

Improved Version   I am happy to be the morning speaker at your four-day conference. However, I am unable to be a workshop leader because of a conflicting engagement on Saturday afternoon.

The second example emphasizes the negative information by position and wording.

Improved Version   Your expense report has been accepted with only one change. We have corrected your conversion of Australian dollars in the business entertainment claim on page 3. The new amount is $42.00

▶ Granting a Claim: Regaining Lost Confidence

Improved Version   The enclosed voucher for a free oil change can be used at any of our dealerships. We hope you'll take advantage of this opportunity for excellent service.

Improved Version   Our employees are trained in the proper way to handle chemicals and we are proud of our reputation for carefulness.

Improved Version   We are now offering the superior ABC model sprayer that has a self-cleaning nozzle and a manufacturer's guarantee.

QUESTIONS FOR DISCUSSION

1. Defend a policy of doing more than asked in answering routine inquiries. Can the policy be carried too far?
2. Discuss why just reporting truthfully may not be enough in handling negative information in letters answering inquiries.
3. Discuss the relationship of positive and negative words to fair treatment in employee evaluation letters.
4. What can acknowledgment letters do to build goodwill?

5. "My company uses a preprinted form to acknowledge orders. How can I build goodwill into that?" Discuss and make suggestions.

6. Discuss how problems (vague orders, back orders) should be handled in letters acknowledging orders.

7. Why is it usually advisable to do more than just grant the claim in an adjustment-grant letter?

8. "If I'm going to telephone or fax a routine response, should I still follow the principles outlined in this chapter? Would an e-mail be different?" Discuss and respond.

9. What makes a goodwill letter different from a persuasive letter or a sales pitch?

CASE 7-1

The scene is the registrar's office of Lewis and Clark University. Eloise Lyon, an administrative assistant, is trying to answer the letter of a prospective student. The letter asked about math requirements for science and technical courses. Because the student is not yet certain about the area of study she wants to pursue, she is concerned to keep her options as open as possible. Her specific concern relates to calculus. From the university calendar, she sees there are several courses offered. What should she take?

Here are the points Eloise thinks she should explain in her reply. Because there are many options, she wants to plan carefully. After studying these notes, suggest the organization Eloise should use. Are all the points needed? Would you include others?

- if you don't have basic calculus, you can take Math 114, and then take Math 115 later
- Math is an important subject for most science programs
- you can't take Math 115 unless you have some previous calculus course

- since Math 114 is not part of the degree program, you will need to take an extra course one semester or take one in the summer to have all the credits you need to graduate
- there are four calculus courses, Math 114, 115, 129, and 133
- only Math 114 and Math 115 are available to first semester students
- Math 115 is required for engineering, computer science, and math specialization programs
- Math 114 and Math 115 are not offered in the evenings or in summer session this year, but Math 115 is planned for next summer. That plan is subject to change, of course
- some boards of education offer basic calculus in their continuing education programs
- consider taking basic calculus in high school before coming to university

LETTER PROBLEMS

▶ Giving Information

1. You, the reservations assistant of the Silver Moon Lodge near Whistler, want the bookings from Fun and Games Travel (see Problem 1, Chapter 6, for background information). From the information given here, prepare an answer to their inquiry.

Concerning the question about discounts, you can make these offers. For a group of 40 or more, you would rent the single rooms (regularly $110) for $96 and the double rooms (regularly $125) for $105. In addition, you would offer your breakfast buffet for $4.50 (normally $5.50) per person. The buffet is an all-you-can-eat meal offering a full range of breakfast foods. As for dinner, you can handle the group in a private dining room at prices ranging from $14.50 to $27.00 per meal, depending on the menu desired. You are sending five sample menus with prices in this range. The prices quoted reflect a 10 percent group discount and include gratuities of 15 percent.

As to the location of the lodge, you can present highly favourable information. It is within walking distance of the lifts; no buses are required. In addition, the

Silver Moon Lodge has even more to offer. A ski rental shop is located at the ground level, and lodge guests get a $4 reduction from the $22 daily rental charge. The price of lift tickets is also reduced for lodge patrons— $24 per day rather than $30.

2. Play the role of the retiring Port Elizabeth pizza cafe owner and answer the letter inquiring about your restaurant (see Problem 2, Chapter 6, for background information). The requested information about operations is perhaps best answered by the operating statements for the past five years, which you will enclose. These statements show gross sales of $567,380, $547,210, $581,340, $603,955, and $577,788 for those years, from the earliest year to the most recent. Net profits for those years were $51,477, $46,519, $55,476, $62,007, and $56,179.

You can help with the financing. If $60,000 is paid down, you would cover the remaining $60,000. You would want interest at the rate of prime plus one percent on a five-year term. Unfortunately, most of the staff will be leaving with you because they are your family. However, your head cook wants to remain. She is especially good, and she has over 20 years of experience. There is one other pizza place in town that has been operating for over 10 years as a takeout and delivery. Since they don't have a dining room, you do not see them as a threat.

Now write the letter that will enable the reader to judge this offer of a business.

3. Your family owns the Wayside Inn. Your uncle wants you to answer the inquiry from Dr. Hertenberger's business manager (see Problem 3, Chapter 6, for background information) showing that the Wayside Inn can meet and in some cases surpass the requirements for Dr. Hertenberger's lecture.

There is a meeting room that can accommodate 100 people. In fact, 136 people were packed into it last week. The rental fee ($750 per day) may be a bit high, but the room is very nice, and the lecture equipment requested (lectern, overhead projector, screen, and white-board) is included.

It is a separate room—not a partitioned section of a larger room. It is your only meeting room, so you can promise that no other gatherings would compete with Dr. Hertenberger's lecture. There is a lounge, however, and it features a pianist-singer for happy hour. It is probably far enough away not to present a noise problem, but to avoid possible objections later, you'll mention it.

The parking lot can accommodate 100 cars, but they would have to be parked in a designated area behind the building. Parking space out front is reserved for the Inn's overnight guests. Valet parking is possible with adequate notice. You have done this before, using students from the local university.

You can provide refreshments for morning and afternoon breaks. The noon meal for a group this large

would have to be served buffet style. Since seating is limited, 90 minutes would be required. You'll include a menu and price list.

Now write a letter that will bring Dr. Hertenberger's lecture to your motel.

4. Play the role of Dana Laing at Mastodon Oil and answer the letter you received from the staff trainer of Beaverbrook Industries. (See Problem 4, Chapter 6, for background information.) You will try to be as honest and helpful as you can.

Your company is pleased with the Niagara Executive Training Program at the University of Niagara. You attended the program the first time and thought it was very good. At the end of each session, you have asked the participants from Mastodon to complete a comprehensive questionnaire on their experiences with the program. Overall, they have given it high ratings. However, there has been some criticism of the overly theoretical emphasis in the organizational behaviour segment.

Because all the people you have enrolled in the program are senior administrators, you cannot be certain that the program would be as useful to middle managers such as those Beaverbrook might send. The benefits would have to be balanced against the high cost. The three-week sessions work out well if participants realize the course is intensive. They will be busy every evening with readings and assignments. There will be no time for office work. Again, the course is too expensive to give it any less than full attention.

One point you can add is that the quality of the instruction was excellent. As the Niagara director explained, only those who get good evaluations from the participants stay on the program faculty.

▶Taking Action

5. For this assignment, your boss, Martin Ellsworth, owner of E. A. Ellsworth Nurseries, wants you to answer the inquiry letter from Old Reliable Insurance Company giving them an estimate for landscaping their new office grounds.

According to Martin, the place is a mess. When he inspected it yesterday, he found severe damage from the summer drought and the lack of care. This estimate includes removing the old growth, buying and planting the replacements, and guaranteeing the work for a year.

Forty-two bushes in the hedges have to be replaced at a cost of $17.95 each. Replacing the three dead junipers would cost $29.95 each. These replacements would be in the 6–8 foot range, somewhat larger than the dead ones being replaced. Seven new cedars about the same size are needed and would cost $17.50 each.

The lawn is almost a total disaster. For $1,870 the nursery would resod completely. A patch job would be cheaper (about $950), but it would take months for the lawn to become the beautiful solid cover that resodding would give immediately.

Mr. Ellsworth wants you to work in the idea of a complete-care contract that would include watering, mowing, fertilizing, spraying, trimming, planting annuals, replacing dead perennials, pruning, and so on. For an annual charge of $5,680, the grounds would be as neat and attractive as each season permits.

6. You are part of a band, and the student association at your school has asked your band to play at the Friday night Rock 'n Talk. They asked the following questions: (1) Is your band available on the last Friday of each month from September to April? (2) Are your amplifiers and speakers powerful enough for a room holding 200 people? (3) How much time do you need to set up? (4) Will you accept an offer of expenses plus $250 per night?

The idea of a steady gig is very attractive. Your band needs the exposure, the experience, and the money. You are available on the dates they want for September to December and February to April, but January is already booked. You could play the third Friday in January instead of the fourth. Your equipment is fine for that size of room. For setup and sound checks, you like two hours. As for the money—expenses plus $250 is fine for September to December, but you'd like the option of changing to a percentage of the gate for January to April because you think there will be good crowds once the word gets around that your band is good.

Write a letter to Tanya Meilen, Activities Director of your student association, accepting the booking with those conditions.

▶ Acknowledgments (of Vague Orders and Back Orders)

7. Today, as manager of mail-order sales for the Damon Company, you received an order from The Great Outdoors (see Problem 9, Chapter 6, for background information). The order specifies "24 of the Woodsman coats, four in size S, eight in size M, eight in size L, and four in size XL; eight each in burgundy, blue, and grey." But it doesn't give the colours wanted in each size category. You'd rather not guess, so you'll delay shipping the coats until you get more specific information.

   The order also included 6 Frontiersman leather backpacks—four in the regular size and two of the oversize model. Unfortunately, you can only send two regular and two oversize backpacks. You'll have to back-order the rest. You have been assured that you will have more in 10 days.

   You are not pleased with the complications in this first order from The Great Outdoors. You'd much prefer to show the store your usual prompt and efficient service. So you'll write an order acknowledgment letter that will explain what has happened, cover the status of the order, and make the store feel positive toward your business.

   Alternate Assignment: Write out or tape-record the telephone conversation between the Damon Company and The Great Outdoors as you (at Damon) clarify the coat order. After that phone call, you discover the shortage of backpacks. Rather than make another call, you want to send a letter to be certain that all the details are on file. Also, you believe that a letter will overcome the poor first impression Damon Company may be giving this customer. Now write the acknowledgment letter to confirm the coat order, explain the back-order situation, and build goodwill.

8. Play the role of owner of Northern Specialties. You are pleased with the order you received today from Gifts Unlimited (see Problem 10, Chapter 6, for background information). Unfortunately, you cannot send all the items ordered right now.

   You have a good supply of the handwoven place mats. But the order was unclear regarding colour choices. You decide to send six of the best seller (light grey and red with white) and three of each of the others. You will exchange them if that choice is not acceptable. You'll offer the helpful information that the grey and red have sold more than twice as many as any other colour combination.

   You will send the dolphin and the totem pole earrings right away. You will also send two pairs of the bells (all you have in stock). The remaining two pairs will be sent next week.

   Write the letter that will acknowledge the order, explain its status, and build goodwill.

9. A few months ago, Seven Seas, your importing company, received its first shipment of jade carvings from the People's Republic of China. Soon afterward, a direct-mail campaign aimed at quality jewellers and gift shops brought in a number of new accounts. The jade carvings sold so well that your stocks of some designs have been exhausted.

   Today you received an order from another new customer, Tina's Treasure House—Tina Marschal, owner. Ms. Marschal requested five carvings, one each of Sea Serpent ($290), Gliding Swan ($195), Running Horse ($370), Flying Dragon ($485), and Guardian Lion ($345). You'll send the first three right away, but Flying Dragon and Guardian Lion are out of stock. You have more on order, but you don't expect them to arrive for another eight weeks. If Ms. Marschal wishes, you'll send the two back-ordered items as soon as they come in.

   In the meantime, you are sending some blown glass (a leopard and a raging bull). If she likes them, she can simply pay the invoice; if she doesn't, they can be returned.

   Now write a letter that combines the functions of welcoming a new customer, back-ordering her jade carvings, and offering the blown glass. Perhaps you can help your cause by emphasizing that brisk sales, including a number of reorders, suggest that these quality products are in great demand.

▶ Personnel References

10. Assume the role of Janic Kvanli, manager of the Pompano Bay Country Club, and write a letter evaluating Thomas Martino (see Problem 12, Chapter 6, for background information). Martino has been your assistant manager for two years.

    Martino is a highly personable man who is very popular with the members. You think he socializes a little too much with them, though this has caused no problems that you know of. Perhaps you are of the old school, which considers such behaviour unwise. You spoke to Martino about it, but he shrugged off your advice good-naturedly.

    Martino is tops in his knowledge of club operations. He knows kitchen and dining room operations. He is an excellent buyer and financial manager. He seems to know just what to look for when hiring people, and he knows how to get good work from the people he hires.

His weakness is that he doesn't play golf! When Martino came to you, he knew very little about golf, groundskeeping, or tennis. He has learned a lot through courses, reading, and practice. The Bonaparte Country Club will have to decide if he has learned enough to move up to the position of manager.

11. You are Charlton Burkhalter, Director of Research for International Foods. Info-Search has requested your evaluation of Cathy Simonini, one of your former research assistants (see Problem 13, Chapter 6, for background information).

    You remember Ms. Simonini well. She came to you with the high recommendations of three professors at Stonehill University, and in time you learned that those recommendations were well founded. Cathy knew research methodology, and was especially competent in the quantitative areas of research. You regarded her as a bright and capable person.

    While at International, Cathy led two project teams. She handled them competently, though you felt that she was reluctant to make decisions on her own. She checked with you frequently when you would have preferred more initiative on her part. Perhaps she was just being cautious, and since that time, she may have gained confidence.

    As for Cathy's work ethic, she willingly put in long hours, and she worked efficiently. She often took work home with her and seldom missed a deadline.

    To answer the question about Cathy's report writing ability, you looked over one of her reports. The organization is logical, and the writing is clear and correct, though a bit wordy. You judge her writing ability to be quite adequate.

    With the preceding information in mind, you will write a letter to answer Info-Search's questions about Cathy Simonini.

▶ Adjustment Grants

12. Frankly, you are embarrassed. Brubaker Sweets takes great pride in the quality of its candy, and candy with rancid pecan nuts most certainly does not meet Brubaker quality standards. (See Problem 14, Chapter 6, for background information.) This will be a challenging letter to write.

    Because situations like this just shouldn't occur, you checked personally to see what might have happened. The best information you could get suggests stale-dated candy taken out of stock for disposal was somehow shipped to the Candy Corner. The good candy that was supposed to be sent to them was somehow destroyed. In other words, someone goofed. (You quickly checked your records to see whether other shipments of bad candy might have been made. You found three possibilities, but you'll check them later.)

    Now you will try to make amends with the Candy Corner. Instead of a credit for the 31 boxes, you will send three dozen boxes of Brubaker chocolates today—guaranteed fresh—at no charge. You will also give a 20 per cent discount on the next two dozen boxes they order. You think that these steps make it unnecessary to reimburse the Candy Corner further if their customers return other boxes of bad candy. You will ask the Candy Corner to carefully dispose of the 31 boxes.

    Now you must write a letter that will respond to the Candy Corner's claim and repair any damages that the bad candy might have caused.

13. Assume the role of Bill Cullum, owner of Cullum's Tropical Fish and Garden. You were surprised to receive the claim letter from the Hi-Tech purchasing agent concerning the tropical fish you sold his company (see Problem 15, Chapter 6, for background information). After checking out the situation, however, you think you know what happened.

    Because emergency surgery was being performed on a close family member that day, you entrusted the delivery to your assistant. Unfortunately, the weather was unsea-sonably cold that morning. In all likelihood, the water in the tanks in which the fish were transported got too cold for tropical fish.

    The error is clearly yours, and you will correct it as soon as possible. It will take three or four days to obtain the replacement fish because you are out of some varieties. But as soon as possible, you will bring them in and make things right. You will follow up with periodic inspections and will promise a tank of healthy, beautiful fish.

    Now write the letter that will make things right with the Hi-Tech people.

14. Apparently, the buyer for B. B. Kennon, Inc., was misled. The material he bought for the warm-up suits was not colourfast despite the supplier's claim. As a result, the turquoise, hot purple, and teal green ran in the wash. To date you have received complaints from three stores—one from the Athlete's Locker (see Problem 16, Chapter 6, for background information).

    After checking with the supplier, you, Kennon's sales manager, find that no explanation can justify what happened. On the positive side, you can say that Kennon learned from this experience. From now on, it will test all materials before they become garments. Another supplier will be found.

    Much as you dislike doing things that reduce profits, you will give money back on every defective garment returned. You will also make a strong effort to explain what happened without just passing the blame. Your goal is to convince every unhappy retail customer that B. B. Kennon is dedicated to making quality clothing, and that if it ever slips up, it makes things right. Your first effort in achieving that goal is an adjustment letter to the Athlete's Locker.

15. For this assignment, as an adjuster in the Consumer Service Department of _____ [a major car manufacturer of your choice], you have received a claim letter from a

salesperson employed by Global Pharmaceutical (see Problem 17, Chapter 6, for background information).

Your check on the facts of the case confirms what the claim letter reported. The dealer's service centre did check the automobile twice. According to the service manager, "We did our best to help, but this customer was too impatient. Just got mad and walked off!" But you know from your records that this service manager has had other disgruntled customers. You suspect that the customer was justified in appealing to your office.

Next you talked with the owner of the dealership by telephone. As a result, the dealership owner will call the unhappy customer, make arrangements to pick up the defective car, leave the customer a "loaner" to use, and deliver the repaired automobile. The dealership owner also assured you that the service manager would give no more trouble and that the unhappy customer would receive VIP treatment from now on.

Now you will write a letter telling the Global salesperson what you have done to correct the problem. It's not exactly what was wanted (the offending dealership is still involved), but the decision is basically positive.

16. You are the owner of Trophy World. The letter you received from the sales manager of the C. E. Greene Insurance Agency contains bad news, and you'll have to take corrective action (see Problem 18, Chapter 6, for background information). Your engraver has made a costly error. He misspelled *Greene* (by leaving off the final *e* on five gold-plated desk sets).

Of course, you'll correct the error. For a special circumstance like this, you will have a courier collect the desk sets. They will be redone and returned to the sales manager by the day before the meeting. You will guarantee the quality and the accuracy.

There's not much you can say to regain the confidence lost as a result of this error. In no way is it typical of your usual work. In fact, your engraver hasn't made such an error in the seven years he has worked for you. But you will require more careful checking in the future.

Write a letter to fax to C. E. Greene Insurance that presents the corrective steps you will take including the details about the courier.

▶ Goodwill Letters

17. Write a goodwill letter to a customer who has just purchased a complete computer system for their home office from you. You want the customer to be satisfied because you know there may be other office equipment needs that you can provide. Also, you want to keep a good relationship with this customer in the hope that you will receive referrals.

8

Indirectness for Bad News

Upon completing this chapter, you will be able to write responses to convey bad news. To reach this goal, you should be able to

1 Use the indirect order to write effective, tactful, bad-news messages.

2 Use the indirect order with tact and courtesy to refuse requests.

3 Write adjustment refusals that cover the refusal positively.

4 Compose credit refusals that are tactful and clear and close with a positive, forward look.

▷ to Bad-News Messages

As property manager for Westridge Mall, Karen Woitas gets to know the owners and managers of her stores quite well. Karen knows, for instance, that owning and operating a Good 'n Nice business has been very satisfying for Doreen Lam. The degree of her success in just two years shows her skills. Despite the slow economy, Doreen expects to see a comfortable profit in the coming year.

Karen knows there is a cloud on the horizon. She has to tell the stores that Westridge Mall is renovating. Many of them will not be pleased with the inevitable dust, noise, and disruption that, in the short term, will translate into fewer people in the mall.

Karen can show the need and the long-term benefit of a modern, attractive mall. For the immediate future, the mall owners are offering a small rent reduction, and the contractors are promising as little disruption as possible. All those things will help, of course, but Doreen's comfortable year will likely be postponed. ▪

SITUATIONS REQUIRING INDIRECTNESS

A bad-news message is one in which you must say no to a request or convey other disappointing news to your receiver. As explained in Chapter 6, when the main message is negative for your receiver, you should usually use the indirect order. Here are three reasons for preferring this approach. First, we have seen that negative points stand out. The indirect order moves the bad news away from the emphatic positions at the beginning and ending of the message. It avoids adding emphasis by position. Secondly, the indirect order provides balance to the message by avoiding emphasis of space. An explanation preceding the bad news gives the bad news itself less space in proportion to the whole message. Finally, the indirect order makes negative messages easier to accept. The explanation that precedes the bad news may convince the receiver that the sender's position is correct and fair. Without the indirect order, the negative message would be unnecessarily harsh. Such harshness damages goodwill and increases the likelihood of resistance and rejection.

* Usually bad-news letters should be in the indirect order.

If we refer to the introductory situation and Karen's task of giving news of the renovations, we can see the potential for anger if Karen starts her letter with

* Consider this example.

Please be prepared for some unavoidable inconvenience and disruption to your businesses. Westridge Mall will be renovating for eight months.

It is reasonable to assume her clients' first reactions will be negative. In that frame of mind, they may continue to read her explanation—or they may not read the rest of the letter at all. Once the resistance begins, Karen's task is much more difficult. If she explains first, the clients are more likely to accept the news with a co-operative attitude. They will not necessarily be happy about the situation, but they will be more likely to make the best of it.

You may consider using directness in some bad-news situations. If, for example, you wish to demonstrate your authority, using the direct order will reinforce your power position. In some cases, you may want your refusal to be emphatic, such as if the request is illegal or unethical. The direct approach would emphasize the steadfastness of your decision. If you know that your reader will appreciate frankness, or if you think that your negative answer will be accepted routinely, you might choose directness. All these instances are possible, but they are not the rule. Usually, you would be wise to use indirectness in giving bad news.

* There are exceptions, as when the bad news is routine or when the reader prefers frankness.

When we must deny a request, what options in wording and structuring do we have . . . ? What could be the consequences?

In business people tend to remember unduly negative or harsh written denials or responses. Sometimes those types of denials may affect the receiver's decision to conduct future business with that company—a decision that may cost that company significant dollars in lost orders or contracts.

Source: http://www.wuacc.edu/services/zzcwwctr/neg-sent.intro.txt

. . . .
THE INDIRECT-ORDER, BAD-NEWS LETTER
The Goals of a Bad-News Letter

- There are two goals for bad-news letters: (1) to give the bad news (2) to minimize negative side effects and maintain goodwill.

There are two goals to be achieved when giving bad news. The first is to give the bad news. That is not too difficult by itself. In combination with the second goal, however, there is a greater challenge. The second goal is to minimize the negative side effects of the bad news and to maintain goodwill. This goal requires that you convince your reader that you are fair and reasonable, that you understand the impact of this news on the reader, and that you have done whatever is possible to limit the damaging effects. How do you convince the reader of these truths?

Developing a Strategy

- Plan a strategy that will be the foundation for your letter.

To develop a strategy, use you-viewpoint and consider how the reader will respond to the bad news. What will the objections be? What impact will this news have? Not just "the reader will be upset," but more specifically, "the reader will be upset because some people seem to receive preferential treatment," or, "the reader will be inclined to reject the idea because it will be expensive to achieve." Once you can imagine how your reader will react, you will know how to focus your explanation. You will address the fears, questions, concerns, and objections of your reader.

Referring to the introductory situation, Karen sees her clients' concerns for profits. In the long term, the benefits of renovation are obvious. Her clients will agree with her on that point, but she anticipates resistance because of the short-term picture. Customers will not want to shop in a noisy, dusty construction area. Her strategy will focus on her clients' concerns about profits in the short and long term.

The following general plan will help you apply your strategy using the indirect order successfully to accomplish your goals for bad-news letters.

- Follow this general plan for giving negative news.

- Begin with a cushioning comment that sets up your explanation.

- Logically present your reasons to prepare the reader for the bad news.

- Clearly give the bad news, either explicitly or implicitly.

- Close cordially or with corrective action (a solution or a compromise) and without further mention of the bad news.

Beginning with a Cushioning Comment

- A cushioning comment establishes rapport and sets up the explanation.

The cushioning comment builds rapport, establishes the tone, and sets up the strategy for the explanation. Examples include referring to the correspondence you are answering, making a general comment that is a point of agreement between you and your reader, using a neutral statement that does not suggest upcoming bad news, or stating a positive point (if there is one). The beginning should be pleasant, but it must not mislead the receiver to expect good news.

Here is an example. A professor's request must be denied because too much work would be required to assemble the information. The best the company can do is permit the professor to go through company records to gather the information herself. The following words set up the strategy:

Your interesting study, described in your July 3 letter, should be a helpful contribution to management literature. It is an ambitious project that will require a substantial commitment of time and effort for data gathering.

Note that these words begin on subject, so the reader recognizes them as a response to the inquiry. Also note that, while positive and pleasant in tone, the words are neutral about the answer. They give no indication of good or bad news. Finally, note that the strategy of the letter is set up by saying that the project will require a large amount of time and effort. The plan of the explanation is to show that, in this case, the company is unable to help to the extent of the request.

A point of agreement Karen might use to begin her letter is

A modern, attractive mall is important for business because it encourages shoppers to come to the mall and, once here, to stay longer.

From this point, Karen's strategy would be to develop the need for renovation at Westridge Mall, emphasizing the benefits for her clients and their customers. Another option she might choose is an opening statement that is neutral and non-committal on the topic of her letter, such as

Westridge Mall is committed to providing the best service and the greatest convenience to our clients and their customers.

Again, she can build on this sentence by showing that the planned renovation is consistent with providing the best service and the greatest (long-term) convenience.

. . . .

A PRACTICE RUN

Identify the strategy that is being introduced in these opening sentences.

Your organization is doing a commendable job of supporting education for needy children. Your cause deserves the help of those who are in a position to give it.

_____

_____

_____

You are correct in believing that a Deep Kold window air-conditioning unit should cool the average three-room apartment.

_____

_____

_____

. . . .

Presenting the Explanation

- The reasoning that supports the bad news comes next.

The explanation behind the bad news should flow logically from your opening and, of course, be presented convincingly. You want your reader to accept that your position is reasonable and carefully thought out.

- Use positive wording, you-viewpoint, and emphasis techniques.

To be convincing, choose your words carefully, avoiding the negative ones. Use the you-viewpoint to show your understanding of the issues from your reader's point of view. Also, draw attention to the brighter parts of your message by skillfully using the emphasis techniques discussed in Chapter 5. All your writing skills will be needed in your effort to sell the reader on your reasoning. Watch for these techniques in the examples given in this chapter.

Handling the Bad News

- The bad news should flow logically from the reasoning. Do not emphasize it.

Your handling of the negative news follows logically from your explanation. If you have built the groundwork convincingly, the bad news comes as a logical conclusion, not as a surprise. If you have done your job well, your reader may even support your position.

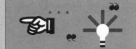

One executive, who asked to remain anonymous, was so concerned to state the bad news positively that the employee whom he fired returned for work the next day! It's a true story.

Even so, because this section is the most negative part of your message, you should not give it too much emphasis.

You may either state the bad news explicitly, or let it be understood implicitly. An explicit example would be

You are not eligible to take scuba diving lessons because you are over the age limit.

The bad news is stated outright in words that leave a clear, strong message. An implicit example would be

Scuba diving lessons are offered to people who are between 18 and 45 years of age.

In this case, the reader, being over 45 years old, realizes that scuba lessons are not possible. The advantage of this method is that the message is a little softer.

Whichever method you choose, you should be brief. Extending the negative for three or four sentences when one would do gives it too much emphasis.

- State the bad news briefly,

You should make certain that the reader will have no doubt about your answer. In trying to soften the blow, writers sometimes become evasive and unclear. Take, for example, someone who attempts to refuse a request by saying, "it would be better if . . ." The reader could take this vague refusal as merely a suggestion to be considered. Attention to clarity is especially necessary when bad news is given implicitly. You must be certain that there can be no other reasonable interpretation than the one you intend.

- clearly, and

Negative words such as *I refuse, will not,* and *cannot* stand out. So do apologies such as "I deeply regret to inform you . . . " and "I am sorry to say . . . ." Unless the situation demands the emphasis of the negative wording, find a positive statement to carry your message. For example, instead of writing, "your insurance does not cover damage to buildings not connected to the house," write, "your insurance covers damage to the house only." Or instead of writing, "We must refuse . . . " a wholesaler could deny a discount by writing, "We can grant discounts when . . . ."

- positively.

You should carefully study the effects of your words. Do not sacrifice clarity to positiveness. Use these questions to check your work.

- Is the bad news stated clearly?
- Have I been positive without misleading the reader?
- Is the overall level of emphasis appropriate or does the bad news stand out too strongly?

Closing with Goodwill

As the news of your letter is disappointing, it is likely to put your reader in an unhappy frame of mind. To reach your goodwill goal, you must shift your reader's thoughts to more pleasant matters.

- Make your closing one that will build goodwill.

Your choice of subject matter for the closing will vary with the facts of the case. Since the closing should be positive talk that fits the situation, it could be almost any friendly remark that would be appropriate if you were handling the case face to face. The major requirement is that your ending words have a goodwill effect.

- Adapt the closing to the case.

A PRACTICE RUN

Make clear statements of the bad news in two ways—explicitly and then implicitly. Remember to be brief, clear, and as positive as you can.

A college course is fully registered. The student's name has been placed on the waiting list.

Explicit _____

_____

_____

Implicit _____

_____

_____

Because of a lack of business, there will be a cut for hourly staff. Each person will work only six hours a day rather than seven. In this way, layoffs may be avoided for the time being.

Explicit _____

_____

_____

Implicit _____

_____

_____

* If you can suggest a solution, you will build goodwill.

If you can suggest a solution, you can use it to conclude your letter. That is, by saying what you can do, you soften the negative impact of what you cannot do without confusing the message. For example, if a student is refused entrance at a college because of low marks, the school could write, "When you have completed your upgrading, please reapply . . ." This makes it clear that although the school cannot admit the student at this time, the door is not entirely closed. If the student takes corrective action, the situation could change. By offering a proposal for changing the negative to a positive, the school is attempting to maintain goodwill.

* Avoid ending with apologetic statements.

Avoid apologies unless you are openly accepting the blame. (If you are accepting blame, you should be offering compensation and considering a direct approach to emphasize the positive outcome for your reader.) In many refusals, there is no blame; the case simply requires the answer no. Therefore, negative apologetic statements, such as "Again, I regret that we must refuse" are inappropriate. Also ruled out are appeals for understanding, such as "I sincerely hope that you understand why we must make this decision." Such words emphasize the bad news.

An Example of a Bad-News Letter

* An example of an indirect-order bad-news letter.

This example of a bad-news letter is based on the introductory situation. The property manager writes to her clients, the shopkeepers renting space in Westridge Mall. She begins by establishing some common ground, showing that mall management has the

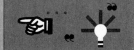
same concerns for profit as the stores. She builds on that reasoning by giving the good news about the rental reductions before the less welcome news about a long period of renovation. Her discussion of the renovation stresses the positive aspects and attempts again to reassure the store owners that their needs are being addressed. The closing is very positive and looks ahead to success in both the short term and the long term.

A modern attractive mall is important for business because it encourages shoppers to come to the mall, and once here, to stay longer. That philosophy quickly launched Westridge Mall to a prominent place among local retailers when it was built in 1982.

Since then, Westridge Mall has continued to be a leader because of its commitment to the well-being of clients and customers alike. In keeping with this principle, the management is pleased to announce the following:
· Store rentals will be reduced by 2 percent for the 1998 calendar year.
· A carefully staged renovation will be undertaken beginning February 15 and continuing for approximately eight months.

The contractors, RJD General Contracting, have been chosen because they are experienced in work of this nature having recently completed the White Pine Mall renovation. They fully understand the needs of retailers and customers during construction and are committed to maintaining a fully functional, comfortable, and safe environment. All stores will have full access to the mall concourse and to delivery bays as usual, although some inconvenience can be anticipated. More details will be released later.

Please join us at a celebration on Saturday, November 3, when a model of the completed mall will be unveiled. We anticipate an exciting year as we continue to lead our city in successful retailing.

The following pages analyze some common letter situations that are usually best handled in the indirect order. As in preceding chapters, the situations reviewed include only the major possibilities. However, if you learn the techniques recommended for these situations, you should be able to apply your knowledge to the others.

* Following are typical letter situations calling for the indirect order.

A word processor's merge feature allows one form letter to be sent to many people and yet appear personal. This organization's form letter is ready to be merged with an address list of applicants for the position. Each entry in the address list contains the items that correspond to the field names used in the letter.

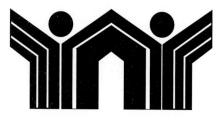

HABITAT FOR HUMANITY EDMONTON

January 24, 1995

FIELD(First Name) FIELD(Last Name)
FIELD(Address)
FIELD(City), FIELD(Province)   FIELD(Postal Code)

Dear FIELD(First Name),

Thank you for applying to Habitat for Humanity Edmonton's recently advertised position of Office Administrator.

A large number of qualified candidates responded to our ad, and it has not been easy to complete our evaluation. After careful consideration, FIELD(First Name), we have decided not to proceed with your application at the present time. Your experience and many of your qualifications would be a valuable asset to the work of Habitat; however, another candidate has been chosen whose background more closely matches our current requirements. This decision does not reflect on your qualifications, but rather on the requirements of the position.

Thank you for your interest in Habitat, and we wish you success in your job search.

For the hiring committee,

Paul Eastwood

Paul Eastwood,
Executive Director.

Building Houses in Partnership with God's People in Need

---

[1] This case example is an actual letter used by Habitat for Humanity. It is reproduced here by permission.

TYPES OF BAD-NEWS MESSAGES

Refused Request

Refusal of a request is definitely a bad-news message. Your reader has asked you for something, and you must say no. Because the news is bad, you should usually write the request refusal in the indirect order. If you begin with the no answer, the reader will not be in the mood to read your explanation. Your best strategy is to explain or justify first. From your explanation or justification, you can move logically to your refusal.

For a refusal, you develop your strategy as discussed under the general plan. Your beginning is one of the types of cushioning comment. It should be linked to your explanation. In your explanation, you must address the objections your reader will have and be clear about why you are refusing.

Sometimes you must refuse because of company policy. When this is the case, you should be careful how you explain the refusal. Do not just say that you are refusing because it is company policy to do so. Instead, justify the policy. For example, take a retailer's policy of refusing to accept the return of goods bought on sale. This policy clearly protects the retailer; but, on closer inspection, it also benefits the customer. Only by cutting the costs of returns can the retailer give the customer the low sale price. Thus, the policy works to the benefit of both the customer and the retailer. A refusal based on that policy should explain its fairness to all concerned.

Sometimes you must refuse simply because the facts of the case justify a refusal. A review of the situation may show the reader had incorrect information or made an invalid assumption. When the facts show that you are right and the reader is wrong, your goodwill goal is hard to reach. Proving someone wrong usually risks anger and defensiveness. In such cases, you can use you-viewpoint reasoning. Review the facts of the case taking care not to accuse or insult. Try to show that although you see and understand the reader's viewpoint, you are confident that yours is correct.

In summary, in request refusals you use the general indirect plan and

- begin with one of the types of cushioning comment.

- address any anticipated objections in your explanation.

- be clear about why you are refusing (justify a policy, rather than only quoting it).

- reduce the reader's defensiveness by being factual and using you-viewpoint.

- ensure your closing is cordial.

Contrasting Refusals.   The advantage of the indirect order in refusal letters is evident from the following contrasting examples. Both refuse clearly, but only the letter that uses the indirect order gains reader goodwill.

Harshness in the Direct Refusal.   The first example is poorly written because it states the bad news right away. Because of this blunt treatment, the reader is less likely to accept the following explanation. The explanation is clear, but note the unnecessary use of negative words (*cannot consider, deeply regret*). Note also how the closing words leave the reader with a strong reminder of the bad news.

> We regret to inform you that we cannot grant your request for a donation to the scholar-ship fund.
>
> So many requests for contributions are made of us that we have found it necessary to budget a definite amount each year for this purpose. Our budgeted funds for this year have been exhausted, so we simply cannot consider additional requests. However, we will be able to consider your request next year.
>
> We deeply regret our inability to help you now and trust that you understand our position.

Tact and Courtesy in an Indirect Refusal.   The second example skillfully handles the negative message. Its opening words are on subject and neutral. They set up the

- Refusing a request calls for the indirect order.

- Do not hide behind company policy. Justify it.

- When the reader is clearly wrong, be factual and use you-viewpoint.

- The directness of this letter makes it harsh.

Tact and strategy mark this refusal in which an office manager turns down a textbook author's request. The author has asked for model letters that can be used as examples in a correspondence guidebook. The office manager reasons that complying with this request would take more time than should be expected.

1417 Burrard Street
Vancouver, British Columbia
V5Z 1V2
(604) 736-4119

October 3, 1997

Dr. Ruth A. Howard
Faculty of Business
University of Southern Alberta
Calgary, AB   T2M 2Y9

Dear Dr. Howard:

The cushioning comment sets up the strategy and remains neutral about the decision.

Your Correspondence Guidebook described in your September 21 letter should be a very practical aid to the business executive.

The practical value of the book, I agree, depends largely on the quality of its examples. Your book demands letter samples that meet all the criteria of good correspondence. However, finding the quality of letter you need will require careful checking by someone who knows good writing. Going through the 40,000 letters in our files will take considerable time and skill. Moreover, most of those letters deal with confidential matters.

The explanation builds on the reasoning from the original letter and presents the practical difficulties.

The bad news is given implicitly through an alternative suggestion.

For these reasons, I suggest that we make copies of all our standard form letters for you. Alternatively, we could provide working space for you if you prefer to come to our Vancouver office to make a selection from those form letters for yourself.

Please let us know how we can help you further. We look forward to co-operating with you in this project and seeing the finished result.

The closing is cordial and supportive.

Sincerely,

René Bossert

René Bossert
Office Manager

RB

This example shows good strategy in turning down a request to speak at a convention.[2]

WILKERSON ASSOCIATES
| Consultants to |
| Management |

7316 Brackenridge Boulevard   P.O. Box 2097   Los Angeles, CA   90005-2097   U.S.A.

January 20, 1998

Mr. T. H. Gooch, Convention Chair
Canadian Association of Administrators
7112 Avon Road
Stratford, ON   N5R 2G6

Dear Mr. Gooch:

The cushioning comment is a point of agreement between sender and receiver.

Your January 13 invitation to address the Canadian Association of Administrators is a distinct honor. I am well aware of the high caliber of CAA's conferences.

The explanation builds upon the suggestion of excellence.

Presenting a major paper to this group deserves a thorough and competent effort. Obviously, such an effort requires time. Because my time is fully committed to a writing project for the months ahead,

The bad news is implicit in the suggestion of an alternate.

I must suggest that you ask someone who has the time to do the job well. May I recommend Ms. Paula Perkins of my staff? Paula is an outstanding speaker and an expert on the subject of women's progress in management.

The closing is positive and supportive.

If I can help you further in your efforts to find speakers, please write me again. My best regards to you and your planning committee in this important endeavor.

Sincerely,

Forrest Y. Wilkerson

Forrest Y. Wilkerson
President

FYW:et

---

[2]Because the writer is from California, American spelling has been retained throughout this example.

explanation that follows. The clear and logical explanation ties in with the opening. Without using negative words, the explanation leads smoothly to the refusal. Note that the refusal is also handled without negative words, and yet is clear. Saying "the best we can do is . . . " implies what we cannot do. The friendly closing fits this one case.

> Your efforts to build the scholarship fund for needy children are most commendable. We are always willing to help worthy causes whenever we can.
>
> That is why every year we budget the maximum amount we believe we can contribute. Then each January, we distribute that money as far as it will go to various deserving groups. As our budgeted contributions for this year have already been made, we are placing your organization on our list for consideration next year.
>
> We wish you good success in your efforts to help educate deserving children.

Adjustment Refusals

Most claims for adjustment are legitimate, and most companies try hard to correct for legitimate damages. But some claims are not well founded. They may be based on wrong information or misunderstanding. When it is necessary to refuse a claim, the situation should be seen as bad news and should be handled indirectly.[3]

The request for an adjustment means something has gone wrong. The refusal of that request will make the customer even more unhappy. This "double negative" emphasizes the need for a carefully worded, clear, and tactful refusal. You must assume you are dealing with people who honestly feel that they are right. Although some of the people may know their reasons are weak, they still hope that you will grant their claims. All the people you deal with are likely to resist your efforts to justify the refusal.

Determining the Basic Strategy. Review and assemble the facts that help you define precisely why a refusal is justified. Then, beginning from your understanding of the reader's knowledge, you should work out what you must say to support your position and convince the reader that your answer is fair. Although variations may be justified, these letters should follow the general plan for bad-news messages. A few modifications are suggested here.

Beginning with a Cushioning Comment. Because you are answering the reader's letter, you should identify this letter. You could use an incidental reference in the opening or a subject-line reference. If you use a subject line, make certain that its wording is neutral. "RE: Your July 22 letter about Order No. 3175A" would meet this requirement, but "Subject: Refusal of your July 22 claim" would not. As in other refusal letters, your opening for the adjustment refusal should be on subject. It should be neutral about the decision and should set up the explanation.

Presenting the Explanation. The explanation that sets up the refusal logically follows the opening. To be successful, the explanation must be believable; to be believable, it must be factual. Support your statements with evidence. For example, you may be able to refer to industry standards, respected authorities, or personal experience.

In presenting your explanation, you should write nothing that questions the reader's honesty, or belittles or insults the reader. Such comments as "If you had read the contract, you would have known . . . " or "Surely anyone would realize . . . " build defensiveness and irritation. They suggest responses such as, "If you had told me clearly, I *would* have realized!" Receivers who are busy defending themselves are difficult to convince. With positive language, the level of tension is reduced and the level of acceptance is increased.

Handling the Bad News. Because of the "double negative" in adjustment refusal situations, the wording of the bad news must be clear and yet as positive as possible. A

---

[3]In problem cases, where the customer is known for frivolous claims or for hostility, the direct order may be justified. Such a case would require special treatment.

clear refusal should leave no doubt in anyone's mind that the answer is no. A positive refusal should leave as little ill-feeling as possible. You may find it possible to refuse without using a single negative word. Perhaps you can clearly imply what you cannot do by explaining what you can do.

Although it is hard to judge refusal sentences without the explanations that precede them, the following three are clear and positive:

For these reasons, only when our employees pack the goods can reimbursement for damages be paid.

Since the warranty ran out on the first of last month, the repair cost coverage has expired.

Because the agreement stipulates the use of XYZ oil, the best we can do under these circumstances is to repair the equipment at cost.

Closing with Goodwill. Because your refusal is bad news, you should follow it with some appropriate comment away from the subject of the refusal. Neither negative apologies nor words that recall the problem are in order.

• End with off-subject, friendly comment.

Tact in a Courteous Refusal. Here is a good example that begins with a point of agreement that also sets up the explanation. Without accusations, anger, or negative words, the writer reviews the facts, which free the company of blame. The refusal is clear, even though it is made by implication rather than by direct words. It uses no negatives, and it does not receive undue emphasis. The closing shifts to helpful suggestions that fit the case. Friendliness is evident throughout the letter but especially in the closing.

Dear Ms. Sanderson:

• This letter is clear and tactful.

Subject: Your May 3 letter about Margot Stewart fabric.
You are correct in your expectation of high quality, value, and service from Margot Stewart. Every product you purchase from us has been developed with years of experimentation and stringent quality controls. We are determined that our products will do for you what we say they will do.

Because we do want our fabrics to please, we carefully ran the samples of Margot Stewart Fabric 103 you sent us through our laboratory. Exhaustive tests show that each sample has been subjected to long periods of direct sunlight. Because our 100 series of fabrics are not designed to withstand exposure to sunlight, we have included the words "For Indoor Use Only" in the catalogue from which you ordered and in a stamped reminder on the back of every yard of the fabric. Under the circumstances, we suggest that you change to one of our outdoor fabrics. All of the fabrics in the 200 series shown on pages 35 to 47 of our current catalogue are recommended for outdoor use.

You may also want to consider the new Duck Back cotton fabrics listed in our 500 series. These vinyl-coated cotton fabrics are economical, and they resist sun and rain remarkably well. If we can help you further in your selection, please call on us.

INTRODUCTORY SITUATION

▶ to Credit Refusal Letters

The renovations have made a difference to Doreen's business. Shoppers do not want to stop for a yogurt cone or a muffin with the hammering and sawing ringing in their ears.

A cappuccino machine would give Doreen's kiosk greater appeal by expanding her menu. She would have had the capital to purchase it if her growth projections had materialized. She still thinks the machine would be a good investment. Without the cash to purchase it, she decides to ask for a higher limit on her line of credit. Another $2,000.00 would allow her to purchase the cappuccino maker and do some minor renovations to her storage and serving areas. ∎

This letter from a mail-order nursery refuses an unjustified claim concerning shrubs that died 14 months after sale. As the nursery's guarantee is for one year, there is no reasonable basis for granting the claim.

GREEN THUMB
N U R S E R I E S
1170 MELVILLE ROAD Penticton, BC V2A 2N9

October 4, 1997

Mr. Clarence S. Huddleston
R.R. 2
Maple Ridge, BC   V2X 7E7

Dear Mr. Huddleston:

The cushioning comment sets up the strategy by building on a point of agreement.

As you said in your September 30 letter, we do want to know about the trees and shrubs you bought from us in June 1996. We want to live up to our guarantees and our reputation for providing quality nursery stock.

The bad news is stated implicitly by referring to the guarantee limitations.

That is why we inspect every outgoing shipment. Of course, after the shrubs leave us, we no longer can give them our personal attention. As you know, proper planting is essential. And so is regular fertilizing and watering, especially during the summer months. Even though this vital care is out of our hands, we guarantee survival for the first year. For a tree or shrub to survive that long, it must have been in good condition when purchased. In view of this explanation, we have decided to stand by the terms of our 12-month guarantee.

The explanation and bad news are combined.

Thank you for this opportunity to explain. If you take a branch of the shrub and some of the soil in which it was planted to a local nursery, they should be able to find the cause of the problem you experienced. We will continue to work hard to provide you with the healthy plants and good service you have come to expect from Green Thumb Nurseries.

The closing offers some corrective action and looks forward to future service.

Sincerely,

Suzanne Ho

Suzanne Ho
Service Representative

SH:me

An out-of-town customer bought an expensive dress and mailed it back three weeks later for a refund, explaining that the dress was not a good fit.

Rue, Ste-Foy, Québec, PQ G1P 2N7

February 19, 1998

Mme. Marie Mercier
117 Riverside Road
Nepean,   ON   K1A 0P9

Dear Mme. Mercier:

The opening identifies the correspondence and introduces the strategy.

We understand your concern about the fit of the DiVella dress you returned February 17. As always, we are pleased to do as much as we reasonably can to make things right.

The explanation appeals to fairness for all concerned.

Exactly what we can do in each case is decided by personal attention to the circumstances. To meet our obligations to customers, all clothing returned for refund for personal reasons of colour, fit, etc., must be unquestionably new. In this way, we can meet our customers' expectations for the best from us. Thus, because the perspiration stains on your dress would prevent its resale, we must return the dress to you and consider the sale final.

The bad news is combined with the explanation and stated explicitly.

The closing attempts to build goodwill by offering an alternative solution.

You will find a special alteration ticket with this letter. When it is convenient, please bring the dress back and let us alter it for you without further charge. In this way, you are assured of the best possible fit.

Sincerely,

Françoise Morin

Françoise Morin
Customer Service

FM:id

Credit Refusals

- Because credit is personal, use tact in refusing it.

- Tact will keep customers for future business.

Letters that refuse credit are more negative than most refusals. The very nature of credit makes them so. Credit is tied to personal things, such as values, acceptance in society, character, and integrity. So, unless skillfully handled, a credit refusal can be felt as an insult.

Some people will argue that you need not be concerned about the reader's feelings in this situation. As you are turning down the opportunity to do business with the reader, why spend time trying to be tactful? Being kind to people is profitable in the long run. People who are refused credit still have needs. They may not be given credit, but if you are friendly to them, they just might pay cash to buy from you. In addition, the fact that people are poor credit risks now does not mean that they will never be good risks. By not offending them now, you may keep them as friends of your company until then. At the very least, you maintain the good reputation of your company.

- Begin by working out the refusal strategy.

Determining the Strategy.   Your first step in writing a credit refusal letter is to work out the reason for the refusal. Perhaps these people have been slow to pay in the past. They may be ineligible because their existing debt load is too high. A bank may refuse to finance a business venture because it is beyond the usual scope of the bank's investment interests.

- Some authorities favour offering an explanation.

Some credit authorities believe that applicants refused credit are entitled to written explanation of the reasons for the refusal. Others disagree. One way of resolving this question is to follow the refusal with an invitation to come in (or telephone) to discuss the reasons. This discussion could be followed by a written explanation, if the applicant wants it.

- Frank discussion is effective with weak financial risks.

If you are refusing because your applicant's credit rating is not fully established, your task is not difficult. Lack of a credit rating is not a reflection on character. It is related less to personal qualities, than to such factors as length of time in business and economic conditions. Thus, with your refusal, you can talk more hopefully about granting credit in the future.

- The opening has three requirements.

- The opening could be thanks for the request.

Beginning with a Cushioning Statement.   The credit refusal is like most bad-news letters in its general organization. The opening is neutral about the bad news, identifies the situation, and sets up the strategy. If possible, it expresses a point of agreement.

Any appropriate comment that fits the situation can make a good opening. An expression of appreciation for the request is one such possibility. Although this approach has been used often, it is almost always appropriate. If you use it, try to vary the wording from the usual "Thank you for your application." Something like this would be better:

Thank you for considering Nova-Tech as a supplier. We appreciate your credit application, Ms. Spangler, and will do all that we reasonably can to help you in getting your business started.

As they should be, these words are on subject and neutral. In addition, they set up the explanation that giving credit for purchases is beyond what the supplier can reasonably do at this time.

Presenting the Explanation and Refusing Tactfully.   The explanation justifies the refusal. Although it may stand alone, in a credit refusal, the explanation is often combined with the bad news of the refusal as the following discussion shows.

- Explanation to a bad risk requires tact.

How you explain depends on why you are refusing. If you are refusing on the grounds of a poor reputation, you need to say little. As bad repayment risks know their records, you need only imply that you also know. You do not need to say anything like "Your credit record is bad." A tactful sentence like this will justify and deliver the refusal:

To keep our prices down, we make every effort to control our operating costs. Credit collections are very costly, so we extend credit to those with 'A' ratings only.

Refusing an applicant who is in a weak financial position allows a more open approach. If you are refusing because the applicant is temporarily overextended, or because his or her credit rating is not yet established, you can discuss the reasons for the refusal with as much frankness as your relationship with the applicant permits.

• Explanation to a weak financial risk can be more open.

In your explanation, you can spell out your credit policy and suggest that the reader may qualify for credit in the future. Of course, your words should be carefully chosen to avoid implying lack of trust. They should be positive and understanding of the reader's credit restrictions. You might recommend corrective actions the reader can take, or you might even be able to offer limited credit in some cases.

• Positive wording is best.

Since you have not yet established your credit rating, we suggest that you approach your bank for a small loan. When you have repaid it, you will have a credit rating that will qualify you for other credit applications.

A PRACTICE RUN

Rewrite the following refusal in positive ways as suggested.

Because of the high likelihood of your defaulting on payments, we must refuse applicants like you whose current assets-to-liabilities ratio falls below 2 to 1.

Suggest future credit options

_____

_____

Suggest limited credit terms.

_____

_____

Closing with Goodwill. Because the refusal is bad news, you should keep it away from an emphasis position. You would do well to follow it with more pleasant information— any goodwill information that fits the case. One often-used but effective closing is a courteous forward look to whatever future relations appear appropriate. Here are two such closings.

• The closing should be pleasant and friendly.

As one of Meyers' cash customers, you will receive our courteous service, quality merchandise, and low prices. We look forward to serving you soon.
For your shopping convenience, we are sending you our new spring catalogue. We look forward to serving you with quality products and services.

Keep the encouragement of future business very gentle—on the public relations level, not selling or reselling. Pushing your product after giving your customer a refusal would be inappropriate.

Courtesy and Tact in a Clear Refusal. Doreen's bank has decided to refuse her application for an extension on her line of credit. The letter, however, is positive. The opening recognizes her success to date and sets up the strategy for the refusal. Industry experience provides good support for the decision to withhold credit at this time. The same experience is used to suggest that more credit will be available in the future. The closing portrays the bank as a concerned partner, working with Doreen for success in her business.

• A clear, positive credit refusal.

This department store's form letter is ready to be merged with an address list that contains items corresponding to the field names in the letter. Large stores ordinarily use form letters because they must write so many similar letters. The word processor allows a general form letter to fit a variety of people and circumstances and yet appear personal.

Sarina
& COMPANY

{Date}

{Field}Personal Title~ {Field}First Name~
{Field}Last Name~

{Field}Company Name~
{Field}Street Address~
{Field}City~, {Field}Province~   {Field}Postal Code~

Dear {Field}Personal Title~ {Field}Last Name~:

The beginning is cordial and neutral about the outcome.

Thank you for your interest in an account with Sarina & Company. We are always grateful for the opportunity to serve our customers in the best way we can.

The bad news is given implicitly and positively.

In determining what we can do for you regarding your {Field}Request Date~ request for credit, we made the routine checks you authorized. The information we have received permits us to serve you as a cash customer.

The explanation is factual, based on routine credit checks.

Cash buying here at Sarina's discount prices means substantial savings for you. We hope you will visit the store very soon to take advantage of our everyday low prices.

The closing points out other benefits to the customer shopping at Sarina's.

Sincerely yours,

Sandy O'Donnell
Sandy O'Donnell
Credit Manager

1013 HEATHER LANE
BLOOMINGTON, IN 47402

Please accept our congratulations on the continuing success of your Good 'n Nice business. The economic conditions at the moment present challenges for any entrepreneur, and especially so for a business as new as yours.

Experience has shown that the first three years of a business are critical for laying the financial foundation for the future. The asset-to-debt ratio during these early stages needs to be monitored carefully to keep a healthy cash flow and to optimize the prospect of long-term success. By examining the enclosed table showing the advisable ratios, you will see that you are already in the highest bracket with your existing line of credit limit. Although an extension is inadvisable at this time, another successful year in business will improve your standing.

We are proud to serve you with financial advice and banking services. You are a valued customer whose success is important to us. If I can advise you on any financial matter, either business or personal, please call me on my direct line at 471-7415.

The types of bad-news letters covered in the preceding pages are the most common ones. You should be able to handle the bad-news situations that you encounter by adapting the techniques explained and illustrated in this chapter.

The next chapter introduces another use for the indirect approach in persuasive messages. Some rather special types of persuasive letters (sales, collections, and job applications) are included in the following chapters as well.

. . . .

A SUMMARY OF LEARNING OUTCOMES FROM THIS CHAPTER

When the main message of your letter is bad news, you should usually use the indirect order. In such situations, you have two main goals: to give the bad news and to maintain goodwill. In approaching these, first you think through the problem, looking for a logical explanation. The opening of your letter sets up this explanation. Then you present the reasoning that supports your strategy. Your reasoning sets up the bad news, which you present clearly yet positively. You may state it explicitly or make it implicitly clear. You end the letter with positively worded goodwill comments.

The refusal of a request is one bad-news situation that you probably will choose to treat indirectly. This type of bad-news letter follows the general plan of beginning with a cushioning comment, presenting the explanation, handling the refusal, and closing with goodwill. You may wish to suggest corrective action that will improve the situation.

Refusals of adjustments follow a similar pattern. After selecting a strategy to use in making such a refusal, you set up this strategy in a neutral opening—one that does not give away the answer. You then present the reasoning that justifies your decision, taking care to build your case in convincing and positive language. Your explanation leads to the refusal. You close the letter with friendly comments that do not recall the refusal to the reader's mind.

For letters refusing credit, your opening words should set up your strategy, be neutral, and tie in with the request being answered. Next you explain. If the refusal is made to a bad risk, you imply the facts rather than state them bluntly. If the refusal is made because of weak finances, you explain more frankly. Your explanation leads to the refusal, which you word tactfully. In refusals because of weak finances, you can look hopefully to credit in the future. You should end the refusal letter with appropriate positive words, perhaps suggesting cash buying or customer services.

ANSWERS TO PRACTICE RUNS

▶Opening Sentence Strategies

Opening Sentence Your organization is doing a commendable job of supporting education for needy children. Your cause deserves the help of those who are in a position to give it.

Strategy The beginning, on-subject comment clearly marks the letter as a response to a request. It implies neither a yes nor a no answer. The second sentence sets up the explanation that will point out that this company cannot afford to help. The request for a donation will be refused.

Opening Sentence You are correct in believing that a Deep Kold air-conditioning unit should cool the average three-room apartment.

Strategy The sentence makes contact on a point of agreement. At the same time, it sets up the reasoning that will justify the refusal: the apartment in question is not an average apartment.

▶Stating the Bad News

Explicit We are unable to accept your application because the course you applied for is already full. Your name has been placed on a waiting list, however, and you will be contacted if an opening arises.

Implicit Because the course is already fully registered, your name has been placed on a waiting list. If an opening arises, you will be contacted.

Explicit Because of a shortage of business at the moment, hourly staff will work one hour less each day. By each person working six rather than seven hours, we hope to keep everyone employed.

Implicit Since there is a shortage of business at the moment, hourly staff will be given six hours each day. In this way, we hope to keep everyone employed.

▶Making Credit Refusals

Answers will vary. These are suggestions only.

Suggest future credit options
Thus, it is in the best interest of both of us if you deal with us on a cash basis until your assets-to-liabilities

ratio reaches 2 to 1 and you qualify for our generous credit terms.

Suggest limited credit.
Until your assets-to-liabilities ratio reaches the standard of 2 to 1, we can offer you credit up to $200.

QUESTIONS FOR DISCUSSION

1. Writing in the indirect order usually requires more words than writing in the direct order. Since conciseness is a virtue in writing, how can the indirect order be justified?
2. What strategy is best in a letter refusing a request when the reasons for the refusal are strictly in the writer's best interest?
3. Including apologies in bad news letters is unwise because they are reminders of the bad news. Discuss.
4. The refusal of a claim was explained by saying that company policy did not permit granting claims in such cases. Was this explanation adequate? Discuss.
5. Why should you try to maintain goodwill when refusing credit? You are not going to sell to the person, so why bother?
6. Discuss the difference between refusing credit to people who do not yet have established credit ratings and to those who are considered bad risks because of their credit history.

CASE 8–1

The library at your college is facing additional funding cuts. The staff has dealt with funding challenges before and has

been resourceful and creative in maintaining an excellent level of service. As in past years, they are seeking input from students. You have been asked to serve on a committee to deal with the question of technology in the library. (Form a committee with several other students to complete this case.)

The Changes That Will Be Occurring

- Reference and technical assistance will have to be reduced by eight hours per week.
- The expansion of the on-line catalogue project to permit searching via modem (from home, for example) has to be postponed. Access from terminals in the library and study halls on campus will be unaffected.

- On-line searching of databases will be replaced by on-disc services. This change means a delay in access to the latest materials, but the cost savings of the CD-ROM format are substantial.

The Tasks of Your Committee

- to decide when reference and technical staff is needed the most. In other words, in which eight hours that the library is open will there be only circulation staff available?
- to suggest ways to present the bad news to the student body. Are there inexpensive alternatives that could soften the blow? What cushioning statements can be used?
- to draft the announcement as a memo, letter, or brochure.

LETTER PROBLEMS

Giving Bad News

1. The Queen City Boat Show is one of the oldest and largest annual shows in Canada. This is your first year as co-ordinator, and it is your task to put the show into the black again after it has run at a loss for a number of years.

   Some of the measures you must adopt will not be popular. Fees for display space have been increased by 25 per cent. To accommodate more displays, the vendors' lounge area has been reduced in size. As well, the entrance fee for the public has also been increased. So as not to discourage the public from attending, this increase has been kept to a minimum.

   You must write a letter to all the vendors who have set up booths at the show in the last two years. The price increases will not be good news because many companies are struggling financially themselves. However, the survival of this boat show depends on increasing revenues this year.

2. For this assignment, you are employed by Kagera Enterprises that manages the real estate holdings of Basilo Kagera. Ben Abell has rented one of Kagera's buildings in Lakeport for the past five years. He and his wife operate Abell Hardware, an independent store offering friendly service and reasonable prices.

   Kagera told you his plans for this building only yesterday. "That location is much too valuable for the use now given it," he explained. "We are going to tear down the building and put up a high-rise office/apartment complex." He went on to say that he already had commitments for much of the new high-rise. Then he told you to give the current tenant the three-month advance notice specified in the contract and offer what help you could.

   After you have selected the best strategy for the case, write the letter that will give the Abells the negative news and explain the situation to help them accept the decision.

3. "This could be my big chance," you say to yourself. You are a recent business grad working for Medico-Tech Equipment Company, manufacturer of medical laser equipment. You have been assigned the job of drafting a

letter to inform the mayor of Saskatoon that efforts to bring Medico-Tech's new plant to that city have failed. The new plant will be built in Regina.

   From asking questions, you know that these two cities have competed vigorously for the past two years. Each one presented convincing facts and figures supporting its case. Both cities met all of Medico-Tech's requirements. Saskatoon appeared to have a slight edge in tax incentives and community support; Regina led in the availability of highly technical labour. Your president and other Medico-Tech executives, very impressed by the excellent presentations of both cities, finally decided in Regina's favour. The key factor was Regina's prestigious Victoria Clinic, with its internationally known research team.

   In talking to you about the situation, Jonah Baedeker (Medico-Tech's president) said, "The Saskatoon team worked very hard to convince us that Saskatoon was the place for us. I think they felt they would win. They will be terribly disappointed."

   Write the letter for President Baedeker's signature, and address it to Mayor Runnels.

Refused Requests

4. You work for King Kola, a leading soft drink manufacturer. Today, on his way out the door to a meeting, your boss said, "You seem to have a way with words. Write a letter for me saying no to Covington."

   Thomas Covington, of Big Bite Burger, wants to promote a Big Bite Burger–King Kola special offer. For a one-month period, his short-order restaurants would offer a regular-size Big Bite Burger and a 12-ounce King Kola for $1.99. He would be willing to absorb a loss on the burger if King Kola will sell him the syrup at a 50 percent discount. "We would both win in the long run," he argues in his letter. "It would be good promotion for both companies."

   "Perhaps," said Emile Fortier, your boss. "Some of our competitors do this sort of thing. But I think that the money would be better spent on other forms of promotion. With this scheme, the cost per impression would be high—much higher than that of conventional advertizing."

   With these thoughts in mind, you will now write a letter for Mr. Fortier's signature refusing Covington's request.

You see three goals: (1) to convince Covington that the decision is fair and logical, (2) to maintain goodwill in the relationship with King Kola, and (3) to make an impression on your boss with a well-composed letter.

5. Lisa Stamps, one of the nation's best-known and most respected motivational speakers, has a very busy schedule addressing business groups (primarily sales organizations). You are her "right hand." In this role, you organize her schedule, make travel plans, and obtain lecture facilities. One of your more difficult duties is handling requests for Ms. Stamps's services on a free or discount basis.

One such request has come from Mary Ellen Yates, president of the Cambrian Region United Way. This quotation gives the gist of her very persuasive message: "As you may recall, you gave one of your motivational messages to the Cambrian Marketing and Sales Executives' Club last August. I was a member of that group, as were a number of other United Way volunteers. I feel that your message would be most useful to our fund-raising committee when we have our annual kickoff banquet next month." She concludes by stating that United Way could pay expenses, if necessary, but that she believes Stamps would not expect compensation from a charitable organization.

Lisa Stamps has been confronted with this difficult situation before and has concluded that she cannot say yes. She gives to charity—and generously. But as with most people, giving in her own area is all she can do. Also as she sees the matter, lecturing is her business. A lecturer giving away lectures is much like a grocer giving away groceries or a shoe store owner giving away shoes. These business people might give goods to the needy in their own area, but they wouldn't go around the country giving their goods away. So why should she?

With Stamps's thoughts in mind, you will now write a letter refusing Yates's request. You will try to explain so that Ms. Yates will see Ms. Stamps, not as a selfish woman, but as a fair, reasonable person with a very logical explanation.

6. The president of the Rumboldt Dads' Club has sent you a persuasive letter requesting that you permit his group to make a dirt biker's trail in a 180-hectare tract of forest land owned by the Wigand Timber Company.

Although Wigand has a policy of maintaining good relations with the people who live nearby, it doesn't allow such activities on its properties. For a time, it did permit groups to make recreational use of its forest land as a goodwill gesture. The resulting damage, however, soon changed this attitude. So although you support the goals of clubs like this, you must say no.

In this case, you will write the Rumboldt Dads' Club (Denis Boissonneault, president) refusing the request and explaining in a way that will keep the group's goodwill and understanding. If there is another service you can offer, you might do so to limit the negative effect of the bad news.

7. You were elated when you learned that Ella Hathaway had been elected to the presidency of the International Association of Administrators. She is a highly qualified business leader and truly deserves this recognition. After learning of her election, you wrote her a letter congratulating her on her victory. A few days later, you received a letter from her asking that you serve as chair of the bylaws committee.

As she explains the assignment in her letter, "This is a very important assignment—especially this year. Our bylaws are terribly out of date. At our directors' meeting, everybody agreed that they need a thorough revision." Her words tell you that this is a work assignment. Normally, you would welcome such an assignment, but this is not a normal year.

Your schedule for the year will be extremely heavy. Your 3-C Manufacturing Company is building a plant in Ireland and is establishing trade offices in various cities in continental Europe. You will have a very heavy travel commitment, and your backlog of work will keep you very busy at the home office.

Because of your heavy workload, you have to say no to Ella's request. So you will write her to say this, and you will explain your decision so that she will consider it completely justified.

Adjustment Refusals

8. You are the manager of the regional service centre for Electro-Tech (Canada), manufacturer of personal computers and printers. You have received a claim from Mr. Matt Hudson concerning the Electro-Tech 21-B printer that he bought 23 months ago.

In the letter he wrote you, Mr. Hudson said that the printer worked well for the first month or two. He then went on an overseas assignment, leaving the printer in a storage warehouse. When he returned a few days ago, he couldn't get the printer to work.

Hudson also said that he couldn't take the printer to the dealer who sold it to him because that dealer had gone out of business. He decided to write you when he saw the address for your service centre in the literature he was given at the time of purchase. He explained his request to you in these words: "Since there is a five-year warranty on the printer, I am sending it to you today and request that you repair it and return it to me. As it is well within the five years, I am assuming that there will be no charge."

Hudson doesn't have his facts straight. Electro-Tech does have a warranty on this printer, but it is an unlimited warranty for the first year only. For the next four years it covers only parts and does not include labour and shipping costs.

When the printer arrived, you had an estimate prepared. The warranty will cover the $76.00 worth of parts, so the machine can be put in first-class working order for the one hour labour charge of $57.50. GST and shipping charges will add $11.40 to the bill, making a total of $68.90.

Now you will let Mr. Hudson know that you must deny his request to repair his printer without charge and give him your estimate for the needed work. You may decide to mention that your warranty is generous (your competitors offer their customers less protection than you do).

9. Assume that you are the business manager of the Henderson Vocational Institute. Today's mail brings a letter from Mr. C. P. Prather, who asks that you refund most of the tuition he paid for his son's 12-week course. Mr. Prather states his case in these words: "The course in computer maintenance and repair you sold me for my son Donald is completely worthless. After attending the course for two weeks, Donald has learned absolutely nothing. He found the instructor to be incompetent and incapable of communicating, so he quit the course. As I see it, I am due back five sixths of the $900 I paid for tuition. That makes $750 you owe me."

    You aren't going to give back the money. You limit your classes to 18 students, and you nearly always have a waiting list. Donald Prather withdrew too late to allow someone else into the course. Allowing insincere people to enroll and then drop out without full payment would not be fair to you or to the people on the waiting list.

    You checked with Al Davenport, the instructor in the course. He made these comments: "I remember him. He was always talking and horsing around in class. I had to call him down a number of times. Not once did he come to class prepared. He took the first examination on the ninth day and made a score of 17. The class average was 83. I haven't seen him since."

    When you told Davenport about Prather's criticism of the course, he gave you some convincing counterinformation: "The course was completed by all 18 students who enrolled in it the last time it was offered, and every one of them went straight to a good job. The student evaluations of the course were good too. On a 10-point scale, I got an average of 8.9—nothing lower than 8."

    With this information in mind, you'll write Mr. Prather. You won't give him his money back. Since Donald is an adult, you will not discuss details of his grades or behaviour with his father, but you decide you can use some of the information you received from the instructor. And in your usual courteous way, you will make your decision seem fair.

10. You were surprised to receive a claim letter from Olga Kushinka, sales manager of Dabney-Farrow, Ltd. Last week, Ms. Kushinka brought her sales force to the Lamplighter Hotel, and you thought all was well when she left. Her letter claims that you mistakenly charged her $496 for six rooms that were not used on the first day of her meeting.

    After checking your records, you found that Kushinka reserved 27 rooms for the meeting—all guaranteed. She doesn't question this fact, but her letter states that on the day involved your office was informed that six rooms would not be used. According to your records, on that day a telephone call from someone at Dabney-Farrow informed your reservations clerk that six rooms would not be used. But the call was made at 8:32 P.M., well after the 6 P.M. deadline for cancelling. The day in question was a busy one for the Lamplighter. The rooms could have been rented if your staff had known earlier that Dabney-Farrow would not use them. As things turned out, only two of them were used.

As you see the situation, this is a ridiculous claim. Your requirement that cancellations be received before 6 P.M. is standard in the hotel industry. The policy is fair to you and your guests.

Regardless of your feelings, you have to write a tactful letter refusing the claim and offering what assistance you can. A corporate client is not one you want to lose.

11. Seven months ago, one of your salespeople sold Mrs. Lucille Tobias the CD-ROM version of your *21st Century Encyclopedia*. She got it at a good discount—$50 off the regular $645 price. Today you received a letter from her saying that she wants to cancel the sale.

    As her letter explains, "The children are not using the encyclopedia as your salesperson said they would. In fact, they have not had one occasion to use it in their homework. With a little effort, they can find everything they need on the Internet. I request that you refund my money. I will return the CD-ROM to you as soon as I get your favourable response."

    For more than one reason, Tobias won't get that favourable response. First, there is no flaw in the product to justify accepting a return. Also, seven months after the purchase, the CD-ROM is unquestionably used. Perhaps Mrs. Tobias doesn't understand the benefits of this product. Unlike many Internet sites, the articles in your encyclopedia are guaranteed for accuracy and reliability. Besides, your encyclopedia is targeted to ages 12 to 18.

    Now you will write Mrs. Tobias, giving her your answer and justifying it so that she will accept it as fair.

12. In your office at the Happy Trails Retirement Home, you have received a letter from Mr. Cornelius Calmes, who moved into your retirement home nine months ago. After six months, Mr. Calmes left the home for a short visit with a daughter in Montreal. Now three months later, he explains his situation:

I left Happy Trails for a brief visit to my daughter's house in Montreal. She insisted that I stay on, which I did. Now she insists that I move in with her permanently. I will ask my friend George Nunn to get my things from my rooms and send them to me. There isn't much there. I want you to send me the money I paid in advance. At $450 a month for six months, that will be $2,700. Thank you for your courtesies while I was with you.

Obviously, Calmes isn't acquainted with the facts of a business operation. He signed a 12-month lease, paid the full 12 months rent in advance, and is obligated for the full 12 months. Since you have a waiting list, you will give him back the rent he paid for the remaining three months. In no way, however, can you justify giving him back the rent for the past three months. You can't believe he expects it. Even though he was away, he had possession of the rooms (his belongings were there). Otherwise, you could have rented them to someone on your waiting list.

You will write Mr. Calmes a letter in which you will deny a part of his claim and grant a part. As is your policy, you will explain your decision and work to maintain goodwill. He should know that you're doing more than you are required to do.

13. In your new position in the applications department of International Card (a major credit card company recognized worldwide), you have been given a special assignment. Your boss said, "In response to our magazine and direct-mail advertising, we receive quite a few applications that we are unable to judge with certainty. They are primarily from people who are self-employed or retired. Take this one, for example—a retired teacher claiming an annual income of $155,000. It could be true; but more than likely it is a joke or someone is trying to bilk us out of some money. We turn down all such applicants initially but try to keep the door open by asking them to submit proof—such as an accountant's or broker's statement or a copy of an income tax form. If they submit the proof and it checks out OK, we grant them a card."

    "We don't have a model letter to cover this type of situation in our office style guide. I have been writing these letters personally, but I'm tired of that. There are getting to be too many of them. I want you to draft a model letter. Make sure that your letter won't offend, because some of the people in this group turn out to be very good credit risks. Still, you'll have to make it clear that we don't issue our card without proof of financial ability. We'll give your draft to a few people in the department for evaluation and feedback. Then we'll take what they say and finalize the letter. That way, when this situation comes up, we can take the general outline of your letter and modify it to suit the situation. That will be a lot easier than starting from a blank page each time."

    Draft the model letter. Exchange letters with one or two classmates for their feedback. Then use their comments to improve your letter. Your instructor may want the original version, the feedback, and the final version, so be sure to keep all the parts of this assignment.

14. For this assignment, you are the developer of Blue Mountain Acres, a beautiful recreational area with access to excellent golf, tennis, fishing, and swimming. Your residential lots sell for $25,000 and up.

    Today's mail brought a letter from Ms. Nadine Chatwin of Hogan City. She wrote: "Last month I visited my sister, who lives in Blue Mountain Acres, and while there I looked over your beautiful development. I especially like Lot No. 271, which is adjacent to my sister's property. It was priced at $30,000. I will buy this lot if you give me the credit I need. I can pay $2,000 down and the rest over 15 years. I am enclosing the names of my banker and of three local retail stores where I have credit."

    You were excited at first, for sales have been slow. However, your check of Ms. Chatwin's references disappointed you. She appears to be a poor credit risk. She has a record of slow payment, and she has extended her indebtedness far beyond safe limits. You will have to write her a letter denying her request for credit. Perhaps she can manage to borrow the money locally, the way most of your customers do it.

    Even though you must say no, Ms. Chatwin is still a prospect for a lot. Besides, her sister is currently one of

your owners. You don't want to cause offense. You will take care to treat her gently, and you will attempt to convince her that your decision is fair.

15. You are the new credit manager for Chauviere's, one of the most exclusive women's clothing stores in the area. Until you came on the job, Mr. Napoleon Chauviere took care of the store's credit applications personally, answering each with an individualized letter. "We're probably getting too big to do it that way in the future," Mr. Chauviere explained to you, "so you may want to write some form letters to make the work easier. Be certain that they project the personal service image I have been building over the years."

    Following Chauviere's advice, you will write a form letter for the first type of applicant to be denied credit. These people, in Mr. Chauviere's words, are "free-spending, high-living social climbers who have some money but not enough to keep their payments current." Because they do shop somewhere, you'll try to keep their goodwill so that they will spend cash at Chauviere's.

16. Assume that you are the owner of Campus Capers, a small clothing store near your campus, and that approving or rejecting credit applications is one of your duties.

    Today, Samantha Muro, a first-year university student selected several garments and then asked her sales clerk whether she could charge them. Following the store's policy, the sales clerk gave her a credit application form to fill out. The sales clerk then marked the garments "On Hold" and put them in the storeroom.

    In reviewing the application, you first note that Samantha is not employed. "I will work if I have to," she wrote in the work space, "but at present I have a $600 per month living allowance above tuition, books, and fees." You suspect that the $600 appears to be a lot bigger to her than it really is. She has no previous credit record. Also, Samantha requested that you bill her directly and left blank the space for the name of her parents or guardians. Experience has shown you that a direct-billing, no-work combination is risky. You will deny the request.

    Even though you won't extend credit to Ms. Muro, you want to keep her as a customer. Your layaway plan seems to be an option. Write a letter to let her know your decision and your suggestion.

17. Your credit check of Adrian Kirschner tells you something that you didn't detect when he applied for credit at your Builders' Supply Company last week. At that time you saw him as a clean-cut, personable, aggressive young building contractor. You thought you would have only to go through the routine of checking his references before granting him credit. But it didn't turn out that way.

    The three credit references Mr. Kirschner listed all told you the same story. He is slow in paying his debts. He is behind in his payments, and he has exceeded his credit limits (which might explain why he is seeking credit from you and not his usual sources). Apparently, he is in a financial bind. Even so, the evidence indicates that he is basically a well-intentioned person who just made some poor decisions in his contracting business. Some of his creditors will be left holding the bag. Your Builders' Supply won't be among them.

Now you will turn down Mr. Kirschner's application for credit. You will state your decision as final in a clear and professional way, but you will try not to offend him. He could be back on his feet in time, and you'll want his business if that happens.

9

Indirectness in Persuasion

C H A P T E R   O B J E C T I V E S

Upon completing this chapter, you will be able to use persuasion effectively in making requests, and composing sales letters and collection letters. To reach this goal, you should be able to

1   Explain the need for indirect presentation of facts and reasoning in persuasion.

2   Use imagination in writing persuasive requests that gain attention, present rational and emotional appeals skillfully, and close with clear action and goodwill.

3   Select the best appeal for the specific reader of the sales letter through audience analysis and skillful use of the you-viewpoint.

4   Compose sales letters that creatively gain attention, persuasively present appeals, and effectively drive for action.

5   Compose letters using the appropriate degree of persuasion and frankness in the middle stage of collection.

6   Use strength and directness to present action in a calm and firm appeal in last-resort letters.

▶ to Persuasive Requests

During the renovations at Westridge Mall, access to the mall has been disrupted. Although customers can always get in, the entrance nearest Good 'n Nice is frequently closed. Doreen believes her business has suffered more than some others because she has lost her impulse buyers. People rarely come to the mall specifically looking for a yogurt cone. However, they are tempted to buy once they see the kiosk.

To help compensate for the decline in business, Doreen wants permission to place colourful signs with tempting pictures of her refreshing foods at strategic places in the mall. These signs would attract customers and direct them to her kiosk. Everyone in her wing of the mall would benefit from the resulting increase in traffic.

Under normal circumstances, such advertizing would not be allowed. As Doreen sees the situation, these circumstances are not normal. She feels the mall management might agree to a temporary change in policy if she can present a convincing case. ▪

USING INDIRECTNESS IN PERSUASION

Letters making requests that are likely to be resisted require a careful, deliberate approach. Persuasion is necessary. By persuasion, we mean reasoning with the reader—presenting facts, logical argument, and emotional reasons to support your case. This supportive material is very effective when it is placed before your objective. Although some writers occasionally use the direct order for persuasion, we will limit our models to the more usual indirect approach.

* Requests that are likely to be resisted require persuasion.

For example, with a letter requesting a favour that will require some personal sacrifice for your reader, your chances for success will be greater if you justify the request before making it. This approach, of course, follows the indirect order. Or, for another example, when you write a letter to sell a product or service, you can anticipate skepticism or resistance from your readers. To succeed, therefore, you have to begin by convincing them that they need what you are offering. You then state your objective—a request that they make the purchase. This approach also follows the indirect order. Such indirect letters involving persuasion are the subject of this chapter.

* Certain requests and sales letters are best written in the indirect order.

The indirect approach for persuasion follows this general plan:

* Generally follow this indirect plan.

- Open with words that (1) set up the strategy, and (2) gain attention.

- Present the strategy (the persuasion), using persuasive language and you-viewpoint.

- Include rational appeals and, when appropriate, emotional appeals.

- Make the request clearly and positively (1) either at the end of the letter, or (2) followed by words that recall the persuasive appeal.

- Make compliance with the request easy for your reader whenever possible.

THE INDIRECT-ORDER PERSUASIVE LETTER

Determining the Persuasion Strategy

Planning the persuasive request letter requires imagination. You begin by thinking of a strategy that will convince your reader. To do this, put yourself in your reader's position. Look at the request as the reader sees it, and determine the reader's objections. Think about what you can say to overcome those objections. From this imaginative thinking, you develop your plan.

* The persuasion is planned to overcome reader objections.

Using your imagination is a dominant factor in successful persuasion. Sometimes you need to take risks and be a little dramatic. Sometimes showing confidence, enthusiasm, and positive energy will draw the receiver to your viewpoint. Sometimes you need to exercise restraint and tact. If you are sensitive to your reader and the circumstances of your persuasive effort, your imagination will generate ideas, and your common sense will help you choose the appropriate ones.

The specific plan you develop will depend on the facts of the case. You may be able to show that your reader stands to gain in time, money, authority, goodwill, or prestige. In some cases you may persuade by appealing to the reader's love of order, excitement, or serenity. In other cases you may be able to persuade by appealing to the pleasant feeling that comes from doing a good turn. Many other possibilities exist. Choose the one that suits your reader and shows the greatest reader benefit.

Gaining Attention in the Opening

In indirect letters one objective of the opening is to set up the explanation. In persuasive letters a second one is gaining attention. The need to gain attention in the opening of persuasive letters is important. You are writing to a person who has not invited your letter and who may not agree with your goal. You could be facing an indifferent, noncommittal, skeptical, or strongly opposed reader. You need to open the door to have the reader consider your request. An interesting beginning gives the reader a reason to continue.

Determining what will catch the reader's attention requires imagination. It might be some controversial statement or a little-known fact that arouses interest. Because questions arouse curiosity, they are often effective openings. The following examples show some possibilities.

From the covering letter of a questionnaire seeking the opinions of medical doctors:

Did you know noise and air pollution are affecting the future of your practice?

From a letter requesting contributions for famine relief:

While you and I dined heartily last week, 31 families became childless because malnutrition claimed their children at the hospital in Khartoum.

From a letter seeking the co-operation of business leaders in promoting a fair:

What would your profits be if 300,000 free-spending visitors came to our town during a single week?

Presenting the Persuasion

Following the opening, you should proceed with your goal of persuading. Your task here is a logical and orderly presentation of the reasoning you have selected. Because your reader may become impatient if you delay your objective unnecessarily, you need to organize your sentences carefully to build your case and lead smoothly to your request for action. As with any argument intended to convince, you should do more than merely list points. You should package the points in convincing words paying careful attention to the meanings of your words and the clarity of your expression. Since you are trying to reach a resistant mind, you need to make good use of you-viewpoint.

Stressing the You-Viewpoint.   In no area of business communication is you-viewpoint writing more important than in persuasive and sales writing. Most of your points depend on reader interest and reader benefit. For example, assume that you are a manufacturer writing a letter to a retailer. One point you want to make is that you will help sell the product by sponsoring an advertizing campaign. You could write, "Star mixers will be advertized in *Canadian Living* for the next three issues." However, to be more persuasive, you would focus on what the campaign means to the retailer: "Your customers will want the new Star mixer when they read about it in the next three issues of *Canadian Living*." For another example, you could quote prices in words such as "The additional beater attachment costs you $12.25, and you can sell it for $18.99." To be more persuasive, you would emphasize the retailer's interest with words like these: "You can sell the additional beater attachment for $18.99—a 55 percent profit on your cost."

. . . .

A PRACTICE RUN

Rewrite the following examples to review you-viewpoint.

We make Aristocrat hosiery in three colours.

_____

The Regal laptop weighs only 1.8 kilograms. It is light and easy to pack.

_____

Lime-Fizz tastes fresh and exciting.

_____

Baker's Dozen is packaged in a rectangular box with a bright, bulls-eye design.

_____

. . . .

Practicing Positive Tone. Using a positive tone is a proven persuasive technique. Readers will opt for solutions to problems that are expressed in positive words. Even if the outcome would be the same, the positive way of describing the process is more attractive.

• Positive tone is persuasive.

. . . .

A PRACTICE RUN

Rewrite the following examples to review positive tone.

Reorganization under Plan A will take three months and cost $500,000. Although it will cost less, Plan B will take twice as long to complete.

_____

Don't forget to mail in your order card.

_____

No one has fewer shipping delays.

_____

. . . .

Including Rational and Emotional Appeals. For convenience in studying persuasive appeals, we can divide them into two broad groups. In one group are rational, logical appeals that, as the name suggests, present reasons that appeal to the mind. With rational

• Use logic to appeal to the mind.

appeals you attempt to show that the request you are about to make is a reasonable course of action for your reader to take. It is something your reader should do.

• Use emotion to appeal to the will and heart.

In the other group are emotional appeals that try to make the reader want to take the action. They use the senses and the emotions to persuade. They describe how something feels, tastes, smells, sounds, or appears. They also appeal to the reader through love, anger, pride, fear, and enjoyment. In other words, the emotional appeal offers subjective reasons while the rational one provides the objective reasons.

As an example, to persuade someone to enrol at your exercise club, you would use rational arguments relating to health, fitness, heart rate, blood pressure, and so on. The emotional arguments would focus on having fun, feeling and looking better, and meeting new people with similar interests. The rational and emotional elements are not always this easy to distinguish. The distinction is less important than the building of a strong case.

A PRACTICE RUN

Identify some rational and some emotional appeals for the following persuasive situations.

To attract people to an alcohol-free, family-oriented First Night entertainment for New Year's Eve.

Rational Appeals: _____

_____

Emotional Appeals: _____

_____

To encourage students to run for office on your student council.

Rational Appeals: _____

_____

Emotional Appeals: _____

_____

To work one day a month without pay, with a promise of no further layoffs for six months.

Rational Appeals: _____

_____

Emotional Appeals: _____

_____

Calling for Action

• Follow the persuasion with the request.

Making the Request Clearly and Positively.   After you have done your persuading, you move to the action you seek. You have prepared the reader for what you want. If you have done that well, the reader should be ready to accept your proposal.

• Keep the request simple.

Make your first statement of the request clear and simple. Extra words or conditions should be handled separately, not with the request. Consider the effect of these two examples. The first one is confusing because of the details. The second one is clear and direct; the important details will be included elsewhere.

Poor example:

Please gather 20 people who can donate four hours of time each and be at the corner of King and Greenwood Streets on Saturday, May 30th, to operate the second water station for our fund-raising run/walkathon.

Improved example:

Please accept the opportunity to operate a water station for our charitable run/walkathon. As well as building positive public relations for your company, you will be helping us win the battle against this mysterious disease.

Because your request may be seen as a negative, you must use positive words. The wording of your request should reinforce the benefits to the reader in fulfilling the request. For example, a reminder of the benefit of positive exposure for the company operating the water station is included in the request example above. Words that might suggest reasons for refusing are especially harmful.

• Be positive.

Poor example:

I am sure that your organizing skills are already much in demand, but will you please consider accepting an assignment to the board of directors of the Children's Fund?

The following positive tie-in with a major point in the persuasion strategy does a much better job.

Improved example:

Your organizing skills are well known in the community. Will you please consider putting them to work on the board of directors of the Children's Fund?

Whether your request should end your letter will depend on the needs of the case. In some cases you will profit by following the request with a few words of explanation. This procedure is especially effective when a long persuasion effort is needed. In such cases you simply cannot present all your reasoning before stating your goal. Even in less involved presentations, you may want to follow the request with a reminder of the appeal. As illustrated in the water station example repeated here, this procedure associates the request with the advantage that saying yes will give the reader.

• The request can end the letter or be followed by a reminder of the appeal.

Improved example:

Please accept the opportunity to operate a water station for our charitable run/walkathon. As well as building positive public relations for your company, you will be helping us win the battle against this mysterious disease.

Making the Action Easy to Accomplish.   You should try to make the first step of the response as simple as possible for the readers. Include a reminder of the telephone number to call, or a preaddressed envelope to mail, or a date and time when you will call again. If you can remove barriers and make the task easy, your reader is more likely to comply.

For example, to encourage preapproved card holders to upgrade to a credit card with more benefits (and higher charges), a short information form is sent. The form is simple to complete, folds and seals into an envelope, and has postage prepaid. Book and music clubs go even further. If the member just waits, the selection of the month and the bill are sent. Even the action to prevent the selection is not difficult. It does, however, require the member to put postage on a preaddressed card and return it.

Magazine subscriptions give an example of breaking down the process into small, simple steps. A potential subscriber is encouraged to begin by removing a seal to qualify for a gift with the subscription. The enclosed card is completed with his/her name and address. Since the card is preaddressed and has postage paid, the subscriber simply drops

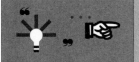
For many years the acronym† *AIDA* has been used to define the stages of one approach to persuasion. Since this text recommends a similar process, you may find AIDA helpful.

In the *A* section you get the receiver to notice your message. The *A*, then, refers to the opening statements that attract the *ATTENTION* of the receiver.

The *I* stands for *INTEREST.* In this section you build on the strategy you established in the opening. The interest section is sometimes referred to as the appeal to the mind. The facts are given to show the good sense in your suggestions.

The *D* stands for building *DESIRE.* Persuading people to take action or to change their opinion requires more than a factual appeal. Most people understand the importance of exercise, but only a small percentage faithfully participates in aerobic activity. To build desire in the receiver, the sender makes an appeal to the heart. The reader should *want* to follow your suggestions.

The final *A* is the *ACTION* stage. A clear action statement or challenge should be issued. After the persuasion process, the receiver wants some direction about the steps to take. The action statement is specific, as in "Call me before Thursday to be a part of this seminar," "Send your cheque today," or "Mark the date on your calendar now."

†A word formed by combining the initial letters of a series of words, such as NATO from North Atlantic Treaty Organization.

it into the mail. After the first issue of the magazine has been received, a bill for the subscription arrives. Several methods of payment are offered (usually credit card, cheque, or money order), and a return envelope is included. When payment has been received by the company, the special subscription gift arrives.

PERSUASIVE SITUATIONS

The Persuasive Request

* The following letters illustrate good and bad persuasion efforts.

The persuasive request is illustrated by contrasting letters that ask business people to donate to Junior Achievement. The first letter is direct and unpersuasive; the second letter, which follows the approach described above, is persuasive and more likely to produce the desired results.

Obvious Failure in Directness.　The weaker letter begins with the request. Because the reader is asked to give away money, the direct beginning makes a negative impression. In addition, the writer tends to lecture as, for example, in the sentence, "As a business leader, you should be willing to support it." Although some explanation follows, the letter has little of the you-viewpoint writing that is effective in persuasion. Perhaps its greatest fault is that the persuasion comes too late. The closing is a weak reminder of the action requested.

Will you please donate to the local Junior Achievement program? We have set $50 as a fair minimum for businesses to give. But larger amounts would be appreciated.

* This letter has poor persuasion strategy.

Our organization badly needs your support. Currently, about 900 young people will not get to participate in Junior Achievement activities unless more money is raised. Junior Achievement is a most worthwhile organization. As a business leader, you should be willing to support it.

If you do not already know about Junior Achievement, let me explain. Junior Achievement is an organization for high school youngsters. They work with local business executives to form small businesses. They operate the businesses. In the process, they learn about our economic system. This is a good thing, and it deserves our help.

We hope to hear from you soon.

Skillful Persuasion Using Indirect Order. The next letter shows good imagination in the use of the indirect pattern described above. Its opening has strong interest appeal and sets up the persuasion strategy. Notice the effective use of you-viewpoint. Not until the reader has been shown the merits of J.A. does the letter make the request. When it is made, the request is clear and direct, with enough detail to make the response easy. The final words leave the reader thinking about the benefit that a *yes* answer will give.

Right now—right here in Brampton—620 teenagers are running 37 companies. These young people run the whole show, their only adult help being advice from some of your business associates who work with them. Last September, they applied for a charter and elected officers. They selected products for manufacture—antifreeze, candles, and chairs, to name a few. They issued stock—and they sold it, too. Now with the proceeds, they are producing and marketing their products. This May, they will liquidate their companies and account to their stockholders for their profits or losses.

• This letter uses positive persuasion strategy.

You, as a public-spirited citizen, will quickly see the merits of the Junior Achievement program. The value of such realistic experience to teach these teens the operations of business is clear. You can see, also, that it's an exciting and wholesome program, the kind young people need and enjoy. After you have considered these points and others you will find in the enclosed brochure, I know you will see that Junior Achievement is a good program.

Like all good things, J.A. needs all of us behind it. During the 13 years the program has been in Brampton, it has had enthusiastic support from local business leaders. But with over 900 students on the waiting list, our plans for next year call for expansion. Can you help make the program available to more youngsters by making a $50 tax-deductible contribution? Please make your cheque payable to Junior Achievement, and send it in the enclosed pre-addressed envelope right away. You will be doing a good service for our youth and our city.

For another example, we return to the situation at Westridge Mall and Doreen's request.

The renovations at Westridge Mall are into their second month now, with four or five more months until completion. Assistance from the contractors and management has been invaluable in keeping our businesses functioning under these conditions. Clearly, we all have a common goal.

Because of the frequent necessity to close Entrance 5, pedestrian traffic in the southwest wing of the mall has temporarily decreased. The businesses along this wing are feeling the effect of losing the impulse shopper. These store managers have made a small initial investment to research a plan to improve this situation for the shoppers, mall management, and store owners alike. We propose placing colourful, free-standing signs at strategic points in the mall reminding shoppers of the stores and services in the southwest wing. The signs would be on pedestals or easels that could be moved easily to allow a free flow of traffic. We would, of course, be responsible for the costs and handling of the signs that would be placed at points approved by mall management.

Would you please meet with our committee to study our proposal and give us your advice? Since this is a matter of some urgency, we have set aside the next three mornings and will accommodate ourselves to your schedule. Please telephone any member of the committee to let us know a suitable time. Our business numbers are listed below.

We look forward to a creative meeting in which we can develop a strategy to meet the temporary challenges created by the renovations.

The Sales Letter

Value of Sales Writing. One special type of persuasive letter is the sales letter. We consider it here for several reasons. One reason is that writing sales letters gives you knowledge of selling techniques that will help you with other types of letters, for in a sense, every letter is a sales letter. In every letter you are presenting something for consideration. It may be an idea, a line of reasoning, your company, or, perhaps, yourself.

• Knowing selling techniques helps you in writing other types of letters.

Secondly, although many large companies contract marketing firms with professional writers to produce sales letters, some businesses cannot afford to hire a specialist. If you

The writer appeals to the reader's pride and generosity to persuade him to comply with this request. She also takes deliberate steps to make the action easy and convenient for the reader.

THE
OFFICE
ADMINISTRATOR
5500 Finch Avenue East   Scarborough, ON   M1S 5R9

November 20, 1997

Mr. Andrew Schuldhaus
Director, Human Resources
Chalmers-DeLouche
7417 Canal Street
Peterborough, ON   L4K 2M8

Dear Mr. Schuldhaus:

The opening is of interest to a personnel administrator.

Young people entering business are eager for any clue that will make their job search successful. They want to know what goes on in your mind, as a personnel administrator, when you are reading, selecting, and discarding application letters. In our column, "Letters That Talk," we want to examine that question for recent graduates. To answer it well, we are drawing our information from highly respected experts in the field.

The strategy of appealing to pride and goodwill is established.

The benefits to the reader are developed.

Through this project, you will be sharing expertise with those who will appreciate it and benefit by it. You will have the opportunity to meet an important need of young people who are trying to find the right job. As well as giving exposure to you and Chalmers-DeLouche, I believe this article will save you time because candidates will write better application letters to your company.

Please recall a recent competition you have directed and answer these questions. I have reprinted them on a separate page with space for your notes.
1. What clues did you find in the application letters that helped you decide on the suitability of applicants for your firm?
2. What specific points did you look for in these letters to select those people you wanted to interview?
3. What fine points enabled you to make your final choice?

The questions are numbered and reprinted for the reader's convenience.

The reader's needs are considered. The request is repeated.

You will see the article before it is published to confirm its accuracy, and your contribution will, of course, be credited. So, will you jot down your comments for me and leave them with your receptionist? I will visit your office on the 27th to collect them. The young people of today are eager to hear from a specialist like you.

Sincerely,

Charlotte Clayton

Charlotte Clayton
Associate Editor

CC:lm

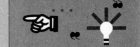
work for a small business, or start your own business, you will need to write sales material.

The third reason is that you will find good use for selling techniques in your daily life. From time to time, all of us are called on to sell something. In the community we are asked to sell everything from raffle tickets to chocolate bars to raise money for worthwhile causes. If we are employed in selling goods and services, our sales efforts will, of course, be frequent. In other areas of business, our sales efforts may consist of selling an idea, our own competence, or the goodwill of the firm. In all these situations, sales writing and selling techniques are very valuable.

Structure of the Sales Letter. As you probably know from experience, most direct-mail efforts consist of more than just a letter. Typically, they include a co-ordinated group of pieces such as brochures, leaflets, booklets, and foldouts. But the letter usually carries the main message, and the other pieces carry the supporting details. The following discussion emphasizes the letter.

- Usually brochures, leaflets, and other support materials accompany sales letters.

Determining the Appeal. As with all writing, you must know your own objective and your audience. For a sales effort, you must know your product or service and be able to explain its merits to prospective buyers. The more you know about your readers, the better you will be able to adapt your sales message.

- Begin work on a sales letter by knowing the goods to be sold, and your readers.

Creating the sales letter involves selecting and presenting persuasive appeals. As we have already seen, there are two major groups—the emotional and the rational or logical. With an emotional appeal, you could stress that your product will provide hours of fun, or that it will be attractive to the opposite sex. A rational appeal that might be used is the product's durability.

- Next, decide what appeals and strategies to use: emotional and/or rational.

How the buyer will use the product may be a major basis for selecting a sales strategy. Cosmetics might well be sold to the final user through emotional appeals. Selling cosmetics to a retailer (who is primarily interested in reselling them) would require rational appeals. A retailer would be interested in their emotional qualities only to the extent that these make customers buy. The retailer's main questions about the product are "Will it sell?" "What turnover can I expect?" and "How much money will it make for me?"

- The prospect's uses of the product often determine which appeal is best.

For greatest success watch for opportunities to use a combined appeal. For tires durability is important, but the look and speed are also important for a sports car owner. The safety factor can be another emotional appeal for parents.

- A combined appeal is often very effective.

Using Imagination and Selling Style. After selecting the appeal, your imagination and creativity are needed. In addition, applied psychology and skillful word use are involved in writing a sales letter. There are as many different ways to handle a sales letter as there are ideas. The only sure measure is the number of sales that the letter creates.

- Writing sales letters involves imagination.

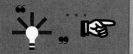

The writer was disappointed. His first sales letter had failed miserably. In discussing the matter with the advertising manager, the writer offered this explanation: "I think I have demonstrated that 'you can lead a horse to water, but you cannot make it drink.' "

"That's not an appropriate explanation," the advertizing manager replied. "Your primary goal is not to make your readers drink. It is to make them thirsty."

* Although sales letters use the general persuasive plan, the writing style is different.

The sales letter usually follows the pattern of the persuasive letter. However, the writing style is quite different from standard business writing. Sales writing is fast moving, conversational, and aggressive. It includes techniques that would be incorrect or inappropriate in most business writing—sentence fragments, choppy paragraphs, slang, and humour. It uses mechanical devices (large print, graphics, colour, font changes) for emphasis. Sales writing has its own style specifically aimed at selling.

* Sales letters may use impersonal salutations or headlines.

Determining Letter Mechanics. The physical layout of a sales letter is different from routine business letters. With some exceptions, sales letters are mass-produced rather than individually processed. To make general letters appear personalized, computer software can insert individual names and addresses. Another technique is to use a salutation such as "Dear Student," or "Dear Pet Owner." Sometimes the salutation and inside address are replaced by the opening words of the letter as shown below.

IT'S GREAT
FOR PENICILLIN,
BUT YOU CAN DO WITHOUT IT
ON YOUR ROOF . . .
We're referring to fungus. Roof fungus, like penicillin, is a mould-like growth. However, the similarity ends there.

* The basic requirement of the opening is to gain attention.

Gaining Attention in the Opening. The opening of the sales letter has one basic requirement: It must gain attention. If it does not, it fails. As sales letters are sent without having been invited, unless the first words overcome the barrier of indifference, the letter will go into the wastebasket.

* The opening should also set up the strategy.

The method you use to attract attention should be relevant to the sales message. That is, it should help set up your strategy and not just gain attention for attention's sake. A small explosion set off when the reader opens the envelope would gain attention, but would not likely assist the selling.

* Sometimes mechanical techniques and gimmicks are appropriate attention-getters.

Sales letters may use a variety of mechanical techniques to gain attention. Pictures, lines, diagrams, and cartoons are common. So is the use of different ink colours. Such devices as coins, stamps, samples, and "scratch-&-wins" have been affixed to sales letters to gain interest and help make the appeal. One letter, for example, was mailed on scorched pages to emphasize the theme of "some hot news about fire insurance." A letter with a small pencil glued to the page used the theme that "the point of the pencil is to make it easy to order" a certain magazine. As you can see, the imaginative possibilities in sales writing are boundless.

* Gain attention by introducing a need.

One effective attention-getting technique is a statement or question to introduce a need that the product will satisfy. For example, a letter to a retailer would clearly appeal to strong needs with these opening words:

Here is a proven best-seller—and with a 9 percent greater profit!

Another example is this first sentence of a letter seeking to place metered personal computers in hotels:

Can you use an employee who not only works free of charge but also pays you for the privilege of serving your clientele 24 hours a day?

Yet another example is this opening for selling a trade publication to business executives:

How to move more products,
Win more customers,
And make more money
. . . for less than $1 a week.

The use of a story is another opening approach. Most people like to read stories, and if you can start one interestingly, your reader should want to read the rest of it and the rest of your letter. This example might be used to begin a letter looking for support for an organization such as Father Murray's Notre Dame School in Saskatchewan, or a youth centre in any inner city.

• Try a story or an anecdote to gain attention.

The boy stood there bored and restless. He had energy, strength, and imagination, but nothing to do. Maybe he would set off the fire alarms and sprinklers at the hotel again. Maybe he would wander through the drug store and "pick up" something to make him feel better. As he thought, he heard a man call to him, "I bet I can beat you at one-on-one basketball." Who was this guy? Not anyone he knew. Not anyone special. And yet, someone to notice.

Thus far, the attention-gaining techniques illustrated have been short. A longer one currently popular in direct-mail selling is to place a summary of the sales message at the beginning. The point of this strategy is to communicate quickly the full impact of the sales message before the reader loses interest. If any of the points presented arouse interest, the reader is likely to continue reading. Illustrating this technique is the beginning of a letter selling subscriptions to a magazine. Notice that the first few lines appear before the salutation.

• Summary messages are also effective.

A quick way to determine whether you should read this letter:
If you are involved in or influenced by higher education—
and if you simply don't have the time to read extensively to " keep up"—
this letter is important to you.
This letter offers you a money-saving shortcut,
PLUS a free gift,
PLUS a money-back guarantee.
CONTACT has the largest readership of any journal among academic people. To find out why 100,000 people now read CONTACT every month, take three minutes to read the following letter.

Dear Educator, Graduate Student, Parent:

As a subscriber to *CONTACT*, the leading magazine of higher learning, you'll have facts and feelings at your fingertips to help *you* make informed decisions on today's topics: tenure, learning on the Internet, open admissions, the outlook for new PhDs—on just about any subject that concerns advanced learning and you.

Presenting the Sales Material.   After your attention-gaining opening has set up your sales strategy, you develop that strategy. The plan of your sales message will vary with your imagination; however, your goal is to present your product or service fulfilling a need for your customer.

- Emotional appeals sell the product based on its effect on the senses.

If you select an emotional appeal, for example, your opening has probably established an emotional atmosphere that you will continue to develop. Thus, you will sell your product based on its effects on your reader's senses. You will describe the appearance, texture, aroma, and taste of your product so vividly that your reader will mentally see it, feel it—and want it.

This paragraph uses an emotional appeal to make a fishing vacation very attractive:

Your line hums as it whirs through the air. Your lure splashes and dances across the smooth surface of the clear water as you reel. From the depth, you see the silver streak of a striking bass. You feel a sharp tug. And the battle is on!

As you can see, the paragraph casts a spell, which is what emotional selling should do. It puts a rod in the reader's hand, and it takes the reader through the thrills of the sport. The reader is ready to learn more.

- Rational appeals stress fact and logic.

If you select a rational appeal, you should describe your product based on what it can do for your reader rather than how it appeals to the senses. You should write matter-of-factly about qualities such as durability, savings, profits, and ease of operation.

Including All Necessary Information.   Whatever plan and appeal you select, make sure that you present enough information to complete the sale. You should leave none of your readers' questions unanswered. Nor should you fail to overcome any likely objections. You must work to include all such basic information in your letter.

- Say enough to answer all questions and overcome all objections.

- Make the letter carry the main sales message. Use enclosures to support your points.

If you use enclosures such as leaflets and brochures, you should take care to co-ordinate all the parts into a unified sales message. As a rule, you should use the letter to carry your basic sales message and the enclosures to supplement the letter. The enclosures might cover descriptions, price lists, diagrams, and pictures. To direct your reader's attention to these helpful details, you can use incidental references at appropriate places in the letter (for example, by saying "as shown on page 3 of the enclosed booklet" or "see page 7 of the enclosed brochure").

- Make a clear drive for the sale. Take the reader through the steps.

Driving for the Sale.   After you have sold your reader on your product or service, the next logical step is to drive for the sale. If your selling effort has been strong, your drive for action may be strong also. It may even be worded as a command. ("Order your copy today—while it's on your mind.") If you have used a milder selling effort, you could use a question. ("Won't you send your order today?") In any event the drive for action should be specific and clear. It also should urge immediate action. You can make the technique especially effective if you give a practical reason, such as "to take advantage of this three-day offer" and "so that you can be ready for the Christmas rush." For best effect the drive for the sale should take the reader through the motions of whatever he or she must do. Here are some examples:

Check your preferences on the enclosed order card. Then drop it in the mail today! No postage needed!

Just pick up the phone and call 1-800-346-8821. Receive your Tabor recorder for a 30-day free trial. Order it now so you can start enjoying Tabor quality right away.

Hurry! Complete and mail the handy order card. We'll pay the postage and bill you later. Send no money now. This is your chance to see how right the *Atlantic Magazine* is for you!

Recall the Appeal.   Make good use of the emphatic last position of a sales letter with a few words that recall the basic appeal. Associating the action with the benefits that the reader will gain by taking it adds strength to your sales effort. Illustrating this technique is a letter selling Easy-Light barbecue starters to retailers. After building its sales effort, the letter asks for action and then follows the action request with these words:

• Recalling the appeal in the final words emphasizes your main point by position.

. . . and start taking your profits from the fast-selling Easy-Light barbecue starter.

The letter selling the fishing vacation follows its action words with a reminder of the joys described earlier:

It's your reservation for a week of excitement with the fightingest bass in the Southland.

Adding a Postscript.   As sales letters are often written in an informal, breezy style, a postscript (PS) is acceptable. Because it stands alone at the very end, a postscript has a very powerful impact. Be sure that the idea you express in the postscript deserves this special attention. Postscripts effectively used by professionals include the following:

• Postscripts are acceptable and effective.

PS Don't forget! If ever you think that *Action* is not for you, we'll give you every cent of your money back. That's how confident we are that *Action* will become one of your favourite magazines.

PS Hurry! Save while this special limited-time offer lasts.

PS Our little magazine makes a distinctive and appreciated gift for someone on your Christmas list.

A PRACTICE RUN

Suggest improvements in this sales letter. It was distributed to homes in a 10-block vicinity of the home for sale. It included pictures of the realtor, the house, and the real estate company's logo.

Dear Neighbour:

This is the house you need. Great price ($129,900). Great location (10 minutes to downtown, near schools, parks, shopping). Great style (3-level split, detached garage, built 12 years ago).
What are you waiting for? You have to see it. This 3-bedroom has semifinished basement, 5 appliances, and much, much more.

Get on the move!

_____

_____

_____

_____

Using a Second Letter in the Mailing.   A currently popular way of adding strength to the sales effort is to use a second letter (or memorandum) as a part of the mailing. This second letter is usually headed with a boldly displayed message saying something like "Don't read this unless you've decided not to buy," which arouses curiosity. An example of such a message follows.

• A second letter is often a part of the mailing.

Accompanying a letter selling subscriptions to a magazine (*The Western Camper*), this second note reviews the main sales message. As you can see, it is really another sales letter. It even ends with a drive for action, and it has a postscript that intensifies the drive.

CASE ILLUSTRATION   **Sales Letter:** *Using an Emotional Appeal to Sell a Vacation in Mexico for Spring Break*

Throughout this letter, the writer tries to make the reader *feel* the benefits of this trip. Note that the call for action is the first step only. It does not spell out details such as visas and inoculations![1]

SUN 'N FUN TOURS

1935 Dorchester Avenue
MIAMI FLORIDA 33151

January 9, 1998

Ms. Katy Maitre
10033 - 93 Avenue
EDMONTON, AB
T4G 3S8

Dear Katy:

The attention of the reader is drawn away from winter and transferred to a holiday.

You sit back in the deep, plush chair. As the snow and cold disappear below you, you climb 30,000 feet to break into the sunshine above the clouds.

You're on your way! Now, for one whole week, you can stay in the sun. You are only a short trip away from the sun and fun of MEXICO!

The excitement builds.

The fast-paced action and varied alternatives are designed to capture the imagination and build the desire.

Choose from sandy beaches, colorful markets, quiet hills. Try sailing or wind surfing, shopping or exploring. Or join the gang for volleyball on the beach. In the evening, find a quiet lounge or a hot spot that parties till dawn.

Pick your style. Pick your fun. Just $999 includes airfare plus 5 days (4 nights) double occupancy. Make that toll-free call to 1-800-491-6700 and Sun 'N Fun will save your spot in the sun this spring break.

The low cost is a rational appeal. The first step is easy to take.

Rather than using a traditional closing, the writer continues the persuasion.

Break away to Sun 'N Fun in MEXICO!

Michael Panousis
Michael Panousis
Sun 'N Fun Tours

[1]Since this letter has Florida as its origin, and since there is debate over the -or and -our endings in Canada, the American spelling has been retained in this example.

The writer depends on rational appeals to attract a business client. He is concerned to establish the credibility of his plan. He shows that it is thorough, professional, and trusted. This is not a get-rich-quick scheme. No attempt is made to get a commitment from this first contact. The opportunity to explain the plan further is the goal.

Your Restaurant Success

October 24, 1997

Watt's for Dinner
165 Citadel Street
Halifax, NS
B2G 3R5

Attn: Ms. Stephanie Collins

Dear Ms. Collins:

The opening testimonial sets up the appeal of increased profits and begins the writer's strategy to stress credibility.

"Russo is adding $5,000 a year to my restaurant's profits!" says Bill Summers, owner of the most popular seafood restaurant in St. John, New Brunswick. He joins many other restauranteurs who can point to proof in dollars that I can help you earn better profits.

My time-proven plan is a product of 28 years of intensive research, study, and consulting work with restaurants all over Canada. I found that where food costs exceed 40 percent, staggering losses slip through. Then I traced down the causes of these losses. And now I can find these trouble spots in your business—and the increased profit dollars you deserve!

The credibility of the writer is established through his experience and knowledge.

The benefits of the plan are given in detail. The process is not complicated or secret.

To make these extra profits, all you do is send me one month's guest tabs, your bills, and a few other items I'll tell you about later. My proven method of analysis will give you an eye-opening report that will tell you how much money your restaurant should make and how to make it. From the report, you will learn in detail just what items are causing your higher costs. And you will learn how to correct them.

Even your menu will receive thorough treatment. You will know what "best-sellers" are paying their way—what "poor movers" are eating into your profits. All in all, you'll get practical suggestions that will show you how to cut costs, build volume, and pocket a net 10 to 20 percent of sales.

A concrete example shows the thoroughness of the plan and, again, its credibility.

The suggested action is the first step of getting more information to reassure the client. No commitment is required yet.

For more details about this service and its cost, you'll want to read the enclosed information sheet. Then let me prove to you, as I have to so many others, that I can add money to your income this year. Just fill out the enclosed form or give our office a call to have me visit you and personally explain how we can improve your future business. That extra $5,000 or more will make you glad you did!

Sincerely,

A. (Tony) Russo
A. (Tony) Russo
Owner

AR:dg
encls.

125 Main Street

Dartmouth, Nova Scotia   B6G 1E8

* Here is an example of a second letter.

Frankly, I'm puzzled.

I just don't understand why every camper and backpacker in Canada doesn't run—not walk—to the nearest mailbox and return the enclosed FREE BOOK CERTIFICATE.

Here's a guidebook that will bring you better times and better holidays each and every time you head for the big outdoors. PLUS, you get a money-saving bargain on a subscription to THE WESTERN CAMPER. Month after month, you'll be in on all the latest tips on equipment, safety and wilderness hideaways. Each issue has superb photographs of breath-taking Canadian landscape, challenging and calling every adventurer.

And Dave Ellison is there each month telling you about the wildflowers and birds that can be seen nowhere else in Canada. Plus many other articles every month. Over 2,000 outdoor lovers are subscribing now. And the yearly renewal rate is just fantastic!

But those 2,000 aren't important this morning. The person I'm thinking about today is YOU. I want YOU as a new subscriber—because I know you'll find more helpful advice here than in any other publication. Do yourself a favour. Send off your FREE BOOK CERTIFICATE today, while you're thinking about it.

PS: Please hurry! We have only a limited supply of the FREE BOOK. Get yours now!

INTRODUCTORY SITUATION

▶ to Collection Letters

Doreen catered for a local bantam hockey club luncheon. This is a nonprofit organization that does an excellent job with kids. There are many fine people in the organization, and she was pleased to work with them. Although it was a busy day for her, she made some good contacts and hopes to see an increase in the catering side of her business. The drawback to this venture is that, except for the deposit, she hasn't been paid.

Realizing that such organizations often run on a shoestring budget and depend heavily on the goodwill of the community, Doreen feels she should approach the situation on the assumption that they will pay as soon as they can. Her difficulty is that she has had to pay her bills, and she needs their payment to make ends meet this month. Somehow she will have to persuade them that her bill should be the very next one they pay. ▪

The Collection Process

* The typical collection procedure consists of a number of progressively stronger efforts.

* The series resembles a stairway.

When your customers do not pay their bills on time, you must try to collect. The typical collection procedure consists of a series of contacts known as early, middle, and final stages. The middle stage is another opportunity to use persuasive techniques.

In a sense the build-up of collection efforts resembles a stairway (see Figure 9–1). Each step represents a collection effort, and each one is stronger than the last. The first steps are called *early-stage* collection efforts. These are mainly reminders. The assumption at this stage is that the debtors intend to pay and *will* pay; the company need only remind them so that payment is received soon.

* The first contacts are reminder efforts.

In the early stage a statement is sent with the specific due date. If this bill is not paid, a second bill may be sent—maybe a third. For added strength, reminder words such as "Please," "May we remind you," or "Past Due" are added to an overdue bill. These reminders may be in various forms—printed enclosures, stickers, stamped words.

* Next comes a series of persuasive letters.

If the reminders fail to bring in the money, the efforts get stronger. Following the early (will-pay) stage comes the *middle stage* of collection. Here the company's attitude is that debtors have to be convinced they *should* pay. This persuasion stage composes the bulk of most collection series. Typically, telephone calls or letters urging payment are sent. The number of contacts depends on company policy.

* A final letter is direct and commanding.

If all persuasive efforts to collect have failed, a *final stage* ends the collection-letter series. In this stage the debtors have to be convinced that they *must* pay. This last-resort stage consists of just one letter that is very direct and firm. Because this letter is so

FIGURE 9–1 Diagram of the Collection Procedure

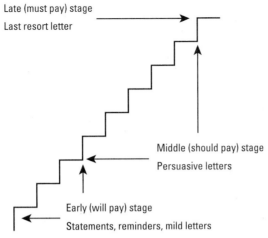

Late (must pay) stage
Last resort letter

Middle (should pay) stage
Persuasive letters

Early (will pay) stage
Statements, reminders, mild letters

Note: The number of steps depends on the policy of the firm.

different from the others, it is treated as a stage in itself. Additional action through collection agencies or the courts may follow.

Using the Telephone to Collect.   As noted previously, the telephone may be used in the collection effort. The companies that use it generally call the debtors after making some unsuccessful mail efforts. Although use of the telephone is time consuming, its users report good results in the middle stage if sound persuasive techniques are used. The telephone is especially effective in cases in which the debtors have good explanations for their delinquency. Such explanations often lead the parties to work out suitable solutions.

• Some companies effectively use the telephone to collect.

Using Computer-Generated Collections.   Most companies use computers in the collection process—to maintain purchase and payment records, to flag delinquent accounts, and to generate appropriate collection letters. Letters can be constructed by selecting standard paragraphs from a "bank" of possibilities written for a variety of situations. Or specific data can be merged into the form letter at designated points. These letters are automatically produced and yet appear to be individually prepared by including personal names and exact amounts owed.

   Since computers have been used as collection tools, a trend toward a shorter collection series and harsher collection letters has been evident. Even so, computer collection policies and procedures can be whatever the company management wants them to be. The wise manager will consider all the possibilities discussed in this chapter.

• Large companies use computers to assist in collections.

Early-Stage Reminder Letters.   As noted previously, the most common early-stage reminders are notes on a bill or statement. If a letter is used, it is a short, direct reminder—sometimes only two or three sentences long. As the account is not long past due, the letter does not need to lecture or persuade. It is written with the assumption that the debtor will pay. Here is an example.

• Such letters remind directly and are short and courteous.

   This is just a friendly reminder that your account with us is now two months past due. No doubt, you just overlooked it. If you're like me, you'll appreciate having the matter called to your attention so that you can bring your account up to date.
   Loren's genuinely appreciates your business. We look forward to serving you again soon.

Middle-Stage Collection Letters.   If your reminders do not collect the money, you will need to write stronger letters to convince debtors that they *should* pay. Here your procedure is to select a basic appeal and then to present this appeal convincingly. That is, you persuade.

• When reminders fail, you should use persuasive letters.

Before the United States had its current postal system, business people placed collection messages in newspapers. The following appeared in the *Norwich* (Conn.) *Packet* in 1779:

BY AUTHORITY

To ALL those who are indebted as a subscriber for Newspapers, whose accounts are one or more years' standing—without even regarding the fashionable substitutes for payment, of IF's, AND's, & WAIT a few Days, VERILY, VERILY, I say unto you, that I have lately had loud and repeated calls for CASH!

Therefore, Nevertheless, Notwithstanding—I now inform all, great or small, young or old, rich or poor, male or female, that are indebted to me for the *Norwich Packet* that I must and will have my due, for this reason: "The Paper makers threaten the Printers, and the Printers threaten the Post." What is to be done? What steps can be taken! All debts must be paid, and I must pay mine;—of course you must pay me, before the expiration of one month from this date, if you wish to keep your accounts out of the hands of an Attorney.

Beriah Hartshorn
Franklin, August 1, 1779

• Debtors do not receive such letters favourably.

As in other cases requiring persuasion, the delinquent customers' wishes run contrary to yours. You want them to pay. They have shown by ignoring your reminders that at best they are not eager to pay. More than likely, they do not want to hear from you at all. In such situations you must gain reader attention at the beginning. If you do not, the odds of getting your message across are slim.

• Select an appeal from these categories: pride, ethics, self-interest, closure, fear.

Analyzing the Strategy. As in other persuasion cases, when persuading debtors to pay, you should begin by looking at the situation as the readers see it. Then you should select appeals that will work with your particular readers. Although the available appeals are varied and may be applied with overlapping variations, they generally fall into the following categories:

Pride. Appeals to pride play on the readers' concern for themselves (self-respect) and for what others think of them (social acceptance).

Ethics. Strategies based on the readers' moral standards fall into this category. The category includes appeals relating to honour, character, integrity, and sense of fair play. In a way it includes all appeals of doing "what is right."

Self-Interest. Persuasion stressing the benefits of keeping a good credit reputation is an illustration of self-interest appeals. Such appeals emphasize the practical benefits of continued credit buying to the consumer. The appeal may be made positively by showing the advantages of having credit, or negatively by stressing the disadvantages of a poor credit rating. These disadvantages might include higher interest rates, lower credit limits, or loss of credit privileges. The person with a good credit record is likely to respond to this appeal.

Fear. In a sense appeals to fear are the negative side of appeals to self-interest. Such appeals stress avoiding the bad things that may result from nonpayment—the consequences of having legal action taken, of being reported to a credit bureau, or of having the account turned over to a collection agency. Among those consequences would be the embarrassment of having a bad credit reputation, the disadvantages of being unable to buy on credit, and the added expense of being involved in legal action.

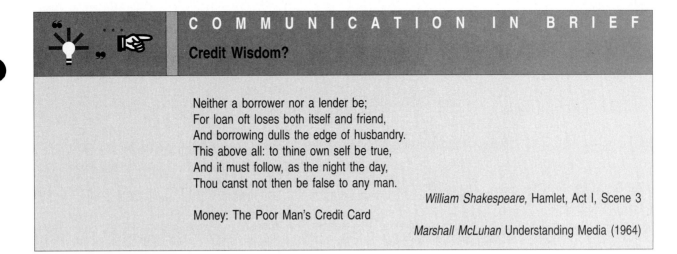

After selecting your appeal, you should develop it by thinking out the reasoning that will convince the debtor to pay. If, for example, you selected the fair-play appeal, you might build a case showing why the debtor should keep his or her end of the bargain. You would go through similar strategies with the other appeals.

• Then develop the appeal to fit the debtor.

How strong you make your appeal depends on how far along in the collection effort you are. Usually, your first persuasion letter is mild and has much goodwill content. The letters that follow get stronger, and their goodwill content decreases. The following detailed description will help you apply the general persuasive plan to these letters.

• Succeeding letters get stronger as goodwill decreases.

Gaining Attention in the Opening.   As your readers have received your reminders, they know that they owe you. More than likely, most of them intend to pay when they find it convenient. If you want them to read this letter rather than throw it away, you must catch their attention immediately. You will need to find some interesting opening words to set up your basic appeal. Some of the many possibilities are demonstrated here.

• The opening should gain attention and set up the strategy.

How are you and your Arctic air-conditioning system making it through these hot summer months?

This opening works on the reader's conscience through a friendly question. The appeal it sets up is that of fair play—of persuading the reader to carry out his or her end of a bargain for goods now being enjoyed. In addition, it is a reminder that being without the air conditioner would be uncomfortable. Payment is the way to keep it.

How would you write to a good friend on an embarrassing subject?

This question is personal and interesting. The appeal it sets up is that of the reader's moral obligation to a friend. The persuasion will build on the need to resolve a situation that could hurt the relationship.

When they ask about you, what should we tell them?

This opening makes the reader want to learn more. Just what is going to be said? How bad is the situation? The appeal of this letter, written late in the collection series, is the danger of losing a good credit reputation.

Persuasively Presenting the Appeal.   Because the opening has set up the appeal, the shift in thought at this point should be smooth. You study the appeal for its you-viewpoint possibilities and then present it adapting to your reader's point of view. The technique is

• Presentation of the appeal comes next.

"What would your neighbours think if we repossessed your car?" the collection letter read.

"I have taken the matter up with them," the delinquent debtor responded. "They think it would be a lousy trick."

Crotchety Mr. Crump received the following collection message from the big-city department store: "We are surprised that we haven't received any money from you."

The gentleman responded, "No need to be surprised. I haven't sent any."

A retailer ordered a large number of refrigerators before paying for the last order. The manufacturer responded with a collection message saying that the goods could not be sent until payment was made for the last order.

"Unable to wait so long," the retailer replied. "Cancel order."

The collection letter was terse: "Please remit the amount you owe us right away."

The response was quick and equally terse: "The amount we owe you is $145.20."

---

much like that of selling. You have searched for reasoning that will move your reader to take the action you want taken. You try to show the advantages to be received from taking it. And you present it all in carefully selected language that will convince.

* Use the right strength for this stage of collection. But keep the tone positive.

In this part your words should carry just the right degree of force for the case. Early in the collection series, the facts of the case usually call for mild persuasion. The further along the collection series you progress, the more forceful you can afford to be. However, take care not to insult, talk down, lecture, or show anger. As we have noted in other situations, an angry reader tends to resist, and resistance leads to failure. Instead, keep in mind that you hope to collect, to maintain cordial relations, and perhaps even to continue business with the debtor.

* End with a clear request for payment.

Closing with a Request for Payment.   After you have made your persuasive appeal, the logical follow-up is to ask for the specific amount in payment. Do not merely hint at payment; state it directly. "Please write a cheque for $77.88 today and mail this first payment to us right away" meets this requirement. "We would appreciate your cheque for $77.88" does not.

In collection letters, as in other persuasive letters, a closing reminder of a benefit resulting from the action strengthens the appeal. For example, a letter stressing the advantages of a prompt-pay record for a business could end with these words:

Will you please mail a cheque for $275.30 right now while you're thinking about it? It's your best insurance for keeping your invaluable prompt-pay record.

* Gradual build-up of strength is evident in the following series.

Build-Up of Appeal in a Good Middle-Stage Series.   Here are examples from a middle-stage collection series. Although each letter contains stronger persuasion than the preceding one, no anger or lecturing tone is evident. The words are calm and reasonable throughout the series.

The first letter begins with an interesting question. The you-viewpoint of the question gives it extra attention value. The letter then moves into a presentation of the fair-play appeal, which it develops skillfully. The writing is strong yet positive. The closing request for money flows logically from the persuasion. Notice how the suggestion of urgency strengthens the request.

Dear Mr. Benoit:

How would you write to a good friend about an embarrassing subject? That's the question we must answer now. You see, you are that friend, and the subject is your overdue account.

As you recall, some time ago you wanted {the item is named}, and we were happy to let you have it simply on your promise to pay 30 days later. Now, since your account is 60 days past due, it's only fair that you should fulfil your end of the agreement right away.

Please send us your cheque for $1,247.81?

Sincerely,

• Good use of the fair-play appeal is shown here.

The second letter begins with an attention-gaining exclamation. The opening words set up an appeal to the reader's pride in having a prompt-pay record. Then the letter develops the appeal convincingly. The request for money logically follows the appeal. The final words link the action with the reward it will bring the reader.

Dear Mr. Benoit:

You don't belong in that group!

Every day Loren's deals with hundreds of charge customers. More than 99 percent of them come through with their obligations to pay. We mark them as "prompt pay," and the doors to credit buying are opened to them all over town. Less than 1 percent don't pay right away. Of course, they sometimes have good reasons, and most of them explain their reasons to us. Then we work something out. But a few allow their good credit records to tarnish.

Somehow, you have permitted your name to be placed in this last group. We don't think it belongs there. Won't you please remove it by writing us a cheque for $1,247.81, now 75 days past due? This would place you in the group in which you belong.

Sincerely,

• This letter skillfully uses an appeal to pride.

The opening question in the third letter is likely to make anyone take notice. The explanation is more negative than in the preceding letters. For the first time in the series, the consequences of not paying are given more space than the advantages of paying. To keep the positive tone, the letter shows that paying can avoid those negative consequences. The final words link the action with a benefit it will give the reader.

Dear Mr. Benoit:

What should we report about you?

As you may know, all members of the Capital Credit Bureau must report their long-past-due accounts for distribution to the members. At the moment, your own account hangs in the balance. And we are wondering whether we will be forced to report it. We are concerned because what we must say will mean so much to you personally.

A slow-pay record would just about ruin the good credit reputation you have built over the years. You wouldn't find it easy to buy on credit from Capital Bureau members (and this includes just about every credit granting business in town). Your credit privileges would probably be cut off completely. It would take you long years to regain the good reputation you now enjoy.

So won't you please avoid all this by mailing a cheque for $1,247.81, now 90 days past due? It would stop the bad report and save your credit record.

Sincerely,

• Frankness and conviction make this letter effective.

Final-Stage Collection Letters (Last-Resort). Some debtors will ignore your most persuasive collection efforts. Because you cannot continue indefinitely, you will need to take last-resort action with these people. You will use the final letter in the collection series to inform them of this action.

• Collection series end with a final (last-resort) letter.

A number of last-resort actions are common. One is to report the account to some credit interchange group, such as a local credit bureau. Another is to sell the account to a collection agency empowered with full authority to take legal steps if necessary. Yet another is to take the delinquent to court. The decision is based on the customs in your field of business, the cost, the nature of the account, and the image of your firm.

- They outline some last-resort action (reporting to credit bureau, taking to court).

Justifying Directness.
Up to this point, you have tried the milder methods. As they have not worked, you must now do something stronger. As you learned earlier, directness produces strength. You did not use it through the middle stage of the series because directness in such cases can destroy goodwill, and until now you have wanted to save the account. But now you are more interested in collecting the money. Thus, you can justify the use of a direct plan for writing the last-resort letter.

- As the direct order adds strength, it is justified for last-resort letters.

Presenting the Action Directly.
You begin the last-resort letter with a clear statement of what you are going to do. Such direct openings are strong, and they gain attention. You might consider bringing in facts that justify the action. Although the reader probably knows these facts very well, mentioning them may prevent a defensive reaction. Something like this would do the job:

- Begin the letter with a statement of the intended action. It is good to justify the action.

The outstanding balance of $378.40, now seven months past due on your account, leaves us no choice but to report your case to the Capital Credit Bureau.

Interpreting the Action.
Your explanation of the effects of the action on the debtor comes next. This is your last effort to persuade. In developing the persuasion, you should place yourself in the reader's position to see how last-resort action will affect him or her. It may, for example, mean the end of credit buying, court costs, loss of prestige, or personal embarrassment. Rather than showing anger, let your words show concern for the debtor's problem. You wish things had not turned out this way, but the debtor's actions leave you no choice.

- Then explain the effects of the action on the debtor. Use you-viewpoint.

Offering a Last Chance in the Closing.
After describing the effects of the last-resort action, you should give the debtor a last chance to pay. Thus, your closing should set a deadline for payment or perhaps for other arrangements. You should urge the debtor to meet this deadline. As in other persuasive efforts, your final words might well recall what the debtor will gain (or avoid) by paying. The following closing meets these requirements well:

- In the closing offer a deadline for paying before action is taken.

We will report your case to the Capital Credit Bureau on March 15. You can help yourself by sending us your cheque for $378.40 before that date. It's the one way you can save your credit reputation.

Strength in a Firm Call for Payment.
This letter gets right down to business with a clear statement of the action that will be taken. Then it moves into a convincing interpretation of this action. Notice the you-viewpoint—how the words emphasize the effects on the reader. Although the message is negative, the overall tone is wholesome. There is no evidence of anger. The closing, a final recall of the disadvantages of not paying, leaves the action in the reader's hands. The letter's calmness and convincing persuasion are likely to get results.

- Following is an example of a good last-resort letter.

Dear Mr. Benoit:

Your failure to respond to our previous attempts to collect your 120 days overdue account of $1,247.81 leaves us no choice but to turn your account over to the Capital Credit Bureau for collection. This is an action we had hoped not to take, for it is unpleasant for both of us—particularly for you. For you it means that you would be forced by the courts to pay the amount of your bill plus legal costs. In addition to being expensive, legal action may be embarrassing to you. Also, your credit record could be permanently injured.

- This letter is strong, yet shows concern.

Both of us want to avoid these bad effects of legal action. We'll do our part by holding off action for ten days until June 4, 1997. To do your part, you must pay us the amount shown below before that date. It's all up to you; only you can save your credit record and the embarrassment of legal action.

Sincerely,

. . . .

A SUMMARY OF LEARNING OUTCOMES FROM THIS CHAPTER

Requests that are likely to be resisted require an indirect approach and a persuasive strategy. Your opening words should set up this strategy and gain the reader's attention. Your convincing persuasion follows. Appeals fall into two broad groups: emotional and rational. Emotional appeals focus on the senses and feelings. Rational appeals are factual and logical. With your reader convinced, you make your request clearly yet positively. You can end with the request, or you can follow it with one more point of persuasion—whichever you think is more appropriate for the given case.

Sales letters are a special type of persuasive request. Typically, a sales mailing contains a number of pieces such as brochures, leaflets, and coupons, with the sales letter as the major item.

You begin work on a sales letter by studying the product or service to be sold. You also study your audience to be able to select the most suitable appeals. Your major goals in the opening of the sales letter are to gain attention and set up the strategy. Next you present the sales message you have decided to use. Throughout the sales presentation, you use good sales language and emphasize the you-viewpoint. When you have completed your sales message, you drive for the sale. You might use a direct question or a stronger command. In any event, your drive for action should be specific and clear.

Collection letters are usually sent in a series, beginning with a simple reminder letter. Next come persuasive letters. The series ends with a last-resort letter. How many letters are used in a series varies. Exclusive shops, for example, would be likely to use a longer, slower series than that used by discount stores. Increased use of computer billings appears to have led to shorter collection efforts and harsher collection letters.

You should begin a collection series on the assumption that the reader will pay. So you write a short, courteous reminder of the past-due bill. Such letters are typically direct and filled with appropriate goodwill talk.

You should write the middle-stage letters on the assumption that the reader *should* pay. Thus, you must persuade. You begin them with attention-gaining words that also set up your strategy. Then you present the appeal convincingly, taking care to use the right strength for the collection stage involved. You would do well to keep the tone wholesome and friendly. You end the middle-stage letters with a request for payment, perhaps linking payment with a benefit to be gained by paying.

If your build-up of middle-stage collection letters fails, you write a final letter. You begin by selecting a last-resort action (reporting to a credit bureau, going to court). Then you write the letter in the direct order because directness adds strength. Your first words tell what action you have decided to take. Then, showing concern rather than anger, you present the effects of this action on the reader in convincing words. You close the letter with a last-chance deadline for paying before you take the specified action.

ANSWERS TO PRACTICE RUNS

▶ You-Viewpoint

Matter-of-Fact Statements

We make Aristocrat hosiery in three colours.

The Regal laptop weighs only 1.8 kilograms. It is light and easy to pack.

Lime-Fizz tastes fresh and exciting.

Baker's Dozen is packaged in a rectangular box with a bright, bulls-eye design.

You-Viewpoint Statements

With Aristocrat hosiery, you have your choice of three lovely shades.

Now you can own a laptop that's *truly* portable! Your Regal will add only 1.8 kilograms to your luggage.

Enjoy the fresh, exciting taste of Lime-Fizz today!

Baker's Dozen's new rectangular package fits neatly in your cupboard. Its bright, bulls-eye design is easy to find on your grocer's shelf.

▶ Positive Tone

For Improvement

Reorganization under Plan A will take three months and cost $500,000. Although it will cost less, Plan B will take twice as long to complete.

Don't forget to mail in your order card.

No one has fewer shipping delays.

Positive

Reorganization under Plan A will be completed in only three months at a cost of $500,000. Although Plan B will take six months, it will cost less.

Mail in your order card today!

We have the best record for on-time deliveries.

▶ Rational and Emotional Appeals

Some suggestions are
To attract people to an alcohol-free, family-oriented First Night entertainment for New Year's Eve.
Rational: reasonable cost, children attend (no babysitting), alcohol-free
Emotional: fun, family time, safe

To encourage students to run for office on your student council.
Rational: importance of good officers, opportunity to learn and develop skills, duty
Emotional: résumé material, fun, networking, prestige

To work one day a month without pay, with a promise of no further layoffs for six months.
Rational: an equal share, fair to all, a necessity
Emotional: job security, standing together as a team

▶ Sales Letter

Answers will vary greatly. Some weak points that should be improved are listed here.

1. The letter lacks focus. Is the purpose to have the reader visit the house (You have to see it), or to move (Get on the move)?
2. The opening and closing sentences are presumptuous and aggressive rather than persuasive.

3. The appeal is mainly rational, describing price, style, age, etc., but without enough detail to be persuasive. Most detail is given on the location which the readers will already know about since they all live within 10 blocks.
4. More emotional appeal is needed. For example, use *home* instead of *house*. The use of descriptive adjectives such as *lovely, new, spacious,* or *cozy.*

QUESTIONS FOR DISCUSSION

1. Explain why a persuasive request letter is usually written in the indirect order. Could the direct order ever be used for such letters? Discuss.

2. What is the role of the you-viewpoint in persuasive request letters?

3. Discuss the relationship between a persuasive request letter and a sales letter.

4. What appeals would be appropriate for the following products when they are being sold to consumers?

    a. Shaving cream
    b. Home repair tools
    c. Fresh vegetables
    d. Calculators
    e. Lubricating oil
    f. Music lessons
    g. Perfume
    h. Fancy candy
    i. Hiking boots
    j. Upgrading courses

5. Should the traditional sales-letter organization discussed in the text ever be altered? Discuss.

6. Most early-stage collections (first reminders) are written in the direct order. Middle-stage letters tend to be written in the indirect order. Why?

7. If the last-resort collection letter is the strongest in the series and, therefore, the most likely to bring in the money, why not use it earlier?

8. Discuss the role of negative and positive wording and the you-viewpoint through the three stages of a collection series.

CASE 9-1

Kim: I hate these pictures of suffering and starving kids. Why do they have to show all that? Why do they describe this awful stuff in such detail? It's horrible!

Chris: That's just it. They want people to feel how horrible it is for those kids.

Kim: Well, frankly, I'd rather not feel it. It just upsets me.

Chris: Maybe they think they have to be descriptive or it wouldn't seem real to people here. People might not believe how bad the situation is for some kids.

Kim: Well, just tell me that and cut out the depressing stuff. I can understand that people need help. I can understand that a donation will help. That just makes sense.

Chris: And have you done something to help?

1. What type of appeal is used by aid organizations? How effective is it?

2. What need has been created in Kim? What do the aid organizations suggest for a solution to Kim's need?

3. What other appeals would work? How effective would each be?

LETTER PROBLEMS

▶Persuasive Requests

1. Last month, you were elected president of the local chapter of the Friends of the S.P.C.A., an organization devoted to bettering the lives of your animal friends. You were pleased because you believe in the organization's goals. Your role as president will help build good public relations for your own company.

   At your first meeting of the society's board of directors, the board decided to attempt something new in this year's fund-raising. The society will seek corporate donations by persuading each company to match the donations of its employees.

   Your job is to write a persuasive letter to the company heads asking them to participate in the plan. Participation means assisting in contacting their employees (you will supply the posters, brochures, and letters to be used for this purpose) and then matching dollar for dollar the money that the employees contribute.

   As you plan your letter, you think of possible persuasive strategies. Will you appeal to humane concerns about animal suffering? Can assisting in this campaign yield business benefits? You will think through the situation carefully, arriving at the best possible strategy for this campaign. Address the letter to any of the company heads on your list.

2. Last week a tragedy occurred at the Electro-Tech (Canada) annual picnic. Billy Proden drowned after saving the lives of two children who had fallen from a boat. Billy's efforts received the praise of newspapers throughout the nation as truly heroic.

   Billy left a wife and two children, aged 10 and 12. He had only a little insurance. Although his widow is working, the future of the Proden family is not bright. In a few years, the children, who have already demonstrated signs of academic brilliance, will be ready for university. There is not likely to be enough money for that.

   Because many Electro-Tech employees were concerned, a group approached management with an idea. It proposed to start a college fund for the Proden children with donations from Electro-Tech employees. Electro-Tech's management responded with a better plan; the company will double the amount donated by employees.

   You, a member of the employee group, were asked to prepare the letter that will be sent to the employees. It will be signed jointly by the company president and the chairperson of the employee group. You want the letter to be the very best persuasive message that you can create. Before writing anything, you will think through the facts carefully, looking for the plan that is most likely to motivate the employees to give money. (If you need additional facts, you may supply them as long as they are consistent with those that have been given.)

3. You are organizing an investment club in response to the appeal of a small group of employees at Central Foods. The goals of the club will be (1) to make money for its members and (2) to assist its members in learning about investing. Membership will be open to any interested employee. Members must invest at least $25 per month and will share in the club's assets on a basis proportionate to their investment. The club will meet monthly to discuss investment possibilities and will make its investment decisions by majority vote. Dr. Marlon McBain, a finance professor at Brandon University, has agreed to serve as the club's advisor without compensation, and Phil Pinnock, the company attorney, has agreed to help work up the club's charter.

To invest effectively, the club will need a large number of members. You will have to send a persuasive letter to the homes of all 457 employees of Central Foods. What appeals are likely to prompt employees to join the club? Should the appeal be to retirement security? To learning about investments? To the reduced risk of pooled investing? To saving taxes? Write a letter designed to persuade employees to join the club and attend the organizational meeting (tell them when and where).

4. A few days ago the management at Goliath Chemical approved a proposal to pay the tuition for all qualified employees who enrol in the M.B.A. (Master of Business Administration) program offered on weekends by the University of Niagara. Forty-three employees appear to be eligible for admission to graduate study. To launch the program, management wants at least ten to enrol.

The task of writing a personalized letter encouraging participation has fallen on your desk in staff training and development. Although you know you'll cover the value of an M.B.A. to job performance and advancement, you want to focus first on the required admissions test. The test will be given on the 12th of next month, and applications to take it must be submitted by next Friday (the forms are in your office). If you can get people to take the first step and write this test, you feel your job of persuading them to take the M.B.A. will be much easier.

Your letter need not say much about the details of the courses, since this information is provided in a brochure that you will enclose. You will refer to the brochure to build interest; however, you don't want to push for a decision about the program yet. Develop the best, most persuasive strategy to get people started with the admissions test.

5. Two months ago, Petro-Plus Energy Company decided to sponsor a fitness program for the company's 715 home-plant employees. You volunteered to help because of your personal commitment to health and fitness.

You began by calling the YMCA who were very helpful indeed. The Y will permit Petro-Plus employees to use the gymnasium, swimming pool, track, tennis and racquetball courts, and weight rooms from 6:30 to 8:30 A.M. every day for the modest charge of $10 per month per participant. This is the only charge that the participants will pay.

Now that you have the facilities and a program, you must convince the employees that they should enrol. You will do this by means of a persuasive letter. In the letter you will announce the program and try to sell it to the employees. In addition to describing the choice of activities, you will use whatever strategy you think will help get people out early in the morning. Don't forget to tell them how to enrol (you may determine the specifics).

6. As an administrative assistant at Chem-Co, Inc., a major chemicals manufacturer, you have a problem. Each month, you collect operating reports from the managers of the company's seven plants around the country. You edit them, consolidate them, analyze them, and then write a final report that ends up in the hands of the president, T. H. Chandler. Mr. Chandler wants your final report on the third working day of the month.

To date you have managed to submit the final report on time every month, but it has been getting increasingly difficult to do so. Some of the seven plant managers are slow. Last month, for example, you got the last plant manager's report on the morning your final report was due. You had a frantic time getting your work done, and you couldn't do your best on it.

You must do something to correct the situation. The plant managers' reports must be in your hands by the first working day of the month—without fail. You know that you are not in a position to demand, for you do not have authority over the plant managers. But you know them all fairly well, and you know them to be reasonable and caring people. Develop a letter that will persuade them to get their reports in on time.

▶Sales

7. Write a letter selling a packaged winter vacation at Club Sun and Sand, a resort in Pirate's Bay, Florida. You will write to business executives and professionals in the Northeastern United States and Eastern Canada.

You'll stress the warm winter weather, of course, with swimming, relaxing on sandy beaches, sailing, and deep-sea fishing. In addition, you'll describe the special facilities at the club: an 18-hole golf course, tennis courts, a swimming pool with hot tub, and six miles of scenic hiking trails. There are two restaurants—the Pirate's Den (restaurant and lounge) and, for gourmet dining, the Captain's Table.

The club's lodge has 112 luxury rooms, all with two king-size beds, outside balconies, and spectacular views. For those wanting more room, there are 22 cottages, each with two bedrooms, two baths, and a combination kitchen, dining, and living area.

From January to March, you are offering special rates for a seven-day, six-night vacation (arrival Sunday, departure

Saturday). Double occupancy in the lodge is $360 per person. A cottage is $400 per person if occupied by two, $300 per person for three or more. Half price is charged for children under 12 who are accompanied by an adult.

All this information and much more about Club Sun and Sand may be found in the descriptive brochure that you will enclose, so you will not need to tell everything in the letter. Your goal will be to describe the physical comfort and enjoyment offered by Club Sun and Sand in a way that will make people who are experiencing cold weather want to go there.

8. You are the manager of the Stephanie Samuels Swimming Camp. The coach of two Olympic gold medal winners, Stephanie is using her record of success to attract girls aged 10 to 16 to her second summer swimming camp.

Swimming instruction with Stephanie serving as the head instructor will be the primary activity at the camp. For six hours each day, the girls who attend the camp will receive instruction in classes for swimmers from intermediate to expert. (Beginners will not be admitted.) The instruction will cover all the strokes recognized in swimming competition. All the participants will work hard, and only girls committed to improving their swimming should attend.

Although the girls will be too tired for many additional activities, there will be some. Two hours each day will be reserved for rest and leisure. Girls who have not used up all their energy in swimming may participate in organized games (softball, volleyball, or whatever the group prefers).

The girls will be housed in Mabrey Hall, a girl's dormitory not used by the university in the summer. They will be assigned two to a room and will eat in the dormitory dining room. The food will be nutritious and delicious, prepared under the direction of sports nutritionist Pauline O'Day. At all times the girls will be under the watchful eyes of the camp staff who will live in the dormitory with them. Each camp session will begin on a Sunday afternoon and end after the noon meal the following Saturday.

The girls are responsible for their own transportation. The total cost of one session is $385. Those who attend more than one session are charged $300 for each additional session. Each of the 10 sessions scheduled for this summer is limited to 40 girls on a first-come, first-served basis. Early enrolment is encouraged.

Your mailing list consists of swimmers participating in various club and school meets in the surrounding 500-mile area. You have deleted the names of all girls who attended last year (a special letter goes to them). Select the strategy that will effectively promote the Stephanie Samuels Swimming Camp. With the letter you'll include a registration form which is to be returned with payment in advance.

9. Assume the role of marketing manager for a major professional sports team (football, hockey, baseball, or your choice). At the moment you are concerned about season-ticket sales for the coming season. They are well below sales for previous years, and you intend to do something about it.

One thing you will do is write a letter to the people who bought season tickets last year but not this year. As you have their addresses, you feel that a good sales letter might be an effective way of reaching a proven group of season-ticket buyers.

You will begin your work on the letter by thinking through why so many people didn't renew their season tickets. Was it the team performance? The local economic situation? The price of tickets? Attitudes toward team members? You'll explore all the possible reasons. When you have completed this task, you'll think about what you can say to counter these reasons. In other words, you'll develop the best possible strategy for getting these people back in the fold. In addition, you'll do what you can to get them excited about the coming season. Even if you don't sell them season tickets, perhaps the interest you kindle will bring them to some of the games.

Consider what enclosures will accompany your letter. As for prices and other information concerning tickets, use actual information about the team you have selected. Address the letter to the first person on your list, Doris Abraham.

10. The North Atlantic Lobster Company has hired Mail Marketers to write a direct-mail letter. The letter will be designed to sell live Nova Scotia lobsters as business gifts to business executives. As lobsters delivered live to distant places are expensive, the mailing list will comprise a highly select group of business executives.

The North Atlantic Lobster Company plans to sell its products in two basic packages. One is the Gourmet Kit, which includes two live lobsters (about 1 ½ pounds each) packed in a traditional black-enamelled cooking pot, with moist seaweed and reusable ice pack. It also includes cooking instructions, two sets of shell crackers, picks, and bibs. The second package is the Super Kit, which includes lobsters, instructions, shell crackers, picks, and bibs. The Gourmet Kit sells for $79.95, the Super Kit for $44.95.

The gift procedure works like this. The purchaser of these kits sends the North Atlantic Lobster Company the names and addresses for the people who are to receive them. North Atlantic sends each recipient a card announcing the good news and giving the recipient North Atlantic's toll-free telephone number. The recipient works out a convenient delivery time with North Atlantic, which sends the kit by courier. The lobsters will arrive live and fresh.

Now you will begin your efforts to sell lobsters by mail. You will think about how to present your sales message—how to gain attention, what appeals to use, and how to press for action. When you have completed your thinking and developed your strategy, you will write the letter.

11. When you got the exclusive dealership for Home Sentry burglar alarms, you were optimistic. You had visions of the public beating a path to your door. It didn't turn out that way. Instead, sales have been so slow that you are making extra sales efforts. Among those efforts is a direct-mail campaign.

Using the Home Sentry brochure as an enclosure, your mailing will feature a sales letter. The letter will develop a protect-your-home-from-burglars appeal. It will bring out the main features of Home Sentry described in the brochure. Your summary notes of these features are as follows:

- A Home Sentry unit can be set to prevent false alarms by allowing for exit and entry time delays.
- Once activated, the unit immediately activates an outlet. Thus, by placing a lamp in this outlet, one can have 15 seconds to turn the unit off before the alarm sounds. An intruder, of course, would be surprised by the sudden appearance of the light.
- After the 15 seconds have elapsed, a 95-decibel alarm sounds.
- One could also attach an outside alarm or other electrical device to the activated outlet—up to 300 watts.
- The alarm can be tailored to one's specifications—from very loud to soft.
- After the alarm has been activated and cut off, it automatically resets. It is ready to protect the home again.
- The alarm can be set at any traffic point in the house—near doors, windows, hallways. Made in a handsome wood-grain vinyl cabinet, the Home Sentry appears to be a part of the home furnishings.
- The selling price is $219.95, well under the price of most security systems.

You'll enclose an easy-to-check order form. Because you believe in Home Sentry, you'll sell it on a 30-day trial basis. You'll accept credit card sales. Address the letter to a person from your mailing list of middle- and upper-income people in the area.

12. As sales promotion manager of the Megadome, Metro city's new domed stadium, you must develop a sales letter that will persuade people in the area to rent or purchase the unsold 38 Skylight boxes. These elegant viewing areas are too highly priced for most individual sports fans, so your letter will be directed toward the big corporations in the area. The boxes should appeal to businesses that want to entertain special customers or friends in an exciting yet refined and luxurious atmosphere.

Here are more details you'll need: A Skylight box rents for $30,000 a year and sells for $350,000. Most businesses can charge the rental or purchase price as an expense. The interior of the boxes is furnished in deep red and blue decor—thick wall-to-wall carpets, blue walls, reclining chairs, and such. Each box contains a built-in bar and a large-screen, colour monitor. The front of the boxes overlooks the playing area and provides the best seats in the house for all events. Each box seats 12 people comfortably. Box patrons may order food ranging from snacks to full-course meals from the special kitchen that serves the boxes during activities. (You may assume that a major football, hockey, and baseball team will play all home games in the Megadome and that boxing, concerts, and other activities will be scheduled there from time to time.)

Your letter will present the Skylight boxes in terms that your special readers will appreciate. Your goal is to make them want this very expensive item enough to pay a high price for it. You'll include a descriptive brochure and a list of some of the other corporations who already have boxes. Mail the letter to any person on your mailing list.

13. As a free-lance writer of direct-mail copy, write a letter for _____ Trust Company [your choice]. The letter will have the goal of inducing people who have recently moved to town to do their banking with this financial institution.

Because you need to know your product before you can sell it, you will first learn things about this trust company—such things as the advantages it can offer, the services it provides, and the security of its investments. You may also include friendliness of personnel; convenient hours and locations; R.R.S.P. and investment services; C.I.D.C. insurance; availability of safety-deposit boxes, traveller's cheques, and low-cost loans; highly trained, understanding loan officers; and so on. Then you'll arrange this information strategically and present it convincingly for a new customer. You'll also enclose a special brochure about the financial planning services you offer. Address the letter to the first person on your list, Ms. Hermina Walzel.

· ·

▶Collections

These problems are arranged by series. The stage in the series is identified at the beginning of each problem.

The Esquire Limited Series

14. Esquire Limited, an exclusive gentlemen's clothing store, has served the high-income buyers of your community for two years. So far, business has been good, and credit sales have been especially good. But recently, to your disappointment, you find that some gentlemen are slow to pay.

You have decided on the following collection plan. (*Early stage*) First, you will send a statement when the payment is due. The month after that, (when the bill is 30 days past due) you will send a statement with a printed reminder. If this reminder does not bring in the money, you will send a first-reminder form letter a month later (60 days past due). The reminder letter will follow a "knowing you have been very busy, we thought you'd appreciate a reminder" theme.

(*Middle stage*) If the first letter doesn't do the job, Esquire will send a second form letter (90 days past due). This one will get down to collection talk, but it will take a positive approach appealing to the rewards of keeping an impeccable credit record. Write this letter. Make some provisions for mentioning the amount owed and the time past due.

15. (*Middle stage continued*) Your collection plan for Esquire is to write a third letter 30 days later and a fourth after another 30 days (5 months overdue). By this time, a stronger appeal is in order. In this fourth letter, you will stress fair play and make strong reference to the amount owed and the time past due. Write this fourth letter.

16. Fifteen days after the fourth letter in the Esquire series comes another persuasive letter. This one talks rather directly about the advantages of maintaining a good credit record, and asks for the money with some force. If it doesn't work in another 15 days, at six months past due, a last-resort letter is sent.

    (*Last resort*) Because Esquire doesn't want the negative publicity associated with forced collection, it sells its long-overdue accounts to the City Collection Agency who has authorization to take legal action. The last letter warns of this impending action with courteous directness. It urges the reader to pay within 15 days and avoid unpleasant consequences. Write this last letter.

Thelma A. Kennedy, D.D.S., Series

17. Assume that Dr. Thelma Kennedy, a friend of yours, has asked you to help her with her collections. Thelma sends bills to her dental patients at the end of each month. And she continues to send bills for months. Before she writes off an account as uncollectable, she turns it over to a collection agency. After discussing the matter with you, Dr. Kennedy agrees that she might improve her collection procedure and asks you to prepare a series of collection letters for her.

    (*Early stage*) The procedure begins with the usual billing on the due date. If payment is not received, a second bill is sent on the first of the following month. Stamped on the bill is a reminder: "Perhaps you have just overlooked this past-due account." If this effort does not bring in the money, a month later a letter is sent. It is short—a courteous, direct reminder of the past-due bill. It encourages the debtor to contact the office if there are extenuating circumstances. Write this letter.

18. (*Middle stage*) If the first letter doesn't work, another month later a persuasive letter is sent. This letter stresses the fair-play appeal—Dr. Kennedy did something for the reader, so isn't it only fair that the reader would now do something for Dr. Kennedy? A partial payment is required with the possibility of a payment schedule. In spite of its strong persuasion, the letter is courteous and positive. Your assignment is to write it.

19. (*Middle stage*) If payment has not been made three weeks after the fair-play letter was mailed, a stronger middle-stage letter is sent. This one appeals to pride, emphasizing the integrity and honour involved in credit dealings. It is more persuasive than the preceding letter, but it does not talk about the negative consequences of not paying.

    After three more weeks of nonpayment, another letter is sent. This last middle-stage effort talks about the value of a good credit record and about the negative effects of losing a good credit reputation. Even though it is strongly persuasive and contains some negative reasoning, the letter is courteous. Write it.

20. (*Last resort*) Dr. Kennedy's collection series ends with a last-resort letter. This letter directly states that unless payment is received in 10 days, Dr. Kennedy will turn the account over to the City Collection Agency, with full powers to take legal action. Although the letter explains the consequences of this action in strong language, it also shows concern for the reader's predicament. Write this final letter.

Best Deal Furniture and Appliance Company Series

21. Best Deal Furniture and Appliance Company is a low-price, high-volume operation catering primarily to low- and middle-income families. It allows purchases to be charged on a selective basis. But because of the limited incomes of its customers, it maintains a vigorous collection procedure. (*Early stage*) If regular payments are not made each month, it sends the next statement with a printed reminder. (*Middle stage*) If this does not do the job, it sends a persuasive form letter. By most standards, this letter, which talks rather directly about the importance and value of maintaining a good credit reputation, would be classified as middle stage. Write the letter.

22. (*Middle stage continued*) If Best Deal's first letter doesn't bring the minimum, the store sends a second persuasive form letter. This letter talks rather directly and negatively about the consequences of late payments. It warns of rising carrying charges and of the danger of losing a credit standing. It makes clear that these bad things are likely to happen to the reader if he or she doesn't pay the now raised minimum payment. Write the letter.

23. (*Last resort*) Best Deal doesn't believe in waiting long. If it doesn't see results this month, it is ready for last-resort action. Its third letter points out clearly that unless payment is made within 15 days, Best Deal is turning the account over to a collection agency who will take legal action. The letter presents convincingly and with concern the consequences of this action for the reader. Write it.

10

Memorandums

Upon completing this chapter, you will be able to compose a variety of memorandums commonly used within organizations. To reach this goal, you should be able to

1 Describe the primary differences between memorandums and letters written for similar situations.

2 Explain the variations of formality in format and style used in memorandums.

3 Describe the primary differences between printed and electronic memos.

4 Write clear and effective memorandums for routine inquiries, routine responses, policies and directives, and indirect messages.

5 Explain the need for and compose memorandums to file.

▶ to Memorandums

Doreen Lam has to go away for a few days. She has appointed an interim manager to be responsible for the Good 'N Nice kiosk while she is away. Now she has to leave this name, address, and telephone number with the management of the mall and the mall security. They will need to know whom to contact in an emergency.

She also needs to tell her staff whom they can call with questions or difficulties. This task is a little more difficult because of the number of part-time employees she has. There about eight people scheduled to work during her absence. She tried to telephone them, but she gave up after getting no answer at two homes and a busy signal at a third. It would take too long to complete all eight calls. Besides, if the employee is out and Doreen has to leave a message, she will be unsure whether the message will be delivered or not. Another complication is that the staff sometimes trade hours after the work schedule has been posted. Doreen may be calling the wrong person.

To get this important information to the people who need it, Doreen decides to write it. A memo is the format she chooses. She will leave copies where everyone can find them and have the information handy in case of trouble. ■

. . . .

THE NATURE OF MEMORANDUMS

Many of the letter-writing instructions presented in the preceding chapters also apply to memorandums. Memorandums (commonly called memos) take the place of letters for most internal communication. Memos are the written messages exchanged within an organization in the daily operation of the business. As you will see in Chapter 13, some longer memorandums communicate factual, problem-related information and are classified as reports. The focus of this chapter will be the shorter memo.

* Memorandums are letters sent within the company.

Similarity of Principles in Memorandums and Letters

As we have noted, the principles for writing memorandums are much the same as those for writing letters. The reason is that the situations for both are very similar. Some memorandums ask for or give routine information; thus, the direct order is appropriate. Others require the communication of negative messages; thus, the indirect order is appropriate. Still others require persuasion; in these cases the indirect order is also appropriate.

* Memorandum writing principles are the same as those for comparable letters because the situations are similar.

Although direct- and indirect-order memorandums are written, memos in the direct order are more common. Memorandums are usually written to someone whose job it is to do the thing you are asking. The information pertains to the organization's operation. Therefore, there is rarely a need for preliminary explanation, justification, or preparation. The writer can best achieve the goal by getting right down to business. The indirect order is still appropriate for bad news or persuasion when the reader will not receive the message favourably. However, such occasions occur less frequently with regular internal communications.

* Most memorandums are direct, because they deal with routine company matters.

Wide Range of Formality

Because memorandums are usually messages among people who work with and know one another, they tend to be informal. Even so, the degree of their informality varies. At one extreme are the highly informal, handwritten messages that workers write to one another. Such memorandums are typically one- or two-line messages—simple requests and responses that require little or no formality. For example, one worker might send another worker this simple, handwritten note asking for certain file information: "Please send me a copy of the latest invoice from the E. Y. Potts Company." Triplicate

* Memorandums can be informal notes.

self-carboning forms are useful here. The sender writes the note and keeps the first copy; the receiver writes a reply and keeps a second copy; the third copy is returned to the sender.

• Memorandums can also be formal messages to top administrators.

At the opposite end of the formality scale are memorandums written for high-level administrators by their subordinates. For example, a department supervisor who sends a memorandum to the company president would obviously give the message more than the minimal degree of formality. A handwritten note would not be appropriate. Since writing in the third person gives an impression of formality, the supervisor might choose it rather than the more usual memo style of first person writing. The typical memorandum falls somewhere between these extremes. It is written in a personal style (with *I* and *you* emphasis) and in conversational language, but is typed on memohead stationery.

Variations in Format

• Printed memo stationery with Date, To, From, and Subject headings is common.

Most large companies have stationery printed especially for memos with the word *Memorandum* at the top of the page in large, heavy type. Some companies prefer other titles such as *Interoffice Correspondence, Office Memo,* or *Interoffice Communication.* Below this main heading come the specific headings common to all memorandums: *Date, To, From, Subject.* The order may vary except that *Subject* comes last just before the text.[1]

• Some larger companies have additional headings.

Large organizations, especially those with a number of locations and departments, often include additional information on their memorandum stationery. *Phone, E-Mail Identifier, Department, Plant, Store Number, File Number,* and *Copies to* are examples. Since in some companies memorandums are often addressed to more than one reader, the heading *To* may be followed by enough space to list a number of names. Another method often used is to put the list of names at the end and *TO: Circulation List* in the header.

A simple arrangement is displayed in Figure 10–1. As this figure shows, memorandums are usually initialled by the writer rather than signed.[2] The initial is placed by the writer's name in the heading, or at the bottom of the page imitating the closing of a letter.

• Memorandum headings can be typed.

Not all companies have printed memorandum stationery. When employees in such companies write memorandums, they simply key in the headings along with the message. Usually they would save a memorandum template with the appropriate headings in their computer and then just fill in the specific information each time. Individually typed arrangements of this kind vary as much as the printed ones. One popular and effective form is displayed in Figure 10–2.

Subject Lines

• Remember to format subject lines correctly.

As in letters, the subject line in a memo consists of a description of the memo's contents. Subject lines appear immediately before the text and use identifying words such as *Subject:, Concerning:,* or *Re:.* The line is underlined, italicized, or capitalized.

Subject: *Expansion of Direct-Mail Opportunities for Members*

RE: *Newly Authorized Direct-Mail Opportunities for Members.*

Electronic Memos (E-Mail)

• Electronic mail is another form for memos.

Many memos are sent electronically now as more and more companies use an e-mail system. Most e-mail systems set up the format and provide the standard information automatically. For example, the sender's name, the e-mail address, and the date would be inserted automatically by the software. The sender would not have to key in these items. The system gives the prompts for the variable components such as the name and e-mail address of the receiver. Another convenience of e-mail is the possibility of attaching an

---

[1]Electronic mail systems sometimes break this convention.

[2]Some writers prefer to sign bad-news memos to show personal attention to the situation. Also, memos carrying official news from management are occasionally signed to add authority. These practices would be a matter of company style.

Maxwell Petroleum, Inc.

MEMORANDUM

To: All Staff   **Date:**   September 12, 1996
From: Nadine Paskaran *NP*
Phone: ext. 4306
Subject: FORMAT FOR MEMOS (IN-HOUSE LETTERS)

Memo Stationery
This is an illustration of our memorandum stationery. It
should be used for all written communications within the
organization.

Salutation and Closing
The memorandum uses no form of salutation (Dear Jane).
Neither does it have any form of complimentary closing
(Yours Truly). You do not need to sign your message. Your
initials, written after your name in the heading or at
the bottom of the page, are sufficient.

Layout
Headings are very helpful to introduce each point as
illustrated here. Notice that the message is single-
spaced with double spacing between paragraphs. Paragraphs
begin...

. . . .

A PRACTICE RUN

Improve the format and wording of these subject lines. You may want to refer to Chapters 6 and 7 for a review of this topic.
CONCERNING: Orders

_____

Subject: *The Correct Tape for Use on Wood and Painted Surfaces to Avoid Damage to the Finish by the Glue on the
Tape*

_____

_____

RE: *NEWLY APPROVED TRAVEL AGENT FOR 1997–98*

_____

. . . .

existing file such as a report or spreadsheet to the message. It is also possible to set up
recipient or distribution lists that will forward messages to each person on the list without
the need for typing the names each time. A sales manager might use this feature

FIGURE 10–2 Illustration of Good Form for the Memo Not on Printed Stationery

Maxwell Petroleum, Inc.

MEMORANDUM

To: William Bartlett
Date: May 3, 1997
From: Marci Davenport MD
Phone: 421-1763
Subject: Agenda for May Meeting of Plant Safety Committee

Please reply by May 15 with any agenda items for the May 23 meeting of the Plant Safety Committee. I will then prepare the agenda and circulate it to all members at least one week before the meeting.

Thanks!

FIGURE 10–3 A Common Layout for E-Mail Messages

Date: September 12, 1997
To: BCOM 501 Recipient List
From: Jan Bamford <janbam@datanet.ab.ca>
Subject: DUE DATE EXTENSION FOR MEMO ASSIGNMENT
Cc: mflatley@edsu.edu
Attachments: c:\bcom501\memorev.doc

Assignment Extension
Because of the conflict of dates between the memo assignment for BCOM 501 and the business writing contest sponsored by the Business Communicators Association of Canada, the due date for the assignment has been extended by one week to Friday, September 20, 1997.
Late Penalty Will Apply
As usual, I will clear my e-mail box at 4:30 P.M. on the new due date. Any assignment not received at that time will be assessed the late penalty.
Updated Assignment Sheet Attached
A revised copy of the complete assignment with the new due date is attached to this e-mail.

effectively to send regular product updates or price changes to all the sales representatives. See Figure 10–3 for an example of an e-mail memo.

Differences between Printed and Electronic Memos

• Electronic memos differ from printed memos.

The speed of reply to an e-mail message is unpredictable. It may be almost immediate, or it may be several days or longer if the recipient forgets to check for mail or overlooks your message. To encourage prompt replies, consider these differences between electronic and printed memos.

• They (1) require greater care in constructing their subject lines,

Electronic memos require greater care in writing their subject lines. Usually the sender's name and the subject line appear in the *In-box* or *New Mail* menu. Readers will judge whether to open a message based on that information only. If the subject line is vague, uninteresting, or too long, the reader may delay opening that message. For example, a memo with the subject line "Information Update" is not one most people would rush to read. "Contract Negotiation Update," however, might receive more attention. Secondly, most menus display between 20 and 25 characters of the subject line. A long line such as "Further to the note of September 12, 1996 regarding progress on contract negotiations" would be cut off on the menu page. "Further to the note of Sep" does not give the receiver the key information.[3]

Electronic memos need to be concise and tightly organized so that all related contents are in blocks the size of one screen or less. Most computer screens display 20 to 25 lines. Take from that the amount used by the software for headings and menus to determine how many lines of text are displayed on a screen. The number is usually somewhere between 18 and 20. Since it is difficult for the reader to view information that is spread over several screens, you should group similar points together. The most important ideas are placed on the first screen to prevent the reader having to scroll through a message looking for key information. The wise e-mail message sender always remembers that a click of the mouse by the reader is all that stands between this message and the next one.

- (2) need to be more tightly organized,

Electronic memos need more titles and subheads within the body to help the reader locate information quickly when scrolling through the memo. The fact that the screen physically divides the message means that the writer must be careful to create unity by giving headings and transitional clues to guide the reader.

- (3) need more subheads, and

For the same reason, electronic memos should include a signal to the reader that more information is found out of sight on the next screen. Symbols such as >> or |more| are used for this purpose. Similarly, symbols such as ### or |END| indicate the last screen.

- (4) need signals to indicate additional pages.

. . . .
MEMORANDUMS ILLUSTRATED

In the following pages, we review the basic types. First, we look at the direct-order forms, specifically at three variations: (1) direct inquiries, (2) direct responses, and (3) policy directives. Policy directives carry work guidelines from administrators to employees. These memos have much in common with other direct-order memorandums, but they also have some unique characteristics. Next we review the indirect-order memorandum. We show an example that conveys bad news and one that is persuasive. Finally, we review a unique form of memorandum—the memorandum written to file.

Direct Memorandums

Standard Inquiries.   The direct-inquiry memorandum that we will review was written by Becky Pharr, an executive in an investment firm. Becky's job is to plan the annual meeting for the financial advisors and brokers. She has tentatively decided to hold the meeting at Timber Creek Lodge, a recreational facility in the Rockies. Before making the final decision, however, she needs cost data. So she has asked Roland Mah, one of her assistants, to get the information for her. She made the initial request orally, but to avoid any misunderstanding, she has decided to put it in writing.

- The problem chosen concerns a request for information about a meeting site.

Becky's memo typifies memorandums that seek information. It follows the direct order, beginning with the overall request and then systematically covering all the vital points. It displays logical arrangement and clear expression. Although the words are courteous, there is no need for delicacy to avoid offending the reader.

- The direct-inquiry memo follows the general pattern of the direct-inquiry letter.

Group Announcements and Requests.   Another type of direct-order memo may be written to a group to solicit input or gather information. An example would be a memorandum asking for holiday requests so that a master schedule can be compiled. This

- Another type of direct-inquiry memo is written to a group.

---

[3]A common error is to type the word *Subject:* rather than beginning with the description immediately. The long subject line in the example would then be truncated at *Subject: Further to the n.*

CORSAIR INVESTMENTS

MEMORANDUM

DATE: April 10, 1998
TO: Roland Mah
FROM: Becky Pharr *bp*
SUBJECT: <u>Request for costs for staff meeting</u>
             <u>at Timber Creek Lodge</u>

The memo begins with the objective followed by the necessary explanation.

As we discussed in my office today, will you please get the necessary cost information for conducting our annual staff meeting at the Timber Creek Lodge, Timber Creek, Alberta. Our meeting will begin on the morning of Monday, June 5, so we should arrange to arrive on the 4th. We will leave after a brief morning session on June 9.

Specifically, I need the following information:

1. **Travel costs** for all 43 participants, including (a) air travel to Calgary and (b) ground travel between the airport and the lodge. I have listed the names and home stations of the 43 staff on the attached sheet.
2. **Room and board costs** for the five-day period, including cost with and without dinner at the lodge. As you know, we are considering the possibility of allowing participants to purchase dinners at nearby restaurants.
3. **Costs for recreational facilities** at the lodge.
4. **Costs for meeting rooms and meeting equipment** (projectors, lecterns, etc.) We will need a room large enough to accommodate our 43 participants.

The requested information is listed in a logical order.

The memo ends courteously with clear final instructions.

If you need additional information, please call me. I'd like to have the information by April 15, if possible, and certainly no later than the 17th.

**WINDSOR-REYNOLDS
WOOD PRODUCTS**

MEMORANDUM

TO: All Support Staff   DATE: March 30, 1997
FROM: J. Barnett, Personnel Officer   PHONE: 555-7747
RE: ANNUAL VACATION LEAVE

The request is made directly with a brief explanation

Please fill in the attached HOLIDAY REQUEST FORM by Monday, April 15 to provide us with your preferred dates for annual leave in June, July, or August 1997. We are currently compiling a master schedule.

Final decisions will be based on the following considerations:
1. a maximum of 25% of any department's staff can be away at one time
2. in the event of competing requests, seniority will be the deciding factor.
The standard three-week holiday may be taken in a block or divided into shorter periods. If you are unsure of how many days' leave you are entitled to, please call my office. The final schedule will be posted on April 30 and each staff member will be given written confirmation of his/her holiday dates.

Important details governing the information are explained. Note the informal, personal tone.

The closing is positive.

We will do our best to fill each person's request.

JR

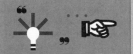
A memo may be informal, but it still needs to be planned and edited. Try following these instructions from a principal's memorandum to the faculty.

First and second periods will meet on regular schedule. At 9:55 those in a one-story building with tickets will go to the auditorium. Those in a one-story building without tickets will report to the cafeteria with study material. At 10:35 those with second period in the main building will report to third period if it is in the main building or to the cafeteria if third period is in a one-story building. At 10:50 those in the auditorium will go to third period in the one-story buildings or to the cafeteria if third period is in the main building. At 11:35 those with second period in a one-story building will report to fourth period class if it is in a one-story building or to the cafeteria if fourth period class is in the main building. At 11:50 everybody will be back on regular schedule.

type of direct inquiry memorandum follows the same basic pattern: (1) the request, (2) any necessary explanation, (3) the detailed information needed, and (4) a courteous closing.

Routine Responses.   The case selected for the routine-response memo is Roland Mah's answer to Ms. Pharr's inquiry. Mr. Mah's goal is simply to present the information requested.

- The direct-response memo should be direct, orderly, and clearly worded.

In this memo the information is work-related and involves no personal feelings. For this reason Mr. Mah appropriately chooses the direct order. He presents his points in an orderly way, arranging them by the general topics found in Ms. Pharr's memo (transportation, room and board, and so on). The writing is simple and clear.

Policy Memorandums and Directives.   Internal written messages giving work rules, pro-

- Company policies and directives may be written in memorandum form.

cedures, and instructions are common in most large organizations. Called *policies* and *directives,* these messages from administrators to subordinates may be written as memorandums, though they sometimes take other forms. Because such messages are more important than most internal communications, they are often compiled in policy manuals—perhaps kept in loose-leaf form in a notebook and updated as new memorandums are issued.

- They should be somewhat formal, direct, clearly written, and well organized.

Policy memorandums and directives are more formally written than most internal communications because of their official nature. Typically, they follow the direct order. They begin with a topic (thesis) statement that repeats the subject-line information and includes the additional information needed to identify the specific situation. The remainder of the message consists of a logical, orderly arrangement of the rules and procedures covered. To make them stand out, the rules and procedures are often numbered or arranged in outline form.

- In writing them, emphasize clarity. Revise to improve.

Because policy memos and directives must be understood by everyone in the organization, the writers must be concerned with adaptation and clarity of expression as we discussed in Chapters 2 and 3 of this text. In addition, since the wording may have legal ramifications, several revisions may be made and reviewed before an acceptable document is produced.

Indirect-Order Memorandums

- Memorandums refusing personal requests are occasionally written.

Bad-News.   As we have seen, most memorandums can be written in the direct order, but there are important exceptions—memorandums carrying bad news that concerns the reader personally require indirect, diplomatic treatment.

- They should be handled indirectly and tactfully.

Like the indirect-letter situations reviewed previously, such personal bad-news messages require tactful handling. This means treating them indirectly—paving the way for

CORSAIR INVESTMENTS

MEMORANDUM

DATE: April 14, 1998
TO: Becky Pharr
FROM: Roland Mah *Rm*
SUBJECT: COST INFORMATION FOR MEETING AT TIMBER CREEK LODGE

This memo begins directly with a statement that sets up the specific detailed answers.

As you requested in your April 10 memorandum, here are the cost details for conducting our annual staff meeting at Timber Creek Lodge, June 4-9.

Air Transportation
Round-trip air transportation for our 43 representatives from their assignment stations to Calgary would be $9,312 (see schedule attached).

Ground Transportation
Ground transportation from Calgary to Timber Creek Lodge could be by chartered bus or by rental car.
By Bus: The White Transport Company would provide round-trip bus transportation from the airport to the lodge for $25 per person, or a total of $1,075.
By Rental Car: Automobile rental costs for a mid-size vehicle for the five-day meeting would be approximately $235 per vehicle, depending on the exact mileage. At one vehicle for four people, we would need 11 automobiles, for a total cost of $2,585. The advantage of automobile rental is that the participants would have transportation throughout the week, although the lodge provides limited shuttle service to Timber Creek.

Accommodation
Corporate rates for private room accommodations at the lodge, including breakfast and lunch, would be $125 per day per person, or $625 for the entire meeting. The total for our 43 attendees would be $26,825.

Meals
Dinners at the lodge could be included for an additional $12 per person per day, making the per person total $685 and the total for all participants $29,405. However, several quality restaurants are in Timber Creek, about 2 kilometres away. We probably would need to budget $15 each for dinners away from the lodge.

Meeting Facilities
The lodge reports that its meeting room will easily accommodate our 43 participants. For a group the size of ours, the lodge would provide the meeting room, projectors, lecterns, and such without additional charge.

Recreation
The lodge recreational facilities (golf, tennis, swimming) would also be available without additional charge, except for equipment rentals.

Headings are used to organize the information logically and clearly.

The closing offers additional resources and help.

I have enclosed the lodge's current descriptive brochure, which should answer other questions you may have. If you need additional information in making your decision, I'll get it for you as quickly as I can.

This example is a policy memorandum that has been written for the company's manual. As indicated in the preliminary information, the memorandum replaces a previous one.

**WINDSOR-REYNOLDS
WOOD PRODUCTS**

MEMORANDUM

This memo is written for the policy book with copies to the employees. It replaces an earlier policy.

DATE:	July 12, 1997
TO:	Policy Manual
COPIES TO:	All Employees, Bayfield Plant
FROM:	J. Barnett, Personnel Officer
SUBJECT:	CHANGE OF OFFICE AND WORKING HOURS, BAYFIELD PLANT
	(Replaces Memorandum Dated May 9, 1995)

Policies concerning office and working hours at the Bayfield plant are as follows, effective today:

The subject line and introductory sentence identify the policy area covered.

1. *Regular working hours.* The normal work week begins at 12:01 a.m. Sunday and ends at midnight the following Saturday. Administrative and department offices will be open from 8 a.m. to 5 p.m. Monday through Friday, except on designated holidays. Offices will remain open during the noon hour each working day, with at least one person on duty. Offices may be open at other times with the approval of the division superintendent concerned.
2. *Service Department.* Service Department personnel will normally work Monday through Friday. Because of the nature of their work, however, they may have a different work schedule and may be subject to call on a standby basis for emergencies. The superintendent of this department will periodically issue a standby schedule, which will be given to each service employee.
3. *Lunch periods.* Employees are entitled to a maximum of one hour for lunch. Supervisors will schedule lunch periods to ensure that work will be done efficiently.
4. *Rest periods.* All full-time employees are entitled to 15-minute rest periods for every four-hour period worked during the workday. Supervisors should schedule all work breaks so that the work is done efficiently. Normally, one break should be taken in the morning and one in the afternoon. When there is an unusually heavy workload or when a crisis occurs, supervisors may request that employees not take their breaks.
5. *Observance of regulations.* Each employee must observe the regular work schedule for his or her work location. Any person who is consistently late for work or who does not return from rest or lunch periods promptly is subject to disciplinary action.

The policy areas are covered clearly and systematically. Numbers and topic captions help organize the contents.

The employee is responsible for notifying the supervisor when he or she will be late or absent. An employee who must leave work early will make the necessary arrangements with the supervisor.

Because the memo is written primarily for the policy manual, there is no personal closing.

The writer has decided to sign rather than initial this memo because of its official content.

JBarnett

the bad news with explanation and justification. It means watching words carefully, trying to emphasize the positive over the negative. It means writing from the reader's point of view with consideration for his or her best interests. These and other points discussed with respect to indirect letters also apply to this type of memorandum.

Illustrating this memorandum type is the case of an administrator who must deny a request for a change in vacation dates. Two reasons support the denial, both of which are specified in the company's contract with the union. First, no more than 25 percent of the workers in any department can be on vacation at one time. Second, seniority determines who gets preference if more than 25 percent ask for the same vacation time.

• A denial of a change in vacation dates illustrates this type of memorandum.

Persuasive Memorandums. Although persuasive memorandums are not common, those that are written are likely to be highly important. Usually they concern a company project or proposal that involves employee participation (a fund drive, a safety campaign, or a total quality management program). In general, they follow the pattern of the persuasive letter. They present a persuasion strategy designed to move the reader to accept whatever is being promoted. Their pattern is indirect, beginning with attention-gaining words that set up the persuasion strategy. Then they present this persuasion strategy, leading to the request for action.

• Persuasive memos follow the pattern of a persuasive letter.

The Memorandum to File

Memorandums to file are memos written for the writer's own file. They are written to document events in a permanent record for future reference and to clarify conversations and decisions. For example, a participant in a meeting might write a memorandum to file to tidy up the quick notes taken as the meeting progressed. This memo would supplement the minutes for the writer. A memo to file might be written after a conference call to provide a clear, concise, and reliable reference for the future. Or, after an employee's performance appraisal, the supervisor would record the event in a memorandum to file. If a copy is placed in the personnel file of the employee, the employee should be allowed to review it and write a response to accompany it. Later, if disciplinary action is needed, memos such as these will give the history of the case.

• People in business write memos to keep in their own files as records or reminders.

The following example illustrates the case of an informal meeting at which no minutes were taken. Here copies of the memo might be routed to all the participants both for personal use and for confirmation of the discussion and/or decisions.

A SUMMARY OF LEARNING OUTCOMES FROM THIS CHAPTER

Most memos are friendly and informal because they carry simple inquiries and responses from and to employees who work in the same organization. Memos to those in high levels of authority, or those that carry serious, official messages are likely to be more formal in tone.

Memorandums (letters written inside a company) usually are processed on special stationery. Typically, *MEMORANDUM* appears at the top of the page and *DATE:, TO:, FROM:,* and *SUBJECT:* follow. Other headings such as *PHONE:, DEPARTMENT:,* or *COPIES:* may be included.

Electronic memos are increasing in importance as more companies adopt e-mail systems. They differ from printed memos primarily because of screen limitations. Electronic memos (1) require greater care in constructing their subject lines, (2) need to be more tightly organized, (3) need more subheads, and (4) need signals to indicate additional pages.

Because the situations for writing memos and letters are similar, memos follow the same basic principles as letters of the same type. They use the direct pattern for routine inquiries and responses, policy memorandums, and directives. For bad news that personally involves the reader and for persuasion, the indirect order is used.

Memorandums to file are written for the writer's own file. They are records of events and activities to help the writer recall the details later.

This memorandum handles the situation indirectly and with concern for the reader's feelings. In general, it follows the principles described for bad-news letters.

**WINDSOR-REYNOLDS
WOOD PRODUCTS**

MEMORANDUM

DATE: May 24, 1998
TO: Jerry Cunningham
FROM: J. Barnett
SUBJECT: Your Request For Change In Vacation
            Dates To July 8-21

The opening is indirect and pleasant. It leads into the explanation.

Your reasons for requesting a change in vacation dates are quite reasonable and certainly deserve consideration.

In evaluating them, I must consider more than merit. I must also follow the rules carefully specified in the contract agreement between the company and the union. These rules specify that no more than 25 percent of any department's workers can be on vacation at one time. This means a maximum of two for your department. The contract also specifies that seniority will determine vacation priorities.

The explanation is positively worded. It is clear and convincing.

The refusal is given in the positive form of an alternate vacation time.

In addition to you, both Rita Gann (18 years) and Bea Lacey (14 years) have requested vacations for July 8-21. Because both of them have more service than your 10 years, the best I can do for you is give you the July 22-August 4 period. These dates would permit you to do at least some of the things outlined in your request.

Please consider these dates. Then let me know whether they are satisfactory. I assure you that I'll do whatever I am permitted to help you with your vacation planning.

The ending is positive and friendly.

JB

This example of a persuasive memo is written to employees of an oil company to encourage participation in the company's education program. The memo is short because the writer's goal was to get the reader to make an inquiry in person.

MASTODON OIL

MEMORANDUM

TO: All Employees
FROM: Cindy Kerr,
            Education Director
DATE: August 12, 1992
SUBJECT: **Your Career Development**

A question catches the attention of the reader.

Do you know any of these people—Linda Campbell, Bob Morris, Charles Huculak, Shannon Bentley?

The success of those named arouses interest and begins the persuasion strategy of showing the benefits of the program for the participants.

They are your fellow employees, and they have two things in common. One, they were recently promoted. Two, they have all been participants in our Career Support Program.

The simplicity of the program and the benefits to the participants attempt to build desire. Your-viewpoint is used extensively.

As you may know, the Career Support Program is Mastodon Oil's way of helping you develop professionally. It offers you the opportunity to participate in continuing education courses and have Mastodon Oil pay all the costs, including tuition, fees and books. All you need to do is (1) follow an approved curriculum designed to help you in your work and (2) satisfactorily meet course requirements (a grade of C or better). It's as simple as that. Mastodon pays. You learn. And we all benefit.

I'd like to tell you more about how the Career Support Program can help you. Just drop by my office (20A, Human Resources Department) any time during the workday. I'll give you the details. Although I won't be able to promise you a promotion, I will promise to help you grow professionally.

The action is clear and easily accomplished. The closing is a reminder of the benefit.

CK

MASTODON OIL

MEMORANDUM

DATE: October 19, 1997
TO: FILE
FROM: Cindy Kerr   *CK*
SUBJECT: <u>Meeting on problems with in-house
             training program</u>

On October 17, 1997, Charles Davison, Diane Kennedy,
and Peter Dominguez met in my office to review the
progress of our in-house management training program.

Diane and Peter reported that their employees
expressed strong dissatisfaction with the first
course conducted. Charles and I reported less
negative (although not entirely positive) experiences
from our employees. The evidence submitted clearly
suggested that the course instructor talked "over the
heads" of the participants. The subject matter, we
concluded, was not too difficult for the employees
involved.

We also agreed that in selecting the next instructor,
we will carefully consider the levels of subject
matter and instruction. In addition, we agreed that
I will monitor the instruction during the next course
to prevent similar difficulties.

cc   C.Davison, D.Kennedy, P.Dominguez

ANSWERS TO PRACTICE RUNS

▶ Subject Lines

Answers will vary. The weaknesses to be improved are listed here.

CONCERNING: Orders
Too vague and lacking correct formatting.

Subject: The Correct Tape for Use on Wood and Painted Surfaces to Avoid Damage to the Finish by the Glue on the Tape

Too long and detailed. The subject line should introduce the message, not contain it.

RE: *NEW APPROVED TRAVEL AGENT FOR 1997–98*
For a direct-order memo, the travel agent could be named, e.g., *Westerra Travel Agency Selected for 1997–98*. The subject line should be emphasized. Italics, capitalization, or underlining are acceptable but not all three together.

QUESTIONS FOR DISCUSSION

1. Compare letters and memos on the following criteria: (1) audience, (2) tone, (3) word choice, (4) format.

2. The need for indirect order in memorandums is rare. Explain.

3. Discuss and justify the use of greater informality in memorandums. Suggest situations where formal language is advisable in memorandums.

4. Describe the special concerns for electronic memos compared to printed ones. How is each concern overcome?

5. Discuss the special need for clear writing and adaptation in policy memorandums and directives.

CASE 10–1

▶ Devendra and Shannon at the Office

Shannon: Devendra, I'm having some trouble writing this memo. Can you take a look at it and make some suggestions?

Devendra: Sure, Shannon. [*Devendra begins reading.*]

Congratulations! We have reached our goal of cutting office expenses by 12 percent. In fact, we have surpassed it! The amount saved here will help us meet our overall budget goals.

Although we don't have any money to spend, there may be changes we can make that will make you more efficient at your job and make your job easier in spite of the cuts. If you have some suggestions, don't hesitate to pass them along.

Devendra: The first paragraph is positive and friendly. It sounds pretty good to me. Could you add what percentage has been saved?

Shannon: Sure. It's 17 percent. It would be encouraging to the staff to know the specific amount, wouldn't it.

Devendra: I think so. And you could add who should get the credit.

Shannon: I thought the "we" made it clear that everyone in our department should share in the credit.

Devendra: Perhaps, but I think some people might feel that "we" means the people writing the memo. You know—just the supervisors.

Shannon: Hmm. I hadn't thought about it that way. Okay, so how about:

Congratulations everyone! Our department has reached its goal of cutting office expenses by 12 percent. In fact, we have surpassed it by an additional 5 percent! That's a great job done by the whole team. The extra amount saved here will help us meet our overall budget goals.

Devendra: I like that opening paragraph much better than the old one. Now, what do you mean in this second paragraph?

Shannon: Well, I want people to make suggestions because I care about them. I know that they are trying to do their job just as well as they did before but with fewer supplies, less photocopying, fewer long distance calls, and so on. I thought there might be things we could do to remove some of the stress.

Devendra: Can you give me some suggestions?

Shannon: Sure. Maybe we could shift the furniture around so more people can see out of the windows, or so the floor plan is more efficient. Or perhaps we could make some scheduling changes that would help people. You know the sort of thing. Some people start a half hour earlier because they want to leave earlier to be home for their kids. Others might want to start a little later to miss the traffic. We could probably do something like that without spending money. We might even have a dress-down, casual day occasionally. But I really want to know what they want, not what I think they might want.

Devendra: I get it now, but I wouldn't have understood that from what you have written. Maybe we can work on that paragraph together.

MEMORANDUM PROBLEMS

►Routine Memorandums (Inquiries, Directives)

1. An unhappy job applicant has threatened to take D'Or Chemical Company to court, claiming discriminatory hiring practices. This female applicant contends that her qualifications are superior to those of the man who was hired over her.

    To be certain that everyone is familiar with D'Or's policy of equal employment opportunities, a memorandum will be prepared. The President, Art Bankston, summarized the policy for you as follows:

    D'Or is an equal opportunity employer—has been for at least 15 years. In every case, we will hire the best-qualified person for the job—and that means we don't look at sex, race, religion, or nationality. Similarly, we don't look at age, but of course all applicants must meet legal minimum requirements; and we don't put people on jobs that they are physically not able to perform.

    It's not just in hiring that we avoid discrimination. The same equality rules apply to promotions, layoffs, and dismissals. When we have to reduce the numbers of employees, we look at qualifications and job performance. If two or more people are equally qualified, seniority is considered.

    Every time somebody is hired, promoted, disciplined, or fired, written justification must be sent to Human Resources giving the decision and supporting it with evidence. The evidence must be factual, though in some cases judgment also has to be given. Nothing should appear in these memos that we couldn't argue logically in court.

    I've rambled quite a bit, but you can organize my thoughts in a better order. I'll check your draft before it is sent to the division supervisors and department managers.

    Your memo will not be concerned with the specific case of the job applicant, but rather with the general review and statement of policy. It should be carefully worded for accuracy and clarity for your wide audience. The tone will be formal as is appropriate for a serious topic of policy.

2. Your office always seemed cold, so one day you brought in a thermometer. Sure enough, the temperature was 17. The thermostat on the wall in the reception area is set at 20, but your office is on the north side of the building and has some large windows. You decide that you need a separate thermostat in your office. You spoke to your boss about it and she said, "Fine, but write me a memo

that I can take to Facilities Management." Now that you know she is agreeable to your plan, write a memo describing the situation persuasively so that she can get the authorization for the purchase and installation of the thermostat.

3. About three weeks ago the home office of Great Lakes Insurance Company established a centralized word processing centre to handle the correspondence and report preparation work of administrators.

    Some confusion has arisen because administrators expect their work to be given immediate attention. And to get quick service, some of them are pressuring the clerical staff. After discussing the matter with Caroline Gunnels, the administrative vice president, you have decided to send a reminder about the procedures for all work submitted to the Word Processing Centre. As recorded in the jumbled, brief notes you took in your discussion with Gunnels, you want to make the following points:

    – 3 categories
       1. – urgent (within 24 hours)
       2. – routine (within 3 days)
       3. – filler (within 1 week)

    – reports and long projects must be category 3
    – rush items with approval of the office manager only
    – complaints to office manager only
    – business work only, no personal work
    – editing for spelling and grammar is provided, but not for content or style
    – letters and memos are category 1
    – provide full information such as addresses, dates, policy numbers, amounts

    Although the administrators may not be happy about these restrictions, you decide to use direct order to organize your message. You want this memorandum to be strong to reinforce the policies implemented almost a month ago but also polite and considerate of your audience. Address it to "All administrators using the Word Processing Centre."

►Routine Memorandums (Information Presentations)

4. For this assignment, you have just hired a new word processor for D'Or Chemical Company (see Problem 1 for background information).

    You received seven applications in response to your advertizement in the local newspaper. Four of the seven applicants (three females and one male) were eliminated because they did not meet the requirement of "one or more years of word processing experience." Of the remaining three, you selected Patrick Ross and rejected

Julia E. Santos and Kerry Pemberton. Your reasons for choosing Ross over the two women are evident in this summary review of credentials:

Patrick Ross. Typing speed, 89 wpm. Experience: 18 months as word processor with Kruger Industries, 3 years and 2 months as executive secretary to senior vice president at Cauble and Barnes Insurance; familiar with Apple/Macintosh, IBM PC, desktop publishing, Windows 95, Word, and on-line services. Education: 2-year business diploma from Mossback Community College, majoring in office administration. Score on office skills test (100-point basis), 89.

Julia E. Santos. Typing speed, 81 wpm. Experience: 14 months with Parke-Shannon, Inc., as word processor, familiar with IBM PC using WordPerfect and Word. Education: diploma from City Secretarial College (six-month course). Score on office skills test (100-point basis), 83.

Kerry Pemberton. Typing speed, 88 wpm. Experience: 21 months half-time work as word processor with Talon and Talon Industries, 9 months with Beaver Manufacturing as administrative secretary; familiar with IBM PC using WordPerfect and Word. Also proficient with Windows and Windows 95. Some on-line experience. Education: word processing courses in high school. Score on office skills tests (100-point basis), 78.

Now write the memorandum that reports and justifies your selection of Ross over the other candidates. Direct it to Glenna Michaels, Manager, Human Resources.

5. You are the assistant to the president of Wasson Industries. A memorandum on conserving energy that you wrote for your boss was distributed to all Wasson employees two weeks ago. In part it said:

> Lights not necessary for work performance are to be turned off. Be especially careful to turn off lights at the end of the workday. In addition, office thermostats will be set at 20 degrees in cold weather and at 24 degrees in warm weather. Employees will not be permitted to bring personal heating or cooling equipment (electric heaters and fans).

Since there has been plenty of time for its message to have taken effect, you were not surprised when your boss left you the following voice message:

> I'm off to Victoria to work out a supply problem. I hope to be back Friday. While I am gone, please check into the effects of our energy-saving program in the office area. Go through the area, check around, and determine what's going on. Report the results to me on my return. Incidentally, that was an excellent memo you wrote for me concerning the energy matter.

You began work on this problem by checking the eight departments in the main office building. You visited them again after working hours and yet again at the beginning of the next work day. You gathered the following data:

You talked with each of the eight department heads. The heads of Departments 1 and 6 felt that they had been complying with the directive generally but admitted that they needed to follow up more closely. The other six department heads claimed that they had been having problems with people who changed the thermostat settings. All eight insisted that they had cautioned their people to follow the directive but admitted that they had been negligent in following up. All eight promised that the next check would find no violations.

You will present this information to your boss, the president, so that he can quickly and easily see the facts of the situation. You will be more concerned with the overall status of things than with a detailed, statistical review.

6. In your position as head of the maintenance department (Department 517) of Hammarstrum-Azel's Morningdale plant, you must respond to a memorandum asking your department members whether they wish to be transferred to the company's Daggetville plant when the Morningdale plant is closed. As requested in the memorandum, you called your people in to hear the news of the company's decision to close the Morningdale plant, and you asked them to inform you within a month whether they wished to be transferred to the Daggetville plant. Today you have answers from all 11 of your people.

Seven of them will not transfer. One of the seven, Amos Stecher, will take early retirement. The other six are Mildred Grabein, Carlos Cato, Beverly Woods, Mike Commons, Gord Zotz, and Naomi Doubilet. You are one of the four who have elected to transfer, of whom you and Brad Theissen have placed conditions on the transfer. You will transfer only if you are given an administrative position no lower than the one you now have. As you feel about ready for a move up the administrative ladder, you would not transfer if that were no longer possible. Theissen, your carpenter, has been getting union wages at Morningdale, but has heard that carpenters are not paid union wages at Daggetville. If the pay difference is significant, Theissen will not transfer. The other two persons who have elected to transfer are Dorothy Cowan and Bert Stinson.

You will present this information in a memorandum addressed to Penny Chang, Hammarstrum-Azel's director of personnel.

Dept. No	Thermostat Setting	Lights Left On	Unnecessary Lights On during Work Hours	Electric Heaters Found
1	19	2	3	5
2	22	7	7	1
3	23	5	5	3
4	23	7	8	1
5	21	6	3	3
6	19	1	1	6
7	24	7	3	4
8	24	8	5	0

▶Indirect Memorandums (Bad News)

7. Every year the Cornwall-Gilbert Company awards $2,000 and an additional week of vacation time to its "outstanding employee." Two runners-up each receive an additional week of vacation time. Candidates for the award are nominated by their fellow workers. A committee of workers and administrators reviews the work records, interviews the nominees, and makes the final selections.

   This year you are serving as chair of the selection committee. In that capacity you have the pleasant assignment of notifying the winners and the unpleasant assignment of informing the losers. You do this by means of memorandums.

   You have already written the good-news memorandums to the three winners. Now you must write the five who didn't make it. You'll try to soften the bad news by emphasizing the honour of being nominated. You want the five to know that the company and their fellow employees appreciate them and recognize their outstanding contributions. Use your good logic and your best writing to achieve your goal.

8. About two months ago, Greg Cobb applied for a transfer from Baccus Manufacturing's production planning department in Detroit to the production planning department of its Toronto plant. He gave two reasons for wanting to transfer: he couldn't get along with his supervisor, and he wanted to be near friends and family in Toronto. In your job as personnel manager, you processed Cobb's application in the usual manner. You sent it along with his personnel records to the supervisor of Cobb's Toronto production planning department. This supervisor would have to certify that a position for which Cobb was qualified existed and that he or she would accept Cobb for that position.

   Today the rejected application came back. A suitable position does exist in Toronto, but the Toronto supervisor is unwilling to put Cobb in it. Apparently, Cobb's performance record is not good enough, perhaps as a result of his current supervisor's evaluations. But you can do nothing about the matter. Your job is to pass on the decision. You'll do this in a memorandum that you will give him in an interview. Perhaps you can suggest alternatives, such as applying for a transfer to another Baccus plant or applying for another type of work in Toronto.

9. Play the role of sales manager for Great Lakes Insurance Company. Your product is the insurance that borrowers from financial institutions can buy to cover payment of their loans in the event of their death. Your sales force sells the insurance to financial institutions, which in turn sells it to their customers.

   In the past few years, you had noticed that some of your salespeople made far more money than others. And you couldn't explain the differences by sales ability alone. So you looked into the matter carefully and found that the sales districts were far from equal in sales potential. Perhaps their sales potential was nearly equal when they were formed, but much has happened since then. Some of the sales districts are now so large that their salespeople can work solely on the larger, more lucrative accounts and ignore the rest. The result, of course, is that Great Lakes is not served adequately in these districts.

   You are, therefore, revising the district boundaries. You will reduce the size of the larger districts by as much as 50 percent. You will increase the size of a few districts. And you will add a few districts. The end result, you feel, will be fair to both Great Lakes and the salespeople. You know, however, that some of the salespeople won't see it this way.

   Now you must write a memorandum informing your salespeople of what you have done and why. You will write it in such a way that they will regard what you have done as fair even if they don't like it. In the memorandum you will refer to an enclosure that describes the recipient's revised district.

▶Indirect Memorandums (Persuasive)

10. You are in the public relations department at the All-Weather Windows plant. Today you were visited by a delegation from the surrounding residential area. These people complained about cars parked in the neighbourhood. As their spokesman explained, "Your employees are parking in the streets in front of our houses. Often they block driveways and park on our lawns. We've noticed that there is plenty of room in your parking lots, but some prefer to park in our neighbourhood because it saves them a few steps."

    You promised the group that you would do what you could to correct the matter—that you'd get the employees to park in the lots provided. But it won't be easy. You can enlist the help of the local police in keeping cars off the driveways and lawns. But parking in the streets is permitted by the city. You conclude that you will have to use persuasion.

    Specifically, you will write a persuasive memorandum to the employees. In it you will use the most effective appeal (or appeals) you can develop. Will it be pride? Fair play? Loyalty? Consider the possibilities, and then write the memo.

11. As regional sales director for Syntex Labs, you firmly believe that paperwork is bogging down your sales representatives. It also holds up orders and, therefore, cash payments. While most representatives have been using laptop computers for a few years, you think it is time to upgrade them by adding fax/modems.

    With a direct link to the main computer, your sales representatives could check on the availability of products or special promotions. They could establish the status of orders for their customers as well as process new orders immediately. In short, with fax/modems built into their laptops, your sales representatives will be more effective at their real job—selling. The weekly and monthly sales reports would be easier to compile and faster to send. Wouldn't having those reports sooner be an advantage for head office? Now write a memo to convince your supervisor who has to approve the funds.

12. The students' council has just come up with a fund-raising idea. They plan to place special containers at strategic places around campus for collecting empty pop cans. If students will put them into these recycle bins instead of into the garbage, the students' council can make quite a bit of money. (Assume each can is worth 5 cents.) And there will be less waste. What is a good approach to take for an open memo to all students encouraging them to participate? The memo will be published on the front page of the student newspaper, so it has to be good. Plan carefully, and then write the memo.

11

Strategies in Job Search and Application

Upon completing this chapter, you will be able to conduct a job search by composing effective job-application documents and participating in job interviews. To reach this goal, you should be able to

1 Develop a network of contacts in your job search.

2 Compile a personal inventory of skills, training, and experience.

3 Compile a résumé that is strong, complete, and well-organized.

4 Write letters of application that skillfully sell your abilities.

5 Explain how you should conduct yourself in an interview.

6 Write application follow-up letters that are appropriate, friendly, and positive.

▶ to Job Search and Application Strategies

Doreen Lam needs two more employees to work at her Good 'n Nice kiosk. The job is not difficult, and Doreen is willing to train her staff in the various food preparation techniques. Reliability and excellent interpersonal skills are required along with honesty and cleanliness, of course. The hours are part-time, and the pay is minimum wage to start.

Doreen first asks her current employees if they know of potential candidates. She then speaks to a few of her friends from college and the guidance counsellor from the local high school. She also places a sign on the counter with application forms. Because it would cost money and might generate more applications than she could handle, Doreen decides not to advertize in the newspaper yet.

▶ Two Weeks Later

Now that the applications have arrived, Doreen finds that some of them can be eliminated immediately. She scans through them looking for neatness, correctness, completeness, and a demonstrated ability to communicate with customers. Although she sees some hints about reliability in the written applications, she had hoped for more. She will have to uncover the characteristics of reliability, honesty, and cleanliness in the interview.

A short list of possible candidates is ready. ■

SOME COMMENTS ABOUT JOB MARKET REALITIES

Of all the things you do in life, few are more important than getting a job. Whether it is your first job or one farther down your career path, the right job is directly related to your success and your happiness.

The traditional picture for finding a job has been for the candidate to locate an advertized position, mail in a standard résumé and letter of application, and answer a few questions at the subsequent interview. Then the employer offers a full-time position with benefits. The candidate, as a loyal, hard-working employee, can expect to be rewarded with raises, promotions, and long-term job security. That picture is close to a fairy tale today.

Because today's economic reality demands lean, pared-down organizations, employees can no longer assume they will build their career in only one or two companies. People with many years of excellent service are being laid off or bought out as companies economize and downsize. Many jobs are never advertized outside the company because there are employees or former employees already known to the company who would like the position. Nor does the assumption of full-time work with benefits hold true. Many positions are filled with part-time employees who receive limited benefits or none at all.

It is important to recognize these changes in the job market. You may find a full-time, permanent position, but if these changes have already taken place in your desired field of work, you may need to look for different rewards from a job. For example, a reasonable expectation is that you will perfect skills or learn new ones while at this job. Instead of security and promotion, the reward for good work may be additional training courses that will leave you in a better position for advancement or for a new job when this one ends. Or perhaps special opportunities will be given that, upon successful completion, will be valuable additions to your portfolio or experience.

A recent advertizing and public relations graduate, who had a four-month contract with a large public utility, was given the opportunity to sit on a community service committee for her employer. Rather than seeing the offer as just another meeting to attend, the graduate correctly saw the potential for building experience and making contacts. When

- Traditional job search methods are not well suited to the present market.

- People change jobs more frequently than in the past.

- Look for different benefits other than job security.

- Make the most of the opportunities given to you.

The Honourable Alfonso Gagliano, P.C., Minister of Labour and Deputy Leader of the Government in the House of Commons, speaking to the Saint-Léonard (Québec) Chamber of Commerce, May 1, 1996.

We are living in a time of major upheaval that is defying our ability to adapt. The rapid pace of technological progress, deregulation, and the dismantling of trade barriers are changing the way we do business and, needless to say, the work environment. The shift from an industrial society to the information age, globalization, demographic changes, and the imperatives of budgetary control are causing tremendous upheaval at all levels of society.

We must all, both collectively and individually, develop new approaches, alter our usual ways of doing things, and face the unknown with imagination and equanimity. But it is within the work environment that this profound change most directly affects our lives. No one can escape it—not employers, or managers, or public servants, or employees, or self-employed individuals.

Older people live in fear of losing their livelihood, younger people are anxiously trying to break into the job market, and everyone else feels vulnerable because of all the changes taking place. There are of course no magic or instant solutions to this general malaise, but we do need to take a serious look at the new realities and try to find equitable, effective solutions to ensure our prosperity in the 21st century.[†]

[†]Source: *Collective Reflection on the Changing Workplace/Réflexion collective sur le milieu de travail en évolution.* http://www.reflexion.gc.ca/speech_e.html (Accessed Aug. 31, 1996).

the committee needed a poster designed, she again took the opportunity and now has an excellent example of her work to show future employers.

* Out-sourcing is a common practice.

The growing trend is toward contract and free-lance work. Rather than hiring employees into the company, many firms are contracting for services. Known as out-sourcing, this trend is evident in areas such as computer support, payroll and benefits management, and advertizing. The popularity of out-sourcing means the search for a job will be a recurring event for many people. While advancement may come within a company, it also may come through completing one job and moving to the next one. In such a job environment, each new skill you learn means the ability to accept larger contracts in a broader field of expertise.

SOME COMMENTS ABOUT THE IMPACT OF TECHNOLOGY

* Technological advances have changed the nature of jobs and of job searches.

As well as downsizing and out-sourcing, the job market is undergoing other changes. The technological revolution means the number of job opportunities for people lacking specialized training and experience is decreasing. It also creates the need for constant upgrading and retraining.

* Technology has changed job search documents.

An offshoot of these technological changes is rapid change in the job search procedure. The use of word processing and specialized résumé writing programs simplify the task of preparing résumés tailored to each job. Applications are now sent by courier, fax, and e-mail, as well as by mail and hand delivery. The creation of a web page for an on-line résumé is a serious option for those looking for a job in the computer field, and probably this option will spread to other job markets soon. Employers may use a computer program to search for key words and spelling errors in submitted résumés to make the first selection automatically. Only those applications containing the key words will be reviewed in more detail.

Consider the impact of the fax machine on your application. Since you cannot know what quality printer the employer has, you have no control over the quality of reproduction when your résumé arrives. To make a favourable impression, you must pay close attention to the spacing and layout of your documents, the clarity of the font you choose, and the type of paper you use for your original. A roman font without italics, printed on smooth, white, bond paper usually sends the clearest copy. Coloured or marbled papers or linen papers with high textures may create many extra spots and marks on the faxed copy.

For example, a faxed résumé needs special development to suit that channel.

If you e-mail a résumé and application letter, the format of your document is even more limited. As we will see in the chapter on technology,[1] the width of the page is not standard in e-mail software. The sender cannot even control the font seen by the receiver of the message. E-mail is a convenient but not particularly attractive format for messages.

An e-mail application has limited flexibility in its format.

Consider the impact of technology on the response to your application. Do you have an answering machine at your home? What type of message does a caller hear? Is it one you would want a potential employer to hear? If not, change it! If you leave an e-mail address, do you check your e-mail regularly?[2] Is your fax machine available at all times or is it on the same line as your telephone? (Sharing a line is a common occurrence with fax modems in a home computer.) If you leave a fax number, make sure it always works. Each channel you open must be properly set up and monitored.

Responses may arrive in many ways. Be ready for them.

THE JOB SEARCH

Building a Network of Contacts

You can begin the job search long before you are ready to find employment. In fact, you can do it now by building a network of contacts with people who can help you find work when you need it.[3] Such people include classmates, professors or instructors, and business people. Remember that many jobs are not advertized and those that are often have an internal candidate whom you must beat. Your contacts can help you by letting you know about the position and helping you plan your strategy.

Begin the job search by building a network of contacts.

Building a network is not as selfish as it sounds. It is not a matter of using people or harassing them until they refer you to someone else. You build a network by helping people. Doing something for someone else puts your action and your name in mind. You might work an extra shift for someone, pass along a book to a fellow student you know is researching that topic, or bring in articles or anecdotes of interest to your instructor. While these gestures are not exactly random acts of kindness,[4] neither are they manipulative favours to make the receiver feel he or she "owes you one." These unsolicited acts of consideration are done not for immediate or direct personal gain, but for the long-term goal of building positive relationships.

Build a network by helping people.

At present, your classmates and friends may not be making or influencing hiring decisions. However, some of them will know of unadvertized job openings. The wider your circle of friends, and the more people who know you are looking for work, the more likely you are to make employment contacts.

(1) Broaden your circle of friends.

Knowing your professors and instructors and making sure that they know you can lead to employment contacts. Demonstrating your work ethic and your ability in the classroom is probably the best way to get your instructors to know you and help you. Taking

(2) Get to know your professors and instructors.

---

[1]See Chapter 18, "Technology in Communication."

[2]If you are looking for work while you are employed, remember that your e-mail and voice mail may not be as private as you think. In addition, there are some ethical questions about using the facilities at one place of work to look for a position elsewhere.

[3]Adapted from John Lucht, "Building a Network before Graduation," *College Edition of the National Business Employment Weekly,* published by *The Wall Street Journal,* Fall 1988, p.9.

[4]As defined by Daphne Rose Kingma in her foreword to the book *Random Acts of Kindness,* by the editors of Conari Press. (Berkeley: Conari Press, 1993).

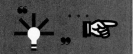
advantage of opportunities such as working on committees outside the classroom can help too. At the very least, get to know the faculty in your major field.

· (3) Meet business people.

Widening your contacts with business people can also lead to employment contacts. You may already know some people through family and part-time jobs. You might meet others through professional clubs and career days sponsored by your college or by attending conferences and seminars.

· (4) Make contacts through internships.

If your school offers an internship or co-op program, do not regard it as just a course requirement. It could be a foundation step in your career plan. The contacts you make in an internship might well lead to your first career position. In addition, this opportunity offers valuable training and experience for your résumé.

· (5) Work with community organizations.

By working in community organizations (charities, community improvement groups, or fund-raising groups), you can meet community leaders. In fact, participation in virtually any activity that provides access to community, business, or political contacts can open doors for you now and well into the future.

Analyzing Yourself

· Begin with a self-analysis covering these background areas:

When you are ready to search for your career job, you should begin the effort by analyzing yourself to develop a personal inventory. In a sense you should look at yourself much as you would look at a product or service that you want to advertize. After all, when you seek employment, you are really selling your ability to work for an employer. For now, write down everything you can. Your goal is to make a complete list of your skills and attributes. When you apply for a job, you will select from this personal inventory the most beneficial points.

A PRACTICE RUN

List specific ways to broaden your contacts. What organizations can you join? Whom can you meet? What workshops or seminars can you attend?

_____

_____

_____

_____

Education.   The analysis might well begin with education. Perhaps you have already selected your career area, such as accounting, finance, or marketing. If you have, your task is simplified, because your specialized curriculum has prepared you for your goal. Even so, you should note special points such as elective courses that have given you additional skills or that show something special about you. You also should look at the quality of your record, including grades, honours, and special awards.

    If you have pursued a general curriculum, you will need to look at it closely to see what it has prepared you to do. Perhaps you will find an emphasis on computers, written communication, human relations, foreign languages—all of which are sorely needed by businesses. Or perhaps you will conclude that your training has given you a strong general base from which to learn specific business skills.

• (1) Education.

A PRACTICE RUN

Note your education and training with the appropriate dates. Be specific about advanced coursework. Include courses such as first-aid training, music certificates, and so on to make this list as complete as possible.

_____

_____

_____

_____

Personal Qualities.   Your self-analysis should cover your personal qualities. Qualities such as team-building skills and leadership skills that relate to working with people are especially important. And if you express yourself well in writing or speaking, note this. Good communication skills are valuable in almost all jobs.

• (2) Personal qualities (people skills, leadership, etc.).

A PRACTICE RUN

List your personal strengths and the evidence you can present to support each characteristic.

_____

_____

_____

_____

From a speech given on June 14, 1996, by the Honourable Alfonso Gagliano, P.C., Minister of Labour and Deputy Leader of the Government in the House of Commons, to the Canadian Employment Research Forum Conference, Ottawa, June 13–15, 1996.

Past generations could rely on their success at university to secure their future. Today, however, young graduates need broader, more diversified knowledge beyond their own specialties in order to meet the needs of our time. To be successful, they must also develop a dynamic attitude toward work. They must master several languages, keep abreast of the latest technology, and pit themselves against the best in their fields, not only here at home, but throughout the world.[†]

[†] Source: *Collective Reflection on the Changing Workplace/Réflexion collective sur le milieu de travail en évolution.* http://www.reflexion.gc.ca/speech_e.html (accessed Aug. 31, 1996).

Of course, you may not be the best judge of your personal qualities. We do not always see ourselves as others see us. You may need to check with friends to see whether they agree with your assessments. You also need to check your record for evidence supporting your assessments. For example, organization memberships and participation in community activities are evidence of teamwork skills. Election to office is evidence of leadership ability. Participation on a debate team is evidence of communication skills. With evidence like this to choose from, you will be able to select your strongest points for each application.

• (3) Work experience, including volunteer activities (with interpretations).

Work Experience.   Because your work experience deserves major emphasis, you should analyze it fully. As you move along your career path, related work experience becomes more and more important. For your first career job, however, you may not have closely related experience. You will have to search out the useful skills you have learned. For example, part-time or menial work can show willingness and determination, especially if you have done it to finance your education.

A PRACTICE RUN

List your paid work experience and the skills learned.

_____

_____

List your volunteer experience and the skills learned.

_____

_____

As well as your paid employment, consider any volunteer experience you have had such as coaching a community sports team or holding an office in student government. Almost any paid or volunteer position can be useful if you analyze it carefully. Look for *transferable skills.* Transferable skills such as teaching, supervising, public speaking, budgeting, organizing, or co-ordinating are useful in almost any job setting. They are, as the name suggests, transferable from one job to the next. Do you work well on a team? Have you learned to handle stress and meet deadlines? These are transferable skills.

Special Qualifications.   As well as looking for transferable skills, you should note any special qualifications that might be valuable to an employer. Analyze your paid employment, volunteer work, studies, hobbies, and interests again. Are you able to speak a language other than English? Do you have athletic experience that would be helpful for a sporting goods distributor? Knowledge gained through a hobby of automobile mechanics would be helpful for work with a parts' wholesaler or retailer, and an interest in music would be helpful for work with a ticket agency or music supplier. Use your imagination and positive thinking skills to find the potential connections.

• (4) Special qualifications (include languages, communication skills, computer skills, etc.).

A PRACTICE RUN

List any special qualifications you may have. These may not have been learned through formal training.

_____

_____

_____

_____

Now that you have completed these steps in your self-evaluation, study Figure 11–1, the actual worksheet of a university student preparing to apply for summer work. In later figures in this chapter, you will see how she selected from this information to tailor her application to different jobs.

A PRACTICE RUN

Select the items from the student worksheet in Figure 11–1 that she should emphasize if she applies to Doreen Lam for the position at Good 'n Nice. (See the introductory situation to this chapter.)

_____

_____

_____

_____

Selecting Your Career Path

With a personal inventory of all your qualifications, you are ready to select the career path that is just right for you. This task involves matching the facts you have listed with the work needs of business. Your education may have narrowed your choice to an area of work such as marketing, information systems, or accounting. A review of your qualifications and personal preferences will indicate what you are best equipped to do. Your goal in this process is to give realistic direction to your search for employment.

• Select your career path.

FIGURE 11-1   A Student's Draft Worksheet: *Looking for a Summer Job*

This is the actual worksheet drafted by a student beginning her search for a summer job. It is used by permission. She has listed as much information as she can think of and has tried to organize it into categories. She has also noted the characteristic that might be demonstrated by her activities. Remember that this is an example of how one student approached the problem and not necessarily the only or best way for you.

General Abilities	
Skill	**Characteristic Shown**
baby-sitting	responsible, work with all ages
summer camp counsellor	leadership
working closely with fellow students at university	teamwork
assisting elderly neighbours (yard work, cleaning, errands)	caring, work with all ages
honours average at university	concentrate, work hard, learn quickly, organized
volunteer leader with the high school youth	time management, work with all ages
Education	
University—Faculty of Science, Math & Physics	1993–Present
R S C High School	1989–1993
Young Life Leader Training Program	date?
YL Work Crew Training Program	date?
Awards and Achievements	
Canada Scholarship	1994, 1993
McKinney Scholarship	1994
Douglas Sheppard Scholarship	1994
U of A Entrance Award	1993
Major Service & Major Curricular Award RSCHS	1992, 1991, 1990? (Check dates)
Possible References	
Christine	Razia
Derek	Pat & Dudley

Continued on page 237.

• Narrow your selection to type of employer.

At this point you may narrow your selection even further. If you are an accounting major, for example, you may decide to look for work with a large firm or in a small, private practice. You may consider work in industry or a government agency. If you are a marketing major, you may narrow your search to wholesaling or retailing, to merchandising giants or smaller operations, or to conservative or aggressive merchandisers.

• Consider location limitations.

In addition, you should consider where you would be willing to work. Are there places where you would not be willing to work? Are you willing to travel around the country? To work abroad? Your answers to such questions are important in your job search, because they affect the job opportunities available to you. Although the availability of work may answer the questions for you, you should answer them based on your preferences as well. Then you can consider the plusses and minuses of each situation to develop a realistic search for a satisfying job.

Finding Your Employer

• Search for potential employers by using these sources:

You can use a number of sources in your search for an employer. Your choice of sources will be influenced by where you are in your career path—just beginning, making a career change, or looking for advancement.

FIGURE 11-1 *Continued.*

Work Experience		
Date	**Job**	**Duties**
July 11-17, 1993	Supervisor, Musicamrose	Counselled junior high school students
September 1992-April 1993	Teacher aide for Department of Music, R S C H S	Coached ensembles, led sectionals, updated music library
September 1991-June 1992	The Muffin Break	Served customers, handled cash, cleaned, opened & closed Worked alone and in teams
September 1991-Present	Math and Physics Tutor	Tutor Junior and Senior High School students (communicate well, explain concepts simply)

Volunteer Experience		
Date	**Job**	**Duties**
August 1994-Present	YL Leader	Counsel at camps, plan weekly activities for high school students
June & July 1994	Office Assistant	Helped plan two large fund-raising events, answered phones, entered info into a database
July 19-25, 1994	Head Cook, Rockies Bike Trip	Planned menu, shopped, cooked (organized) Supervised, co-ordinated team Motivated volunteer workers
check dates	Camp work crew	Worked with teens and adults (teamwork) Physical work (healthy)

Network of Personal Contacts. As has been noted, the personal contacts you make can be extremely helpful in your job search. In fact, personal contacts are becoming the leading means of finding employees. It is always worthwhile to let people know that you are looking for a job.

• (1) your network of personal contacts,

College and University Placement Centres. If you are just beginning your career, one good possibility is the placement centre at your school. Most of the large schools have placement centres, and these attract employers who are looking for suitable applicants. Many placement centres offer excellent job-search counselling and maintain files on registrants (containing school records, résumés, and recommendation letters) for review by prospective employers.

• (2) your school's placement centre,

Government Employment Centres. The federal and provincial governments provide many services to job seekers through career development and employment centres. Services include help with career guidance, résumés, application forms and letters, and interview techniques. As well, these employment centres keep files on potential employers with contact names and type of employment opportunities. Sometimes they also arrange on-campus interviews and alert job seekers to new jobs as they become available.

• (3) federal and provincial employment centres,

The federal and provincial governments also offer many publications with helpful tips suited to your type of work and region.

• (4) on-line services,

On-Line Services.   A few moments on the Internet will lead you to many companies looking for employees. It is particularly helpful if you are willing to relocate to other parts of Canada, the United States, or other continents.[5] Both large and small companies have established web pages to tell the world about their business. Before you respond electronically to advertized positions, you should be aware that computer networks can turn private information into public information in milliseconds. Since the degree of security varies from one system to the next, you would be wise to check out the measures you need to take to protect yourself.

The Canadian Association of Career Educators and Employers (CACEE—pronounced Casey) has an exceptional site on the World Wide Web. Their Work Web pages give very useful information about making applications, locating companies, and competing in interviews.[6] For more Canadian information, look at CanWorkNet,[7] and The Canadian Job Source.[8]

• (5) prospecting techniques,

Prospecting.   Some job seekers approach prospective employers in person to try to introduce themselves to the company they would like to work for. Personal visits to drop off résumés are effective. Of course, the opportunity to meet someone who will influence a hiring decision is more likely with a smaller company.

There are also many résumés posted on the Web. If developing a web site could be part of the requirements for the type of job you want, an on-line résumé is an obvious plus. Once your résumé has been posted, it is available worldwide; however, having it seen by the appropriate people is still a challenge. You have to invite employers to visit your site. Since many employers still depend on paper formats, a printed résumé should be prepared as well.

• (6) classified advertizements, and

Classified Advertizements.   Career sections and help-wanted advertizements in newspapers and professional journals list employment opportunities for many kinds of work. Although they are limited in the opportunities they provide for new college graduates, they can be good sources for experienced workers seeking to improve their positions or change their career field.

• (7) employment agencies.

Employment Agencies.   Companies that specialize in finding jobs for employees can be useful, especially if you seek to change employment later in your career. Of course, such companies charge for their services. But because many now use on-line database systems for listing the job opportunities, they are up-to-date. In a tight job market, this timeliness makes paying a fee worthwhile. The employer sometimes pays the charges, usually if qualified applicants are scarce. Employment agencies are commonly used to place experienced people in managerial positions.

Studying the Audience

• Study prospective employers to know what they want.

As with any persuasive presentation, you need to study the audience. In this case studying the audience means learning as much as you can about the company's history, plans, policies, and operations. Refer to standard business reference works, the annual report of the company, recent newspaper or magazine articles about the company, and, of course, the World Wide Web. At the same time, learn as much as you can about the requirements for any job you are considering. Ask questions of the people in your network and, if

---

[5]You may also wish to consult Jena-Marc Hackey's book *The Canadian Guide to Working and Living Overseas.* The second edition printed in 1995 is available from Intercultural Systems/Systèmes interculturels (ISSI), PO Box 588, Station B, Ottawa, K1P 5P7.

[6]You can visit their site at http://www.cacee.com (accessed Aug. 20, 1996).

[7] http://canworknet.ingenia.com/canworknet (accessed Aug. 31, 1996).

[8] http://www.irus.rri.uwo.ca/~jlaw/job_can.html (accessed Aug. 31, 1996).

possible, the people in the company. You then compare this information with your personal inventory and select the points that match the employer's criteria.

Research supports the need for adapting your application to the employer. A study by Zane Quible showed that information considered important by one company is not the same for another. Differences also existed between departments of the same company. This study supports the necessity for researching prospective employers and jobs to know what to include in your application.[9]

THE RÉSUMÉ

The résumé is a formal listing of the relevant details of your background and qualifications drawn from your personal inventory. You will want to include in the résumé all background information you think the reader should have about you. Designed for quick reading, the résumé usually has concise points arranged under keyword headings.

Two basic types of résumés are common. One type, the *general* résumé, covers a variety of jobs. It is the type you would send to a placement centre. The second type, the *targeted* résumé, is written for one company and one job. The wording, information, and organization are targeted toward this one position. Because it is personalized, the targeted résumé is more effective and worth the effort. We will consider two patterns of targeted résumés, the chronological and the functional.

* The résumé lists facts in some orderly way.

* The general type of résumé fits several companies and jobs. The targeted résumé is personalized to fit one company and one job.

Differences in Format and Content

The correct format and content for résumés and application letters is a hotly debated issue. Most employers and communication experts have strongly held opinions on what they would like to see in these documents. Unfortunately, many of these opinions are different. Why do these differences exist, and why are they so strongly defended? The primary reason is that résumés and application letters are personal documents. They are written by a specific person for a specific job. They try to represent that person to the employers in a way that shows the close match between the candidate and the job. Moreover, they try to accomplish the task in a way that the employer will notice favourably and that the candidate will recognize as true and accurate.

* Preferences for job search documents vary.

Does this mean that any approach is acceptable? Yes and no. While there may be no one standard that is correct for all résumés, there is a correct way to write a particular résumé. Because it is a personal document written within a context for the purpose of getting an interview, the correctness of style in a résumé is defined by the circumstances. However, the correct approach will follow certain principles. Therefore, our discussion of job search documents will focus on guidelines rather than the details that may vary from one situation to another.

* Let the context influence how you shape your job search documents.

Four Guidelines for Résumé Writing

Guideline One. *Prioritize the contents of your résumé for each employment opportunity.*

Organize your résumé based on what qualifications best suit you for this job. Your strongest qualification may be your education, or you may have experience that sets you apart from other graduates. Alternatively, you may need to summarize skills learned from both your training and your work experience to show your qualifications for this position.

Put enough relevant information on the first half page to have your résumé selected for further consideration. If it is being scanned by a person, the first half of the first page is the most important. Ten to fifteen seconds is all an experienced employer will take to decide whether your application makes the first cut. If it is being scanned by computer,

---

[9]Zane K. Quible, "The importance of résumé content items as perceived by those who make the final hiring decisions about recent business graduates." Paper presented at the 57th Annual Convention of the Association for Business Communication, November 7, 1992.

the key words chosen by the employer must be found. If very few of them appear on the first page, the résumé may be rejected.

Guideline Two. *Make the résumé truly representative of your skills and personality.*

If an interview is granted, the person the employer wants to talk to is the one seen in the résumé. Therefore, be sure that the picture is as true as possible. If you model your résumé after others you have seen, be very careful to personalize it enough to be representative of you and not the model. For the same reason, professionally prepared résumés may give disappointing results.

Guideline Three. *Make your résumé as complete and accurate as possible within the space limitations.*[10]

- Be sure to include all of your qualifications and not to minimize or exaggerate them. A false claim on a résumé can be reason for dismissal.
- Make sure your dates, addresses, and postal codes are accurate and complete. If you include telephone numbers, use the area codes as well. Partial information is not useful to the interviewer and just takes up space that should be better used.
- Check and recheck for spelling and grammar corrections. Be particularly careful with the spelling of names that will not be detected by your word processor.

Guideline Four. *Make your résumé attractive and professional looking.*

Since you are applying for a job in business, you want your résumé to give a professional, business-like impression.[11] Here are some ideas to help you achieve this goal.

- Choose your paper carefully. Usually white or off-white is best.
- Use a bubble jet or laser printer.
- Keep the fonts simple and clear.
- Balance the page attractively. (Avoid too much or too little white space.) A crowded page is difficult to scan and read; an empty page gives the impression of having nothing to say.

FAQs (Frequently Asked Questions) about Résumés

Question: If my name and address is on the envelope and on the covering letter, do I need it on the résumé too?

- Display your contact information prominently.

Your name, address, and telephone number should be on the résumé because documents often become separated. Make it as easy as possible for the interviewer to contact you and call you by name by displaying this information prominently at the top of the page. The most common location is at the left margin or centred. If you need to include a permanent address and a current (school term) address, place them side by side rather than underneath one another. Two columns will use fewer lines and avoid empty space along the sides. Remember that the beginning is a position of emphasis that needs careful planning for the best use.

Question: Do I have to use a job or career objective?

- Consider a statement of your objective.

Although not all authorities agree on its value, a statement of your objective may be appropriate. Since the objective uses prime space at the top of the résumé, its content must be important enough to justify the prominence given to it. For example, an accounting graduate who writes, "My objective is to find a job where I can use my accounting skills and

---

[10] For additional hints, see the box "Making Your Résumé Attractive."

[11] An exception might be an application for a position such as a graphic artist when innovation and creativity are appreciated.

make a contribution to the company," is wasting time and space in stating the obvious. Compose a concise statement of your goal, being specific and realistic, to give the recruiter a clear picture of how you would fit into the company. The accounting student applying to a large firm for a temporary position in the personal income tax department might write

Job Objective: To use this temporary position to apply and develop my recent training in the taxation field and to demonstrate my abilities to accept responsibility and work efficiently as part of a team.

Question: Do my points have to be arranged under Education and Work Experience?

The background facts you have assembled about yourself need to be arranged into logical groups. The most conventional is this four-part grouping: experience, education, personal qualities, and references. However, many other arrangements are possible.

- Organize the facts into logical groups.

In a functional résumé, you organize your points around the skills or qualifications you have. For example, you may want to stress your leadership skills. These were learned through courses in organizational behaviour, coaching a community sports team, and chairing meetings for your student council. In this example, the traditional four groupings would limit your ability to express the strengths you have in leadership.

Question: What is the difference between a chronological and a functional résumé?

In a chronological résumé, you list your qualifications under standard headings in a reversed time order. That is, for work experience, you start with your present or most recent job and move back in time to earlier jobs. A chronological résumé works well if you have systematically moved along a path from high school to college to work. It allows you to show clearly any promotions or advancements you have made from year to year in your work experience or education.

- Chronological and functional résumés serve different purposes.

If you have a mixed background, perhaps changing programs in college, returning for retraining in a new field, or returning to the work force after a period away, the chronological résumé is limiting. A functional résumé allows you to arrange your points under the qualifications you wish to stress. Perhaps you have strong transferable skills. These are often best disclosed in a functional résumé.

In some instances other organization plans may be effective. One possibility is organization by the job requirements stated in the advertisement (for example, proven interpersonal skills, training, and related experience). Another possibility is to use a strict time basis integrating education and experience into one sequence. You may be able to work out other plans. A general principle is to strive for simplicity and clarity. Any plan that favourably presents and clearly communicates the information is all right.

Question: Can I combine the functional and the chronological formats?

With care the functional and the chronological formats can be used together in a combination résumé. Special groupings such as *Achievements* and *Qualifications* highlight information drawn from the more conventional groupings. For example, points covered under *Qualifications* may bring together information from the three areas of education, experience, and personal qualities. Typically, this arrangement emphasizes your most impressive background facts that pertain to the work sought, as in this example:

- Special groupings may be used to highlight extraordinary performance.

Qualifications

Experienced:	Three years of practical work as programmer/analyst. Designed and developed financial software for the banking industry.
Highly trained:	B.Sc. degree with honours in computer science.
Self-motivated:	Proven record of successful completion of independent work on major projects.

Although such items may overlap other categories in the résumé, using them again in a separate group emphasizes your strengths. The concern with a combination résumé is the challenge of stating the information clearly and concisely.

Making Your Résumé Attractive

The attractiveness of your résumé will create the first impression readers have of you. Before they begin to read the words, they will notice the appearance of the information. That appearance plays a part in the decision about your suitability. If there are hundreds of applications, what easier way to begin the selection process than to make a quick check of neatness and correctness. To be sure that your application makes that first cut, make your letter and résumé attractive and correct.

Designing the résumé for eye appeal is no routine matter. There is no one best arrangement, but a good procedure is to approach the task as a designer would in planning a magazine layout. Your goal is to work out an arrangement of type and space that appears pleasing to the eye.

- The résumé should be complete in not more than two pages and the application letter in one.[†]

- Heavy, crowded arrangements appear difficult to read and are often ignored, whereas line spacing and indentations make the contents easy and attractive to read. Therefore,

  - Margins should be at least 2.5 centimetres at the top and sides of the pages and at least 3.5 centimetres at the bottom to frame your text.

  - Each factual item should have its own line. This practice keeps the lines short and easy to scan.

  - Descriptive items of information are more appropriately set up in longer lines to keep related thoughts together.

  - If there is too much white space in some parts, such as in the list of references, you may find a two-column layout more attractive.

- Be absolutely certain that spelling, grammar, and punctuation are correct. Pay close attention to personal names that will not be recognized by spell-checking software.

[†] Experts have varying opinions on the exact length of résumés. From personal observation, many U.S. communication texts strictly require a one-page résumé while Canadian sources usually advise not more than two pages. There is strong agreement on the principle that your résumé should be short, clear, and easy to read.

---

* Headings should be grammatically parallel and emphasized by some mechanical means.

Question: How do I write the headings?

By far the most commonly used form is the topic heading, which identifies the subject covered in a word or two. For example, *Education, Experience, Objective,* and *References* are suitable topic headings for the parts of a résumé. *Interests, Achievements,* and *Qualifications* are also frequently used. There are two rules about headings.

1. Headings should be grammatically parallel in structure.

The headings on the left do not use grammatically parallel structure. The first two headings are nouns modified by adjectives, the third is an adjective alone, and the fourth is a noun alone. The errors have been corrected in the example to the right.

HEADINGS ARE NOT PARALLEL	HEADINGS ARE PARALLEL
Specialized Training	Specialized Training
Related Experience	Related Experience
Personal	Personal Attributes
References	Qualified References

2. Headings should be formatted in the same way for easy identification.

Consistently use the same mechanical device to emphasize headings at the same level. Choose a method of emphasis that is attractive and properly shows the relative importance of the information. If you choose capital letters and boldface for **EDUCATION,** other headings at the same level of importance should also be in capital letters and boldface, such as **EXPERIENCE** and **REFERENCES.** The illustrations in the chapter give more examples for you to study.

Question: Can I make the headings more interesting?

Although talking headings are unusual in an entry-level résumé, some authorities suggest them because they are interesting. Talking headings use additional words to draw favourable attention to the items covered. Their form is best explained by illustration. Instead of *Education,* you would write *Specialized Training in Accounting.* Instead of *References,* you would use *Supervisors and Instructors Who Know My Work.* Be selective about using this method because some employers would be unhappy with this non-standard approach.

> • Topic headings are interesting but unusual.

Question: Should I use sentences or point form in my résumé?

As the résumé is a listing of information, you should write in point form for the most part, making your points grammatically parallel. Remember that your résumé does not stand alone. The application letter and the interview give you opportunities to explain points more fully.

> • List the information under the headings in point form.

Question: Guideline three says to be complete. What is "complete information" about my work experience?

Your coverage of working experience should include dates, position held, company, and skills or duties that show your accomplishments. For recent jobs you could consider including a telephone number or address, but only if your supervisor is still there and is willing to talk to your potential employers. If there is someone at your last place of work you would prefer not talk to a potential employer, you can direct the recruiter to someone who will speak well of you by including a name and telephone number here. Student jobs should be listed as *part-time* or *summer* to prevent confusion.

> • As a minimum for job experience, include dates, position, firm, and accomplishments.

You will want to present your work experience in words that do the most for you. Try to bring out skills or accomplishments that will apply to the job you seek. For example, you could write "1991–94: Office manager for Carson's." But it would be better to give this fuller description that points out your accomplishments: "1991–94: Office manager for Carson's, supervising a staff of 14."

Question: Do I include dates for my education as well?

Education gets less emphasis in your application as you gain related experience. If, however, you are applying for your first career job, you will cover your education in some detail. At a minimum your coverage should include institutions; dates; diplomas, certificates or degrees; and major areas of study. On occasion, you may want to list advanced courses if your course work has uniquely prepared you for the job.

> • For education, include schools, dates, diplomas, certificates or degrees, and areas of study.

Education and experience begin with the most recent and work back as shown here.

EDUCATION

1993–1995	Great Lakes Community College Business Administration Program Diploma in Accounting
1991–1992	Huron University Faculty of Arts and Science Completed 1 year
1987–1991	West Glen Composite High School Advanced (Matriculation) Diploma with honours

Question: Should I say that I will work very hard because I am an immigrant to Canada and it is part of our culture to work hard?

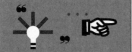

Résumé software programs are on store shelves everywhere. Since both their price and their quality vary widely, your decision about these programs is twofold—should you use one? and which one?

Résumé programs help with the selection and layout of résumés. They give ideas on what should be included by posing questions. After you complete a template, the program arranges the information into an attractive format. Some of these programs include a spell checker and/or a thesaurus to help you describe yourself accurately. A few of them have small databases for you to keep track of names and addresses of references and contacts. A few even include a calendar feature, allowing you to keep track of interview times and dates.

Although they can be helpful, résumé programs can limit the amount of flexibility you have. When considering a résumé writing program, you will want to check

- How many layouts are possible?
- Can headings be customized and subdivided?
- How much space is available under each heading?
- Is this program compatible with my computer, printer, and software?

When deciding whether to use résumé generating software, you should carefully evaluate all the features you intend to use. If you are competent with your full-featured word processing software, you probably can manage without one. On the other hand, some of the well-done programs can make your entire job search process easier. If the package you are evaluating serves you well, use it!

- Some personal information (race, religion, age, etc.) should probably not be listed.

Are there other ways that you could show your personal characteristic of dedication?

The trend is that personal information, such as marital status, height, weight, health, race, religion, and age should be omitted. First, current human rights legislation prohibits hiring decisions being based on such information. If it is not included, the question of favouritism or discrimination cannot arise. And secondly, it takes up precious space with details. In a survey of *Fortune 500* companies, personnel directors indicated that this type of personal information was unimportant. They reported more interest in education, job-related information, and a willingness to relocate.[12]

Personal information that is generally appropriate supports your personal qualities. Information on your professional memberships, civic involvement, and social activities is evidence of experience and interest in working with people. Hobbies and athletics tell of your balance of interests. Such evidence can be quite useful.

Question: Should I list my references or not?

- You may list references, or you may postpone them.

Whether to list the names and addresses of references on the résumé is another matter of debate. Although some authorities think that references should not be given until negotiations are further along, others recommend including references because employers want to check them early in the screening process. Your decision will have to be based on the circumstances.

- Be ready to provide reference information when it is requested.

If you decide not to list your references, you should acknowledge the absence. You can do this with a comment such as "References will be provided on request." Be sure to keep your promise by having a prepared reference sheet that you can produce as soon as requested. If your reference list has not been requested before the interview, take it with you.

- Make your reference information complete.

When you do list your references, either in your résumé or on a separate sheet, be sure that the information is complete. The reason a reference is listed is to allow the employer

---

[12]Jules Harcourt and A.C. Krizan, "A Comparison of Résumé Content Preferences of *Fortune 500* Personnel Administrators and Business Communication Instructors," *Journal of Business Communication*, Spring 1989: 177–191.

THAT'S NOT WHAT WE MEANT BY AN ELECTRONIC RÉSUMÉ

to contact the person. Therefore, you should include a complete mailing address with the postal code. If available, a telephone number and an e-mail address are also useful.

Question: Whom should I choose as a reference?

Generally, employment or education references are preferred over character references, but whom to list may vary from one application to another. Choose people who can verify the points on which your appeal for the job is based. If you base your application on your education or personal qualities, you should include those who can vouch for you in those areas such as professors, clergy, or community leaders. If you have work experience, you should include a name from your latest job or from recent major jobs. Relatives are not acceptable as references.

• Select references that cover your background. Have their approval before you use their names.

Standard letters of reference—the type addressed *To Whom It May Concern* and given as a matter of course when an employee leaves a job—are not effective and are usually not considered because they are too general and do not address the issues that are important to the current job.

Be sure that you have the permission of your references to use their names. You also should give them permission to release information about you. As a courtesy give them a recent copy of your résumé and keep them informed of your progress. At the very least, let them know when your job search has been successful.

Examples of Résumés

The résumé by Len Darcus is attractively arranged. The information is neither crowded nor strung out, giving good balance to the page. The content shows the quality of Mr. Darcus's work experience and education. The words emphasize points that make this man suited for the work he seeks. This résumé excludes trivial personal information and has only the facts that tell something about Darcus's personal qualities. Complete mailing addresses let the reader contact the references easily. Job titles tell how each is qualified to evaluate the subject.

The second case illustration is the work of the student looking for a summer position. Her worksheet appears in Figure 11–1. She has decided that neither her education nor her work experience are strong qualifications for the job. Therefore, she begins with transferable skills that will give strong support to her application. She emphasizes her experience in working with youth and with seniors. This experience is an obvious asset for a co-ordinator of teen volunteers in a seniors' residence. She was the successful candidate from about 90 applicants.

LEN DARCUS

3177 North Hawthorne Boulevard   (604)967-3117 (home)
Vancouver, BC V6E 2K3   (604)938-4449 (work)

Employment Goal: To obtain entry-level work in labour relations that will build on my training and experience and lead to work as a labour relations specialist.

Experience

1988-1993   Equipment repair worker, Davidson Electric Company, North Vancouver, BC

1986-1988   Driver, Wayland Trucking Company, Kelowna, BC, active member of union Local 714

1984-1986 (part-time)   Greenhouse worker, Kiawa Growers Penticton, BC

Education

1993-1997   Lakeland University
Bachelor of Business Administration, labour relations major
Grade-point averages: 3.9 in major field, 3.7 overall

1983-1986   C.H. Aldridge High School, Penticton, BC

Personal Qualities

Interests: Active in sports such as tennis, fishing, jogging
Avid reader

Activities: Lakeland University Alumni Association
served as secretary, presently serving as vice-president
Delta Community League
served as membership chairman

References

Ms. June Rogers
Davidson Electric Company
7114 East 17th Street
North Vancouver, BC V6E 1S5
Telephone: (604)342-1171

Mr. Todd Frankle, Manager
Wayland Trucking Company
477 Bleaker Street
Kelowna, BC V2J 1R3
Telephone: (604)466-9101

Professor Helen Robbins
Department of Management
Lakeland University
North Bay, ON P1B 1A9
Telephone: (705)392-6673

Professor Carl Schmidt
Department of Economics
Lakeland University
North Bay, ON P1B 1A9
Telephone: (705)392-7879

CASE ILLUSTRATION   A Student's Résumé: *Applying for a Paid Summer Job as Co-ordinator of Teen Volunteers at a Seniors' Lodge.*[†]

Name   permanent address
current address
telephone

Skills and Abilities:

<u>Interpersonal skills</u>: I work well with people of all age groups, baby-sitting young children, counselling high school students at summer camps, working closely with fellow students at university, and assisting elderly neighbours.

<u>Time Management skills</u>: I am an organized worker and have maintained an honours average at university. I manage my time effectively so that I can be involved as a volunteer leader with the high school group, Young Life.

Education:

University of Alberta, Faculty of Science   1993-Present[†]
Entering third year Math and Physics

Young Life of Edmonton   1990 and 1994
Leader and Work Crew Training Programs

Work Experience:

July 11-17, 1993   Supervisor, Musicamrose
                         Counselled junior high school students

Sept.1992-April 1993   Teacher aide, Ross Sheppard High
                         School Music Department
                         Coached ensembles, led sectionals,
                         updated music library

Sept.1991-June 1992   Muffin Break, Jasper Gates Square
                         Served customers, handled cash, opened
                         and closed
                         Worked alone and in teams

Sept.1991-Present[†]   Math/Physics tutor for High School and
                         Junior High students

Related Volunteer Experience:

August 1994-Present   Young Life Leader
                         Counsel at camps, plan weekly
                         activities for teens

July 19-25, 1994   Head Cook, Young Life Rockies Bike Trip
                         Supervised, co-ordinated, and motivated
                         teen volunteers

1990-1993   Work crew at summer and winter camps
                         Worked in teams with teens and adults

Activities and Achievements:

<u>Music</u>:
Since 1990, I have been an active member of several orchestras, ensembles, and bands including the Youth Orchestra and the Conservatory of Music Academy Program. I also participated in the Centennial Singers (EPSB honour choir) from 1991 to 1993. My music training from the Royal Conservatory of Music includes Grade 10 French Horn, Grade 3 History, and Grade 3 Harmony.

<u>Academic</u>:
Canada Scholarship   1994, 1993
McKinney Scholarship   1994
Douglas Sheppard Scholarship   1994
University of Alberta Entrance Award   1993

References will be supplied upon request.

[†]Note: This résumé was completed in 1995 by the student who prepared the worksheet in Figure 11-1. It is used by permission.

A PRACTICE RUN

Critique the following résumé by contrasting it with the case illustration of Mr. Darcus's résumé. There are *many* faults to note.

LEN DARCUS
3177 North Hawthorne Boulevard
Vancouver, V6E 2K3

My Experience in Labour

1988–1993	Equipment repair, Davidson Electric, North Vancouver, BC
1986–1988	Driver, Wayland Trucking, Kelowna, BC
1984–1986	Helper, Kiawa Growers, Penticton, BC

My Education in Labour

1993–1997   Lakeland University, Bachelor of Business Administration degree, major in labour relations, 24 semester hours in labour and management courses, a 3.7 grade-point average, 3.9 in major field
1983–1986   C.H. Aldridge High School, Penticton, BC

My Personal Qualities

Age:27, Married, One child, age 1
5 ft. 11 in., 165 pounds
Interests: tennis, fishing, reading
Active in sports

Memberships:

Lakeland University Alumni Association
Delta Community League

People Who Know His Abilities

Ms. June Rogers	Prof. Helen K. Robbins
Davidson Electric	Lakeland University
N. Vancouver, BC	North Bay, Ont.
Mr. Todd Frankle	Prof. Carl Schmidt
Wayland Trucking Co.	Lakeland University
477 Bleaker Street	North Bay, Ont.
Kelowna, BC	

THE APPLICATION LETTER

* The application letter is a persuasive letter that accompanies the résumé.

The application letter is a covering letter to accompany your résumé. Its purpose is to present your application in a persuasive way. You want to highlight your strengths for this job so that the employer will give attention to your résumé over the many others received. Since a job application is a competition, you will have to win the time and attention of this employer by fitting the facts from your background to the work you seek. The following general plan will be discussed in detail below.

* Follow this general plan for writing a letter of application.

- Begin with words selected to gain attention appropriately and to set up the review of information.

- Present your qualifications, keeping like information together and adapting to the company and the job.

- Use good persuasive strategy, especially the you-viewpoint and positive language, to show how you can fulfil the requirements of the job.

- Ask for the appropriate action (request an interview, invite reference checks, ask to be kept on file).

After reading a student's application letter, Professor Sneer made this comment to the business communication class: "This is positively the worst letter submitted. It violates just about every writing principle I have emphasized in this course."

"That's my letter," an angry student responded. "I'll have you know that I copied it from one a friend wrote. And *it got the job* for my friend!"

"I was just getting to the letter's strong point," replied Professor Sneer. "The salutation overcomes all the letter's weaknesses. Can you imagine anything more effective than 'Dear Dad'!"

Gaining Attention in the Opening

As in persuasive writing, the opening of the application letter has two requirements: It must gain attention, and it must set up the review of information that follows.

> • Gain attention and set up the information review in the opening.

Gaining attention is especially important in prospecting letters (application letters that are not invited). Such letters are likely to reach busy people who have many things to do other than read application letters. Unless the letter gains favourable attention right away, the potential employer probably will not read it. Even invited letters must gain attention because they will have to compete with many other applications. Many possibilities exist. There is no need to use the dull, overworked beginnings such as "This letter is to apply for. . . " and "Please consider this my application for. . . . "

The application letter should be a creative effort with your imagination being guided by the work you seek. Take, for example, work that requires an outgoing personality and a vivid imagination, such as sales or public relations. In such cases you could show these qualities in your opening words. Work in a more conservative field, such as accounting or banking, requires openings that are more conservative.

> • Make the opening fit the job.

You can gain attention in the opening in many ways. One way is to use a topic that shows understanding of the reader's operation or of the work to be done. Employers are likely to be impressed by applicants who have made the effort to learn something about the company, as in this example:

> • You can gain attention by showing an understanding of the reader's operations.

Now that Taggart has expanded operations to Central America, can you use a business administration graduate who is fluent in Spanish and is familiar with the culture of the region?

Another way is to make a statement or ask a question that focuses attention on a need of the reader that you can fill. The following opening illustrates this approach:

> • You can stress a need of the reader that you can fill.

As a recent business college graduate with retail experience in two dynamic stores, I can quickly become a productive part of your sales team.

If you learn of a job possibility through a company employee, mentioning the employee's name can gain attention as in this opening sentence:

> • Using the name of an employee makes your letter stand out.

At the suggestion of Ms. Martha Hawkes of your staff, I submit the following summary of my banking experience for work as your loan supervisor.

Your opening paragraph or a subject line should clearly identify the position or the type of work for which you are applying. As early as possible begin to show your qualifications for the work to be done. The following example structures the review of qualifications around two areas—education and experience.

> • Your opening should also identify the job and begin to show your qualifications.

As an honours graduate in accounting with experience in the petroleum industry, I believe I meet your qualifications for the position you listed in today's *Post*. (Competition A-1151M)

Selecting Content

• Present the key points from your résumé that fit you to the job.

Following the opening, you should present more information that qualifies you to do the work. Since an application letter should be only one page long, carefully select the facts about you that best match the requirements for the job. Remember that the application letter does the selling and the résumé summarizes the significant details. The letter should contain the major points around which you build your case, and the résumé should include these points plus supporting details. As the two are parts of a team effort, you should refer the reader to the résumé somewhere in the letter.

Writing for Impact

• Select an order that complements and highlights your résumé.

The application letter gives you an opportunity to repeat some ideas from your résumé in a different way. For example, you may want to show that your education and summer jobs fit together to build your qualifications. It also gives you the opportunity to say things you could not bring out in your résumé. If communication skills and time management skills are listed in the job requirements, you can briefly describe specific situations in which you have used these skills. You may have learned to prioritize and balance your time among studies, a part-time job, and family commitments, for example.

• Avoid the tendency to overuse *I*'s, but use some.

Since you will be writing about yourself, you will need to use *I* and *my*. However, overuse of these words will make your letter sound egotistical. On the other hand, stripping the letter of all *I*-references would rob it of its personal warmth. Thus, you want a balance. This version has too many *I*- and *my*-references.

I have an aptitude for mechanics that I have developed by working on farm machinery. Because of my aptitude, I am sure I will fit into one of your technical manufacturing operations. I submit my experience in the service department of Massey Container Company as evidence that I am interested in and diligent about my work. I was commended by Susan Lee, my supervisor, because I had energy and I worked hard.

• Use the you-viewpoint wherever practical.

You can help your case by presenting your facts in reader-viewpoint language wherever this is practical. You should work to interpret the facts based on their meaning for your reader and for the work to be done. Here is a better version of the example.

My aptitude for mechanics developed by working on farm machinery will help me fit into one of your technical manufacturing operations. As evidence of my interest and diligence, I submit last summer's experience in the service department of Massey Container Company. I was commended by my supervisor, Susan Lee, for my energy and hard work in machine repair.

Asking for Action in the Closing

• In the closing ask for whatever action is appropriate.

The presentation of your qualifications should lead logically to the action that the closing of the letter proposes. You should ask for whatever action is appropriate in your case. It could be a request for an interview, an invitation to call the references, or a request to be notified of any job openings. Rarely would you want to ask for the job in a first letter. You are concerned mainly with opening the door to further negotiations.

• Make the action words clear and direct.

Your action words should be clear and direct. As in the sales letter, the request for action may be made more effective if it is followed by words recalling a benefit that the reader will get from taking the action. The following closing illustrates this technique:

These highlights of my training and experience show my preparation for a human resources career. May I have an appointment to discuss beginning this career with you? A collect telephone call (817-921-4113) or a letter will bring me to your office at your convenience.

Sample Application Letters

Figures 11–2 and 11–3 are application letters prepared by the student whose draft worksheet appears in Figure 11–1. Each letter begins with an interesting paragraph that sets the stage for the following presentation. The review of experience is interpreted by showing how the experience would help in performing the job sought. Similarly, she shows that she understands what each job requires. Reader-viewpoint is stressed throughout, but a moderate use of *I*'s gives each letter a personal quality. The closing request for action is clear, direct, and courteous. The student, offered both positions, chose to accept the co-ordinator's job.

THE APPLICATION FORM

Some employers like to use an application form to simplify the task of comparing candidates. They feel that using a standard form gives each applicant an equal chance. By their nature, forms stress information and appear more objective and less personal. Since you want to make a strong, positive impression, you should follow these tips for completing application forms.

- Read carefully before you write to avoid crossovers and corrections. Each form is a little different. Does the address go above the line or below? Is there a separate space for the province and postal code?

- Type or print neatly in ink. Take your time. A neat, accurately completed form is easier to scan, avoids confusion, and makes a good first impression.

- Fill in the categories such as *Other comments* and *Interests* to let your personality and unique talents show and to overcome the impersonal style of the form.

- Be concise, clear, and accurate in the information you give. Remember that the company's purpose for using a form is to get the facts.

- Know your rights and weigh the costs and benefits of demanding those rights. Decide beforehand whether you will supply personal information such as your age, marital status, and social insurance number. This type of information should only be required *after* you are hired (for income tax, pension, etc.), but many application forms ask for it.

- Compare the information on the completed application form with what you have included on your résumé to be sure the facts are consistent, accurate, and complete.

> • Here are suggestions for making good use of an application form.

THE INTERVIEW

As we have said, your initial contact with a prospective employer can be in writing or by a personal (face-to-face) visit. A successful contact is one that results in an *employment interview*. So we now turn our attention to the interview.

In a sense, the interview is the key to the success of the application—the "final examination" so to speak. You should carefully prepare for the interview, as the job will likely be lost or won there. The following review of the employment interview and some additional information about interviews in Chapter 17 should help you succeed.

> • The interview is essential. For good results, follow this procedure.

Investigate the Company

Before arriving for an interview, you should learn even more about the company—its products or services, its personnel, its business practices, its current activities, and its management. What better way to decide if this is a good place to work? Secondly, company knowledge will help you talk with the interviewer. And finally, the interviewer is likely to be impressed because you took the time to investigate the company thoroughly. That effort might even place you above your competitors.

> • Find out what you can about the employer.

FIGURE 11-2 A Student Application Letter (see the worksheet in Figure 11-1): *Applying for a Paid Summer Job as Co-ordinator of Teen Volunteers at a Seniors' Care Centre.*[†]

The student writes with enthusiasm and respect that are both true to her personality.

return address

April 27, 1995

inside address

Dear Ms. MacDonald:

Thank you for considering my application for your Teen Volunteer Co-ordinator position. Because I enjoy working with teens and seniors, I hope I can be a part of a great summer at the Continuing Care Centre.

Through my experience with Young Life I have had many opportunities to supervise high school students. This summer, as head cook for forty cyclists on a Rocky Mountain bike trip, I lead a crew of six teen workers. Since none of the work crew were paid, I learned a lot about how to motivate and encourage the volunteers. I used my communication skills to solve conflicts and give constructive criticism. This past year I have been a volunteer leader for Young Life, counselling at camps and leading weekly activities, and have gained valuable insight into the world of high school students. I've also had the opportunity to organize events for up to seventy people, again working alongside volunteer leaders.

The time I spend with my elderly grandparents, shopping with them, taking them to the doctor, and cleaning for them, helps me understand the special concerns of seniors, their need for independence, and their right to make choices in a secure environment.

Please refer to my résumé for a more complete description of my experience, skills, and achievements. May I have an interview for this job opportunity? My number is 444-2222 if you have any questions about my application. I look forward to discussing this summer job with you.

Yours truly,

signature and name

[†] This application letter was written in 1995. It is used by permission.

FIGURE 11-3 A Student Application Letter (see Figures 11-1 and 11-2): *Applying for a Paid Summer Job as Camp Cook*[†]

The student selects and emphasizes points that suit this employment opportunity.

return address

May 1, 1995

inside address

Dear Ms Mathison:

A camp cook who loves cooking, camping and children is what I could be at the Bee Gee Club Camp this summer. I enjoy planning and preparing meals, and I appreciate the important role that delicious and nutritious food plays in a positive camp experience.

I have had many wonderful camping experiences myself while volunteering at camps in the past, and I am familiar with commercial kitchens. This summer I was head cook for a bike trip and prepared meals for forty cyclists during their trip through the mountains. I enjoyed the challenge of cooking outdoors, responding to the variable working conditions and the changing needs of the cyclists. As well as cooking, my responsibilities included planning and shopping within a food budget. I was also responsible to supervise a work crew of six high school students to ensure that meals were well prepared and on time.

My work with the youth group Young Life has given me camping experience with junior and senior high students. I have counselled at camps, and worked in food preparation kitchens and dishwashing pits at camps for up to 300 campers. In addition, work crew and leader training programs have helped me learn about hard work, dedication, and leadership.

May I have an interview with you to discuss my application for this job? My number is 444-2222. I would love to be a part of the excitement of camp this summer.

Yours truly,

signature and name

[†] This application letter was written in 1995. It is used by permission.

Make a Good Appearance

How you look to the interviewer is a part of your message. Unfortunately, interviewers differ to some extent on what style is best. In principle, however, the interviewer will be watching to see whether you fit into the role you are seeking. Your clothing should suit the nature of the company. If you have the opportunity, observe the clothing style of the employees before your interview. If in doubt, you would be wise to present a conservative appearance. Your appearance is important to make an impression, to help establish your credibility, and to identify you as a professional.

* Make a good appearance (conservative dress and grooming).

Put Yourself at Ease

Being at ease throughout the interview is difficult because you are being inspected. However, the interviewer should see a poised and collected person. Appearing calm and collected involves talking in a clear and strong voice. It also involves controlling your facial expressions and movements. Developing such controls requires self-awareness, self-discipline, and, above all, practice.

* Be at ease—calm, collected, confident.

Many people are not aware of their nervous habits. Ask your friends, parents, or someone else who cares about you to draw them to your attention. Then practise eliminating them. It may be easier to find a less obvious substitute. If you have a habit of saying "um," for example, you may try to take a breath in its place. If you scratch your eyebrow or adjust your glasses frequently, try resting your hand under the other one. You may find it helpful to remind yourself that the stress experienced during an interview is normal. Or, you may find you can reduce excessive stress by looking at the interview as a conversation.

* Try to find a substitute behaviour.

A word of caution. If you eliminate all stress reactions, you may look so calm that you appear bored or sleepy! Also, avoid becoming so relaxed that you slip into very casual slang as if you were talking to friends at a football game. Your goal is to control your emotions so you present the best possible appearance to the interviewer.

* Some stress is useful.

Anticipate Questions

You should be able to anticipate some of the questions that the interviewer will ask. Questions about your education (courses, grades, honours, etc.) are usually asked. So are questions about work experience, interests, career goals, location preferences, and activities in organizations. You should prepare answers to these questions in advance. Your answers will then be thorough and correct, and your words will display poise and confidence.

* Anticipate the questions; plan the answers.

Prepare for Tough Questions

In addition to the general questions noted above, interviewers often ask more complicated ones. Some are vague and open-ended. These are designed to test you—to learn your views, your interests, and your ability to deal with difficult problems. Others seek more specific information about your ability to handle the job in question. Although such questions are more difficult to anticipate, you should be aware that questions of this kind are likely to be asked:

* Think ahead to answer difficult questions.

* What can you do for us?
* Would you be willing to relocate? to travel?
* Do you prefer to work with people or alone?
* What do you expect to be doing in 5 years? in 10 years?
* What income goals do you have?
* Why should I rank you above the others I am interviewing?
* Why did you choose_____ as your lifework?

- How do you feel about working overtime? nights? weekends?
- Have you done the best work you are capable of in college?
- Is your college record a good measure of how you will perform on the job?
- What are the qualities you look for in the ideal boss?
- What are your beginning salary expectations?

• Know the facts; support your answers; turn negatives to positives.

To answer these questions, you need to know certain facts such as a reasonable salary range for the position you want. Your investigation of the company and the job market will have given you this information. You also need to think about your experience and education in terms of this job to be able to emphasize your strengths. Whenever possible, support your answers with evidence.

Interviewer:	Would you be willing to relocate within Canada?
Candidate:	Yes. Several of my summer jobs have been out of province and I enjoyed getting to know other parts of the country, so I would look forward to relocating.

Finally, look for the positive results or lessons learned through a failing or a weakness. If your grades were not the best, you will need to shift the emphasis to your stronger points—your willingness to work, or your experience, for example. You might show what other benefits you had from college.

Interviewer:	Do your school grades accurately reflect your ability?
Candidate:	My grades were solid passes but not outstanding because I had to work while I was studying. I had to learn to manage my time very well to accomplish all that needed to be done each day.

Prepare for Inappropriate Questions

• Decide ahead of time how to respond to questions that violate your human rights.

Sometimes interviewers will ask questions that contravene human rights legislation. Although you are within your rights to refuse to answer such questions, your refusal should be planned and polite. The question may not be intended to discriminate, so your response should not make that accusation. A simple statement, such as "I prefer not to answer that question," should be sufficient. Or, you may prefer to respond with another question such as, "I can give you that information, but would you explain why it is important to this job?" As with questions on application forms, you may choose to answer the question rather than raise an objection. The key here is that you need to plan because under the stress of an interview, you may have difficulty finding an appropriate response. Questions such as these could be considered to violate your human rights:

- How old are you?
- Do you plan to have children?
- What language do you speak at home?
- How long has your family been in Canada?
- Are you religious?

Prepare for Behavioural or Hypothetical Questions

• New questioning techniques are being used to reveal more about the candidate.

As companies count the cost of the hiring exercise, they are becoming more concerned to find the right person the first time. Some new interviewing techniques have been developed to reveal the behavioural and personality qualities of the candidate and help determine whether the fit between the candidate and the company is a good one.

• Behavioural questions ask for examples from the candidate's experience.

Behavioural questions ask the candidate to describe a time when he or she used certain skills or faced a particular situation. Many interviewers feel the answers to these questions are revealing because candidates are so busy choosing an example and applying it that they do not have time to fabricate or exaggerate. The questions are difficult to answer, so the interviewer sees the candidate under stress. And finally, these questions test the candidate's ability to select and organize information by applying critical thinking and communication skills. Some examples of behavioural questions are

- Describe a time when you were faced with an ethical choice. What steps did you use to reach your decision and what was the outcome?

- I'd like you to discuss a time when someone in authority corrected or disciplined you. Describe the circumstances. Then tell me what you liked and disliked about the way the supervisor handled the situation.

- Give me an example of your ability to work under pressure. How did the time constraint or deadline affect your work style and performance?

A related type of question is the hypothetical one. Here, candidates are asked to project themselves into a possible situation and describe the likely response. Many of the skills needed to answer behavioural questions are also needed to answer hypothetical questions. However, hypothetical questions seem a little easier because they do not require the candidate to provide a true example. Nevertheless, a strong answer would include a personal example, such as "In that situation, I would . . . because I have learned from my experience in . . . . " Here are some examples of hypothetical questions:

> • Hypothetical questions look ahead and ask candidates to visualize their behaviour.

- If you found that a co-worker was taking money from the company, what would you do?

- Read this customer complaint letter and suggest what response you would make and why.

- Your department has been struck by the flu and five of your co-workers have been absent for a week. The supervisor, rather than hiring temporary help, has told the remaining staff to cope. Your workload is impossible. What would you do?

A PRACTICE RUN

Choose one of the questions above and draft an answer for it. Then, role-play with a partner to experience giving the answer orally without looking at your notes.

_____

_____

_____

_____

_____

Help Control the Dialogue

Just answering the questions asked is often not enough. As one authority explains, "It's important to establish a dialogue with the recruiter by asking a few good questions and playing off the responses."[13] The questions you ask and the comments you make should bring up what you want the interviewer to know about you. Your self-analysis has revealed to you the strong points in your background. Now you want to make certain that the interviewer knows those points.

> • Help bring up the questions that show your qualifications.

---

[13]Kevin Collins and Patricia B. Carr, "A Short Course on Landing a Job," _The College Edition of the National Business Employment Weekly,_ published by _The Wall Street Journal,_ Fall 1988, p.38.

<table>
<tr><td>

• Here are some examples.

</td><td>

How to bring up points about you that the interviewer does not ask is a matter for your imagination. For example, a student seeking a job in advertizing believed that a certain project should be brought to the interviewer's attention. So she asked, "Did you notice in the portfolio of my work the advertizing campaign I did for ABC Company as one of my class projects?" Whether the interviewer had noticed it before or not, the candidate now has the opportunity to direct attention to her portfolio and speak about those examples of her work. For another example, a student who wanted to bring out his knowledge of the prospective employer's operations did so with this question: "Will your company's expansion at the Malton plant create new job opportunities there?"Because the number of questions you can ask is limited, try to work some of these points into your answers as well. Your goal is to give the interviewer all the information you consider important.

</td></tr>
</table>

THE CLOSE OF THE APPLICATION

<table>
<tr><td>

• Keep notes to stay on track and to increase the benefits of each application procedure.

</td><td>

During the application process, it is helpful to keep a record of the documentation you sent, who interviewed you, the tough questions you were asked, your impressions of the company, and so on. As the application process comes to an end, make a few more notes about what you handled well, what you would do differently another time, and what you learned. Then, whether the application is successful or not, you have gained from the experience.

</td></tr>
<tr><td>

• Follow up the interview with thank-you, status-inquiry, job-acceptance, or job-rejection messages.

</td><td>

The interview is not the final step in the application process for the candidate. Conveying a brief thank-you message by letter is an appropriate follow-up step. It shows interest, and because some of your competitors will not do this, it can give you an advantage. If you do not hear from the prospective employer within a reasonable time, it is appropriate to ask about your application. You also may need to inquire if you are in the enviable position of having a deadline to decide about another offer.

</td></tr>
</table>

Application Follow-Up Letters

<table>
<tr><td>

• You may write a thank-you letter following an interview.

• Use a direct-order, good-will format.

</td><td>

Writing a Thank-You Letter. After an interview, you may write a thank-you letter if you feel it is appropriate. Once considered essential, this letter is less common today. A thank-you letter can help your case by showing your interest in the job.

Such letters are usually short. They begin with an expression of gratefulness. They say something about the interview or the job, and they take care of any additional business (such as submitting information requested). They end on a goodwill note—a hopeful look to the next step in the negotiations.

</td></tr>
<tr><td>

• When employers do not respond, you may write a follow-up letter. It follows the order of the routine inquiry letter.

</td><td>

Constructing a Follow-Up Inquiry. When a prospective employer is slow in responding to an application, you may need to write a follow-up letter. The delay may be because the employer is very busy, but it could be that your application went astray. Whatever the explanation, a courteous follow-up letter may help to produce action.

Such a letter is a form of routine inquiry. As a reason for writing, you can use the need to make a job decision, or some other good explanation. The following letter is an example:

</td></tr>
</table>

> Because I soon must make a job decision, may I please know the status of my application with you?
> You may recall that you interviewed me in your office November 7. You wrote me November 12 to say that I was among those you had selected for further consideration.
> Barrow, Inc., remains one of the organizations I want to consider in my career decision. I will very much appreciate an early response.

<table>
<tr><td>

• You may need to write a letter accepting a job. Write it as you would a favourable response letter.

</td><td>

Writing a Letter Accepting a Job. Job acceptances in writing are merely favourable response letters with an extra amount of goodwill. As the letter should begin directly, a yes answer in the beginning is appropriate. The remainder of the letter should contain a

</td></tr>
</table>

confirmation of the starting date and comments about the work, the company, the interview—whatever you would say if you were face-to-face with the reader. The letter need not be long. This one does the job well:

> I am very pleased to accept your offer of employment as a marketing representative. After my first interview with you, I was convinced that Allison-Caldwell was the organization for me. It is good to know that you think I am the right person to represent Allison-Caldwell in the Kingston area.
> Following your instructions, I will be in Toronto on May 28, ready to begin training for a career with you.

Writing a Letter Refusing a Job.   Letters refusing a job offer follow the normal refusal pattern. One good technique is to begin with a friendly comment—perhaps something about past relations with the company. Next, explain and present the refusal in clear yet positive words. Then end with more friendly comment. This example illustrates the plan.

• To refuse a job offer, use the normal refusal pattern (indirect).

> Meeting you and the other people at Northern was a genuine pleasure. All that I saw and heard impressed me most favourably.
> In considering your job offer, I naturally gave some weight to these favourable impressions. Although they remain strong in my mind, I have accepted a job with another firm where, I believe, my skills and training will be better suited to the company's needs.
> Thank you for the time and the courteous treatment you gave me.

. . . .

A SUMMARY OF LEARNING OUTCOMES FROM THIS CHAPTER

A first step in a good job-search procedure is to build a network of contacts consisting of friends, professors or instructors, and business people who may help you find a job.

When you are ready to find work, analyze yourself. Specifically, analyze your education, personal qualities, work experience, and special qualifications to find out what work you can do. Then, plan and conduct your job search based on this personal inventory.

Next, find prospective employers by using your school's placement centre, your personal contacts, or job advertizements. If these do not produce results, prospect by personal visits or on-line. Watch for news of businesses opening or expanding in your area.

The résumé lists the major facts about your background. A general résumé is useful for giving to a placement centre; a targeted résumé is created for a particular job opportunity.

In preparing your résumé, you should keep four guidelines in mind.

· Prioritize the contents of your résumé for each employment opportunity.

· Make the résumé truly representative of your skills and personality.

· Make your résumé as complete and accurate as possible within the space limitations.

· Make your résumé attractive and professional looking.

You organize the facts for your résumé under headings. For your job experience, give at least dates, firms, and duties, skills or accomplishments. For your education, you should include dates, schools, diplomas or degrees, and fields of study. You may list references, or you may postpone listing them.

The application letter is a persuasive letter. You begin the presentation with an attention-gaining opening—one that makes the letter stand out while setting up the persuasion. Make the tone and content fit the job you seek. You then present your qualifications, fitting them to the job you seek. In doing so, choose your words carefully to enhance your ability to do the work. After you have presented your case, ask for specific action.

Some companies require applicants to complete a standardized form. Use the application form to communicate your qualifications concisely and clearly. Neatness makes a positive impression, so take the time to print legibly. Use areas such as "Other comments" to say something unique about yourself and your suitability for the job.

Your major contact with a prospective employer is the interview. For best results, research the employer in advance so you can impress the interviewer. Present a good appearance through appropriate dress and grooming and by being relatively at ease. Try to anticipate the interviewer's questions and to plan your answers. Help the interviewer establish a dialogue with your own questions and comments.

You will have various contacts with the prospective employer following the interview. A thank-you letter and inquiries about the status of the application are appropriate. You may need to write other letters about the job, such as an acceptance letter or a job refusal letter. You write an acceptance letter in the direct order, just as you would write any other favourable response letter. You write a job refusal letter in the indirect order, just as you would write other letters containing negative news.

ANSWERS TO PRACTICE RUNS

Because most of the practice runs in this chapter are for your personal use and involve your own personal information, no standard answers can be given.

▶ The Résumé of Len Darcus

There are many shortcomings in the poor résumé example. First, the form is not pleasing to the eye. The weight of the type is heavy on the left side of the page. Grouping many points together makes reading difficult. A key emphasis position is wasted on trivial information. These are not the points that will get an interview for the applicant.

This résumé also contains many errors in wording. Information headings are not parallel in grammatical form. All are in talking form except the first one. The items listed under *Personal Qualities* are not parallel either. Throughout, the résumé coverage is scant, leaving out many of the details needed to present the best impression of the applicant. Under *Experience,* little is said about specific tasks and skills in each job, and under *Education,* high school work is listed needlessly. The references are incomplete without street addresses and job titles.

QUESTIONS FOR DISCUSSION

1. "Building a network of contacts to help one find jobs appears to be selfish. It involves acquiring friendships just to use them for one's personal benefits." Refute this view.

2. Discuss the value of each of these sources for finding jobs to a finance major (*a*) right after graduation and (*b*) after twenty years of work in the field: (*i*) a university placement centre, (*ii*) a network of personal contacts, (*iii*) classified advertizements, (*iv*) employment agencies, and (*v*) prospecting.

3. The most popular arrangement of résumé information is the four-part grouping: education, experience, personal details, and references. Describe other arrangements. When would each be used?

4. Distinguish between the general résumé and the targeted résumé. When would each be most appropriate?

5. What is meant by parallelism of headings?

6. Describe the application letter and résumé you would write (*a*) immediately after graduation, (*b*) 10 years later, and (*c*) 25 years later. Point out similarities and differences, and defend your decision.

7. Describe the effect of beginning an application letter with these words: "This is to apply for . . . " or "Please consider this my application for the position of . . . "

8. "In writing job-application letters, just present the facts clearly, without analysis and without interpretation. The facts will tell the employer whether he or she wants you." Discuss this viewpoint.

LETTER PROBLEMS

1. Move the calendar to the time you will complete your education. Find an advertizement for a job for which you would be qualified. Write the application letter that would present your qualifications for this job. Attach the advertizement to the letter.

2. Write the résumé to accompany the letter for Problem 1.

3. Project yourself five years past your graduation date. During those years, you have had good experience working for the company of your choice in the field of your choice. (Use your imagination to supply this information.)

   Unfortunately, your advancement in the company hasn't been what you had expected. You think that you must look around for a better opportunity. Find an advertizement for a suitable job and write an application letter that skillfully presents your qualifications for it. (You may make logical assumptions about your experience over the

five-year period.) For class purposes, clip the advertizement to your letter.

4. Write the résumé to accompany the letter in Problem 3.

5. Assume that you are in your last term of school and that graduation is just around the corner. Your greatest interest is in finding work that you like and that would enable you to support yourself now and to support a family as you win promotions.

   No job of your choice is revealed in the want ads of newspapers and trade magazines. No placement bureau has provided anything to your liking. So you decide to approach some companies directly. Write a prospecting application letter.

6. Write the résumé to accompany the letter for Problem 5.

7. Move the calendar to your graduation date so that you're now ready to sell your working ability in the job market.

Besides canvassing likely firms with the aid of prospecting letters and diligently following up family contacts, you've decided to look into anything especially good in the ad columns of newspapers and magazines. The latest available issues list the following jobs that you think you could handle. Instructions follow the list.

a. **Accounting Majors**   Large international company seeks hardworking, personable, mature beginning accountants. Start in training program. Must have sound knowledge of principles and theory and be willing to learn our way. Must be computer knowledgeable. Excellent communication and interpersonal skills needed. Apply by letter and résumé to Accounting Office, Box 1717, _____[your city].

b. **Banking Trainee**   Major chartered bank seeks recent graduates for training program in all phases of bank operations. Finance majors preferred. Must be familiar with computerized banking systems. Good communication skills desirable. Willingness to work and ability to get along with people essential. Send résumé and letter to Personnel Director, P.O. Box 4172, _____ [your city].

c. **Management Trainee**   Graduate of a two-year postsecondary program with a major in business administration for career administrative work with major manufacturing company. Knowledge of administration important. Must have drive and leadership potential and strong interpersonal skills. Good written and oral communication skills a must. Should have working knowledge of personal computers. Send letter and résumé to Recruiting Manager, Box 7714, _____ [your city].

d. **Sales Trainee**   Worldwide leader in pharmaceuticals offers challenging sales career to business graduates. Company recognizes and rewards individual effort. Preference given to applicants who have attained high level of academic excellence, who thrive in a competitive environment, and who can work independently. College training in marketing preferred. Interest in life sciences or medical community important. Sales experience a benefit but not required. Outstanding training program. Send résumé and letter to P.O. Box 69117, _____ [your city].

e. **Office Manager**   Person with training or equivalent experience in appropriate area of business administration to take over office of seven employees. Must have ability to work with and handle older workers. Current knowledge of office procedures and computer technology essential. Must be hard worker, personable, and intelligent. Ability to communicate orally and in writing important. Interested people should apply to Vice President for Administration, P.O. Box 99391, _____[your city].

f. **Administrative Assistant**   Executive in large manufacturing company wants recent college graduate in a business field to serve as assistant. Ability to communicate (orally and in writing) highly important. Knowledge of modern administrative techniques and procedures essential. Must be familiar with micros, including knowledge of spreadsheet applications. De-

pendability, pleasing personality, and intelligence important. If interested, send letter and résumé to Personnel Officer, P.O. Box 555, _____[your city].

g. **Executive Secretary**   Private secretary for top executive in insurance industry. Prefer graduate of a two-year diploma program. Must have necessary skills in word processing and transcribing. Knowledge of office procedures required. Pleasing personality, good telephone skills, professional image, and language knowledge important. Familiarity with wordprocessing software necessary. Desktop publishing and spreadsheets helpful. Liberal pay and benefits. Send résumé and letter to Personnel Director, P.O. Box 2135, _____[your city].

h. **Department Store Management**   College grads wanted for training program. Majors in marketing preferred but all majors considered. Good personality and willingness to work essential. Must be willing to relocate throughout career. Should be computer literate. Communication and interpersonal skills important. Write Recruiting Director, P.O. Box 7748, _____[your city].

i. **Computer Science Grads**   We train you for challenging career in business computer market. We design, develop, and support business applications of micros, minis, and mainframes. Applicants should have excellent oral and written communication skills, ability to learn quickly, and knowledge of current languages, and programming techniques. If interested, send résumé and application letter to P.O. Box 2391, _____[your city].

j. **Management Training Program**   Dynamic corporation in the wholesale satellite electronic business has opening in its management training program. High-energy, results-oriented individual required with excellent organizational and communication skills. Opportunity for advancement based on demonstrated abilities. Qualified candidates must be mature and demonstrate a professional image and appearance. University or college grads with computer literacy preferred. Send résumé and letter to P.O. Box 11876, _____[your city].

k. **Customer Service Trainee**   International sports manufacturing and distribution company has unusual opportunity for college-trained person. Position will lead to management of our customer services department. Work involves resolving customer service issues. Excellent communication skills, a strong customer service orientation, and a take-charge attitude tempered with professional demeanour are required. Should be able to interface effectively with upper management and all other areas of the company. Interested people should write P.O. Box 2122, _____ [your city].

l. **National Finance Company** needs candidates to learn finance business. Thorough training program. Knowledge of lending, loan administration, and general office administration helpful. Must have working knowledge of personal computers. Good opportunity for intelligent, hardworking, and personable people. Finance majors or business graduates with some finance emphasis desired. If interested, write Personnel Director, P.O. Box 346, Station F, _____[your city].

m. **Assistant Accountant** to work with chief accountant of small manufacturing company—a growth company. College work with concentration in accounting required. Must work long hours during peak periods. Excellent chance for advancement. Must be knowledgeable, personable, and dependable. Good interpersonal and communication skills desirable. Should be familiar with micros, and have experience with a standard computerized accounting package. Write P.O. Box 8449, _____[your city].

n. **Transportation Majors** Regional airline has career openings for recent college grads. Transportation majors preferred but other majors considered. Start in company training program, rotate assignments, work up. Aggressive, personable hardworking individuals wanted. Able to work well under pressure. Should be computer knowledgeable. Write Personnel Search, P.O. Box 313, _____[your city].

o. **Human Resources Trainee** International management consulting firm seeks a qualified person to train for work in local office. Candidates must display a knowledge of human resources, including compensations, benefits, selection, job analysis, employee surveys, and human resource planning. College training in human resource management or industrial psychology necessary. Must be willing to travel for extended periods of time. Good communication skills a must. Knowledge of information systems helpful. If interested, write Trainee Search, Box 4842, _____[your city].

p. **Production Trainee** Major local manufacturer seeks recent college graduates with production-operations management training. Selected candidates will be trained for supervising production employees; maintaining good employee relations; ensuring plant safety; implementing good manufacturing, sanitation, and quality assurance practices. Salary competitive.

Excellent benefits program. Send letter and résumé to Personnel Department, Box 5455, _____[your city].

q. **Credit and Claims Correspondent** A nationwide leader in the automotive aftermarket has a position available for a credit and claims correspondent. Working with the Finance Department, this person will be responsible for resolving customer disputes concerning billing, shipping, and returns and allowances. Excellent communication skills are required to interact with customers and sales and management personnel. Good math aptitude and experience in retail credit and customer claims an asset. Send letter and résumé to Personnel Manager, P.O. Box 181, Ajax, ON, L1N 2R3.

r. **PC Support Co-ordinator** A premier environmental consulting firm is seeking a PC Support Co-ordinator for one of the largest, most state-of-the-art information centres. This person must have strong end-user support experience in both IBM compatible PCs and Apples. Additionally, familiarity with LANs and communication software is preferred. Most of the work will involve configuring and installing new systems and trouble-shooting hardware/software problems. Knowledge of major user software packages is important. Excellent communication skills and the ability to relate well to people. Please fax your résumé to Eleanor Batten, 604-489-2323.

Select the ad describing the job you would like most or could do best. Study it for what it says and even more for what it implies. Weigh your own preparation even more thoroughly than you weigh the ad. You may imagine far enough ahead to assure completion of all the courses that are blocked out for your program of studies. Sort out the things that line you up for the job, organize them strategically, and then present them in a letter of application that will get you that job. Assume that you've attached a résumé.

8. Write the résumé to accompany the letter for Problem 7.

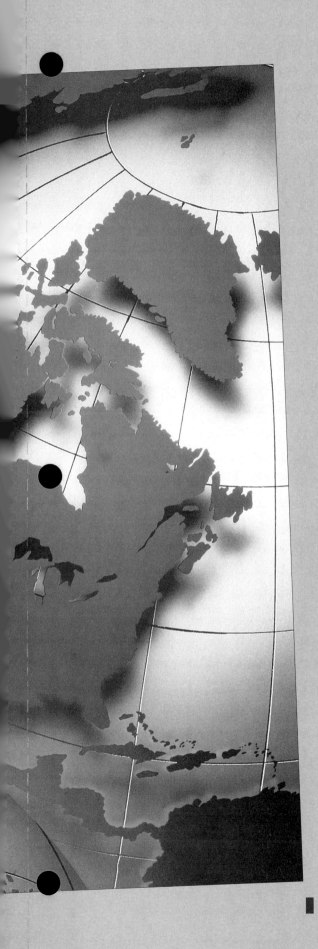

WRITING FOR BUSINESS: REPORTS

12

Basics of Report Writing

Upon completing this chapter, you will be able to prepare well-organized, objective reports. To reach this goal, you should be able to

1 State a purpose in writing and list the factors to be investigated.

2 Interpret and apply information to develop the report plan.

3 Organize detailed information in outline form by further refining the plan.

4 Construct topic or talking captions that outline reports logically and meaningfully.

5 Maintain objectivity and consistency in viewpoint when writing reports.

6 Use transitions effectively to achieve smoothness and coherence in written reports.

▶ to Report Writing

With the growing success of her franchise, Doreen Lam has come to the attention of the owners of Good 'n Nice. A representative from national headquarters, Tony Averinos, was sent to visit her. He was so impressed with Doreen's ideas and tips that he asked her to write a report for the president. He assured her it didn't have to be a long report, but a full description of the steps she took to reach this level of success so quickly was what he wanted. Her ideas might be incorporated into future training for Good 'n Nice franchisees.

After being flattered by the request, Doreen began to panic. What could she remember about planning and organizing reports? The importance of writing for the audience had been stressed in her report writing class, so she checked the library and the Internet for information about the president right away. She also looked at some examples of short reports prepared for executives at this level.

Another point she remembered from class was the need to write the purpose statement clearly and succinctly. She began to think about the purpose.

"Tony wants me to tell my story. I want to impress the president. And then, there are the people who want to learn from my report during their orientation and training. I'd forgotten about that secondary audience. I wonder how much I should focus on them? Maybe I could write a section on what should be covered in orientation based on my experience. Whoa! I'd better make some notes and check with Tony again. I guess I do need to write out my purpose statement. If I can't tighten up my purpose, this report is going to get way off track." ▪

DEFINING REPORTS

Whether or not you have a good idea of what reports are, you will likely have a hard time defining them. Some people define reports broadly to include almost any presentation of information; others limit reports to only the most formal presentations. For our purposes a middle-ground definition is best. A *business report* is an orderly and objective communication of factual information that serves a business purpose. We will look at this definition more closely.

As an *orderly* communication, a report is prepared carefully. Care and time in preparation distinguish reports from casual exchanges of information. The *objective* quality of a report is its fairness in approach. Reports seek to uncover truth. Although a report expresses a clear point of view, it does not mislead the receiver. The word *communication* is chosen for its broad meaning. It covers speaking and writing, of course, and in some reporting circumstances artistic and nonverbal channels as well. Reports can be presented using any of these means. The basic ingredient of reports is *factual information*. Factual information is objective, quantitative, and accurate. And finally, since research scientists, medical doctors, politicians, students, and many others write reports, a report must *serve a business purpose* to be classified as a business report.

This definition is specific enough to be meaningful, yet broad enough to take into account the variations in reports. For example, some reports only present information. Such factual, descriptive reports offer little interpretation or evaluation and are called *informational reports*. Other reports that include interpretations, conclusions, and recommendations are known as *analytical reports*. Both types fit within the suggested definition. Reports sometimes are classified by their style rather than their content. A *formal report* is formal both in writing style and in physical appearance. It is usually bound in some type of cover, has a title page and table of contents, and is quite long. An *informal report* uses more casual language and has a variety of presentations from a memorandum report to a short report with a title page attached, much like a student paper. Our definition permits all of these variations.

* A business report is an orderly and objective communication of factual information that serves a business purpose.

PLANNING THE REPORT

Planning a report is not unlike planning other forms of communication. To write an effective report, you must know your audience, know your purpose, and select the structure and order to suit those realities.

Knowing the Audience

As we have seen in earlier chapters, your receiver or audience has specific needs and characteristics. The more you know about them, the more you can tailor your communication. Here are some simple examples. A report can be written for an internal audience. If your reader is within your company, your structure would be affected. Likely, you would choose a memo report format. If the report carries negative news, and you anticipate a resistant, skeptical, or hostile audience, you would choose the indirect order and consider persuasive strategies. If your audience is an authority figure, you might decide that a more formal approach would be best. In that case a title page and covering letter could be used to enhance your message. Your choice of language might be more formal as well. The knowledge level of your audience will influence your choice of words. The technical language suitable for a knowledgeable expert would not communicate to a naive beginner. None of these ideas are new. They are repeated here because reports can and should be modified to meet any of these conditions.

- Reports often have a secondary audience to consider.

One challenge that arises in report writing that is less evident with letter writing is the need to consider a secondary audience. The secondary audience consists of people who will read the report for another reason or under different circumstances from the person for whom the report was intended. As Doreen in the Introductory Situation found, a report may be put to more than one use. If you know that your report will have a secondary audience, you should try to provide for their needs too as long as your major focus remains on your primary audience. To help you distinguish your primary and secondary audiences, think about children's television shows. The producers aim the entertainment to the primary audience of the children, but they also include educational segments about safety tips, sharing, fair play, and so on. These segments have in mind the secondary audience, the parents. Parents feel more comfortable if programs have some educational value as well.

A PRACTICE RUN

As a class discussion, consider the advertizers who sponsor children's television programs. Would you consider them as primary or secondary audiences of the writers and producers?

_____

_____

_____

Determining the Report Purpose

- Your task is to get the purpose clearly in mind.

Your work on a report logically begins with a need. Someone or some group needs information for a business purpose. You may need to solve a problem, promote an idea, present background data as the basis for a decision, or report on progress to date. One of your first tasks will be to get that purpose clearly in your mind. Elementary and basic as defining the purpose may appear, all too often a report fails to reach its goal because of inaccuracy and haphazardness in this step.

Writing a Working Statement of the Purpose

After you understand your purpose, your next step is to state it clearly in a working statement of purpose. This statement may not be the final one you use in your report. It is a working version to get your work underway. Writing the purpose statement is a good practice for several reasons. A written statement is preserved permanently for you to refer to time and again as your report progresses. It is more difficult to ignore, forget, or distort a purpose statement when it is written down. In addition, a written statement can be reviewed, approved, and evaluated by other people whose assistance may be valuable. Most important of all, writing the statement forces you to think through the situation and put yourself on the right track.

- Then you should write a clear, complete purpose statement.

Since this statement will guide your research, it is important to develop it as fully as you can. If your purpose is to solve a problem, you should say more than, "My purpose is to find out about the sales problem." Are you going to investigate only, or investigate and decide on major causes? Will you also recommend solutions? Be as specific as you can be at this stage.

The statement normally takes one of three forms: infinitive phrase, question, or declarative statement. To illustrate each, we will use the problem of determining why sales at a certain store have declined:

- Purpose statements may be (1) infinitive phrases, (2) questions, or (3) declarative statements.

1. *Infinitive phrase:* "To determine the major causes of decreasing sales at Ali Baba's."

2. *Question:* "What are the major causes of decreasing sales at Ali Baba's?"

3. *Declarative statement:* "The major causes for decreasing sales at Ali Baba's must be found."

. . . .

A PRACTICE RUN

Write purpose statements for the following reports. Try to use each type at least once.

1. A breakfast cereal manufacturer wants to know the traits of its consumers.

_____

_____

2. A supervisor must prepare an evaluation of the department's secretary at the end of a three-month probation period.

_____

_____

3. A bakery wants to compare its products and service with a competitor.

_____

_____

. . . .

Conducting a Preliminary Investigation

Once you have a clear statement of purpose, begin to gather preliminary information. Make note of what background knowledge you have already and what more you need to find out. Then begin with general sources that will help you become familiar with the history, terminology, and methodology associated with your report topic. You may need material from company files or a library collection. The Internet may be a valuable source

- Begin by gathering preliminary information to understand the situation.

for current information. You should continue this investigation until you have the information you need to understand the background of your situation.

Organizing the Plan

- Next, you should identify the factors of the case.

After stating the purpose or problem and gathering preliminary information, you should have enough understanding to identify the factors or subject areas you must research and develop more fully to achieve your goal. You may not yet have information to place under all the subject areas, but you should be able to identify them. The three common ways to organize a report are subtopics of the overall topic, hypotheses (theories to test), and bases for comparison. We will consider each of these in turn.

. . . .

A PRACTICE RUN

Suggest subtopics for organizing this report.

Purpose: To outline the business diploma program at Cambrian College to attract graduating high school students.

_____

_____

_____

_____

_____
. . . .

- Use subtopics of the overall topic in informational reports.

Subtopics for Information Reports.   If the purpose of the report concerns a need for information, the organization would be based on the logical subdivisions or subtopics of the overall subject. Illustrating this type of situation is an informational report that reviews and summarizes the last three month's activities of Dewar Manufacturing. A plausible set of subtopics is shown in this example.

Purpose statement: To review operations of Dewar Manufacturing from January 1 through March 31.

Factors:

1. Production.
2. Financial status.
3. Product development.
4. Sales and promotion.
5. Plant and equipment.
6. Personnel.

Hypotheses for Problem-Solving Reports.   Some reports concern why something is happening and perhaps how to change it. In analyzing problems of this kind, you should seek explanations or solutions. Such explanations or solutions are termed *hypotheses.* Once formulated, hypotheses are tested, and their applicability to the problem is either proved or disproved.

• Hypotheses (possible explanations of the problem) may be the factors in problems requiring solution.

To illustrate, assume that you have the problem of determining why sales at a certain store have declined. In preparing this problem for investigation, you would think of the possible explanations (hypotheses) for the decline. You could come up with such explanations as these:

Problem statement: Why have sales declined at the Melton store?

Hypotheses:

1. Activities of the local competition have caused the decline.
2. Changes in the economy of the area have caused the decline.
3. Merchandising deficiencies have caused the decline.
4. Changes in the environment (population shifts, political actions, etc.) have caused the decline.

In the investigation, you would test these hypotheses and weigh their importance, perhaps by assigning point values to each. You might find that one, two, or all apply. Or you might find that none is valid. If so, you would have to advance additional hypotheses for further evaluation.

. . . .

A PRACTICE RUN

Suggest hypotheses for organizing this report.

Problem: Why are older students returning to class? (The average student age has risen from 22 in 1988 to 25 in 1996.)

_____

_____

_____

_____

_____

. . . .

Bases of Comparison in Evaluation Reports.   When the report concerns an evaluation, you must decide on the bases for that evaluation. That is, you should select the characteristics you will evaluate. The procedure may involve setting the standards for each of the characteristics as well. For example, a speed of at least 100 kilometres per hour is required, or a credit rating not less than AA must be maintained.

• For evaluation problems, the criteria for evaluating are the factors.

Illustrating this technique is the problem of a company deciding which of three cities would be best for a factory. Such a problem obviously involves a comparison of three locations. The bases for comparison are the factors needed for the success of the factory involved. After careful thought, you might come up with a plan such as this:

Problem statement: To resolve whether Y Company's new factory should be built in City A, City B, or City C.

Factors:

1. Availability of labour.
2. Abundance of raw material.
3. Local tax structure.
4. Transportation facilities.
5. Power supply.
6. Community support.

· ·

A PRACTICE RUN

Suggest bases of comparison for the following report.
Problem: Which long-distance telephone carrier should I choose?

_____

_____

_____

_____

_____

· ·

• The subtopics sometimes can be divided again.

Need for Subdivisions.   Each of the subtopics selected for investigation may have factors of its own. In the last illustration, for example, the comparison of transportation in the three cities may need subdivisions such as water, rail, road, and air. Labour may be compared by using subcategories such as skilled and unskilled labour. Subdivisions of this kind may go still further. Skilled labour may be broken down by specific skills: machinists, plumbers, pipefitters, welders; unskilled could be full-time, part-time, seasonal, and so on. Continue to subdivide as long as the divisions are helpful.

• Try using a diagram to illustrate the relationships between ideas.

Diagrams Help Interpretation.   At this early stage of organization, many people find it helpful to use a diagram to illustrate their ideas. While diagrams may be helpful at many other stages as well, here the more visual representations serve the purpose of showing links and relationships. A pyramid with the goal at the top and contributing factors fanned out below is an example. A wheel with spokes, a series of bubbles joined by lines, and a set of stair steps are others. An example of one such diagram follows in Figure 12–1.

• A personal system is best.

Some complex diagramming systems have been developed and used with varying degrees of enthusiasm and success. The possibilities include clustering, tree models, and mind maps. These systems give helpful suggestions, but you should feel free to adapt and modify them to suit your needs. The system you develop for yourself will be the most powerful and effective for you.

· ·

GATHERING THE DETAILED INFORMATION NEEDED

• The next step is to conduct the research needed. A personal investigation is usually appropriate.

You are now ready to begin your research in earnest. For most business problems, you will need to conduct a personal investigation. A sales problem, for example, might require collecting information through discussions with customers and sales personnel. A

FIGURE 12-1 A Simple Bubble Sketch

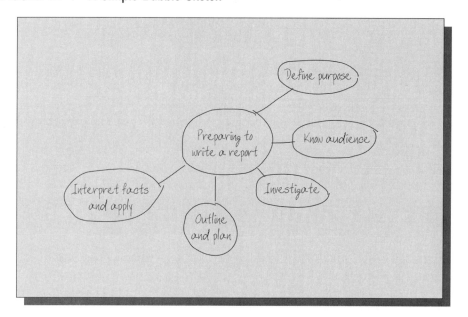

computer problem might require extensive reading in manuals as well as interviews with users, programmers, and hardware suppliers. Conducting these investigations intelligently requires knowledge of the field, which is why your preliminary investigation is important.

Some business reports require a more formal type of research, such as an experiment or a study. Except in the area of product design and development, the experiments used in business are not the laboratory experiments of the sciences. Business uses field experiments. Field experiments are conducted primarily in areas related to marketing or management. The impact of a new advertizement could be measured by a field experiment comparing sales in two similar communities, one of which saw the new commercial. Once again, knowledge gathered during preliminary research will prove invaluable for obtaining undistorted results.

• Experiments or studies are sometimes needed.

Another method of business research is the survey. Surveys are useful for gathering current information that is specific to the question at hand. Consumer surveys are common in service businesses such as banks, restaurants, and retail stores that want to improve customer satisfaction. Specialized training is required for designing a valid survey. Since this training is beyond the scope of business communications, only a summary of the basic concepts is presented in Chapter 19.

• Surveys are used to gather current information.

In some cases you may use library research to find the information you need in printed sources. Classroom assignments may have already prepared you to use the techniques of library research. If not, you will find them summarized in Chapter 19. Using the findings of library research involves citation techniques such as referencing and bibliography construction that are covered in Appendix C.

• Sometimes library research is used.

INTERPRETING AND APPLYING THE FINDINGS

With your research complete, you weigh the evidence you have found, select the relevant points, and apply this new understanding to achieve the purpose of your report.

• Next you interpret the information gathered and apply the findings to the problem.

Careful thought is needed to consider both the obvious and the not-so-obvious factors. Apply your critical thinking skills (see Chapter 2) to develop a logical and reasonable interpretation.

• Use careful thought and judgment to find logical meanings.

Use the test of experience and reason by asking, "Does this interpretation appear reasonable in the light of all I know or have experienced?" If your work passes this test, try

• Test your interpretations.

FIGURE 12-2 An Expanded Bubble Sketch

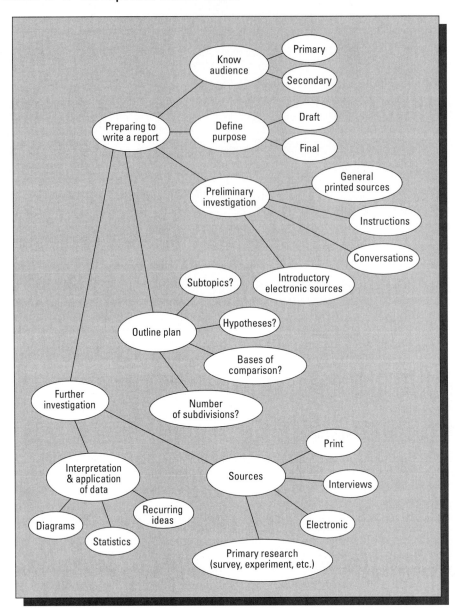

the negative test. In this test you try to support an opposing interpretation. When you have studied your interpretations from as many angles as you can and found reasonable answers for the objections you have raised, you will have more confidence in your findings.

Diagrams Again Help Interpretation

- Try adding to your diagram to develop the relationships between ideas.

Faced with many pages of data from your research, you will find your diagrams helpful again. As Figure 12-2 illustrates, you can add the new information you have to your existing diagrams or sketch out new ones. They will help you select, edit, and find relationships. They bridge the gap between your unorganized research results and the logical, linear outline you need to develop your report and present it to someone else.

Statistics Help Interpretation

- Statistics permit one to examine a set of facts.

If the information you have gathered is quantitative (expressed in numbers), statistical techniques will help you analyze and communicate it. By knowing basic statistical methods, you can improve your ability to interpret. Your job as an analyst is to help your audience interpret the information too. Therefore, whatever statistical analysis you do to reduce the volume of data deserves careful explanation so that the audience will receive the proper meaning. Although a thorough review of statistical techniques is beyond the scope of this book, you should know the more commonly used methods described in the following paragraphs.

Possibly the greatest use to you in writing reports are *descriptive statistics*—measures of central tendency, dispersion, and probability. Measures of central tendency—the mean, median, and mode—will help you find a common value of a series that appropriately describes a whole. The measures of dispersion—ranges, variances, and standard deviations—should help you describe the spread of a series. Ratios, which express one quantity as a multiple of another, and probabilities, which determine how many times something will likely occur out of the total of possibilities, can also help you convey common meaning in data analysis. Inferential and other statistical approaches are also useful, but they go beyond these basic elements. You will find descriptions of these and other useful techniques in any standard statistics textbook.

* Descriptive statistics should help the most.

ORGANIZING THE REPORT INFORMATION

When you have finished interpreting your information and you know the message of your report, you are ready to organize this message for presentation. Organizing the report message, of course, is the procedure of grouping your findings into categories and then sorting those categories into a linear argument that accomplishes your purpose and suits your audience.

* After you know what your findings mean, you are ready to construct the working outline.

Deciding on the Approach

As with other forms of communication, you choose between the direct and indirect approach.

Deciding whether to use the direct order is best based on a consideration of your readers' likely use of the report. If your readers need the report conclusion or recommendation as a basis for an action that they must take, directness will speed their effort by enabling them to receive the most important information quickly. If they have confidence in your work, they may choose not to read beyond this point and to take the action that the report supports. Should they want to question any part of the report, however, the material is there for their inspection.

* Use the direct order when the conclusion or recommendation will serve as a basis for action.

The direct arrangement presents right off the most important part of the report. This is the answer—the achievement of the report's goal. Depending on the problem, the direct beginning could consist of a summary of facts, a conclusion, a recommendation, or some combination of summary, conclusions, and recommendation.

* The direct order gives the main message first.

Whatever introductory or background material is needed usually follows the direct opening. Sometimes little or none is needed in the everyday, routine report. Next come the details of the report findings organized in good order. These facts and analyses support the conclusion already given. A brief summary or closing statement ends the direct-order report. Illustrating this arrangement is the following report outline of a short and simple personnel problem. Only the key parts are shown.

* Then it covers introductory material (if any), findings and analyses, and closing.

 I. Recommendation that C. A. Knudson not receive merit pay.
 II. Background
    A. Thorough investigation
    B. Authorized by department head
III. Findings
    A. Late to work seven times.
    B. Absent without acceptable excuse for seven days.
    C. Made two serious errors in his work that were costly for the company.

The following checklist should help you maintain objectivity and integrity in your report.

1. *Report the facts as they are.* Do nothing to make them more or less exciting. Adding colour to interpretations to make the report more interesting amounts to bias. Stock prices may fall or even fall sharply by several points, but seldom do they plummet or nose-dive.

2. *Do not force a conclusion that cannot be defended by the evidence.* When the facts do not support a conclusion, remain true to the evidence and state that there is no clear conclusion. Avoid statements such as "Although our survey found few shoppers who could recall the recent advertizing campaign, we are confident it will have a positive impact on this month's sales."

3. *Do not interpret a lack of evidence as proof to the contrary.* The fact that you cannot prove something is true does not mean that it is false. Similarly, not being able to prove something false does not automatically make it true. Beware of statements that begin with "There is no evidence to show."

4. *Do not compare data without a common basis.* When you look for relationships between sets of data, make sure they do have characteristics in common. For example, are prices all in Canadian dollars and not a mixture of Canadian and American?

5. *Do not draw illogical cause-effect conclusions.* Just because two sets of data appear to affect each other does not mean they actually do. A rooster may crow at sunrise but does the rooster cause the sun to rise? If world oil prices rise, should the credit for a favourable trade balance be claimed by the newly elected government?

6. *Beware of unreliable and unrepresentative data.* Information found in secondary sources may be incorrect to some extent because of collection errors or recording mistakes. Beware especially of data collected by groups that advocate a position (political organizations, special-interest groups).

7. *Do not oversimplify.* Most business problems are complex. Looking only for quick, simple solutions will mean some important points are overlooked. Raising prices to increase profits is a simple answer that may not give the desired results.

IV. Conclusion that his work is unsatisfactory
V. Summary and Closing

> • Use the indirect order when you need to take the readers through the analysis.

On the other hand, if there is reason to believe that your readers will want to arrive at the conclusion or recommendation only after a thorough review of the analysis, you should organize your report in the indirect order. This arrangement is especially preferable if the topic of your report is controversial, or likely to be met with skepticism. The indirect order will help you persuade the readers to accept your conclusion or recommendation.

> • The indirect order has this sequence: introduction, facts and analyses, conclusions, and recommendations.

The indirect arrangement begins with whatever introductory material is needed to prepare the reader for the report. Then comes the presentation of facts, with analyses when needed. Next comes the part that accomplishes the goal of the report. If the goal is to present information, this part summarizes the information. If the goal is to reach a conclusion, this part reviews the analyses and draws a conclusion from them. And if the goal is to recommend an action, this part reviews the analyses, draws a conclusion, and, on the basis of the conclusion, makes a recommendation.

Using the personnel example again, the indirect arrangement would be as follows:

I. Introduction
   A. Identification of employee.
   B. General concern of supervisor.
   C. Thorough study conducted.

A PRACTICE RUN

The following captions are in random order. Rearrange them to complete a direct approach outline.

Purpose: To recommend buying or leasing company cars.
   To date, the company has bought cars.
   Maintenance costs would be included in the lease.
   Leasing requires only a small initial cost outlay.
   Long-term costs are slightly higher with leasing.
   Research shows the company image would be improved with newer cars.
   The benefits of leasing outweigh the drawback of the extra expense.
   The current cars are aging and need replacement.
   Lease cars for the company fleet rather than buying them.

I. Recommendation

_____

II. Background Information

_____

_____

_____

III. Findings

_____

_____

_____

IV. Conclusion

_____

II. Findings
   A. Late to work seven times.
   B. Absent without acceptable excuse for seven days.
   C. Made two serious errors in his work that were costly for the company.
III. Conclusion that his work is unsatisfactory
IV. Recommendation that C. A. Knudson not receive merit pay

Formatting the Outline

Constructing an outline forces you to think in a linear fashion before you write. Although your plan may be clear in your mind, writing it is advisable. The reasons are similar to those given for writing the statement of purpose. A written plan keeps you on target, reduces the chance of serious omissions, allows others to work with you more easily,[1] and helps you think through the problem to get your writing under way. A working outline is the plan for the writing task that follows. At first, it is a working document, a draft that can be changed as you write. Later, it becomes what the blueprint is to the construction engineer or what the pattern is to the dressmaker. In a longer report, the outline forms the basis for the table of contents. Also, in most long reports, and even in some short ones, the outline topics may be used as guides by placing them within the text as captions or headings.

* Outlines should usually be written. With later modifications, they may become tables of contents and captions.

[1]The topic of collaborative writing is covered in more detail in Chapter 18, "Technology in Communication."

A PRACTICE RUN

The following captions are in random order. Rearrange them to complete an indirect approach outline.

Purpose: To recommend buying or leasing company cars.
   To date, the company has bought cars.
   Maintenance costs would be included in the lease.
   Leasing requires only a small initial cost outlay.
   Long-term costs are slightly higher with leasing.
   Research shows the company image would be improved with newer cars.
   The benefits of leasing outweigh the drawback of the extra expense.
   The current cars are aging and need replacement.
   Lease cars for the company fleet rather than buying them.

I. Background Information

_____

_____

_____

II. Findings

_____

_____

_____

III. Conclusion

_____

IV. Recommendation

_____

• You may view outlining as a process of division into parts and subparts.

The outlining procedure described in the following pages is based on the idea that outlining is a process of dividing. The subject you are dividing is all the information you have gathered and interpreted. You may continue to divide and organize your information as you did at the beginning of your research, or you may find another way that makes a simpler explanation of those findings to someone else. In short reports one level of division may be enough. Long reports, however, may require further subdivision. You may continue to subdivide as long as it is useful to do so (Figure 12–3). Each division makes a step in the outline.

• The conventional and decimal systems are used in marking the levels of an outline.

In constructing your outline, you probably will use either the conventional or the decimal system to mark the levels. The conventional system uses Roman numbers to show the major headings. Capital letters and Arabic numbers are used for the second and third levels respectively. To show the lesser headings, lowercase letters and lowercase Roman numbers are used. The decimal system uses whole numbers to show the major sections. Places of decimal (digits to the right of the decimal point) show each successive step in the outline. Illustration best explains these systems.[2]

Whatever system you use, when you begin producing the final report, you also will show differences in the levels of headings by placement and form (font, size, or style) as reviewed in Chapter 14.

---

[2]You may also see periods between all the numbers in the decimal system.

FIGURE 12-3 Procedure for Constructing an Outline by the Process of Division

Conventional System	Decimal System
I. First-level heading	1 First-level heading
A. Second-level	1.1 Second level, first part
B. Second-level	1.2 Second level, second part
1. Third-level	1.21 Third level, first part
a. Fourth-level	1.211 Fourth level, first part
b. Fourth-level	1.212 Fourth level, second part
2. Third-level	1.22 Third level, second part
a. Fourth-level	1.221 Fourth level, first part
i. Fifth-level	1.2211 Fifth level
ii. Fifth-level	1.2212 Fifth level
b. Fourth-level	1.222 Fourth level
II. First-level heading	2 First-level heading

To develop the topic of outlining, we will focus on the part of the report commonly called the *body*. The body presents the information gathered, with analyses and interpretations where needed. Therefore, special attention needs to be given to its organization. We have already discussed the three most common types of subdivisions—subtopics, hypotheses, and bases for comparison. It is now time to consider other methods and some refinements of these three.

> • The following discussion of outlining deals with the body of the report.

Division by Conventional Relationships

In dividing your information into subparts, you have to find a way of dividing that will produce about equal parts. Whenever the information you have to present has some time aspect, consider organizing it by *periods of time*. The periods you select need not be equal in duration, but they should be about equal in importance.

> • When the information has a time basis, division by time or sequence is possible.

A report on the progress of a research committee might be broken down into the following comparable periods:

Orientation, May–July.

Planning the project, August.

Implementation of the research plan, September–November.

If the information you have collected has some relation to geographic location, you may use a *place* division. A report on the sales program of a national manufacturer might be broken down by major geographic areas. Note that these areas are not the same size, but are approximately equal in sales volume for this company.

> • When the information is related to geographic location, a place division is possible.

Maritimes

Quebec

Central and Eastern Ontario

Southwestern Ontario

Prairies

British Columbia

Another illustration of organization by place is a report on the productivity of a company with several manufacturing plants. A major division of the report might be devoted to each plant. The information might be broken down further, this time by sections, departments, or divisions within the plant.

Quantity divisions are possible for information that has quantitative values. To illustrate, an analysis of the buying habits of the population could be divided into income groups such as the following:

> • Division based on quantity is possible when the information has a number base.

Under $20,000.

$20,000 to under $40,000.

$40,000 to under $60,000.

$60,000 and over.

A second example of division on a quantitative basis is a report of a survey of men's preferences for shoes, in which an organization by age groups might be appropriate:

Youths, under 18.

Young adults, 18–30.

Adults, 31–50.

Senior adults, 51–70.

Elder adults, over 70.

Multiple Division Possibilities

* Multiple organization possibilities can occur.

* This plant-location problem is organized by place.

Some problems can be organized in more than one way. For example, take the problem of determining the best of three towns for locating a new manufacturing plant. The report could be organized by towns or by the bases of comparison. Organized by towns, the bases of comparison would probably be the second-level headings.

I. Introduction
II. Town A
    A. Availability of workers.
    B. Availability of raw materials.
    C. Sources of power.
    D. Transportation facilities.
    E. Taxation.
    F. Public support and co-operation.
III. Town B
    A. Availability of workers.
    B. Availability of raw materials.
    C. Sources . . . (etc.).
IV. Town C
    A. Availability of workers.
    B. Availability . . . (etc.).

* Here it is organized by the bases of comparison.

Organized by bases of comparison, towns would be the second-level headings:

I. Introduction
II. Availability of workers
    A. Town A.
    B. Town B.
    C. Town C.
III. Availability of raw materials
    A. Town A.
    B. Town B.
    C. Town C.
IV. Sources of power.
    A. Town A.
    B. Town B. (etc.).

* The second plan is better because it makes comparison easy.

At first glance both plans appear logical. Close inspection, however, shows that organization by towns separates information that has to be compared. For example, three different parts of the report must be examined to find out which town has the best labour pool. Furthermore, to be fair to each town, the reader must try not to make a decision until the very end. In the second outline, the information that has to be compared is close together. The comparisons are made point by point and then compiled together in a summary. This order allows decisions on each factor along the way and a final decision simply by combining all the earlier ones. These two plans show that some problems can be organized in more than one way. In such cases you must compare the possibilities carefully to find the one that makes the clearest presentation for your reader.

. . . .

A PRACTICE RUN

Give two possibilities for organizing a report that analyzes three different servers (A, B, and C) offering access to the Internet. Consider the speed and number of telephone lines, the costs, the hours of access, and the technical support of each server.

Which method would you recommend in this case? _____

_____

_____

_____

_____

_____

_____

. . . .

Wording of the Headings

Since the headings are an important part of the report, you should word them very carefully. Your working outline can be modified so that in its finished form it becomes the table of contents. Its parts serve as headings to the sections of the report (which is why we refer to these parts as *headings* in the following discussion).

* Word the headings carefully based on your working outline.

Topic or Talking.   In selecting the wording for headings, you have a choice of two general forms—topic headings and talking headings, as illustrated in Figure 12–4. *Topic headings* are short constructions, frequently consisting of one or two words. Because they merely identify the topic of discussion, they are suitable for both direct- and indirect-approach reports.

* You may use topic or talking headings. Topic headings give only the subject of discussion.

Talking headings also identify the subject matter covered. However, they go a step further to indicate what will be said about the subject. In other words, talking headings summarize the material they cover. Therefore, they are more suited to direct-approach reports than indirect reports. If you want to explain and build your case before telling the reader your position, your heading must not describe too much. It should identify the subject and be neutral about your position. If it summarizes the following paragraph or section, then your opportunity to explain first has been lost. Figure 12–4 shows a report outline using topic headings in comparison with headings that talk.

* Talking headings identify the subject and tell what is said about it.

Parallelism of Construction.   The principles for using parallelism in report headings are the same as in résumés and in sentences. You should write the headings for each level in the same grammatical form. In other words, equal-level headings should be parallel in structure. For example, all first-level heading could be sentences; all second-level headings could be noun phrases (a noun with its modifiers).[3] This segment of an outline violates parallelism:

* Headings making up a level of division should be parallel grammatically.

A. Machine output is lagging. (sentence)
B. Increase in cost of operations. (noun phrase)
C. Unable to deliver necessary steam. (decapitated sentence)

---

[3] Some authorities permit varying the form from one part of the report to another.

FIGURE 12-4 A Comparison of Topic and Talking Headings

Topic Headings	Talking Headings

I. Introduction
  A. Authorization
  B. Purpose
  C. Sources
  D. Preview
II. Community attitudes
  A. Plant location
  B. Labour policy
III. Factors of labour
  A. Skilled workers
  B. Unskilled workers
  C. Wage rates
IV. Softwood supply
  A. Adequate areas
  B. Inadequate areas
V. Utilities
  A. Water
  B. Natural gas
  C. Electricity
  D. Waste disposal
VI. Transportation
  A. Surface
  B. Air
VII. Conclusions
  A. First choice
  B. Alternative choice
  C. Other possibilities
	I. Orientation to the problem
	  A. Authorization by board action
	  B. Problem of locating a pulp mill
	  C. Use of miscellaneous government data
	  D. Logical plan of solution
	II. Community attitudes toward the pulp and paper industry
	  A. Favourable reaction of all towns to new mill
	  B. Mixed attitudes of all towns toward labour policy
	III. Labour supply and prevailing wage rates
	  A. Concentration of skilled workers in Athabasca
	  B. Largest pool of unskilled labour in Athabasca
	  C. Generally confused pattern of wage rates
	IV. Nearness to the softwood supply
	  A. Location of Ballinger, Coleman, and Athabasca in the logging area
	  B. Relatively low production near Big Spring and Littlefield
	V. Availability of utilities
	  A. Inadequate water supply in all towns but Athabasca
	  B. Unlimited supply of natural gas in all towns
	  C. Electric rate benefit of Athabasca and Coleman
	  D. General adequacy of all towns for waste disposal
	VI. Adequacy of existing transportation systems
	  A. Surface transportation advantages of Athabasca and Ballinger
	  B. General equality of airway connections
	VII. A final weighting of the factors
	  A. Selection of Athabasca as first choice
	  B. Recommendation of Ballinger as an alternate
	  C. Rejection of Big Spring, Coleman, and Littlefield

A PRACTICE RUN

Change the following topic headings into talking headings.

Availability of workers

_____

Availability of raw materials

_____

Transportation facilities

_____

Change the following talking headings into topic headings.

Taxation rates are high.

_____

Severe weather conditions prevail.

_____

Industrial land costs are reasonable.

_____

You may correct this violation in any of three ways—by making all the headings sentences, noun phrases, or decapitated sentences (a sentence fragment that lacks an expressed subject). If you choose noun phrases, your headings could be

A. Lag in machine output
B. Increase in cost of operations
C. Inability to deliver necessary steam

A PRACTICE RUN

Make the headings above grammatically parallel by writing them as sentences.

_____

_____

_____

Variety in Expression. In the report headings, as in all other forms of writing, you should use a variety of expressions. Repeating words too frequently is monotonous and unpleasant for the reader. The following outline excerpt illustrates this point:

• Repeating words in headings can be monotonous.

A. Chemical production in Ontario
B. Chemical production in Alberta
C. Chemical production in Nova Scotia

The headings in the previous example can be improved simply by making them talk:

A. Ontario leads in chemical production.
B. Alberta's production is in second place.
C. Nova Scotia is close behind in third.

If using topic headings, another level would remove the monotonous repetition:

I. Chemical production
   A. In Ontario
   B. In Alberta
   C. In Nova Scotia

A PRACTICE RUN

Write these headings as talking headings and as topic headings.

	Talking Headings	Topic Headings
Print quality of dot matrix printers	_____	_____
Print quality of bubble-jet printers	_____	_____
Print quality of laser printers	_____	_____

WRITING THE REPORT

After you have collected and organized your information, you are ready to begin writing. Much of what you should do in writing the report was covered in the review of writing techniques in Chapters 2 to 5. However, you should be aware of some additional characteristics of good report writing. These are writer objectivity, consistent time viewpoint, smooth transitions, and appropriate formality.

Requirement of Objectivity

• Good report writing is objective.

Good report writing presents fact and logical interpretation of fact. It avoids presenting preconceived ideas, biases, and personal attitudes. You will approach the problem with an open mind, look at all sides of the issues, and fairly review and interpret the information you have uncovered. In other words, you will be objective.

Being objective does not mean being neutral. It means reaching a position after fairly examining all the evidence. It means presenting your conclusion and that of others as long as these positions can be supported by the evidence. Because reports are important documents that may be published, used as references, and kept for a long time, you as the writer should feel an increased sense of accountability. Your role will be much like that of a fair-minded judge presiding over a court of law. Your opinions, conclusions, and recommendations are reached only after careful consideration of all the facts because many people over many years will depend on the accuracy and reliability of your words.

• Objective writing is believable.

Objectivity as a Basis for Believability.   An objective report has an ingredient that is essential to good report writing—believability. Biased writing in artfully deceptive language may at first glance be believable, but if bias is evident at any place in a report, the reader will be suspicious of the entire report. Painstaking objectivity is, therefore, the only sure way to make report writing believable.

• Historically, objective writing has required writing in the third person.

Objectivity and the Question of Person in Writing.   Recognizing the need for objectivity, early report writers worked to develop a style of writing that demonstrated objectivity. Since the source of bias in reports was people, they reasoned, objectivity was best achieved by emphasizing facts rather than the people involved in writing and reading reports. They concluded that objectivity could be shown by writing in the third person—without *I*'s, *we*'s, or *you*'s. Use of the third person became compulsory.

• Some writers argue that first-person writing is more interesting and just as objective.

Then some writers questioned the required use of third-person writing. They believed that objectivity is an attitude—not a matter of person—and that a report written in the first person could be just as objective as a report written in third person. These writers pointed out the advantages of first-person writing, such as its directness, forcefulness, and interesting conversational style. These benefits, they felt, were too important to lose. Moreover, they argued that third-person writing often led to an overuse of the passive voice and a dull, long-winded writing style.

• There is merit to both sides.

As in most controversies, the arguments on both sides have merit. In some situations first-person writing is more spirited and direct. In rebuttal, however, one can look at the lively style of writers for newspapers, news magazines, and journals. Most of this writing is in the third person—but it is usually not dull. In some formal situations, third-person writing is better. And in still other situations, either type of writing is fine. In your decision you should consider the expectations and preferences of those who will read the report as well as your purpose. Do you want to emphasize that "I did it," or that "the study supports"? Comparing the following examples will help you in your choice.

PERSONAL USING FIRST PERSON

I have completed a study of the advantages and disadvantages of using discount coupons. My recommendation is that your company should not adopt this practice. If you use the coupons, you will have to pay for them to be printed and distributed. Secondly, your profits from increased sales will not compensate for the extra staff you will need.

IMPERSONAL USING THIRD PERSON

A study of the advantages and disadvantages of using discount coupons supports the recommendation that the Mills Company should not adopt this practice. The coupons themselves would cost extra money to print and distribute. Also, the profit from the projected increase in sales would not compensate for the cost of the additional staff required.

Consistency in Time Viewpoint

Presenting information in the right place in time is a major problem in keeping order in a report. Not doing so confuses the reader and creates barriers to communication. Thus, it is important that you maintain a proper time viewpoint.

You have two choices of time viewpoint—past and present. Although some authorities favour one or the other, either viewpoint can produce a good report. The important thing is to be consistent—to select one time viewpoint and stay with it. In other words, you should view all similar information in the report from the same position in time.

The present time viewpoint describes all that is current at the time of writing in the present tense. For example, a present viewpoint report would say, "Our study *shows* that 22 percent of the managers *favour* a change." In referring to an old survey, you would write: "In 1988 only 12 percent *held* this opinion." And in making a future reference, you would write: "If this trend continues, 30 percent *will hold* this opinion by 1999."

If you adopt the past time viewpoint, you treat the research, the findings, and the writing of the report as past. Thus, you would report the results of your survey in the past tense: "Our study *showed* that 22 percent of the managers *favoured* a change." You would write a reference to another part of the report this way: "In Part III this conclusion *was reached*." Your use of the past time viewpoint would have no effect on references to future happenings. It would be proper to write a sentence like this: "We have predicted that if the current trend continues, 30 percent will favour a change by 1999."

* Keep a consistent time viewpoint throughout the report.

* There are two time viewpoints—past and present. Select one, and do not change.

* The present viewpoint uses present tense for everything current at the time of writing.

* The past time viewpoint views the research and the findings as past.

Need for Smooth Transitions

As we have seen in Chapter 4, communication needs coherence. A well-written report reads as one continuous story because the parts connect smoothly. Much of this smoothness is the result of good, logical organization with transitions used to connect the ideas and guide the reader.

To review, a *transition* is a bridge between ideas made by words or sentences that show the relationships between parts. Whether you use a transition in a particular place depends on need. At the beginning of a section, a transition links the new section with preceding ones. At the end of a section, a transition is an outlook or overview of points to come. A transition is placed in the middle to help move the flow of information. Since transitions are meant to help the reader understand your message by making your logical progression clear, you should use them when they are needed—when leaving them out would produce abruptness or make extra work for the reader.

* You should use transitions to connect the parts of the report.

* *Transition* means a "bridging across."

Transitional Words.   We have already seen in our discussion of paragraphs that transitions are needed to connect clause to clause, sentence to sentence, and paragraph to paragraph. Single words or short phrases generally serve to make such connections. The following list shows some transitional words and phrases that are useful in reports. With a little imagination to supply the context, you can easily see how these words relate ideas.

* Transitional words show relationships between lesser parts.

* This partial list shows how words explain relationships.

RELATIONSHIP	WORD EXAMPLES
Listing of subjects	In addition First, second, and so on Besides Moreover
Contrast	On the contrary In spite of On the other hand In contrast However

RELATIONSHIP	WORD EXAMPLES
Likeness	In a like manner
	Likewise
	Similarly
Cause-result	Thus
	Because of
	Therefore
	Consequently
	For this reason
Explanation or elaboration	For example
	To illustrate
	For instance
	Also
	Too

• For connecting large parts, transition sentences may be used.

Sentence Transitions.   For connecting larger parts of your report, use transitional sentences. They will show the connecting network of thought throughout the report. The following example shows the use of transitional sentences. Part A of the report deals with the cost of gasoline, Part B with the cost of oil, and Part C with the cost of repairs and maintenance. The example begins with the conclusion for Part B. Then, with a smooth tie-in, the next words look back to Parts A and B (gasoline and oil costs) and introduce Part C. The relative importance of the three parts is also established.

[Part B concludes] Thus, the results show only negligible differences in the cost for oil consumption.

[Part C begins] Even though the costs of gasoline and oil are the more consistent factors of operation expense, the picture is not complete until the costs of repairs and maintenance are considered.

Then, Part C is concluded and the next subject is set up in a smooth and logical step.

This research clearly shows that Edmund's machines are the most economical. Unquestionably, their low gasoline consumption and their record for low-cost maintenance give them a decided edge over competing brands. *Before a definite conclusion about their merit is reached, however, one more vital comparison should be made.*

Appropriate Level of Formality

• Write formally (1) if the situation requires it or (2) if your reader prefers it.

And finally, you should choose the appropriate level of formality. Consider the formality of the situation and the preferences of your readers. If the situation is a formal one, you should write formally. Convention favours third-person writing for the most formal situations. Secondly, if those who will receive the report expect formality, you should write that way. If they expect informality and the situation permits it, you should write informally. However, even if you decide to write informally, your language and tone will not be casual or colloquial. These are business documents you are preparing.

. . . .
MAINTAINING INTEREST

• Report writing should be interesting. Interesting writing is necessary for best communication.

Like any other form of writing, report writing should be interesting. Actually, interest is as important as the facts of the report, for communication is not likely to occur without interest. Readers cannot help missing parts of the message if their interest is not held—if their minds are allowed to stray. Interest in the subject is not enough to ensure communication. The writing must be interesting. This should be evident to you if you have ever tried to read dull writing in studying for an examination. How desperately you wanted to learn the subject, but how often your mind strayed away!

If writing interestingly is an art, it is one that you can develop with practice. To practice the art of interesting writing, avoid jargon and make your words build concrete pictures. Try to cultivate a feeling for the rhythmic flow of words and sentences. As you do, you will find that you automatically vary the length and structure of your sentences. If you remember that behind every fact and figure there is life—people who negotiate, repair, finance, operate, sell, and so on—you will be able to bring that life to the surface. Of course, efforts to make writing interesting can be overdone. If your reader's attention is attracted to how something has been said rather than to what has been said, you need to revise your work. A well-written report will prompt readers to say, "Here are some interesting facts," rather than, "Here is some beautiful writing."

* Interesting writing can be developed with practice.

A SUMMARY OF LEARNING OUTCOMES FROM THIS CHAPTER

A business report is an orderly and objective communication of factual information that serves a business purpose. Your work on a report begins with a purpose. You get the situation clearly in mind by studying the audience and gathering preliminary information you need to understand the background. It is wise to write out a purpose statement or a problem statement to guide you in your work. Phrase the statement as an infinitive, a question, or a declarative statement.

From this statement, you try to predict the factors you will need to study. These factors may be subtopics in information reports, hypotheses in problems requiring a solution, or bases of comparison in problems requiring evaluations. As you research, you may refine these factors or add more.

With the purpose or problem clearly determined, you then do your detailed research to gather information. Next, you apply this information to the situation, looking for trends and developing interpretations. Diagrams and descriptive statistics should help you interpret and present your findings, while critical thinking skills and tests such as the test of experience and the negative test should help you assess your work.

Finally, you construct an outline of the report contents. You may use the conventional outline symbols (I, A, 1, a) or the decimal system (1, 1.1, 1.11). You organize the body through a division process using time, place, or quantity, and you continue to subdivide as far as is necessary. The result is your outline.

Next, you take the completed outline and construct headings for each part. Either talking headings or topic headings are appropriate. But make certain that the headings are grammatically parallel and that words have not been repeated monotonously.

After you have organized your information, you write the report. You should follow the rules of clear writing discussed in earlier chapters. In addition, you should strive to give your report objectivity, consistent time viewpoint, clear transitions, appropriate formality, and interest.

Objectivity means reporting without bias. Historically, the effort to achieve objectivity required writing in the third person. Some writers have questioned that requirement, arguing that using the first-person can be more interesting and just as objective. Most formal writing uses the third person.

Since a report should have a consistent time viewpoint, select one of the two time viewpoints and stay with it.

Good transitions connect the report parts smoothly. While transitional phrases and words are enough to link simple ideas, full sentences may be needed to guide the reader's thoughts from one section or major idea of the report to the next.

To make the report interesting to read, practise the techniques of good writing (selecting words carefully, developing a rhythmic flow of sentences, and so on). Remembering the people behind the facts will help bring life to your writing. However, your style of writing should not draw attention away from the information you present.

QUESTIONS FOR DISCUSSION

1. Explain the concept of outlining as a division process.
2. Although both the conventional and the decimal system are used for marking the divisions of a report, are there times when one is better than the other? Would some readers prefer one method over the other?
3. Using Doreen Lam's experience in the Introductory Situation, explain the value of writing a one-sentence purpose statement.
4. You are writing a report on the progress of the Frost Company's efforts to increase sales of its five products through extensive advertizing in newspapers, on television, and in magazines. Discuss the possibilities for major headings. Evaluate each possibility.

5. Is it necessary to use third-person writing to be objective in a report?
6. Is it incorrect to have present, past, and future tense in the same report? in the same paragraph? in the same sentence? Discuss.
7. "Transitional sentences are unnecessary. They merely add length to a report and thus are contrary to the established rules of conciseness." Discuss.
8. "Reports are written for business executives who want them. Thus, you don't have to be concerned about holding your reader's interest." Discuss.

CASE 12-1

The Community Relations Department of your college has an interesting challenge. They want to develop a web site for the Internet to promote higher education in general and your college in particular. Several students have been asked to participate in the planning. Here is part of the conversation.

"We have to start with a home page that has links to all the other pages. What areas should we list on that first page?"

"For sure we have to have a heading like 'Cool Stuff.' I've seen that a lot on other web sites."

"O.K., but we have to have the serious stuff too. You know. Stuff like programs, financing, and accommodation."

"I think people will want an overview of the campus and maybe something about our history."

"What about the programs we have that no one else does? Or some of the special awards and accreditations the college has?"

"These are all good ideas. Let's get them on paper. Should we start with a sketch? Then we can turn it into an outline and show the links to the other pages on the web site."

ANSWERS TO PRACTICE RUNS

▶ Purpose Statements

Answers may vary. These are suggestions only.

1. What are the common characteristics of the people who eat Crunchie Munchies?
   To determine the market profile for Crunchie Munchie eaters including demographic and psychographic characteristics.
2. This report is a fair evaluation of J. Pferschy after three months of employment.

How well is J. Pferschy performing her duties after three months of employment?
To assess the job performance of J. Pferschy after three months of employment.

3. To compare our products and service with those of Far Side Bakery.
   Our products and services need to be measured against those of Far Side Bakery.

▶ Subtopics

Answers may vary. These are some suggestions only.

Purpose: To outline the business diploma program at Cambrian College to attract graduating high school students.

Length of Program; Cost; Compulsory Subjects; Optional Subjects; Flexibility of Study Programs (part-time, evening, summer, etc.); Social and Recreational Facilities of the College; Scholarships and Bursaries; Transferability of Credit

▶ Hypotheses

Answers may vary. These are some suggestions only.

Problem: Why are older students returning to class? (The average student age has risen from 22 in 1988 to 25 in 1996.)

The changing technology requires retraining.

The tight job market creates high unemployment.

The declining economy forces people to look for higher-paying jobs.

People prefer jobs with responsibility that offer higher job satisfaction.

Divorce often results in the need for upgrading or training for single parents.

As people live longer, they want to pursue their interests.

A combination of all of these reasons.

▶ Bases of Comparison

Answers may vary. These are some suggestions only.

Problem: Which long-distance telephone carrier should I choose?

Basic costs; Rate of discount; Numbers to which the discount applies; Time restrictions; Overseas restrictions; Calling card restrictions

▶ Direct Approach

Purpose: To recommend buying or leasing company cars.

I. *Recommendation*

Lease cars for the company fleet rather than buying them.

II. *Background Information*

To date, the company has bought cars.

The current cars are aging and need replacement.

III. *Findings*

Maintenance costs would be included in the lease.

Leasing requires only a small initial cost outlay.

Long-term costs are slightly higher with leasing.

Research shows the company image would be improved with newer cars.

IV. *Conclusion*

The benefits of leasing outweigh the drawback of the extra expense.

▶ Indirect Approach

Purpose: To recommend buying or leasing company cars.

I. *Background Information*

To date, the company has bought cars.

The current cars are aging and need replacement.

II. *Findings*

Maintenance costs would be included in the lease.

Leasing requires only a small initial cost outlay.

Long-term costs are slightly higher with leasing.

Research shows the company image would be improved with newer cars.

III. *Conclusion*

The benefits of leasing outweigh the drawback of the extra expense.

IV. *Recommendation*

Lease cars for the company fleet rather than buying them.

▶ Multiple Division Possibilities

Which arrangement would you recommend in this case?

Bases of Comparison

Arranged by Server
  Server A
  Speed and number of lines

Arranged by Bases of Comparison
  Speed and Number of lines
  Server A

Arranged by Server
  Costs
  Hours of access
  Technical support

Server B
  Speed and number of lines
  Costs
  Hours of access
  Technical support

Server C
  Speed and number of lines
  Costs
  Hours of access
  Technical support

Arranged by Bases of Comparison
Server B
Server C

Costs
  Server A
  Server B
  Server C

Hours of Access
  Server A
  Server B
  Server C

Technical Support
  Server A
  Server B
  Server C

▶ Talking and Topic Headings

Answers may vary. These are suggestions only.

Availability of workers
Availability of raw materials
Transportation facilities
Taxation rates are high.
Severe weather conditions prevail.
Industrial land costs are reasonable.

Both skilled and unskilled workers are available.
Raw materials would have to be imported.
Air, road, and rail connections are excellent.
  Taxation
  Climate
  Land Prices

▶ Parallel Headings: Sentences

Answers may vary. These are suggestions only.
A. The machine output is lagging.

B. Our cost of operations is increasing.
C. The boiler cannot deliver necessary steam.

▶ Variety in Expression

Answers may vary. These are suggestions only.

Talking Headings
Dot matrix printers have near-letter-quality printing.
Bubble-jet printers are the next best.
Laser printers have the highest print resolution.

Topic Headings
Print Quality
  Dot matrix
  Bubble-jet
  Laser

13•

Report Structure:
The Shorter Forms

Upon completing this chapter, you will be able to write well-structured, short reports. To reach this goal, you should be able to

(1) Determine the appropriate approach and style for short reports.

(2) Understand the uses of three short report formats: memo; letter; and familiar short reports.

(3) Write concise and well-organized memorandum and letter reports.

(4) Employ organizational skills to write effective short reports.

(5) Adapt report writing skills for such special reports as progress and audit reports.

(6) Write complete, well-organized, and persuasive proposals.

▶ to the Structure of Short Reports

Doreen has a working outline for her report, but she still has to decide on some stylistic and structural points. Since this report is going to someone in her company, she considers a memo report format. However, she is a long way from head office and she has never met the president. A letter report might be better.

Then again, she wants to make a good impression. The short report with a title page might be more impressive.

"Yes," she decides, "that's my best choice. And I'll include a letter to introduce it and summarize the highlights. This is going to be a report to be proud of!" ■

AN OVERVIEW OF REPORT STRUCTURE

From the definition of reports given in Chapter 12, you will have realized that reports come in many shapes. Before you can put your information into its final form, you will need to choose the structure for your report.

The needs of the situation dictate the report structure. The more complex the problem and the more formal the situation, the longer and more involved the report structure is likely to be. The simpler the problem and the more informal the situation, the shorter and less involved the report structure is likely to be. There is no set rule, however, that defines whether a report is classified as long or short, formal or informal.[1]

This chapter will discuss shorter, written reports such as the memorandum report, the letter report, and the familiar short report.[2] Chapter 14 will discuss longer written reports, and Chapter 16 will cover oral reports.

The shortest of reports is usually the fill-in-the-blank printed form. This structure is used for registration, inventory, sales records, expense records, and so on. On a well-designed form, routine information can be gathered quickly in a consistent format for easy comparison. Although these fill-in reports are very common in business, they are not considered here in detail because they are generally self-explanatory.

The shortest, most informal report we will discuss is the memorandum report. Its layout is similar to a memo, but its text is longer. The style tends to be informal because the intended audience is within the organization. The second type, the letter report, is short like the memo report but slightly more formal because it is prepared for an external audience. As its name suggests, the layout is similar to a letter, except that the letter report is a longer document. Memo and letter reports are usually only a few pages long.

The third type is the familiar short report, a very popular form in business. This report has a title page[3] and 10 or more pages of text. In this type of report, the purpose, because of its complexity, is given a more thorough discussion than a memo or letter report permits. If the report is longer than about 12 pages, a table of contents should be considered. It is also appropriate to consider a covering letter or initial summary outlining the key points of the report. If these items are added, they make the report appear more formal.

- Choose the report's structure based on the needs of the situation.

- A printed form is the simplest report.

- The first step is the memo report, and after that is the letter report.

- The familiar short report has a title page.

---

[1] Figure 14–1 shows the continuum of report styles and types.

[2] In distinguishing memo and letter reports from familiar short reports, we do not mean to suggest that memo and letter reports are uncommon or unusual. All three types are regularly seen in business. However, students likely will have more experience with the familiar short report because of its similarity to class assignments.

[3] The title page is a very useful cover page containing the most important identifying information of title, author, intended audience, and date.

Before we discuss these reports in more detail, we will consider some characteristics common to most short reports.

CHARACTERISTICS OF SHORTER REPORTS

While the techniques for organizing discussed in the preceding chapter cover all forms of reports, the following discussion will apply these more specifically to the shorter reports.

Predominance of the Direct Order

- The shorter report usually begins directly—with conclusions and recommendations.

Because the shorter report usually gives information or solves routine problems, it is likely to be written in the direct order. To review, *direct order* means that the report begins with its most important information. It begins with the answer—the achievement of the report's goal. Whatever explanatory background material is needed usually follows the direct opening. Sometimes little or none is needed in the short, routine report. The facts are organized to show support for the conclusion, and a brief summary or closing statement ends the direct-order report. You use this order if you know that your readers are receptive and that their main concern is to get the information right away.

- Use titles and headings to suit the direct order.

A direct-order report should have titles and headings that are direct. For example, a report on the use of temporary help in the office written to a receptive audience would use the direct order. If the recommendation is to hire temporary staff, the title of the report could be "A Recommendation to Hire Temporary Office Help." Internal headings might be phrases such as "Excessive Use of Overtime" or "Cost Benefits of Temporary Help." All of these titles and headings indicate the answer to the receptive audience.

- The indirect order is possible in a short report.

Although the direct order is more usual, a short report can be written in the indirect order if you believe the explanations are critical to your audience's acceptance of the information or recommendation. The situation would have to be simple and noncontroversial to permit the use of a short report. A more difficult, sensitive issue would be handled in a longer document.

- The indirect order has this sequence: introduction, facts and analyses, conclusions, and recommendations.

Again, to review, the indirect-order report begins with whatever introductory material is needed to prepare the reader. Then the facts are presented with analysis when needed. Next comes the part that accomplishes the goal of the report. It could be a summary of the information, a conclusion, or, on the basis of the conclusion, a recommendation.

- Use titles and headings to suit the indirect order.

An indirect-order report must not use direct titles and headings. If the title "A Recommendation to Hire Temporary Staff" is used, your reader knows the outcome before reading the facts and analysis—the very circumstance you want to avoid. An indirect-order report would have a title such as "An Investigation of Office Staffing Needs." Headings such as "Overtime Statistics for January to June" and "Cost Estimates for Temporary Help" guide your reader but are neutral about the final recommendation.

More Informal Writing Style

- More informal writing is popular in the shorter reports.

Although the writing for all reports is similar, shorter reports tend to be more informal in tone. For example, shorter reports are likely to use the personal pronouns, *I, we,* and *you* rather than only the third person. Short forms, acronyms, first names, and conversational language may also be appropriate.

- They usually (1) involve personal relationships, (2) concern a personal study, and (3) are routine.

The reasons for informal writing in the shorter reports should be noted. First, short reports tend to be from and to colleagues who know each other and who normally address each other informally when they meet. In addition, the shorter reports are apt to involve personal investigations and to represent the observations, evaluations, and analyses of their writers. Finally, the shorter reports tend to deal with day-to-day, routine problems. It is logical to discuss these situations in everyday language.

A PRACTICE RUN

For each situation suggest the form (memo, letter, or familiar short report), the order (direct or indirect), and the style (formal, informal).

1. The department head asked Eva Campbell to inspect the work area and report on safety conditions. Eva has about two pages of information to present.

_____

_____

2. A research organization has completed a survey of consumer attitudes for the Alto Company. The results, including nine charts and tables, will be presented to the president.

_____

_____

3. Karen Belamonte, a stock clerk at Edmunds Plumbing Contractors, was asked by Doug Edmunds for current inventory information (quantity on hand, part number, manufacturer, list price, and description of the item) on a number of basic products.

_____

_____

4. Bryan Chao, a sales manager for Brownlee Shoes, was asked by the vice president for marketing to analyze the results of a promotional campaign conducted in Chao's district. The report is six pages long, including one chart.

_____

_____

. . . .

Less Need for Introductory Information

Most shorter reports require little or no introductory material because they concern day-to-day situations already known to the readers. This holds true for weekly sales reports and inventory reports. Deciding whether introductory material is needed is simply a matter of answering one question: Is there more background information my reader needs to know before reading this report? An incidental reference to the problem or the authorization for the report may be all you need. Here is an example.

* Shorter reports have less need for introductory material.

This second progress report is submitted in agreement with the conditions of our contract, RT706-96, Renovations to Westridge Mall.

. . . .

FORMS OF SHORTER REPORTS

Memorandum Reports

A memo report format is chosen for internal reports about important but routine topics. Topics for a memo report include progress reports, informative reports, and solutions for simple problems. A very complex topic could not be handled effectively in this format. Figure 13–1 illustrates a memorandum report.

* Memo reports are used for important but routine topics.

Memo reports are similar in format to memos except that they are longer. Because of their length, memo reports are usually divided into sections with headings that follow the rules for outlines. A second level of heading is seldom needed in a report of this length.

* They resemble long memos.

FIGURE 13-1   Illustration of a Memorandum Report

This memorandum report summarizes progress a sales manager has made in opening a new sales district. It begins with highlight information—all the busy reader may need to know. Following comes the report of what was done in the period covered, organized by the categories of activities. Because of the close relationship of writer and reader, an informal style is used.

MEMORANDUM   **The Marchand Co. Inc.**

To: Claudette Tremblay
          Director of Sales
From: James Gagnon _JAG_
          Trois Rivières Sales District
Date: July 5, 1997
Topic: _Report for Trois Rivières Sales District_
          Second Quarter, April 1 to June 30, 1997

SUMMARY HIGHLIGHTS

After three months of operation, I have secured office facilities, hired and developed two sales-people, and contacted about half the customers available in the Trois Rivières Sales District. Although the district is not yet showing a profit, at the current rate of development it will do so this year. Prospects for the district are unusually bright.

OFFICE OPERATION

In April, I opened the Trois Rivières Sales District as authorized by action of the board of directors last February 7th. Initially, I set up office in a motel on the outskirts of town, and remained there three weeks while looking for permanent quarters. These I found in Laurentides Park, a downtown office structure. The office suite selected rents for $940 per month. It has two executive offices, both opening into a single secretarial office, which is large enough for two secretaries. Although this arrangement is adequate for the staff now anticipated, additional space is available in the building if needed. We have purchased or leased the necessary pieces of basic office furniture and equipment.

COMMUNICATIONS

Our voice mail system is running smoothly at last. During the unfortunate period of delay, we used an answering machine. The paging company will be compensating us for our inconvenience by extending our service. Our 1-800 number has been operational for a week and has already proven its worth. The e-mail addresses, the last links in our communication system, have been finalized today. We have a six-month contract that can be extended at any time.

PERSONNEL

In the first week of operation, I hired an office secretary, Mme. Marie Cournoyer. Mme. Cournoyer has good experience and has excellent credentials. Her computer skills are excellent and she is comfortable with customer service and secretarial duties. She has been very effective in both capacities.

In early April I hired two salespeople—M. Charles Petain and Mlle. Georgette Dionne. Both were experienced in sales, although neither had worked in apparel sales. I still am searching for someone for the third subdistrict. Currently I am investigating two good prospects and hope to hire one of them in the next week. Until then, I will continue to spend two days a week in the area to make initial contacts with prospective customers.

PERFORMANCE

After brief training sessions, which I conducted personally, the salespeople were assigned the territories previously marked. They were instructed to call on the accounts listed on the sheets supplied by your office. During the first month, Dionne's sales totalled $17,431 and Cournoyer reached $13,490, for a total of $30,921. With three salespeople working the next month, total sales should reach $60,000. Although these monthly totals are below the $95,000 break-even point, current progress indicates that we will exceed this volume within ten months. As we have made contact with only about one half of the prospects in the area, the potential for the district appears to be unusually good.

Again, as with memos, the usual tone for memo reports is informal. In writing to top management at head office, you might choose more formal wording; however, if formality is important, another format, such as the short report, should be considered. One final similarity is that the indirect approach is less frequently used than the direct approach. Because the audience is likely to be receptive, the direct approach is commonly used in memo reports.

One example of an appropriate use of the indirect approach in a memo report would be an application for funding for a department. The reasons for the needed funds would probably be given in a persuasive manner before the specific request is made. In such a case, the subject line must be carefully worded to be neutral about the subject.

The Use of E-Mail for Memorandum Reports

The Expansion of Electronic Mail Usage.
The use of electronic mail is increasing rapidly as the number of people comfortable with e-mail increases. Some companies use it almost exclusively for written, internal communication. In addition to short notes and memos, e-mail networks now carry longer reports. We have already seen in our discussion of memos that the e-mail format has benefits and limitations. Because these benefits and limitations are more obvious in longer memo reports, another review of e-mail is included here.

- E-mail is frequently used for memo reports.

The Convenience of This Channel.
Electronic mail is a convenient medium because every step can be handled from the desktop. E-mail is particularly convenient for memo reports because of the ease with which existing files can be attached to an e-mail message without retyping or reprinting the document. There is no need for the sender to duplicate or deliver the message. There is also no discernible delay in delivery. In addition, to encourage the receiver to open mail, most systems provide a warning sound such as a bell or announcement when new mail arrives.

The Importance of Subject Lines.
If you find a consistent pattern of slow responses, check your subject lines. Remember that people decide whether to open your e-mail message based on your subject line as it appears in a menu. You must do your best to make your subject line reflect the importance of the document. Using URGENT only when the message is urgent is a common courtesy. If the report is provided only as a courtesy, you might consider including FYI (For Your Interest) to show its status.

The Variance in Appearance.
Because a computer screen displays only about 20 lines of text, your thoughts need to be well organized so that the reader will scan through to the following screens. You must do your best to set the stage and make your points before your reader skips ahead to another message waiting in the mailbox.

Some technical points include controlling the length of lines. Some e-mail software wraps the lines while others do not. Some have narrower viewing screens. Read the following examples carefully.

If your sending lines are long, your reader may be faced with lines that disappear off requiring them to scroll the screen sideways to read the full line.

Another example is the narrower viewing screen that puts the last word or
two
on a line of its own and then begins at the left margin again. Over the
course
of an entire document, this annoyance becomes a major distraction for the
reader.

There are many guides to effective use of e-mail in print and on the Internet. They are worth reading for the basics of "netiquette"—the courteous use of electronic mail and other on-line services.

- Invest in a guide if you use e-mail regularly.

A PRACTICE RUN

Suggest ways to improve these messages to make them more suitable for e-mail.

First e-mail message:

SUBJECT: Investigation as requested
Last month at a staff meeting, it was requested that an investigation be made of the causes of the delays that have occurred. The investigation is now complete, and the results have been compiled. Some of the recommendations have already been implemented, so there should be less trouble in the future. Now that a new helper has been hired, there should be no more trouble. This was the cause of the problem.

Follow-up e-mail message

SUBJECT: A clarification of yesterday's message URGENT
FYI, I am sending this message today to clarify yesterday's e-mail message. There was no problem with the sales staff or the warehouse and there was always enough stock to deliver the items within a reasonable time. The truck was not in for repairs either. None of these reasons caused the problem. A temporary helper was found with the help of the driver. The helper gave some help in the unloading work, but he got behind and couldn't seem to catch up. He could have caught up by working overtime, in the opinion of the writer, but he refused to do so. Of the 36 deliveries, all were completed within two days. And now that the temporary helper has been replaced by a permanent helper, there should not be any more delays.

Letter Reports

* Letter reports are reports in letter form.

The second familiar shorter report form is the letter report. Letter reports are used primarily to present information to persons outside the organization, especially when the information is to be sent by mail or fax. For example, an outside consultant may write a report of analyses and recommendations in letter form. Or the officer of an organization may report certain information to the membership in a letter.

* They are usually written in a personal style.

The letter report format is chosen over the short report because it allows personally addressed communication. The personal touch continues with the use of the first and second person (*I, you,* and *we*). The writing style recommended for letter reports is much the same as that recommended for letters. Clear and meaningful expression, conciseness, and a professional manner is a requirement for all business documents.

* Most letter reports begin directly.

Although letter reports follow the usual organizational plans for direct or indirect order, most letter reports use the direct approach. Considering the personal nature of the letter format, most letter report writers assume the audience is receptive and prefer the direct approach. Sometimes a subject line gives the answer before the text of the letter report even begins.

Re: Endorsement of Pro-Green Landscapers for Commercial Sites

The routine letter report usually needs little background information or introduction. For example, a direct beginning could be followed by background information such as this:

These are the major outcomes of the special meeting of your board of directors last January. As they concern information vital to all of us in the association, they are presented here for your confidential use.

* On occasion, letter reports may use the indirect approach.

If the news is negative, the personalized letter report format may be chosen to show concern and personal attention to the situation. The indirect approach would then be a reasonable choice. A letter report written to a member of an organization, for example, might appropriately begin as follows:

As authorized by your board of directors last January 6, this report reviews member company's use of discount selling.

With either the direct or indirect order, a letter report closes with whatever friendly, goodwill comment fits the occasion.

The Short Report

The short report consists of only a title page and text. Its popularity may be explained by the middle-ground impression of formality and thoroughness that it conveys while still being short enough to be read completely at one sitting. This report format is ideally suited for the short but important problem.

> • The short report consists of a title page and the report text.

As previously discussed, the direct order is more usual in the short report. On occasion, the basic direct order may be modified by repeating a summary of the conclusions and recommendations at the end. Such a review of the opening material is used to reinforce the important ideas and overcome a feeling of abruptness in the closing.

> • It is usually in the direct order, beginning with the conclusion.

The mechanics of constructing the short report are simple. The title page includes the report title, the author, the receiver, and the date. For the formatting of this page, see Chapter 21. The short report uses the standard page layout for reports, also discussed in Chapter 21. Because of the report's brevity, two levels of headings are usually adequate. In fact, one level of division is common. A table of contents is a recommended option if the report's length goes beyond 12 or 15 pages. Like any other report, the short report may use graphic aids, an appendix, and a bibliography when these are needed.

> • Short reports have one or two levels of division.

Figure 13–2 illustrates a short report written in the direct order (recommendation and summary first). This report compares service providers for access to the Internet. It begins with a statement of the recommendation and a summary of the supporting information and analysis. In a sense this section appears to be tacked on, but it may be all a busy reader needs to know. Next comes the traditional introduction, which is followed by a detailed analysis of the criteria and each of the providers under consideration. Notice that the tables are introduced in the text, and their contents are interpreted. As the report conclusion is evident from these analyses, it is not repeated. In accordance with the conventions of the company, the writing style of the report is informal.

> • See Figure 13–2 for an example of this report form.

SPECIAL REPORT FORMS

As noted previously, this review describes the report forms most commonly used in business. Many variations exist, a few of which deserve emphasis.

> • Some special report forms deserve mention.

The Progress Report

As its name implies, a progress report presents a review of progress made on an activity. For example, a fund-raising organization might prepare weekly summaries of its efforts to achieve its goal. Or a building contractor might be required as part of the contract to prepare a report on progress towards completing a project—is it on time, within budget, etc. Typically, the contents of these reports concern progress made, but they may also include such related topics as problems encountered or anticipated, and projections of future progress.

> • Progress reports give an accounting of progress made towards a goal as of a certain date.

Progress reports are grouped together because of their content rather than their format. Many are informal, narrative reports like the memo report example in Figure 13–1. Others are quite routine and structured, involving filling in blanks on forms devised for the purpose, as with a weekly sales report. However, progress reports can also be quite formal, as when a researcher is reporting to a sponsoring agency. They can be elaborate works including drawings, pictures, or videos to provide tangible evidence of progress.

> • Progress reports take many shapes.

FIGURE 13-2   Illustration of a Short Report

(Please note that all names and data in this report are fictitious and for illustrative purposes only.)

**A RECOMMENDATION OF AN INTERNET PROVIDER
FOR PERSONAL OR SMALL COMPANY USE
PROPOSED FOR THE E-Z RESEARCH COMPANY**

Submitted to
Mr. Nadir Kazin
E-Z Research Company
312 Dauphin Street
Winnipeg, MB R2L 2H2

Prepared by
Nick Vourakis
Owl Computer Resources
743 Portland Street
Winnipeg, MB R3L 4M9

April 7, 1996

**A RECOMMENDATION OF AN INTERNET PROVIDER
FOR PERSONAL OR SMALL COMPANY USE
PROPOSED FOR THE E-Z RESEARCH COMPANY**

FIGURE 13-2 *Continued*

I. *Recommendations and Conclusions*

Following the criteria established, we recommend Datanet Central as the best provider of service to the Internet for the needs of our client, E-Z Research.

Datanet Central's wide variety of subscription plans offer competitive rates and connect hours. Their support services surpass those of most of their competitors, and during their two years of operation, they have an enviable record of system reliability.

II. *Background of the Problem*

Authorization of the Study.

On March 29, 1996, Owl Computer Resources was requested to conduct a comparative study and make a recommendation on Internet providers for E-Z Research by Ms. Benita Shaffer and Mr. Nadir Kazim, co-owners.

Statement of Purpose.

Our purpose was to compare available service providers and make a recommendation based upon a set of criteria agreed upon by E-Z Research.

Method of Solving the Problem.

In our discussion on March 30, 1996, we agreed upon the following criteria for comparison:

- full graphical access to the Internet, plus e-mail
- reasonable setup fees and hourly rates
- generous connect hours
- local support services
- system reliability.

Two providers were eliminated from the study because they were new to the market and therefore unproven. If they perform well over the next year, a subsequent review might include these providers.

Two others were not considered seriously because, although they provide e-mail services, they do not offer full graphical access to the Internet.

Steps in Analyzing the Problem.

A preliminary comparison of providers resulted in a short list of four to be studied in detail. These four were Datanet Central, SuperGate, Worldnet, and Smartserve.

For these four providers, a full study was made of the plans offered. Costs were compared for six-month and one-year periods with an average usage of 70 hours connect time per month. If a provider offered more than one plan, each plan was evaluated separately.

Additional information was gathered about these four companies by telephone request or by downloading information from their sites on the Internet.

Finally, users of the services were surveyed for assessments of reliability, expertise of operators, and customer service.

III. *A Summary of Findings*

Costs and Hours.

The Worldnet offers unlimited hours for a set rate. SuperGate has the highest overtime hourly rate and competitive basic rates. Smartserve has only a monthly plan with no reduction for six-month or one-year terms. Datanet Central has a lower-than-average overtime rate and the highest number of hours included in the basic rate.

The following table summarizes the setup costs, monthly rates and connect hours, overtime charges, and special rates if available. Only the four providers with proven reliability and full graphical access to the Internet have been included.

FIGURE 13-2 *Continued*

Table 1   Costs and Hours for Internet Providers

	Datanet Central	Smartserve	SuperGate	Worldnet
Setup fee	$25	$20	$30†	$30
Monthly rate	$30	$35	$30	$40
Hours included	40	35	40	unlimited
Overtime hourly rate	$1.50	$1.00	$1.50	n/a
Six-month rate	$180		$180	$200
Hours included/month	50	n/a	45	unlimited
Overtime hourly rate	$1.00		$1.50	n/a
One-year rate	$360		$360	$360
Hours included/month	60	n/a	50	unlimited
Overtime hourly rate	$0.50		$1.50	n/a

†Setup fee waived on one-year purchase.

Support Service and System Reliability.
Customers are least satisfied with Worldnet. Comments included slow response time and inadequate help-line hours. SuperGate is rated second. Help-line hours are more extensive than Worldnet, but some staff lack the appropriate expertise. Customer satisfaction is highest for Smart Serve and Datanet Central. Datanet Central has the longest help-line hours with Smart Serve only slightly behind.

A copy of the questionnaire sent to subscribers of each service by electronic mail (e-mail) is included in Appendix A. The individual replies to the survey are available on the diskette that accompanies this report. The results have been tabulated and are summarized in Table 2.

Table 2   Service and Reliability of Internet Providers

	Datanet Central	Smartserve	SuperGate	Worldnet
# of complete surveys	25	30	20†	20
Reliability of connection†	9.0	9.0	9.0	7.5
Expertise of help-line staff†	9.0	9.5	8.5	7.0
Availability of help line	24 hours daily	9–9 M–F‡ 24 hr S–S	9–5 M–F‡ 9–11 S–S	9–9 M–F‡
Overall satisfaction†	9.0	9.0	8.0	7.0

† 1 = low, 10 = high
‡M–F Monday to Friday; S–S Saturday and Sunday

Additional Documentation.
Additional documentation, including technical information about the hardware each system uses and the software provided to each subscriber, is included in Appendix B. This material was obtained from the promotional literature sent by the service providers, or from telephone discussions with their representatives. Some supplementary material was printed from the service providers' own web sites.

FIGURE 13–2 *Concluded*

IV. *Analysis and Conclusions*

Based on the information obtained from each provider, the six-month and one-year costs for E-Z Research to subscribe to the services with an average usage of 70 hours per month have been calculated in Table 3. For six months of service, World Net is the least expensive and Datanet Central is the second least expensive. For one year, World Net is again the least expensive and Datanet Central is second.

Table 3 Analysis of Costs for Six Months and One Year

	Datanet Central	Smartserve	SuperGate	Worldnet
6 months				
Setup charge	25	20	30	30
Basic charge	180	210	180	200
Overtime charges	120	210	225	0
TOTAL COST	$325	$440	$435	$230
1 year				
Setup charge	25	20	0	30
Basic charge	360	420	360	360
Overtime charges	60	420	360	0
TOTAL COST	$440	$860	$720	$390

From the survey and our study of the additional documentation, Datanet Central gives the best overall service and reliability. Although SmartServe received a comparable customer service rating, its cost is significantly higher and the help line has fewer hours of operation. World Net is less expensive, but its customer rating on service was unsatisfactory.

In summary, Datanet Central meets the criteria set by E-Z Research. It offers a full graphical access to the Internet, plus e-mail. Its fees and hourly rates are competitive. For seventy hours of service over a six-month or one-year period, Datanet Central is significantly more economical than providers of similar quality. Support services and system reliability are rated highly by current users.

V. *Closing Remarks*

If, after reviewing this report and its appended materials, you have further questions, I will do all I can to answer them. Because of recent improvements in fibre optic connections and the availability of Internet service through cable operators, a new study should be undertaken within a year to re-evaluate the service market. Owl Computers will, of course, be pleased to undertake this additional study for you.

FIGURE 13-3   A Short Audit Report

```
                    KENT, YOUNG & CRAGG
                    Chartered Accountants
                     743 Portland Street
                    Winnipeg, MB R3L 4M9


     We have audited the financial statements of_____
[company] as at _____ [date].  These financial state-
ments are the responsibility of the Company's management.  Our
responsibility is to express an opinion on these financial
statements based on our audit.

     We conducted our audit in accordance with generally accepted
auditing standards.  Those standards require that we plan and
perform an audit to obtain reasonable assurance whether the
financial statements are free of material misstatement.  An
audit includes examining, on a test basis, evidence supporting
the amount and disclosures in the financial statements.  An
audit also includes assessing the accounting principles used
and significant estimates made by management, as well as
evaluating the overall financial statement presentation.

     In our opinion, these consolidated financial statements
present fairly, in all material respects, the financial position
of the Company as at _____ [date] in accordance with
accounting principles generally accepted in Canada.




Kent, Young & Cragg
Chartered Accountants
```

The Audit Report

- Short-form audit reports are well known in business.

The short-form, audit report is perhaps the most standardized of all business reports. It is a statement verifying the inspection and approval of a firm's financial records by anaccountant. Figure 13–3 shows a typical example. If problems are found, a special, longer report would be prepared. Because these special reports are tailored to the situation and the client, they vary greatly in their format and content.

The Proposal

- Proposals vary in length.

Placing proposals in a discussion of shorter reports is debatable, since they are not always short. They range in length from a few pages to several volumes with videos, slides, and demonstrations. We discuss them here primarily as a matter of convenience.

Proposals Defined. By definition, a *proposal* is a presentation for consideration of something, such as an opportunity, an initiative, a solution, or a new method. Examples of proposals include one company's offer to merge with another company, an advertizing agency's suggested plan for promoting a product, or a city's attempt to induce a business to locate within its boundaries. Other proposals are appeals or bids for grants, donations, or contracts. To illustrate, a university professor with an idea for research submits a request for funds to a government agency, a community organization submits a request to a foundation to finance a proposed drug rehabilitation facility, or an architectural firm responds to a call for bids to build a new arena. See Figure 13–4 for an example of a simple proposal.

- A proposal is a presentation for consideration of an idea or offer.

Most proposals cover larger topics and involve a major financial commitment. The total dollar value involved means the proposal will be unique and specifically adapted to the reader's business. The written documents may be accompanied by oral presentations or multi-media productions.

Invited or Uninvited (Prospecting) Proposals. Proposals may be invited. By *invited* we mean that the awarding organization announces to interested parties that it is soliciting proposals. In their announcements the awarding organizations typically specify the unique requirements that the proposal should cover. To illustrate, a business might want computer repair companies to bid on a three-year service contract for all desktop and laptop computers owned by the business.

- Proposals may be invited.

Uninvited or prospecting proposals, on the other hand, are descriptions of what the writer could do for the reader's organization. The idea has originated with the writer rather than as a request from the reader. Architectural firms have approached city councils in recent years with proposals to redevelop downtown warehouses or hospitals as loft apartments. The architects with the vision and expertise approach those in authority to obtain permission.

- Prospecting proposals are like sales letters.

Format and Organization. The physical arrangement and organization of proposals vary widely. The simplest internal proposals resemble formal memorandums. The more complex proposals may take the form of full-dress, long reports, including prefatory pages (title pages, letter of transmittal, table of contents, executive summary), text, and an assortment of appended parts. They can be quite elaborate with supporting visual aids. In preparing a proposal for a large contract, a company could spend thousands of dollars. Most proposals have arrangements that fall somewhere between these extremes.

- Their formats vary from memorandums to long report forms.

Because of the wide variations in the makeup of proposals, you would be wise to investigate carefully before designing a particular proposal.[4] In your investigation try to discover what format is conventional among those who will read it. Look to see what others have done in similar situations. Your design should be the best for the situation if you are to win the contract.

- Select the format after careful thought and research.

In the case of an invited proposal, review the announcement thoroughly, looking for clues concerning the preferences of the inviting organization. It is very important that you follow any guidelines carefully. In competitive situations the selection procedure frequently involves a checklist and a rating system for each required element. One omission could put your proposal out of the running.

- Follow the guidelines of an invited proposal very carefully.

If you are making an uninvited proposal, you will have to imagine what your readers need to know. As each case will involve different needs, you will have to use your best judgment in making your choices.

- If the proposal is uninvited, use judgment in anticipating the readers' needs.

Content. Although the number of content possibilities is almost limitless, you should consider including the eight topics listed below. They are broad and general, and you can combine or subdivide them as needed to fit the facts of your case.

- Consider including these eight topics:

1. Purpose and Problem. An appropriate beginning is a statement of the purpose (to present a proposal) and the problem (for training Dunn Company sales personnel in

- 1. Purpose and problem, and gaining attention (in uninvited proposals);

---

[4] Figure 14–1 "A Progression of the Adjustments in Report Structure" will help you in your choices.

FIGURE 13–4   Illustration of a Short Proposal

THE CROOKED SIXPENCE
123 Main Street
Four Mile House, MN R2V 4T4

A Proposal to Supply
Crafts on Consignment

KATY-DID KRAFTS
Four Mile House

August 31, 1997

PROPOSAL SUMMARY
    Katy-Did Krafts has two skilled crafters who will create
dried flower arrangements, wreaths, trinkets, personal items,
bows, and gift bags for sale by consignment through your gift
shop, The Crooked Sixpence. You will have final approval over
the quality of the products placed in your shop. By agreeing
to our proposal, you will be guaranteed an adequate variety
and quantity of unique gift crafts to meet the needs of your
customers.

BACKGROUND
    Kathleen Moore and Hazel Smeed are gifted crafters with over
50 years of experience between them. They have sold their
crafts through bazaars, farmers markets, flea markets, and house
parties very successfully for many years. They also have made
items to customer specifications. They take pride in their skill
and their work.

    With the current interest in simpler living styles, the demand
for handcrafted gift items is growing. The natural materials used
in Katy-Did crafts reflect this trend. In addition, Katy-Did
Krafts proudly supports the concern for the environment by using
recycled papers. Samples and pictures are included with this
proposal.

BENEFITS
As a local supplier, we can be responsive to the needs of your
business.
• Our products will be delivered to your location on a regular
  basis at your convenience.
• Your stock will be rotated to maintain the interest of your
  regular customers.
• You will be provided with a variety of items unique to your
  shop.
As a smaller producer, we can accept custom orders and small
order quantities.
• You will be provided with order forms for special requests from
  your customers.
• You can restock with small or large quantities. No order is too
  small. Consider the advantage you will have with seasonal
  items—no more stock overruns.
As experienced crafters, we have gathered ideas and patterns for
a wide variety of products.
• You will have a choice of seasonal items from many countries and
  traditions.
• Your customers will be delighted by nostalgic items from the
  pioneer days, the Roaring Twenties, and art deco periods.
• You will be able to offer modern items that are artistic and
  exciting in both colour and style.

CONCLUSION
Please examine the samples customer comments, and reference letters
attached to this proposal. By accepting our proposal, you will
offer your customers a wider selection of quality items with a
minimum of effort, and that makes good business sense.

A PRACTICE RUN

For the following situation, identify the type of proposal (invited or prospecting) and comment on the format and content you would recommend.

Chad Benton has an idea for improving a work procedure in his department at the Preston Manufacturing Company. His department head suggested that Chad present his idea in a report to the production superintendent. His draft report is almost five pages long, including a full-page diagram.

_____

_____

_____

_____

Renata Burdick, as secretary of her condo association, has sent out a number of letters to landscaping companies. The association believes that some extra work will have to be done this year to restore the grounds, trees, shrubs, and perennial gardens to their former quality. The landscaping companies are being asked to inspect the property, assess the needs, and provide a detailed plan with cost estimates.

_____

_____

_____

_____

· ·

demonstration techniques). If the report is in response to an invitation, that statement should tie in with the invitation (as described in the July 10 announcement). The problem should be stated clearly, in the way described in Chapter 12. Your clear statement of the purpose and problem may be the most important aspect of the proposal. To be willing to award you a contract, your reader must be confident that you have a clear understanding of the situation.

If a proposal is submitted without invitation, its beginning has an additional requirement: It must gain attention and overcome the reader's reluctance. One way of doing this is to begin by emphasizing the benefits for the reader as you briefly summarize the highlights of the proposal. This technique is illustrated by the beginning of an unsolicited proposal that a consultant sent to restaurants:

A review of your operations using our proven methods will give you the strategies to (1) reduce your food costs, (2) strengthen your menu offerings, (3) increase efficiency in your kitchen, (4) improve customer service and satisfaction, and (5) increase your profits. We can offer you these benefits with no disruption to your customers or staff. We will analyze guest cheques and invoices and observe your kitchen and serving staff. You are guaranteed a positive result from our study.

2. Background. A review of background information sometimes promotes an understanding of the problem. Thus, a company's proposal of a merger with another company might review industry developments that make the merger desirable.

· 2. Background;

3. Need. Closely related to the background information is the necessity for what is being proposed. The need may be established through the background information or

· 3. Need;

presented separately. This description of the need is an important step in the persuasive process because the reader must understand the reasons for the proposal to give it serious consideration. In the restaurant situation, a brief discussion of rising costs, trends in food tastes, and new competition would set the stage for review and improvement in even a successful restaurant.

• 4. Overview;

4. Overview.   The heart of the introduction is the description of what the writer proposes to cover in the report and in what order. The overview should present the report's plan in a clear and orderly manner. This description should be complete and concise to give the reader the overall picture. While always honest, the writer can already begin to emphasize the positive benefits of the proposal.

• 5. Proposal;

5. Proposal.   It is now time to explain the proposal both in general and in detail. After laying out the plan in overview, you now give the details of how it will work. Try to anticipate and answer the readers' questions by giving all the particulars. By *particulars* we mean the specific details of costs, time schedules, performance standards, personnel requirements, equipment and supplies, performance evaluations, guarantees, and so on.

• 6. Reliability;

6. Reliability.   The proposing organization must sometimes establish its credibility and reliability. Information on the qualifications of personnel, success in similar cases, the adequacy of equipment and facilities, operating procedures, and financial status are outlined to show the organization's ability to carry out what it proposes.

• 7. Benefits; and

7. Benefits.   The proposal report must describe the positive results the client would realize. The greater the need to persuade, the more you should stress reader benefits. Proposals are persuasive, but unlike sales presentations, they are more objective and less flamboyant in style. The proposal for a consulting service to restaurants could stress such benefits as improved work efficiency, increased customer satisfaction, savings in food costs, and increased profits.

• 8. Concluding comments.

8. Concluding Comments.   The proposal should end with words directed to the next step—acting on the proposal. One possibility is to invite the prospective client to contact previous clients for references. Another is to offer a personal interview to explain the proposal more fully. Yet another is to urge action on the proposal to meet a deadline such as the potential increase in business over an upcoming holiday.

• Business thrives when proposals are presented well.

   With the increase in entrepreneurship and small business ventures and the growing competition among corporate players, the proposal is an important key to success. The prospecting proposal brings attention to a company and generates business.

A SUMMARY OF LEARNING OUTCOMES FROM THIS CHAPTER

The shorter report forms are by far the most common in business. The shorter reports typically begin directly with the conclusions and recommendations first, and they are written in a personal, informal style. Because they often deal with routine matters, they require only brief introductory material.

   Memorandum reports are written for and by people within an organization. They are widely used in business for routine problems and information. Direct-order and informal language are common.

   Letter reports are another popular shorter form. Usually written in the direct order, they are a little more formal than the memo report because they are intended for an external audience.

The familiar short report, made up of a title page and text, usually begins with a summary or conclusion and continues with findings and analyses. It combines some features of a more formal document with the efficiency of a short, narrowly focused one.

Among the special report forms used in business, three deserve mention. (1) The progress report gives an accounting of progress made towards a goal. (2) The short audit report presents the results of an audit in a few prescribed paragraphs. (3) By definition, a proposal is a presentation for consideration. Proposals may be invited or uninvited (prospecting). They vary widely in form, ranging from simple memorandums to long, full-dress reports. They may be formal or informal, as the situation dictates.

The contents of proposals vary with need, but you should consider including these eight topics: (1) purpose, (2) background, (3) need, (4) plan description, (5) particulars, (6) ability to deliver, (7) benefits, and (8) concluding comments.

QUESTIONS FOR DISCUSSION

1. Explain why some routine report problems require little or no introduction.

2. Why is the direct order generally used in shorter reports? When is the indirect order desirable for such reports?

3. Give examples of short report forms that are appropriately written in personal style. When would a more formal style be used in a short report?

4. What types of problems are written up as letter reports? as memorandum reports? Explain the differences.

5. Describe the organization of the conventional short report.

6. Identify possible topics for (a) invited and (b) prospecting proposals that might be received by the administration of your school.

7. "To be successful, a business must be able to prepare excellent, persuasive proposals." Discuss.

CASE 13-1

"Reports to write; reports to read! Who ever thought there would be so many reports?"

"What did you expect in business?"

"I thought we were a lot closer to the paperless office where everything was done on voice mail, or e-mail, or conference telephone calls."

"Those technologies have brought big changes, for sure, but people still are people. We don't listen all that well. We forget things. And it's good to write things down to work out our ideas. Besides, voice mail and e-mail messages still need to be planned and carefully scripted."

"That's not the same thing at all. Putting something on paper is different."

Discussion

Think of the advantages and disadvantages of electronic copies.

What are the differences between e-mail and paper documents? Are they as substantial as the speaker believes?

What legal considerations are raised by electronic communication?

ANSWERS TO PRACTICE RUNS

▶Choosing the Best Report Form

1. An internal document would usually follow a memo format. The direct order would be appropriate since she is not required to make recommendations. She is asked only to observe and report. Since safety matters have legal repercussions, she might be wise to make her report objective and a little more formal.

2. A research report of this size should be handled in the short report format with a title page and text. Because it is an external report from the research organization to the Alto Company, it will be somewhat formal in its use of language. Since it would be scientific in its methodology, the reporting of the results should be objective. Since Alto requested the report and is paying for it, the direct order would be best. They should receive their answers right away.

3. While accuracy is important in this report, it would not be necessary to phrase the information in formal language. A simple memo including a table with the desired information would be enough. The order should be direct so that Mr. Edmund gets the data he needs as soon as possible.

4. Depending on the circumstances, this report could be written as a memo report, a letter report, or a short report with a title page. If the sales manager and the V-P Marketing work together closely, a memo report would be fine. The language could be reasonably informal, but not so casual that Mr. Chao would be embarrassed if the V-P Marketing handed it on to the President.

If the Brownlee company is very large with many sales managers under a national V-P, a letter report would be more appropriate. The style would be more formal than for the memo report.

A short report is possible if Mr. Chao knows that the reports from all the districts will be combined to make one major report. There would have to be careful consideration before this format was chosen.

The direct order would be appropriate, because this report has been requested and the audience is interested and receptive.

▶E-Mail Documents

The first memo is much too vague. Nothing stands out to remind the reader of the exact situation. What was the problem? The subject line is likely to be ignored as something that means little to the reader (and, therefore, must be intended for someone else). The very short lines make the memo seem long and choppy.

The clarification memo is not a clarification at all. Many irrelevant facts are included. People will soon learn to ignore mail from this sender. The use of URGENT in the subject line is also inconsiderate. Someone will remind the sender about the story of the children who called "Wolf!" so often that people learned to ignore these cries for help. The lines are now the full width of the screen. This length may create inconvenience for the reader.

. . . .

▶Proposals

Chad Benton and the Preston Manufacturing Company. This proposal is a prospecting proposal. His department head suggested that Chad write it, but the production superintendent to whom it is addressed did not invite it. A memo report format would be fine. He should take care with the level of language he chooses, because his proposal may be passed along to other important people in the company. He will also be able to give greater credibility to his proposal if he expresses his ideas well.

Renata Burdick and the landscaping of her condo development. These proposals would be invited. The landscape companies would submit them to Renata as requested. The content should cover all of the items she mentions—grounds, trees, shrubs, and gardens. It would include an assessment of the current state, a plan of action to restore the property, and a detailed estimate. A letter format would be suitable, with some appended photos and letters to show the company's earlier work.

REPORT PROBLEMS

Memorandum and Letter Reports

1. Determining the Effects of Giving Product Samples. As advertizing manager of Leo's Pizzas, Inc., you conducted the following experiment to determine the effectiveness of giving free samples to shoppers in grocery stores.

First, you selected two comparable cities, Ableton (67,000 population) and Bentley (71,000 population). As well as you could determine, the two cities were about as alike as two cities could be, even in sales of Leo's pizzas. In each city you selected five comparable stores that sold your product. You used the stores in Ableton as test stores and the stores in Bentley as control stores. You hired five servers, selected for their outgoing personalities, to give free samples to shoppers in the Ableton test stores for a two-week period. During this period, Ableton and Bentley shoppers were exposed to the company's normal national advertising (mainly by television and magazine). Thus, the give-away program was the only apparent difference in the sales efforts of Leo's Pizzas in the two cities.

In order to determine what influence the sample-giving program had on sales, you kept records of sales in the five stores in each city. Since all other factors were relatively similar, you reasoned that any differences in sales could be attributed to the give-away. You also reasoned that the effects might be short-lived; so you checked the sales records over time to see whether there were any long-term effects. Now, you have tabulated your results in Table 1.

It is now your task to analyze these results and to report your analysis to Tammy DuBois, vice president for marketing.

TABLE 1 (Problem 1)   Pizza Sales in Ableton and Bentley

Time Periods	Pizzas Sold Ableton	Pizzas Sold Bentley
Two-week period before give-aways	2,320	2,345
Two-week period of give-aways	3,873	2,260
Two-week period after give-aways	3,014	2,326
Two-week period month later	2,823	2,395
Two-week period half-year later	2,566	2,288

2. Selecting the Best Outlet for Gentry Suits. Assume the role of assistant sales manager for Gentry, Ltd. Your assignment is to investigate two stores and recommend to Mr. Gentry the one you think should be awarded the Gentry dealership. Both stores have indicated an interest in handling Gentry's quality products, but the Gentry dealership policy permits only one retail outlet in a city the size of Markston (population 113,000).

For the past two days, you carefully inspected the stores. As you conducted your investigation, you kept foremost in mind that Gentry's enviable sales record and its reputation among quality-conscious gentlemen have been attributed to careful selection of retail outlets. Gentry's customers are men of means, usually coming from the upper-middle-income and high-income groups. So Gentry has traditionally selected retail outlets catering to these groups. You are also seeking a retail outlet that gives the kind of service for which Gentry dealers are noted. In addition, you will consider a number of other factors—store location, growth potential, physical plant, and so on. Now you are ready to begin your analysis of the facts. In the garbled form in which you noted them, they look like this:

BARRINGTON'S

An exclusive store for men, catering to style-conscious, successful business executives and professionals. Stocks three other brands of suits—Bates (high quality), Corrigan (middle to high quality), and the popular Rover (middle quality). Would drop Bates if given exclusive Gentry dealership. Store is owned by Scott A. Barrington, son of the founder. He is quiet, courteous. Likes to wait on customers personally. Two other salespeople, both in early 30s. Little or no sales pressure is used—very leisurely atmosphere. Annual sales approximately $900,000. Advertizes weekly—usually about half page in local daily. No TV or radio advertizing. Ads stress quality and style. Store interior is conservative and elegant. Sales floor is small—about 10 metres by 25 metres. It is neat but appears a little crowded with merchandise. Store opened about 42 years ago—moved to current location in Southside Mall 21 years ago. Although it is the oldest shopping centre in town, it has been renovated to keep up with the times. It continues to prosper despite the opening of Maple Leaf Mall about a year ago. Continued success appears to be result of its nearness to downtown and to McMurray Heights, probably city's most prestigious residential area.

THE CLOTHES HORSE

A new store (less than a year old) in a prime location of the Maple Leaf Mall. Floor space about 15 metres by 30 metres. Store is modern, bright, and attractive. Merchandise is neatly arranged, giving spacious appearance. Store owned by Hardy A. Soilleau, a former sales representative for a clothing manufacturer, now in retail selling for the first time. Soilleau is personable, outgoing, excellent conversationalist. Three other salespeople, all young (in 20s). Selling is somewhat aggressive—some pressure. But service is also stressed. Merchandise ranges from high quality to upper low quality—conservative to mod. Store now carries three brands of men's suits: T.C. Smith (high quality), Waymond-Ward (middle quality), and Dandy (upper low to middle quality). This year's sales about $1.1 million (projected). Customers are all ages—with fairly wide range of incomes (high to lower middle). Heavy advertizing—about a quarter page three times a week in local daily plus heavy use of spot ads on local radio. Ads stress style and low price.

3. Correcting the Parking Problem at Neo Instruments.   At today's staff meeting at Neo Instruments, Inc., discussion centred on the parking situation at the local plant. A spokesman for the middle managers pointed out, "The present system discriminates against the middle managers and the highly skilled professionals. The top five administrators have their reserved parking space, which we all consider appropriate. But 17 middle-level managers, 9 highly skilled professionals, 228 production workers, and 15 maintenance workers must compete for parking space on a first-come, first-served basis. Because the maintenance and production workers begin work earlier than the managers and the professionals, they get the choice locations."

After lengthy discussion, the plant manager, Gloria Mather, agreed to "look into the matter." Following the staff meeting, she assigned the task of "looking into the matter" to you, her administrative assistant. And she asked that you propose a specific plan for solving the problem if you found that one existed.

As you begin the investigation, you review the pertinent information concerning plant parking. One of the plant's two parking lots is adjacent to the main entrance. This lot has 56 spaces, of which 5 are reserved for the top administrators and 5 are reserved for handicapped workers. The second lot, with spaces for 266 automobiles, is about 250 metres from the plant. About 190 automobiles are parked in the two lots on a typical day.

Your investigation also finds that the present arrangement does indeed inconvenience the middle managers and the professionals. The maintenance workers begin work at 5 A.M., and the production workers begin at 8 A.M. Although the managers and professionals have no specific work hours, most of them arrive around 8:30 or 9 (and leave quite late). Moreover, they frequently have cause to leave the plant for short periods during the day for appointments, meetings, etc.

Having assembled this key information, you work out a parking plan appropriate for the situation. You will present your plan, along with a review of the pertinent facts, to Ms. Mather in a memorandum report.

4. Comparing Customer Traffic at Two Fast-Food Restaurants.
For the past 11 years Burger Supreme and Burger DeLite have been competing vigorously in the city of Bannerville. Every time one of these fast-food restaurants does something, the other follows suit. When Burger Supreme began offering a breakfast menu, Burger DeLite followed. When Burger DeLite conducted a contest, Burger Supreme followed. When Burger Supreme opened a drive-through window, Burger DeLite followed. And so it has been over the years.

As a management trainee for Burger Supreme, you have become a part of this competition. Penny Kahler, manager of the Burger Supreme restaurant and your training supervisor, assigned you the job of getting sales comparison data for the two restaurants. "I know you can't get dollar information," she said, "but you can get traffic counts. Get traffic counts for key hours of the day—for inside and drive-through customers. Then let me know how we're doing. Point out anything significant you see in the results."

You began the assignment by selecting six periods that cut across the business day. Then you planned your observation procedure. Because day of the week, weather, and such could affect sales, you decided to observe each restaurant at alternating periods on two successive days. On Wednesday, you observed Burger Supreme the first period, Burger DeLite the second period, Burger Supreme the third period, and so on. On Thursday, you observed Burger DeLite the first period, Burger Supreme the second period, Burger DeLite the third period, and so on. You stationed yourself in the parking lot outside each restaurant so that you could see all entrances and the drive-through lane. You recorded the number of people who entered the restaurants and the number of automobiles that went through the drive-through lane. Table 2 summarizes your observations:

TABLE 2 (Problem 4)   A Comparison of Customer Traffic

Time	Burger Supreme		Burger DeLite	
	Walk-In	Drive Through	Walk-In	Drive Through
7–8 AM	73	13	114	31
9–10 AM	23	5	39	11
12–1 PM	255	32	207	30
3–4 PM	14	3	13	7
7–8 PM	210	41	337	66
9–10 PM	97	11	187	39

Now you will present your findings to Ms. Kahler in a memorandum report. You'll include the table, but you'll also present your main findings in words. And of course you'll "Point out anything significant." (You may supply additional details about your procedures or findings as long as they are consistent with the above information.)

5. Reporting an Accident Resulting from Employee Horseplay.
As safety officer for the Harbour City plant, you have the task of writing a report on any accident whose cost exceeds $100. Yesterday such an accident occurred in Department 212. It seems that the horseplay of two employees near the time clock led to the breakage of a water cooler (damage $130) and cuts on the arm of Todd Flannigan (one of the employees involved). Flannigan was taken to the emergency room of St. Joseph's Hospital where he was given emergency treatment and released. Eleven stitches were required. Follow-up treatment will require a half-day off work. You obtained a copy of the doctor's report, which you will submit with your report. Now you go to Department 212 and interview the participants and witnesses. Following are the highlights of your interviews.

Eddie Masterson: Right after quitting time, Todd and I were running down the hall toward the time clock. I was ahead of Todd. He tried to pass me, but there wasn't room. He ran into the water cooler. The cooler broke as he fell into it. The broken glass cut his left forearm pretty bad. Abe Clements and Joe DuBois took him to the hospital.

Todd Flannigan: Eddie and I were trying to see who could check out first. We do it almost every day—kind of a game we play. I was about to pass him when he gave me a hard shove with his hip and knocked me into the cooler. It cut me pretty bad. Abe and Joe took me to emergency. I was sewed up and released in a couple of hours.

Abe Clements: I was cleaning up my work area, getting ready to check out. Then I heard all this noise—like people running and hollering. I looked up and saw Todd and Eddie horsing around on the way to the clock. Seems like they were trying to hold each other back. Eddie was a little ahead, and Todd grabbed him to slow him down. They scuffled, and Todd went right into the cooler. Broke it and got cut. Both of them fell into the cooler, but only Todd was hurt. Joe and I took Todd to the hospital.

Alice Shumate: Those two have acted like kids for months, each trying to clock out before the other. They're always scuffling and roughhousing. This time they got a little too rough. Eddie was in front trying to keep Todd from passing. Todd grabbed Eddie, and they scuffled around—right into the cooler. Both were at fault, but only Todd got hurt.

With the evidence you have collected, you must now write your report on the accident. Your report will set out clearly what happened, and it may include a recommended action, if the evidence supports it. As you do with all accident reports, you will write this one in memorandum form and you will direct it to the plant manager, Evan Kansky.

6. Presenting the Effects of Promotion of One Brand on Sales of Others in the Same Category.

Take over as a management trainee in the west end store of Super Saver Groceries. Soon after you began your training under the supervision of Evelyn A. Benedict, the store manager, she gave you your first challenging assignment. As Ms. Benedict explained it to you, "At the grocery retailers' convention last month, I heard something very interesting. In one of the presentations, a store manager said that promoting one of the brands in a category caused the sales of all the brands in that category to increase. He said that he had tested this, but most of the audience doubted him. But I've been thinking that he may have something there. Testing it would be a good training project for you."

You saw the assignment as a chance to show Ms. Benedict and Super Saver's management that you were a capable person and a promising future administrator. You began to search for a product category to use for the test. After considering a number of possibilities, you concluded that spaghetti would be ideal. The store carried six brands, and sales of those brands could be easily counted.

For two weeks you kept records of spaghetti sales to get a measure of normal activity. Then, in another two weeks, you promoted one brand, Milan, with point-of-sale advertizing featuring a reduction from $0.90 to $0.75, in the price of the 500-gram package. For the next two weeks, you stopped the promotion, selling all spaghetti brands at regular prices. Then you introduced another two-week promotion of Milan spaghetti, this one with point-of-sale advertizing featuring the 500-gram package at $0.60. After that, you returned again to normal selling of spaghetti, continuing to keep records for two more weeks. Now you are ready to analyze and report your findings. They are in summary form in Table 3.

You will write your report to Ms. Benedict in memorandum form. Because you suspect that she will forward a copy to Mr. Thomas A. Keane, Super Saver's director of training, you want to do a very good job. You may decide to include the summary table, but your words will carry the highlights of the report and any analyses and conclusions that the data support.

7. Writing an Evaluation Report on Wilma Rundell.

As sales manager of District III, Biz-Serv Office Supply, Inc., you are now writing your annual evaluation reports on your subordinates. Biz-Serv's evaluation reports are frank and honest. They praise when praise is deserved, and they criticize when criticism is in order. Their goal is to be constructive. Of course, the originals are sent to the persons rated.

At the moment you are working on the report for Ms. Wilma Rundell, your newest salesperson. Your garbled notes on her are as follows:

Hard worker. Excellent personality for selling—outgoing, good conversationalist, pleasant mannerisms, sharp wit. Have received three reports (investigated and confirmed) that she is too aggressive—more concerned with sales than service. Sales volume for year was $379,144, which is above the $350,000 quota set for her. Obtained 9 new accounts; lost 13 accounts (mainly small ones). Appears to go after big-ticket items and big orders. Her calls on smaller accounts are less regular than her calls on larger accounts. Manner of dress could be improved—not in line with conservative image company seeks to present. [You may add additional specific details to support the points given above.]

Now using the company's standard memorandum form, you will organize this information into an orderly and meaningful report. Identify the subject as "Annual Evaluation Report," and note in the report that you will discuss Ms. Rundell's evaluation with her within the next few days.

TABLE 3 (Problem 6)   Effects of Sale Prices on Other Brands

Week	Milan Price	Milan Units Sold	All Brands Total Units Sold
1	$0.90	33	211
2	0.90	37	232
3	0.75	59	288
4	0.75	68	299
5	0.90	44	224
6	0.90	47	219
7	0.60	311	377
8	0.60	186	301
9	0.90	31	190
10	0.90	38	209

8. Recommending a District Sales Manager for Moore Pharmaceutical, Inc.   As sales manager for the Central Region of Moore Pharmaceutical, Inc., you must recommend your best salesperson for the vacant position of district sales manager for the Metro City area. After carefully screening the records of your seven candidates, you determine the top three. Now you have to evaluate them, rank them for the job, and pass on your recommendation to M. Maurice Cuenod, Moore's marketing vice president. You know the three top candidates fairly well. They are all personable, ambitious people. Judging from your impressions, they would all do an excellent job. Your recommendation will be based on the factual information you have assembled from their personnel records (Table 4). You will write up your analysis and recommendation in the standard memorandum form used for all internal Moore reports. And you will use the conclusion-first approach that you know M. Cuenod prefers.

9. Reporting on the Extent of Highway Litter.   As an employee in the Environmental Protection Commission of the province of your choice, you have been assigned the task of gathering information on the extent and nature of litter along the highways. The Commission plans to use this information in an anti-littering campaign. The information should also help the commission identify problem areas to work on.

To obtain the desired information, in late June you carefully collected all the litter that the eye could see from a randomly selected section of a major highway. At the end of July, you repeated the process. The first pickup, of course, contained litter accumulated over the winter or longer. The second pickup consisted of litter accumulated over a one-month period of peak vacation travel. You have assembled your findings in a simple table (Table 5).

You have been assigned to present your data to the commission in report form. Because the report is relatively simple and an in-house project, you will use the memorandum report form.

TABLE 4 (Problem 8)   Summary of Information on Applicants for District Sales Manager Position

	Felix Duehy	Shannon Kyle	Fred Dabny
Age	33	28	35
Sales experience	3 1/2 years, Glad Publishing Company; 4 years, Moore Pharmaceuticals	6 years, Moore Pharmaceuticals	4 years, Central Insurance; 5 years, Lund Pharmaceutical; 4 years, Moore Pharmaceuticals
Education	High school diploma; Great Lakes Community College, Diploma in general business	B.Comm., Georgian University, major in marketing	B.Sc., University of Ontario, major in psychology
Record with Moore Pharmaceuticals (percent of sales quota)	1st yr, no quota 2nd year, 117 3rd year, 106 4th year, 121	1st yr, no quota 2nd year, 105 3rd year, 98 4th year, 121 5th year, 107 6th year, 137	1st yr, no quota 2nd year, 137 3rd year, 141 4th year, 140
Score on Management Potential Test (60 = pass, 70 = above avg., 80 = outstanding)	81	88	77

TABLE 5 (Problem 9)   Content of Litter on Highway

	First Pickup		Second Pickup	
	Items per Kilometre	Percent of Total	Items per Kilometre	Percent of Total
Beer cans	710	21.59	153	11.72
Soft-drink cans	143	4.35	40	3.06
Food cans	33	1.00	8	0.61
Other cans	43	1.31	11	0.84
Total cans	929	28.25	212	16.23
Returnable beer bottles	103	3.13	35	2.68
Returnable soft-drink bottles	79	2.40	28	2.14
Other bottles	45	1.37	13	1.00
Total bottles	227	6.90	76	5.82
Total paper items	1605	48.81	776	59.42
Total Styrofoam™ items	123	3.74	56	4.29
Total plastic items	155	4.71	75	5.74
Total miscellaneous	240	7.29	107	8.19
Total special interest	9	0.27	4	0.31

Common Short Reports

10. Determining Changes in Eating-Out Practices for a Restaurant Association.   You
have completed a survey for the Lakehead Restaurant Association to determine changes
in the eating-out practices of people in the area. Five years ago you conducted a similar
study for the association. A comparison with your current findings will measure the
changes that have taken place over that time.

In your surveys you used a simple questionnaire to gather data from which you made calculations about the way respondents spent their food dollars. You recorded this information by age of the household head, by household income, and by household size. These classifications tell restaurant owners about their customers. The comparison of the current findings with the findings made five years ago should point clearly to any changes in the customer base.

In both surveys you mailed the questionnaires to a random sample of 3,000 families in the area. You got back 1,127 questionnaires the first time and 1,007 this time. You feel that these returns were reasonably good. You have tabulated the returns and created Table 6 to make the comparison with the first survey. At first glance you can see that some interesting changes have occurred, but you will need to study them carefully to determine what has happened and what this means to the area restaurant owners.

After studying the data, write a report to present your findings to the association.

TABLE 6 (Problem 10)   Weekly Household Expenditures Eating Out

Household Characteristics	Five Years Ago		This Year	
	Amount	Proportion of Total	Amount	Proportion of Total
Age of household head[†]				
Under 25	$16.25	42.7%	$23.01	48.0%
25–34	24.14	35.6	31.50	38.6
35–44	29.00	32.7	37.89	35.2
45–54	27.44	33.1	38.55	34.3
55–64	19.11	29.0	30.46	34.0
65 and older	11.01	23.9	15.55	26.9
Household income				
Under $10,000	10.96	24.2	15.89	30.7
$10,000–19,999	18.11	31.3	26.25	36.9
$20,000–29,999	22.37	31.6	29.59	37.1
$30,000–39,999	32.27	33.0	34.75	32.8
$40,000–49,999	40.01	37.9	42.84	36.8
Over $50,000	49.79	41.7	50.94	40.3
Household size				
One	15.06	44.5	21.21	50.5
Two	21.19	35.2	30.30	37.8
Three	23.14	30.7	29.29	31.6
Four	26.74	29.6	40.96	33.3
Five	28.31	26.7	36.87	27.6
Six and over	25.88	20.4	31.68	22.5
All Households	21.25	32.5	29.40	35.9

[†]Determined by respondent.

11. Which Commercial Is Best for Glass Kleen?

The research department of the T. Timothy Kinney Advertizing Agency has completed an experiment with two 60-second TV commercials for Glass Kleen, a liquid window cleaner. This Canadian-made product is new to the U.S. market. Being unable to decide between two approaches for launching this product, the agency decided to try out each commercial in a different test city. Columbus, Ohio, and Indianapolis, Indiana, were selected for the test. After the commercials were run, a representative sample of viewers were interviewed by telephone in an attempt to determine the effectiveness of the ads.

One of the commercials (Commercial A) utilizes popular comic-strip characters. It depicts an animated mouse gleefully cleaning a large pane of glass with an "old-fashioned" glass cleaner. Then he runs into the next room, attracts the attention of a cat, his perpetual adversary, and gets the cat to chase him. His plan to get the cat to run into the glass pane fails when the cat sees dirt on it. The cat then lectures the mouse of the virtues of Glass Kleen and walks away. Walking out of the room, however, he runs into a glass door and knocks himself out. The commercial ends with the mouse standing by the door, holding Glass Kleen, and winking at the TV viewers.

In the second commercial (Commercial B), a conventional family scene shows a husband and wife looking out of the "largest picture window in town." Their view is limited, however, by dirty streaks on the window. They try everything—ammonia, water, other products—but nothing does the job until they try Glass Kleen. At the end of the commercial, they are watching a parade as it passes by their clean window.

The results of the test are now in (see results in Tables 7 and 8), and it's your job to study them and to report your analysis and conclusions to the agency. Your conclusions will be based on which ad is likely to sell more Glass Kleen. Of course, you will present your work in good report form.

12. Writing a Status Report on Adult Education.   Place yourself in the position of research director of the Council for Adult Education, an organization dedicated to elevating the educational level of people past the usual age for formal schooling. The council's membership includes most of the leading U.S. and Canadian organizations and practitioners in the field of adult education. Among these organizations are schools that are primarily engaged in providing formal education but have special adult programs—high schools, community colleges, universities, and vocational schools. Here adult education is provided in somewhat traditional school settings. Also included in the council's membership are organizations that provide adult education in non-school settings—for example, business training departments, professional and labour associations, and government agencies.

At the last monthly meeting of the council's board of directors, you were instructed to gather information and report on four questions concerning the membership's activities

---

TABLE 7 (Problem 11)   Commercial A

	Percent
Remembered commercial 24 hours after viewing	88.3
Product story recall	72.3
Video (recall of specific incidents)	
Mouse cleaning window with old-fashioned cleaner	68.5
Cat lecturing to mouse about Glass Kleen	64.3
Mouse gleefully viewing scene	60.2
Cat running into glass door	71.3
Mouse holding can of Glass Kleen	36.4
Audio (recall of specific appeals)	
Simple/easy to use	8.3
Not messy	2.3
Gets glass clean, cleaner, cleanest	11.7
Cleans well, is best cleaner	3.2
Glass stays clean, clear longer	6.3
Leaves no film, leaves glass clear	6.1
Glass seems to disappear	16.1

TABLE 8 (Problem 11)   Commercial B

	Percent
Remembered commercial 24 hours after viewing	68.4
Product story recall	56.4
Video (recall of specific incidents)	
Demonstration: Saw window being cleaned by couple	45.1
Window cleaned with Glass Kleen	21.1
Window cleaned with "old-fashioned" cleaners	18.8
Saw couple in living room—couldn't see out of dirty windows	21.8
Saw outdoor scene, parade, through Glass Kleen windows	12.0
Different sizes of Glass Kleen	5.3
Spray pump	3.8
Audio (recall of specific appeals)	
Simple/easy to use	36.8
Not messy	7.5
Gets glass clean, cleaner, cleanest	28.6
Cleans well, is best cleaner	11.3
Glass stays clean, clear longer	10.5
Leaves no film, leaves glass clear	9.8
Glass seems to disappear	5.3

TABLE 9 (Problem 12)   Adult Education

Type of Operation	Courses Offered	Percent	Percent Job Related
School setting	14,107	53.9	58.5
High school	1,785	6.8	23.2
1-year college	4,921	18.8	53.2
4-year college	5,012	19.2	67.3
Vocational / technical school	2,389	9.1	77.0
Non-school setting	12,059	46.1	62.4
Consultants	1,146	4.4	32.9
Business training departments	3,583	13.7	89.9
Professional / labour groups	1,301	5.0	95.0
Government agencies	2,220	8.5	16.2
Other	1,755	6.7	53.5
TOTAL	26,166	100.0	60.3

last year: (1) what types of organizations provided instruction to adults, (2) how much of that instruction was job related, (3) what subject matter was offered, and (4) how many males and females were enrolled.

Fortunately, council members submit a somewhat detailed annual report on their activities, so you had little difficulty in gathering and tabulating the facts you needed (Tables 9 and 10). Now you must write the report that will present your data in clear and meaningful fashion. Direct the report to the board, as it will be used primarily in the board's planning activities.

TABLE 10 (Problem 12) Adult Education

Type of Course	Total Courses		Taken by Men		Taken by Women	
	Number	Percent	Number	Percent	Number	Percent
Agriculture	314	1.2	228	2.0	86	0.6
Arts	1,661	6.3	403	3.6	1,258	8.5
Business	5,994	22.9	2,920	25.8	3,076	20.7
Education	2,047	7.8	628	5.4	1,420	9.6
Engineering	2,558	9.8	2,080	18.4	478	3.2
Health care	2,794	10.7	865	7.6	1,930	13.0
Health education	805	3.1	253	2.2	553	3.7
Home economics	872	3.3	59	0.5	813	5.5
Language and literature	1,529	5.8	569	5.0	960	6.5
Life sciences	844	3.2	416	3.7	428	2.9
Personal services	499	1.9	207	1.8	292	2.0
Philosophy and religion	1,824	7.0	723	6.4	1,101	7.4
Physical education	1,664	6.4	435	3.8	1,229	8.3
Social sciences	1,350	5.2	750	6.6	599	4.0
Interdisciplinary studies	236	0.9	92	0.8	144	1.0
Other	1,175	4.5	699	6.2	476	3.2
TOTAL	26,166	100.0	11,327	100.0	14,839	100.0

Note: Details may not add to totals because of rounding.

13. Comparing Laurier Heights' Crime Statistics with Those of Its Neighbours.

Play the role of a research associate employed by J. Andrew Research, Inc. About a week ago, you were called to the office of Pat Yamamoto, Laurier Heights City Manager, to help with a problem that the city faces. It seems that a few days earlier the Laurier Heights City Council held a meeting marked by stormy citizen protest. The citizens were outraged by the recent increase in criminal activity in the city. Demands were expressed for an investigation, for sweeping changes in police procedures, for the resignations of police administrators, and so on. In the end, however, the council concluded that before taking any action, it needed more information. Thus J. Andrew Research was hired to get this information, and you were assigned the task.

As you discussed the matter with Ms. Yamamoto, you learned that some members of the city council thought that the Laurier Heights police had been maligned. "Some of them feel that what is going on here is a regional problem and not exclusively our problem," she told you. "We want you to investigate the question for us. Get crime statistics for the other major cities in the region, and compare those statistics with ours. If what is happening here is happening elsewhere, then instead of being harsh on our police, maybe we should strengthen regional co-operation. But if the sharp crime increase is exclusively ours, we need to take action locally."

With these words in mind, you began your investigation. You took the Laurier Heights' crime statistics that Ms. Yamamoto gave you, and you gathered comparable statistics for Worthington, Alden, Lewiston, and West Hill, the four other major centres in the region. These statistics covered each of the seven conventional crime categories (homicide, rape, robbery, aggravated assault, burglary, theft, and auto theft) for last year and the year before. You made some quick computations to determine the percentage changes from one year to the next. You know that these comparisons do not tell the whole story, but they do pinpoint areas of rapid change.

Now your findings are neatly arranged in a general table (Table 11). Because the centres are not equal in size, reporting the crimes on a per-1,000-population basis might

TABLE 11 (Problem 13)   Crime in Laurier Heights and Neighbouring Centres

City (Population) and Crime Category	Last Year	Year Before	Change (%)
Laurier Heights (108,000)			
Homicide	6	5	+20
Rape	18	17	+6
Robbery	55	14	+292
Aggravated assault	59	85	−30
Burglary	1,372	1,183	+16
Theft	4,140	3,974	+4
Auto theft	165	130	+30
TOTAL	5,815	5,408	+8
Worthington (424,000)			
Homicide	32	28	+14
Rape	123	101	+22
Robbery	373	120	+210
Aggravated assault	238	121	+97
Burglary	6,257	5,873	+6
Theft	14,334	10,877	+32
Auto theft	554	456	+21
TOTAL	21,911	17,576	+25
Alden (229,850)			
Homicide	22	18	+22
Rape	120	105	+14
Robbery	518	299	+73
Aggravated assault	190	169	+12
Burglary	2,275	1,502	+51
Theft	9,763	10,280	−5
Auto theft	247	174	+42
TOTAL	13,135	12,547	+5
Lewiston (174,550)			
Homicide	15	13	+15
Rape	71	94	−24
Robbery	230	142	+43
Aggravated assault	34	37	−8
Burglary	1,286	934	+38
Theft	3,991	4,344	−8
Auto theft	151	113	+33
TOTAL	5,751	5,677	+2
West Hill (143,600)			
Homicide	18	11	+63
Rape	75	82	−9
Robbery	269	203	+32
Aggravated assault	324	347	−12
Burglary	2,105	2,047	+3
Theft	5,136	4,783	+7
Auto theft	235	196	+20
TOTAL	8,162	7,659	+7

be logical, but there may be other approaches. You will give the matter your best thinking, remembering that your goal is to tell the Laurier Heights City Council how Laurier Heights' crime problem compares with that of other cities in the region.

This is a professional report, so you will make appropriate use of graphic aids to emphasize the report highlights, and you will include an executive summary so that the busy reader can get the major facts quickly. Address the report to the Laurier Heights City Council.

14. Presenting Physicians' Views on Advertizing by Physicians.

As a student researcher employed by the Association of Physicians in Canada (APC), you have been assigned to prepare a report for its board of directors based on a study to determine the membership's views on advertizing by physicians.

Historically, physicians have viewed the advertizing of their services as unprofessional and have generally taken a stand against such advertizing. The Association has supported this view and has endorsed only what it classifies as public announcements and educational advertizing by its members. Recently, however, some APC members have stretched the limits of these guidelines, and others have questioned their logic. Thus, the board wants to know what the entire APC membership thinks about advertizing by physicians and has assigned you the task of getting this information.

After receiving the board's letter of authorization, you met with Patrick McCartney, chair of the APC board to get a clearer picture of what you must do. As Dr. McCartney explained it, "We have all this data. We want to know what it means. What do the members think about advertizing by physicians? Can we find any trends in their thinking? Are there any differences between older and younger doctors? Or between specialists and family doctors? If they want to advertize, what would they promote? How much use do they think physicians would make of advertizing if advertizing were permitted? What would be the effects on the profession? And there is also the matter of ethics."

Following your meeting with Dr. McCartney, you received 500 usable returns, 100 for each of the experience categories. In tabulating the answers (Tables 12 and 13), you concluded that age (measured by years of experience) was significant only for the questions concerning ethics and whether one would advertize. For the other questions, you felt that only the overall totals were meaningful.

Now you are ready to begin the review and analysis that will lead to the final report. It will present not only the information but also what that information means to the APC and its members. You will address the report to the Board of Directors, Patrick A. McCartney, Chair. Although the report probably won't be very long, the situation is somewhat formal and the report should reflect that.

15. Reporting on Hunting Interests of North American Males.

For this assignment you are employed by Martin-Meadows, publisher of a variety of popular magazines. You are working on a new magazine called *Hunters' Companion*.

Martin-Meadows needs to know the characteristics of its potential readers. Ms Bobbie Raskin, vice president for marketing, wants to know where hunters live, how old they are, how much they earn, and what kinds of work they do. This information will help focus marketing on those most likely to buy *Hunters' Companion*.

With the help of Susan Kettering-Brown and Don Lam, you developed and mailed a questionnaire to a random sample of adult males throughout the United States and Canada. (For class purposes, you may supply any additional details of your research methodology that you may need.) Now 1,288 usable returns are in. The respondents comprise 198 frequent hunters (five times or more a year), 270 moderate hunters (one to four times a year), and 811 nonhunters. Your quick initial examination of the tabulated responses (Table 14) tells you that you have obtained some interesting and useful data.

Now you are ready to begin analyzing these data to focus Martin-Meadows' efforts to promote its new publication. The result will be a profile of potential *Hunters' Companion* readers.

After finishing your analyses, you will write the report that presents your findings and conclusions. Because the information in the report is quantitative, you plan to use tables and charts wherever they seem helpful. Although others will probably read the report, you will address it to Ms. Raskin.

TABLE 12 (Problem14)   Advertizing by Physicians

	Years of Experience				
Issues	Under 5	5–9	10–14	15–19	20 & Over
If allowed, would you advertize?					
Yes	31	28	17	9	5
No	60	65	72	85	91
Undecided	9	7	11	6	4
If others advertized, would you?					
Yes	35	32	21	18	14
No	37	40	49	51	64
Undecided	28	28	30	31	22
Does restricting you from advertizing violate your rights as a citizen?					
Yes	29	25	18	9	4
No	57	62	68	82	89
Undecided	14	13	14	9	7
Do you believe that advertizing by physicians is ethical?					
Yes	37	34	20	9	6
No	38	42	68	82	90
Undecided	25	24	12	9	4

16. Advising a Widow on Investments.   (Requires research.) Place yourself in the office of Financial Planners, Inc., your own consulting company. You are its president.

At the moment, you are working on the problem presented to you by Kathleen Lee Barrington, a recent widow with $320,000 in insurance money. Ms. Barrington wants you to advise her on how to invest her money.

She wants to invest some of the money in trust for her children's education. They are 10 and 12 years old now. She also wants to put something into a retirement plan. The rest she wants to invest to supplement her income from a part-time teaching job.

You'll present the report to Ms. Barrington in an appropriate form. The report will be largely informational, but it will include your expert advice wherever necessary.

17. Recommending an Amount Needed for Scholarships.   (Requires research.) For years the Amos Justin Foundation gave five full scholarships to deserving students in the business program at your school. These scholarships modestly covered all the costs of an education in business (tuition and fees, books, room, board, and miscellaneous items). In recent years, however, as a result of inflation, some holders of Justin scholarships have had to take part-time jobs in order to make ends meet.

As the foundation directors want the scholarships to fully support each of the students selected, they have hired you to recommend a revised scholarship amount to them. More specifically, they want you to report actual cost data to them by major categories of expenditure. The sum of these categories will give the recommended amount. (For class purposes, you will assemble, for an appropriate period, your cost-of-living records and those of a sample of your friends.) You may consider living in residence or off-campus.

TABLE 13 (Problem 14)   Advertizing by Physicians Part II

Issue	Respondents	
If Advertizing Were Allowed, ...	**Number**	**Percent**
... what would you advertize?		
Price	12	10.7
Service	62	55.4
Hours of operation	81	72.3
Location	87	77.7
Professional membership	51	45.5
Other	9	8.0
... would the demand for physicians' services be increased?		
Yes	48	9.6
No	428	85.6
Undecided	24	4.8
... would more price competition result?		
Yes	131	26.2
No	381	66.2
Undecided	38	7.6
... would prices be lower?		
Yes	62	12.4
No	403	80.6
Undecided	35	7.0
... would more quality of service competition occur?		
Yes	32	6.4
No	449	89.8
Undecided	19	3.8
... would the quality of service be higher?		
Yes	13	2.6
No	474	94.8
Undecided	13	2.6
... would it be used much?		
Yes	57	11.4
No	415	83.0
Undecided	28	5.6
... would much price advertizing be used?		
Yes	46	9.2
No	425	85.0
Undecided	29	5.8
... could the public evaluate the relative value of service through advertizing?		
Yes	11	2.2
No	485	91.0
Undecided	4	.8
... would significant false or deceptive advertizing result?		
Yes	342	68.4
No	114	22.8
Undecided	44	8.8

TABLE 14 (Problem 15) Demographics of Male Hunters and Nonhunters

	Frequent Hunters* (Base - 198)	Moderate Hunters† (Base - 279)	Nonhunters (Base - 811)
Age			
Under 25	8%	10%	6%
25–34	34	36	14
35–44	28	29	20
45–54	19	17	23
55 & over	11	8	37
Occupation			
Professional	6	13	17
Managerial	19	21	21
Clerical-sales	23	20	27
Craftsperson	52	46	35
Income‡			
Under $15,000	27	19	18
$15,000–24,999	41	43	35
$25,000–34,999	22	21	31
$35,000 & over	10	17	16
Population density			
Rural	35	37	11
2,500–49,999	29	28	12
50,000–499,999	16	14	26
500,000–1,999,999	11	9	34
2 million & over	9	12	17
Geographic division			
United States			
New England, Mid-Atlantic	16	18	28
South Atlantic	20	22	12
Northwest Central	19	17	25
East South Central	9	10	5
West South Central	9	9	4
Mountain	6	6	3
Pacific	9	7	14
Canada			
Eastern provinces	3	3	2
Central provinces	4	4	4
Western provinces	3	3	2
Territories	2	1	1

*Frequent hunters, five or more times per year.

†Moderate hunters, one to four times per year.

‡Adjusted for difference in value of U.S. and Canadian currency.

Use your own tuition, fees, and book costs. An analysis of the cost data you report should enable you to recommend a revised amount for Justin scholarships. Remember that the foundation wants the scholarships to cover all the holders' costs but that it expects a somewhat modest standard of living.

Address the report to Cindy O. Gerrard, executive director of the Amos Justin Foundation.

18. Selecting a Business Publication as a Gift.   (Requires research.) Play the role of special assistant to the president of Malcolm G. Primer Industries. Mr. Primer wants to give 117 Primer administrators a subscription to a business publication that will help keep them up-to-date with current trends and issues. Your task is to select two or three of the best possibilities from business publications such as *Business Quarterly (University of Western Ontario), Canadian Business, The Wall Street Journal,* and the *Harvard Business Review.* Then rank them for him on the basis of the factors that appear important in this case.

Present the report in a form appropriate for the situation.

19. Reporting on the Condition of a City Park.   (Requires research.) Assume that as an assistant to the director of your city's Parks and Recreation Department, you have been assigned the task of inspecting one of the city's parks (your instructor will select it), reporting on its condition, and making recommendations for correcting any problems you find.

Your inspection will cover whatever can be observed by visual inspection: cleanliness, condition of equipment and facilities, extent of use, condition of landscaping upkeep of grounds, and such. You will present the report orally to the Parks Board (made up of city council members). But you will also write it for the record in formal report form. Address the report to the Parks Board, Mimi Knauth, Chairperson. Ms. Knauth is also the director of the Parks and Recreation Department, which makes her your boss.

Proposals

20.   As a member of SIIR (Students for Improving International Relations), you have been assigned to chair a committee that will develop a scholarship at your school for a student from _____ [a foreign country of your or your instructor's choice].

Today, at SIIR's monthly meeting, you discussed your committee's objective with the guest speaker, Mr. Roger Yousef, a vice president of Dearman Import/Export Company. He appeared interested. "Write up a proposal for me," he said. "I'll take it to our executive committee. I can't promise anything, but I think it has a good chance of being approved. Make sure that you include the important points—things like selection procedures, costs, monitoring of progress, benefits, and obligations of the scholarship holder."

Now you must comply with Yousef's request. Use your imagination to logically develop the facts you will need, but be realistic. Your proposal will be in a form appropriate for this situation.

21.   As a delegate of _____ [a campus organization of your choice], you have just returned from the annual regional meeting. At the meeting you proposed that the next meeting be held on your campus. Two other offers to host the meeting were made.

The regional board of directors was interested in all three offers. So it requested that written proposals be submitted by each of the three chapters whose delegate had made the offers. It would then review the proposals and select what seemed to be the best site.

The leaders of your chapter appear to like the idea. But since the idea was yours, they assigned you the task of preparing the proposal. You will begin the task by thinking through the matter carefully. What attractions can your school and community offer visiting students? Where would the delegates stay for the two nights required? What transportation is available? What free-time activities are available? How can your chapter help make the meeting a success? What expenses would be incurred?

After you have worked out answers to these and other pertinent questions, you'll write up the proposal. (You may assume that your school and your chapter will go along with it as long as it is reasonable.)

22.   Assume that you are a member of BLOT (Business Leaders of Tomorrow), a business club at your school. You chair a committee appointed to organize a Career Day program in which major employers of your school's graduates will be invited to meet students.

You and your committee began work on this project by developing a three-part plan. The first part, Meet Your Employers, is an assembly of employers. These employers will each have booths where they can hand out company literature, show videos, or just talk with interested students.

The second part is the Job Search Forum, a two-hour seminar conducted by two or three employment experts. The seminar, open to all students, will address questions about finding the right job.

The third part, I Did and You Can, is an informal gathering of graduates who have recently found work. They will share their job search strategies and their experiences as new members of the working world.

Now you and your committee must work out the details and the arrangements necessary to conduct the Career Day program on your campus. Then you will write these up in a proposal directed to the dean of students (or the appropriate authority on your campus). The proposal will explain precisely how BLOT will conduct each part of your plan. And it will specify the facilities that the school will have to furnish.

As you develop the proposal, you will bear in mind the following BLOT decisions.

· The program will be available without cost to all interested students at your school.

· All the program participants will serve on a volunteer basis.

· BLOT will arrange and promote the program.

· The school will furnish facilities without cost.

Now you must write the proposal and present it in a form appropriate for the occasion.
23.   You and two friends want to set up Helping Hands, a food bank for students who are in financial distress. Recent policy changes in tuition structures have hit international students particularly hard, but many others are having trouble making ends meet.

You plan to use volunteer student help to staff the centre but you need some funds from the Student Union to pay a student to be co-ordinator (10 hours per week). You also need help from your school administration to provide the space, some shelving, and some basic furniture.

You may use your imagination to furnish whatever additional information you need, but make certain that it is consistent with the facts given above. Write a proposal that can be taken to both the Student Union and the administration to get support for this project.
24.   Submit a proposal on a job sharing plan to an employer who is positive towards job-sharing and has asked for people to make suggestions of areas where it could apply.
25.   Write a proposal to the curriculum committee for your program suggesting an improvement in the way your business communications course is taught (or graded).

Long, Formal Reports

Upon completing this chapter, you will be able to construct long, formal reports for important projects. To reach this goal, you should be able to

1 Describe the roles and contents of the prefatory parts of a long, formal report.

2 Construct an executive summary that accurately represents the report.

3 Organize an introduction by considering the readers and selecting the appropriate contents.

4 Determine, based on the goal, how to end a report—with a summary, a conclusion, a recommendation, or a combination of the three.

5 Describe the roles and contents of the supplementary parts.

6 Use a structural coherence plan.

▶ to Long, Formal Reports

Doreen can relax. Her report was a success. She had put in many hours to make sure her short report was accurate, interesting, and impressive. A few days after sending it to Good 'n Nice's head office, she received a letter from the president commending her on her work. It had been an exciting experience.

The following week Doreen learned that the experience was not yet over. Dale Mudrick, the head of recruiting and training, had read Doreen's report and wanted her to turn it into a much larger work. Instead of just talking about how to get a new franchise on its feet, Dale wanted the complete story about the benefits of Good 'n Nice over other companies, the financing, the qualifications of a franchise owner, and so on. The idea was to create a reference work that would stay on file to be updated periodically. Then it could be given to serious applicants as part of the screening and training process. Dale also had visions of putting selections of it on the Internet to advertize the potential of a Good 'n Nice franchise.

Dale had lots of ideas, but Doreen's first step was to expand her short report into a much longer and more formal document. ∎

Although not often required, long, formal reports are highly important in business. They usually concern major investigations, which explains their length. They are usually prepared for high-level administrators, which explains their formality. As the trend to out-sourcing continues, an increase in the use of the long, formal report can be expected. The hiring of external agents creates an increased need for well-written and well-presented reports between the parties.

* Long, formal reports are important but not numerous in business.

ORGANIZATION AND CONTENT OF THE LONGER REPORTS

The level of formality in a report can be adjusted depending upon the needs of the situation. You have a number of parts available to you such as the title page, executive summary, and index. Your task as the author is to design a report by selecting parts appropriately to meet your specific needs.

* Needs should determine the level of formality in reports.

As noted in Chapter 13, short, informal reports will have only a title page and text. If they are a little longer, a table of contents may be added. There are other prefatory and supplementary pages that can be included as the report length and the formality of the situation increase. For convenience in the following discussion, the report parts are organized by groups: the prefatory parts, the report proper, and the supplementary parts.

The following classification plan, illustrated by the diagram in Figure 14–1, arranges business reports in a stairway. At the top of the stairway are the most formal, full-dress reports. Such reports have covers, making the longest of them almost like books. They also have several *prefatory pages* that come before the text material. These pages serve useful purposes, but they also dress up the appearance of the report. The full arrangement of prefatory pages includes these parts: title fly, title page, letter of transmittal, letter of authorization, letter of acceptance, table of contents, and executive summary. Flyleaves and end papers (blank pages at the beginning and end that protect the report) may also be included especially if the report has a cover.

* Report structure may be pictured as a stairway. Long, formal reports are at the top.

To decide which arrangement of parts meets the length and formality requirements of your situation, you need to know the roles and contents of these parts. As you read the following descriptions, trace the parts through the sample report at the end of this chapter, and consult Chapter 21 for additional illustrations and instructions on format.

* Know the roles and contents of the prefatory parts to select the ones you need.

This stairway plan does not account for all the possible variations in reports, but it provides a general
picture to help you construct reports that are appropriate for the situation.

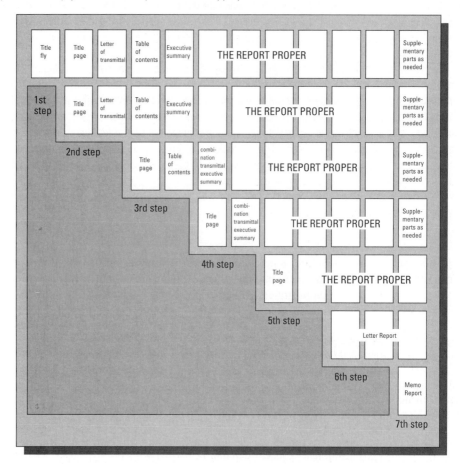

THE PREFATORY PARTS

Title Fly

- The title fly contains only the report title.

The printed prefatory pages begin with the title fly. Since it contains only the report title,
which appears again on the following page, the title fly does not add content, but it does
make an impression. It is included solely for reasons of formality. Most books have one,
and so do most formal reports.

Title Page

- The title page displays the title, identification of the writer and authorizer, and the date.

The title page presents information essential to the identification of the report: the report
title, the author's name, the receiver's name, and the date. In addition, the affiliation of
the author and/or of the receiver may be included. The affiliation might be a company or
a committee name. The position the person holds may also be shown. For example, the
person who asked for the report might be the Vice President of the Overseas Division.
The construction of this page is illustrated in Chapter 21 and in the report at the end of
this chapter (Figure 14–5).

Letter of Authorization

A *letter of authorization* is a letter or a memo that assigns the report-writing task to the author and gives the authority to conduct the necessary research, have access to existing documentation, spend funds, and so on. Its presence in a report is not determined by formality or length but by whether the report was authorized *in writing*. If such written authorization exists, a copy should be included after the title page. Because it is not written by the author of the report, this letter is not included in Figure 14–1.

• Include the letter of authorization if the report was authorized in writing.

Letter of Acceptance

A *letter of acceptance* is the author's reply to the letter of authorization. It was written before the work of the report was undertaken and is included here only to complete the documentation about this report project. A letter of acceptance expresses agreement with the task and the terms set down in the authorization letter. If there is no letter of authorization, there will be no letter of acceptance.

• If there is a letter of authorization, it should be answered with an acceptance.

Letter of Transmittal, Preface, or Foreword

In less formal situations a report is delivered personally with a spoken transmittal message. In formal situations a letter usually does the job. In business reports the *letter of transmittal* hands over the report from the writer to the reader. It is written at the completion of the report-writing process.

• The letter of transmittal is a personal message from the writer to the reader.

The message in a transmittal letter is much like what you would say if you were face-to-face with the reader. It begins directly, without explanation or other delaying information, saying, in effect, "Here is the report." After that, there is a statement of the goal. The rest of the content depends on the situation. It might be something about the report—how to understand, use, or appreciate it. It might be suggestions about follow-up studies, disclaimers about limitations, or comments about side issues that will help the reader appreciate the report. Typically, the letter of transmittal ends with goodwill comments. An expression of appreciation for the assignment or an offer to do additional research if necessary makes good closing material.

• Its main goal is to transmit the report.

In some cases, particularly where the report is written for a group of readers, a preface is used instead. Although a preface is a little more formal than a letter of transmittal, it accomplishes the same task. Both are preliminary messages from the writer to the readers to help them appreciate and understand the report.

• For large audiences, a preface is used.

One more step up in formality takes us to a foreword. This document is usually not written by the author but by another authority or well-known personality. Besides introducing the report, a foreword adds the credibility of its writer to the work. Although forewords do not formally transmit the report, they do many of the other things done by letters of transmittal. They may, for example, include helpful comments about the report's use, interpretation, follow-up, and so on.

• Forewords do not transmit the report—they comment about it.

Table of Contents, List of Illustrations

If your report is long enough to need a guide to its contents, you should include a *table of contents*. This table is an outline of the report with page numbers. As noted in the discussion of outlining in Chapter 12, the outline headings appear in the text of the report as headings of the various parts. Thus, a listing showing the pages where the headings appear helps the reader find the parts of the report. A table of contents is especially helpful to the reader who wants to see only a few specific parts of the report.

• Include a table of contents when the report is long enough to need a guide to its contents.

The table of contents lists everything that follows it, including the executive summary, the text contents, and the supplementary parts (bibliography, appendix, index). It does not list itself. The major illustrations, figures, charts, and tables appear in a separate *list of*

• The table of contents lists everything that follows it and gives page numbers.

illustrations. If there are only a few, they can be included as headings within the table of contents at the appropriate page. More detailed instructions for constructing the table of contents appear in Chapter 21.

Executive Summary

- The executive summary summarizes the report.

The executive summary (also called *synopsis, abstract, epitome, précis, digest*) is the report in miniature. It concisely summarizes whatever is important in the report and serves as a preview to the report. It is useful for people who lack the time or the interest to read the whole report. Perhaps they can get all they need to know by reading the executive summary. At least they will know whether the report covers the points they are interested in. If they want more details, they can find the specific section through the table of contents or index.

- The executive summary is used in key word indexing.

A second importance of the executive summary is its use as the basis for automated indexing. Machine-readable databases now frequently include the text of the executive summary, as well as the author and title of the report. Key words for the index are drawn automatically from the entire summary and not just from the title. Since this type of indexing gives more complete and accurate search results, it is becoming increasingly popular with researchers.

- It includes highlights of the facts, analyses, and conclusions in proportion to the text.

You construct the executive summary simply by reducing the parts of the report in order and in proportion. More specifically, you go through the report, selecting whatever is essential. You should include the purpose and the major items of information—the bottom-line facts and figures of the report. You should include a summary of all the major analyses and, if appropriate, the conclusions and recommendations derived from these analyses. The executive summary is a miniature of the whole, generally less than an eighth as long as the writing it summarizes and often only one or two pages in total.

- To write an executive summary well requires practice.

From the description of the executive summary, you will realize that, although it is placed at the beginning of the document, it is written after the report is completed. As your goal is to overview the report in a fraction of its length, you need to exercise word economy; however, you must not sacrifice accuracy to conciseness. Because you are so familiar with the contents of the report and the original wording, you may find it beneficial to draft your executive summary from the table of contents rather than from the report itself. The points you remember under each heading are likely the key ones that are needed. Moreover, your word choice will be fresh, which will help to maintain interest. Once you have completed the draft, check it against the full report for accuracy and completeness. A clear, concise, and correct executive summary is only achieved through careful writing and editing.

- Either the direct or indirect order is appropriate.

The traditional executive summary reviews the report in the indirect order (introduction, body, conclusion). In recent years, however, the trend has been to follow the order of the report. If the report is in direct order with the major findings, conclusions, and/or recommendations at the beginning, then the executive summary echoes that order. But if you have carefully built a persuasive case by using the indirect order in your report, your executive summary also needs to be indirect. On occasion, a clear statement of conclusion and of recommendation in the executive summary may be deferred entirely if the need for the indirect order is strong enough to justify delaying the outcome until after all arguments are read. Diagrams of both arrangements appear in Figure 14–2. An example of an executive summary is included in Figure 14–5.

- The executive summary and the letter of transmittal may be combined.

When you want a less formal approach, you may combine the letter of transmittal with the executive summary. This arrangement shortens the report slightly and is more efficient if your report topic is not complex. In this combined document you begin with the usual transmittal statement. Then you summarize the report highlights and close with other appropriate information about the report as you would in a letter of transmittal.

- This progression of structure is general.

Our review of the prefatory parts is complete. This general analysis has simplified the structure of reports to help you picture the relationship of formality and length to the parts of a report. As you increase the number of these parts included in your report, your work becomes more formal in format.

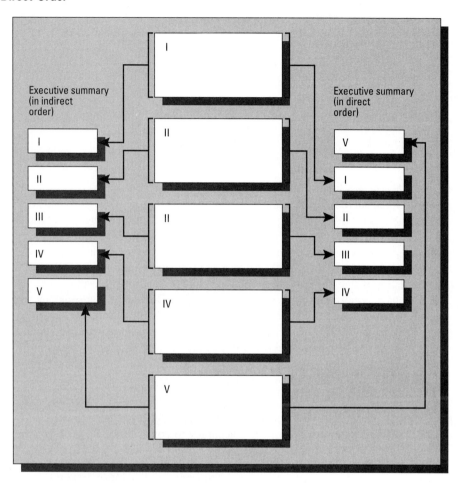

THE REPORT PROPER

As noted in Chapter 13, the content of most longer reports is written in the indirect order (introduction, facts and analysis, conclusion, and recommendation). Therefore, the following review of the makeup of the report proper follows that order.

• The parts of the report proper will be reviewed in the indirect order.

Title

Composing a title is not as easy as it first seems. In fact, on a per word basis, the title typically requires more time than any other part of the report. Titles should be carefully worded to fit the approach and content of your report. If your report uses the direct approach, your title should indicate your results. If your report is indirect, your title should not give away your position. A good title fits its report like a glove.

• Construct titles to make them describe the report precisely.

For complete coverage of content, you should compose your titles around the five Ws (*who, what, where, when, why*) and sometimes *how.* As shown here, they serve as a good checklist even if you decide not to use them all in your final wording.

• As a checklist, use who, what, where, when, why, and sometimes how.

Who: Allied Distributors, Inc.

What: Recommendation to purchase Brand X cars for replacement of sales fleet.

Where: City Motors

When: 1998

Why: Economy, reliability, warranty.

How: Comparison of four subcompacts.

From this analysis comes the title "Recommendations for 1998 Replacements for Allied Distributors' Sales Fleet Based on a Comparison of Four Subcompact Automobiles." In a direct approach your title could be even more specific: "A Recommendation to Purchase Brand X for Allied Distributors' 1988 Sales Fleet."

For a report about an advertizing campaign, this analysis would be appropriate:

Who: Lane Company.

What: Analysis of advertizing campaign.

Where: Southern Ontario.

When: 1997.

Why: Implied.

How: Survey.

Thus, the title emerges as "Results of a Survey Measuring the Effectiveness of the Lane Company's 1997 Advertizing Campaign in Southern Ontario." This title indicates the content of the report without giving away the results of the analysis and, therefore, suits a report written in indirect order. Consider the difference if the first word is changed to *Recommendations,* as in "Recommendations Based on a Survey Measuring the Effectiveness of the Lane Company's 1997 Advertizing Campaign in Southern Ontario." The subtle suggestion is that changes are needed to improve next year's results.

• Subtitles can help balance completeness and conciseness.

You may have noticed that these titles are quite long. Obviously, you sometimes have to balance completeness with conciseness. Titles that are too long are boring and confusing. Extremely short titles tend to be broad and general, covering everything and touching nothing. So you must seek the most economical word pattern consistent with completeness. A subtitle can often help. Here is an example: "Measuring Employee Morale at Pfeiffer's Mossback Plant: A Comparative Study, 1996 and 1998."

Introduction

• The introduction should prepare the readers.

An introduction should prepare readers to receive the report. As we noted earlier, most short reports need very little introductory material because the readers are already familiar with the problem. But such is not the case for the longer reports. A more extensive introduction is needed for several reasons. First, the situation or problem is more complex, and so is the document. Secondly, long reports usually have a wider audience, with varying levels of knowledge about the problem. And finally, because these reports are kept for many years, they may be read outside the current context. A strong introduction will promote understanding and order.

• Then determine what those readers need to know. Use the following checklist.

In determining what should be included, consider all the likely readers of your report. Ask yourself what they need or want to know about the problem. The following checklist will be helpful. Use it to remind yourself of the possibilities and select from it the pieces that are appropriate for your report.

• 1. Origin.

Origin of the Report.   The first part of your introduction might include a review of the report's origin. If you decide to include it, you should present such facts as when, how, and by whom the report was authorized; who wrote the report; and when the report was submitted. Information of this kind is particularly useful in reports dealing with controversial or sensitive issues that need to be understood within a context. That the report has been authorized by someone in a power position will add to its credibility.

• 2. Purpose.

Purpose.   A vital part of a report is its statement of purpose. Often called by other names (*objective, problem, aim, goal*), the *purpose* is whatever the report seeks to do. You may want to state secondary goals that will be reached in the process of achieving your purpose. This section is also the place to explain why you are conducting this study.

A PRACTICE RUN

Set out the following information in the charts and then write effective titles that balance completeness with conciseness. Assume that the reports are in the indirect order. A recent consumer survey on the popularity of video games showed MegaJoy's new game, TNT, well back in sixth place.

Who	
What	
Where	
When	
Why	
How	

FINISHED TITLE _____

_____

The Winston Institute made a detailed comparison of strategies used in Canada and the United States for economic recovery after a recession. They found that encouraging small business was critical.

Who	
What	
Where	
When	
Why	
How	

FINISHED TITLE _____

_____

Scope. By *scope,* we mean the boundaries of the problem such as dates, geographical areas, and so on. If the scope is not clearly covered anywhere else, you should create a separate part to describe what is and what is not included in the problem.

* 3. Scope—the boundaries of the problem.

Limitations. In some reports you will need to explain the *limitations* you face. Circumstances beyond your control may impair the quality of your report. For example, you may have to work under strict time constraints. Or perhaps the budget has prevented you from doing the testing you needed to do. Limitations are not excuses for less than satisfactory work. Nor are they appeals for pity. They are unavoidable conditions that have affected the outcome of your work.

* 4. Limitations—conditions that impair the quality of the report.

Historical Background. Knowledge of the history of the problem is sometimes essential to understanding the report. Your general aim in this part is to acquaint the readers with how the problem developed and what has been done about it so far. You review what past investigations have uncovered, and how your work will complement that knowledge.

* 5. History—how the problem developed and what is known about it.

Sources and Methods of Collecting Information.   You need to tell the readers how you collected the information for your report. That is, you explain your research methodology. You may have conducted library research, a survey, an experiment, or some combination. You describe the steps you took in enough detail to give your readers the confidence that your work was performed competently.

In a case in which you conducted only library research, your references are probably explanation enough, although you may want to direct your reader's attention to your bibliography. If most of your findings come from one or two sources, you can give them additional credit here.

More complex research is described later in detail to show its validity and reliability. If you conducted a survey, for example, you would explain all parts of the investigation including selecting the sample of people, designing the questionnaire or interview, and tabulating and checking the results. Providing a copy of the questionnaire in an appendix would also add to the credibility of your work.

Definitions and Acronyms.   Every subject has its jargon. If you use initials, acronyms, or words that are likely to be unfamiliar to readers of the report, you must define them. Short forms and initials need to be spelled out in full at least once before they are used alone. A common method is to include the explanation in context.

Most sites on the World Wide Web (WWW) begin with an overview of the site. Headings might include FAQs (Frequently Asked Questions), Recent Additions to This Site, and subject headings.

An *acronym* is a word formed from the first letters or syllables of other words, such as *radar* (*RA*dio *D*etecting *A*nd *R*anging), *modem* (*MO*dulate and *DEM*odulate), and *Yahoo!* (*Y*et *A*nother *H*ierarchical *O*fficious *O*racle, a subject guide to the World Wide Web). These short forms also need explanation.

If you use words in a very narrow or specific sense, perhaps not the commonly understood meaning, you should explain your special interpretation. You can do this in either of two ways: you can define each word in the text or as a footnote when it is first used in the report, or you can define all unfamiliar words in a separate part of the introduction. If the list is long, you may choose to arrange the words alphabetically. As well, you may choose to include a glossary in the supplementary parts as discussed later.

Report Preview.   In very long reports a final part of the introduction should preview the report presentation. In this preview you give your readers a clear picture of the road ahead by telling them what topics will be taken up first, second, third, and so on. You also give your reasons for choosing this report plan. As you will see later in the chapter, this part of the introduction is a basic ingredient of the coherence plan of the long report. Examples of report previews appear in the coherence discussion and in Figure 14–5.

The Report Body

In the report body the information collected is presented and related to the problem. Normally, this part of the report comprises most of its content. This part, plus the conclusion or recommendation, is what is commonly thought of as the report, because the other parts are attached to it.

Although the body makes up most of the report, practically all that we need to say about it is covered in other chapters. It is written in clear, concise business style as discussed in Chapters 2 to 5. Its organization and format follow the patterns discussed in Chapter 12. Its presentation style includes graphic aids and captions as discussed in Chapter 15. Its format is described in chapter 21. All the major elements of business writing are applied in the body of the report.

Side notes (left margin):

• 6. Sources and methods—how you got the information.

• Major sources can be given additional credit here.

• More complex research requires thorough description.

• 7. Definitions of unfamiliar words used.

• 8. Preview—a description of the route ahead.

• The report body presents and analyzes the information gathered.

Technical Writer's Report on Humpty Dumpty†

A 72-gram brown Rhode Island Red country-fresh candled egg was secured and washed free of feathers, blood, dirt, and grit. Held between thumb and index finger, about 3 feet or more from an electric fan (GE Model No. MC-2404, Serial No.JC23023, nonoscillating, rotating on "Hi" speed at approximately 105.23 plus or minus 0.02 rpm), the egg was suspended on a pendulum (string) so that it arrived at the fan with essentially zero velocity normal to the fan rotation plane. The product adhered strongly to the walls and ceiling and was difficult to recover. However, using putty knives a total of 13 grams was obtained and put in a skillet with 11.2 grams of hickory-smoke Armour's old-style bacon and heated over a low Bunsen flame for 7 min. 32 sec. What there was of it was of excellent quality.

†Source: "The DP Report," DuPont Explosive's Department, Atomic Energy Division, Savannah River Laboratories, July 12, 1954.

The Ending of the Report

You can end your report several ways: with a summary, a conclusion, a recommendation, or a combination of the three.

* Reports can end in various ways.

Ending Summary. When the goal of a report is to present information, the logical ending is a review of the major findings. Such reports usually have short summaries at the end of each section. When this arrangement is followed, the ending recapitulates these summaries.

* Informational reports usually end with a summary of the major findings.

You should not confuse the ending summary with the executive summary. The executive summary is a prefatory part of the report; the ending summary is a part of the report text. Also, the executive summary is more complete than the ending summary. The executive summary previews the entire report, including authorization, methodology, strategy, findings, and in some reports, conclusions and recommendations.[1] The ending summary reviews only the highlights of the report's content.

* The ending summary is not as complete as the executive summary.

Conclusions. Some reports must do more than just present information. They analyze the information in light of the problem, and from this analysis, they reach a decision. Such reports typically end with this conclusion.

* Reports that seek an answer need a conclusion.

The makeup of the conclusion section varies from case to case. In problems for which a single answer is sought, the conclusion section normally reviews the preceding information and analysis, and from this review, selects the one answer. In problems with more than one goal, the report plan may treat each goal in a separate section and draw simple conclusions in each section. Then at the end of such a report, a conclusion section might well summarize all the previous conclusions and draw them together.

* The structure of the conclusion varies by problem.

Recommendation. When the goal of the report is not only to draw conclusions but also to present a course of action, a recommendation is in order. Whether you include a recommendation should be determined by whether the readers want or expect one. Do not offer advice for action unless you have been asked for it. A recommendation gives the readers a direction for solving the problem.

* Include recommendations when the readers want or expect them.

As we have seen in Chapter 12, a recommendation (or recommendations) must grow logically from the conclusions you have drawn. You may present it in a separate section

---

[1]Informational reports will not have recommendations to include in the executive summary. The executive summaries for indirect analytical reports may defer the conclusions and recommendations on occasion.

following the conclusion; however, sometimes the conclusion so clearly leads to a recommendation that you may want to present them both in one section. If you do use only one section, be careful not to move directly to the recommendation omitting the conclusions. Conclusions and recommendations may belong together, but they are not the same.

Supplementary Parts

- Add an appendix, bibliography, glossary, or index as needed.

When the report proper is finished, there are some supplementary pages that may be added. These pages all have important roles to play in helping your reader explore your report. The standard supplementary parts include an appendix (or several appendices), some form of documentation for sources such as a bibliography, a glossary, and an index. As with the prefatory pages, not all the supplementary parts are needed all the time.

- The appendix contains information that indirectly supports the report.

Appendix. The appendix, as its name implies, is a tacked-on part. You use it for supplementary information that supports the body of the report but has no logical place within the body. Possible appendix contents are questionnaires, working papers, statistical or other summary tables, and related reports. These materials would interrupt the flow of your argument and take your reader off target if they were placed in the report proper. Instead, they are referred to in the text and included in appendices for readers who want more information.

- Information that directly supports the report belongs in the text of the report.

Anything that directly presents the content information of the report should be in the body. As a rule, the appendix should not include the charts, graphs, sketches, and tables that directly support the report. For clarity and for the convenience of the readers, such illustrations should accompany the findings they reinforce. Obviously, it is not convenient for readers to have to look in the appendices for all the graphs and illustrations. So if the material is crucial to your argument, include it in the body. Use the appendix for background and peripheral material of interest.

- Document the sources you have used.

Documentation of Sources. When your investigation makes use of secondary sources in any format, you include a list of them to give credit to the originator of the ideas. Preparing this list[2] is one of the steps you must take to avoid the serious error of plagiarism. On the positive side, your list of sources adds credibility to your report by showing the depth of your research. Since documenting your sources involves more than constructing a list, and since there are several methods of referencing, the topic of documentation is discussed separately in Appendix C of this book.

- A glossary is a convenient tool for the reader.

Glossary. A *glossary* is an alphabetical list of terms with their definitions. As mentioned earlier, it provides a quick reference for the meanings of short forms, initials, acronyms, and words. Readers appreciate the convenience of having the definition readily available all the time rather than only the first time the term is used.

- An index is a search tool that makes the contents of a report more accessible.

Index. Some long reports require an index for the convenience of the reader who wants to find a particular topic quickly. A report intended for long-term use, one that is expected to be a standard for future reference, is a strong candidate for an index. Indexes are included more often now because full-featured word processors can generate them automatically, thus reducing the cost and time involved.

. . . .
STRUCTURAL AIDS TO COHERENCE

- Longer reports need structural aids to coherence.

As we have noted, the instructions for writing given in earlier chapters apply to the longer reports. But there is one point that needs to be stressed. Special attention must be given to the coherence of long, complex reports.

---

[2]This list has several names (bibliography, list of references, works cited, etc.), and a variety of formats based upon the documentation system you are using.

Structural aids to coherence are explanations, introductions, conclusions, and summaries to guide the reader through the report. This network is an expansion of the techniques for coherence introduced in Chapters 5 and 12. You should use these aids wherever they will help to link parts of the report or move the message along. Although you should not use them mechanically, you will find that they are likely to follow the general plan described in Figure 14–3. Another way to visualize the coherence plan is as a jigsaw puzzle (see Figure 14–4).

• A network of explanations, introductions, conclusions, and summaries guides the reader.

The coherence plan begins with the preview in the introduction. As you will recall, the preview tells the readers what lies ahead. It covers three things: the topics to be discussed, their order, and the logic behind that order. With this information in mind, the readers know how the parts of the report relate to one another. They know the overall strategy of the presentation. The following paragraphs do a good job of previewing a report comparing automobiles.

• The coherence plan begins with the preview, which describes the route ahead.

The decision on which light car the company should buy is reached by comparing the cars on the basis of three factors: cost, safety, and reliability. Each of these factors is broken down into its component parts, which are applied to the makes being considered.

Because cost is the most tangible factor, it is examined first. In this section, the four makes are compared for initial and trade-in values and operating costs such as fuel, oil, and maintenance. In the second section, safety is considered. Driver visibility, special safety features, brakes, steering quality, acceleration rate, and traction are compared. In the third major section, dependability is predicted based on the three previous model years. Repair records and time lost because of automobile failure are considered. In the final major section, weights are assigned to the foregoing comparisons, and the automobile brand that is best suited to the company's needs is recommended.

FIGURE 14–3 Diagram of the Structural Coherence Plan of a Long, Formal Report

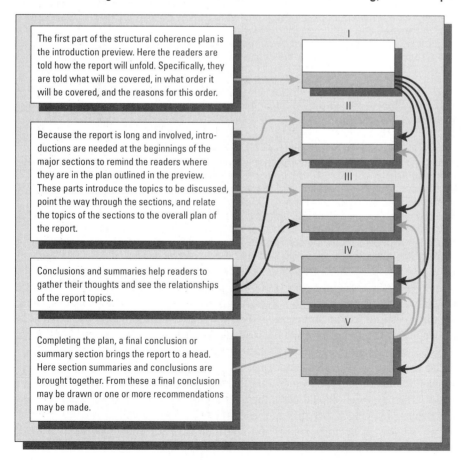

FIGURE 14-4 A Representation of the Coherence Plan

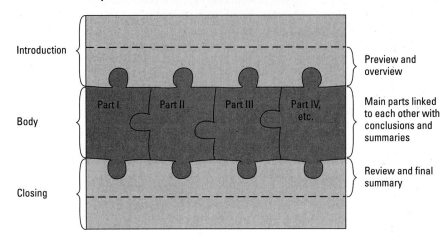

In addition to the review in the introduction, the plan uses introductory and summary sections at convenient places throughout the report. Typically, these sections are at the beginning and end of each major division, and at other points as they are needed. Such sections remind the readers where they are in the report by telling them where they have been and where they are going. Illustrating this technique is the following paragraph that introduces a major section of a report. Note how the paragraph ties in with the preceding discussion that concerned industrial activity in three centres. Note also how it justifies covering secondary areas.

• Introductions and summaries in each section tell readers where they are in the report.

> Although the great bulk of industry is concentrated in the three centres of Grandin, Lacombe, and Port Sturgeon, a thorough industrial survey needs to consider the secondary areas. In the rank of their current industrial potential, these areas are the Southeast, with Hartsburg as its centre; the Central West, especially the community of Barrington; and the North Central, where Pine Lake is the centre of activities.

The following summary-conclusion paragraph is a good ending to a major section. The paragraph brings to a head the findings presented in the section and points the way to the subject of the next section.

> These findings all lead to one obvious conclusion. The small-business executives are concerned primarily with subject matter that will aid them directly in their work. That is, they favour a curriculum slanted toward the practical subjects with some coverage of the liberal arts. They are also convinced of the value of studying business administration. On all these points, they clearly differ from the positions of the big-business leaders. Moreover, business administration professors would find it difficult to support such an extremely practical concept. Nevertheless, as the small-business executives are the consumers of the business-education product, their opinions should be considered. Likewise, their specific recommendations on curriculum (the subject of the following section) deserve careful review.

• The final major section of the report reviews the information and applies it to the goal.

Completing the coherence plan is the final major section of the report. In this section you achieve the goal of the report. Here you recall all the major findings and analyses from the preceding section summaries. Then you apply them to the problem and present the conclusion. Thus, you complete the strategy explained in the introduction preview and recalled at convenient places throughout the report.

• Use coherence aids naturally—when they are needed.

Wise use of coherence aids can form a network of connections throughout the report. You should keep in mind, however, that these aids should be used only when they are needed. That is, you should use them when your readers need help in seeing relationships, knowing where they are, and where they are going. If you use them well, they will appear as natural parts of the report story. They should never appear to be mechanical additions.

THE LONG ANALYTICAL REPORT ILLUSTRATED

Illustrating the longer analytical report is the report presented in Figure 14–5 (pages 342-359). The report's structure parallels that of the formal type described in the preceding pages.

• Figure 14–5 is an illustration of a longer, formal report.

A SUMMARY OF LEARNING OUTCOMES FROM THIS CHAPTER

Long, formal reports have several prefatory parts before the body of the report. The first of these is the title fly, a page displaying only the title. In constructing the title, use as a checklist the five Ws: *who, what, where, when, why;* and *how.*

The title page is the next prefatory part. It displays the title, identifies the writer and the recipient (and perhaps the authorizer), and shows the date of submission.

If the report was authorized in writing, you should include a copy of the memorandum or letter of authorization as a prefatory part. This part is written by the authorizer of the report. A letter of acceptance is the writer's response to the letter of authorization. A copy of the acceptance is also included.

The letter of transmittal is the next prefatory part. In more formal presentations a preface or a foreword may be used. In this letter you transmit the report and make any helpful comments you would make if you were presenting it in person. Some reports include a summary in the letter of transmittal.

The next prefatory part is the table of contents, which lists the report outline in polished form with page numbers. It also lists other report parts that follow it, such as the executive summary, appendices, and bibliography.

The executive summary is the report in miniature. It includes everything that is important in the report. The purpose statement, major facts, analyses, and conclusions are included in their correct proportion to reflect the emphasis each has in the full report. Either the direct or indirect order is appropriate, whichever is used in the report itself.

The report introduction prepares the readers to receive the report. Consider the following items as a checklist of the introduction contents: purpose, scope, limitations, historical background, methodology, definitions, and preview. The preview is especially useful in the longer, involved reports. It tells the readers what the report will cover, the order of the presentation, and the reasons for this order.

The ending of the report achieves the report goal. It may be a summary (if the goal is to review information), a conclusion, and/or a recommendation (if the goal is to arrive at an answer).

Appendices, a bibliography, a glossary, and an index can follow the report text. The appendices contain support items that have no specific place in the text, such as questionnaires, working papers, and summary tables. The bibliography is a list of the sources used in the investigation. The glossary is an alphabetical list of terms and their definitions, while the index is an alphabetical list of topics with page references.

The longer reports need a network of explanations, introductions, conclusions, and summaries to give them coherence and to guide the readers. You begin the coherence plan with the introduction preview, which presents the structure of the report. Then through the skillful use of introductions and summaries in the following parts, you tell the readers where they are in the structure. Completing the coherence plan, in the ending of the report, you bring together the preceding information to reach the report goal (conclusion or recommendation). The aids to coherence should be an inconspicuous, natural part of the message.

FIGURE 14–5 A Long, Formal Report The illustration that appears in the following pages represents an orderly, thorough, and objective solution to a somewhat complex problem.

Title fly

The title includes the essentials of the 5 w's

RECOMMENDATIONS FOR 1998 REPLACEMENTS

IN ALLIED DISTRIBUTORS' SALES FLEET

BASED ON A COMPARISON OF FOUR SUBCOMPACT AUTOMOBILES

FIGURE 14–5 *Continued*

Title page

RECOMMENDATIONS FOR 1998 REPLACEMENTS

IN ALLIED DISTRIBUTORS' SALES FLEET

BASED ON A COMPARISON OF FOUR SUBCOMPACT AUTOMOBILES

Prepared for

*Here the essential
facts of authorization
are provided*

Mr. Norman W. Bigbee, Vice President
Allied Distributors, Inc.
3131 Speedall Street, Akron, Ohio 44302

Prepared by

George W. Franklin, Associate Director
Midwestern Research, Inc.
1732 Midday Avenue, Chicago, Illinois 60607
April 13, 1998

FIGURE 14–5 *Continued*

Letter of transmittal

April 13, 1998

Mr. Norman W. Bigbee
Vice President in Charge of Sales
Allied Distributors, Inc.
3131 Speedall Street
Akron, Ohio 44302

Dear Mr. Bigbee:

The letter of transmittal begins directly, with the authorization.

Here is the report on the four makes of subcompact automobiles you asked me to compare last January 3.

Pertinent comments help the reader understand and appreciate the research.

To guide you in deciding which of the four makes you should buy as replacements for your fleet, I gathered what I believe to be the most complete information available. Much of the operating information comes from your own records. The remaining data are the findings of both consumer research engineers and professional automotive analysts. Only my analyses of these data are subjective.

A goodwill comment ends the letter.

I sincerely hope, Mr. Bigbee, that my analyses will help you in making the correct decision. Thank you for this assignment. And should you need any clarification on my analyses, please call on me.

Sincerely,

George W. Franklin

George W. Franklin
Associate Director

FIGURE 14–5 *Continued*

FIGURE 14–5 *Continued*

*Table of contents
(continued)*

LIST OF TABLE AND CHARTS

TABLES

*Separate lists of
tables and charts
follow the text
content. The report
has no appendix or
bibliography.*

FIGURE 14–5 *Continued*

*Executive
summary*

*Following the
direct-order plan,
this executive
summary places the
recommendations first.
Highlights of the
introduction follow.*

*The remaining
paragraphs summarize
the major facts,
analyses, and
conclusions of the
report.*

*A summary of the
analyses and
conclusions logically
leads to the overall
conclusion.*

Executive Summary

The recommendation of this study is that Gamma is the best buy for Allied Distributors, Inc. Authorized by Mr. Norman W. Bigbee, Vice President, on January 3, 1998, this report is submitted on April 13, 1998. This study gives Allied Distributors an insight into the problem of replacing the approximately 50 two-year-old subcompact cars in its present sales fleet. The basis for this recommendation is an analysis of cost, safety, and construction factors of four models of subcompact cars (Alpha, Beta, Gamma, and Delta).

The four cars do not show a great deal of difference in ownership cost (initial cost less trade-in allowance after two years). On a per-car basis, Beta costs least for a two-year period—$3,216. Compared with costs for the other cars, Beta is $370 under Gamma, $588 under Alpha, and $634 under Delta. For the entire sales fleet, these differences become more significant. A purchase of 50 Betas would save $18,500 over Gamma, $29,400 over Alpha, and $31,700 over Delta. Operation costs would favor Gamma. Cost per mile for this car is $0.13970, as compared with $0.14558 for Alpha, $0.14785 for Delta, and $0.15184 for Beta. The totals of all costs for the 50-car fleet over the two-year period show Gamma to be least costly at $385,094. In second place is Alpha, with a cost of $400,208. Delta is third at $406,560, and Beta is fourth with a cost of $417,532.

On the qualities that pertain to driving safety, Gamma is again superior to the other cars. It has the best brakes and is tied with Alpha for the best weight distribution. It is second in acceleration and is again tied with Alpha for the number of standard safety devices. Alpha is second overall in this category, having the second best brakes of the group. Beta is last because of its poor acceleration and poor brakes.

Construction features and handling abilities place Gamma all by itself. It scores higher than any other car in every category. Alpha and Delta are tied for second place. Again Beta is last, having poor steering and handling qualities.

FIGURE 14–5 *Continued*

*Report text
(introduction)*

RECOMMENDATIONS FOR 1998 REPLACEMENTS
IN ALLIED DISTRIBUTORS' SALES FLEET
BASED ON A COMPARISON OF FOUR SUBCOMPACT AUTOMOBILES

I. ORIENTATION TO THE PROBLEM

A. The Authorization Facts

*These authorization
facts identify the
participants in the
report.*

This comparison of the qualities of four brands of
subcompact automobiles is submitted April 13, 1998,
to Mr. Norman W. Bigbee, Vice President, Allied
Distributors, Inc. At a meeting in his office January
3, 1998, Mr. Bigbee orally authorized Midwestern
Research, Inc., to conduct this investigation. Mr.
George W. Franklin, Associate Director for Midwestern
Research, served as director of the project.

B. Problem of Selecting Fleet Replacements

*Here the writer
explains the problem
clearly and precisely.*

The objective of this study is to determine which
model of subcompact automobile Allied Distributors,
Inc., should select for replacement in its sales
fleet. The firm's policy is to replace all two-year
old models. It replaces approximately 50 automobiles
each year.

The replacements involve a major capital outlay, and
the sales fleet expense constitutes a major sales
cost. Thus, the proper selection of a new model
presents an important problem. The model selected
must be economical, dependable, and safe. Allied is
considering four subcompact automobiles as
replacement possibilities. As instructed by Mr.
Bigbee, for reasons of information security, the cars
are identified in this report only as Alpha, Beta,
Gamma, and Delta.

FIGURE 14-5 *Continued*

Report text (continued)

2

C. Reports and Records as Sources of Data

This review of methods and sources permits the reader to judge the research.

The selection of the replacement brand is based on a comparative analysis of the merits of the four makes. Data for the comparisons were obtained from both company records and statistical reports. Operating records of ten representative cars of each make provide information on operating costs. These reports are summaries compiled by salesperson-drivers and represent actual performance of company cars under daily selling conditions. Additional material enumerating safety features, overall driving quality, and dependability comes from the reports of the Consumers Union of the United States, Inc., Automotive Industries, and Bond Publishing Company's periodical, Road and Track. Mr. Bigbee furnished the trade-in allowance granted on the old models. From this material, extensive comparisons of the four makes are presented.

D. A Preview to the Presentation

A description of the presentation prepares the reader for what follows.

In the following pages of the report, the four cars are compared on the basis of three factors: operating costs, safety features, and total performance. Operating costs receive primary attention. In this part the individual cost items for each car are analyzed. This analysis leads to the determination of the most economical of the four cars.

Safety features make up the second factor of comparison. In this part the analysis centers on the presence or absence of safety features in each car and the quality of the features that are present. From this analysis, comes a safety ranking of the car. The third factor for comparison is total performance and durability. As in preceding parts, here the analysis produces a ranking of the cars.

II. THE MAJOR FACTOR OF COST

From this point on, the presentation of facts and analyses pursues the report goal.

As cost analysis is an obvious and generally accepted requirement of any major purchase, it is a logical first point of concern in selecting a car to buy. Here the first concern is the original cost—that is, the fleet discount price. Of second interest in a logical thinking process is the cash difference after trade-in allowance for the old cars. These figures clearly indicate the cash outlay for the new fleet.

FIGURE 14–5 *Continued*

Report text
(continued)

3

A. <u>Initial Costs Favor Beta</u>

Note how the sections begin with introductory comment.

From Table I it is evident that Beta has the lowest window sticker price before and after trade-in allowances. It has a $634 margin, which must be considered in the light of what features are standard on Beta in comparison with those standard on the other cars. That is, the Beta may have fewer standard features included in its original cost and, therefore, may not be worth as much as the Alpha, Gamma, or Delta.

Note the use of tables and of text references to them at proper times.

	Table I ORIGINAL COST OF FOUR BRANDS OF SUBCOMPACT CARS IN 1998		
Make	Window Sticker Prices	Trade-in Value for Two-Year-Old Makes*	Cash Costs after Trade-in Allowance
Alpha	$7,318	$3,514	$3,804
Beta	$6,716	$3,500	$3,216
Gamma	$7,140	$3,552	$3,588
Delta	$7,700	$3,850	$3,850

*Trade-in value for Alpha and Beta are estimates
Sources: Primary and <u>Road and Track</u>, 1998

It is clear that where features are listed as standard they do not add to original cost, but where listed as options they do. As will be shown in a later table, the Delta has many more standard features than do the other makes. In addition to a study of standard features, a close look at trade-in values and operating costs will also be necessary to properly evaluate original cost.

FIGURE 14–5 *Continued*

Report text (continued)

4

Further discussion of standard features of the cars appears in the following discussions of safety and per-mile operating costs.

B. Trade-in Values Show Uniformity

Original costs alone do not tell the complete purchase-cost story. The values of the cars at the ends of their useful lives (trade-in values) are a vital part of cost. In this case, the highest trade-in value is $3,850 for Delta, and the lowest is $3,500 for Beta (see Table I). Only $350 separates the field.

Although fairly uniform, these figures appear to be more significant when converted to total amounts involved in the fleet purchases. A fleet of 50 Betas would cost $160,800. The same fleet of Gammas, Alphas, and Deltas would cost $179,376, $190,222, and $190,500, respectively. Thus, Allied's total cost of purchasing Betas would be $18,550 lower than Gammas, $29,216 lower than Alphas, and $31,676 lower than Deltas.

C. Operating Costs Are Lowest for Gamma

Gamma has the lowest maintenance cost of the four, 1.970 cents per mile. But Delta is close behind with 2.0650 cents. Both of these cars are well below the Beta and Alpha figures of 2.7336 and 2.7616, respectively. As shown in Table II, these costs are based on estimates of repairs, resulting loss of working time, tire replacements, and miscellaneous items.

It should be stressed here how greatly repair expense influences the estimates. Actually, two expenses are involved, for the expense of time lost by salespeople must be added to the cost of repairs. Obviously, a salesperson without a car is unproductive. Each hour lost by car repairs adds to the cost of the car's operation.

The time lost for repair is the same for each car—five hours. Thus, the important consideration is the number of repairs and the cost of these repairs. On this basis, the Gamma has the lowest total cost burden at $1,086 (see Table II). Delta ranks second with $1,038. Beta is third with $1,506, and Alpha is last with $1,520.

FIGURE 14–5 *Continued*

5

Table II
COMPARISON OF REPAIRS AND RELATED
LOST WORKING TIME FOR FOUR MAKES
OF CARS FOR TWO YEARS

Make	Number of Repairs	Repair Expense	Working Hours Lost*	Total Burden
Alpha	8	$820	40	$1,520
Beta	8	806	40	1,506
Gamma	6	560	30	1,086
Delta	6	612	30	1,138

*Based on hourly wage of $17.50
Sources: Allied Distributors, Inc., Operating Records

Alpha has the best record for oil and gas economy with a per-mile cost of 6.228 cents (see Table III). Second is Gamma with a cost of 6.654 cents. In third and fourth positions are Beta, 6.910 cents, and Delta, 7.336 cents. Figured on the basis of the 55,000 miles Allied cars average over two years, Alpha's margin appears more significant. Its total margin over Delta is $610.22 per car—or $30,512 for the fleet of 50 cars. Compared with

Table III
COST-PER-MILE ESTIMATE OF OPERATION

	Alpha	Beta	Gamma	Delta
Depreciation	$.05566	$.05540	$.05344	$.05384
Gas	.05800	.06482	.05800	.06482
Oil	.00428	.00428	.00854	.00854
Tires	.00452	.00326	.00168	.00122
Repairs	.01450	.01446	.01054	.01278
Miscellaneous	.00862	.00962	.00750	.00666
Total	$.14558	$.15184	$.13970	$.14786

Source: Allied Distributors, Inc., Operating Records

FIGURE 14–5 *Continued*

*Report text
(continued)*

6

Gamma, Alpha's margin is $1,034 per car and $11,742 for
the fleet total. Alpha's per-car margin over Beta is
$356.12, and its fleet margin is $17,806.

D. <u>Cost Composite Favors Gamma</u>

*A summary conclusion
ends the review of
costs*

Gamma is the most economical of all cars when all cost
figures are considered (see Table III). Its total cost
per mile is 13.970 cents, as compared with 14.558 cents
for Alpha, 14.786 cents for Delta, and 15.184 cents for
Beta. These figures take on more meaning when converted
to total fleet cost over the two-year period the cars
will be owned. As shown in Chart 1, a fleet of 50 Gammas
would cost Allied a total of $385,094.

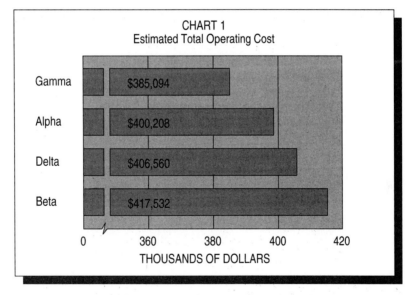

CHART 1
Estimated Total Operating Cost

This figure is under all other car totals. It is $15,114
below Alpha's $400,208, $21,466 below Delta's $406,560,
and $32,436 below Gamma's $417,532.

III. EVALUATION OF SAFETY FEATURES

*This introductory
paragraph makes a
good transition from
one section to the
next.*

Even though cost receives major emphasis in this
analysis, safety of the cars is also important. How much
importance safety should receive, however, is a matter

FIGURE 14–5 *Continued*

Report text (continued)

7

for Allied management to decide. Allied salespeople spend a large part of their working time driving. And unquestionably, driving is a hazardous assignment. Certainly Allied management wishes to minimize these hazards. Thus it may be willing to sacrifice some cost benefit in order to get safer vehicles.

A. Delta Is Best Equipped with Safety Devices

Note how headings help organize the information for the reader.

Only Delta has as standard equipment all five of the extra safety devices considered desirable by The Consumers Safety Council. The Delta is fully equipped with front disc brakes, vacuum brake assist, adjustable seatbacks, flow-through ventilation, and anti-glare mirrors, as shown in Table IV. The Delta's braking system differs from that of the Alpha and Gamma in that it provides vacuum assistance. The Beta does not equip its cars with either disc brakes or vacuum assistance.

TABLE IV
LIST OF STANDARD
SAFETY FEATURES

FEATURE	Alpha	Beta	Gamma	Delta
Front Disc Brakes	Yes	No	Yes	Yes
Vacuum Brake Assist	No	No	No	Yes
Adjustable Seatback	No	No	No	Yes
Flow-through Ventilation	Yes	No	Yes	Yes
Anti-glare Mirror	No	No	No	Yes

Source: Road and Track

Alpha and Gamma are tied in the field of safety features with two out of the possible five shown in Table IV. The Beta, although offering three of these features as options, does not provide any of the possible five.

Now that the federal government has legislated the basic safety requirements such as seat belts, padded dashboards, collapsible steering column, and shatter-proof windshields, the extra safety features of the Delta are even more welcome.

FIGURE 14-5 *Continued*

*Report text
(continued)*

8

B. <u>Acceleration Adds Extra Safety to Delta</u>

A life-saving factor that differs greatly among the
four makes is acceleration. It is important as a safety
"on-the-spot" need—something to have when in a pinch.
It is especially important in low-powered subcompact
automobiles. When needed, acceleration should be
available in the safest car. It should never be
depended on by drivers to the extent of their taking
chances because they know that it is available. But
acceleration must be included in any brand comparison.

While Gamma's acceleration time from 0 to 30 miles per
hour is the fastest in the group, the Delta leads in
both 0 to 60 and in the 1/4 mile acceleration runs. As
shown in Chart 2, Gamma reached 30 mph .3 seconds
sooner than Beta, and .5 and 1.5 seconds sooner than
Delta and Alpha, respectively. Delta reached 60 mph .4
seconds sooner than Gamma, which is not a very significant
length of time. The Delta, however, achieved this same
speed a full 3 seconds faster than Alpha, and 4.5 seconds
sooner than Beta.

*Charts add interest
and emphasize the
importance of the
data.*

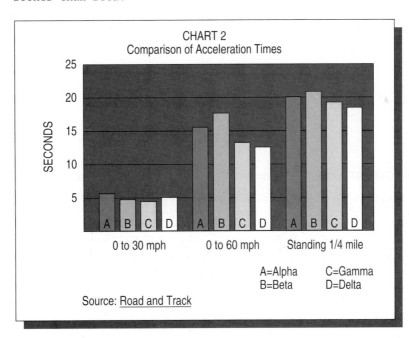

CHART 2
Comparison of Acceleration Times

A=Alpha   C=Gamma
B=Beta   D=Delta

Source: <u>Road and Track</u>

FIGURE 14–5 *Continued*

*Report text
(continued)*

9

C. Weight Distribution Is Best in Alpha and Gamma

Weight distribution affects not only the acceleration of
an automobile, but also the effectiveness of its brakes
and its handling abilities. The correct proportion of
weight on the rear wheels balances the car. In doing so,
it controls body movements in cornering and braking. The
problem is generally caused by the placement of the engine
in the front of the automobile. The arrangement of the
other essential heavy items at the best places on the
chassis results in the best distribution.

*Here text and table
work closely together
to present the
information.*

As shown in Table V, Alpha and Gamma are tied in this
category.

TABLE V
COMPARATIVE WEIGHT DISTRIBUTIONS,
BRAKING DISTANCES, AND CORNERING ABILITIES

	Alpha	Beta	Gamma	Delta
Distribution, rear, %	47	45	47	43
Braking, 80-0 mph, ft.	330	331	321	390
Brake fade, % increase in pedal effort	30	33	14	43
Control, panic stop	good	fair	excel	fair
Lateral acceleration, in g units	0.680	0.685	0.611	0.614
speed achieved, mph	32.0	32.1	30.2	30.3

Source: Road and Track

Their 47 percent is near the 50 percent automotive experts
consider best. In contrast, Delta carries a relatively low
proportion (43 percent) of its weight on the rear wheels.
This low proportion of weight is not good from the
standpoint of traction on slippery roads that seem to be
common throughout the Allied sales territory. The Beta is
between the two extremes with 45 percent of its weight on
its rear wheels.

FIGURE 14–5 *Continued*

Report text (continued)

10

D. Gamma Has Best Braking Quality

At speeds of 80 miles per hour, Gamma stops in the shortest distance (321 feet); but Alpha (330 feet) and Beta (331 feet) are not far behind. Delta is well back (390 feet). In tests simulating panic-stop situations, Gamma's brakes also prove superior to the others, ranked "excellent" by test standards. On the same test scale, Alpha's brakes rank "good" and Beta's and Delta's brakes rank "fair." Gamma's brakes are also more resistant to fade than are the other three. In stops from 80 miles per hour, all makes exhibit good braking control except Beta. Its stops are far less consistent than the others.

A summary conclusion paragraph brings this section to a close.

An overall review of safety features shows Gamma to have a very slight advantage over the other cars. Its brakes, weight distribution, and stopping distance lead to this conclusion. Alpha is second, scoring high in all categories except acceleration and standard safety features. Delta is third with the best acceleration but poor braking action. Beta is last, having only scored highly in cornering ability.

IV. RIDING COMFORT AND OVERALL CONSTRUCTION

An introduction fits the next topic into the report plan.

Few things affect the day's work of a traveling salesperson more than the ride in the car. Thus, the factors of handling ease and general riding quality should be considered in selecting a car. Somewhat related to these factors are the overall qualities of construction of the cars in question.

A. Gamma Ranks First in Handling

The Gamma, with near perfect steering, is overall the best handling car of the group. As shown in Table VI, Gamma exceeds all of the other makes when values are assigned to each category. Alpha, which is second in the area, is quick and predictable in handling. During emergency situation tests, however, it jarred and rocked severely around bumpy corners. Delta, while exhibiting normal handling characteristics during routine driving, performed miserably when subjected to emergency handling tests. Beta suffered from being knocked off course by almost any small bump. When smoother roads were encountered, Beta's handling was judged somewhat below average.

FIGURE 14–5 *Continued*

Report text (continued)

11

	Front Seating	Rear Seating	Ride Light Load	Ride Full Load	Handling	Steering Effort
Excellent						
Good					Gamma	
Fair-to-good	Gamma Alpha Delta	Gamma	Alpha		Delta Alpha	
Fair	Beta		Gamma		Beta	
Fair-to-poor		Delta	Delta	Gamma Delta		
Poor		Alpha Beta	Beta	Beta Alpha		
Low						
Low-to-moderate						Beta Alpha Gamma
Moderate						Delta

**TABLE VI
COMPARATIVE COMFORT AND RIDE**

Source: Consumers Union of United States, Inc.

B. <u>Gamma Gives Best Ride</u>

A thorough yet concise review of facts moves the report along systematically.

While it is true that Alpha's ride has been judged
superior to Gamma's when loaded lightly, Gamma comes
out first overall because of the quickly deteriorating
ride Alpha exhibits when its load is increased. Gamma's
superior ride and directional stability are the best in
the group primarily because of its fully independent
suspension. A rarity in any front-engine car, much less
a car in this price field, Gamma's front bucket seats
are judged fair—to-good in comfort—a relatively high
rating in economy car circles. As shown in Table VI,
Gamma's rear seating is the best in the group.

FIGURE 14–5 *Continued*

12

C. Gamma Is Judged Most Durable

The Gamma is assembled with better-than-average care. In fact, Consumer Research engineers have found only 16 minor defects in the car. In addition, the Gamma has a better-than-average record for frequency of repairs. Delta, second in this category, has only 20 problems. Some of these problems are judged serious, however. For instance, in the test run the starter refused to disengage after a few hundred miles had accumulated on the car. The car's ignition timing, idle mixture, and idle speed were incorrectly set. An optically distorted windshield and inside mirror were discovered. In spite of all these defects, the Delta ranks above Alpha and Beta on durability.

Again, a summary conclusion closes a section.

Clearly, Gamma leads in all categories of riding comfort and overall construction. It handles best. It gives the best ride. And it has some definite construction advantages over the other three.

V. RECOMMENDATION OF GAMMA

Normally, a conclusion cannot be drawn from a count of rankings on the evaluations made, for the qualities carry different weights. Cost, for example, is the major factor in most such decisions. In this instance, however, weighting is not necessary, for one automobile is the clear leader on all three of the bases used for evaluation. Thus, it would lead in any arrangement of weights.

A final section recaps and weighs the preceding conclusions and makes the recommendation.

From the data presented, Gamma is the best buy when all cost are considered. The total difference on a purchase of 50 automobiles is a significant $15,114 over the second-place brand. Gamma has a slight edge when safety features are considered. And it is the superior car in handling ease, ride quality, and construction. These facts point clearly to the recommendation that Allied buy Gammas this year.

QUESTIONS FOR DISCUSSION

1. If you decide to use the indirect sequence to write a persuasive report because you anticipate some resistance in your readers, what parts of the report will be affected by that decision?

2. Discuss the relative importance of the title fly and the title page in a report.

3. Distinguish between the letter of transmittal, the preface, and the foreword.

4. What is the basis for deciding if a report should have a table of contents?

5. The executive summary has been described as the report in miniature. What elements of the report are reflected in the executive summary?

6. Why do long, formal reports need more introductory material than short reports?

7. Using as a guide the diagram in Figure 14–2, summarize the coherence plan of the long, formal report.

CASE 14–1

BOSS: Why doesn't this report have a decent cover?

CHESTER: I thought you were just interested in the contents.

BOSS: Well, where's the Table of Contents, then?

CHESTER: Doesn't the index do the same thing?

BOSS: NO! And is this what you call a glossary?

CHESTER: I kept it concise because I thought most of the words and short forms were common jargon.

BOSS: (Groan.) Where are all the tables, maps, and charts you refer to?

CHESTER: They're all together in Appendix B.

BOSS: Wrong! Take this thing away and bring me back a REPORT!

Despite his sarcastic attitude, Chester's boss has raised some valid points. However, he has not given Chester any guidance. Rewrite or role-play the conversation to give Chester the specific and constructive input he needs to bring his report up to professional standards.

ANSWERS TO PRACTICE RUNS

▶Report Titles

Since the wording of the titles will vary, only the components are listed here.

Who	MegaJoy
What	TNT's popularity
Where	n/a
When	Recent (current month & year)
Why	Determine share of market and improve (implied)
How	Consumer survey

Who	Winston Institute
What	Strategies for recovery after recession
Where	Canada & United States
When	n/a
Why	Implied
How	Detailed comparison

REPORT PROBLEMS

1. *Determining the Advertizing Practices of a Discount Store and Its Competition.* (Requires research.) As a management trainee of a major city discount store (you or your instructor will choose it), you have been assigned to conduct a study comparing your store's newspaper advertizing with that of two competitors (you or your instructor will choose these, too).

   As your boss, Carmen Vilas, explained, your store wants a thorough comparison of its print advertizing with that of its competition. You will gather the information you need by carefully inspecting over a two-week period all the newspapers and flyers that carry the advertizing of the three stores. You will systematically measure, examine, and evaluate all the advertizing to obtain the facts you need. Include space measurements, the types of merchandise advertized, the presentation (size of print, use of pictures, colour, glossy or newsprint paper), and the advertizing appeals.

You will present the results of your study in a formal report addressed to Ms. Vilas.

2. *Comparing Two Fitness Centres.* (Requires research.) Your company is willing to subsidize memberships in a fitness club for your employees. It has already been determined that using existing clubs is more feasible than buying equipment and hiring trainers for an on-site club. Investigate at least two clubs in your area, and make a recommendation about which one the company should approach first. Consider accessibility, hours, staff, equipment, facilities and cost of each club. Look for any additional benefits, such as child care, massage services, or special events.

   When you have completed your analyses, you will write a formal report appropriate for the situation. You will organize your material so as to provide the best possible build-up for your recommendations. You will use tables, charts, or graphic aids wherever they help communicate the report story. Address the report to Ms. JoAnne Timmons, Wellness Co-ordinator.

3. *Getting the Facts about Living in Your Area for DeVillier Instruments.* (Requires research.) DeVillier Instruments, a major international manufacturer of electronic equipment, is considering a move of its corporate headquarters to _____ [an appropriate area of your city]. If the move is made, DeVillier wants as many of its 1,800 employees to move here. Before these employees can decide, they will need information.

   The company will help by putting together information about the quality of life in two areas within reasonable commuting distance of the new headquarters. Since they want their staff to move, the presentation of the information is important. First impressions count. But the information must be fair and objective.

   The issues they want investigated include the availability and quality of housing, the accessibility of all levels of education, the availability of recreational and cultural opportunities (parks, athletic facilities, theatres, restaurants), and the variety of shopping facilities. Since many of the employees' spouses will seek employment, the job market should also be investigated. Make some general comments about the weather, the proximity to cottage or wilderness areas, and other geographic points of interest.

   As a management trainee with Leo Romanowski, manager of human relations with DeVillier, you have been given the task of gathering the needed information. You will organize it in an order that conveys your message quickly and easily, and you will present it in a report appropriate for the somewhat formal situation.

4. *Comparing Pharmacies and Pharmacy Departments in Grocery Stores.* You have been asked to prepare a report for a consumer watch organization on the benefits and drawbacks to consumers of having pharmacy departments in grocery chains.

   You will investigate quantitative factors such as selection and cost, as well as qualitative factors such as convenience and knowledgeable staff. You decide to investigate two grocery chains and two drug store chains. You visit four stores, one from each chain, to gather primary data. Your cost comparison is based on five items, one from each of these categories: toothpaste, shampoo, cold remedy, pain reliever, and first aid (antiseptic) cream.

You know that the consumer watch organization may use your report in media presentations, so you carefully plan not only its content but its appearance. Graphic aids are part of your plan, and you choose a formal approach which includes the appropriate prefatory parts. At the end you state your recommendation to consumers on where to shop.

5. *Determining Whether a Discount Store's Prices Are in Line with Those of the Competition.* (Requires research.) Assume that the manager of a local discount store (you or your instructor will select the store) has hired you, an independent research specialist, to compare its prices with those of its two main competitors. For some time she has been hearing that the prices of this or that product are much lower at other stores in town. Such products could, of course, be largely advertized loss leaders—that is, products advertized at low prices merely to attract customers. But the manager isn't sure, and the fact that sales have dropped recently makes her want to investigate the matter. So she has hired you to investigate it for her.

   To get the information you need, you will first select the major departments common to all three stores. Then, from each of these departments, you will select a number of items that all three stores carry. You will take care to select items that adequately represent the products sold in each department and that are easy to check. You will specify these items by grade, quantity, and/or brand. After selecting the items, you will record their prices during visits to the three stores. As you are concerned primarily with normal prices, you will note which prices result from special promotions.

   Your next chore will be to evaluate the data you have collected. Then you'll report the results in a manner appropriate for this somewhat formal situation. You will probably use graphic aids to help your words communicate your major findings. As you prepare the report, bear in mind that the store manager wants you to pinpoint the departments and products that are out of line. Address the report to the store manager.

6. *What Will Your Team Be Like Next Year?* (Requires research.) Assume that you are doing a bit of advance research for a rival school (you name it). Your assignment is to collect, analyze, and report the information available on each of the senior teams (football, volleyball, or whatever your instructor specifies) on the schedule. One, of course, is your own school's team; and that's the one you'll work on first.

   You will begin your work by collecting all the available information on who the players will be—who is returning, who is coming up from the junior teams, and the like. Then you'll collect all the available information on abilities and performance records. Next you will systematically analyze this information. Your analysis will lead to a conclusion on the team's overall strength.

   Of course, you will present the report in an appropriate form.

7. *Solving a Problem on Your Campus.* (Requires research.) From the following list of topic areas, select one that you think needs attention at your college:

   Campus security / Campus crime
   Admission requirements

Faculty-student relations
Curriculum improvement
Decreasing funding and program cuts
Scholastic honesty
Improving cultural atmosphere on campus
Parking, traffic control
Operation of bookstore, library, food service, etc.
 [choose one]
Emphasis on athletics

You will first gather all the significant facts regarding the problem you select. When you are thoroughly acquainted with them, you will gather authoritative opinions concerning the solution. Obtaining such information may involve looking through bibliographic sources to find out what has been done on other campuses. It may involve interviewing people on campus who are attempting to deal with the problem. Next you will carefully analyze your problem, draw your conclusions, and recommend a solution.

Write a formal report addressed to the appropriate administrator.

8. *Determining What Business Will Be Like in the Months Ahead.* (Requires research.) Roland Anderson, president of Northern Lights, an oil and gas exploration company, wants you to write a business forecast for presentation at next Wednesday's meeting of the board of directors.

Since Anderson's instructions were quite vague, much of what you do will depend on your good judgment. All Anderson said was that he wanted you to survey the current business periodicals for the predictions of the leading economic forecasters and to present your findings in a clear and meaningful report to the board. And he wanted the forecasts consolidated—that is, he did not want a mere succession of individual forecasts. Your report will give special emphasis to forecasts pertaining to the oil and gas industry over the next six months to a year.

The report will be in a form appropriate for the board. Because the board members will want to get at the most important material quickly, be sure to include a fast-moving executive summary. Address the report to President Anderson, who also chairs the board.

TOPICS FOR INTERMEDIATE-LENGTH AND LONG REPORTS

▶Accounting

1. Design an inventory control system for Company X.
2. Report to Company X executives on how new tax regulations in the past year will affect their firm. You may limit this topic by level of government, e.g., municipal tax changes.
3. What accounting software should Company X use with its computer?
4. Advise the managers of Company X on the accounting problems that they can anticipate when the company begins overseas operations in _____ [country].
5. For accounting students at your college, develop information that will help them choose between careers in public accounting and careers in private accounting.
6. Report to a group of independent business owners on the status of professional ethics in accounting.

▶Business Education

7. Which business skills should colleges teach, and which should companies teach?
8. Examine and compare the curricula of two postsecondary business education programs.
9. Report on the pros and cons of business internships in a business program.
10. Evaluate the contribution that campus business and professional clubs make to business education.
11. Should business education be specialized, or should it provide a generalized, well-rounded education?

▶Labour

12. For the executives of the National Association of Manufacturers (or some such group), report on the outlook for labour–management relations in the next 12 months.
13. Report on the successes or failures of self-directed (or self-managed) teams.
14. Report on the potential impact of total quality management on Company X.
15. Layoffs based on seniority are causing a disproportionate reduction in the number of women and minority workers at Company X. Investigate alternatives that the company can present to the union.
16. Report on the role of unions (or management) in politics, and recommend a course for them to follow.

▶Finance

17. As a financial consultant, evaluate a specific form of tax shelter for a client.
18. Compare the customer-relations practices of banks, trust companies, and credit unions.
19. Give estate planning advice to a client who is in a unique personal situation.

20. Advise Company X on whether it should lease capital equipment or buy it.
21. Advise Company X on whether it should engage in a joint venture with a company overseas or establish a wholly owned foreign subsidiary.

▶Management

22. Develop a guide to ethics in its highly competitive business situation for Company X.
23. Report on the behavioural and psychological effects of downsizing at Company X as a means of coping with reduced product demand and reduced profits.
24. The manufacturers of automobile and truck tires want a report on the recent increase in demand for recycling of old tires after the serious fires at tire dumps. Include any recommendation that your report justifies.

25. Develop an energy conservation plan for your college.
26. Evaluate internal communications in Company X and make specific suggestions for improvements.
27. As a consultant for an association of farmers, evaluate the recent past and project the future of growing or raising _____ (your choice of farm product).

▶Personnel/Human Resources Administration

28. Prepare a report on the human rights concerns around personality testing for employees and potential employees for Company X.
29. Report on what personnel executives look for in application letters and résumés.

30. Report on the advantages and disadvantages of providing on-site daycare for children of employees.
31. Report on the role of formal wellness programs for employees. Investigate their popularity, their scope, and their success rate.

▶Marketing

32. Review the ethical considerations involved in advertizing directed to children and advise Company X on the matter.
33. For a national department store chain, discover and describe the changing trends in the services that customers expect.
34. Determine the trends in packaging in the _____ industry and the impact the environmental ("green") movement is having.

35. What should Company X include in its site on the World Wide Web?
36. Select the best channel for distribution for new product Y and justify your choice.
37. Report to Company X on telemarketing, direct-mail marketing, or catalogue marketing [choose one] and make a recommendation about its use by the company.

▶Computer Applications

38. Advise Company X about the steps it can take to protect its computerized files from sabotage.
39. Explain for Company X the advantages and disadvantages of the Internet, and advise the company on whether to establish a site.
40. Report to the president of Company X the copyright and contract laws that apply to the use of computer programs.

41. What are the advantages and disadvantages of allowing employees of Company X to do computer-related work at terminals installed in their homes rather than requiring them to do all computer-related work at the office?
42. Report to the International Organization of Business Communication on the impact of electronic technology on business communication in Canada.
43. Determine the future of robotics in the _____ industry.

The Construction and Use of Graphics

15

Upon completing this chapter, you will be able to use graphics effectively in written reports. To reach this goal, you should be able to

1 Determine which parts of your report should be supported by graphics and where in the report they should appear.

2 Explain the general mechanics of constructing graphics—size; layout; borders, lines, and shading; colour and cross-hatching; numbering; titles; title placement; and notes and acknowledgments.

3 Select and construct the best type of graphic for displaying the information.

4 Recognize the potential of computers to assist in the creation of graphics.

▶ to Graphics

Doreen realizes that some of the points she wants to make in her report would be clearer if she included some illustrations. She will also need tables to summarize statistical data. She selects her graphics carefully because she knows they will have a big impact on her readers. Also, she remembers that each type has its own strengths and weaknesses.

For example, one of her innovations is a new type of storage cabinet that saves space and doubles as a work surface. It is not difficult to describe the advantages of the storage unit, but it is difficult to describe its appearance in detail. A photograph, a colour photocopy, or the technical drawing used by the millwright would be possible as illustrations. Doreen decides to make a colour photocopy from a photograph because it will fit into the report easily. If her innovation is adopted for the entire franchise, she can provide the technical drawings. For now, the concept is more important.

Now, what would be best for showing the growth of her business? ■

In many of your reports you will need to use graphic aids. By *graphic aids* we mean any form of illustration: charts, pictures, cartoons, diagrams, maps, tables. Although tables are not truly graphic, they are included in this definition because they perform the same function. They make complex data more easily understood through an arrangement that makes a visual impact.

* A graphic aid is any form of illustration.

PLANNING THE GRAPHIC AIDS

In a report the physical arrangement of data in graphic aids has many benefits. Good graphic aids can

* Graphics are planned to communicate first, impress second.

* display data efficiently for scanning,
* simplify the presentation of complex information,
* show the relationships between various pieces of information,
* reinforce information by repeating it (in textual and graphical format), and
* summarize the content of the message.

In other words, they communicate. Of course, well-constructed graphic aids may also enhance the attractiveness of a report, but this benefit is secondary. Your graphic aids should be rooted in your goal of communicating effectively.

You should plan the graphics for a report soon after you make and organize your findings. In selecting graphic aids, you should review the information that your report will contain, looking for any possibility of improving the message of the report through the use of graphics. Specifically, you should look for complex information that visual presentation can make clear, for information too detailed to be covered in words, and for information that deserves special emphasis.

* In planning their use, look for points in the text that they should support.

As you plan the graphics, remember that they should supplement the writing, not take its place. Graphics must not be allowed to overpower the text. Neither are they a substitute for a clearly worded explanation. Although they can help the writing by summarizing and emphasizing the message, graphics cannot stand alone. The words carry the main message.

* Graphics supplement not replace the writing.

PLACING THE GRAPHICS IN THE REPORT

As well as carrying the main message, your text should introduce and explain the graphic. For the best communication effect, you should place each graphic just after the place where it is covered in writing. Exactly where on the page you should place it, however,

* In the text before the graphic, introduce and explain it.

should be determined by its size. If the graphic is small, place it within the text that covers it. If it is larger than one-half page, place it by itself on the following page.

• Placing graphic aids at the end of the report does not help the readers.

Some old reports have all the graphics at the end, usually in an appendix. Although this arrangement was practical when reports were prepared on typewriters, it is a misuse of the appendix. Moreover, it is comparable to giving a speech about travel in Europe and showing all the slides at the end. Integrating the graphics into the text is much more helpful to your readers. If they have to flip through pages every time they want to see a chart, many will not take the trouble. Your effort to integrate the graphics into your text will be well worthwhile.

• Invite the readers to look at the graphic aids at the right place.

Graphic aids communicate most effectively when they are seen at the right moment because much of their impact comes from their context. Thus, you should refer the readers to a graphic at the most relevant point in the report. When this point is reached, direct the readers to the graphic by saying something like

> Refer to Table 5 on the next page.
> See Figure 16–6 for an example of . . .
> Please consult Chart 4 now to compare the results of . . .

For variety you can use an incidental reference. Of the many possible wordings, here are a few of the most common:

> . . . , as shown on Map 2, . . .
> . . . , indicated in Table 5, . . .
> . . . , as a glance at Chart 1 reveals, . . .

• Explain the graphic.

It is appropriate to explain the graphic to integrate it fully into the flow of the textual material. The explanation highlights the main points, clarifies details, emphasizes connections, and guides the reader through your argument. Consider the following discussion:

> In Chart 6 the large red section of the pie chart shows that more than 60% of our students come directly from high schools in this province. The blue slice shows another 30% coming from the work force or other post-secondary institutions in the western provinces. Only 8% of our students come from other regions of Canada. Based on this evidence, we are a long way from having a national reputation for excellence.

. . . .

A PRACTICE RUN

Using the bar chart in Figure 15–5, write a description to integrate that graphic into a report. Assume that the point you are building towards is that, on a per capita basis, the Vancouver store outperforms any of the others. Your report will have a second graphic to show that point clearly.

_____

_____

_____

_____

_____

. . . .

. . . .

GENERAL MECHANICS OF CONSTRUCTION

In constructing graphics, you will be concerned with various mechanical matters. The most common of these are summarized in the following paragraphs.

Size Determination

One of the first decisions you must make in constructing a graphic is determining its size. This decision should not be arbitrary, and it should not be based on convenience. You should give the graphic the space its content justifies. If a graphic aid is simple (with only two or three quantities), a full page would be too much. However, if a graphic is to display complex or detailed information, a full page would be justified.

    If you must go to a second page for a long table, use carefully constructed headings to show the continuation. With maps or drawings, you may need to use a large page that is inserted and folded. The folds you select will be determined by the size of the page. You simply have to experiment until you find a convenient fold that the readers can open easily.

* Make each graphic the size its content justifies.

* Graphics larger than a page need special treatment.

Layout Arrangement

You should decide on the layout (shape) of the graphic by its size and content requirements. Sometimes a tall, narrow rectangle (referred to as *portrait*) is the answer; sometimes the answer is a short, wide rectangle, possibly with the page turned sideways for greater width (known as *landscape*). You consider the logical possibilities and select the one that allows you to display the information the best.

* Size and content determine the shape of graphic aids.

Borders, Lines, and Shading

Borders, lines, and shading help the appearance of graphics. As a general principle, you should place borders around a graphic that occupies less than a full page to set it off from the text. You can also place borders around full-page graphics, if they improve the appearance, but you should not extend the borders beyond the normal page margins. The internal lines guide the readers' eyes across wide tables and charts. With bubble jet or laser printers, shading is possible. The shaded sections also make a table easier to read at a glance. See Figure 15–1 for examples.

* Use borders, lines, and shading when they help appearance.

Colour and Cross-Hatching

Contrasting colour and/or cross-hatching help the readers see comparisons and distinctions. In addition, they give the report a boost in physical attractiveness. Colour is especially valuable for this purpose, and you should use it whenever practical.

    Cross-hatching is shading with lines that are diagonal, crossed, vertical, and so on, to distinguish areas of a diagram or chart. If your graphics are computer generated and you have a black and white printer, you should select cross-hatching patterns that are easily distinguished from one another. Sometimes this clarity is obvious on the colour monitor but less satisfactory in the printed version. You can only be sure by printing a sample of a graphic.

* Colour and cross-hatching can improve graphic aids.

Numbering

Except for minor tabular displays that are part of the text, you should number all the graphics in the report. Many schemes of numbering are available to you, depending on the makeup of the graphic aids.

    If you have many graphics that fall into two or more categories, you may number the items in each category consecutively. For example, if your report is illustrated by six tables, five charts, and six maps, you may number them Table 1, Table 2, . . . Table 6; Chart 1, Chart 2, . . . Chart 5; and Map 1, Map 2, . . . Map 6.

    But if your graphic aids are a mixture of types, you may number them in two groups: tables and figures. By convention, tables are not grouped with other types of graphic aids. Figures, a miscellaneous grouping, may include all types other than tables. To illustrate, consider a report containing three tables, two maps, three charts, one diagram, and one photograph. You could number these graphics Table 1, Table 2, and Table 3 and Figure 1, Figure 2, . . . Figure 7. Even if there are enough graphics of the same type to permit

* Number graphic aids consecutively by type.

* Figures are a miscellaneous grouping of types. Number tables separately.

FIGURE 15–1   The Use of Shading and Lines in Tables for Clarity

Table 3   Analysis of Costs for Six Months and One Year

	Datanet Central	Smart Serve	Super Gate	World Net
6 months				
set-up charge	$ 25	$ 20	$ 30	$ 30
basic charge	180	210	180	200
overtime charges	120	210	225	0
TOTAL COST	**$325**	**$440**	**$435**	**$230**
1 year				
set-up charge	$ 25	$ 20	0	$ 30
basic charge	360	420	360	360
overtime charges	60	420	360	0
TOTAL COST	**$440**	**$860**	**$720**	**$390**

Table 3   Analysis of Costs for Six Months and One Year

	Datanet Central	Smart Serve	Super Gate	World Net
6 months				
set-up charge	$ 25	$ 20	$ 30	$ 30
basic charge	180	210	180	200
overtime charges	120	210	225	0
TOTAL COST	**$325**	**$440**	**$435**	**$230**
1 year				
set-up charge	$ 25	$ 20	0	$ 30
basic charge	360	420	360	360
overtime charges	60	420	360	0
TOTAL COST	**$440**	**$860**	**$720**	**$390**

separate numbering, it would not be wrong to group them as figures (except, of course, for the tables).[1]

Construction of Titles

- The titles should describe content clearly.

Like the other headings in a report, the title of a graphic should concisely cover the contents. As a check of content coverage, you could use the five *Ws* and *how* again. A title of a chart comparing the annual sales volume of the Toronto and Montreal branches of the Brill Company for 1997 and 1998 might be constructed as follows:

Who: Brill Company

What: Annual sales

Where: Toronto and Montreal branches

When: 1997 and 1998

Why: For comparison

---

[1]Note that a three-dimensional object, model, or display would normally be referred to as an *exhibit*. More commonly used in oral reports and presentations, exhibits are now included with some written reports such as proposals. Exhibits would be numbered separately from the two-dimensional graphics such as charts, tables, and illustrations.

A PRACTICE RUN

How would you number the graphics in these reports?

Report A has five tables, four charts, a diagram, and a map.

_____

_____

Report B has six charts and seven tables.

_____

_____

Report C has two charts, one map, one diagram, and three tables.

_____

_____

The title might read, "Comparative Annual Sales Figures for the Brill Company, Toronto and Montreal Branches, 1997 and 1998." As conciseness is also desired, not all these elements may be necessary in the title. For an internal report, the title could be simplified to "Annual Sales for Toronto and Montreal Branches, 1997 and 1998."

Placement of Titles

Titles of tables conventionally appear above the tabular display; titles of all other types of graphics conventionally appear below. It is also traditional to use a higher type for table titles (usually solid capitals or boldface) than for the titles of other graphics. These conventions are not followed universally except in more formal reports.

* The usual placement of titles is at the top for tables and at the bottom for charts.

Notes and Acknowledgments

Parts of a graphic sometimes require special explanation or elaboration. When this happens, you should use a concise note placed below the graphic. For example, you would include a note to explain that some of your information is a projection based on a

* Use footnotes to explain or elaborate.

FIGURE 15-2 Good Arrangement for the Parts of a Typical Table

TABLE NUMBER AND TITLE				
	Spanner Head		Spanner Head	
	Column Head	Column Head	Column Head	Column Head
Stub	data	data†	data‡	data
Stub	"	"	"	"
Stub	"	"	"	"
Stub	"	"	"	"

†Note of explanation

‡Note of explanation

Source:

partial year's data. Link the note to the part being explained by means of a superscript (raised) number or symbol such as an asterisk, dagger, or double dagger (* † ‡). The notes themselves are usually in a smaller font than any words in the graphic. If the title is under the graphic, the note goes between them. See Figure 15-2 for an illustration.

- Acknowledge the source of the data with a note.

A source acknowledgment is the last note made under the graphic. By *source acknowledgment* we mean a reference to the person or group that deserves the credit for gathering the data used in the illustration. If you created a pie chart using data from Statistics Canada, you can take credit for the design, but Statistics Canada must be acknowledged for the data. The entry consists of the word *Source* followed by a colon and the name. Source notes might read like these:

Source: Canadian Direct Marketing Association

Source: Based on Unemployment Insurance Statistics for June from Statistics Canada.

Because sources for graphics are not usually listed in the bibliography or list of works cited, you should make your source note as specific as you can. For example, if you have drawn the information from one publication, give the full bibliographic information for that source.

Source: Statistics Canada, Industry Division, *Electric Power Generating Stations*, Ottawa: Minister of Supply and Services, 1995:3-6.

- "Source: Primary" is the proper note for data you gathered.

If you collected the data, you may either omit the source note or give the source as "Primary," in which case the note would read:

Source: Primary.

. . . .
CONSTRUCTION OF TEXTUAL GRAPHICS

Tables

- A table is an orderly arrangement of information.

A table is an orderly arrangement of information in rows and columns. As we have noted, tables are not truly graphic because they are not pictorial. They are included because they communicate visually. Moreover, they have many of the requirements of graphics such as titles, notes, and source designations as previously discussed.

- See Figure 15-2 for details of table arrangement.

A table contains columns and rows of data. It has a title and number to identify it. The columns and rows are labelled by *stubs, column heads,* and *spanner heads* as shown in Figure 15-2. Stubs are the titles of the rows of data, and heads are the titles of the columns. Spanner heads are used if the columns are grouped together.

The construction of text tables is largely influenced by their purpose. Nevertheless, a few general construction rules may be listed:

- If rows are long, the stubs may be repeated at the right.

- The *em dash* (—), double hyphen (- -), or the abbreviation *n.a.* (*n/a or NA*), but not the zero, is used to indicate data not available.

- In a numeric table, symbols or lowercase letters are best for linking notes to items in the table because numbers followed by note reference numbers may cause confusion.

- Totals and subtotals should appear whenever they help the purpose of the table. The totals may be for each column and sometimes for each row. Row totals are usually placed at the right, but when they need emphasis, they may be placed at the left. Similarly, column totals are generally placed at the bottom of the column, but they may be placed at the top when the writer wants to emphasize them. A ruled line (usually a double one) separates the totals from their components.

- The units in which the data are recorded must be clear. Unit descriptions (millions of barrels, hectares, kilometres, etc.) appropriately appear above the columns, as part of the headings. If the data are currency, however, placing the currency mark such as $ or £ with the first entry in each column and in the total is sufficient.

A PRACTICE RUN

Complete the following table using the information provided.

Spanner Head:	% of Population by Age Group
Title:	Population of Major Urban Centres by Age: A Projection for the Year 2000
Table Number:	3
Column Heads:	Toronto, Montreal, Vancouver, Calgary, Halifax
Stubs:	City, Total Population†, Median Age, 18–24 Years, 25–40 Years, 40–65 Years, Over 65
Note:	Source: Statistics Canada, 1998
Note:	†Includes metropolitan and surrounding areas

In-Text Displays

Tabular information need not always be presented in formal tables. In fact, short arrangements of data may be presented more effectively as part of the text. Such arrangements are generally made as either leaderwork or text tabulation.

Leaderwork. Leaderwork is the presentation of tabular material in the text without titles or lines. (Leaders are the repeated dots.) Appropriate introductory words precede the tabulation as in this illustration:

* Tabular information can also be presented as (1) leaderwork,

The August sales of the representatives in the Western Region were as follows:

Glenn Eveland $13,517
Ann Lypka 19,703
Toby Reid 18,198

These figures show an average increase of 1.5% over this month last year.

• as (2) text tabulations,

Text Tabulations.   Text tabulations are simple tables, usually with column heads and some lines. They do not have titles because they are made to read with the text, as in this example:

In August the sales of the representatives in the Western Region increased sharply from those for the preceding month, as these figures show:

Representative	July Sales	August Sales	Increase
Glenn Eveland	$12,819	$13,517	$ 698
Ann Lypka	17,225	19,703	2,478
Toby Reid	16,838	18,198	1,360

• and (3) as bullet lists.

Bullet Lists.   Bullet lists are listings of points arranged with bullets (·) to set them off. These lists can have a title that covers all the points, or they can appear without titles. There are examples at various places throughout this book. When you use this arrangement, make the points grammatically parallel. If the points have sub-parts, use sub-bullets for them. Make the sub-bullets different by colour, size, or weight. The filled circle is commonly used for the primary bullets and darts, check marks, squares, and triangles for the secondary ones.

A summary of sales in the Western Region for August, 1997 shows the following information:
· Sales increased by 1.5% over August, 1996.
· Sales increased by $4,536 over July, 1997.
· Ann Lypka accounted for almost 55% of the July to August increase with $2,478 in additional sales.
· Other high producers for August, 1997 included
   · Toby Reid ($1,360)
   · Glenn Eveland ($698)

PICTORIAL TYPES OF GRAPHIC AIDS

• Many of the same rules apply.

The truly pictorial types of graphic aids include a variety of forms. As with tables, these graphics should be introduced in the text, should have a source note to credit the originator of the information, and should be placed at the most relevant point in the text. Titles and labels should be kept horizontal for clarity. Of the many forms available to you, the following are the most widely used.

Organization and Flow Charts

• Various specialized charts are useful in reports.

Various specialized charts are useful in reports. Perhaps the most common of these for business is the organization chart (Figure 15–3) and the flow chart (Figure 15–4). Organization charts show hierarchy of positions, divisions, and departments in an organization. A flowchart, as the name implies, shows the sequence of activities in a process. Technically, flowcharts have specific designs and symbols to represent process variations, but the name is used freely for any diagram showing the direction or flow of a process.

Bar Charts

• Simple bar charts compare differences in quantities by varying bar lengths.

Simple Bar Charts.   Simple bar charts illustrate quantities by the lengths of the bars representing those quantities. You should use them primarily to show the situation at different times or in different locations. Bar charts cannot distinguish fine differences but they are excellent for giving a "snapshot." As shown in Figure 15–5, they are simple to read and give an impression of the situation.

FIGURE 15-3 An Organization Chart

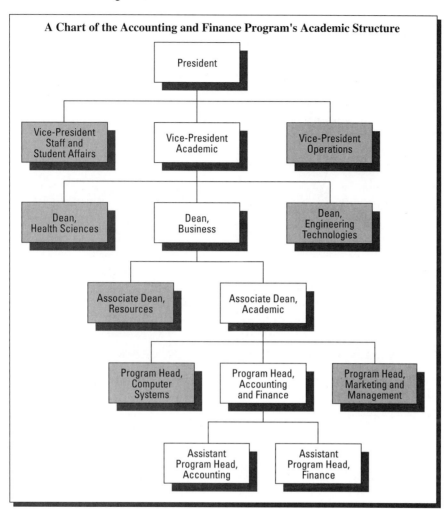

A Chart of the Accounting and Finance Program's Academic Structure

The main parts of the bar chart are the bars and the grid (the field on which the bars are placed). The bars may be arranged horizontally or vertically as long as they are of equal width and clearly labelled. Grid lines may be added to show the magnitudes of the bars. The units (dollars, units sold, kilometres, etc.) are identified by a scale caption.

Multiple Bar Charts.   When you need to compare two or three different kinds of quantities in one chart, you can use a multiple bar chart. In such a chart, bars show the values of the quantities compared. Cross-hatching or colours on the bars distinguish the different kinds of information (see Figure 15-6). Somewhere within the chart, a legend gives a key to the interpretation of the bars. Because multiple bar charts can become cluttered, usually you should not compare more than three kinds of information.

> • Multiple bar charts are useful in comparing two or three kinds of quantities.

The type of information to be compared should be fixed at a certain point in time. That is, a bar chart does not show flow or trends as well as a line chart does. A suitable topic for a bar chart would be the total number of sick leave days taken by two departments in each quarter of the year. A line chart could compare the two departments each month and show the developing trends as seasons change, for example.

Bilateral Bar Charts.   When you need to show positive and negative values, you can use bilateral bar charts. The bars of these charts begin at a central point of reference and may go either up or down, as illustrated in Figure 15-7. Bar titles appear either within, above, or below the bars, depending on which placement fits best. Bilateral bar charts are

> • When you need to show positive and negative values, bilateral bar charts are useful.

FIGURE 15–4   A Simplified Flow Chart

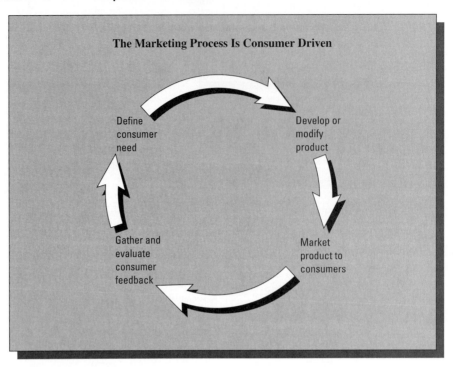

FIGURE 15–5   A Simple Bar Chart

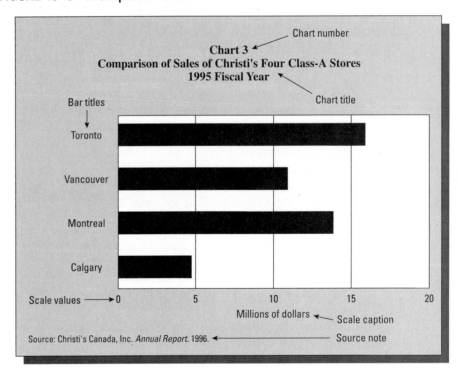

especially good for showing percentage changes, but you may use them for any series in which plus and minus quantities are present.

• To compare the parts of an item, use a subdivided bar chart.

Subdivided Bar Charts.   If you need to compare the parts of an item, you can use a subdivided bar chart. As shown in Figure 15–8, such a chart divides each bar into parts.

FIGURE 15-6 Multiple Bar Chart

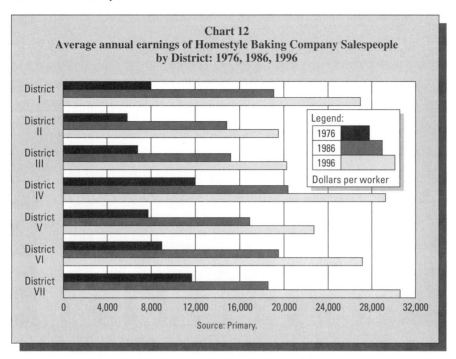

Chart 12
Average annual earnings of Homestyle Baking Company Salespeople
by District: 1976, 1986, 1996

Legend:
1976
1986
1996
Dollars per worker

Source: Primary.

FIGURE 15-7 Bilateral Bar Chart

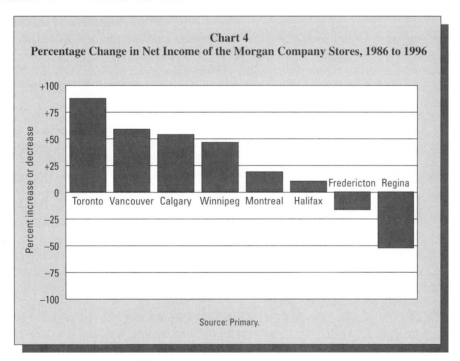

Chart 4
Percentage Change in Net Income of the Morgan Company Stores, 1986 to 1996

Source: Primary.

By using several bars, you can compare these parts over time. You distinguish the parts by colour or cross-hatching and explain them in a legend.

A special form of subdivided bar chart is used to compare the subdivisions by percentages. In this form, because each bar represents 100 percent, all the bars are equal in length. Only the subdivisions within the bars vary. This type of chart might be used to

* You can also use such a chart for comparing subdivisions of the whole by percentages.

FIGURE 15–8   Subdivided Bar Chart

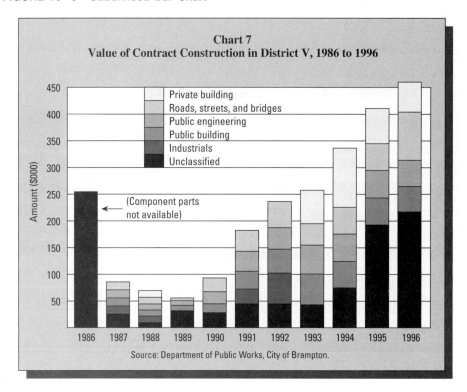

Chart 7
Value of Contract Construction in District V, 1986 to 1996

Source: Department of Public Works, City of Brampton.

compare how tax money was spent by a province over several years. For example, if 4 percent of tax revenue was needed to service the debt ten years ago and 30 percent two years ago, subdivided bars would show which sectors suffered when more money was needed for interest payments. The advantage of the subdivided bar chart is that it allows comparison in how whole items are divided.

Pie Charts

- Pie charts show subdivisions of a whole.

Also important in comparing the divisions of a complete unit is the pie chart (see Figure 15–9). As the name implies, pie charts show the information being studied as a pie (circle) with the parts as slices of the pie. Because well-constructed pie charts are visually appealing and quickly comprehended, they are excellent for oral presentations.

A good rule to follow is to arrange the slices from largest to smallest clockwise around the pie, with the largest slice either beginning at the 12 o'clock position or centred there. For clarity, a maximum of six or seven segments, distinguished by colour or pattern (cross-hatching), is best. As it is hard for the reader to judge the comparative sizes of the slices, their values must be labelled. Percentages are useful; however, including the hard numbers as well gives completeness and accuracy. Again for clarity, it is necessary to keep the labels horizontal.

- If pie charts are to be compared, keep them the same size.

It is possible to use more than one pie chart so that two units and their divisions can be compared. For example, to compare the budgets of two provinces last year, you could use two pie charts side by side. One important point is to keep the circles the same size. If you vary the sizes of the pies, the comparisons are distorted. An alternative to using several pies is to use the subdivided bar chart discussed previously.

Line Charts

- Line charts show changes over time.

Line charts are useful to show trends—changes in information over time. For example, changes in prices, sales totals, employment, or production over a period of years can be shown well in a line chart.

FIGURE 15–9 Pie Chart

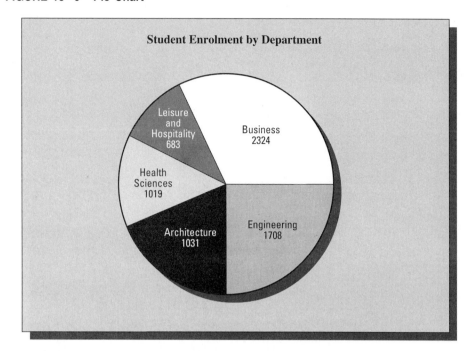

In constructing a line chart, you plot points on two axes and join them to draw a continuous line on a grid (see Figure 15–10). The grid is scaled to show time changes from left to right across the chart (X-axis) and quantity changes from bottom to top (Y-axis). You should clearly mark the scale values and the time periods.

* The line appears on a grid (a scaled area) and is continuous.

You may also compare two or more series on the same line chart (Figure 15–11). In such a comparison, you should clearly distinguish the lines by colour or form (dots, dashes, dots and dashes, etc.). You should clearly label them by a legend somewhere in the chart. As a practical rule, the maximum number of series that you can represent clearly on one line chart is four or five.

* Two or more lines may appear on one chart.

Line charts are simple to construct, but you should guard against three common errors in their construction. The first is the error of violating the zero beginning of the series. For accuracy, you should begin the vertical scale at zero. But, when all the information shown in the chart has high values, it is awkward to show the entire scale from zero to the highest value. For example, if the quantities compared range from 1,320 to 1,350 and the chart shows the entire area from zero to 1,350, the line for these quantities would be almost straight very high on the chart. Starting the scale at a high number (say, 1,300) could distort comparisons with other charts. Your solution is to begin at zero and show a scale break. The following two ways of showing scale breaks are recommended:

* Avoid these errors: (1) failure to start the Y-axis at zero (you can show scale breaks).

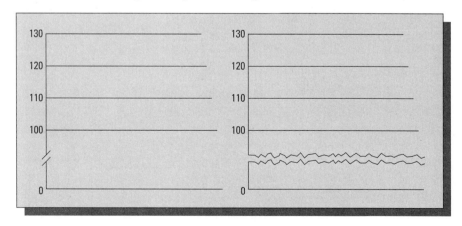

FIGURE 15–10   Line Chart

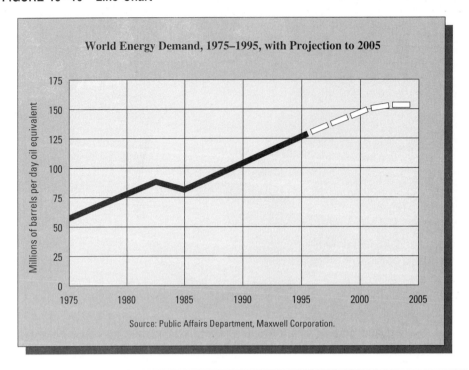

World Energy Demand, 1975–1995, with Projection to 2005

Source: Public Affairs Department, Maxwell Corporation.

FIGURE 15–11   Line Chart with Multiple Lines

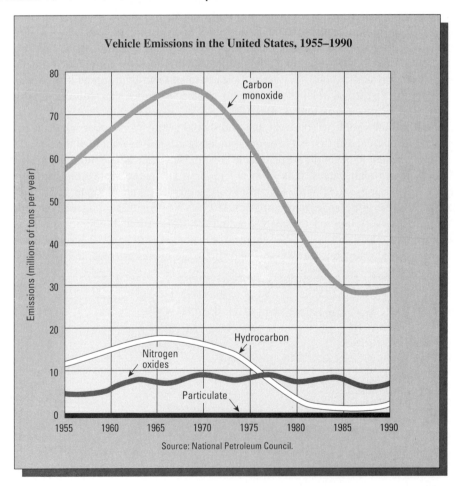

Vehicle Emissions in the United States, 1955–1990

Source: National Petroleum Council.

A second error in constructing line charts is failing to keep the chart's scale uniform. All the dimensions from left to right (X-axis) should be equal, and all those from bottom to top (Y-axis) should be equal. Otherwise, an incorrect picture would be shown.

• (2) failure to keep scales uniform,

A third error is to use grid distances that do not give a true picture of the information. Expanding a scale can change the appearance of the line. For example, if the values on a chart are plotted 5 millimetres apart instead of 20 millimetres, the changes appear to be much more sudden. Determining the distances that present the most favourable and yet still accurate picture is a matter of judgment.

• (3) use of distances on the grid that do not show the true picture.

Variance Charts

Charts that show a range of data for particular times are called *variance* or *hi-lo* charts. As shown in Figure 15–12, some variance charts show high and low points as well as the mean, median, and mode. When used to chart daily stock prices, they typically include the closing price in addition to the high and low. When you use points other than high and low, be sure to make clear what these points are.

• Variance charts show high and low points.

Scatter Diagrams

In a *scatter diagram,* as in a line chart, points are plotted on two axes; however, the points in a scatter diagram are not joined by a line. The locations of the individual points give a visual cue about the relationship between the variables. If the points are scattered randomly, the two variables are unrelated. If the points group towards a line, the pattern tells you the variables are related. An example of a scatter diagram is shown in Figure 15–13.

• Scatter diagrams are used to find trends.

Statistical Maps

You may also use maps to illustrate quantitative information. They are useful primarily when a comparison is by geographic areas. On such maps the areas are clearly outlined and some mechanical technique such as colour or shading is used to show the differences between areas. Of the many techniques available to you, these are the most common:

• You can show quantitative information for geographic areas in a statistical map.

1. Showing quantitative differences of areas by colour, shading, or cross-hatching is perhaps the most popular technique (Figure 15–14). Of course, maps using this technique must have a legend.

• Here are some specific instructions for statistical maps.

FIGURE 15–12   A Variance (Hi-Lo) Chart

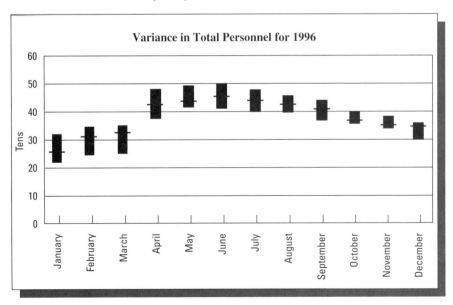

2. Some form of chart may be placed within each geographic area to depict the quantity for that area, as illustrated in Figure 15–15. Bar charts and pie charts are commonly used in such statistical maps.

3. Placing the quantities in numerical form within each geographic area, as shown in Figure 15–16, is another widely used technique.

4. Symbols, each representing a definite quantity (Figure 15–17), may be placed within the geographic areas in proportion to the quantities for those areas.

Pictograms

- Pictograms are charts made with pictures.

- In constructing pictograms, follow the procedure for making bar charts.

A pictogram is a chart that uses bars made of pictures. The pictures are typically drawings of the items being compared. For example, a company's profits over a period of years, instead of being shown by ordinary bars, could be shown by drawings of stacks of coins or lines of dollar signs (see Figure 15–18).

In constructing a pictogram, you should follow the procedures you used in constructing bar charts plus two special rules. First, you must make all the picture units equal in size. That is, you must base the comparisons wholly on the number of picture units used rather than on a variation in the size of the pictures. This rule is a practical one because

FIGURE 15–13 A Scatter Diagram

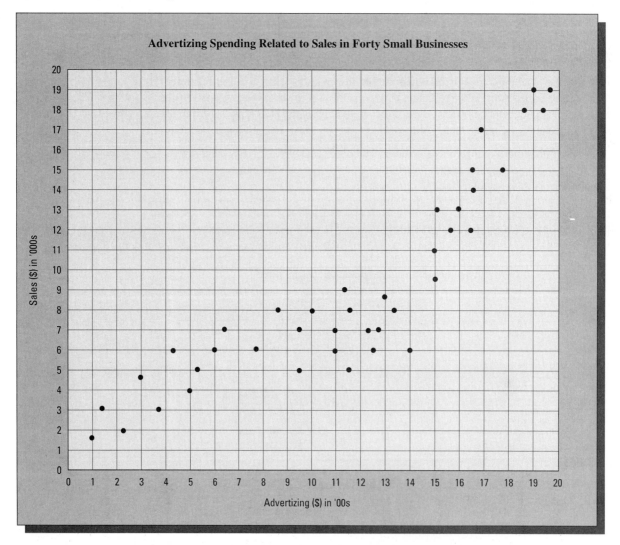

FIGURE 15–14   Statistical Map Using Shading

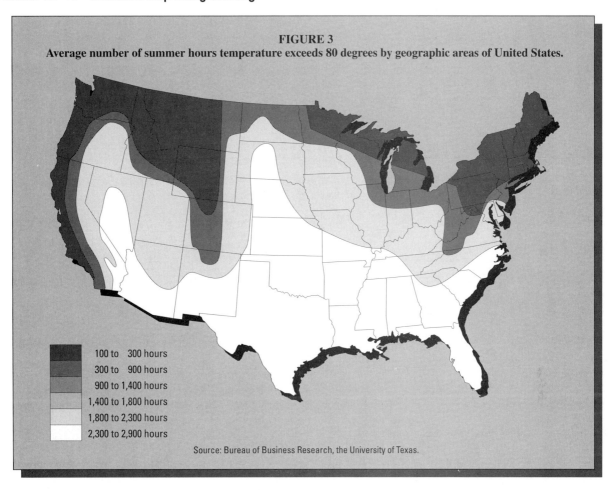

FIGURE 3
Average number of summer hours temperature exceeds 80 degrees by geographic areas of United States.

100 to   300 hours
300 to   900 hours
900 to 1,400 hours
1,400 to 1,800 hours
1,800 to 2,300 hours
2,300 to 2,900 hours

Source: Bureau of Business Research, the University of Texas.

FIGURE 15–15   Statistical Map Showing Comparisons by Charts within Geographic Areas

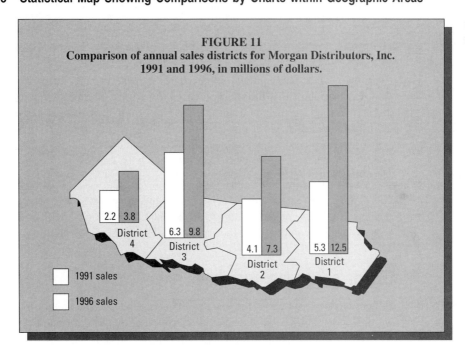

FIGURE 11
Comparison of annual sales districts for Morgan Distributors, Inc.
1991 and 1996, in millions of dollars.

2.2 3.8
District 4

6.3 9.8
District 3

4.1 7.3
District 2

5.3 12.5
District 1

1991 sales

1996 sales

FIGURE 15–16 Statistical Map Showing Quantitative Differences Numerically within Geographic Areas

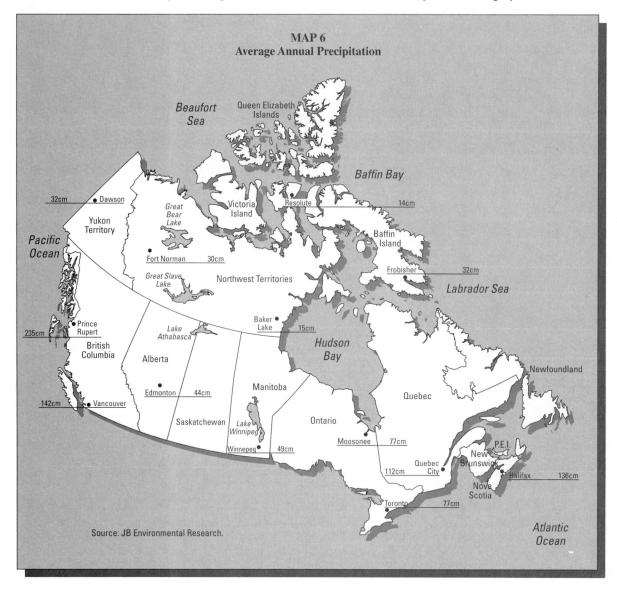

MAP 6
Average Annual Precipitation

Source: JB Environmental Research.

the human eye cannot compare geometric designs accurately. Second, you should select pictures or symbols that fit the information to be illustrated. In comparing the number of flights an airline has to certain destinations, for example, you might use jets. In comparing the wheat production of various provinces, you might use sheaves or grain elevators. The symbolism of the drawings you use should be immediately clear to the readers.

Miscellaneous Graphic Aids

- Other graphic aids available to you are diagrams, drawings, and photographs.

There are many other types of graphics available to you. Photographs, diagrams, sketches, cartoons, models, and videos are just a few. Any graphic aid is acceptable as long as it helps communicate the true story. The possibilities are almost unlimited.

USE OF COMPUTER GRAPHICS

- Computer programs offer many graphics options.

If there is any doubt about the truth of the old saying, "One picture is worth a thousand words," it can quickly be dispelled by considering modern computer programs. Not only are there specialized graphics packages, but almost all full word processing packages have

FIGURE 15-17   Statistical Map Using Symbols to Show Quantities within Geographic Areas

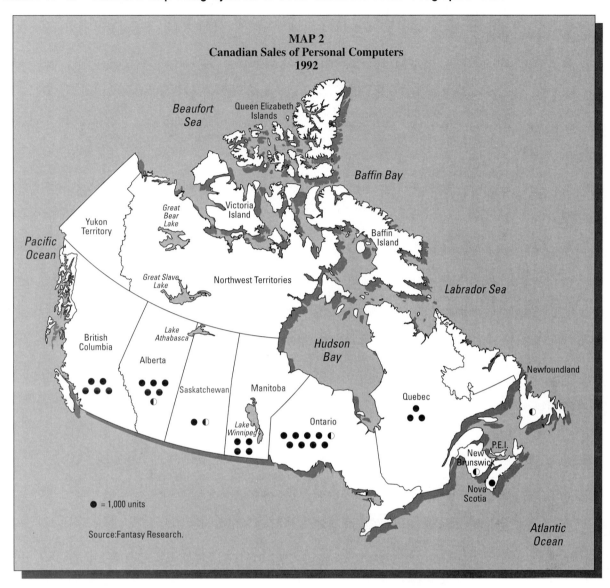

MAP 2
Canadian Sales of Personal Computers
1992

● = 1,000 units

Source:Fantasy Research.

graphics options—some are approaching the level of desktop publishing. Even spreadsheet and database programs have graphics options to display quantitative data conveniently and effectively. Don't overlook these options. If you spend a little more time with a computer package, you can reap the benefits of graphic support for your presentations.

If you have access to the appropriate computer, printer, and software, you can use them to prepare graphics quickly and easily. With some graphics software programs, you need only choose the form of graph you want and then supply the information the program requests. For example, when using one popular program to construct a bar chart, you simply respond "Bar" to the initial request for chart type. Then you answer on-screen questions about the number of bars, the labels for each bar, and the value each bar represents. As you supply the answers, the results appear on the screen. After producing the bar chart on the screen, you can manipulate its design until it meets your ideal requirements. When you are satisfied with the design you see on the screen, you print the chart in black and white or in colour.

Technology makes it easy to reproduce charts or illustrations from books or databases. A moment with a scanner is all it takes. However, you are liable if you infringe on

* Specialized computer graphics programs are not complicated to operate.

* Avoid plagiarism and copyright infringement.

A PRACTICE RUN

For each of the areas of information described below, select the appropriate form of graphic. Be prepared to explain your decision.

a. Record of annual sales for the Kenyon Company for the past 20 years.

_____

b. Comparison of Kenyon Company sales, by product, for this year and last year.

_____

c. Monthly production of minivans by the big three automakers.

_____

d. Breakdown of how the average middle-income family in your province disposes of its income dollar.

_____

e. Comparison of sales for the past two years for each of the B&B Company's 14 sales districts. The districts cover all of Canada, the continental United States, and Mexico.

_____

. . . .

someone else's copyright. Read carefully before you scan or download! And, of course, document your sources.

* Ease of use can encourage overuse.

Because computer graphics are easy to make and can be exciting and colourful, you may be tempted to overuse them. Keep in mind that the one requirement for including a graphic aid in a report is usefulness in communicating the report message. Too many charts can clutter the report, delay the message, and cause confusion.

FIGURE 15–18   Illustration of the Pictogram

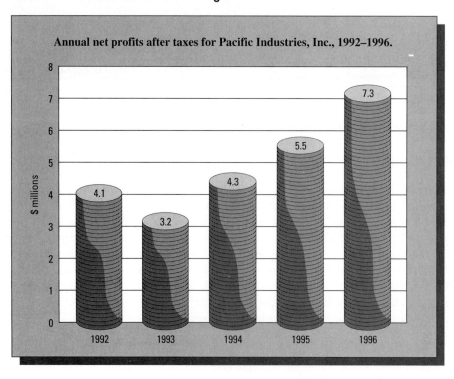

Also keep in mind that clarity is a major requirement of communicating with graphics. The possibilities for changing and enhancing graphics can lead to interesting, beautiful, exciting, but confusing results. Even though the software package will do much of the planning and thinking for you, the guidelines presented in this chapter should be in your mind as you construct graphics by computer.

A SUMMARY OF LEARNING OUTCOMES FROM THIS CHAPTER

You should plan the graphics for your report, remembering that they supplement the words rather than replace them. You use them whenever they help communicate.

You should place the graphics closely following the text messages they cover, and you should introduce them at the appropriate place in the text by inviting the readers to look at them. In constructing graphic aids, give each the size and arrangement its contents justify; and use lines, borders, and shading when they help. Number the graphics consecutively by type. Using the five Ws (*who, what, where, when, why*) and *how,* construct appropriate titles. If notes and acknowledgments are necessary, place them below the graphics.

Tables are orderly arrangements of information in columns and rows. They use titles, stubs, column heads, and, sometimes, spanner heads to identify information. You will sometimes want to present tabular information as a part of the text rather than in a formal table. You may do this as leaderwork or as text tabulations.

The truly pictorial types of graphic aids include a variety of forms. For instructions on the mechanics of each form, review the illustrations in the chapter. Table 15–1 presents the primary uses of each form.

TABLE 15–1 Common Charts and Their Uses

Simple bar chart	to compare quantities at different times or geographic locations
Multiple bar chart	to compare two or three kinds of quantities on one chart
Bilateral bar chart	to show positive and negative values, especially percentage changes
Subdivided bar chart	to compare differences in the division of wholes
Pie charts	to show how wholes are divided
Line charts	to show changes over time
Variance charts	to show high and low points
Scatter diagrams	to uncover trends and relationships
Statistical maps	to show quantitative differences by geographic areas
Pictograms	to show quantitative differences in picture form

Computer graphics packages are very helpful in producing attractive, accurate graphic aids, but the same rules for appropriate and effective use apply.

QUESTIONS FOR DISCUSSION

1. "My report was too short. It didn't look very important. So I put all the graphics on separate pages and expanded them to the full size of the page." Comment on the success of this action to gain credibility.

2. "I have placed the charts carefully in the body of my report. The reader can see them without any introduction in the text." Evaluate this comment.

3. "My computer program lets me put eight lines on a line chart. I guess the rules have changed from the times when people drew charts by hand." Discuss the advantages and dangers of using graphics software.

4. The data you gathered for a graphic came from three places. You created the graphic yourself to allow your readers to compare the facts. Do you need a source note? If so, how would you word it and where would you place it?

5. Both Jennifer and Christina chose multiple bar graphs to display the following data. However, Jennifer put the dates on the *y* axis while Christina put the taxation areas on the *y* axis. What different comparisons would be shown by these methods? Which way is standard?

6. Why is it important to select an appropriate scale for constructing a chart grid? Explain the logic of showing scale breaks in a chart.

Share of Real Estate Tax Payments by Area for Shelburne in Thousands of Dollars			
	1989	1994	1999†
Area 1	27.1	17.6	11.8
Area 2	23.4	21.8	20.4
Area 3	21.5	21.1	20.8
Area 4	20.2	21.3	20.2
Area 5	7.8	18.2	26.8
City Total	100	100	100

†Projected

7. Discuss the techniques that may be used to show quantitative differences by area on a statistical map.

8. Select data that are ideally suited for presentation in a pictogram. Explain why use of a pictogram is good for this case.

9. Discuss the limitations of pictograms.

CASE 15–1: CAUGHT IN THE NET

Mehran: Hey, Rod! I was surfing the net last night and dug up some great information for my report. Just look at all these stats I can throw into a table or a chart. And here's a graphic I found. I won't have any trouble getting a top mark on this one.

Rod: Wow! Yeah. That's pretty neat stuff. How recent is it?

Mehran: Up to the minute, I guess. After all, it was on the net.

Rod: So who did the research? Is it a reliable source?

Mehran: I don't know. I got so into it. I just jumped from one place to the next. Who knows where I ended up. That's the fun of surfing, eh?

Rod: So, how are you going to credit the sources?

Mehran: I thought about that a bit this morning, but then I thought, hey, people know when they put something on the web that it is available all around the world. I figure the web is public, so I can use anything I want. Besides, it's not like

I'm going to make any money here. This report is just for my economics class, and no one's going to care about a few numbers. The tables and charts will be mine 'cause I'll have to set them up. As long as they fit with the graphic, who'll know?

Discussion

Take the role of the following people and give an answer to Mehran.

· The web site creators
· Mehran's friend, Rod
· The marker of the paper
· The college administration
· The future employer of Mehran

ANSWERS TO PRACTICE RUNS

►Describing a Graphic

Answers will vary widely. You will refer to the chart and present the figures for the four stores. You will also need to make a transition to add the population factor. A simple transition would be, "Although Toronto and Montreal have the highest sales volume, their success is related to the size of their market. As Chart 4 shows, Vancouver is the most successful store on a per capita basis."

▶Numbering Graphics

Report A
Table 1, Table 2, ... Table 5; Chart 1, Chart 2, ... Chart 4;
Figure 1, Figure 2
or Table 1, Table 2, ... Table 5; Figure 1, Figure 2, ... Figure 6

Report B
Chart 1, Chart 2, ... Chart 6; Table 1, Table 2, ... Table 6

Report C
Figure 1, Figure 2, ... Figure 4; Table 1, Table 2, Table 3

▶Completing a Table

TABLE 3   Population of Major Urban Centres by Age: A Projection for the Year 2000

City	Total Population†	Median Age	% of Population by Age Group			
			18–24 Years	25–40 Years	41–65 Years	Over 65
Toronto						
Montreal						
Vancouver						
Calgary						
Halifax						

†Includes metropolitan and surrounding areas.

Source: Statistics Canada. 1998

▶Choosing the Form of the Graphic

a. Line Graph

b. Subdivided Bar Chart with two bars or two pies in one Pie Chart

c. Line Graph with three lines

d. Simple Bar Chart with a bar for each category, Subdivided Bar Chart, or Pie Chart

e. Map

▶Exercises

1. A table showing total attendance at home football games at your school for every second year from 1988 to 1998 requires an explanation for the years 1992 to 1996. In those years one extra home game was played. Write the note for the necessary explanation. Explain how it should be formatted for inclusion with the table.

2. For each of the following sets of facts, (*a*) determine the graphic aid (or aids) that would be best, (*b*) defend your choice, and (*c*) construct the graphic aid.

   (*a*) Average (mean) amount of life insurance owned by Fidelity Life Insurance Company policyholders. Classification is by annual income.

Income	Average Life Insurance
Under $20,000	$ 5,245
$20,000–24,999	14,460
$25,000–29,999	26,680
$30,000–34,999	35,875
$35,000–39,999	41,440
$40,000 and over	56,390

   (*b*) Profits and losses for D&H Foods, Nova Scotia by store, 1992–96, in dollars.

	Store			
Year	Annapolis	Digby	Yarmouth	Total
1992	13,421	3,241	9,766	26,428
1993	12,911	(1,173)	11,847	23,585
1994	13,843	(2,241)	11,606	23,208
1995	12,673	2,865	13,551	29,089
1996	13,008	7,145	15,482	35,635

(c) Percentage change in sales by employee for 1994–95 at Abbot, Inc.

Employee	Percentage Change
Joan Abraham	+7.3
Helen Craig	+2.1
Todd Johnson	–7.5
Clifton Nevers	+41.6
Wilson Platt	+7.4
Clara Ruiz	+11.5
David Schlimmer	–4.8
Phil Veitch	–3.6

3. The basic blood groups are O, A, B, and AB. These can be either positive or negative. With some basic research, determine what percentage of people in Canada have each type. Choose an appropriate graph type and create it to convey the data.

4. Through research, find the approximate number of milligrams of caffeine in the following items and create an appropriate graphic to illustrate your findings.

> a cup of coffee (drip brewed)
> a cup of tea
> a glass of cola with caffeine
> 1-oz. semi-sweet dark chocolate

5. Choose four or five exercise machines. In a graphic identify each machine and show whether it gives cardiovascular or muscular workout. If it helps to build muscle, specify upper body, lower body, back, or abdominal areas. You can assume a machine will affect more than one fitness zone.

SPEAKING IN BUSINESS

16

Oral Communication

Upon completing this chapter, you will be able to lead and participate in meetings, conduct interviews, dictate messages, and communicate by telephone using good speaking techniques. To reach this goal, you should be able to

1 Discuss the techniques for conducting and participating in meetings.

2 Practise good interviewing techniques as both an interviewer and an interviewee.

3 Dictate letters and reports in an organized and effective manner.

4 Describe good procedure for courteous and efficient handling of business telephone calls and voice mail.

▷ to Oral Communication on the Job

Doreen was unhappy with herself. She had called a meeting of all her Good 'n Nice employees to deal with some problems relating to customer service. Because there were only a few points to discuss, she didn't plan an agenda. What she needed to say was clear in her own mind. However, in the meeting, the situation was quite different. Someone asked a question right at the start that put her off track. Then there was a lot of informal chatter in small groups. To bring the meeting back to order, Doreen raised her voice. Needless to say, the reaction from her staff was less than positive! She closed the meeting without accomplishing all her goals.

To complete her less than ideal day, Doreen answered the telephone while she was still upset and was dismayed to hear her frustration coming out in her tone of voice with a customer. Of course she knew better, but everything seemed to happen so quickly.

"Next time, I'm going to be more careful," she promised herself. "I can't afford careless words that alienate my staff and my customers." ▪

THE IMPORTANCE OF ORAL COMMUNICATION

As a student looking ahead to a business career, you will probably see written communication as a major challenge, but oral communication will be just as challenging. On the job, you will spend large portions of each day speaking and listening. In fact, you will likely spend more time in oral communication than in any other work activity. While the old saying "Practice makes perfect" undoubtedly holds some truth, practice can also lull us into a state of overconfidence or carelessness. Rather than taking speaking skills for granted, we need to examine and develop them.

- You will spend more time talking than writing in business.

In preparation for this chapter, you may need to review the sections on nonverbal communication and listening from Chapter 2. Those topics are integral to effective oral communication skills.

- Review the sections on nonverbal communication and listening.

Much of the oral communication that goes on in business is the informal, person-to-person conversation that takes place whenever people get together. While not unimportant to business, the topic of casual communication will not be dealt with in these chapters. We will focus on the various kinds of structured oral communication for business. These include formal presentations such as speeches, lectures, and oral reports, and interactive communication such as meetings, group discussions, and interviews. The topic of interviews will be expanded from the job interview situation to include other types such as exit interviews or personnel evaluations. This chapter covers participating in meetings, conducting interviews, dictating, and using the telephone and voice mail. The following chapter covers public speaking and oral reporting.

- Oral communication has two sides, the casual and the structured.

CONDUCTING AND PARTICIPATING IN MEETINGS

From time to time, you will participate in business meetings. They will range from formal conferences and committee meetings to informal discussions with groups of fellow workers. The participants may include people you have lunch with every day and people who are complete strangers to you. There may be people with high status and power within the company, as well as the newest junior recruit. The level of success of any of these meetings will be determined by the quality of the communication that occurs.

- Meetings involve oral communication.

Whether your role in a meeting is that of leader or participant, there are techniques that will help you make the meeting a success. Of course, the leader plays a primary role, but good participation is also vital. The following paragraphs review the skills for performing well in either role.

- A successful meeting needs a skillful leader and good participants.

Meetings of formal committees, boards of directors, and professional organizations usually follow generally accepted rules of conduct called *parliamentary procedure.* These very specific rules are too detailed for review here. When you are involved in a formal meeting, you would do well to study one of the books covering parliamentary procedure before the meeting. For less formal meetings, you can depart somewhat from parliamentary procedure, but you should keep in mind that every meeting has goals and that informality should never hinder reaching them.

- In formal meetings, you need to know parliamentary procedure.

Techniques of Conducting Meetings

Maintaining discreet but firm control of a meeting is not an easy task. Each participant is a unique personality who may be bringing a particular concern to the meeting. Some participants may not be on friendly terms. Issues may be hotly debated, and positions vehemently defended. Chairing a meeting effectively is a skill developed by observation and practice. These notes will be a beginning.

Plan the Meeting.   A key to conducting a successful meeting is to plan it thoroughly. Know what the goal or purpose is for the meeting and be able to state it concisely. Then, develop an *agenda.* An agenda is a list of topics to be included in the meeting for discussion and/or decision. Only those items that are needed to achieve the goals of the meeting should be included.

- The leader of a meeting should plan the agenda.

An agenda is not haphazard. Careful planning goes into the arrangement of the items. When assigning an item's place on the agenda, consider the relationship between items. Does one item depend upon the decision of another? Does a positive vote about one item mean there is no need for discussion about a second?

- Arrange the selected items in an intentional order. Consider the relationship between items,

The complexity of the item also helps to determine its place. A complex topic is not a good beginning for a meeting because the group has not yet settled into working together. It is usually best to begin with one or two simple items to set a tone for the meeting. A complex item should not be left until last either because there may not be time for the thorough discussion it needs. A good place for a difficult topic is somewhere in the middle, possibly immediately before a break. Then, having solved the complex issue, people can stretch, relax, and refocus in the short break.

- the complexity of the topic,

A very controversial issue is similar to the complex one in that it is not a good beginning or closing for a meeting. If it is placed at the beginning and tempers flare during the discussion of this topic, the rest of the meeting will be hindered. If it is placed at the end, there may not be adequate time and people may leave feeling frustrated and angry. The grapevine will be very busy after such a meeting.

- the degree of controversy surrounding the item, and

Some agenda items have traditional places. Housekeeping issues such as establishing a quorum (being sure that enough members of the committee are present to hold a meeting), reading and approving the minutes, and approving the agenda come at the beginning of the meeting. A miscellaneous *Other Business* category appears at the end. A break is normally scheduled a little over halfway through the allotted time in a long meeting.

- the traditional procedure.

An agenda does more than list the topics for discussion. It also tells who will speak to the item, that is, who is responsible for the presentation of that item. An estimated time is also included so that those who wish to comment will know how long they have. This time limit can be adjusted with the agreement of members at the meeting.

- Include the person responsible and the estimated time beside each item.

The purpose of the agenda is not just to regulate the running of the meeting. It is also to allow participants to be prepared to discuss the items listed. Therefore, after preparing the agenda, make it available to those who will attend. As a rule the agenda should be distributed a week before the meeting.

- Distribute the agenda early.

Select the Participants.   The participants for some meetings are easy to select. The members of the committee are those who will attend a committee meeting. The selection of participants for other meetings is more complex. There may be guests who need to be invited to provide information or make a report. If the meeting's purpose is to solve a problem, a representative from each area affected by the problem will need to attend. In addition, those who have the power to make the changes needed to solve the problem should be involved. The leader must try to anticipate the needs of the meeting, and, usually in consultation with others in authority, select the appropriate participants.

• The leader confirms who should attend the meeting.

. . . .

A PRACTICE RUN

Suggest who should be invited to participate in a meeting on the following topics at your school.

Changing the entrance requirements for your college.

_____

_____

Making changes to the curriculum in your program.

_____

_____

Making changes in the scheduling of assignments in this course.

_____

_____

. . . .

Follow the Plan.   The leader is responsible for seeing that the meeting accomplishes its goal. That means following the agenda. If people discuss items out of order or introduce new items, you must step in. A statement such as "That issue will be addressed under agenda item 6. We need to complete our discussion of this item first," will usually bring the meeting back to order. For a new item, you can suggest that it be taken up at the end under *Other Business,* or perhaps noted for the agenda of a future meeting. For this present meeting, follow your plan.

• The leader directs the meeting by following the plan item by item.

Move the Discussion Along.   As leader, you should manage the agenda. When one item has been covered, bring up the next item. When the discussion wanders off subject, move it back on subject. If the discussion becomes repetitive, ask if the participants are ready to make a decision. If there are no new points being added, people are probably ready to vote. If one person is monopolizing the floor, direct the discussion to someone else. In general, do what is needed to proceed through the items efficiently, remembering that participants need time to make and consider all the important points. You will have to use your listening skills and your good judgment to allow complete discussion on the one hand and to avoid unnecessary repetition, excessive detail, and useless comments on the other hand.

• The leader manages the discussion.

Encourage Participation from Those Who Talk Too Little.   Just as some people talk too much, some talk too little. Sometimes people are shy or hesitant. In a business meeting, those who hold lower positions in the organization may be reluctant to speak. Your job as leader is to encourage these people to participate by asking them for their viewpoints, by showing respect for the comments they make, and by acknowledging their contributions.

• The leader encourages everybody to take part in the discussion.

Control Time.   At the beginning of your meeting, you need to agree on the time limits suggested on the agenda. Once that is done, you need only remind the members of the time status during the meeting. If the meeting runs overtime, you should ask the participants if they can stay longer or if another meeting needs to be scheduled.

• The leader maintains control of the time for discussion.

Technology is making its way into meetings, assisting in numerous ways, and changing the basic structure of meetings to some degree. Electronic Meeting Systems (EMS) is one example. EMS software links the participants electronically through their computers. The participants take part by typing on their keyboard and reading the responses of others on the screen. They may be in the same room or at a distance. They can be typing their ideas together at the same time or, for less urgent matters, at a different, later time, convenient to the individual.

When the EMS is used within the context of a traditional meeting, the technology is usually combined with oral communication. For example, the discussion breaks for a few moments while everyone brainstorms, typing their ideas into the system. Research has shown that appropriate use of the various components of the EMS toolkit helps meeting participants improve their performance and accomplish their goals in half the time of the traditional meeting. EMS is faster because everyone can be on-line together, "talking" all at once. The slow turn taking of the traditional meeting is eliminated.

This tool also changes the nature of meetings. Most electronic meeting systems elicit equal participation, preventing one person from dominating the meeting. Additionally, some systems allow participants to maintain anonymity, entering their ideas through the network without others knowing whose idea it is. This removes the effects of status and personal bias. Many people claim this feature alone improves quality by allowing participants to respond to the idea, not who said it. Others attribute the increased quality to the ability of the system to force an agenda and keep people focused on the task at hand. Finally, this tool keeps a record of all the ideas entered; no thoughts are lost as they often are in traditional meetings.

A variation of the EMS is the meeting held on-line over a period of time rather than at a precise time. While not quite the same as the traditional meeting, the performance of groups meeting on-line this way has been good. Electronic meetings can also be held in geographically dispersed settings. A major benefit of this feature is its ability to allow groups access to experts otherwise unable to attend a face-to-face meeting.

As more is learned about the effectiveness of technology in assisting with different tasks, these tools will certainly be enhanced and further developed. Using these tools appropriately makes group work and group tasks seem easier.

A PRACTICE RUN

Because group meetings are meaningful only when they concern problems that the participants know about and understand, the following topics for meetings involve campus situations. For one of these topics, develop a specific problem that would warrant a group meeting. Then lead a section of the class (or participate) in a meeting on the topic. After the meeting, evaluate its success.

a) Scholastic dishonesty
b) Library
c) Attendance policies
d) Parking
e) Homework requirements
f) Student evaluation of faculty
g) Student government
h) Grading standards
i) Intramural athletics
j) Examination scheduling
k) Tuition and fees

Summarize at Appropriate Places. As the leader of the meeting, you should give a summary whenever it will help the group members understand their accomplishments. After a key item has been discussed, you should review what the group has covered and concluded before moving ahead to the next agenda item. If the group makes a decision, recording the vote would be the conclusion. At the end of the meeting, summarize all the progress made. For formal meetings, minutes kept by the secretary provide another summary.

• At appropriate places, the leader summarizes what the group has covered and concluded.

Closing and Follow-Up. The official closing of a meeting is just as important as calling it to order. As mentioned above, a summary of the progress made is usually a part of the closing. A second part is the clarification of the duties assigned during the meeting. Finally, thanks to the participants and acknowledgment of special contributions are appropriate. After the meeting is adjourned, informal discussion may continue, but the participants are free to leave. The minutes will record the time the meeting ended.

• The leader closes the meeting and provides follow-up.

The end of the meeting is not the end of the leader's work. A record of the meeting should be distributed. Although you do not prepare these notes, you must ensure that the job is done. For formal meetings, the secretary of the meeting will prepare minutes. For informal meetings, the task of recording can be on a voluntary or rotating basis. A record of decisions made and action required is usually sufficient. The minutes need to include the names of the people responsible for the action and the deadlines to be met. Each participant should receive a copy within a few days of the meeting.

Techniques for Participating in a Meeting

From the preceding discussion of the techniques that a leader should use, you know something about the things that a participant should do. The following review emphasizes them for you.

• As a participant in a meeting you should

Be prepared. The agenda was prepared for you. Use it well before the meeting to plan what documents you need to bring, what points you want to make, and what questions you want answered. Be sure you can discuss each topic intelligently and concisely.

• (1) be prepared,

Follow the Agenda. When an agenda exists, you should follow it. Specifically, you should not bring up items not on the agenda or comment on such items if others bring them up. When there is no agenda, you should stay within the general limits of the goal for the meeting.

• (2) follow the agenda,

Participate.   The purpose of meetings is to get the input of everybody concerned. Thus, you should participate. Your participation, however, should be meaningful. You should talk when you have something to contribute; you should talk only when you have something to contribute.

Do Not Talk Too Much.   Although you should speak up whenever you have something to say, you need to be sure that what you say will contribute useful information to the discussion. Then when you do speak, the remarks you make should be concise and to the point.

Co-operate.   A meeting by its very nature requires co-operation from all the participants. So keep this in mind as you participate. Respect the leader and his or her efforts to move through the agenda efficiently. Respect the other participants and work with them in every practical way.

Be Courteous.   Courtesy might be included as a part of being co-operative, but specifically mentioning this trait is useful. Pay attention to the rights and feelings of others. Show respect for the other participants by permitting them to speak and listening carefully to their ideas. Keeping your comments on the topic and staying away from personal grudges or clashes is also polite and considerate.

INTERVIEWING PEOPLE

In your work in business, you may need to participate in a variety of types of interviews. Perhaps the best-known type is the employment interview discussed in Chapter 11, but there are others. Interviews are often involved in the periodic evaluations that some companies make of their workers. These interviews are primarily a means of communicating the evaluations. When workers leave a company, they may be interviewed to determine their reasons for leaving. Interviews are sometimes conducted to gather information on such matters as worker attitudes, working conditions, managerial effectiveness, and worker plans.

Interviewing is not a precise activity—that is, few hard-and-fast rules exist. It is a flexible activity that requires the good judgment of the people involved. Nevertheless, well-established guidelines exist for both the interviewer and the interviewee.

Guidelines for the Interviewer

If you are the interviewer, the success of the interview is in your hands. Thus, it is especially important to know and follow these general guidelines.

Plan the Interview.   Most interviews are conducted because of a need for information. So as a starting point, you should determine your information needs. You can usually express these needs in a list of specific questions leading to your goal. You should make such a list and use it as the outline for the interview.

Put the Interviewee at Ease.   The chances are that the interviewee will be nervous. As nervous people are unlikely to give information freely, you should try to put the interviewee at ease. How you should do this varies with the person involved and with your social skills. You could, for example, begin with some friendly talk on a point of common interest. Or you could begin with simple, non-threatening discussion about the interviewee's hometown, sports interests, or hobbies.

Make the Purpose Clear.   The interviewee should know the purpose of the interview from the beginning. Sometimes the purpose is obvious, as in an employment interview. Nevertheless, the purpose should be stated clearly. If the interviewee has any doubt about the purpose, the interviewer should give a more detailed explanation about the goal and the possible outcomes.

Let the Interviewee Do Most of the Talking. You can get the information you seek only when the interviewee talks. Thus, you should manage the process so that the interviewee does most of the talking. You should talk only to guide the course of the interview—to carry the discussion through specific questions. The commonly quoted ratio is interviewee, 80 percent, and interviewer, 20 percent. As some interviewees are reluctant to talk, you will sometimes need to encourage them to speak freely. But you should never put words in their mouths.

• (4) allow the interviewee to do the talking,

Guide the Interview. Even though the interviewee does most of the talking, your task is to guide the interview so as to obtain the needed information. That is, you follow the plan you set up in the beginning. You ask specific questions, and you summarize answers when you have the information you need. In guiding the interview, you will need to handle moments of silence. Brief periods of silence are acceptable if the interviewee is considering an answer, but too much silence can be awkward for all concerned. A long silence indicates that the interviewer needs to rephrase the question or take a different approach.

• (5) guide the interview through the plan,

Listen. You should listen carefully to all that the interviewee says. In addition to listening, you should give the appearance of listening. Your interviewees will be more relaxed and will talk more if they feel that they have your undivided attention.

• (6) listen and make it apparent that you are listening,

Keep a Record. You will need to make a record of the interview. How you record the information may vary with the situation. When you need detailed information, you may have to take notes during the interview. Because your writing may be disturbing to the interviewee, you should explain at the beginning why you must take notes. Even after explaining, you should write as quickly and briefly as possible. Try to avoid writing notes immediately after a damaging or negative admission. Wait for a good point, and then write your notes about both points. In this way your note-taking will not inhibit the interviewee from giving you the complete information you want.

• (7) record information either during the interview or soon after, and

Even if you decide not to write during the interview, you should make notes soon after the interview is over. Few people can accurately remember detailed information for very long.

End the Interview. As you are in charge of the interview, you should end it. If the situation justifies it, some friendly talk can follow the questioning. However, you should avoid letting the conversation trail off to meaningless talk. One good way of ending interviews is to ask a finalizing question—one that tells the interviewee that the interview is over. This one does the job well: "Is there anything else you would like to tell me?" After the response and discussion, you can say, "Well then, thanks for giving me your time."

• (8) end the interview, perhaps with a finalizing question.

Guidelines for the Interviewee

When you are the person being interviewed, you may have little control over the situation. Nevertheless, you can help make the interview successful by following these guidelines.

• Here are some guidelines for the interviewee:

Prepare for the Interview. When you know the nature of the interview, prepare for it. Do enough preparation so that even if you become angry, nervous, or upset, your points will still be clear. Your feelings must not dominate the interview.

• (1) prepare (anticipate questions and plan your answers),

Your preparation should consist mainly of thinking about the questions you are likely to be asked and formulating answers to them. It may also include gathering additional information. For a job interview, for example, you would be wise to learn what you can about the company—its history, its current activities, its plans. For an exit interview you should plan a concise statement about why you are leaving and put it as positively as possible while still being honest.

You should also plan the questions you want to ask. In an exit interview, you might ask how long your records are kept, or when you can expect severance or holiday pay.

Preparation will impress the interviewer and contribute to the success of the interview. However, even if you prepare diligently, you are not likely to cover all that will be asked. So be prepared for the unexpected.

- (2) make an appropriate appearance,

Make an Appropriate Appearance. What the interviewer sees is a part of the message that he or she receives. You should do what you can to make an appearance appropriate for the situation. You will find that the conventional standards of neatness and dress are desirable in most cases. In addition, you will usually want your posture, facial expressions, and physical movements to give favourable impressions.

- (3) show interest (look at the interviewer and pay attention),

Show Interest. You can improve the impression you make in most interview situations by showing interest. You should look at the interviewer and give your undivided attention to the discussion.

- (4) answer correctly and completely, and

Answer Correctly and Completely. If a question in the interview serves a legitimate purpose, it deserves correct and complete answers. If you do not know the answer, or if you decide not to provide the requested information, you are usually better to state your position. Inaccurate or vague answers only confuse the situation and prolong the interview process.

- (5) be courteous.

Practise Courtesy. Once again you should remember the value of courtesy in business. Courtesy plays a major part in the impression you make. The interview situation is no exception, so be courteous throughout the interview.

. . . .

A PRACTICE RUN

Working with a classmate, assume that you are a researcher conducting a survey on career goals of business students. You want to consider their previous education, background, and experience; their expectations upon graduation; and their expectations five years after graduation. Conduct a personal interview to gather your information. Be sure that the interviewee is at ease so that he/she will answer freely. Listen carefully for the full meaning. Use appropriate encouragers and open-ended questions to get as much relevant information as possible.

. . . .

. . . .

DICTATING LETTERS AND MEMOS

- Dictating letters onto tape is a convenient time saver.

With increased travel, many business people find keeping notes on a hand-held tape recorder is an effective time saver. On airplanes, in automobiles, in quiet restaurants, letters, notes, and reminders are being dictated for later transcription. Others are discovering the convenience of voice-activated computers that accept voice dictation as well as keyboard input. The ability to dictate is also useful for dictating a motion to be put before a meeting. In all these circumstances, clear dictation requires that you follow these guidelines.

Techniques of Dictating

- You should (1) get all the information you need, to avoid interruptions later;

Gather the Facts. Your first logical step in dictating is to get all the information you need for the message. This step involves such activities as getting past correspondence from the files, consulting with other employees, and finding out company policy. Unless you get all the information you need, you will be unable to complete the work.

- (2) plan the message;

Plan the Message. With the facts of the case before you, you next plan the message. You may prefer to do this step in your mind or to jot down a few notes or an outline.

Whatever your preference, your goal in this step is to decide what your message will be and how you will present it. Apply the procedures covered in our earlier review of writing letters and memos.

Give Preliminary Information and Instructions.   Your first step in the actual process of dictating is to give the stenographer specific instructions. These include instructions about special handling, enclosures, and page layout. For example, "This letter will be sent with a copy of our annual report, so it will require a large envelope." They also include all the necessary additional information about the message—such information as the mailing address, subject line, attention line, and salutation. When this information is easily available, you need only refer to the source (for example, "Get the address from our supplier database").

* (3) dictate instructions, such as form, enclosures, inside address, and subject line;

Make the Words Flow.   Your next step is to talk through the message. Simple as this step appears, you are likely to have problems with it. Thinking out loud to a machine unsettles most of us at first.

* (4) talk through the message forcing the words to flow if necessary;

Overcoming this problem requires self-discipline. You should force yourself to concentrate and to make the words flow. Your goal should be to get the words out—to talk through the message. A rough draft is fine. You need not be concerned with producing polished work on the first effort. After you have forced your way through enough messages, the speed and quality of your dictation will improve.

Speak in a Strong, Clear Voice.   As your dictation must be heard over the sound of a keyboard, you should dictate in a strong, clear voice. Speak at a speed slow enough to separate the words clearly. Words that do not stand out clearly can cause delays for the typist as well as errors in the message. Be especially careful to eliminate or compensate for extraneous background noise.

* (5) speak so that the stenographer can understand each word;

Give Paragraphing, Punctuation, and Other Mechanics as Needed.   How much of the paragraphing, spelling, punctuation, and other mechanics you should include in your dictation depends on your stenographer's ability. You may leave these matters to a stenographer who is competent in writing correctness and form. For clarity, however, it would be wise to dictate most such information. Your dictation might well sound like this. (The instructions are indicated by italics.)

* (6) give as much instruction on paragraphing, punctuation, and mechanics as is needed; and

"Dear Ms. Schmidt *S-C-H-M-I-D-T colon and new paragraph* On Friday *comma* November 12 *comma* your order for 18 cases of Nu-Mix *comma* with 12 500 *hyphen* gram packages per case *comma* should reach your loading docks *period*."

Avoid Asides.   Asides (comments not intended to be a part of the message) should be avoided. They tend to confuse the stenographer, who must decide which words are part of the message and which are not. As proof, imagine the stenographer's difficulty in handling the following dictation (asides in italics):

* (7) avoid asides.

Dear Mr. Dobbs: *Well, let's see. How about this?* The attached cheque for $19.45 . . . *Is that the right amount?* . . . is our way of showing you that your good faith in us is appreciated. *That should make him happy.* Our satisfaction-or-money-back policy means what it says.

Use Play-Back Intelligently.   Although you should try to talk through the message without interruption, you will sometimes need to stop and get a play-back of what you have said. But do this only when necessary. For a smooth-flowing letter, it is preferable to complete an entire draft letter before using the play-back.

* Use play-back when this helps you.

Once the draft is completed, begin the editing process with play-back. Your dictated letter will need editing just as much as, or perhaps more than, your written letters. It is a simple matter to re-record a paragraph or a new letter that more nearly achieves your goal.

Letter Dictation Illustrated

• Here is an illustration of the dictation of a letter.

Many of the foregoing techniques are illustrated in the following example of the dictation of a routine letter. This example shows all the dictator's words, with instructions and asides in italics.

Let's acknowledge the Key Grocer Company order next. Get the address from the order. It's no. 9. Dear Mr. Key Colon. First paragraph. Three crates of orchard *hyphen* fresh Tex-acates should be in your store sometime Wednesday morning as they were shipped today by Greene *that's G-R-E-E-N-E* Motor Freight *period.* As you requested in your August 29th order *comma* the $61.60 *open parenthesis* Invoice 14721 *close parenthesis* was charged to your account *period. New paragraph* Your customers will go for these large tasty avoca-dos *comma* I am sure *period.* They are the best we have handled in months *period. New paragraph* Thanks *comma* Mr. Key *comma* for another opportunity to serve you *period.* Sincerely *comma and type it for my signature.*

. . . .

A PRACTICE RUN

Working with a classmate, select a letter problem from the "Letter Problems" sections following Chapters 5, 6, or 7. Then dictate the letter to your classmate. After you have finished your dictation, exchange roles with your classmate. (If possible, try a tape-recorded message as well.)

. . . .

. . . .

USING THE TELEPHONE

• Many business people are discourteous and inefficient in telephone communication.

A discussion of business telephone techniques may appear trivial at first thought. After all, most of us have had long experience in using the telephone and feel that we have little to learn about it. Although some of us have excellent telephone skills, you have only to call a few businesses to learn that some users of the telephone are less proficient. You will get some gruff, cold greetings; you will be subjected to a variety of discourtesies. Almost certainly you will find costly instances of inefficient use of time.

Most progressive businesses are aware of the need for good telephone habits, but awareness is only the first step to improvement. Training, practice, and reinforcement are necessary to ensure friendly, professional telephone skills. Too many employees are told to be business-like on the phone but not told how to accomplish this style.

Excellent telephone techniques are critical because very often the first and sometimes the last contact a customer has with the company is on the phone. Effective telephone usage is especially important in Canada because of the convenience and speed with which telephones bridge the geographic distances. Canadians are among the heaviest phone users in the world. The following pointers are intended to help you get positive results from your telephone contacts.

Need for Appropriate Voice Quality

• Because only sound is involved, friendly voices are important.

In reviewing good telephone techniques, keep in mind that a telephone conversation is a unique form of oral communication. Only voices are heard; the speakers are not seen. Impressions are received only from the words and the quality of the voices. Thus, when speaking by telephone, it is extremely important that you work to make the sound of your voice match the purpose of your message.

• So talk as if you were in face-to-face conversation.

One often suggested way of improving your telephone voice is to talk as if you were face-to-face with the other person. If you want your voice to sound cheerful and friendly, try smiling and gesturing as you talk. Even though the receiver will not see the smile, it will help you speak more naturally. If you want your voice to sound assertive, try standing to help you feel in control of the situation. You may want to look ahead to Chapter 17 to the section about improving the quality of your voice, varying your pitch, and changing the pacing of your words to make your voice match your message. Perhaps the best instructional device for this problem is to record some practice telephone conversations. Then judge for yourself how you sound and how you can improve.

Need for Vocalized Encouragers and Regulators

Because telephone communication has no visual cues, all encouragers (the cues that encourage the speaker to continue or elaborate) have to be audible. Just nods or smiles will not work. Use words and sounds such as "Yes," "I see," and "Hmmm" to show that you are listening, are interested, and want the conversation to continue. Similarly, regulators (the cues that help speaker and listener pace the conversation and change roles) also have to be audible. In face-to-face conversation, eye contact is the key regulator. On the telephone use short questions, such as "What do you think?" Interrogative tags also work well. For example, "Your policy is to ship within three days, isn't it?" And, of course, be sure to pause long enough for the other person to begin to speak.

* All cues must be audible.

Effective Telephone Procedures

If you have worked in business for any length of time, you have probably experienced most of the common telephone discourtesies. You probably know that most of them are not intended as discourtesies but are the results of lack of knowledge or lack of concern. The following review should help you avoid them.

* Be courteous.

The recommended procedure when you are calling is to introduce yourself immediately and then to ask for the person with whom you want to talk:

* When calling, immediately introduce yourself and ask for the person you want (or explain your purpose).

"Good morning. This is Wanda Tidwell of Tioga Milling Company. May I speak with Mr. Martinez, please?"

If you are not certain with whom you should talk, explain the purpose of your call:

"Hello. This is Wanda Tidwell of Tioga Milling Company. I have a question about your service warranty on our photocopiers. Whom should I talk to about it?"

At the beginning of a telephone conversation that you have initiated, it is good practice to state the purpose of the call. Then you should systematically cover all the points involved. For important calls, you should plan the points you want to cover, even to the extent of making notes. Then you should follow your notes to make certain that nothing important is left out.

* State your purpose early. Then cover your points systematically. Plan important calls.

When a secretary or someone else who is screening calls answers the telephone, the recommended procedure is first to identify the company or office and then to make a cheerful offer of assistance:

* When receiving a call, identify your company or office; then offer assistance.

"Rowan Insurance Company. How may I direct your call?"
"Ms. Santo's office. May I help you?"

When a call goes directly into an office instead of through a switchboard, the procedure is much the same, except that the person identifies herself or himself:

"Bartosh Realty. Toby Lenuik speaking. May I help you?"

When calls are screened, special care should be taken not to offend the caller. The following exchange leaves the impression that Mr. Gordon may be in but does not want to talk with this particular caller.

* Avoid offending callers by asking misleading questions, by making misleading comments,

"Cowan and Smith. May I help you?"
"Mr. Gordon please."
"Who is calling?"
"This is Pat Yamamoto."
"I am sorry, but Mr. Gordon is not in."

A better procedure would be to state directly, "Mr. Gordon is not in right now. May I ask him to return your call?" Or perhaps "Mr. Gordon is away from his desk at the moment.

Can someone else help you?" could be used. Ask for the caller's name only when the action has been stated.

> "Cowan and Smith. May I help you?"
> "Mr. Gordon, please."
> "Mr. Gordon is away from his desk. Can someone else help you?"
> "No, I need to talk to him."
> "I see. May I have him call you when he returns?"
> "Yes, that will be fine."
> "And your name please?"

• or by being inconsiderate in placing callers on hold. Let the callers choose, and check on the hold status continually.

With long distance calls becoming more and more common, being put on hold can become expensive. Especially irritating to callers is being put on hold for unreasonable periods of time. If the person being called is on another line or involved in some other activity, it may be desirable to place the caller on hold. The choice, however, should be the caller's. ("Mr. Gordon is taking another call. Would you like to hold?") If the hold continues for a period longer than anticipated, the receptionist should check back with the caller, showing concern and offering assistance. ("Mr. Gordon's line is still busy. Would you prefer to have him call you when he is free?") Equally irritating is the practice of having a secretary place a call for an executive and then put the person called on hold until the executive is free to talk. While it may appear efficient to use secretaries for such work, as a matter of courtesy, the executive should be ready to talk the moment the call goes through.

• Be considerate, listen, and do not dominate. Use time efficiently.

Courteous procedure is much the same in a telephone conversation as in a face-to-face conversation. You listen when the other person is talking. You refrain from interrupting. You avoid dominating the conversation. And perhaps most important of all, you cover your message quickly, saving time (and money) for all concerned.

Effective Voice Mail Techniques

• Voice mail is growing in popularity with business.

Many companies are installing voice mail systems to help them keep in touch with their customers and clients as economically as possible. The advantage of voice mail systems over simple answering machines is that they have a password to protect access to the messages. While this is not a foolproof protection, it is enough to discourage the curious. The first advantage for you as the caller is the ability to leave a voice message in an electronic voice mailbox for a person who is not in to receive the call. Not only do you save the time of having to call back, but also you can leave a more detailed message than is practical to leave with a receptionist.

• A voice mail message follows the principles of any other telephone call,

You need to be prepared with a message that is complete, concise, and clear. You begin the message by stating your name and affiliation. Try to speak naturally while being careful to enunciate clearly. A taped telephone message is more difficult to hear than the original. Begin with an overview of the message and continue with details. If you want the listener to take action, call for it at the end. If you want the listener to return your call, state that precisely, including your number and the time when you can be reached. Close with a brief goodwill message. For example, as a volunteer for your local symphony, you might leave this message in the voice mailbox of one of your sponsors:

> This is Linda Wang from the Tri-City Symphony. I'm calling to remind you about the Summer Pops special concert for sponsors. The concert will be on Friday, June 25, at 7:30 P.M. at Mayfair Park on LaSalle Road and 24th Avenue. Fireworks will begin immediately after the concert. To attend, please call the symphony office between 10 A.M. and 4 P.M. Monday through Friday for tickets. You can reach us at 764-0017. We look forward to hearing from you.

• Voice mail handles routine orders and requests.

In combination with touch phone technology, voice mail systems allow you to do more than leave a message. They usually offer a menu of activities to help you get to the right department or even place credit card orders. Many long distance telephone calls are now handled electronically by voice mail. The recorded instructions guide you. They might begin:

"Thank you for calling your long distance service. If you wish to place a calling card call, press 1. If you want to call collect, press 2." If you press 2, you are asked to state your name. The person who must accept the charge hears a taped message with your name inserted. "You have a collect call from _____ If you wish to accept the charge, press 1 or say "yes" after the tone. . ."

The limitations in current voice recognition technology create frustration for people who find "Ah, yes" not accepted by the system as a positive answer. Similarly, "No, thanks," "Yes, fine," and "O.K." will not be understood. The responses must be exactly as asked for in the message. Because it has limitations and is still resisted by those who object to talking to a machine, voice mail systems must include the option of talking to a live operator.

Telephone companies are rapidly adopting the "Talking Yellow Pages" concept. This, too, is a voice mail system. By dialling the number and selecting the appropriate department, you can obtain information about swimming pools, current news, or a soap opera update. Some television channels and newspapers conduct polls through this system asking people to register their opinion about an issue.

Another common voice mail activity is registering at a college or university. As long as each student has a student number and each department has a department number and each course has a course number, the procedure can be handled automatically using the tones of a touch telephone. To use these systems, you simply listen carefully to the instructions and key the appropriate response number. If you do not respond, most systems will give you another opportunity. For example, "Your response has not been registered. If you want to . . . " From these examples and from your own experience, you will realize that the voice mail concept is rapidly changing the way we conduct business.[1]

In this chapter we have discussed many of the everyday communication activities that sometimes are overlooked or taken for granted. Because most of your workday will be spent on these activities, your attention to these skills will help you in your efforts to become a consistently good communicator.

A PRACTICE RUN

Make a list of voice quality traits including both positive and negative features. Call some businesses after hours to get their recorded telephone answering message. (Or call a voice mail system such as Aeroplan or the Talking Yellow Pages if one is available in your area.) Evaluate the message based on the traits you have listed. Record the company name and the telephone number for verification.

A SUMMARY OF LEARNING OUTCOMES FROM THIS CHAPTER

In your work in business, you are likely to participate in meetings often. The more formal meetings follow parliamentary procedure, but many business meetings are more informal.

When you are in charge of a meeting, plan it carefully. Develop an agenda, and circulate it in advance. At the meeting, follow the agenda. Keep the discussion moving. Control those who talk too much, and encourage participation from those who talk too little. Also control time, making sure that the agenda is covered within the time limit. At appropriate places, summarize what has been done.

When you are a participant in a meeting, you also have responsibilities. You need to be prepared for the meeting. You should follow the agenda and not those who stray from it. You should participate fully without talking too much, and you should be co-operative and courteous.

---

[1]Most telephone companies offer answering systems for residential telephones as well with separate mail boxes for each member of the household. As an example, the recorded answer might include "To leave a message for Jeremy, press 1. For Amy, press 2. For Val, press 3."

Interviewing is another form of oral communication in which you are likely to participate. There are various types of interviews, such as employment interviews, interviews for performance reviews, and interviews on job exits. In conducting them, you should follow these guidelines: (1) Plan the interview to get the information you need. (2) Begin by putting the interviewee at ease. (3) Make certain the interviewee knows the purpose. (4) Let the interviewee do most of the talking. (5) Guide the interview, making sure to get all the information you need. (6) Listen carefully, and give the appearance of listening. (7) Keep a record (take notes). (8) End the interview, perhaps with a finalizing question.

When you are being interviewed, you need to follow these guidelines: (1) Prepare by anticipating possible questions and gathering the information needed to respond. (2) Make a good impression through dressing suitably for the occasion and being aware of posture, facial expression, and other nonverbal cues. (3) Show interest. (4) Answer correctly and completely. (5) Be courteous.

The ability to dictate is a useful skill. To do it well, first gather all the information you will need so you will not have to interrupt your dictating to get it. Next, plan (think through) the message. Begin the dictation by giving the stenographer any special information or instructions needed (enclosures, form, special handling, address, etc.). Then talk through the message. Until you are experienced, force the words—then revise. Remember to speak in a strong, clear voice. It is usually good to include punctuation and paragraphing in the dictation. Avoid asides (side comments). Use play-back only when necessary.

Good telephone technique is not so easy as one might think, but it is very important to the success of a business. To give a favourable impression, you should work to make your voice sound pleasant, and you should take care to be courteous. When calling, introduce yourself and ask for the person you want. When receiving a call, identify your company or office and offer assistance. Take care not to offend by asking questions or making comments that might give a wrong impression or by neglecting callers who have been placed on hold.

Desired procedures are much the same in telephone conversation as in face-to-face communication. Listen when the other person is talking, and do not interrupt or dominate. In addition, state your purpose early in the conversation, and cover the points systematically. When the conversation is long or important, plan it before calling, and then follow the plan.

For good communication using voice mail, follow these suggestions:

· Deliver a complete and accurate message, giving important information slowly

· Speak naturally and clearly

· Close with a brief goodwill message

· Listen to instructions carefully and follow the menu steps.

QUESTIONS FOR DISCUSSION

1. The people attending a meeting—not the leader—should determine the agenda. Discuss.
2. As meetings should be democratic, everyone present should be permitted to talk as much as he or she wants without interference from the leader. Discuss.
3. Assume that you are a local politician, business leader, or celebrity. What questions would you anticipate being asked by a reporter in an interview. How would you answer them?
4. Justify each dictating technique suggested in the chapter.
5. "I think receptionists are underpaid for what they do. The receptionist answering the telephones and greeting clients at the front desk has one of the most important jobs in the office." Discuss.
6. Discuss the benefits of voice mail for a busy office. Can you think of any disadvantages?

CASE 16-1

Julie: I have a chance to interview Dr. Managré, the chairman of this year's United Way Campaign, for the staff newsletter.

Vince: Are you looking forward to it?

Julie: Yeah, but I'm not sure how to go about it. He's only giving me 20 to 30 minutes. I'm taking him for coffee at the Bagel Café. They have nice, quiet booths there, and it isn't too expensive for me. I have a small tape recorder that I hope he'll let me use. Or maybe I'll just keep it hidden. [Sigh.] I don't know. It's just hard to know what to do so I don't get the glossy brochure kind of answers.

Vince: What do you mean?

Julie: Well, I want a fresh approach. You know, the inside scoop kind of thing. And I want specific information that gives people a clear idea of what the United Way does. I don't just want a list of the non-profit, service organizations they helped last year, or the amount they collected. We're pretty important to United Way, you know. I got the interview because our staff raised the largest amount per capita of

any company in the region last year. I want to write something that will put us on top again this year.

Vince: I'll help you write out some questions if you like. What if you telephoned his office ahead of time to let him know what kind of information you want? Maybe they would want you to fax him the questions.

Discussion

Pick out ideas from this discussion that you think are good tips to someone preparing for such an interview. What are the benefits to be gained from these tips?

What advice would you give Julie that would help her improve her approach to Dr. Managré? Defend your suggestions.

Help Julie focus her expectations for a fresh approach by suggesting some questions for her to ask.

ANSWERS TO PRACTICE RUNS

▶Meeting Participants

Changing the entrance requirements for your college.
    This type of meeting would require high level officials from your college. Guests from the Board of Education, from high schools, and from government could be included. Students, instructional staff, and industry representatives should also be invited to give input.
Making changes to the curriculum in your program.
    This meeting would require representatives of the administration for the department or faculty as well as for the program. Instructors in the subject areas, students, and industry representatives should be included.

Making changes in the scheduling of assignments in this course.
    This meeting may include only student representatives from your class and your instructional staff. In other schools all who currently teach the course, or the co-ordinator or chair for the course may need to be consulted. Some schools attempt to co-ordinate assignment dates across the program. In that case the meeting participants would include a much wider representation.

17

Public Speaking and Oral Reporting

CHAPTER OBJECTIVES

Upon completing this chapter, you will be able to use good public speaking and oral reporting techniques. To reach this goal, you should be able to

1 Appreciate the differences between oral and written presentations.

2 Explain the role of a speaker's confidence, sincerity, friendliness, thoroughness, and nervousness in an oral presentation.

3 Explain the effect of nonverbal cues from the speaker's environment, personal appearance, facial expressions, eye contact, and gestures.

4 Make use of pitch, speed, and volume to add interest and emphasis when speaking.

5 Create a structure for impromptu speeches.

6 Use visual aids to support speeches and oral reports.

7 Select and organize a subject for effective formal presentation to a specific audience.

8 Work effectively with a group in a team presentation.

▷ to Formal Speaking

Doreen set aside the letter from head office. "A trip to Toronto with travel, accommodation, and meals paid. All I have to do is make an oral presentation of my report. That should be pretty easy since the report is written already," she mused.

As the days passed, Doreen reflected more on the opportunity she had. Gradually, she realized the task was not easy. There were many important details to consider. Her list began:

• What will I wear?

• Who will be in the audience?

• What will they want to know?

• Should I read my report, memorize it, or speak from notes.

• Should I have visuals to show while I speak?

• ... ■

DIFFERENCES BETWEEN ORAL AND WRITTEN PRESENTATIONS

Oral presentations have many similarities with written reports, so rather than repeating much of the previous material on reports, we will focus on the most significant differences between oral and written reports. Three in particular stand out.

• Oral presentations differ from written works in these ways:

Visual Advantages of the Written Word

The first significant difference between oral and written reports is that writing permits greater use of symbols for clear communication. A writer can use paragraphing and headings to show readers the structure of the message and to make the thought units stand out. In addition, punctuation shows relationships, subordination, and qualification. These techniques improve the communication effect of the entire message.

• (1) writing uses symbols such as paragraph indentions and punctuation while speaking uses inflection, pauses, and gestures;

To accomplish the same tasks in an oral presentation, a speaker uses inflection, pauses, volume emphasis, and changes in the rate of delivery. Clearly, both oral and written reports have techniques that are effective in communication. But the techniques are different, and the appropriate skills must be learned.

Reader Control of Written Presentation

A second significant difference between oral and written reports is the degree of control the receiver has. The readers of a written report control the pace of the communication. They can pause, reread, change their rate of reading, or stop as they choose. Since the readers set the pace, the report can contain complex and difficult information and still communicate. On the other hand, the listeners to an oral report cannot control the timing or the pace of the presentation. They cannot choose to listen at another, more convenient time. They cannot review unless the speaker does. The listeners must grasp the intended meaning as the speaker presents the words. Because of this limiting factor, good oral reporting must be relatively simple.

• (2) the speaker controls the pace of an oral report, and the reader controls the pace of a written report; and

Emphasis on Correctness in Writing

A third significant difference between oral and written reports is the different degree of mechanical correctness that they require. Because written reports are likely to be read without the presence of the writer to explain anything, the writer must follow the recognized rules of punctuation, paragraphing, and spelling. In oral reports, while correct grammar is required, mechanics are less evident. However, a speaker must pay close attention to correct pronunciation, both for clarity and for the comfort of the audience.

• (3) written reports place more stress on correctness in mechanics.

CONSIDERATION OF INTANGIBLE ASPECTS

* A logical preliminary to speech-making is to analyze yourself as a speaker.

A preliminary to good speech-making is to analyze yourself as a speaker. In oral presentations you the speaker are a very real part of the message. The members of your audience take in not only the words you communicate but also what they see in you. And what they see in you can significantly affect the meanings that develop in their minds. Thus, you should carefully evaluate your personal effect on your message. You should do whatever you can to sharpen your strengths and overcome your shortcomings.

Confidence

* Having confidence in yourself is important. So is having the confidence of your audience.

A primary characteristic of effective oral reporting is confidence—your confidence in yourself and the confidence of your audience in you. The two are complementary. Your confidence in yourself tends to produce an aura that gives your audience confidence in you, and your audience's confidence in you can give you a sense of security that increases your confidence in yourself.

* You must establish your credibility and earn the confidence of your audience.

Typically, you earn your audience's confidence by proving your credibility. As your presentation progresses, you show your knowledge of the topic, your objectivity and fairness, and your accuracy and thoroughness. But there are things you can do right away to project an image of credibility. For example, thoroughly preparing and practising your opening will help you deliver it with a confidence that will be reassuring to both you and your audience. Another technique is to create an appropriate impression through your physical appearance. Unfair and illogical as it may seem, clothing, accessories, and hairstyles create strong images in people's minds. Your choices can project an image to your audience that will reinforce your trustworthiness. Yet another technique is simply to talk in strong, clear tones. Such tones help to establish you as an authoritative speaker on the topic. Your audience will hear confidence even if you are feeling nervous. If you are nervous, your confident voice will help you too.

* Helpful techniques and hints abound.

There are many "secrets for success" used by different speakers. Some speakers picture the audience in pyjamas, some imagine they are talking to a non-threatening person such as their best friend or partner, and some use meditation or deep-breathing techniques. People who are nervous about making eye contact will look at the bridge of the nose if the listener is far enough away not to notice the strategy. If a particular method works, by all means use it, but the best protection against nervousness is thorough preparation. By knowing your material, by learning what good speaking techniques are, and by practising those techniques, you will build the confidence that allows you to handle nervousness.

A PRACTICE RUN

What aspects of public speaking make you nervous? Are you concerned about dropping your notes, forgetting the points you want to make, repeating points you have already made, stuttering or mispronouncing words, looking at a sea of faces, shaking, perspiring? In a group with your classmates, share some of the ideas you have for taking action against these concerns. Make a note of the ones that you think will help you.

_____

_____

_____

Sincerity

* Sincerity is vital. Pretence of sincerity is rarely successful.

Sincerity is valuable in persuasion. Many audiences will accept unpopular viewpoints if they see sincerity in the speaker. But it must be genuine. Insincerity is quickly detected by your listeners. And if they detect it, they are likely to dismiss your entire message, not just the point you pretended to believe.

Friendliness

A speaker who projects an image of friendliness has a significant advantage in communicating. People respond more positively to friendly people and to what they say. Some speakers find it difficult to project friendliness, especially when they are nervous. With self-analysis and practice in front of a mirror or a video camera, most speakers can find ways to appear more friendly. A smile is a good start. Then consider posture, gestures, and tone of voice. As we saw in Chapter 2, the nonverbal cues should not be underestimated.

* Projecting an image of friendliness helps the communication effort.

Thoroughness

Generally, a thorough presentation is better received than a scanty or hurried one. Thorough coverage gives the impression that time and care have been taken, and that the presenter is an authority on the topic. However, the key is careful selection of material. Too much detail can drown your listeners in a sea of data. You need to edit as thoroughly as you research, focusing on what your listeners need to know. Thoroughness means giving your listeners all the information they need—not necessarily all the information you can find.

* Thoroughness means giving your listeners all the information they need.

Nervousness

The last intangible aspect to consider is one to overcome. It is nervousness. If you are nervous about speaking in public, you have something in common with the vast majority of people in North America. Fear of speaking has been identified as a primary concern of people from all walks of life including professional performers and speakers.

* Many people experience stage fright.

People who frequently have to speak in public learn to use the adrenaline that nervousness releases to add enthusiasm and energy to their presentations. Although it is difficult to explain, the technique involves focusing outward on the concerns of the audience rather than inward on the butterflies inside. Speakers who become more concerned about the benefits for the audience than about their own fears of failure or embarrassment find their nervousness dissipating after a few moments of speaking.

* Nervous energy can be put to good use.

. . . .
IMPACT OF APPEARANCE AND PHYSICAL ACTIONS

There are some tangible aspects of speaking to be considered as well. In your efforts to improve your formal oral presentations, you should review the communication effects of the nonverbal factors seen by your listeners.

The Speaking Environment

For the best communication results, the factors in the environment should contribute to the message, not detract from it. For the first speech of her 1991 tour of the United States, Queen Elizabeth II stood at a podium with media microphones set on top of it. However, since the Queen is not tall, all that was visible from the audience was her hat on top of the microphones. The resulting lack of eye contact meant that the audience found it very difficult to listen to an otherwise excellent speech. The words of goodwill were undermined by the distraction created by a podium that was too tall.[1]

* Check the nonverbal cues of (1) your environment,

Personal Appearance

Your personal appearance is a part of the message your audience receives. Posture is likely to be the most obvious of the things that your audience notices in you. Even listeners not close enough to detect facial expressions can see the general form of the body. If you lean back too far, you will appear slightly aloof. If you lean forward over the podium, you will appear intense and perhaps over-eager. If you stand gripping the podium, or shifting your weight from one foot to the other, you will appear nervous and

* (2) your personal appearance,

---

[1] From then on Her Majesty was provided with a stool to stand on!

tense. What should you do to appear poised, alert, and communicative? Choose a natural stance that is neither overly casual or theatrical. You could try walking a few steps to the left or right of the podium if the sound system will permit movement. You should at least stand straight without appearing stiff, and be comfortable without slouching.

Facial Expressions

• (3) facial expressions (smiles, frowns),

Probably the most expressive physical movements are facial expressions. A smile, a grimace, and raised eyebrows all convey strong messages. Without question, you should use these effective communication devices. The problem, however, is that you may unconsciously use facial expressions that convey unintended meanings. For example, if, during a serious speech, a nervous speaker tightens the jaw and unconsciously begins to grin, the effect can be completely contrary to the intent of the words.

Eye Contact

• (4) eye contact, and

Eye contact is important. Looking at the audience, as we have already discussed in Chapter 2, is an excellent source of feedback for the speaker. Moreover, the eyes, which have long been considered "mirrors of the soul," give most listeners their impression of the speaker's sincerity, goodwill, and open-mindedness. Speakers who do not look at their audience may appear to have something to hide. They are also harder to listen to because they seem to be speaking to no one in particular. Indeed, they may find that no one in particular is listening!

Gestures

• (5) gestures.

Gestures contribute to the message you communicate. Just what they contribute, however, has to be carefully investigated. Most gestures have no definite, simple meaning. A clenched fist, for example, certainly adds emphasis to a strong point. But it can also be used to show defiance, make a threat, or signify respect for a cause. A kiss blown through the air can communicate affection or be an insult as in kissing someone off. And so it is with other gestures. They often register multiple meanings.

• Gestures have imprecise meanings, but they communicate.

Even so, gestures are strong, natural aids to speaking. It appears natural, for example, to emphasize a plea with palms up. Raising first one hand and then the other reinforces opposing points. How do we know? It is the context that helps us. The combination of words *and* supporting gestures communicates the appropriate meaning. Although we may not all use them in exactly the same way, gestures are generally clear in a given context.

• In summary, your physical movements can support your speaking.

In summary, it should be clear that physical movements can help your speaking. The appropriateness of physical movements is related to the personality of the speaker, the content of the message, and the size and nature of the audience. Once again, the mirror or the video camera is the key to developing skill in this area. Professional speakers and politicians study their video tapes carefully. You should too.

. . . .

USE OF VOICE

Proper Breathing

• Support your voice with proper breathing techniques.

Good voice is an obvious requirement of good speaking. Like physical movements, the voice should not hinder the listener's concentration but rather help focus attention on the message. One of the best pointers for maintaining good vocal quality is simply to breathe. Lack of breath causes the throat to constrict, and the voice to quiver and lose volume. Your audience will not see you as someone who is in charge if you sound out of breath. If being out of breath is a problem for you, study and use the breathing exercises of singers or actors. With practice you can learn to breathe fully and use the diaphragm for support.

There are three major areas to consider in discussing the use of the voice: (1) variation in pitch, (2) variation in speed, and (3) vocal emphasis.

A PRACTICE RUN

Give at least two interpretations of the following nonverbal cues.

Someone in the audience has his eyes closed.

_____

_____

Someone in the audience is fidgeting in her place.

_____

_____

A section of the audience is fidgeting.

_____

_____

Variation in Pitch

Speakers who talk in monotones are not likely to hold the interest of their listeners for long. As most voices are capable of wide variations in pitch, the problem can usually be corrected with practice. The failure to vary pitch is generally a matter of habit—of voice patterns developed over years of talking without being aware of the effect.

> • Variation in pitch adds interest and meaning.

While English is not a tonal language in the way other languages such as Mandarin are, a variation in pitch does change the meaning of words in some cases. The speaker's pitch indicates questions, feelings, and certainty, for example. Since pitch goes up at the end of a question, even one word said with a rising pitch is understood as a question. The single word *No?* asks for clarification. It could mean something like "Are you sure you won't go?" The same word said with a slight decline in pitch becomes the answer, *No.*

Some people end almost every phrase in a narrative with a rise in pitch as if checking if the listener understands the story so far.[2] Try reading the following example out loud, observing the question marks as a rise in pitch.

What did I do this summer? Well, I went to Europe? With my parents? And we got a rail pass? So we travelled all over? But I liked Paris the best?

It becomes obvious quite quickly that if the practice continues too long, most listeners will have tuned out.

Variation in Speaking Speed

Just as a long car trip at a set speed becomes tiring, so too does a long speech delivered at the same speed. A constant slow speed is boring; there is too much time for the listener's mind to race off to another train of thought. A constant fast speed is confusing and tiring; there is no time to sift and digest the information. In general, for best comprehension, you should present the easy parts of your message at a fairly fast rate and the harder parts at a slower rate. The excitement of a quick-paced section makes an interesting contrast with the thoughtfulness of a slower one. Variety is the key.

> • Variation in speed adds interest and emotion, and indicates relative importance.

---

[2] This practice has been given the clever colloquial name *uptalking.*

Vocal Emphasis

• Vocal emphasis is the punctuation of speaking.

A secret of good speaking is to give words their proper emphasis by varying the manner of speaking. In written work we emphasize by underlining or italicizing; in spoken work, we emphasize by pitch, pacing, and volume. As we have seen, as well as being more interesting to listen to, a speech given with variations in pitch is easier to understand.

Pacing, and especially pausing, clarifies the meaning and draws attention to the parts the speaker thinks are important. Introducing a pause between sections is a useful cue to your listener and provides a change. Surrounding key phrases with a brief silence emphasizes the subject matter and gains attention. Be careful to keep your pauses short and silent. Long pauses are irritating, but they become even more so when the speaker fills them in with distracting repetition of *uh, you know,* or *O.K.*[3]

And finally, vary the volume of your voice. You must always talk loudly enough for your entire audience to hear you, but raising and dropping voice volume is good for interest and emphasis. Some speakers incorrectly believe that the only way to show emphasis is to get louder and louder. But you can also show emphasis by going from loud to soft. The contrast with what has gone on earlier provides the emphasis. Again, variety is the key to making the voice more effective.

CHOICE OF THE PRESENTATION METHOD

• Choose one of these presentation methods:

With the speech organized, you are ready to prepare its presentation. At this time, you need to decide on your method—that is, whether to present the speech extemporaneously, to memorize it, or to read it.

Presenting Extemporaneously

• (1) extemporaneous presentation,

Extemporaneous presentation is by far the most popular and effective method. With this method you first thoroughly prepare your speech. You may write it out in full. However, you then make notes of the key points and present the speech from those notes alone, not the full speech. You rehearse, making sure that your notes remind you of all the important points and that you have the explanation for them all clearly in mind. You might revise your notes and practise some more, but you make no attempt to memorize your presentation. Because you have only brief notes in front of you when you speak, you are free to watch and respond to the audience most of the time. Your speech takes on the knowledgeable, natural, and spontaneous qualities of a good conversation. In fact, the most natural extemporaneous presentations are the product of careful planning and practice.

Memorizing

• (2) memorizing, or

The most difficult method is memorizing. If you are like most people, you find it hard to memorize a long succession of words. And when you do memorize, you are likely to memorize words rather than meanings. Thus, when you make the speech, delivery tends to be mechanical and flat. Moreover, if you miss a word or two, you become confused—and so does your speech. You may even become panic-stricken and then recovery is very difficult.

Probably few of the speakers who use this method memorize the entire speech. Instead, they memorize key passages and use notes to help them through the rest of the speech. A delivery of this kind is a cross between an extemporaneous presentation and a memorized presentation.

Reading

• (3) reading.

The third presentation method is reading. Although there is little danger of leaving out key points (unless the pages are lost or out of order!), there are several difficulties with

---

[3] Other examples are *umm, ahh, like,* and short coughs.

PART 4 Speaking in Business

this method. First, oral and written communication have differences in style. Most speeches that are written out in full and then read aloud, sound more like written reports than speeches. Secondly, without extensive practice, most people read aloud in an uninteresting monotone. Most reading is done silently for the entertainment or education of the reader. It is a different skill to read out loud for communicating that content to others. Thirdly, when reading out loud, people easily miss punctuation marks, fumble over words, or lose their place. (Even experienced news broadcasters have this difficulty occasionally!) When reading silently, the reader can go back over a sentence or paragraph if it was misread. That is a poor option for the reader of a speech.

These are all serious drawbacks to reading a speech, but perhaps the most serious is the loss of eye contact with the audience. Readers are tempted to watch their notes rather than looking at the audience. The audience is tempted to look at other things in the room more interesting than the top of the speaker's head. Then, of course, their minds wander, and an opportunity for effective communication is lost.

Those who successfully use the reading method usually combine it with extemporaneous or memorized passages so that they can look at their audience more. The variety of presentation methods can be helpful for emphasis and for pacing. An important point can be stressed by adding a few impromptu comments. Other parts can be read to move the speech along more directly to its conclusion.

. . . .
ORGANIZATION OF AN IMPROMPTU SPEECH

An impromptu speech is one that must be made at short notice. There is little time to plan and no time to research. The speech comes from your head and your heart. Sometimes there is so little warning that you do not even have an opportunity to make notes. You must simply stand up and make a speech. The occasions for impromptu speaking are numerous. The discussion in a meeting is one example. Introducing or thanking a speaker at short notice is another. Even the request to show a visitor around your office is an impromptu presentation.

In the absence of an abundance of time for planning, you need a system that you can keep in your head, or at least, count on your fingers. One outline system is *Past-Present-Future*. In this system you begin with a statement about the past.

* Try the *Past-Present-Future* system to help you organize your thoughts.

We used to handle all the accounts for Northern Ontario from this office. That required . . .

You then explain the current situation.

We now have another office in Sudbury to . . .

And you close with a comment about the future.

By 1999, if the growth pattern continues, we will open another office in Thunder Bay to handle the western part. Sudbury will continue to . . .

* Another system is *Statement-Explanation-Example-Summary.*

A second system for organizing your thoughts is *Statement-Explanation-Example-Summary.* Under this plan you make a statement, elaborate on it by explanation and by example, and close with a summary.

The statement:
At the Bagel Café, they serve the best bagels in all of Western Canada, I'm sure.

The Explanation:
By best, I mean the tastiest and the healthiest.

The Example:
For example, they use more grains in their multigrain bagel than any of the other bagels I've tried. They also have the widest selection with 37 varieties, and all their bagels are fat free. With flavoured cream cheese spreads that are lower in fat than butter or margarine, and a salad or some fruit, I can have a satisfying light lunch.

The Summary:
I like the Bagel Café for good taste and for good health.

* A third method is *State the purpose, Accomplish the purpose, Review the purpose.*

In a situation such as thanking or introducing a speaker, you may want to try another method. In this example, you state your purpose.

Ladies and gentlemen, it is my pleasure to express our thanks to our speaker, Bob Vandersloot.

You now accomplish the purpose that you have given.

Bob, thank you for your excellent presentation on . . .

To close, you review your purpose.

Please join me, Ladies and Gentlemen, in showing thanks to Mr. Vandersloot this evening. [*Begin the applause.*]

A PRACTICE RUN

Working in small groups, assign one another topics for impromptu speeches. Select the appropriate plan for organizing the speech and give the points you would make at each step. Here are some suggested topics to get you started.

Why do you think communication is an important course in the business program?

What political party do you support and why?

What do you understand about [marketing, accounting, economics] now that you have taken a course in it that you did not realize before?

What course do you think will be the most important to you when you graduate? Did you always think so?

Why do you [jog, swim, walk, work out] each day?

USE OF VISUAL AIDS

* Visual aids can sometimes help overcome the limitations of spoken words.

The spoken word is severely limited in communicating because sound is here briefly and then gone. A listener who misses the vocal message may not have a chance to hear it again. Because of this limitation, speeches often need strong visual support to reinforce the message. Visual aids may be as vital to the success of a speech as the words themselves.

As with written reports, graphics and visuals support the message. They are aids to more effective communication. Some of the functions they serve in an oral presentation are

- to clarify complex material
- to emphasize major points
- to summarize details
- to show relationships and trends
- to keep the audience's attention
- to keep the speaker on track.

Proper Use

Effective visual aids are drawn from the message. They are designed to fit the speech and the audience. In selecting visual aids, you should search through your presentation for topics that need clarification or emphasis. If a visual aid will help eliminate vagueness or confusion, you should use it. Visual aids are truly a part of your message, and you should look at them as such.

• Use visual aids for the hard parts of the message.

Types to Consider

Because no one type of visual aid is best for all occasions, you should have a flexible attitude toward visual aids. You should know the strengths and weaknesses of each type, and you should know how to use each type effectively. You should select your visual aids primarily on the basis of their ability to communicate. Simple and obvious as this injunction may appear, people violate it all too often. They select visual aids more for appearance and dramatic effect than for communication effect.

• Use the type of visual aid that communicates the information best.

You will mainly consider these types of graphic aids—charts, graphs, tables, diagrams, and pictures. Each of these types can be displayed in various ways—for example, by projection from transparencies, computer screens, or slides; by flip chart; or on a chalkboard. In addition, you will consider supporting your speech with videos, models, samples, or demonstrations.

Your choice of visuals should be influenced by the audience size and composition, the cost of preparing and using the media, and the ease and time of preparation. The following table illustrates how the different media fare on these dimensions.

Presentation Media Comparison			
Media	Image Quality	Audience Size	Cost
Photos	Good–Very good	2–20	Low
Slides	Very good	20–200	Low
Overhead transparency	Good–Very good	2–200	Low
Video monitors	Good	2–50	Medium
Hi-Res television	Very good	2–100	High
LCD screens	Poor	2–20	Medium
Video projection	Good	20–200	High
Video tape	Very good	2–200	High
Film	Very good	2–200	High
Computer graphics	Very good	2–200	High

Source: G.A.Marken, "Visual Aids Strengthen In-House Presentations,"*Office Systems* (February 1990), p. 34.

Techniques in Using Visual Aids

• Make the visual aids points of interest in your presentation.

Visual aids are used to reinforce key parts of the presentation. You blend them in with your words to communicate the message. Some pointers to help you develop your personal technique are in this list of *do's* and *don'ts*.

• Here are specific suggestions for using visuals.

1. Make certain that graphics are well produced. A lack of contrast between colours, or too many lines on a chart, for example, can be difficult for the audience to see. An illustration that is too small can be meaningless to people far from the speaker.

2. Select an appropriate format for the conditions and the audience. If the room cannot be darkened, a slide presentation will not be successful. If the audience is very large, a flip chart is inadequate.

3. Fit the visuals into the presentation at appropriate points just as you would place them in a written report. Avoid grouping your visual aids all together as a review at the end. This is comparable to placing them in an appendix in a written report and is an ineffective use of visual aids.

4. Draw the audience's attention to the visuals. Point to them with physical action and words.

5. Talk to the audience—not to the visual aids. Look at the visual aids only when the audience should look at them, and avoid talking to the screen.

6. Avoid blocking the listeners' view of the visual aids. Make certain that lecterns, pillars, chairs, and such do not block anyone's view. Take care not to stand in anyone's line of vision.

PREPARATION OF SPEECHES AND ORAL REPORTS

Selection of the Topic

• Your topic may be assigned.

Your first step in speech-making is to determine the topic of your presentation. In some cases your choice of topic will be determined by the purpose of your assignment, as when you are asked to welcome a group or introduce a speaker. In other cases you will be assigned a topic, usually one within your area of specialization. In fact, when you are asked to make a speech on a specified topic, it is likely to be because of your knowledge of the topic. But usually the suggested topic is vague and broad. You will need to define it more carefully so that it will suit your audience and the occasion just as you would if you were selecting the topic yourself.

• If you must select a topic, consider (1) your knowledge, (2) your audience, and (3) the occasion.

If you are not assigned a topic, then you must find one on your own. In your search for a suitable topic, you should be guided by three basic factors. The first is your background and knowledge. Any topic you select should be one with which you are comfortable— one within your area of proficiency. The second basic factor is the interests of your audience. Selecting a topic that your audience can appreciate and understand is vital to the success of your speech. It is also essential to look at your topic and your examples from the point of view of the audience to be sure none of your comments will cause unnecessary offense. The third basic factor is the occasion of the speech. Is the occasion a meeting commemorating an historic event? a monthly meeting of an executives' club? a sports awards banquet for the district? The topic you select should fit the occasion. A speech about the lessons we can learn from history is appropriate for the commemorative event, while a talk that could form part of a series would suit the monthly meeting of executives. Your selection should be justified by all three factors: your background and knowledge, the interests of your audience, and the occasion of the speech.

Analysis of the Audience

• You should find out about your audience.

One requirement of good speech-making is to know your audience. You should study your audience both before and during the presentation.

Preliminary Analysis.   As soon as you are asked to speak somewhere, you should begin to ask questions about the expected audience. Knowing their characteristics can help you select your data, choose your words, prepare your visuals, and decide on your presentation style.

> • Analyze the expected audience to help you prepare the speech.

For example, the size of your audience is likely to influence how structured or casual your speech should be. As a rule, speeches for large audiences require more structure. It will also affect what type of visuals you can use. If a microphone is needed, your freedom to move away from the podium may be restricted. The personal characteristics such as age, education, experience, and knowledge of the subject matter should also influence your choices. Again, these factors should affect the words, illustrations, and level of detail you use. All of these adaptations depend on knowing the audience first. The more you know about the expected audience, and the sooner you know it, the better you can adapt your presentation for them.

Analysis during Presentation.   Your audience analysis should continue as you make the speech. Your eyes and ears will give you feedback information. For example, facial expressions will tell you how your listeners are reacting to your message. Smiles, blank stares, and frowns will give you an indication of whether they are comfortable with it. You may need to soften your style or repeat some difficult concept. Shuffling and movement usually indicate boredom or fatigue and may be your cue to wrap up quickly. The sounds coming (or not coming) from the audience will give you clues about their interest. Yawns, laughter, and applause are all measures of audience response. If questions are in order, you can learn directly how your message is coming across. Feedback from your audience during your speech allows you to adjust your presentation to improve the communication result.

> • Watch for nonverbal feedback during the speech.

Preparation of the Presentation

After you have decided what to talk about and analyzed the audience, you should gather the information you need for your speech. This may involve searching through your mind for experiences or ideas, conducting research in a library or in company files, consulting people in your own company or other companies. Give yourself time to think about the ideas you uncover so that associations and patterns can emerge.

> • Conduct research to get the information you need.

When you have that information, you are ready to begin organizing your speech. Although variations are sometimes appropriate, you should usually follow the indirect order in a speech: *introduction, body, conclusion.* This is the order described in the following paragraphs.

> • Then organize the information.

The first words usually spoken are the greeting. Your greeting, of course, should fit the audience and the situation. Some speakers choose not to use a greeting. They begin immediately with the speech, especially in the more informal and technical presentations. If you decide to use a greeting, it should be brief and should move naturally into the introduction of your topic. Consider this example: "Thank you, Mr. Chairman, for your invitation to speak today. I am pleased to be here and to bring greetings from Mayor Buchanan and your representatives on city council. Ladies and Gentlemen, the economic life and vitality of our city . . . " This type of smooth tie-in does not happen by chance. It needs planning and practice, which again requires thought and time.

> • The greeting usually comes first.

Introduction.   The introduction of a speech has much the same goal as the introduction of a written report: to prepare the receivers for the message. In addition, the introduction to a speech usually has the goals of focusing the interest of the audience and establishing rapport.

It should be an interesting beginning to help the audience focus their attention on what promises to be an excellent speech. Unless you can arouse interest at the beginning, you are unlikely to achieve the objective of your presentation. The situation is somewhat like that of the persuasive letter. You can assume that at least some of the people will think they are not interested in your topic. Others would normally be interested, but today they

> • Gain attention in the opening.

are having difficulty focusing their attention. There is no question about it: you, the speaker, will have to work to gain and hold the attention of your audience. In the introduction you want to prove to the audience that this speech will be worth their time.

The greeting and the opening both work to build a relationship between you as the speaker and your audience. The audience will be forming impressions of you—about your personality, your professionalism, your consideration for others, and your level of preparedness. These impressions are formed within minutes. To ensure that they are positive, prepare your opening well.

The techniques of arousing interest are limited only by the imagination. One possibility is a human interest story. For example, a speaker presenting a message about the opportunities available to people with original ideas might open this way: "Nearly 150 years ago, an immigrant boy of 17 walked the streets of our town. He had no food, no money, no belongings except the shabby clothes he wore. He had only a strong will to work—and an idea." The story is suited to the topic, the audience, and the situation. The audience immediately senses a well-prepared presentation that will be interesting. They are prepared to listen.

Humour, another possibility, is probably the most widely attempted technique. However, to be successful, humour must be relevant to the topic, appropriate for the audience, and well delivered. The embarrassment over a failed joke has undermined many otherwise competent speakers. When well done, a humorous beginning gets attention, introduces the topic, and sets a positive tone.

Causing offense is not good business. There are many books of jokes and humour that have speech openers. Just be sure to check them against the current guidelines of political correctness and consideration so that you avoid jokes that are told at the expense of others. If in doubt, find something else.

Yet another possibility is the startling statement, which presents facts and ideas that awaken the mind. Illustrating this possibility is the beginning of a speech to an audience of merchants on a plan to reduce shoplifting: "Last year, right here in your stores, shoplifters stole over $3.5 million of your merchandise! And almost nothing was done about it." If this statement is made with the correct intonation and emphasis, these merchants are alert and ready to hear more.

A quotation from a source known and respected by the audience will gain attention and begin your speech with credibility. A debatable quotation will arouse interest and thought. Two standard collections of quotations are *Colombo's Concise Canadian Quotations* and *Bartlett's Familiar Quotations*. For more recent quotes, check the lead articles in magazines, in newspapers, and on the Internet. You may want to begin your own collection of quotations related to your areas of interest. Always be sure to note the reference to give credit.

A question that touches most people personally such as "Who wants to be freed from the weight and responsibility of financial debts?" will encourage each member of the audience to identify with the topic and to listen to the suggestions you offer. Another type of question gives you background information as well as getting attention. If you ask, "How many of you are regular users of bulletin board services?" your audience becomes involved by answering with a show of hands. You are then able to comment about the services to gauge your audience's knowledge level and feelings, either positive or negative. Now you can adjust your approach to your topic of user and discussion groups on the Internet. Making these adjustments on the spot is less difficult for an experienced speaker. A novice should think ahead about the possible responses and plan for them.

In addition to arousing interest, your opening should lead into the theme of your speech in both its subject and its tone. Each method suggested has its strengths. If your talk is motivational, a human interest story is a good beginning because it engages the emotion. A startling statement makes your audience think and suits the serious topic of a speech calling for remedial action. Select the type of opening that best sets up the message.

In most business-related presentations, you should make a direct statement of your theme early in the speech. In cases where your audience already has an interest in what you have to say, you may use a very short opening just to establish rapport and reach this theme statement quickly. Presentations of technical topics to technical audiences typically begin directly with the theme, giving the impression that a detailed, no-nonsense presentation is underway.

If your speech is persuasive, you may find it undesirable to reveal your position this early. In that case give a neutral statement of your subject. You might say you want to explore the topic, or review the evidence pro and con, or consider the facts about it. Then you can build your case before revealing your position. This pattern is especially desirable when you need to move the views of your audience from one position to another.

- Withhold your position on the subject if your goal is to persuade.

- -

A PRACTICE RUN

Assume that you must prepare a speech on the importance of making good grades for an audience of college students. Develop some attention-gaining ideas for the introduction of this speech.

- -

Body.   Organizing the body of your speech is much like organizing the body of a report (see Chapter 12). You take the whole and divide it into comparable parts. Then you take those parts and divide them. In most speeches, your presentation will be built around subtopics of the subject. In other words, you will have only one, or at most two levels of headings. Any more becomes too difficult for an audience to visualize. They will become lost in the multiple levels of your hierarchy.

- Organize most speeches by factors, as you would a report.

In your planning remember that a listener cannot review in the way a reader can. It is your responsibility as the speaker to provide clear guidance for the audience by building in transition words and sentences. You might say, "A second type of RRSP . . ." or "If a self-directed RRSP seems too complicated, there is another type that is easier to manage. . . ." The clear transition makes sure your audience is applying the points you are making to the right type of RRSP.

- Make obvious transitions and

A second important device is to occasionally summarize the points you have covered, as in the following example.

- mini-summaries to guide the listener.

We have seen the importance of an RRSP for your retirement security and the benefits you can realize right now in tax deferrals, so we now turn to getting an RRSP started.

Mini-summaries or reviews will help a listener in at least three ways: (*a*) to remember key points, (*b*) to consolidate facts into patterns, and (*c*) to pick up your train of thought again if his/her mind wandered.

Conclusion.   You should consider including these three elements in your close: (1) a restatement of the subject, (2) a summary of the key points developed in the presentation, and (3) a statement of the conclusion or a call to action (recommendation). Like most reports, the speech usually ends by drawing a conclusion. Here you bring all that you have presented to a head, and achieve whatever goal the speech has. Making the conclusion the high point of the speech is usually effective. A well-chosen quotation or humorous anecdote can be used to create that high point. In any case present the concluding message in strong language—in words that will make a positive impression and will be remembered. The following close is for a speech encouraging adoption of total quality management. Its layout is deliberate and is intended to help the presenter deliver it forcefully. Read it aloud, adding emphasis where it is indicated.

- The ending usually (1) restates the subject, (2) summarizes key points, and (3) draws a conclusion.

If we want profit, . . .
    if we want longevity, . . .
        if we want success, . . .
then . . . we want *T Q M.*

To do the right job—consistently—the first time—
is a goal we *can* achieve through **Total Quality Management.**

A Summary List of Speaking Practices

1. Organize the speech so that it leads the listeners' thoughts logically to the conclusion.
2. Move surely and confidently to the conclusion. Do not appear unable to close.
3. Use language specifically adapted to the audience.
4. Articulate clearly, pleasantly, and with proper emphasis. Avoid mumbling and the use of vocalized pauses such as *ah, er,* and *uh.*
5. Speak correctly, using accepted grammar and pronunciation.
6. Maintain an attitude of alertness, displaying appropriate enthusiasm and confidence.
7. Use body language well to emphasize points and to help clarify concepts and ideas.
8. Avoid stiffness and unnatural actions. Similarly, avoid excessive movements, fidgeting, and other signs of nervousness.
9. Look the listeners in the eye and talk directly to them.
10. Punctuate the presentation with reference to visual aids. Make them a part of the report story.

A PRACTICE RUN

For the speech on the importance of making good grades (see the previous practice run), plan an effective, memorable close. This closing should be co-ordinated with the introduction you developed earlier.

_____

_____

_____

Reporting Orally

* The oral report is a form of speech.

A special form of speech is the oral report. Oral reports are common in business, and the ones you make are likely to be important to your career. Since they are a specialized form of oral presentation, they are covered separately in the following review.

* An oral report is defined as an oral presentation of factual information.

A Definition of Oral Reports.   In its broadest sense, an oral report is any presentation of factual information using the spoken word. A business oral report would logically limit coverage to factual business information. By this definition, oral business reports cover much of the information exchanged daily in the conduct of business. They vary widely in formality. At one extreme they cover the most routine and informal reporting situations, such as a progress report given in a conversation with a superior. At the other they include highly formal, structured presentations, such as one given to shareholders at an annual meeting. The emphasis in the following pages is on the more structured ones because they require the most preparation and the most care and skill in delivery.

* Planning is the first step in preparing oral reports.

Planning the Oral Report.   As with written reports, planning is the logical first step in your work on oral reports. For short, informative oral reports, planning may be a few notes or a quick review of relevant data. But for the more formal oral reports, particularly those involving large audiences, proper planning is as complex as that for a comparable written report.

Determination of Report Objective.   Logically, your first task in planning an oral report is to determine your objective. Just as was described for the written report in Chapter 12, you should state the report objective in clear, concise language. Then you should clearly state the factors involved in achieving this objective. Doing these things gives you a guide to the information you must gather and to the framework around which you will build your presentation.

In the process of determining your report objective, you must be aware of your general objective. That is, you must decide on your general purpose in making the presentation. Is it to persuade? to inform? to recommend? This decision will have a major influence on your development of material for presentation and on the order of the presentation itself.

* First, determine the objective and what must be done to reach it.

Organization of Content.   The procedure for organizing oral reports is similar to that for organizing written reports. You have the choice of using either the direct or indirect order. Even so, the same information is not necessarily presented in the same way orally and in writing. Time pressure, for example, might justify direct presentation for an oral report on a problem that, presented in writing, might be better arranged in the indirect order. Remember, readers in a hurry can always skip to the conclusion or ending of the report; listeners do not have this choice. Moreover, you can watch your audience's reactions and adjust your approach to a more indirect order if you sense resistance.

* Next, choose the approach and organize your content.

Although oral reports may use either the direct or indirect order, the indirect is the more logical order and by far the most widely used. Introductory remarks are needed to prepare the audience to listen to your message. You may need to arouse interest, stimulate curiosity, or impress the audience with the importance of the subject. Secondly, the introduction is important in the oral report because it tells the listener what to expect. The outline headings are essential for the listener to be able to organize, understand, and remember the contents of the presentation. Since listeners have little control over pacing and reviewing, a clear introduction is very helpful to them. As in the written report, the introductory remarks state the purpose, define unfamiliar terms, explain limitations, and describe the scope.

* The indirect approach is more common.

In the body of the oral report, you should work toward the objective you have set. Here too, the oral report closely resembles the written report. The subject matter is divided into parts and discussed in a logical order. However, remembering again that the listener has only one chance to listen, the speaker must use clear signposts to guide the listener. Transitional words and phrases which develop the argument help the listener stay on track. Small reviews of key points also help the listener. A one-sentence review such as "As already noted, the profit picture has improved by 1.5 percent over the last 18 months," will remind the listener of the key point that forms the basis for the next idea.

* Oral reports need more transitional words

Another difference in the organization of the written and oral report is in the ending. Both forms may end with a conclusion, a recommendation, a summary, or a combination of the three. But the oral report almost always has a final summary of the main points. The audience will remember the beginning and the ending best because these are the positions of emphasis. The speaker uses these times to best effect to achieve the goal of the report.

* Oral reports usually have a closing summary.

. . . .
CO-ORDINATION OF TEAM PRESENTATIONS

Another type of presentation you may be called on to give is the group or team presentation. While the skills you use for individual speeches are also needed here, team presentations require additional skills. In order to present a cohesive group image, extra planning is needed.

* Group presentations require individual speaking skills plus planning and co-ordinating.

Teams must determine the content of each member's part to prevent omitting points, repeating points, and wasting time. In addition to dividing the content, the team must decide on the order of presentation. Each member then begins with a transition from the last person's part and closes with a lead-in to the next person's part. To achieve these smooth transitions, the order must be settled early in the development of the presentation.

* Plan the individual roles in the presentation early in your preparation.

Knowing the order of speaking and how to make the transition between one speaker and the next makes each team member and the team look well prepared.

• Develop a plan for unity.

It is just as important to unify the content as it is to divide it. The whole team must keep the purpose clearly in mind to ensure that each member's part moves the presentation smoothly toward its goal. One way to create unity is to use supporting examples. Sometimes each member can add to the same example to build from one part to the next. Another way is to be consistent in terminology. Yet another way is to be sure there is no undue delay or confusion between speakers. If each speaker is prepared to begin without faltering, the continuity of the message will be strengthened.

• Plan for the physical factors.

Groups need to plan the physical arrangements carefully. Planning the layout of the stage area and the access to it is important. Remember, several people have to be able to move around at the same time. And then, are the chairs well placed? Can every member of the team adjust the microphone? Preparing the team, the room, and the equipment all contribute to making a good impression.

• Plan the closing.

The team needs to plan how to close, who will close, and what will be said. If a summary is used, the member concluding should attribute the points to the appropriate group member. The team should smile or nod in agreement when the closing member expresses thanks or appreciation to the audience. If the team members decide to have a question-and-answer session, they need to know how it will be handled. Will one person act as a chairperson? Who will keep an eye on the time? While these might seem like minor points, paying careful attention to them is necessary to deliver a polished, co-ordinated team presentation.

A SUMMARY OF LEARNING OUTCOMES FROM THIS CHAPTER

In pursuing your career, you will probably spend some time making speeches and oral reports. These are not likely to be the most time consuming of your oral communication activities, but they are likely to be high in difficulty and importance.

Written and oral reports differ in these significant ways: (1) written reports permit more use of symbols for communication; (2) written reports give greater control of the pace of presentation to the receiver; and (3) written reports place more emphasis on correctness.

In improving your speaking, consider how you rank on each of the following characteristics: confidence, sincerity, friendliness, thoroughness, and nervousness.

Be concerned about what your listeners see, for what they see affects the communication. Be especially concerned about these factors: (1) the environment (stage, lighting, etc.), (2) personal appearance, (3) posture, (4) walking, (5) facial expressions, and (6) gestures.

Work to acquire an effective speaking voice. Do this by varying pitch, varying speed, and giving vocal emphasis.

You can present a speech extemporaneously, memorize it, or read it. Extemporaneous presentation is by far the best method in most cases. Memorizing is difficult and risky; and reading in a natural, interesting way is difficult.

Opportunities for impromptu speaking arise unexpectedly. The content of your speech must be organized simply so that you can remember it in your head. Three plans are suggested: *Past-Present-Future; Statement-Explanation-Example-Summary;* and *State the purpose, Achieve the purpose, Review the purpose.*

Visual aids are often effective in speaking. Use them whenever they help communicate, and select the types that do the best job. Blend the visual aids into your speech, making certain that the audience sees and understands them. Organize them as a part of your message. Emphasize the visual aids by pointing to them; but talk to the audience, not to the visual aids. Take care not to block your audience's view of the visual aids.

You can reduce the difficulty of making speeches by learning and implementing good speaking techniques. You begin by selecting an appropriate topic—one in your area of specialization and of interest to your audience. Then you research it thoroughly. Next, you organize the message, probably using the traditional speech order of introduction, body, and conclusion.

You should know your audience. Before the speech, size up the audience, looking for characteristics that affect your presentation (sex, age, education). Continue analyzing your audience during your presentation, paying attention to facial expressions, noises, and so on so that you can adapt to the reactions of your listeners.

Although not really a part of the introduction, an appropriate greeting often begins the speech. Along with the introduction, the greeting focuses the audience's attention and establishes rapport. The introduction itself usually has three goals: to arouse interest, to present the topic to be discussed, and to prepare the listeners to receive the topic. You can arouse interest in many ways—through human interest stories, humour, startling statements, quotations, or questions. In addition, your introduction tells the subject (theme) of your speech. It is good if your interest-gaining words tie in closely with your subject.

You have a choice of the indirect or direct order of presentation for your message. You will probably choose the indirect order when your goal is to persuade and the direct order in most other cases.

Organizing the body of a speech is much the same as organizing the body of a report, involving dividing and subdividing by time, place, quantity, or factor. A factor division is usually best.

To achieve its goal, the typical speech ends with a restatement of the subject, a summary of the key points, and a conclusion or recommendation. Normally, it is good to make the closing the highlight of the speech.

Business oral reports are spoken communications of factual business information. As with written reports, planning is the first step in preparing oral reports. You determine the objective. Then you organize the content, using either the indirect or direct order. The procedure for organizing oral reports is similar to that for organizing written reports (organization by division), but there are more transitional links required. The oral report typically has a final summary to remind listeners of the key points.

Group presentations require all the skills of individual presentations plus extra planning to demonstrate unity, reduce overlap, and improve transitions between speakers.

QUESTIONS FOR DISCUSSION

1. What are the differences between a report written to be read by the audience and one written to be heard by the audience?

2. An employee presented an oral report to an audience of 27 middle- and upper-level administrators. Then she presented the same information to three top executives. Note some of the probable differences between the two presentations.

3. What are the advantages and disadvantages associated with (a) reading a speech, (b) reciting a speech from memory, (c) delivering a speech without notes, and (d) giving a speech from brief notes or cue cards.

4. Describe appropriate uses for each of the impromptu plans suggested.

5. What should be the determining factors in the choice and use of visuals? What additional functions do they have in an oral presentation that they do not have (or have to a lesser degree) in a written presentation.

6. What can a speaker do to keep him- or herself at the centre of the audience's concentration.

7. Give examples of ways a team could provide continuity between members during the presentation. Be specific.

8. Identify new broadcasters, politicians, business leaders, or sports personalities whom you consider good speakers. Which trait in particular do you admire in their presentation style?

CASE 17–1

Stephanie: Tanya, your impromptu speech in class today was just awesome. Mine was a disaster. If there's one thing I have to learn before I start my business career, it's how to speak in public without being so nervous.

Jonathan: What's the big deal?

Stephanie: I don't know. My knees knock, my voice quivers, and my hands get clammy. Sometimes I start to cough and can't stop. One look at the sea of faces in an audience and I lose all my confidence.

Jonathan: Come on. Just jump in and start talking! It doesn't matter whether everything's perfect or not. Hey, don't worry. You'll do fine when you get a job and have to speak for real. It won't come up very often anyway. I have to go to work now so I'll see you tomorrow, eh?

Stephanie: I wish I could be so confident. It just isn't that easy for me.

Tanya: Well, actually, it isn't that easy for Jonathan either. He may think he isn't nervous, but when he starts talking in front of an audience, he just keeps going on and on. Sometimes he talks in circles as if he doesn't know how to stop. I think he's nervous whether he knows it or not.

Discussion

1. When giving a speech, would you identify more with Stephanie or Jonathan?

2. Is Jonathan correct in saying Stephanie won't have to speak in public very often in her business career? Will it be easier for her when it is part of her job rather than a class assignment?

3. What tips might help Stephanie? What would you suggest to Jonathan?

ANSWERS TO PRACTICE RUNS

▶ Critical Thinking

Attention-Gaining Ideas
   Answers will vary widely. If you are uncertain, check with your instructor.
Closing
   Answers will vary widely. If you are uncertain, check with your instructor.
Nonverbal Cues
   Many answers are possible. Here are some suggestions.
Someone in the audience has their eyes closed.
   They are thinking. They are tired. They are meditating.

Someone in the audience is fidgeting in her place.
   She is uninterested in your presentation. She has an uncomfortable chair. Her foot has fallen asleep.
A section of the audience is fidgeting.
   Perhaps they sense something that others don't. Maybe someone is ill or a draft makes their side of the room too cold. They have lost interest in your presentation because they cannot see you or the visuals you are using. Perhaps you are ignoring that side of the room and need to make more eye contact with them.

SUGGESTED TOPICS FOR SPEECHES AND ORAL REPORTS

▶Speeches

Since a speech can be made on almost any topic, the suggestions here are very general in nature. Before giving the speech, you will need to determine the goals clearly, to work out the facts of the situation, and to set a time limit.

1. "Dress for success" is (is not) a valid concept in business.
2. . . . is a career for 2000 and beyond.
3. Techniques for successful time management are . . .
4. Exercise (a hobby, a pet) is an effective defence against stress.
5. Seniors over 70 years old should (should not) have restrictions on their driving licenses.
6. For their first three years of driving, people should (should not) have restrictions on their driving licenses.
7. The Canadian health care system is (is not) a model the world should copy.
8. People who volunteer in their community gain as much as they give.
9. Canada's contribution as a peace keeper needs to be reconsidered.
10. Environmental protection should be achieved through legislation (co-operation, incentives).
11. For success in the 21st century start applying Total Quality Management principles now.

▶Oral Reports

Most of the written report problems presented in the problem section following Chapter 13 can also serve as oral report problems.

1. (Requires research.) Survey the major business publications for information about the outlook for the national (or world) economy for the coming year. Then present a summary report to the directors of Allied Department Stores, Inc.
2. As a student leader on your campus, you have been asked by the faculty senate (or a comparable faculty group) to report to its members on the status of faculty-student relations. You will include recommendations on what can be done to improve those relations.
3. (Requires research.) Report to a meeting of a wildlife-protection organization on the status of an endangered species in your area.
4. The Future Business Leaders Club at your old high school has asked you to speak on the nature and quality of business studies at your college. You will cover all the factors that you think high school students need to know.
5. (Requires research.) As representative of a travel agency, present a travel package on . . . (place or places of your choice) to the members of the Adventurer Travel Club.
6. (Requires research.) Gather the best available information on the job outlook for this year's business graduates in Canada. Present your findings in a well-organized and -illustrated oral report.
7. Present a plan for improving some phase of operation on your campus (registration, scholastic honesty, housing, grade appeals, library, cafeteria, traffic, curricula, athletics, etc.).
8. (Requires research.) Present an objective report on some legislation of importance to business (right-to-work laws, environmental controls, taxes, etc.). Take care to present evidence and reasoning from all the major viewpoints.
9. Prepare and present an informative report on how individuals may reduce their income tax payments. You will probably want to emphasize the most likely sources of tax savings such as registered retirement savings plans and avoiding common errors.
10. Make a presentation to a hypothetical group of investors that will get you the investment money you need for a purpose of your choice. Your purpose could be to begin a new business, to construct a building, to develop land—whatever interests you. Make your presentation as real (or realistic) as you can.
11. As a buyer of men's (or women's) clothing, report to the sales personnel of your store on the fashions for the coming season.

THE WORLD OF BUSINESS COMMUNICATION

Technology in Communication

Upon completing this chapter, you will be able to describe the role of technology in business communication. To reach this goal, you should be able to

1. Trace the technological developments through the traditional office to the modern office.

2. Discuss the various ways now available to transmit messages.

3. Identify appropriate computer software used in the different stages of the writing process.

4. Explain how word processing impacts modern-day business.

5. Describe the ways technology assists collaborative writing.

▶ to Technology in Communication

Doreen has been out of school for several years now. She has been concentrating on developing her business, and her efforts have been rewarded with good results. With a strong team of employees, Doreen has a little more free time. She feels she would like to spend at least some of it on personal development and upgrading her education. Of the several options open to her, she chooses to take some university courses through a distance learning program. That way she can work at her own pace and still have the time she needs for her work and her hobbies.

She was sure she was making the right decision, but she was astonished to find out how quickly her knowledge of communication technology had become out of date. To receive the lectures, to send in her assignments, and to consult with her professors, Doreen needed to upgrade her computer and learn some new skills. She also wanted to buy some new software to help develop her planning and time management skills. In the process of researching her needs, she found some other new technologies that could help her.

"How did I get so far behind? I've missed out on some great things. The prices have come down so much! I could have had some of this hardware a long time ago." ▪

THE EVOLUTION OF THE TRADITIONAL OFFICE

To meet the communication needs described in earlier chapters, business has used the best communication technology available. Throughout most of business history, the best technology was paper, quill and ink, or pencil. In the 1800s, however, some major technological developments changed the nature of business communication.

The first of these developments was the telegraph, which permitted almost instant communication of abbreviated, coded messages between places that were connected by telegraph lines. Then came various forms of "writing machines" that in time developed into the typewriter. This major technological development vastly improved the quality and preparation speed of written work in day-to-day business communication. Finally came the telephone that, for the first time, gave instant oral communication over a distance. Now, because of the convenience of immediate responses and feedback, more complete messages could be exchanged without the necessity of travelling to meet face to face.

* After centuries of primitive writing technology, three revolutionary innovations appeared in the 1800s: (1) the telegraph, (2) the typewriter, and (3) the telephone.

The development of communication technology accelerated in the first half of the 20th century. The radio brought the ability to send messages through the air without a physical line link. Message duplication techniques progressed from carbon paper to mass duplication methods, such as mimeographing and photocopying. The dictating machine, first developed by Thomas Edison in the late 1800s, was greatly improved, and the manual typewriter was displaced by the electric one. Telephone technology, including switchboards and multiple lines, made people almost instantly accessible.

* In the first half of the 20th century, technological improvements made the traditional office more efficient.

By the 1950s office tasks could be performed more efficiently and with better results than ever before. However, these technological developments did not radically change the patterns of business. Business was still centred in the downtown cores of major cities in the world. The postal service delivered most written messages, business representatives spent months each year in travel, and the current status of a company took several days or weeks to compile. More recent technological advances have revolutionized the world of business.

REVOLUTIONARY ELECTRONIC INNOVATIONS

Foremost among the revolutionary technological developments was, first, the computer, and then miniaturization. Following these advances came the introduction of other office equipment such as photocopiers, cellular telephones, and fax machines. The creation of networks allowing electronic mail systems and the World Wide Web are also part of the computer revolution.

Charles Babbage, an English mathematician, is generally recognized as the first person to propose the concept of the modern computer. He designed and partially built a steam-driven mechanical calculator called the *difference engine* with the help of a grant from the British government. In 1833 he outlined in detail his plans for an "analytical engine," a mechanical steam-driven computing machine that would accept punch-card input, automatically perform any arithmetic operation in any sequence under the direction of a mechanically stored program of instructions, and produce either punch-card or printed output. Before his death in 1871, he produced thousands of detailed drawings, but the machine was never built. His ideas were too advanced for the technology of his time.

Many of Babbage's ideas were recorded and analyzed by Lady Augusta Ada Byron, the daughter of Lord Byron, the famous English poet. She is considered by some to be the world's first computer programmer. The programming language Ada was named in her honour.[†]

[†]Source: James A. O'Brien. *Information Systems in Business Management.* (Burr Ridge, IL: Richard D. Irwin, 1988) p. 52.

The Effect of Computers and Miniaturization

- The computer brought about an electronic revolution.

The computer was to have a major impact on business. By current standards the first computers were gigantic and slow. One of these, the ENIAC, occupied a space the size of a family home and weighed over 25 tonnes. Although it could process only simple problems that any inexpensive pocket calculator now handles, it was a beginning.

- Personal computers were an outcome of miniaturization in computer technology.

Business communication activities felt the effects of the computer revolution when miniaturization made possible the development of the personal computer. Personal computers were an outcome of the development of the silicon chip that replaced the wiring, tubes, transistors, and extensive circuitry of the older computer models. Especially significant is the fact that miniaturization was accompanied by increased processing speed, greater memory capacity, and substantially decreased costs. Commenting on output improvements and cost decreases, one observer noted that if the automobile industry had made the progress that the computer industry has made, a Rolls-Royce would cost only a few dollars and run about 1 million kilometres on a litre of gasoline. The trend continues. Laptop and notebook computers are powerful, fast, and affordable.

- Advances in software also contributed to the impact of the personal computer.

Equally significant in the impact of personal computers were the advances in software technology. By *software* we mean sets of electronic instructions called programs that tell a computer what to do. The software enables users to perform a wide variety of operations, including calculations, three-dimensional designing, and word processing. Simplified, "user-friendly" software has made the personal computer usable by virtually anyone.

- Personal computers can be linked together to form a communications network.

Now that it is feasible to have a personal computer at almost every desk, and a laptop in almost every briefcase, it is reasonable to develop a communications network. A *computer communication network* is the linking of two or more computers for the purpose of sharing information. The network usually consists of personal computers physically linked by cables with a main computer in a *local area network* (LAN). This computer usually links with other more distant computers via telephone lines in a wide area network. In a network, information can be protected or released by the use of passwords. An authorized user is given access to the files needed for the job at hand. Since the users can communicate with other computers in the network, they can draw on the capabilities of all these computers to do many vital tasks.

Through computer network connections, a stockbroker can use a laptop to check current prices on stock exchanges around the world, retrieve historical data from archival files, review a client's portfolio including up-to-the-minute changes, and send instructions to buy or sell stocks. Information that used to take several hours or days to compile, analyze, and transmit is now handled in minutes. In addition, the broker can use e-mail to send messages to clients and other brokers, or word processing to develop professional-looking letters, including graphs and charts. Clearly, the computer and computer networks are changing the way business people work. They now have the best information available at their fingertips, and they can retrieve it unaided.

> * This example shows some possibilities.

Another area of interest to business communicators is voice activation of the computer. *Voice activation* refers to having computers respond to the human voice. Systems are currently being developed to allow dictation of documents directly into the computer. The computer "learns" the tone, pronunciation, and vocabulary of the user and changes the sound it "hears" into machine readable input. Voice systems are particularly promising for accessing numerous databases from remote locations.

> * Voice activation of computers is under development.

However, the process is still quite limited because of the many variations in voices. For example, fatigue can affect voice quality, and a tired person often does not enunciate clearly, creating recognition problems for the computer. New discoveries in equipment and software rather than greater refinements of existing technology may be needed for voice-activated systems to progress and gain acceptance. Interest and research continue because voice activation has so much potential for saving time and effort in the practice of business communication.

All the electronic technology we have reviewed has altered the way businesses communicate. Additionally, it has moved us away from the traditional office described earlier and into the development of offices without walls. Many small entrepreneurs operate a successful business from their homes or cars with a cellular telephone, a calculator, and a computer that includes a fax and a modem to link to other computers.

> * Electronic technology is moving us away from the traditional office.

Of course, some jobs are most efficiently done by those specifically trained to do them. Word processing specialists continue to do the bulk of written communication processing. They receive information, usually as dictation on some form of voice recorder, or as a rough draft on a computer diskette, and produce the final documents appropriately and attractively formatted. Here again, local area networks are cost effective because files and software can be shared. Also, since security systems to protect files from unauthorized use or copying can be maintained from the central server, LANs provide greater protection from computer viruses and computer theft.

> * Word processing specialists still handle written communications.

Expanded Role of Copiers, Telephones, and Fax Machines

Microchip technology has been the basis for many other technological developments affecting business communication practices in the electronic office. We will examine three of them: advanced copiers, telephones, and fax machines.

> * Microchip technology has other effects in the electronic office.

Copiers. Photocopiers have been with us too long to be considered innovations, but revolutionary improvements have been made in recent years, especially in combination with fax machines or computers. Modern copiers offer an amazing array of options and yet some are small enough to be hand-carried. The larger ones can reduce or enlarge original pages, duplicate both sides automatically, collate the pages and staple the finished document. They can copy onto a wide variety of materials including paper, peel-off labels, and plastic sheets for overhead transparencies. In addition, high-quality colour copiers are now economical for most businesses. Once the copier is integrated into the company's communications network, there is very little in the way of printing that cannot be done in-house.

> * Modern copiers give users many options.

Telephones. As we have noted, the telephone was a major technological development that changed the nature of business communication. As a result of revolutionary

> * Modern telephone service has influenced the electronic office.

advances, its impact persists today. Modern telephone service includes such features as listed here:

automatic redialing	allows you to press one key to redial the last number you called
number storing	keeps frequently called numbers in memory for rapid dialing
call waiting	alerts you to another caller trying to reach you on the same line, lets you put the first caller "on hold," talk to the second caller, and then return to the first
call-tracing	discourages prank calls by allowing you to trace a call very quickly
call-display	displays the number and name of the person calling you
conference calling	allows three or more parties in different locations to participate in a telephone conversation
call return	alerts you when the number you want to call is free (not in use)

Moreover, the telephone can serve as an intercom, as a transmission link for electronic mail, and as an input device for voice mail systems.

Cellular Telephones. Although not a new technology, the wide popularity of the cellular telephone has had a significant impact on business. The cellular technology was developed over 50 years ago. However, only recently have cellular telephone systems been fully developed to allow instant communication from almost any location at any time of day or night.

- The wide use of cellular telephones is a significant development.

- Cellular telephones depend on computer technology.

Large-city areas are divided into smaller geographic areas called *cells*. These cells are connected to one another through antennas, transmitters, and individually assigned frequencies. As vehicles (in which cellular telephones are most commonly found) move from one cell to another, a computer transfers the call automatically to successively adjacent cells without the awareness of the caller or receiver. Obviously, cellular telephones have changed the business communication environment. The owner of a cellular phone is always just a call away, ready to deal with the latest, up-to-the-minute information.

- Voice mail allows the caller to make selections.

Voice Mail. Voice mail is an automated answering system that allows the caller to do more than simply leave a message. By using a touch telephone, the caller can respond to instructions given in a taped message to do tasks such as (*a*) leave a message; (*b*) have the call transferred to the appropriate department; (*c*) speak to an operator or receptionist; (*d*) hear a taped message with information the caller needs; and (*e*) input choices to, for example, make purchases, register for courses, or record responses to a questionnaire. The possibilities are almost limitless. Voice mail offers 24-hour service to the caller and greater efficiency to the business by giving standard information to customers, limiting the need for telephone callbacks, and reducing the number of missed calls. Automated procedures save the cost of labour and usually return the cost of the system to the company in a short time.

- Voice mail systems differ. Most use a menu option to guide the caller to the information or service needed.

A call to your neighbourhood movie theatre or a government office will show that voice mail is being used extensively. Although each voice mail system is customized for the needs of the company, most of them use menus that give the caller several choices. The caller can select one of these options or exit the voice mail system to speak to the receptionist. After hours when a receptionist is not available, voice mail systems can allow the caller to key in an extension number to be transferred to the voice mailbox for the person being called. Some systems have a helpful feature that allows the caller to key in the person's last name if the extension number is not known. When using voice mail to leave messages, remember that you have no guarantee that the intended person has received the message until you have a reply. If an urgent deadline is involved, it is wise not to depend on voice mail alone.

As well as handling incoming calls, voice message systems have many other features that are helpful for internal communications. For example, the same message can be delivered to several voice mailboxes at one time. Furthermore, a message of interest to someone else can be forwarded to another person's mailbox. Many systems allow messages to be retrieved by various categories such as date, sender, or subject. Learning all the features of your company's voice mail system will help you be efficient and productive.

* Some features can strengthen communication within the company.

Facsimile (FAX) Machines. A *facsimile machine* (or fax) is a machine that scans a document, converts the information into electronic impulses, and sends the impulses along telephone lines to another facsimile receiver. The receiver converts the impulses back and prints a copy of the original document. A fax machine is fast, inexpensive, and simple to use. It can transmit the printed word, pictures, charts, and other graphics. In fact, a new experimental technology has been developed to transmit replicas of three-dimensional objects.

* Document scanners send impulses to facsimile receivers.

The stand-alone fax machine is quickly becoming obsolete as integrated technologies now allow the insertion of a fax card into a computer. The electronic impulses are received and stored in the computer in machine-readable form. Then the message is available at any time for viewing, printing, editing, or forwarding.

* The stand-alone fax machine is becoming obsolete.

The Impact of Electronic Mail

Business communication practices have also been changed by the increased use of electronic mail. As we have seen, *electronic mail* refers to the sending of messages through a network of computers usually joined through telephone lines. E-mail systems can be set up on a company's own computer, on a bulletin board system, or on a private subscriber information system. In addition, most World Wide Web browser systems also include e-mail software and support.

* Increasing use of electronic mail has affected business communication.

The increasing use of electronic mail means that we write more than we ever used to before.[1] Information that used to be handled by long-distance telephone is now often sent via the more economical e-mail system. The tone of voice, which can carry so much of the true meaning of a message, is lost. As a result, a special language of symbols has been developed. While not always appropriate for business communication, *smileys* (also known as *emoticons*) are useful for clarifying the intent of the writer. Some examples are included in the "Communication in Brief" inset box on page 436.

* E-mail has fewer nonverbal cues than voice communication.

E-mail lacks not only the cues of oral communication, but also some of the cues of written communication. Bold, italics, and even underlining are not available with most e-mail systems. Capitalization is the easiest way to add emphasis, but it is not popular with regular e-mail users. If capitalization is overused, the reader feels uncomfortable as if the sender is shouting. Once again, users have developed codes to help. An important word may be enclosed in asterisks. To show underlining, the underline character is inserted before and after the words. (See the e-mail example in Figure 18–1.)

* E-mail has fewer nonverbal cues than most written communication.

The organization of the message and the selection of words must be considered carefully to be sure the intended message is clear. It is advisable for e-mail users to be positive in their language choices in recognition of the greater possibility for misunderstanding.

The Potential of the World Wide Web

Perhaps the most far-reaching technological change for business and business communication is the evolution of the Internet. The theory behind the Internet was developed to protect sensitive government and military information in the United States during the cold

* The Internet began as a protective strategy for sensitive information.

---

[1] For more on e-mail messages, see Chapter 10, "Memorandums," and Chapter 12, "Report Structure: The Shorter Forms."

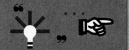
FIGURE 18-1   An Example of an E-Mail Message

From:	jbamford@gpu.srv.ab.ca[†]
To:	eveitch@usernet.com
Date:	May 14, 1997
Subject:	Travel to April Marketing Meeting

FLIGHT ARRIVAL

My flights for the marketing meeting on April 29th and 30th are booked. I will arrive at the International Airport at 1:00 p.m., April 28th, on Canadian Airlines flight 695.

GROUND TRAVEL

Should I rent a car to get to your offices? If so, please SEND DIRECTIONS from the airport to your office. BTW, is the reception on the 30th formal dress?

RESEARCH FOR YOUR REPORT

The book I mentioned is called _Marketing for Business in Canada_. It gives examples that may fit into your report. Of course, the federal government pages on the world wide web are worth checking. HTH.

[†]These are realistic but not real addresses. They have been created for this example.

war tensions with the USSR. Rather than being held in one central location, all this information was divided among computers scattered about the country. In the event of an attack by a hostile force, at least some of the information would be safe. To provide access for everyone who needed the information, a communication network was established using the existing telephone lines and new communications software.

The early Internet was difficult to use and required special codes and clearance. However, the idea of sharing information was attractive to researchers and academics. Gradually, more and more people became aware of the usefulness of this technology.

* Easier access through new software made the World Wide Web popular.

When Swiss researchers developed a simpler and more attractive way to access the Internet, now also called the World Wide Web, the system flourished.

Until recently, the most active parts of the World Wide Web have been the discussion groups. Thousands of people find others with similar interests and share their ideas by typing and sending messages through user groups or chat lines. The standards and rules for these groups vary widely, and their content ranges from the serious to the silly. Some of these groups are *moderated* or reviewed to see that the messages are on topic and appropriate for this discussion group. Others are live or on-line with several people sending messages at the same time. Now, however, the more passive side of the Web is attracting attention.

* User groups and chat lines are popular.

Surfing the net is a very popular pastime. The Web sites created by individuals and companies to tell the world about themselves are being visited in record numbers. As well as a readily available source of entertainment, the World Wide Web is now also an easily accessible source for current information. The variety of information is as great as the variety of people creating the sites. Some of the information is reliable, but some of it is incorrect, out-of-date, misleading, or false. Knowing the source is just as important with information from the Web as it is for information from an interview, a book, or a magazine. "I saw it on the Web" is no more reliable a credit than "I overheard it on the bus."

Despite the misinformation that can be found on the World Wide Web, the value of this communication link to the world is just beginning to be realized. Through a Web site, even the smallest business can economically reach a huge audience. Along with giving information, businesses advertize and entertain to get exposure and to sell products. Once some questions of channel security are solved, the ability to perform complex transactions from any computer in the network will change the way we handle business and the way we conduct our lives.

* The Web impacts every aspect of business.

. . . .
USE OF COMPUTERS TO IMPROVE WRITING

Knowledge of the electronic technology reviewed in the preceding pages is important to your understanding of how people in business communicate. Perhaps even more important to you are the ways in which this technology can help you improve your written communication.

* Software programs for improving writing have been developed.

When you think of enhancing the writing process through technology, you probably first think of using word processing software. While that is one important tool, there are

* Computer tools can be used throughout the writing process.

many others that can help improve your messages. Writers can get assistance from computer software at each of the different stages in the writing process—planning, gathering data, analyzing and organizing information, writing, editing, and checking. There are also products to help with the construction, presentation, and transmission of messages written collaboratively.

Computer Tools for Planning

Whether you are writing a short letter or long report, you can use a computer to help you plan both the document and the writing project. In planning the content of the document, *outlining* or *idea processing* software is useful. You can brainstorm, listing your ideas as they occur to you. Once you've captured your ideas and grouped related ideas together, you can rearrange items into a meaningful order, organizing with the reader in mind. Outlining software comes with some word processors, or it comes alone and can be used with a variety of word processing software.

One way to use an outliner is with a split screen. In one part of the screen, you will see your outline, and in another part, the document you are writing. Another way you can use an outliner is as a pop-up window. In this case your outline is held in memory; you can pop it up over your document to view it and put it away when you are done. You can also collapse or expand the outline to see as few or as many levels as you want. This lets you look at the overall structure of your document or the detailed breakdown for checking the consistency at all levels.

Finding time for writing, of course, is one of the major challenges for business people. By using *personal information management software,* you can plan time for completing writing projects. These time management tools are annotated electronic calendars. They will remind you of today's tasks or the number of days remaining before a project needs to be completed.

Computer Tools for Gathering Data

Gathering data is an important part of a writer's work. Factual data is usually stored in databases that are searchable either by subject or by keyword. For efficiency you need to use electronic searches, supplemented by manual searches, to find the facts you need. Much of the printed information is available electronically, and some kinds of information are only available electronically.

If you need the current inventory of a product your company manufactures, you could connect to your company's computer and download (copy to your computer system) the most recent data before completing your report. If you also want to project the number of units to be completed by the end of the month, you may need to connect to your supplier's computer to check their inventory of the parts. For information about the economy of your province, you could connect to the statistical databases of the provincial or federal governments. This information is available almost instantly without your leaving your desk.

Some libraries are now allowing their catalogue databases to be accessed both in the library and from remote locations. This means you can check the library holdings from your home or office. Many commercial services offer on-line searching while others provide their indexes on compact disk for computer searching. As mentioned earlier, the World Wide Web is another important resource. Further discussion on how to search the Web for research is found in the research chapter.

Computer Tools for Analyzing and Organizing Information

If the facts you've gathered have some characteristics in common, database software will help you store, organize, and sort them. Data such as library references to books and articles, parts inventories, client lists, and sales records are easily handled by a database. Once you enter the information, you can search and sort it on any of the categories (called fields) you used in your design. In a client list, for example, you could sort the records alphabetically or by postal code, you could search for the name and address of a client from the telephone number, or you could get a list of clients who have not made purchases in the last six months. A well-organized database allows you to find what you need when you need it.

Three tools that writers find useful in analyzing data are statistics, graphics, and spreadsheet software. Combining raw numbers or viewing them in different ways gives you a clearer picture of their meaning. Some very sophisticated *statistical software* has been made user-friendly, allowing those with little computer expertise to use them easily. Some programs will even query you about the nature of your data and recommend which statistical tests to use. Also, most *spreadsheet software* will compute basic statistics that allow writers to give some basic but meaningful interpretations to data.

* Computer software helps analyze and interpret data with statistics and graphics.

Graphics software helps writers in a couple of ways. First, graphs reveal trends and relationships in data that may be hard to recognize from raw data. This helps writers interpret the meaning of their data. Second, graphics software helps writers explain more clearly to readers what the data mean. For example, you can direct the reader to look at the red and blue lines for the last five years, noting the trend of increasing rate of profits. You can create graphics easily with both spreadsheet and graphics software. Also, a large variety of graphics software is available for creating special symbols and illustrations. You no longer have to be an artist to create clear, good-looking graphics.

Computer Tools for Writing

Word Processing Functions.   *Word processing software* is clearly the favourite writing tool of most writers. The purpose of word processing, of course, is to help writers transform ideas, information, and opinions into readable messages. By liberating the writer from tiresome chores, word processing software gives more time for revising and editing. The process involves four basic functions: input, processing, storage, and output.

* Word processing helps you manipulate, edit, and revise your messages.

The process begins when someone chooses the words by writing on paper or by composing directly on the keyboard. Devices such as the mouse and scanner are available to help with input of data, but keyboarding skills still are needed. In the end, by some means, the words have to be converted into the electronic impulses of machine-readable form and placed into the memory of the computer.

* Four parts of word processing are (1) Input (originating the message),

Once the message is in machine-readable form, it can be viewed, edited, corrected, changed, and arranged into the desired form. In the process various forms of text-editing aids, such as spelling checkers, punctuation and grammar checkers, and automatic formatting tools, can be used. These aids are discussed in a later section.

* (2) processing (modifying the message),

In the input stage, material is stored in the computer memory for temporary use. It should also be given a name and filed more permanently on disks or other secondary storage media for easy retrieval at a later date. Another copy should also be saved as a backup in case of damage to the first one. The goal is to store the information so that it can be retrieved easily and quickly.

* (3) storage (filing the message for easy retrieval), and

The final function of word processing usually involves printing the message on paper, and then sending the printed document to its destination. A machine-readable copy can be physically transferred by diskette to another computer. Another possibility is to transfer the message by e-mail or some other telecommunication channel.

* (4) output (printing and delivering the message).

Processing Features of Word Processors.   Word processors have many features to help the writer construct clear, correct messages. Take the time to find out how to accomplish the following tasks on your word processor.

Since revising and editing are extremely important to turning out well-written business documents, the insert, delete, and copy/move features are tools you will use often. With a few keystrokes, the shape and emphasis of the document can be changed for greater audience appeal, impact, and clarity.

* Investigate the power of your word processor. Be able to use features such as insert, delete, and copy/move;

Two other useful features of word processing are basic math and simple sorting features. The basic math feature lets the writer enter columns or rows of numbers, leaving the calculation job for the software. The sorting feature lets the writer enter columns or

* basic math and sort functions;

* tables and column creation; and

* footnoting and indexing.

rows of words, leaving the alphabetic sorting for the software. While these are useful features of word processing software, the writer has to be careful to enter or make the copy exactly the way the software needs it to do the proper calculating or sorting.

The table feature allows formatting of individual cells, rows, and columns. It is useful for presenting numeric data as well as textual material in rows and columns. Most word processors offer several automatic format features to enhance the appearance of tables. See Figure 18–2 for some typical examples.

Two other word processing features that make the writing job easier are footnoting and index building. The footnoting feature inserts a marker in the text where the writer chooses and then prompts the writer to create the note. The software adjusts the text to leave enough room at the bottom of the page for the footnote even if material is added or deleted later. It also will move and renumber the note appropriately if the text associated with it is moved.

An index is a vital asset to an information-rich report. However, because the task of indexing used to take many days, only formal reports and published works had indexes. Now, word processing software can create indexes quickly, economically, and accurately. The writer simply tags the words in the text to be indexed, and the software builds an alphabetic index with associated page numbers. The processing time for preparing the index for a long document may be an hour or two, but it is considerably less than the time required for a manually created index.

* Using advanced word processing features saves time.

Advanced Features of Word Processors.   Word processing also has three other features which save the writer from having to re-enter the same information. These features are merge, macros, and headers and footers. Merge is particularly useful in

---

FIGURE 18–2   Automatic Formatting of Tables

The following examples were generated automatically by a word processing package. The data was input only once.

	Jan	Feb	Mar
North			
South			
East			

	Jan	Feb	Mar
North			
South			
East			

	Jan	Feb	Mar
North			
South			
East			

One special word of advice—*Backup frequently!*

Some programs will create an automatic backup file, but the final responsibility is with the user. Most writers know how difficult it is to create a document much less recreate it, so they are willing to spend a few seconds regularly to protect their investment. Some writers backup every fifteen minutes or so while others backup every page. To decide how often you should backup, think about how much you can remember. Can you recreate from memory the work you have done since your last backup? If not, it's time to save your work.

For added protection, alternate the backup floppies you use. Then, if one disk should be lost, damaged, or infected with a virus, you will still have another copy. Using different-coloured floppies for different days and making grandparent files by giving each revision a new name are tips some writers use. The goal is to make it as easy as possible to recreate the document from earlier drafts should the current file become unusable for any reason.

Ask anyone who has ever lost a file. Backup copies are the least expensive insurance you can buy.

adding personal information to a form letter. It permits you to combine a form document with a file containing variable data. The macro feature allows you to record a complex sequence of commands and, from then on, to activate that sequence with only a few keystrokes. These are useful for special formatting styles as well as for creating memo headings. The feature for creating headers and footers repeats information at the top and/or bottom of each page automatically. The information in headers and footers might include the date, time, page number, shortened title, or reference number.

Graphics and Drawing Packages. Because readers appreciate clear graphics in a report, writers are turning to *graphics and draw software packages.* With word processors that can import files smoothly, graphic support for text is both economical and easy. Graphics packages can be used to generate graphs of all types and most come with ready-made pictures (called clipart) that can be edited for size, position, and shape. Moreover, low-cost scanners that transfer printed graphics and pictures into machine-readable form have made it easier to supplement text with high-quality illustrations.

• Graphics and draw programs are used to add visuals.

Word processing and graphics packages are quickly advancing, but people who regularly prepare reports may prefer specialized software. Referred to as *desktop publishing,* this technology goes beyond word processing and allows the user to choose from a variety of type sizes and faces, to create attractive graphics, and to vary column widths and add borders for a customized format. Laser printers are required to take full advantage of this software.

• Desktop publishing is now available.

Computer Tools for Editing and Checking

Other attractive computer tools are spelling checkers, electronic thesauruses, and grammar and style checkers. In recent years, these software packages have been developed to check writing for correctness and for certain principles of style. Thus, you can draft a document on your word processor and then use the editing and checking packages to test your rough draft. From the programs you then receive analyses of your work with suggestions for improvement.

Spelling Checkers. Among the most useful of these programs are *spelling checkers.* The early spelling checkers were separate programs, but now they are an integral part of the word processing and desktop publishing packages. Spelling checkers contain large

• Spelling checkers use large dictionaries.

You may have seen examples like this one before. The spell checker gives this paragraph full marks!

The sail of spell checking soft wear witch cheques yore spelling has raisin in the lost years. There us has maid letters mower simple to right. They can knot ketch every arrow, through, bee cause hours is an complicated language.

dictionaries of words (50,000 and more). Most offer a British or American version and allow the user to customize the dictionary by adding words. Each word in your document is tested against this dictionary. If there is no match, the word is flagged and alternatives appear on the screen. You then decide whether to make a change. Because not all the words you use will be in the spelling checker's dictionary, some flagged words will, in fact, be correct.

- Some errors will not be detected. The writer must proofread carefully.

Although spelling checkers do a very good job, do not expect more than they can deliver. The error of a correctly spelled word used incorrectly will not be flagged. For example, both *there* and *their* are correctly spelled words. Use of one in place of the other would be incorrect, yet the spelling checker would not catch that error. Many other types of errors such as missing words or improperly placed words will only be caught through careful checking by human eyes. Beware of a false sense of security, and check your writing carefully.

- Spell checkers are convenient and should be used regularly.

A spell checker is only an effective tool if the writer uses it. Research has found that 75 percent of the spelling errors in student letters could have been caught by the spell checker if the student had used it.[2] These findings clearly show the value of a few moments spent with the spell checker.

- The electronic thesaurus gives easy access to synonyms.

Thesaurus Software.   A *thesaurus* lists words along with their synonyms and antonyms. Serious writers usually have a thesaurus in their collection of reference books. However, most writers find popping up a window in their word processors so easy that they use an electronic thesaurus more frequently than the bound one. Another mouse click searches the thesaurus again or inserts the suggested word into the text. Most of the suggested words can be looked up as well until you are satisfied that you have found the best word for your purpose. The thesaurus is a powerful tool, and the computer has made it faster and easier to use.

- Software has been developed to check style and grammar.

Style and Grammar Checkers.   Several software programs have been developed for checking the style and grammar of documents. They let you select from a variety of writing styles such as business, technical, fiction, or general. You can modify the rules the checker uses, having it overlook sentences beginning with *And* or *But,* for example. Some allow an interactive approach in which you correct the mistakes as the checker goes through the documents. Others make a new copy of the document marked with comments for you to consider.

- They also check punctuation, spacing, abbreviations, and capitalization.

Programs can check a variety of mechanical elements that are standardized into set patterns. For example, they can check the spacing before and after punctuation marks, the correctness of abbreviations, capitalization, double words (unintentionally repeated), and incorrectly expressed numbers (such as $7,35.55). As with spell checkers, the writer still has to know the exceptions and fine points, since the final responsibility does not lie with the program, but with the person using it.

---

[2]Berle Haggblade, "Has Technology Solved the Spelling Problem?" *The Bulletin of the Association for Business Communication* March 1988: 23.

Most of these programs have been designed to analyze the readability of your writing. They measure sentence length and calculate the percentage of long words. With this information they estimate the reading level for your document. In addition, they search for other possible weaknesses such as the passive voice, long paragraphs, clichés and jargon, and vague words.

* Some software programs analyze readability.

As with other checkers, grammar and style checkers will produce *bad hits* (identifying as an error something that is correct) and will miss other errors. Although the frequency is declining as the programs are improved, the user must understand grammar and style to know whether the program is giving good advice or not. Some programs now explain the rule being applied to help the user decide if changes are necessary.

* "Bad hits" will occur.

Computer Tools for Collaborative Writing

A large, complex project requires a team of experts working together to complete the task. Projects such as contract proposals and research activities are time consuming and costly. Unless they are done well, a company can suffer a major setback. Team projects such as these require collaborative writing. Other common group writing tasks are policy manuals, instruction guides, and annual reports. Although the need for collaborative writing in business occurs regularly, most people find it difficult to do well. Fortunately, the job can be made easier by a wide range of computer tools that support the various stages of the process.

* Computer tools assist groups on a wide variety of tasks.

The outlining, time management, and database tools already discussed can be used for collaborative projects. But for a long writing project, several simultaneous projects, or a task shared with a team, *project management software* is an excellent tool. It allows you to identify all the tasks needed to complete the project, to estimate how much time each task will take, and to generate a time and task chart (commonly called a Gantt chart). Also, it helps you to keep track of your progress and to decide how to allocate your resources to complete the project on time or within budget.

* Project management software assists in identifying tasks and allocating resources.

Turning to computer tools to support the group writing process, an interesting study divided them into two classifications—asynchronous and synchronous.[3] Asynchronous tools allow the user to work at any time, independently of other team members. The work is shared at a later time convenient to the other members. Synchronous tools, on the other hand, are used by all group members at the same time and thus create a new kind of group writing environment.

* Computer tools to support the collaborative process of writing in groups fall into two categories.

---

[3]Annette Easton, George Easton, Marie Flatley, and John Penrose, "Supporting Group Writing with Computer Software," *The Bulletin of the Association for Business Communication* June 1990: 34.

- Several computer tools assist the traditional group.

Asynchronous Computer Tools.

Asynchronous tools include word processing, conferencing systems, electronic mail systems, and group authoring systems. Word processing features useful in group writing include commenting, strikeouts, and redlining. Commenting allows you to insert comments in a document written by someone else. Strikeout and redlining allow you to identify text you would like to delete or insert. A lead writer in a group might distribute a document draft to members of the group; they would use these features of their word processor and return the file to the leader. The leader would then review the documents and edit the original.

- Computer conferencing gives time and place flexibility to the writing team.

Another group writing tool is computer conferencing. This tool is useful when groups have a difficult time meeting due to distance or time. The lead writer would enter some text to begin. Others would access the system at their convenience, review the comments, and enter their own. All comments stay in the system to be reviewed by all members of the group whenever they sign on. In some systems group members have anonymity, but others maintain audit trails so comments can be attributed to specific group members.

- E-mail is convenient for two writers.

If two people are collaborating on a project, they could use their existing e-mail accounts. If more than two people are involved, conferencing is better because access to standard e-mail boxes is private. Only the person addressed can retrieve the message. With the use of distribution lists, e-mail could be used for a small team, but other methods are more convenient.

These tools are designed to work the way groups have traditionally worked. The planning, writing, and revising activities occur much the way they always have in traditional groups. However, the tools improve the speed and convenience for writers.

- New computer tools change the group process and improve its output quality.

Synchronous Computer Tools.

Synchronous computer tools are used by all group members at the same time. They allow multiple users to work on the document; they also allow users to view the comments of other users immediately. These programs contain a variety of tools from brainstorming tools, to organizing and analyzing tools, to writing tools.

One group member starts with a question or a statement; other members comment on the statement anonymously. Perhaps a proposed new policy is entered. Members comment, review all comments, gather related comments, rank them, and write the final policy statement. This kind of group writing tool reduces meeting time significantly and produces high quality documents. A review of research indicates that this electronic meeting technology improves group work in four ways: (1) by providing an equal opportunity for participation, (2) by discouraging behaviour that negatively impacts meetings, (3) by enabling a large number of ideas to be managed effectively, and (4) by permitting the groups to use the tools as needed.[4]

Technology has enhanced collaborative or group writing. From simple disk-sharing programs to sophisticated network-based programs, computer support for group writing improves both the process and product.

. . . .
A LOOK TO THE FUTURE

Revolutionary changes are coming. To take advantage of them, we will need strong communication skills. In fact, the increasing complexity of our technological world will require that our communication skills become even more effective.

- High-tech tools will continue to enhance the communication process.

In addition to the technical developments discussed thus far, you can expect to see user-friendly systems and the integration of computer tools in a way that is transparent to the user. For example, the integration of spell checkers and grammar checkers into word processors is now common. Because the transition from one tool to the next is almost seamless, we think of them as a unit. The smooth transfer of data from a spreadsheet to a word processor is another example. In the next few years, we can expect technologies

---

[4]J. F. Nunamaker, Alan R. Dennis, Joseph S. Valacich, Douglas R. Vogel, and Joey F. George, "Electronic Meeting Systems to Support Group Work," *Communications of the ACM* July 1991: 40.

such as fax, voice mail, and e-mail to become more closely linked. Increasing reliability in voice and handwriting input will allow even further integration of a variety of communication tools.

You can expect to be using networks with an even broader range of information easily accessible. However, some people are concerned about the future of the World Wide Web. Will technology advance quickly enough so that the millions of people who want access to this network will not overwhelm it? For example, will there be so many users that the system becomes too slow? How long will users be willing to wait for a connection to be made before they decide to abandon the search and use another resource? The Internet could be weighed down by its own success. The question of security is also a major concern. How can a company protect its files while still allowing employees to access the Internet? How can a user safely send personal information via the World Wide Web?

It is important to emphasize again that the ability to communicate must advance along with the technology. For example, as more business decisions are made via conference calls rather than in face-to-face meetings, all the nonverbal cues that can be read on a face are lost. Participants need to listen very carefully for the nuances of meaning carried in the tone of voice, the speed and volume of speaking, and the choice of words. They need to choose words and sentences carefully to construct clear, efficient messages. They need to use encouragers, door-openers, and feedback more than ever before. The future will bring more of the same. There is an urgent need to write, speak, and listen more effectively than ever before. Whatever form new technology takes, human minds will continue to control message formulation and interpretation.

* Effective communicators are needed more than ever.

A SUMMARY OF LEARNING OUTCOMES FROM THIS CHAPTER

For many years business has benefited from the use of technology to streamline the operation of the traditional office. However, since the introduction of computers and miniaturization, the traditional office has been revolutionized. Technology has changed the way businesses manage their records, market their products, pay their bills, and transmit their messages.

The integration of copiers, telephones, and fax machines with computers has led to new capabilities. An office no longer needs a building. It can be completely mobile. It can be in a remote location without being isolated.

The networking of computers has given rise to the extensive use of e-mail as a quick, convenient, and inexpensive channel of communication. Users must, however, be aware of the limitations of e-mail caused by the absence of important nonverbal cues. The availability of information through networks and especially through the Internet allows business people to make decisions quickly and accurately.

There are many computer tools to support planning, writing, and collaborative work. Tools such as word processors, graphics packages, spell checkers, and grammar and style checkers help the user to improve the accuracy and appearance of documents. Collaborative writing and project management systems improve the quality of the work produced by (1) providing an equal opportunity for participation, (2) discouraging behaviour that negatively impacts meetings, (3) enabling a large number of ideas to be managed effectively, and (4) permitting the groups to use the tools as needed.

QUESTIONS FOR DISCUSSION

1. What is a business office?

2. What are the strengths and limitations of the following channels of communication that have been made possible through advances in technology: (*a*) voice mail, (*b*) e-mail, (*c*) conference telephone calls, and (*d*) electronic meetings.

3. Select a typical business procedure such as writing a letter, circulating a memorandum, or preparing a pay cheque. Describe the accomplishing of this task in 1950 and 2000.

4. What impact has the World Wide Web had on (*a*) your education, (*b*) your recreation, and (*c*) your future career in business?

5. What impact has the World Wide Web had on business to date? What can we expect in the next 10 years?

19

Business Research Methods

Upon completing this chapter, you will be able to design and implement a plan for conducting the research needed for a business-report problem. To reach this goal, you should be able to

1. Construct and conduct a search for library information.

2. Construct a search for use on the World Wide Web.

3. Describe the procedure for a search through company records.

4. Describe an experiment for a business problem.

5. Describe an observational study for a business problem.

6. Describe the steps in planning a survey, including selecting an appropriate sample and designing a clear and effective questionnaire.

▷ to Business Research Methods

Doreen was just leaving the library when she met a friend from college.

"Hi Doreen. What are you doing here? I thought that now you have your own business, you wouldn't be in a library any more. Remember how many hours we spent here trying to get information to answer those questions for our business communications report?"

"Sure do! It doesn't take me so long to find the information I need any more, but I still have a lot of questions to answer. The big difference is that now they're my own questions. I think I've had to work harder and learn more since I graduated than I ever had to in school."

"With all that work, does the successful entrepreneur have time to go for a coffee?" ∎

You can collect the information you need by using two basic forms of research—secondary and primary. Secondary research is research utilizing material that someone else has presented—most often in printed or electronic form through periodicals, brochures, or books. Commonly called *library research,* it usually is the first form of research that you use to get background information, define the terms of your study more closely, and identify areas for further research. Primary research is your own research that uncovers information firsthand or produces new findings.

- Two basic forms of research are secondary research (getting information from someone else's research) and primary research (getting information firsthand).

SECONDARY RESEARCH

Secondary research materials are potentially the least costly, the most accessible, and the most complete source of information. However, to take full advantage of the available materials, you must know what you are looking for and how to find it. Assuming that you have defined your problem adequately, you can turn to libraries and other collections of information such as the World Wide Web. First, we will consider libraries. As different types of libraries offer different kinds of collections, it is helpful to know what types of libraries are available and to be familiar with their contents.

- Secondary research can be a rich source of information if you know what to look for and where to look.

Finding Publication Collections

General libraries are the best known and the most accessible. General libraries, which include college, university, and most public libraries, are called *general* because they contain materials on a wide range of subjects. The basic collection is broad rather than deep in its coverage of most subjects. Beyond that basic collection, many general libraries also have substantial collections in certain specialized areas. Usually the libraries within close proximity will try to co-operate so that their specialized collections are shared and not duplicated.

- General libraries offer a wide variety of information sources.

Libraries that limit their collections to one type or just a few types of material are considered *special libraries.* These libraries will have in-depth coverage of narrowly defined subject areas. Some special libraries are open to the public for consultation but not for borrowing. Others are completely private. The private libraries develop collections principally for members, employees, or research staff.

- Special libraries have limited collections and limited circulation.

Examples of special libraries include *The National Film Board Library* (specializing in NFB productions), the libraries of provincial legislatures such as the *Alberta Legislature Library* (specializing in government publications and topical materials used in the development of legislation), and the libraries of private businesses (serving the sponsoring company in the specialized area of its operations).

Now, how do you determine what these research centres and special libraries offer and whom to contact for permission to use their collections? In general, government libraries of all levels of government are open to the public for use of materials in the library. Some

- Access to special libraries varies with the type of library.

will also allow borrowing if adequate identification is produced. Universities and research centres often charge a fee for external users, especially for materials from specialized collections, but rarely is this fee prohibitive. Libraries of private corporations are seldom open to the public, but a specific question may be answered over the telephone or by e-mail. On occasion, the resources may be made available for research if requested.

- Ask for help in a general library to locate special collections, and use the published guides.

If you need leads for locating special libraries in your area, ask the reference librarian of your college or public library. Directories of libraries are available, and the librarian will know how to use them effectively. Although most of these guides concentrate on the United States, some Canadian libraries are included. Ask about *The Directory of Special Libraries and Information Centers* and *The Research Centers Directory*. Both of these publications are updated periodically and have excellent indexes by subject.

Conducting the Search

- Begin your research using the reference collection.

When you have found the appropriate library for your research, you are ready for the next challenge. With the volume of material available, how will you find what you need? The reference section of your library is where you should start. There, either on your own or with the assistance of a research librarian, you can discover any number of timely and comprehensive sources of facts and figures. Although you cannot know all these sources, as a business researcher you should be familiar with certain basic ones.

To lead you to reference sources, try consulting listings such as *Access Canada: Micromedia's Directory of Canadian Information Sources,* Barbara Brown's *Canadian Business and Economics: A Guide to Sources of Information/Economique et Commerce au Canada: Sources d'information,* and Gale Research Company's *Encyclopedia of Business Information Sources.* Browsing the shelves in the business reference section will also help you find sources.

- Encyclopedias offer both general and detailed information.

Encyclopedias. Encyclopedias are particularly valuable when you are just beginning a search. They offer background material and other general information that give you a helpful introduction to the area under study. Articles are written by experts in the field and frequently include a short bibliography which is useful for further research. Of the general encyclopedias, two worthy of special mention are *The Canadian Encyclopedia* for Canadian coverage and the *Encyclopaedia Britannica,* published in the United States, for completeness and for historical material. Both of these publications are now available in machine-readable form. *The Canadian Encyclopedia Plus* is available on CD-ROM and *Encyclopaedia Britannica* is available for a fee through the World Wide Web.[1]

- Specialized encyclopedias offer a specific focus but may lack Canadian content.

Specialized encyclopedias are useful because of their narrow focus. However, most are produced in the United States and refer to American law and practice. Subjects such as accounting practices, the banking system, trade regulations, labour laws, and human rights are handled differently in Canada. Therefore, *The Encyclopedia of Accounting Systems, Encyclopedia of Banking and Finance, The Encyclopedia of Management, The Encyclopedia of Professional Management,* and *Facts on File Encyclopedia of Management Techniques* are helpful but need to be used with caution. Unfortunately, there are not always Canadian equivalents available. Sometimes an international publication such as Johannsen's *International Dictionary of Management* is useful for a broader perspective.

- Biographical directories offer information about influential people.

Biographical Directories. A source of biographical information about leading figures of today or of the past is a biographical directory. The best-known biographical dictionaries are *Who's Who in Canada, Who's Who in America,* and *Who's Who in the World,* annual publications that summarize the lives of living people who have achieved prominence. Specialized publications will help you find information on people in particular professions. Among the most important of these for business are *Standard & Poor's Register of Corporations, Directors, and Executives;* and *Dun & Bradstreet's Reference Book of Corporate Management.* Nearly all business and professional areas are covered by some

[1]www.eb.com

form of directory: *Who's Who in Labor; Who's Who in Economics; Who's Who in Finance and Industry; The Rand McNally International Bankers Directory; Who's Who in Insurance;* and *Who's Who in Computer Education and Research.* Some of these publications have Canadian equivalents such as *Who's Who in Canadian Business, Who's Who in Canadian Finance,* and the Financial Post's *Directory of Directors.*

Almanacs.   Almanacs are handy guides to factual and statistical information. Simple, concise, and selective in the presentation of data, they should not be underestimated as quick references. Because almanacs are published annually, their contents are regularly updated. *The World Almanac and Book of Facts,* published by the Newspaper Enterprise Association, is an excellent general source of facts and statistics.

   Standard Canadian almanacs include two publications from Statistics Canada: *Canada Yearbook,* a factual and concise overview of Canada based on statistics gathered by Statistics Canada; and *Canada: A Portrait,* a readable, well-illustrated publication, aiming at a more popular audience. Another resource, *The Canadian Global Almanac,* includes Canadian as well as some international data. And finally, there are two almanacs that include directory material as well: *The Canadian Almanac and Directory* and *The Corpus Almanac.*

Trade Directories.   For information about individual businesses or the products they make, buy, or sell, directories are the references to consult. Directories are compilations of details in specific areas of interest and are variously referred to as *catalogues, listings, registers,* or *source books. The Blue Book of Canadian Business, The Canadian Book of Corporate Management,* the *Canadian Key Business Directory,* and the *Financial Post 500* all profile leading Canadian companies, giving information such as ranking and size (in annual sales and number of employees), names and titles of officers and managers, products, and locations. Literally thousands of directories exist—so many, in fact, that there are at least two directories of directories (*Trade Directories of the World* and *Directory of Directories*).

Government Publications.   Governments at all levels publish hundreds of titles that are invaluable in business research. Surveys, catalogues, pamphlets, periodicals—there seems to be no limit to the information that various bureaus, departments, and agencies collect and make available to the public. Statistics Canada publishes a wealth of information in a variety of formats. Each provincial government also has statistical, financial, and regulatory information available in attractive, easy-to-read publications. The challenge of working with government publications, therefore, is finding your way through this wealth of material to the specifics you need.

   Federal and provincial government publications are listed in many indexes and bibliographies, but these three are the major guides to current government documents: (1) The Canadian Government Publications Centre has published *The Government of Canada Publications Catalogue* since 1979. This catalogue has weekly checklists, quarterly compilations, and an annual index. From 1954 to 1979, its title was *Canadian Government Publications Catalogue.* The Centre also publishes inventory lists and selected subject lists on an irregular basis. (2) *Canadiana,* published by the National Library of Canada, lists federal and provincial documents. Because it began about 1950, it is a useful source for identifying older materials. (3) *Microlog Index* (formerly *Publicat Index*) lists federal and provincial documents from the late 1970s to the present. It is published monthly with annual cumulations by Micromedia Limited of Toronto.

   For U.S. documents, it may be helpful to consult the *Monthly Catalog of U.S. Government Publications.* Issued by the Superintendent of Documents, it includes a comprehensive listing of annual and monthly publications and an alphabetical index of the issuing agencies. The Printing Office also issues *Selected United States Government Publications,* a monthly list of general-interest publications that are sold to the public.

   Some libraries keep government publications in a separate section with a unique system of organization; others catalogue them and place them with other books and

* Almanacs provide factual and statistical information.

* Canadian almanacs and yearbooks are available.

* Trade directories publish information about individual businesses and products.

* Governments publish extensive research materials.

* Guides are available to federal and provincial government publications.

* The U.S. government publishes guides to its publications.

* Government publications may receive special treatment in your library.

magazines on the same topic. In either case knowing the department that publishes the document is a key to finding it, for example Statistics Canada, or The Department of Labour.

Some larger libraries are designated *depository libraries* and automatically receive copies of government publications. If your library does not have what you need, you might ask for the location of the nearest depository library. Current Canadian government publications may be purchased from the Canadian Government Publications Centre[2], from provincial centres, and from designated bookstores. Sales locations are available from Supply and Services Canada.

- Private business services collect and publish data. Many such reports are available in public and university libraries.

Business Services.   Business services are private organizations that supply a variety of information to business practitioners, especially investors. Libraries also subscribe to their publications, giving business researchers ready access to yet another source of valuable, timely data.

Moody's Investors Service, one of the best known of such organizations, publishes a weekly *Manual*. These reports summarize financial data and operating facts on all the major American companies, providing information that an investor needs to evaluate the investment potential of individual securities or of fields as a whole. *Corporation Records,* published by Standard & Poor's Corporation, presents similar information in loose-leaf form. More financial information on Canadian companies is available in the *Financial Post Investors' Guide* and the *Blue Book of CBS Stock Reports* included in the weekly *Canadian Business Service.* Financial Post also publishes surveys such as the *Survey of Industrials* and the *Survey of Mines and Energy Resources,* which give financial information on Canadian public corporations in those sectors. CCH Canadian publishes several services in loose-leaf format, including *Canadian Tax Reports, Canadian Small Business Guide,* and *Canadian Corporation Law Reports.*

Two other organizations whose publications are especially helpful to business researchers are Predicasts, and Gale Research Company. Predicasts provides seven separate business services, although it is best known for publications featuring forecasts and market data by country, product, and company (*Predicasts, World-Regional-Casts,* and *Expansion and Capacity Digest*). Similarly, Gale Research provides numerous services to business researchers. Two of its most useful publications for business researchers are *Statistical Sources* (a subject guide to data on business and related topics) and *Encyclopedia of Business Information Systems.*

- Take advantage of work already done by others; try to find a prepared bibliography.

Prepared Bibliographies.   You may find a *bibliography*[3] that has been compiled by an association, government agency, or library. Finding such a list may save you time and trouble. If the bibliography has been published as a reference book, it will often include a description of the scope and contents of each source the bibliographer listed. Another way to discover resources is to consult the bibliographies included in encyclopedia articles, texts, magazine articles, and theses that deal with your subject. These bibliographies will be more selective, but will usually include the most important works in the subject area—the standard references and authorities.

- The library catalogue is another resource for developing a bibliography.

The Library Catalogue.   The library catalogue itself will give you more clues to follow. Part inventory and part index, the catalogue is the key to the resources of the library. It offers three distinct ways of identifying and locating desired references: by author, by title, and by subject. Do you know the author but not the title? Just look up the author's last name to find the title and the location of that work in the library. You may find additional publications by the same author that relate to your topic. Or, if you know the title, you will be able to identify the author and the location of the work. Because libraries

---

[2]Supply and Services Canada, Ottawa, Ontario, K1A 0S9.

[3]A list of resources on a particular subject, such as "Personal Financial Planning." It may sometimes have additional limitations of authorship, time, or place, such as "Sources of Information for Personal Financial Planning in the Gatineau Hills Library System."

shelve their materials by subject, once you know the location of one title, you can scan the shelves nearby for similar works.

A catalogue search by subject is frequently the most productive route. Most computerized catalogues offer keyword searches. You enter words that describe your topic and the computer searches for those words in the titles, assigned subject headings, or abstracts and notes. The resulting list will include some peripheral material as well as material relevant to your topic. The success of the search depends upon your choice of distinctive keywords and phrases. Again, once you have identified a useful resource, you can use it to lead you to others. Somewhere in the catalogue entry for that work, you will find the subject categories that have been assigned to it. If you pursue them, you will find similar sources by other authors. A third way to conduct a subject search is to consult the *Library of Congress Directory of Subject Headings,* a volume readily available in the general reference section of most libraries. This list helps you find the subject heading that most closely defines your subject.

• A subject search will identify possible sources of information.

Each entry has a code for locating the item. For books, the first part of the code is the classification number that groups materials on a similar subject together. The next part is usually the author number, beginning with the first letter of the author's last name. A third part indicating the publication date of the book may also be included. This number notes the specific shelf address of the book. Again, if you find a book on your topic, be sure to check other books with a similar classification number since libraries shelve books by subject.

• Each catalogue entry has a code which classifies the item and indicates its location.

Periodical Indexes. The catalogue will tell you the titles of newspapers, magazines, and journals located in that library. To identify specific articles within those publications, you will need to consult an index. Regularly updated indexes are available in the reference section of most libraries. They may be general or specialized in the field you are researching.

• To identify articles for your list of prospective sources, consult a periodical index.

The general ones are a good place to start. Try the *Business Periodicals Index* and the *Canadian Business Index* (formerly the *Canadian Business Periodicals Index*). Issued monthly and cumulated yearly, these indexes cover the major business periodicals. Articles on a wide variety of business areas, industries, and trades are indexed by subject, author, and company. Two other indexes that you may find useful are the *United States Predicasts F & S Index,* which covers business-oriented periodicals, newspapers, and special reports, and the *Public Affairs Information Service Bulletin,* which lists information relating to economics and public affairs. *Canadian Business and Current Affairs,* available on CD-ROM, gives more complete coverage of Canadian materials.

These indexes are available in printed form; however, most libraries prefer the machine-readable form for computer searching. Sometimes several indexes are included on one CD-ROM, making your search process very efficient. If the index allows multiple-term searching, you can focus your search very specifically. With the author and title of the article, and the title and issue of the magazine, you can now locate the article if your library subscribes to that periodical title. Knowing that an article on your subject exists is only helpful if you can get a copy of it. If your library does not subscribe to that magazine, you may have to go to another library or request a copy on inter-library loan. Both of these procedures take additional time. A database search can overcome this problem.

Database Searching. The advantage of a database over an index is that the database has not only the author and title of the article, but an abstract or, in some cases, the whole text of the article. As you know, the search and storage capacity of computers has been expanding phenomenally. Much of the information routinely recorded in printed form and accessed through directories, encyclopedias, bibliographies, and indexes is now collected and stored in computer files as well. When these *databases* are accessed by computer, the result is faster, more extensive, and more complete research than any conducted through traditional means.

• Databases are organized files of information that can be sorted and accessed by key terms.

Databases, many of which are produced by private information services, offer a variety of materials essential to business research. Some are on-line services, while others use CD-ROM. To find on-line resources, consult *Business Online: A Canadian Guide,* which is designed to help business users determine which services are most useful for their needs. One example is Dialog Information Systems. DIALOG includes in its selection the *American Statistics Index,* the *Encyclopedia of Associations,* a number of Predicasts services (*PTS, F&S Indexes, International Forecasts,* and *Prompt*), and *Standard & Poor's News.*

• Many libraries offer facilities for computer searches of databases.

An increasing number of public, college, and university libraries offer on-line database searching service, usually for a fee that reflects the cost of the computer time employed and the number of items identified. They also usually require you to work closely with trained staff to design a search strategy that will use computer time effectively and retrieve only relevant information. Because of these costs, some libraries prefer to purchase CD-ROMs. These files are then available without further cost except for the personal computer needed to search them. The disadvantage is the time lag between the publication of a magazine and the CD-ROM index.

• Gather all available publications. Check each systematically for the information you need.

The next two steps are elementary, but nonetheless important. As you identify resources that match your topic, record all the pertinent information in your personal bibliography so that you will be able to identify the source later. Then gather the publications and systematically check them for the information you need. In a thorough search, you may need to use inter-library loan services or to send away for company or government documents. Your check of the sources you gather also must be thorough. For each source study the pages cited in your bibliographic reference. Then take some time to learn about the publication. Review its table of contents, its index, and the endnotes or footnotes related to the pages you are researching. For key sources, you may want to locate reviews or annotated bibliographies that comment on the reliability of the source you are using. You should be familiar with both the source and the context of all the information you plan to report; they are often as significant as the information itself.

The World Wide Web.   To access the World Wide Web (WWW), you will need to subscribe to a server that will provide you with access to the many networks that are linked together into the WWW. Because of the function it performs, the server is called a *service provider* or an *access provider.* If the link is established using a modem and telephone lines, it may be called a *dial-up service.* Researching several providers to find the one offering the best plan for your needs is worthwhile. Most will provide a certain number of hours of service for a flat rate, with additional time charged at an hourly rate. Many WWW users find they enjoy the Web experience and quickly increase the number of connect time hours in their subscription.

• Using the World Wide Web requires access to a server and to browser software.

• Service providers offer browsers, e-mail packages, and more advanced software.

The service provider you choose will advise you on the communications software you need and the hardware requirements for the best operation of your link to the WWW. In addition, the provider will offer you browser *software* (such as *Netscape*) to allow you to search the Web, and an additional e-mail package (such as *Eudora*). Some providers will offer you more advanced options and training.

• Find information by using a catalogue, a keyword search engine, or a worm.

Once your connection is established, you will use a catalogue, a keyword search engine, or a worm to find the information you need. A catalogue takes information from the Web and categorizes it into subject areas much like a library does. Typical areas might be Arts and Entertainment, Business, Computers, Government and Politics, and so on. A catalogue is useful for narrowing the search area, increasing the "good hits," and reducing the time spent searching. For example, by narrowing the search to the subject area *Computers,* a search for *engines* will avoid information about locomotives.

A catalogue is usually associated with a keyword search engine. Once you select the general subject category from the catalogue, you use a keyword search to find the specific references. A keyword search engine looks for matches between the words you enter and the words found in the titles, abstracts, or full text of the sites listed with that particular search engine. Because directories and search engines may not look at every document on the WWW, it is wise to use several different ones in your search. *Yahoo!, AltaVista,* and *Infoseek Guide* are popular examples.

A *worm* is another tool used for searching the Web. It is sometimes referred to as an *automated robot* program or a *web crawler.* This program searches through the Web looking for new sites to index. A Web site does not have to be registered to be found in this search.

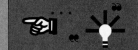
Although the worm is working all the time, its index is usually updated once a week or less. When you enter terms for it to match, it looks at the index it has created and lists site addresses for you to check. *Lycos* and *WebCrawler*[4] are examples of this type of search software.

Because of the size of the WWW, it is not unusual to find 100,000 hits from a search—far more than you want or can use. To limit the references found, you must be careful to use as specific a search strategy as you can. Use the catalogue or subject index first; then enter words or phrases with narrow meanings. If the search engine you are using allows it, group several words together and require that they all appear in the document before it is listed for your consideration. Be sure to check the *help feature* for instructions and short cuts. Once you find the type of information you want, use the links in that document to lead you to other similar items.

* Be specific with your search terms to create a successful search.

The World Wide Web is an invaluable source, but it comes with no guarantees about the accuracy, currency, or reliability of the information it provides. Many sites give only personal opinion. Others give biased or one-sided opinions. Still others give out-dated or incorrect information. As we said earlier, "I saw it on the Web" is no more reliable a credit than "I overheard it on the bus."[5]

* Be alert to the credibility and reliability of the source.

PRIMARY RESEARCH

When you cannot find the information you need in secondary sources, you must get it firsthand. You may find it useful to discuss your work with others. In that case *Sources: The Directory of Contacts for Editors, Reporters and Researchers* could guide your networking efforts. You should also check newsgroups and e-mail lists for people who are working in a similar area. Be careful not to divulge information that is private or useful to competitors on these public forums. After you have exhausted those routes, you consider four basic methods of primary research:

* Primary research employs four basic methods.

1. Searching through company records
2. Experimenting
3. Observing
4. Surveying and Interviewing

---

[4]For more information on WebCrawler, see http://www.webcrawler.com/WebCrawler/Facts/HowItWorks.html.
[5]See also Chapter 18, "Technology in Communication."

Searching through Company Records

- Company records are an excellent source of firsthand information.

Since many of today's business problems involve various phases of company operations, a company's internal records—production data, sales records, merchandising information, and accounting records—are frequently an excellent source of firsthand information. To clarify why these records are considered a primary research source, remember that you are looking at raw data. Someone else kept these records, but no one has compiled or interpreted them for you. You will analyze them for new information. A report written by someone else using the same raw data would be considered as a secondary source to you. If you use its ideas, you would give credit to the original author of the report.

- Make sure you (1) have a clear idea of the information you need, (2) understand the terms of access and confidentiality, and (3) co-operate with company personnel.

There are no set rules on how to go about finding and gathering information through company records. Record-keeping systems vary widely from company to company. However, you are well advised to keep the following standards in mind as you conduct your investigation. First, as in any other type of research, you must have a clear idea of the information you need. Undefined, open-ended investigations which inconvenience the staff of the department are not appreciated—nor are they particularly productive for the researcher. Second, you must clearly understand the ground rules under which you are allowed to review materials. Matters of confidentiality and access should be resolved before you start. And third, if you are not intimately familiar with a company's records, you must co-operate with someone who is. The complexity and sensitivity of such materials require that they be reviewed in their proper context.

Conducting an Experiment

- The before–after design is the simplest experiment. You use just one test group.

The Before–After Design. The simplest experimental design is the before–after design. In this design you select a test group of subjects, measure the variable in which you are interested, and then introduce the experimental factor. After a specified period of time, during which the experimental factor has presumably had its effect, you again measure the variable in which you are interested. If there are any differences between the first and second measurements, you attribute them to the experimental factor. Figure 19–1 illustrates the before–after design.

Consider the following application. Assume that you are conducting research for a retail store to determine the effect of point-of-sale advertizing. Your first step is to select a product for the experiment—Cameo bath soap. Second, you record sales of Cameo soap for one week, using no point-of-sale advertizing. Then you introduce the experimental variable—the Cameo point-of-sale display. For the next week, you again record sales of Cameo soap; and at the end of that week, you compare the results for the two weeks. Any

FIGURE 19–1 The Before–After Design

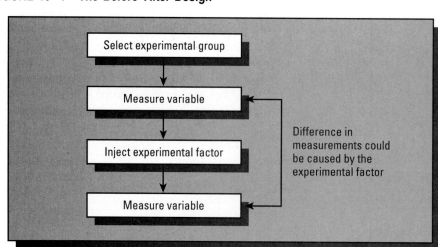

increase in sales would presumably be explained by the introduction of the display. Thus, if 500 bars of Cameo soap were sold in the first week and 600 were sold in the second week, you would conclude that the 100 additional sales can be attributed to point-of-sale advertising. For validation, you may repeat the experiment at other times or in other locations.

You can probably recognize the major shortcoming of the design. It is simply not logical to assume that the experimental factor explains the entire difference in sales between the first week and the second. The sales of Cameo bath soap could have changed for a number of other reasons—changes in the weather, holiday or other seasonal influences on business activity, other advertising, and so on. At best, you have determined only that point-of-sale advertising *could* influence sales.

> • The changes recorded in a before–after experiment may not be attributable to the experimental factor alone.

The Controlled Before–After Design.
To account for influences other than the experimental factor, you may use designs more complex than the before–after design. These designs attempt to measure the other influences by including some means of control. The simplest of these designs is the controlled before–after design.

In the controlled before-after design, you select not one group, but two—the experimental group and the control group. Before introducing the experimental factor, you measure in each group the variable to be tested. Then you introduce the experimental factor into the experimental group only.

> • In the controlled before–after experiment, you use two identical test groups.

When the period allotted for the experiment is over, you again measure each group on the variable being tested. Any difference between the first and second measurements in the experimental group can be explained by two causes—the experimental factor and other influences. But the difference between the first and second measurements in the control group can be explained only by other influences, for this group was not subjected to the experimental factor. Thus, comparing the "afters" of the two groups will give you a measure of the influence of the experimental factor. The controlled before–after design is diagrammed in Figure 19–2.

In a controlled before–after experiment designed to test the point-of-sale application, you might select Cameo and Pearl bath soaps and record the sales of both brands for one week. Next you introduce point-of-sale displays for Cameo only, and you record sales for both soaps for a second week. At the end of that week, you compare the results for the two brands. Whatever difference you find in Cameo sales and Pearl sales will be a fair measure of the experimental factor, your point-of-sale display.

For example, if Pearl soap sales increase 12.5 percent from week one to week two, the increase must be due to factors other than the experimental factor. (Remember, there was no point-of-sale display for Pearl soap, the experimental control.) If sales of Cameo soap

FIGURE 19–2 The Controlled Before–After Design

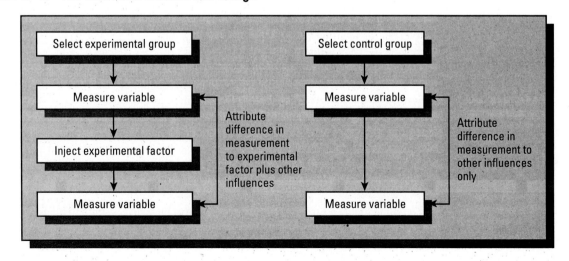

increase by 20 percent, the increase can be attributed to both the experimental factor (Cameo's display) and other influences. You use the increase in sales of Pearl soap to calculate how much of Cameo's increase was due to other influences. That is, since Pearl soap had an increase, you reason that Cameo would have experienced a similar increase without the special advertizing. However, Cameo's additional increase can be attributed to point-of-sale advertizing. Again, for validation, you may repeat the experiment at other times or in other locations.

Using the Observation Technique

Like the experiment, observation is a technique perfected in the sciences that is also useful in business research. Simply stated, observation is seeing with a purpose. It consists of watching the events involved in a problem and systematically recording what is seen. In observation, you do not manipulate the details of what you observe; you take note of situations exactly as you find them.

Note that observation as an independent research technique is different from the observation you use in recording the effects of variables introduced into a test situation. In the latter case, observation is a step in the experiment, not an end in itself. The two methods, therefore, should not be confused.

To see how observation works as a business technique, consider this situation. You are a grocery supplier who wants to determine how shoppers are responding to a new line of foods. A review of sales records would certainly give some information, as would a survey of store patrons. However, observing customers as they shop may reveal important information that you might overlook if you used alternative techniques.

Like all primary research techniques, observation must be designed to fit the requirements of the problem being considered. However, the planning stage generally requires two steps. First, you construct a recording form; second, you design a systematic procedure for observing and recording the information of interest.

The recording form may be any tabular arrangement that permits quick and easy recording of that information. Though observation forms are hardly standardized, one commonly used arrangement (see Figure 19–3) provides a separate line for each observation. Headings at the top of the page mark the columns in which the observer will place the appropriate mark. The recording form identifies the characteristics that are to be observed and requires the recording of such potentially important details as the date, time, and place of the observation and the name of the observer.

Collecting Information by Survey

The premise of the survey as a method of primary research is simple: You can best determine certain types of information by asking questions. Such information includes personal data, opinions, evaluations, and other material that is important in and of itself. It also includes information necessary to plan for an experiment or an observation or to supplement or interpret the resulting data.

Once you have decided to use the survey for your research, you have to make decisions about a number of matters. The first is format. The questions can range from spontaneous inquiries to carefully structured interrogations. The next is the matter of delivery. The questions can be posed in a personal interview, asked over the telephone, or presented in printed form.

Most important is the matter of whom to survey. Except for situations in which a small number of people are involved in the problem under study, you cannot reach all of the people involved. Thus, you have to select a sample of respondents who represent the group as a whole as accurately as possible. There are several ways to select that sample, as you will see.

Sampling theory forms the basis for most research by survey, though it has any number of other applications as well. Buyers of grain, for example, judge the quality of an entire shipment by examining a few scoops of it. Quality-control supervisors spot-check a small

FIGURE 19–3 Excerpt of a Common Type of Observation Recording Form

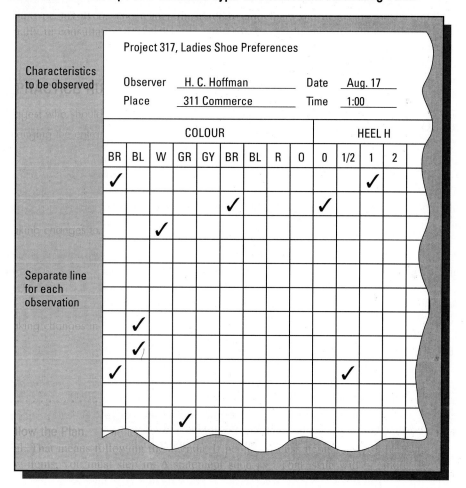

percentage of products ready for distribution to determine whether production standards are being met. Judges at country fairs take a little taste of each entry of homemade jam to decide which entry will win a blue ribbon.

The premise for these and all other sampling cases is the *general law of sampling:* a sufficiently large number of items taken at random from the larger number of items in a group will have the characteristics of the group as a whole. *Sample representativeness* means that the selected sample reflects the composition of the larger group in every way possible. For example, if you want to determine the opinion of the general public on a political issue, you should not use a sample consisting entirely of people who sign petitions or write letters to government officials because such people are not representative of the general public. Instead, you must make certain that your sample proportionately represents all the different kinds of people in the total population.

The methods for determining the reliability and representativeness of a sample involve statistical techniques beyond the scope of this book. For information on this subject, consult any general statistics textbook.

Designing the Sample. The techniques most commonly used to construct representative samples are random sampling, stratified random sampling, systematic sampling, and area sampling. Each of these techniques has advantages in certain situations and limitations in others. Your first task in designing a representative sample, therefore, is to decide which sampling technique is best suited to your research problem.

• The sample must have the characteristics of the group from which it has been selected.

Random Sampling.

Random sampling is the technique assumed in the general law of sampling. By definition it is the sampling technique that gives every member of the group under study an equal chance of being included. To achieve this equality, you must first identify and record every member of the group. Then, through a chance method, you draw the members for your sample.

For example, if you are studying the job attitudes of 200 assembly-line workers and determine that 25 interviews will give you the information you need, you might make out a name card for each worker, place the 200 cards in a container, mix them up, and draw out 25. Since each of the 200 workers has an equal chance of being selected, your sample will be random and can be presumed to be representative.

Stratified Random Sampling.

This special form of random sampling subdivides the group under study and makes random selections within each subgroup. The size of each subgroup is proportionate to that subgroup's percentage of the whole. If a subgroup is too small to yield meaningful findings, however, you may have to select a disproportionately large sample. (Of course, when the study calls for statistics on the group as a whole, the actual proportion of such a subgroup must be restored.)

Let us say that you want to survey a college student body of 4,000, using a 10 percent sample. As Table 19–1 illustrates, you have a number of alternatives for determining the makeup of your sample, depending on the focus of your research. Keep in mind, though, that no matter what characteristic you select, the quotas the individual segments represent must total 100 percent and the number of people in the sample must total 400 (10 percent of 4,000). Keep in mind also that within these quotas you will use an equal-chance method to select the individual members of your sample.

Systematic Sampling.

Systematic sampling, though not random in the strictest sense, is random for all practical purposes. It is the technique of taking selections at constant intervals (every nth unit) from a list of the items under study. The interval used is based, as you might expect, on the size of the list and the size of the desired sample. For

TABLE 19–1 Stratified Random Sampling: Some Possible Divisions of a Student Population

	Number in Universe	Percent of Total	Number to Be Interviewed
Total student enrolment	4,000	100	400
By Gender			
Male	2,400	60	240
Female	1,600	40	160
By Faculty			
Arts	1,600	40	160
Science	1,400	35	140
Education	760	19	76
Medicine	250	6	24
By Marital Status			
Married	400	10	40
Single	3,600	90	360
By Years of Study			
First	1,600	40	160
Second	1,000	25	100
Third	800	20	80
Fourth	400	10	40
Graduate studies	200	5	20

example, if you want a 10 percent sample of a list of 10,000, you might select every 10th item on the list.

If the original list was compiled according to a certain criteria such as length of service or alphabetically by surname, the designated place on the list means the items do not have an equal chance of being selected. To correct that problem, you might use an equal-chance method to determine what *n* to use. Thus, if you selected the number 7 randomly, you would draw the numbers 7, 17, 27, and so on to 9,997 to make up your sample. Or, you might first scramble the list and then select every 10th item from the now randomly ordered list.

• Select the interval randomly or scramble the order of the subject group if you want your systematic sample to be random.

Area Sampling.   In area sampling the items for a sample are drawn in stages. This sampling technique, also known as *random cluster sampling,* is appropriate when the area to be studied is large and can be broken down into progressively smaller components. For example, if you want to draw an area sample for a certain city, you may use census data to divide the city into homogenous districts. Using an equal-chance method, you then select a given number of districts to include in the next stage of your sample. Next, you divide each of the selected districts into sub-districts—city blocks, for example. Continuing the process, you randomly select a given number of these blocks and subdivide each of them into households. Finally, using random sampling once more, you select the households that will constitute the sample you will use in your research.

• For an area sample, draw items from the subject group in stages. Select randomly at each stage.

Area sampling is not limited to geographic divisions, however. It is adaptable to any number of applications. For example, it is an appropriate technique to use in a survey of the workers in a given industry. An approach that you may take in this situation is to randomly select a given number of companies from a list of all the companies in the industry. Then, using organization units and selecting randomly at each level, you break down each of these companies into divisions, departments, sections, and so on until you finally identify the workers you will survey.

Constructing the Questionnaire.   Most orderly interrogation follows a definite plan of inquiry. This plan is usually worked out in a printed form, called the *questionnaire.* The questionnaire is simply an orderly arrangement of the questions, with appropriate spaces provided for the answers. But simple as the finished questionnaire may appear to be, it is the subject of careful planning. It is, in a sense, the outline of the analysis of the problem. In addition, it must observe certain rules. These rules sometimes vary with the problem. The more general and by far the more important ones follow.

Avoid Leading Questions.   A leading question is one that in some way influences the answer. For example, the question "Is Cameo your favourite bath soap?" makes a suggestion which influences the respondent to choose Cameo. Some people who would say yes to that leading question would name another brand if they were asked, "What is your favourite brand of bath soap?"

• Avoid leading questions.

Make the Questions Easy to Understand.   Questions not clearly understood by all respondents lead to error. Unfortunately, it is difficult to determine in advance just what the respondents will not understand. As will be mentioned later, the best means of detecting the difficult questions in advance is to test the questionnaire before using it, but you can be on the alert for a few general sources of confusion.

• Word the questions so that all the respondents understand them.

One source of confusion is vagueness of expression. Does the question "How do you bank?" mean "at a chartered bank or a trust company," "in person or by automated teller," "weekly or monthly," etc. Who other than its author knows what information the question is meant to uncover? Another source of confusion is using words not understood by the respondents, as in the question "Do you read your house organ regularly?" The words *house organ* have a specialized, not widely known meaning, and *regularly* means different things to different people. "Do you read every issue of your monthly newsletter, *The Workline*?" is much clearer. Combining two questions in one is yet another source of confusion. For example, "How frequently do you read books and magazines?" actually

• Vagueness of expression, difficult words, and two questions in one cause misunderstanding.

asks two questions: "How frequently do you read books?" and "How frequently do you read magazines?" Someone who reads magazines but not books would find it difficult to answer.

• Responses to direct personal questions may be inaccurate.

Control for Inaccurate Responses to Questions on Personal Matters.

Because of prejudices or pride, people cannot be expected to answer personal questions accurately even if the surveys are anonymous. These personal areas include age, income status, morals, and personal habits. How many people, for example, would answer no to the question "Do you brush your teeth twice a day?" How many people would give their ages correctly? How many citizens would admit to fudging a bit on their tax returns? Many people will choose to answer based on favourable appearances rather than accuracy.

But one may ask, "What if such information is essential to the solution of the problem?" The answer is to use less direct means of inquiry. To estimate age, for example, investigators could list 10-year intervals. (What is your age group: 21–30, 31–40, 41–50, 51–60, over 60.) For approximating income, they could ask for such non-threatening information as occupation, postal code, or type of dwelling. Admittedly, such techniques do not give precise data, but they can provide more reliable information than direct questioning. Secondly, they can be used in combination with direct questions to check on the accuracy of the answers given.

• Seek facts as the basis for conclusions.

Seek Facts as Much as Possible.

Most people are not accurate reporters of their opinions. They may find it difficult to describe their feelings in words, they may prefer to present a "best case scenario" of their opinions, or they may invent an answer to complete the questionnaire when they have never considered the matter before. Although some studies require opinions, it is best to seek facts whenever possible.

Even when opinions are needed, it is still more reliable to record facts. The opinion behind the fact is revealed through the investigator's judgment. Although this is not a perfect method, the logical analysis of fact made by trained investigators is preferable to a spur-of-the-moment opinion from the interviewee.

A frequent violation of this rule results from the use of generalizations. Respondents are sometimes asked to generalize an answer from a large number of experiences over time. The question "Which magazines do you read regularly?" is a good illustration. Aside from the confusion caused by the word *regularly* and the fact that the question may tax the respondent's memory, the question forces the respondent to generalize. A better wording is this: "What magazines have you read this month?"

• Ask for information that people will remember, such as recent or significant events.

Ask Only for Information That Can Be Remembered.

Since the memory of all human beings is limited, the questionnaire should ask only for information that the respondents can be expected to remember. In order to make sure that this is done, a knowledge of certain fundamentals of memory is necessary.

Recency is the foremost fundamental. People remember events that occurred within the past few hours. By the next day, they will forget some. A month later they may not remember any. One might well remember, for example, what one ate for lunch on the day of the inquiry, and perhaps one might remember what one ate for lunch a day, or two days, or three days earlier. But one would be unlikely to remember what one ate for lunch a month earlier.

The second fundamental of memory is that significant events may be remembered over long periods of time. One may long remember the first day of school, an automobile accident, or a Christmas Day. In each of these examples, there was an intense stimulus—a requisite for retention in memory.

A third fundamental of memory is that fairly insignificant facts may take on significance and be remembered over long periods of time through association with something significant. Although one would not normally remember what one ate for lunch a year earlier, for example, one might remember if the day happened to be one's wedding day. Obviously, the memory is stimulated, not by the meal itself, but by the association of the meal with something more significant.

Plan the Physical Layout with Foresight.

The overall design of the questionnaire should be planned to facilitate recording, analyzing, and tabulating the answers. Three major considerations are involved in such planning.

• Plan the layout for clarity and accuracy.

First, answers should be allowed sufficient space for recording. When practical, a system for checking answers may be set up. Such a system must always provide for all possible answers, including conditional answers. For example, a direct question may provide for three possible answers: Yes _____, No _____, and Don't Know _____.

Second, adequate space for identifying and describing the respondent should be provided. In some instances the age, sex, and income bracket of the respondent is vital to the analysis of the problem and should be recorded. In other instances little or no identification is necessary.

Third, the best possible sequence of questions should be used. In some instances starting with a question of high interest value may have psychological advantages. In some other instances, it may be best to follow an order of progression from general to specific. Frequently, some questions must precede others because they help explain the others. Whatever the requirements of the individual case may be, however, careful and logical analysis should be used in determining the sequence of questions.

Use Scaling When Appropriate.

It is sometimes desirable to measure the intensity of the respondents' feelings about something (an idea, a product, a company, etc.). In such cases some form of scaling is generally useful.

• Use scaling to rank or rate an answer.

Of the various techniques of scaling, ranking and rating deserve special mention. These are the simpler techniques and more practical. There are various more complicated methods[6], but the more sophisticated techniques are beyond the scope of this book.

The ranking technique consists simply of asking the respondent to rank a number of alternative answers to a question in order of preference (1, 2, 3, etc.). For example, in a survey to determine consumer preferences for toothpaste, the respondent might be asked to rank toothpastes A, B, C, D, and E in order of preference. In this example the alternatives could be compared on the number of preferences stated for each. This method of ranking and summarizing results is reliable in spite of its simplicity.

The rating technique graphically sets up a scale showing the complete range of possible attitudes on a matter and assigns number values to the positions on the scale. Respondents must then choose the position on the scale that best represents their attitudes on that matter. Typically, the numeral positions are described by words, as the example in Figure 19–4 illustrates.

Because the rating technique deals with the subjective rather than the factual, it is sometimes desirable to use more than one question to cover the attitude being measured. Logically, the average of a person's answers to such questions gives a more reliable answer than does any single answer.

FIGURE 19–4   An Example of Rating Using Words and Numeral Positions

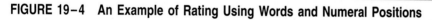
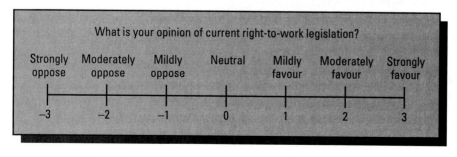

---

[6]Equivalent interval techniques (developed by L. L. Thurstone), scalogram analysis (developed by Louis Guttman), and the semantic differential (developed by C. E. Osgood, G. J. Suchi, and P. H. Tannenbaum) are more complex techniques.

Selecting the Manner of Questioning.

- Select the way of asking the questions (by mail, personal contact, or telephone) that gives the best sample, the lowest cost, and the best results.

Selecting the Manner of Questioning.   You can get answers to the questions you need answered in three primary ways: by personal (face-to-face) contact, by telephone, or by mail. You should select the way that in your unique case gives the best sample, the lowest cost, and the best results. By *best sample,* we mean respondents who best represent the group concerned. *Lowest cost,* of course, refers to dollars spent. And *results* are the information you need. As you can see, such factors as geographic distances, difficulty of contacting respondents, time available, and need for explanations will influence your selection.

- Develop a working plan that covers all the steps and all the problems.

Developing a Working Plan.   After selecting the manner of questioning, you should carefully develop a working plan for the survey. As well as you can, you should anticipate and determine how to handle every possible problem. If you are conducting a mail survey, for example, you need to develop an explanatory message that motivates the subjects to respond, tells them what to do, and answers all the questions they are likely to ask. If you are conducting a personal or telephone survey, you need to cover this information in instructions to the interviewers. You should develop your working plan, test that plan in a pilot study, and then revise it based on the knowledge you gain from the pilot study.

- Test the questionnaire and the working plan. Make any changes needed.

Conducting a Pilot Study.   Before doing the survey, it is advisable to conduct a pilot study on your questionnaire and working plan. A pilot study is a small-scale version of the actual survey. Its purpose is to test what you have planned. Based on your experience in the pilot study, you modify your questionnaire and working plan for use in the full-scale survey.

. . . .

A SUMMARY OF LEARNING OUTCOMES FROM THIS CHAPTER

You can get the information you need for a report by secondary (library) or primary (firsthand) research. You conduct secondary research in either a general library (usually public) or a special library (often private). If you need quantitative or factual information, you may be able to go directly to it, using such sources as encyclopedias, biographical directories, almanacs, trade directories, government publications, or business services.

When you cannot go directly to the source, you use indirect methods. You may begin by searching for an already prepared bibliography. You may consult the catalogue of a library. If the information you need is likely to be in periodicals, you can consult various indexes in printed or machine-readable form.

The World Wide Web is a very large resource. Construct a specific search strategy using catalogues and keyword searches to find information on your topic.

You can conduct primary research in four major ways, depending on the information you need. If the information involves company operations, you will need to look through company records.

For some problems, you may need to conduct an experiment (an orderly form of testing). The simplest design for an experiment is the before–after design. It involves selecting a group of subjects, measuring the variable, introducing the experimental factor, and measuring the variable again. The difference between the two measurements is attributed to the experimental factor. The controlled before–after design involves selecting two groups, measuring the variable in both groups, introducing the experimental factor in one group, and then measuring the variable again in both groups. The second measurements enable you to determine the effect of the experimental factor and of other factors that might have influenced the variable between the two measurements.

The third primary research method is observation, which may be defined as seeing with a purpose. It consists of watching the events involved in a problem and systematically recording what is seen. The events observed are not manipulated, as in an experiment.

The fourth method is the survey, in which the needed information is obtained by questioning a sample of people—a group representative of a larger group that holds the information needed. The procedure for selecting the sample is based on the general law of sampling: a sufficiently large number of items taken at random from a larger number of items in a group will have the characteristics of the group as a whole. A good sample is both reliable (of sufficient size) and representative (having the characteristics of the whole).

You may use any of a variety of sample designs. A random sample involves pure chance selection, giving every member of the group under study an equal chance of being selected. A stratified random sample involves proportionate and random selection from each major subgroup of the group under study. In systematic sampling, selections are taken at constant intervals (every fifth one, for example) from a complete list of the group under study. In area sampling you first divide the entire group under study into parts. Then you select some of these parts by some chance means. Next you subdivide the parts selected; and you make chance selections from the subparts. You continue to subdivide and select until you have the units (households, offices, etc.) that contain the people you will interview.

You should construct the questionnaire carefully, following these general rules:

1. Avoid leading questions.

2. Make the questions easy to understand.

3. Control for inaccurate responses to questions on personal matters.

4. Seek facts as much as possible.

5. Ask only for what can be remembered.

6. Plan the layout with enough space and a proper sequence of questions.

7. Use scaling when appropriate.

You get answers to the questions by personal contact, telephone, or mail, depending on which will produce the best sample and the best information at the lowest cost. You develop a working plan for conducting the questioning—one that covers all the possible problems and clearly explains what to do. It is usually advisable to test the questionnaire and the working plan through a pilot study. This enables you to make changes in the questionnaire and improve the working plan before conducting the survey.

QUESTIONS FOR DISCUSSION

1. Select a major Canadian company and use your library to find the following information. For this question, do not use the World Wide Web. Be sure to record your sources.

   a. The full company name.
   b. The name of the current CEO or principal.
   c. The number of employees.
   d. The value of the company's shares.
   e. The names of parent or subsidiary companies.

2. For the same company, locate the home page on the World Wide Web. Find the information asked for in Question 1 using one of the search engines available to you.

3. Evaluate the two searches you did for Questions 1 and 2. Consider ease of use, amount of time required, accuracy of the data, completeness of the data, and so on.

4. Using your knowledge of how to conduct primary research, evaluate the results and conclusions you have drawn in Question 3. Should you generalize from this one experience to draw conclusions about these sources of information?

Intercultural Communication

Upon completing this chapter, you will be able to describe the major barriers to intercultural communication and how to overcome them. To reach this goal, you should be able to

1 Explain the nature of cultural differences.

2 Give examples of cultural differences in body language, and attitudes toward time, space, frankness, and intimacy.

3 Explain how the communication problems caused by cultural differences can be overcome.

4 Discuss the problems of equivalency in translation.

5 Communicate in words that people whose first language is not English will understand.

▶ to Intercultural Communication

Doreen sat up with a start. Suddenly things began to make sense. For several weeks now, she had been having some difficulty with two of her employees at her Good 'n Nice kiosk. They seemed very sensitive and easily hurt. If she told them to do something, they did the task but in a way that told Doreen they were upset.

At last she was beginning to understand. From her background and culture, Doreen had learned to be direct and concise when dealing with routine matters. She tended to be very brief in her instructions. "Stop doing that. Do this instead." These two employees, on the other hand, were used to a less direct approach. They preferred a suggestion rather than a direction.

In discussing the matter with the employees the next day Doreen said, "This is going to take some work. I can't change overnight, and neither can you. But if we can reach some understanding we can make the work atmosphere more pleasant for us and for others around us." ▪

THE IMPORTANCE OF UNDERSTANDING CULTURE

There are two good reasons to develop a culturally sensitive approach to business. First, technological advances in communication, travel, and transportation have made business increasingly international. This trend is expected to continue in the foreseeable future. Second, we live in a multicultural society. Almost every day in Canada, you will have opportunities to learn something about cultures, languages, and values different from your own. Almost every day in Canada, you will need to put that knowledge to use.

* Business communication has to become more culturally sensitive.

Culture has been defined in many ways. The definition most useful in this discussion is one derived from anthropology: *Culture* is "a way of life of a group of people . . . the stereotyped patterns of learning behaviour, which are handed down from one generation to the next through the means of language and imitation."[1] In other words, people living in different geographic areas have developed different ways of life. Groups have developed habits, values, traditions, and ways of relating to one another that are different from other groups. These distinct traits have been taught to succeeding generations as their cultural and ethnic heritage.

* Culture is the way people in an area view human relationships.

CULTURAL DIFFERENCES AFFECT COMMUNICATION

If not understood, these differences can be sources of misunderstanding when people of different cultures try to communicate. Some people find differences frightening or confusing. Others view their own ways as normal, natural, and right while seeing the ways of others as bad, wrong, or peculiar. Still others may attempt to ignore the differences or to isolate themselves from them by associating only with people from similar backgrounds. None of these responses will promote successful cross-cultural communication.

* People respond differently to cultural variations.

In preparing to communicate with those from other cultures, you might well begin by reviewing the instructions given in the previous chapters in this book. Most of the general principles fit most people. Using adaptation, for example, is appropriate across cultural lines[2]. However, some of the specific instructions, such as the techniques for persuasion, need to be considered carefully in the context of a specific culture. You must study your own culture and that of others to be a successful communicator in the modern, Canadian business world. In addition, you must look at the special problems that the English

* Successful cross-cultural communication involves understanding differences and overcoming language problems.

---

[1]V. Barnouw, *Culture and Personality* (Chicago: Dorsey Press, 1963) 4.

[2]Remember that adaptation means communicating in a way that suits the receiver. Therefore, it is the essence of being culturally sensitive and aware. To review adaptation, see Chapter 2.

1971   Multiculturalism becomes the official government policy.
1972   A minister of state for multiculturalism is appointed.
1977   The *Canadian Human Rights Act* is passed.
1982   The Canadian Charter of Rights and Freedoms, including multiculturalism and equality rights, are included in the Constitution.
1988   The *Canadian Multiculturalism Act* is passed.

The Act states its own purpose: to "encourage and assist the social, cultural, economic and political institutions of Canada to be both respectful and inclusive of Canada's multicultural character."[†]

[†]Source: Canada Department of Foreign Affairs and International Trade, *Multiculturalism.* http://canada.gc.ca/canadiana/faitc/fa26.html (viewed May 24, 1996).

language presents to those who use it as a second language. It is around these two problem areas that this review of intercultural business communication is organized.

- Two major kinds of cultural differences affect communication.

It is impossible to discuss all cultures; however, we will try to give some guidelines to make cultural adjustments easier. Communication between people of different cultures is affected by two major kinds of differences: (1) differences in body positions and movements and (2) differences in attitudes toward various factors of human relationships (time, space, intimacy, etc.).

Body Positions and Movements

- Body positions and movements differ among cultures. For example, in some cultures, people sit; in other cultures, they crouch.

At first, one might think body language is so natural that it is much the same for all people, but such is not the case. Not only do actions differ from culture to culture, they have different meanings. These differences can affect communication. For example, to indicate a direction, many Canadians would point with the index finger. This very rude gesture is replaced by pointing with the thumb in Indonesia. In Canada most people sit when they wish to remain in one place for some time, but in much of the world people crouch. Those who sit may view crouching as primitive or childlike. But how correct is this view? Who is to say that one way is better or more natural than another? Biases such as this one obviously would affect communication.

- Manners of walking differ among cultures.

For another example, people from colder climates who visit tropical countries are likely to view the slower, measured gait of the inhabitants as a sign that they lack drive or ambition. People who live in tropical conditions realize that a fast-paced lifestyle is physically exhausting in such hot climates. Similarly, people in some cultures see standing up as the appropriate thing to do on certain occasions (as when someone enters the room) whereas people from some other cultures do not.

- Communicating by body language varies with culture.

As you know, movements are a vital form of human communication. Some of these movements have no definite meaning within a culture, but some have clear meanings. In Canada an up-and-down movement of the head means *yes,* and a side-to-side movement of the head means *no.* Thrusting the head forward, raising the eyebrows, jerking the head to one side, or lifting the chin are used to convey similar meanings in other countries. Nodding or shaking the head may mean nothing at all or something quite different to people from other cultures.

- A smile can be a sign of weakness, and the left hand may be taboo.

In some cultures smiles are viewed positively; but, in certain situations such as bargaining, other cultures regard a smile as a sign of weakness. Accepting something in the left hand is a serious breach of etiquette among some groups who view the left hand as unclean. Most North Americans attach no such meaning to the left hand, but they are very particular about saying, "Thank you," and they spend many hours teaching children to "mind their Ps and Qs." And so it is with other body movements—arching eyebrows, crossing legs, putting hands on hips, and many more. All cultures use body movements in communicating, but often in different ways.

A PRACTICE RUN

Take a common gesture such as nodding, rolling the eyes, smiling, or glaring, and use it inappropriately in a conversation with another student or small group. Use it often enough for the others to try to guess the new meaning you have attached to the gesture. Once they have deciphered your meaning, ask them how they felt when you used the gesture inappropriately. Change roles and try the exercise again.

Attitudes toward Factors of Human Relationship

Because they are more visible, differences in body language may be overcome quite quickly. Differences in attitude toward human relationships are harder to recognize and, therefore, may create deeper problems. For illustrative purposes, we will review four major factors: time, space, frankness, and intimacy.

- Differing attitudes toward various factors of human relationships cause communication problems.

Time.   In Canadian business circles, people tend to regard time as something that must be planned for the most efficient use. They strive to meet deadlines, to be punctual, to conduct business quickly, and to work on a schedule. In some other cultures, people view time in a more relaxed way. They value spontaneity and see planning as unwise and unnecessary. It is more important to stop to speak to a friend than to arrive at a meeting or a social function on time. In fact, arriving late is considered appropriate for important people to show that they are busy. It is easy to see how different views of time could cause people from different cultures to have serious communication problems.

- Views about time differ widely. Some cultures stress punctuality; some do not.

Rather than becoming irritated, it is better to realize the differences in outlook and make allowances for them. Perhaps more time needs to be allotted for these meetings. Certainly, both sides must refrain from assigning negative value judgments based on these attitudes to time. Punctuality does not necessarily mean the person is brash, rude, or pushy; tardiness does not necessarily mean lack of interest, thoughtlessness, or negligence.

A PRACTICE RUN

Work out a role-play for a business negotiation between two groups with different attitudes to time. One group is punctual, task-oriented, and matter-of-fact. The other group moves at a deliberately slow pace and engages in many polite formalities before getting to the main issue.

Discuss ways to recognize this situation in real life. Have you encountered some similar experiences in everyday life such as getting service at a store?

Space.   People from different cultures often vary in their attitudes toward space. North Americans tend to view space as personal and, therefore, prefer about half a metre of distance between themselves and those with whom they speak. In other cultures people view space as belonging to all. They stand closer to each other; not following this practice is considered impolite. For another example, it is common in Canada to stand in line and wait for a turn in order. In other traditions people jostle for space and crowd together when boarding trains, standing at ticket counters, or shopping in stores. In encounters between people whose cultures have such different attitudes toward space, friction may occur unless there is an understanding of these different views.

- Space is viewed differently by different cultures. In some cultures people want to be far apart; in other cultures they want to be close.

A PRACTICE RUN

Review the section on personal space in the chapter on non-verbal cues. Make a list of situations and your expectation of how close or distant people would stand from you. Compare your list with another student of a different cultural or ethnic origin.

· ·

* Some cultures are more direct, more blunt than others.

Frankness.   Depending on the cultural background, the North American tendency to be frank in relationships with others might be appreciated as efficient and honest, or it might be criticized as blunt and disrespectful. Southeast Asians tend to be far more reticent and sometimes go to great lengths to soften a message so as not to offend. Should this practice be taken as evidence for evasiveness and indecisiveness, or as proof of good manners and consideration? With the application of *adaptation,* you would see good manners. Even though your preference might be to be told something more directly, your understanding of this practice would make you appreciate the behaviour that is rooted in that culture. As an interesting side note, telephone customs appear to be an exception. On the telephone, Southeast Asians are more likely to end calls abruptly after their purpose has been accomplished while North Americans tend to move on to friendly talk and clearly prepare the listener for the end of the call. No culture is completely logical or consistent!

· ·

A PRACTICE RUN

Canadians are not always as frank as we might think. Experiment with ways to say *Yes* but mean *No.* Use any form of the positive response accompanied by other cues to let the listener know that you mean something other than what you say in your words.

· ·

* Intimacy among people varies in different cultures.

Intimacy and Respect.   In many cultures strict social classes exist and class status determines how intimately people are addressed and treated in communication. A person from such a culture might make assumptions based on occupation, income, or position. People from cultures that stress equality are apt to take offense at the notion of class status.

A similar but less obvious attitude is illustrated by differences in the familiarity of address. In some parts of the world, people are quick to get on a first-name basis, while in other regions such a practice would be considered disrespectful or too forward. This practice may also be offensive to older people who expect such intimate address only from long-standing acquaintances.

Effects on Business Communication Techniques

* Cultural differences affect communication.

We have given only a few illustrations of the many differences among cultures. However, these examples are enough to show that communication techniques need to be modified in the light of cultural differences. Because it is not possible to cover all the alternatives, you will have to combine your knowledge and understanding of the culture with a meticulous application of the adaptation principle.

Cultural differences cause communication problems among people using the same language. For example, even though Canada and Australia have a common language, communication can be challenging because of the cultural differences between the two countries. For similar reasons, a British writer comments about American business communication textbooks: "It is almost impossible to recommend them to students for reasons other than academic interest, because the 'cultural gap' is so great that, for example, the language and tone advocated are frequently inappropriate for an English reader."[3]

---

[3]Nicki Stanton, "Business Communication in England," in *International Business Communication,* ed. Herbert W. Hilderbrandt (Ann Arbor: Division of Research, Graduate School of Business Administration, University of Michigan, 1981) 16.

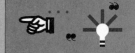

Saburo Haneda and Hirosuke Shima, authorities on international correspondence, comment:

> For international business, Japanese businessmen write mostly in English. But their mother tongue, customs and manners concerning communication in general, and cultural background are so different from those of English-speaking people that they cannot get away from their native ways even when they communicate in English, unless they have thoroughly mastered English and other Western habits of saying things.[†]

Haneda and Shima note that the Japanese tend to use a yes answer to signify agreement with an earlier statement. Therefore, if the original statement is positive, the yes means yes. If the original sentence is negative, a yes in agreement results in a negative. For example, in response to the question "You are not Chinese, are you?" "Yes," means "I am not."

Haneda and Shima also point out that the Japanese culture frowns on the hard-sell style of sales writing. For this reason alone, much that is acceptable in our business communication must be modified for Japanese readers.

[†]Saburo Haneda and Hirosuke Shima, "Japanese Communication Behaviour as Reflected in Letter Writing," *Journal of Business Communication* 19 (Winter 1982) 19.

Although cultural differences can cause confusion, there is a way to overcome those communication breakdowns. You can become a student of cultures. That is, you can ask questions about your own cultural background and assumptions and then, taking advantage of Canada's multicultural heritage, ask questions about the cultures of the people with whom you study and work.

• Learn about cultures from the people around you.

The WWW is an excellent resource for experience in cross-cultural communication and knowledge about other cultures. There are many lists of pen-pals and many usenet groups[4] willing to have new participants. Take advantage of such opportunities to discuss ideas with people from other parts of the world or other ethnic and cultural backgrounds.

• Use the World Wide Web to learn about and experience cross-cultural communication.

And, of course, take advantage of the opportunity to travel. As you experience and understand your own and other cultures, you will recognize that cultural differences are highly complex. Be careful not to overgeneralize or oversimplify the many variations and exceptions within cultures. On the other hand, you must also take care not to exaggerate the effects of cultural differences. Not all miscommunications between people of different cultures result from cultural differences. Noise, inattention, and interruptions could be the cause. Intercultural communication is not easy. Even using the suggested techniques, you may not be completely successful, but with practice and experience you will find yourself more comfortable communicating in a culturally diverse setting.

• Take advantage of travel opportunities.

PROBLEMS OF LANGUAGE

The people on earth use more than 3,000 languages. Because few of us can learn more than one or two other languages well, problems of miscommunication are bound to occur in international communication.

• Communication problems are caused by the existence of many languages.

Unfortunately, wide differences among languages make precisely equivalent translations difficult. One reason for such differences is that languages are based on the concepts, experiences, and views of the cultures that developed them. That is, language

• Differences among languages make equivalent translations difficult.

[4]On-line, worldwide discussion groups on a wide variety of topics.

If you want to know what is happening in Canada, visit the Canadian government sites at *http://canada.gc.ca/main_e.html*. The Department of Foreign Affairs and International Trade has an article that discusses multiculturalism at *http://canada.gc.ca/canadiana/faitc/fa26.html*. Or you might explore what The Department of Canadian Heritage is doing (*http://www.pch.gc.ca/pch/intro-e.html*). The Community Learning Network, part of the British Columbia Ministry of Education, Skills and Training, has a list of links to other sites related to multiculturalism. This excellent resource can be found at *http://www.etc.bc.ca/coop2/mc.html*. An example of a provincial body concerned with the topic is The Multicultural Council of Saskatchewan (MCoS). Their web site is *http://www.unibase.com/~chatabi/mcos.html*.[†]

[†]Although these sites were checked in May 1996, some of them may have changed. The World Wide Web is a rapidly evolving medium.

reflects a way of thought and life. As we have seen, different cultures have different concepts, experiences, and views. For example, in Canada, a *florist* is someone who sells flowers and related items in a store. In some cultures, however, a florist's shop does not exist since flowers are sold by street vendors. Obviously, our word *florist* does not have a precise equivalent in the language of such cultures. Similarly, our *supermarket* has no equivalent in some languages. And so it is with words for many other objects, actions, and concepts, such as *highway, interview, labour strike, tough, snow, domestic, feminine, senator,* and *aloof.*

Translating into English can also be problematic because other languages express some concepts very exactly while English groups them together. Consider the importance of snow to the Inuit. Their language must be able to distinguish many varying conditions of snow with distinct terms. For other cultures shade of colour must be precisely named. Again for others the concepts of ownership and sharing must be carefully defined. Translating these terms into English requires descriptive phrases because no true equivalent exists.

* Grammar and syntax differences add to the difficulty.

Another explanation for the lack of language equivalency is the grammatical and syntactic differences among languages. Not all languages deal with verb mood, voice, and tense in the same way. Some languages (Indonesian, for example) have no verb tenses; Urdu does not use gerunds. The obvious result is that even the best translators often cannot find literal equivalents between languages.

* So do the multiple meanings of words.

Adding to these equivalency problems is the problem of multiple word meanings. Like English, other languages have more than one meaning for many words. Think of the possible meanings for the word *run* (to move fast, to compete for office, a score in baseball, a break in a stocking, a fading of colours, and many more). Or consider the multiple meanings of such words as *fast, cat, trip, gross, ring,* and *make.* Unless one knows a language well, it is difficult to know which of the meanings is intended.

* Overcome such language problems by knowing languages well and by questioning.

Overcoming such language problems is difficult. The best way, of course, is to know more than one language well. If fluency is beyond your reach, your awareness that translation problems exist will help you listen carefully and ask questions to gauge what the other person understands. For very important messages, you might consider using a procedure called *back translating.* Two translators are needed. To translate an English document into Japanese, a native Japanese speaker translates from English into Japanese. To check the accuracy of the work, a second translator with English as a first language translates the Japanese version back into English without having seen the original. If the translations are good, the second translation matches the original.

Difficulties in Using English

English is the primary language of international business, and its leadership continues to grow. However, obviously, when business executives from different countries have a common language, they are likely to use it. For example, an executive from Venezuela would use Spanish in dealing with an executive from Mexico. However, when business people have no common language, they are likely to use English. Since many of these users have had to learn English as a second language, they are likely to use it less fluently than a first language speaker and to experience problems in understanding it. Because some people will be reluctant to admit their confusion, the speaker has a heavy responsibility to make the meaning clear.

> • English is the primary language of international business.

Two-Word Verbs. One difficult problem for non-native speakers of English involves the use of two-word verbs. By *two-word verbs* we mean a wording consisting of (1) a verb and (2) a second element that, combined with the verb, produces a meaning that the verb alone does not have. For example, take the verb *break* and the word *up*. When combined, they have a meaning quite different from the meanings the words have alone. Note how the meaning changes when the same verb is combined with other words: *break away, break out, break in, break down, break through.*

> • Two-word verbs are hard to understand.

There are so many two-word verbs that a special dictionary has been compiled.[5] Here are a few examples.

Away	give away, keep away, lay away, pass away, put away, throw away
Back	cut back, feed back, keep back, lay back, play back, take back, turn back, win back
Down	calm down, die down, hand down, keep down, let down, lie down, mark down, pin down, play down, put down, run down, shut down, sit down, wear down
In	cash in, cave in, close in, dig in, give in, run in, sign in, take in, turn in
Off	break off, brush off, buy off, check off, clear off, cool off, cut off, finish off, let off, mark off, pay off, run off, send off, show off, shut off, sound off, start off, take off, write off

---

[5]George A. Meyer, *The Two-Word Verb* (The Hague, Netherlands: Mouton, 1975).

Out	burn out, clean out, clear out, crowd out, cut out, die out, dry out, even out, figure out, fill out, find out, give out, hold out, lose out, pull out, rule out, speak out, tire out, wear out, work out
Over	check over, do over, hold over, pass over, put over, read over, run over, skim over, stop over, take over, talk over, think over, win over
Up	blow up, build up, call up, catch up, cover up, dig up, end up, fill up, get up, hang up, hold up, keep up, look up, mix up, pick up, save up, shake up, shut up, slow up, split up, wrap up

Miscellaneous words such as:

> bring about, catch on, drive on, get across, knuckle under, pass on, put across, put forth, set forth, stop over

* Use two-word verbs sparingly. Find substitutes as shown here.

Of course, students of English learn some of these word combinations, for they are part of the English language. But many of them are not covered in language textbooks or listed in dictionaries. Whenever possible, replace them with words that do appear in standard dictionaries, such as:

TWO-WORD VERBS	SUGGESTED SUBSTITUTES
give up	surrender
speed up, hurry up	accelerate
go on, keep on	continue
put off	defer, delay
take off	depart, remove
come down	descend
go in, come in, get in	enter
go out, come out, get out	exit, leave
blow up	explode
think up	imagine
figure out	solve
take out, take away	remove
go back, get back, be back	return

* Some two-word verbs have noun and adjective forms. Use these sparingly.

Additional problems result from the fact that some two-word verbs have noun and adjective forms. These also tend to be confusing. Examples of such nouns are *breakthrough, cover-up, drive-in, hook-up, turn-off,* and *sit-in.* Examples of such adjectives are *going-away* (a going-away gift), *cover-up* (cover-up tactics), and *clean-up* (clean-up work). Fortunately, some nouns and adjectives of this kind are commonly used and appear in standard dictionaries.

A Note on Dictionaries.   When writing for an international audience, remember that the unfamiliar words you use will be checked in dual language dictionaries (Thai–English/ English–Thai for example). Many of these dictionaries are old and, therefore, do not contain the modern words or the modern meanings of words. Gradually, these words will develop into standard language from the colloquial, but multi-language dictionaries are likely several years behind. The English language is changing rapidly. To be understood clearly, use common, standard English and define carefully any new technical terms.

* Culturally derived words may be difficult to translate.

Culturally Derived Words.   New words derived from one culture may present problems in intercultural communication. Slang expressions may be new words, or they may be old words with new meanings. Although some slang expressions eventually find a place in our dictionaries (*brunch, hobo, blurb*), most are used for a short while and then disappear from the language. Examples of such short-lived slang expressions are *twenty-three skidoo* and *oh you kid* from the 1920s and *ritzy, scram, natch, lousy, all wet,* and *groovy* from the 50s, 60s, and 70s. More recent ones that are probably destined for the same fate include *awesome, pig out, no way,* and *couch potato.* Since most slang words are not in dictionaries used to study English, the obvious conclusion is that you should not use slang.

Colloquial expressions are also difficult for foreign-language speakers to understand. Since colloquialisms are on the developing edge of language, they do not have universal meanings. Some of them carry regional colour and emphasis that may not be understood outside the area. Others will have special meaning within a technology, sport, or industry. As with slang, some colloquialisms will gradually become established; others will disappear, or take on new meanings. Colloquialisms are important to the life of a language; however, because of their informal, changing nature, they are not effective in international communication.

* Avoid colloquialisms in international correspondence.

. . . .

A PRACTICE RUN

Discuss the meanings of these expressions. (You may not be familiar with all of them.) For as many as you can, substitute appropriate terms.

to sign on the dotted line	a bomb
to be in over my head	a wheeler-dealer
to wipe out	an educated guess
to be in the red	a hot deal
to shoot from the hip	a workaholic

. . . .

The words and expressions that we derive from sports, social affairs, and work should be carefully considered before they are used in intercultural business situations. Some sports words are so widely used that we may forget that they come from a specialized background. Words such as *kickoff* (from football),[6] *strike out, touch base, off base, right off the bat* (from baseball), *below the belt* (from boxing), and *offside* and *face-off* (from hockey) are examples. While these terms add colour to language for those familiar with the sport, they confuse or obscure the meaning for those who are not.

* Words derived from sports, social activities, and trends cause problems.

A General Suggestion

In addition to the specific suggestions for improving your communication in English with non-native speakers, you should follow one general suggestion: talk (or write) simply and clearly. Talk slowly and enunciate each word, while keeping a normal speaking volume. Remember that as most international business people learned English word meanings from vocabulary lists, they are acquainted mainly with the primary dictionary meanings. They are less likely to understand the shades of meanings we give words. Thus, they will understand you better if you use simple, basic English.

* Use simple, basic English.

. . . .

A SUMMARY OF LEARNING OUTCOMES FROM THIS CHAPTER

Cultural differences affect communication in two major ways: (1) through body positions and movements (sitting, walking, gesturing, smiling) and (2) through attitudes toward factors of human relationships (time, space, frankness, intimacy). People tend to view the ways of their own culture as right and normal and those of other cultures

---

[6]The term *football* itself will cause confusion since, in many countries, football refers to soccer, not the North American football game.

as peculiar or wrong. Such views impede communication, so beware of them. Cultural differences probably make our letter-writing techniques ineffective with some cultures and even with some English-speaking peoples.

Communication is difficult not only because of cultural differences but also because of wide differences in the 3,000 languages used on earth. These languages differ in grammar and syntax. Like English, most of them have words with multiple meanings. The result of such differences is that equivalency in translation is difficult to achieve. You can help overcome the equivalency problem by thoroughly mastering the languages of the people with whom you deal. Because such mastery is unusual, you should be aware of the problems caused by language differences. You should ask questions to make certain you are understood. For important communications, consider back translating (using two translators—the first to translate from one language to the other and the second to translate back to the original).

English is the primary language of international business, but you should be aware of some special problems in using it. As two-word verbs are especially troublesome, substitute for them (*remove* instead of *take away, explode* instead of *blow up*). Also troublesome are culturally derived words, especially slang (*no way, nerd*), words derived from sports (*off base, time out*), and colloquialisms (*to be under fire, on the beam, in orbit*). You should avoid such words and write in simple, basic English.

QUESTIONS FOR DISCUSSION

1. What is culture?

2. What recent events in Canada and the world emphasize the need for strong cross-cultural communication skills?

3. "In intercultural communication, a verbal mistake may cause confusion, but a nonverbal mistake may cause even bigger problems." Discuss.

4. What is an accurate translation? (Hint: remember the criteria of shared meaning and understanding for successful communication.) What are the challenges that have to be met to achieve the best translation?

5. Give some examples of English language structure and vocabulary that cause difficulty for those whose first language is other than English.

6. List some ways to make an English language message more easily understood by those whose first language is other than English.

21

Physical Presentation
of Letters and Reports

CHAPTER OBJECTIVES

Upon completing this chapter, you will be able to produce business letters, letter and memorandum reports, and formal reports using good form. To reach this goal, you should be able to

(1) Determine the appropriate layout, type, and media for business documents.

(2) Select and construct an effective layout for business letters.

(3) Explain the requirements of each part of a business letter and a mailing envelope.

(4) Use business-letter format in writing letter reports and conventional memorandum format in writing memorandum reports.

(5) Select and construct all the necessary parts for a formal report.

(6) Choose a logical combination of type and position in designing and placing headings.

▷ to the Importance of Presentation and Layout

In her mail today Doreen found two letters from suppliers who wanted her business. Both Alliance and Best offered a variety of single-use products such as paper cups, Styrofoam™ bowls, and plastic cutlery for takeout foods. Although their prices were comparable and their promises of dependable service and delivery were similar, Doreen knew almost immediately which supplier she would investigate. The presentation of the information made her willing to believe the claims made by Alliance. She might give them a small order to see how they compare with her current supplier.

The letter from Best went into the wastebasket. ▪

The appearance of a letter or a report plays a significant role in communicating the message. Attractively displayed messages reflect favourably on the writer and the writer's company. They give an impression of competence and care. Moreover, their attractiveness tells the readers, "You're important and deserving of a good-looking document." On the other hand, sloppy work reflects unfavourably on the writer, the company, and the message itself. Thus, you should want your messages to be attractively displayed.

• The appearance of your reports and letters affects your readers' response to them.

Recent advances in word processing have finally relieved us of much of the tedious, repetitive tasks involved in presenting documents. Yesterday's hot feature in word processing software was a feature called styles. Styles allowed writers to define and apply a set of commands or keystrokes to a single style just once and then reuse the style. Writers could format a level-one heading once and reuse its style each time they needed to format a level-one heading. Also, if a writer decided to change the level-one formatting, only the style needed to be changed for the software automatically changed all occurrences linked to the styles. While styles let writers create formatting for use anywhere within a document, today's templates let you create the formatting for the entire document.

Templates have several advantages. Since they let you create documents from a previously defined shell, your documents will be consistent over time. Also, templates enable a company to be consistent across the company. They help assure that a professional image is being presented through the look of all types of documents the company uses. This continuity helps show the reader that a company is stable and probably reliable, too.

In addition to creating a professional image consistently, companies that use templates usually are more productive. Not only will the company save time formatting documents, but the templates also can act as prompts to the writer. This can help ensure that all components are included. Most major word processors include a full range of templates, but templates can be customized to serve the precise needs of a business. The templates can include text, graphics, macros, styles, keyboard assignments, and custom toolbars. Furthermore, templates are easy to use because of the help features that accompany them.

BASICS FOR ALL DOCUMENT PREPARATION

All documents you present will require decisions on layout, type, and media. Your choices will depend on the circumstances and the nature of the document you are writing.

• Document preparation requires decisions on layout, type, and media.

Layout

White space should be a careful part of the design of your document. To make your document look its best, you must consider both external and internal spacing. The commonly accepted ratio of white space to text is 1:1. That means half of your page is devoted to white space and half to text.

• Plan the white space for best effect.

FIGURE 21-1 Recommended Layout for a Normal Double-Spaced Page

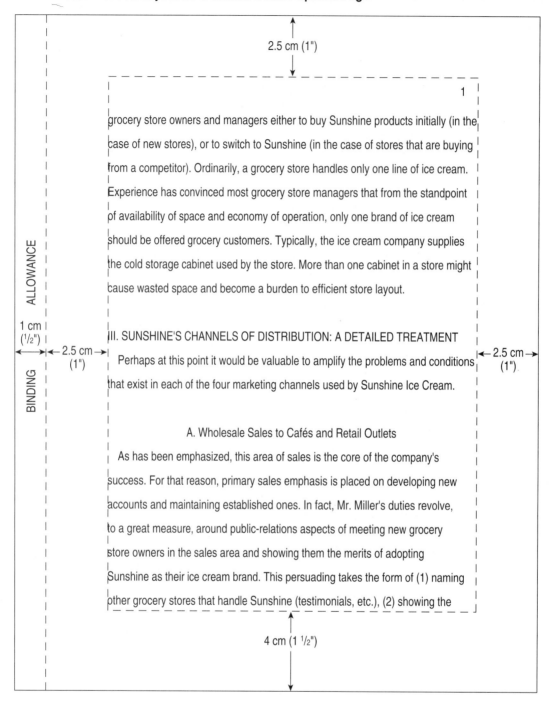

2.5 cm (1")

1

grocery store owners and managers either to buy Sunshine products initially (in the case of new stores), or to switch to Sunshine (in the case of stores that are buying from a competitor). Ordinarily, a grocery store handles only one line of ice cream. Experience has convinced most grocery store managers that from the standpoint of availability of space and economy of operation, only one brand of ice cream should be offered grocery customers. Typically, the ice cream company supplies the cold storage cabinet used by the store. More than one cabinet in a store might cause wasted space and become a burden to efficient store layout.

III. SUNSHINE'S CHANNELS OF DISTRIBUTION: A DETAILED TREATMENT

Perhaps at this point it would be valuable to amplify the problems and conditions that exist in each of the four marketing channels used by Sunshine Ice Cream.

A. Wholesale Sales to Cafés and Retail Outlets

As has been emphasized, this area of sales is the core of the company's success. For that reason, primary sales emphasis is placed on developing new accounts and maintaining established ones. In fact, Mr. Miller's duties revolve, to a great measure, around public-relations aspects of meeting new grocery store owners in the sales area and showing them the merits of adopting Sunshine as their ice cream brand. This persuading takes the form of (1) naming other grocery stores that handle Sunshine (testimonials, etc.), (2) showing the

ALLOWANCE

1 cm (1/2")

BINDING

←2.5 cm→ (1")

←2.5 cm→ (1")

4 cm (1 1/2")

External Spacing. External spacing is the white space around text or graphics. It includes margins and blank lines—the space some never think about carefully. White space denotes importance. Surrounding a heading or a graphic with white space sets it apart, emphasizing it to the reader. Used effectively, external white space has also been shown to increase the readability of your documents by giving your readers' eyes a rest.

For the typical text page in a report, a conventional layout appears to fit the page as a picture fits a frame (see Figure 21-1). Remember that your goal is to give the page vertical and horizontal balance. This eye-pleasing layout must take into account the margin needed for binding the report. If the report is to be bound, you need to allow a

* There are standard measurements for margins.

FIGURE 21–2   Recommended Layout for a Normal Single-Spaced Page

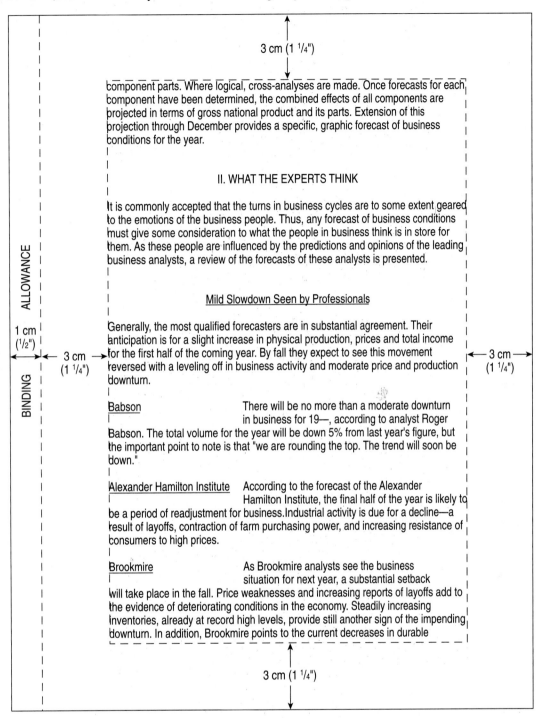

little extra width on that edge. In manuscript, then, the effect will be less pleasing, but once the report is bound, the page layout will appear balanced.

As a rule, top, left, and right margins are equal and uniform. For double-spaced manuscripts, margins of about 2.5 centimetres (1 inch) are recommended. Bottom margins may be the same size or slightly larger, i.e., between 2.5 and 4 centimetres (1–1 1/2 inches). Margins about 3 centimetres (1 1/4 inches) are considered ideal for single-spaced work (see Figure 21–2). However, rather than strictly following these conventions, some businesses set the margins to line up with the design features on their letterhead.

FIGURE 21-3 The Effect of Justification and Proportional Spacing

This is an example of left justification.

Left justification aligns every line at the left; full justification aligns every line at both the left and the right. Full justification takes the extra spaces between the last word and the right margin and distributes them between the words across the line. Proportional spacing adjusts the spacing according to the width of the character.

This is an example of full justification.

Left justification aligns every line at the left, full justification aligns every line at both the left and the right. Full justification takes the extra spaces between the last word and the right margin and distributes them between the words across the line. Proportional spacing adjusts according to the width of the character.

This is an example of full justification with a proportional spacing.

Left justification aligns every line at the left; full justification aligns every line at both the left and the right. Full justification takes the extra spaces between the last word and the right margin and distributes them between the words across the line. Proportional spacing adjusts according to the width of the character.

The left margin is defined by the characters that begin the line. The right margin is formed by the average lengths of the full lines. Although the right margin may be ragged or straight, most unpublished reports leave it ragged. If the ragged right margin is distracting, you may want to turn on the hyphenation feature of your word processor or manually hyphenate words at the end of lines to smooth it out. Full justification aligns every line at both the left and the right. Unless you are using a proportional font,[1] full justification takes the extra spaces between the last word and the right margin and distributes them across the line. With a proportional font, the spacing between characters is also adjusted so that no extra spaces are noticeable to the reader. In both cases, the right and left margins are straight.

- Consider effects of spacing between letters (kerning) and between lines (leading).

Internal Spacing.   Internal spacing refers to both the horizontal and vertical spacing between letters and lines. Standard type allows the same amount of space for each character. Proportional type recognizes that a w is wider than an i and sets the spacing according to the width of the letter. Compare the effects of justification and spacing in Figure 21-3. The spacing between letters on a line is called kerning. With desktop publishing software and some word processing software, you can adjust how close the letters are to each other. For example, in the word *The* a publishing system would allow the T to overhang, moving the h in for an even-appearing spacing. A standard printer, on the other hand, would place the h after the overhang, appearing to leave more space between the T and h than between the h and the e. If copy doesn't quite fit the page, you can squeeze it or stretch it by tightening or loosening the kerning.

Publishing software also allows you to adjust the leading—the vertical distance between the lines. Currently, many are still referring to line spacing in business documents as single- or double-spaced. However, this is a carryover from the typewriter era. Today's software and hardware give you much greater control and flexibility in this aspect of your document. Deciding the best spacing to use is dependent on the degree of clarity achieved with the typeface and size you are using. In any case you have choices and, therefore, decisions to make about the spacing aspect of your documents.

Type

- Select type suited to your purpose.

The type size and font you choose may influence the appearance of your document more than any other aspect. Based on the type in a document, readers will form an impression

---

[1] For more information about standard and proportional spacing, see the section on internal spacing.

FIGURE 21–4 Serif and Sans Serif Typefaces

This typeface has serifs (feet) attached to the letters.

This is a sans serif typeface (without feet).

The letter on the left has serifs and the letter on the right is sans serif.

R   R

Times Roman (Serif)   Helvetica (Sans Serif)

of the difficulty of the subject matter and the level of the intended reader. Think of the number of times you have decided to check out a book from the library based on the size and style of print on the pages. Although there are hundreds of fonts available, they are generally classified as serif or sans serif. Serif typefaces have feet (cross lines) at the end of the main strokes; sans serif do not. You can see this clearly in the examples in Figure 21–4.

Since readers use the visual cues they get from the serifs to form the words in their minds, most people find the text of documents easier to read if a serif typeface is used. Sans serif typefaces are particularly good for headings where clear, distinct letters are important.

Type size is measured in points, with 72 points per inch. (One inch is about 2.5 centimetres.) Generally, body text is between 9 and 14 points, and headings are 15 points and larger. While this is a standard measure, different typefaces in the same size often appear to be a different size. You need to consider your typeface in choosing size for your documents.

- Type size is measured in points.

Type style refers to the way a chosen font can be modified. The most basic styles include normal, **bold,** *italic,* and ***bold italic.*** Depending on your software and printer, you may have other options such as outline or shadow. You'll usually decide to use modifications for specific reasons. For example, you may want to bold all actions you want the reader to take. Or you may decide to apply different styles to different levels of headings. In any case use of type styles should be a planned use, not a random or haphazard use.

- Style refers to type modification, such as normal, bold, italic, outline, shadow.

Media

The media you choose to transmit your documents also communicates. Most electronic transmissions today are perceived as informal media that emphasize content over appearance. Choosing to send your message by fax may also imply your appreciation of speed and timeliness. However, because you cannot be assured of the quality of the fax output at the other end, your document may suffer in either print quality or paper quality. By choosing paper as your medium, you'll have control over the appearance but you relinquish control over the delivery to couriers or the post office.

- Transmission by electronic mail, fax, or paper can affect image.

Today paper is still the top choice of media. In Canada and the United States standard business paper size is 8 1/2 by 11 inches; in international business its measurements are metric, resulting in paper sized slightly narrower and slightly longer.[2] As well as size, you have a variety of choices in the colour, weight, and texture of the paper.

- Paper is top choice, usually of standard 8 1/2 x 11 inch size.

You want your paper to represent you and your business but not distract your reader from the message. The colour you choose for the paper is usually chosen for the envelope as well. The most common colour choice is any of the many variations of white. Pastel colours are next, with almost any colour or tint available.

- White paper is most conservative, but other colours can be effective.

---

[2]Paper that is 8 1/2 by 11 inches is known as letter-size paper. Sheets 8 1/2 by 14 inches are legal size. Metric sheets are referred to as A4 and B5.

Although the ancient Greeks wrote letters in a fixed pattern of salutation and closing, as well as in a standard jargon, the credit for our conventional letter pattern goes to Professor Buoncompagno, Master of Rhetoric at the University of Bologna. In 1231 a trend-setting manual by Professor Buoncompagno established the basic pattern of heading, inside address, salutation, body, complimentary close, and signature that has survived to this day. Perhaps the deep roots of the pattern explain why recent efforts to change it have made slow progress.

- Recycled paper is becoming popular and more economical.

Recycled paper is becoming more popular, reflecting the growing environmental concerns of the Canadian consumer. Recycled paper is not available in a true white because of the bleaching that would be required to remove the old inks. But a full range of colours and weights are available. Some recycled papers have a light fleck which many consider attractive. Growing demand for recycled papers has reduced the cost so that corporations now see it as a viable alternative. The message of corporate responsibility the recycled logo sends makes the cost of recycled paper a public relations investment.

- Paper weight and texture communicate an image.

The weight and texture of your paper also communicate. While "cheap" paper may denote control of expense to one reader, it may denote financial instability and belt tightening to another. Usually businesses use paper with a weight of 16 to 20 pounds and a rag or cotton content of 25 to 100 percent. The higher the numbers the higher the quality. And, of course, many readers often associate a high-quality paper with a high-quality product or service.

- Consider all the messages your medium choice sends.

The choice of medium to use for your documents is important because it, too, sends a message. By being aware of these subtle messages, you'll be able to choose the most appropriate medium for your situation.

THE BUSINESS LETTER

Ideal Layout

- The ideal letter layout has the same shape as the space available for typing.

As discussed earlier, the ideal letter layout is one that fits that space much as a picture fits a frame (see Figure 21–5). That is, a rectangle drawn around the processed letter has the same shape as the space under the letterhead. The layout is best placed a little high on the page because this looks better to the eye. (See the form of the letter of transmittal, Figure 21–16 on page 502.) While these requirements may sound difficult to achieve, many of them are the default settings on word processors. Others can be accomplished with only a few keystrokes. The resulting impression is worth the effort.

Style Preferences

- Block and modified block types are the most popular.

As to the style of the layout, any generally recognized one is acceptable. Some companies prefer one style or another, and you may even have your own preferences. But these choices are best made in context. Since appearance is a key factor, choose a style that looks attractive with the company's letterhead. Generally, the most popular styles are block, modified block, and simplified. These are best explained by illustration (see Figures 21–5, 21–6, 21–7, and 21–8). In all styles single-spacing is the rule for all but very short letters, which are appropriately double-spaced. Agreement has not been reached on all the practices for setting up the parts of the letter. The suggestions below, however, follow common practice.

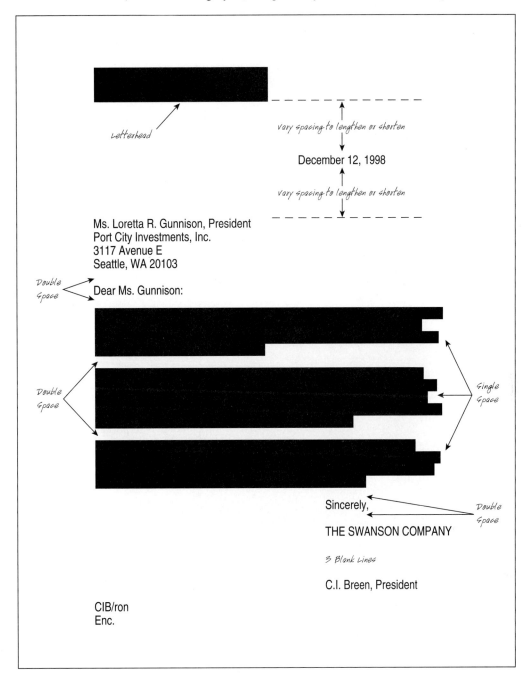

Elements of the Business Letter

Return Address.   In most cases your return address is printed on the letterhead. However, if you are writing a personal business letter, you would not use company letterhead. Therefore, you insert your street address, city, province, and postal code single-spaced directly above the dateline. For example, in a full block letter your return address would be blocked at the left margin like this:

> 64 Lennox Avenue
> West Hill, ON
> M1S 5A2

* Use a return address on paper without a letterhead.

FIGURE 21-6 Block Style, Fixed Margins Using Subject Line

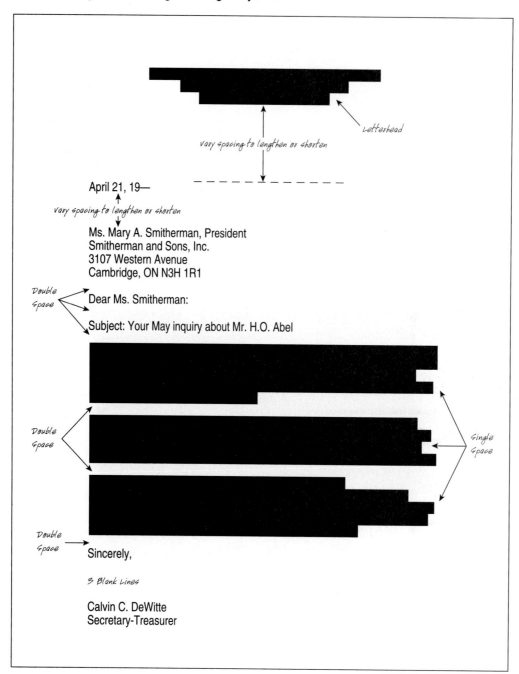

• Dateline includes the complete date.

• The International System of Units may be used for the date.

Dateline. You should use the conventional date form, with day, month, and year (December 19, 1998). Abbreviated forms such as Dec. 19/98 or 19/12/98 are too informal for business letters. The latter may also cause confusion since the Canadian style follows the day-month-year order and the American style, also frequently used in Canada, follows the month-day-year order. Thus, 5/12/98 could be read as December 5 or May 12, 1998.

SI (for *Le Systeme International d'Unites* or International System of Units) was adopted by almost all the countries in the world in 1960 and by Canada in the Weights and Measures Act of 1971. Despite this official acceptance and the simple, logical style of SI, Canadian companies seldom use it for dates. Perhaps the influence of the United States, which still follows the Imperial system, is too strong. Nevertheless, SI style should

FIGURE 21-7   Modified Block, Indented Paragraphs, Fixed Margins

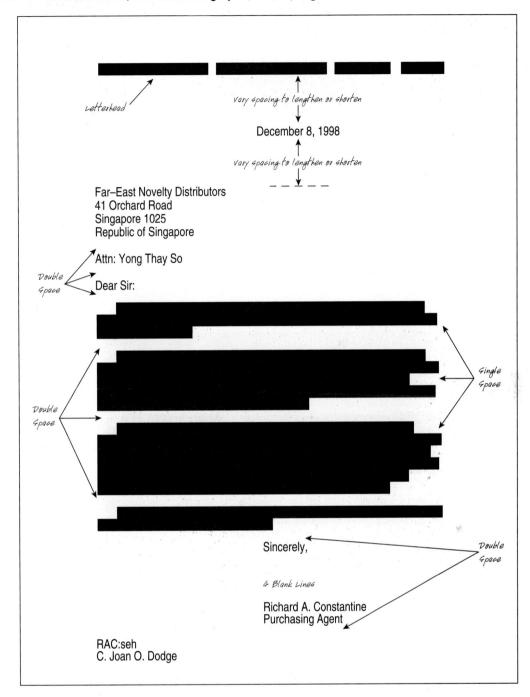

be recognized. An SI dateline uses year, month, day on the logical pattern of hierarchy, as in 1998 12 05 for December 5, 1998.

Inside Address.   The name and the title of the person being addressed, the company, and the mailing address complete with postal code make up the inside address. Include the country if the letter is going outside Canada.

- The inside address is the letter's destination.

Attention Line.   Some executives prefer to emphasize the company address rather than the individual. Thus, they address the letter to the company in the inside address and then

- Use an attention line to route a letter to the correct reader.

FIGURE 21–8 American Management Society Simplified Style

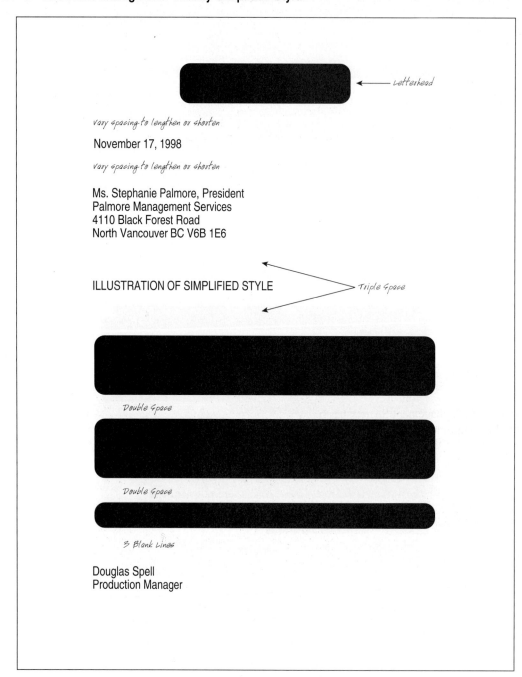

Letterhead

vary spacing to lengthen or shorten

November 17, 1998

vary spacing to lengthen or shorten

Ms. Stephanie Palmore, President
Palmore Management Services
4110 Black Forest Road
North Vancouver BC V6B 1E6

ILLUSTRATION OF SIMPLIFIED STYLE

Triple Space

Double Space

Double Space

3 Blank Lines

Douglas Spell
Production Manager

use an attention line (Figure 21–7) to direct the letter to a specific office or department. The attention line is placed a double space below the inside address and a double space above the salutation. Typical forms of such attention lines are as follows:

Attention: Mr. William O'Brien, Vice President
Attention of Mr. Clayton E. Haney, Office Manager
For Ms. Clara Blake, Director

• Select the salutation based on your familiarity with the reader.

Salutation. The salutation you choose should be based on your familiarity with the reader and on the formality of the situation. As a general rule, if the writer and the reader

Recommended salutations:

"After my hartie commendation to you" (to an inferior)

"After my hartie commendation unto your Lord" (to a nobleman)

Recommended closes:

"Acknowledging myself deeply bounde unto your Lord for many sundry favours, I do remaine in all humbel reverence."

"Finding myselfe many ways beholding unto your exceeding courtesies, I ende."

SOURCE: Angel Day, *The English Secretarie* (London, 1595).

know each other well, the salutation may be by first name (*Dear Joan*); however, a salutation by last name (*Dear Mr. Baskin*) is appropriate in most cases. In formal or impersonal situations, the salutations *Dear Sir* and *Dear Madam* are considered correct, but they are becoming obsolete. If you do not know and cannot find out the name of the person to whom you are sending the letter, use a position title. By directing your letter to Director of Personnel or Public Relations Manager, for example, you are helping your letter reach the appropriate person.

The Administrative Management Society has for some time attempted to eliminate the salutation and the complimentary close (see the example of their simplified style, Figure 21–8). Although the AMS should be commended for promoting these logical changes, its style has gained only modest support in business.

• AMS style eliminates the salutation and the complimentary close.

The use of *Mrs.* and *Miss* is rapidly declining in favour of *Ms.* Although some people oppose using *Ms,* the term is gaining widespread acceptance and, as you may have noticed, appears throughout this book. Unless you know that your reader has other preferences, you would be correct to use it when addressing women.

• *Ms* is taking the place of *Mrs.* and *Miss.*

The punctuation following the salutation and the closing is either mixed or open. Mixed punctuation uses a colon after the salutation and a comma after the complimentary close (discussed below). Open punctuation uses no punctuation after the salutation and complimentary close. Either method is acceptable, but do not combine them by, for example, using a colon after the salutation and no punctuation after the complimentary close.

• Use mixed or open punctuation.

Subject Line. So that both the sender and the receiver may quickly identify the subject of the correspondence, many offices use the subject line in their letters. As illustrated in Figure 21–11 and Figure 21–16, the subject line tells what the letter is about. In addition, it contains any specific identifying material that may be helpful—date of previous correspondence, invoice number, file number, and the like. It is usually placed on a line below the salutation, though some companies prefer to place it higher—often in the upper right corner of the letter layout. In simplified style (Figure 21–8), it appears in all-capital letters after the inside address. The block may be headed in a number of ways, such as:

• Subject lines are useful identification parts.

Subject: Your July 2nd Inquiry About

RE: Your File H-320.

Reference your October 17 order for . . .

About your invoice No. 721-A dated . . .

Second Page Heading.   When the length of a letter must exceed one page, you should set up the following page or pages for quick identification. Always use plain paper (no letterhead) and a header such as:

Ms. Helen E. Mann   2   May 7, 199x

Ms. Helen E. Mann
May 7, 199x
Page 2

Complimentary Close.   By far the most commonly used complimentary close is *Sincerely*. It suits the friendly but professional tone of business letters today. *Yours truly,* probably the next most popular closing, is used in letters with a slightly more formal tone. Such closes as *Cordially* and *Respectfully* are appropriate when their meanings fit the particular writer-reader relationship. A long-standing business acquaintance, for example, might use *Cordially;* the writer's respect for the position, prestige, or accomplishments of the reader would justify *Respectfully.*

Signature Block.   The writer's name is printed about four lines below the complimentary close to leave room for the signature. A short name and title may appear on one line, separated by a comma. More usually, however, the title appears on the following line, blocked under the name. If there is a preferred form of address, such as *Miss* or *Dr.,* that preference is indicated here. Consider the following four examples:

(Mrs.) Lily Schneider   (Dr.) J.S. McNicoll
Payroll Clerk   Medical Officer

(Ms) K.A. McAllister   G.A. (Art) Moore
Personnel Administrator   Computer Systems

Some people prefer to have the company name appear in the signature. The conventional form for this arrangement places the company name in solid capitals and blocked on the second line below the closing phrase. The typed name of the person signing the letter is on the fourth line below the company name (see Figure 21–5).

Information Notations.   In the lower left corner of the letter may appear abbreviated notations of enclosures (*Encl., Enc.-3,* and so on) and the initials of the writer and the typist (*WEH:ga*) which are useful for office checking. Indications of photocopies prepared for other readers may also be included (*pc A.E. Gibbings, Copy to A.E. Gibbings, xc A.E. Gibbings*). Sometimes *cc A.E. Gibbings* is still seen—a carry over from the days of carbon copies.

Postscripts.   Postscripts, commonly referred to as the PS, are placed after any notations. While rarely used in most business letters because they look like afterthoughts, they can be very effective for added punch in sales letters.

Preparation for Mailing

Folding.   The carelessly folded letter is off to a bad start with the reader. Neat folding will complete the planned effect by (1) making the letter fit snugly in its envelope, (2) making the letter easy to remove and handy to unfold, and (3) making the letter appear neat when opened.

The two-fold pattern is the easiest. It fits the standard sheet for the long (Number 10) envelope as well as some other envelope sizes.

As shown in Figure 21–9, the first fold of the two-fold pattern is from the bottom up, taking just less than a third of the sheet. The second fold goes from the top down, to leave the recipient a narrow thumbhold for easy unfolding of the letter. Thus folded, the letter should be slipped into its envelope with the second crease toward the bottom.

The three-fold pattern is necessary to fit the standard sheet into the commonly used small (Number 6 3/4) envelope. Its first fold brings the bottom edge of the sheet up

FIGURE 21-9   Two Ways of Folding and Inserting Letters

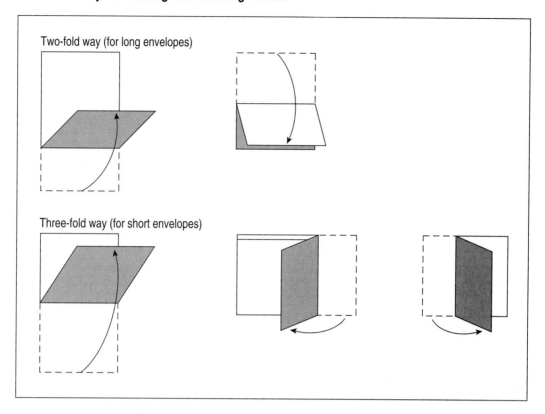

almost to the top edge leaving a narrow thumbhold. (If the edges are exactly even, they are harder to separate.) The second fold is from the right side of the sheet toward the left, taking slightly less than a third of the width. The third fold matches the second: from the left side toward the right to leave a thumbhold at the right for the user's convenience. So that the letter will appear neat when unfolded, the creases should be parallel with the top and sides, not at angles that produce "dog-ears" and irregular shapes.

The three-fold letter is inserted into its envelope with the third crease toward the bottom and the loose edges toward the stamp end. (From habit most recipients of business letters slit envelopes at the top and turn them facedown to extract the letter. The three-fold letter inserted as described thus gives its reader an easy thumbhold to pull out the letter, and a second one at the top of the sheet for easy unfolding.)

• Properly inserting a letter into the envelope aids the reader.

Addressing the Envelope. So that optical character recognition equipment may be used in sorting mail, Canada Post requests that all envelopes be typed as follows (see Figure 21-10):

• Canada Post requests that we follow this procedure in addressing envelopes.

1. On the Number 10 envelope (large), start the address 10 centimetres (about 4 inches) from the left edge. On the Number 6 3/4 (small) envelope, start 5 centimetres (2 inches) from the left edge.

2. Use a block address format.

3. Single-space.

4. Do not use punctuation.

5. Use all uppercase letters for the city, postal code, and country (if other than Canada); use uppercase and lowercase for the rest of the address, including the province if written in full.

Joseph Langley
3504 Kennedy Road
SCARBOROUGH, ON M5N 2B4

PERSONAL

        Mr. Grady E. Cromwell
        1062 - 22 Street
        LETHBRIDGE, Alberta
        T1H 3E9

6. Use these two-letter abbreviations for the provinces, territories and states:

CANADIAN PROVINCES and TERRITORIES

BC (British Columbia)	PQ (Province of Quebec)
AB (Alberta)	NB (New Brunswick)
SK (Saskatchewan)	NS (Nova Scotia)
MB (Manitoba)	PE (Prince Edward Island)
ON (Ontario)	NF (Newfoundland)
NT (Northwest Territories)	YT (Yukon Territories)
LB (Labrador)	

STATES OF THE UNITED STATES

AL (Alabama)	MD (Maryland)
AK (Alaska)	MA (Massachusetts)
AZ (Arizona)	MI (Michigan)
AR (Arkansas)	MN (Minnesota)
CA (California)	MS (Mississippi)
CO (Colorado)	MO (Missouri)
CT (Connecticut)	MT (Montana)
DE (Delaware)	NE (Nebraska)
DC (Washington, D.C.)	NV (Nevada)
FL (Florida)	NH (New Hampshire)
GA (Georgia)	NJ (New Jersey)
HI (Hawaii)	NM (New Mexico)
ID (Idaho)	NY (New York)
IL (Illinois)	NC (North Carolina)
IN (Indiana)	ND (North Dakota)
IA (Iowa)	OH (Ohio)
KS (Kansas)	OK (Oklahoma)
KY (Kentucky)	OR (Oregon)
LA (Louisiana)	PA (Pennsylvania)
ME (Maine)	RI (Rhode Island)

SC (South Carolina)	VA (Virginia)
SD (South Dakota)	WA (Washington)
TN (Tennessee)	WV (West Virginia)
TX (Texas)	WI (Wisconsin)
UT (Utah)	WY (Wyoming)
VT (Vermont)	

7. Put the postal code on its own line, and separate the first three characters from the second three with a space. Always use uppercase letters. For example, use T5N 3R4, not T5N-3R4 or t5n 3r4. For reasons of space, the postal code may be included on the same line as the city and province, but it must be separated by two spaces. The U.S. zip code normally is placed on the same line as the city and state.

8. When the return address is printed in the top left corner, begin on the second line from the top of the envelope about 1 centimetre (1/2 inch) from the left edge of the envelope.

9. Place any post office stickers such as "Special Delivery" and any on-arrival instructions such as "Confidential" or "Personal" about 7 millimetres below the return address and still above the centre line.

10. Leave about 2.5 centimetres (1 inch) blank at the bottom of the envelope. This space is the code band for the machine sorting code.

THE MEMORANDUM

Memorandums have basic components in common, but their form varies widely from organization to organization. The basic components are the heading and body. The heading has four elements: *To:*, *From:*, *Date:*, and *Subject:*. Most large companies have memo stationery printed with the conventional heading information. Some variations in order exist depending on the circumstances, but these are the standard elements. The body of the memo is usually single-spaced with double spacing between paragraphs. First-level headings are frequently used in memos for conciseness and clarity. Because memos tend to be informal, notations for writer, typist, and enclosures may or may not be included. For examples and more detail on the format for memos, see Chapter 9.

* *To:*, *From:*, *Date:*, *Subject:* are basic parts of memo headings.

THE LETTER REPORT AND THE MEMORANDUM REPORT

Very little needs to be said here about these two report formats since the basic information is covered elsewhere. As letter reports resemble long letters, the review of letter form applies to them. Memorandum reports begin with the conventional memorandum form (Figure 21–11). The report text follows the introductory information just as in a standard memo. Both letter and memorandum reports may use headings to display the topics covered. The headings are usually printed in the margins, or on separate lines, and are emphasized by underlining or boldface type. Memorandum and letter reports may also have illustrations (charts, tables), an appendix, and/or a bibliography.

* Letter reports are typed in letter form. Memorandum reports have *To:*, *From:*, *Subject:*, *Date:* at top.

THE FORMAL REPORT

You are likely to prepare formal reports on desktop publishing or word processing equipment. These packages are very helpful for producing professional-looking reports, but you still need to know the general mechanics of manuscript preparation. Even if you

FIGURE 21-11 Good Form for the First Page of a Memorandum Report

---

Campus Correspondence

UNIVERSITY OF NORTHERN ONTARIO

TO: All Faculty Members
           Faculty of Business Administration
FROM: Committee on Courses and Curricula
           J. William Hughes, Chairperson
SUBJECT: Report of progress and plans on the study of the business administration curricula
DATE: December 15, 1998

Progress for the Period October 1 to December 15

On October 10 the Committee mailed questionnaires (copy attached) to the deans of 24 selected colleges of business administration. To date, 21 of the deans have returned questionnaires.

Professors Byrd, Calhoun, and Creznik have tabulated the replies received and are now analyzing findings.

Future Plans

Professors Byrd, Calhoun, and Creznik will present their analyses to the Committee at its February 4th meeting. At this time, the Committee expects to study these analyses and to make final recommendations.

Professor Byrd will record the recommendations in a written report. The Committee will distribute copies of this report to all voting members of the faculty at least one week before the faculty meeting scheduled for May 9.

---

do not have to keyboard your own reports, you are responsible for the final product. Therefore, you have to know enough about report presentation to be sure your work is done right. The following points about report preparation are supplementary to the basic information for all documents given earlier in this chapter.

General Format Information

- Single-sided printing is standard, but duplexing is gaining in popularity.

Single- and Double-Sided Printing.   Most reports are printed on one side of the paper only, but as corporations become more environmentally concerned, they are printing on both sides. Because recent advances in technology have made double-sided printing easier and more economical, informal and internal reports are more frequently duplexed. Formal reports are still printed on one side only.

- Pages displaying major titles may have special layouts.

Special Page Layouts.   Certain text pages may have individual layouts. Pages displaying major titles (first pages of chapters, tables of contents, executive summaries, and the like) conventionally have extra space at the top (see Figure 21-12). Some also have special graphics or colour for emphasis and attractiveness.

- Indent double-spaced text; block single-spacing.

- The distance of indentation is optional, but should be consistent.

Patterns of Indentation.   You should indent the paragraph beginnings of double-spaced typing. On the other hand, you should block single-spaced typing, because its paragraph headings are clearly marked by extra line spacing.

No generally accepted distance of indentation exists. Some sources suggest 4 spaces, some prefer 5, some like 8, and others like 10 and more. The decision is up to you, though you would do well to follow the practice established in the office, group, or school for which you write the report. Whatever your selection, you should be consistent.

FIGURE 21–12 Recommended Layout for a Double-Spaced Page with Title

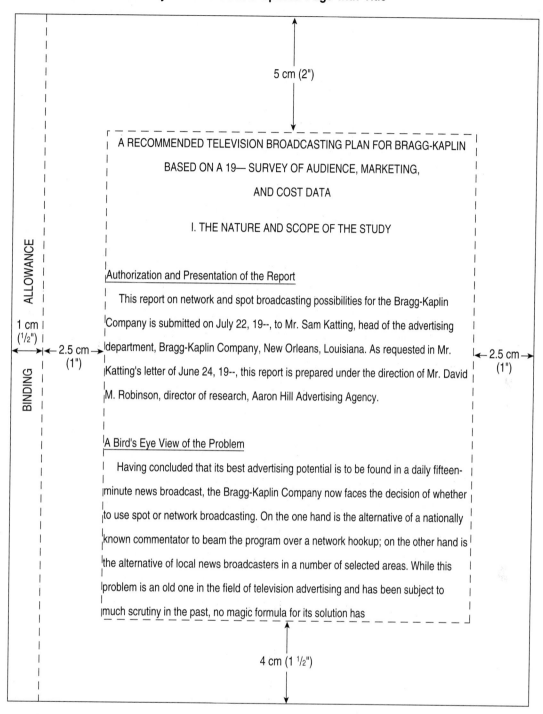

Neatness in the Finished Report.   As keyboarding mistakes, misspellings, and other signs of sloppy work reflect on your letters or reports, you should work for a neat end product. With word processing equipment this goal is more easily reached than it used to be. Nevertheless, the final editing and proofreading of a report is a tedious, time-consuming task which cannot yet be entrusted entirely to a machine.

* Neatness is a requirement in business reports.

Numbering of Pages.   Two systems of numbers are used in numbering the pages of the written report. Arabic numerals (1, 2, 3, etc.) are conventional for the text portion, normally beginning with the first page of the introduction and continuing through the

* Number prefatory pages in small Roman numerals, text pages in Arabic numerals.

appendix. Small Roman numerals (*i, ii, iii,* etc.) are standard for the pages preceding the text. Although these prefatory pages are all counted in the numbering sequence, the numbers generally do not appear on the pages before the table of contents. See the following sections on the format of these prefatory pages for more details.

In reports bound at the top of the page, you should centre all page numbers at the bottom of the page, a double or triple space below the text. For left-sided binding, it is convenient to place the numbers in the upper right corner, a double or triple space above the top line and in line with the right margin. If the report is duplexed, the page numbering should alternate between top right for odd-numbered pages and top left for even-numbered pages. Exceptions to this placement are customarily made for special-layout pages that have major titles and an additional amount of space displayed at the top. Numbers for these pages are centred a double or triple space below the imaginary line marking the bottom of the layout.

Display of Headings. Headings are the titles of the parts of the report. Designed to lead the readers through the report, they must show at a glance the importance of the information they cover.

In showing heading importance by position, you have four main choices. As shown in Figure 21–13, the most important position is centred between left and right margins. Next in importance is the marginal heading on a line by itself. The box heading ranks third. It is on the left margin, and it is surrounded by a box of space. (The boxes should be of equal width, but they can vary in height.) Fourth is the run-in heading (also called the *paragraph heading*). It runs into the line and is distinguished from the text by underlining.

There are also type choices to show levels of importance. If you are using word processing equipment, you have many choices such as capital and lowercase letters, boldface, italics, large print, and underlining. There is no set hierarchy pattern except that solid capitals are more important than a combination of capitals and lowercase. Establish your own pattern, and use it consistently throughout your report. The following table gives some possible choices.

NORTH AMERICA	capitals, bold, underlined
CANADA	capitals, bold
MANITOBA	capitals
Winnipeg	capitals and lowercase
NORTH AMERICA	capitals, bold, underlined
CANADA	capitals, bold
Manitoba	capitals and lowercase, bold
Winnipeg	capitals and lowercase
NORTH AMERICA	capitals, underlined
CANADA	capitals
Manitoba	capitals and lowercase, underlined
Winnipeg	capitals and lowercase

By combining position and typeface, you have numerous options. You can even use any combination of type and position that clearly shows the relative importance of the headings. You can use the same type for two successive levels of headings as long as the positions vary. And you can use the same position for two successive levels as long as the types vary. You can also skip over any of the steps in the progression of type or position.

Mechanics and Format of the Report Parts

The foregoing notes on physical appearance apply generally to all parts of the report, but special notes are needed for some of the specific report pages. A part-by-part review of the physical construction of the formal report follows.

FIGURE 21-13   Heading Positions in Order of Importance

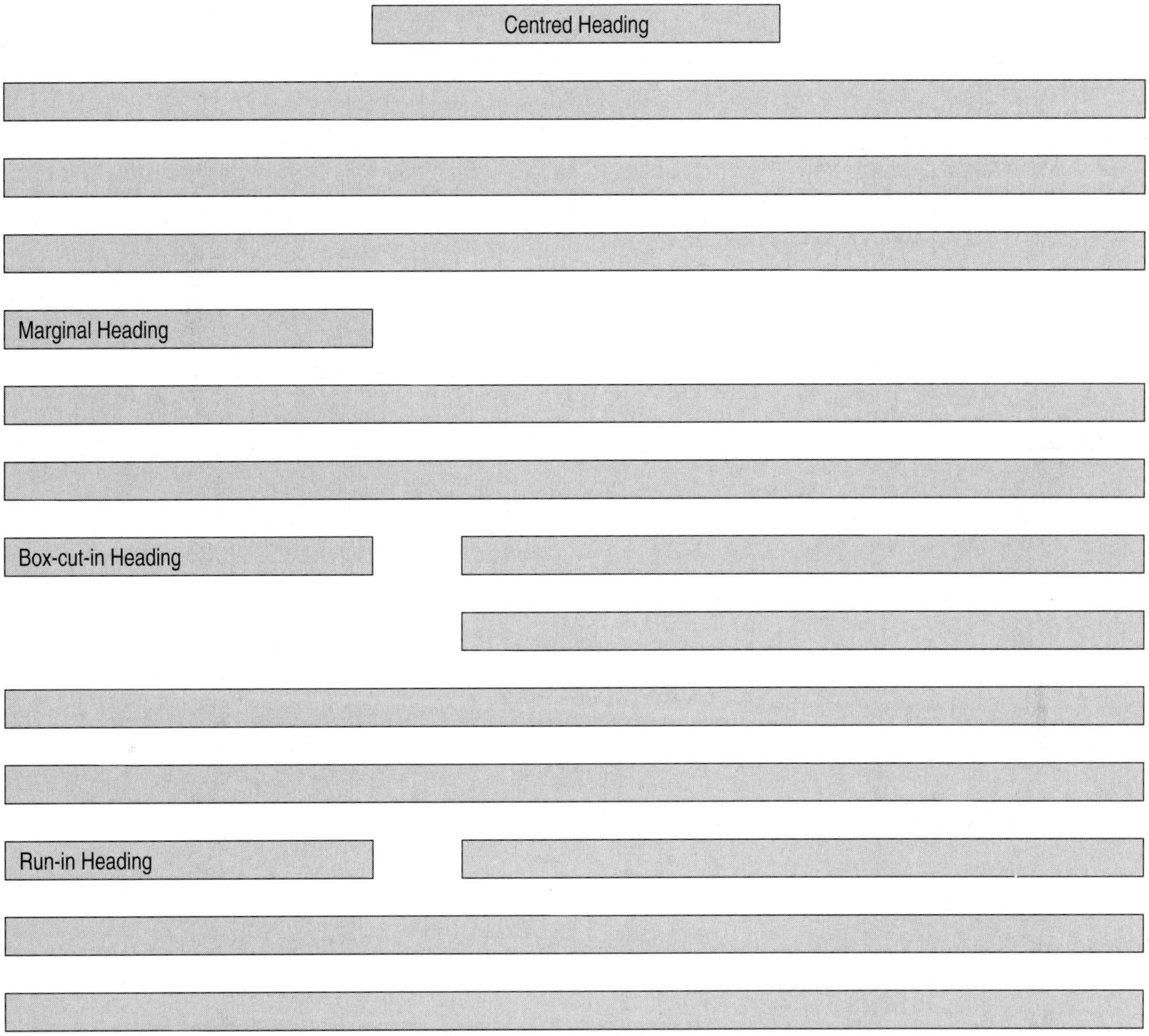

Centred Heading

Marginal Heading

Box-cut-in Heading

Run-in Heading

Title Fly.   The title fly contains only the report title. In constructing the page, place the title slightly above the vertical centre of the page in an eye-pleasing arrangement. Centre all lines with regard to left and right margins. Type the title in the highest-ranking type used in the report (such as boldface, solid capitals), and double-space it if you need more than one line.

A very formal report may also have an end fly or fly leaf. This is a blank page, sometimes of a different weight of paper from the rest of the report. It precedes the title page.

* The title fly contains only the title, centred and a little high on the page.

Title Page.   The title page normally contains four main areas of identification (Figure 21-14), although some forms present this information in three spots on the page (Figure 21-15). In the typical four-spot title page, the first area of identification covers the report title. Preferably, type it in the highest-ranking type used in the report, usually boldface and solid capitals. Place it at least 2.5 centimetres (1 inch) down from the top of the page, centred from left to right. If the title requires more than one line, break the lines between thought units and double-space the lines.

The second area of information begins with an identifying phrase such as "Prepared for" or "Submitted to." Set off this identifying phrase from the line below it by a double

* The title page typically contains (1) the report title,

* (2) authorizer identification,

FIGURE 21–14   Good Layout for the Four-Spot Title Page

RECOMMENDED SALES DISTRICT BOUNDARIES
FOR REGINA, SASKATCHEWAN
BASED ON AN ANALYSIS OF 1985 CENSUS ESTIMATES

Prepared for
Mr. Jerome M. Hightower
Sales Manager, Fourth Region

Prepared by
Elaine W. Leggarson
Director, Division of Research

Great Midwestern Life Insurance Company
3147 Newport Road
Winnipeg, Manitoba R2C 0T8

April 10, 1992

space. Then, name the individual (or group) for whom the report has been prepared. In addition to the recipient's name, include other appropriate identification such as title or role, company, and address. If three or more lines are required, use single space; otherwise, use double space.

• (3) writer identification, and

The third area of identification names you, the writer of the report. It begins with an identifying phrase, such as "Prepared by," "Written by," or similar wording describing your role in the report. After a double space, include your name, and below that, your title or role, company, and address if needed.

• (4) the date and optional address.

As a final part of the title page information, you should include the date of publication. It should be written in full form including the month, date, and year, as in July 7, 1992. Place the date about 5 centimetres (2 inches) from the bottom of the page, or at least a double space below the last line of the writer information. Sometimes it is appropriate to include an address as Figure 21–14 shows. Placement of the four areas of identification on the page should make for an eye-pleasing arrangement.

Another possible arrangement uses only three areas of information as shown in Figure 21–15. The title begins about 3 centimetres (1 1/4 inches) from the top of the page. The final area of information, combining the author's name and the date, appears about 5

FIGURE 21–15 Good Layout for the Three-Spot Title Page

A RECOMMENDED TELEVISION BROADCASTING PLAN FOR BRAGG-KAPLIN
BASED ON A 1992 SURVEY OF AUDIENCE, MARKETING,
AND COST DATA

Submitted to

Ms. Joanna Katting
Head of Advertising Department
Bragg-Kaplin Company
Vancouver, B.C.

Prepared by

David M. Robinson, Director of Research
Aaron Hill Advertising Agency
New Westminster, B.C.

July 22, 1992

centimetres (2 inches) from the bottom. The centre spot of information appears to split the space between the top and bottom units in a 2:3 ratio, the bottom space being the larger. As before, the lines are broken at logical thought units.

Letters of Authorization, Acceptance, and Transmittal. As their names imply, the letters of authorization, acceptance and transmittal are actual letters. The letter of authorization contains the instructions requesting that the report be written. Since it is prepared by the authorizer of the report, you should include it without change. If you, as the person who prepared the report, wrote a reply accepting the task, include that letter of acceptance as well as the letter of transmittal. The letters you write should be in an acceptable letter form as discussed earlier. In the example transmittal letter (Figure 21–16), a modified block form is used. Note that the letter fits into a rectangle the same shape as the space in which it is typed.

* Include the letter of authorization in its original form; letters of acceptance and transmittal are typed in any accepted letter form.

Acknowledgments. When you are indebted to others for assistance, it is fitting that you acknowledge them somewhere in the report. If the number of names is small, you may include them in the introduction of the report or in the letter of transmittal. In the rare

* Include a special page for acknowledgment of help.

FIGURE 21–16 **Letter of Transmittal Fitted to the Shape of the Space in Which It Is Typed**

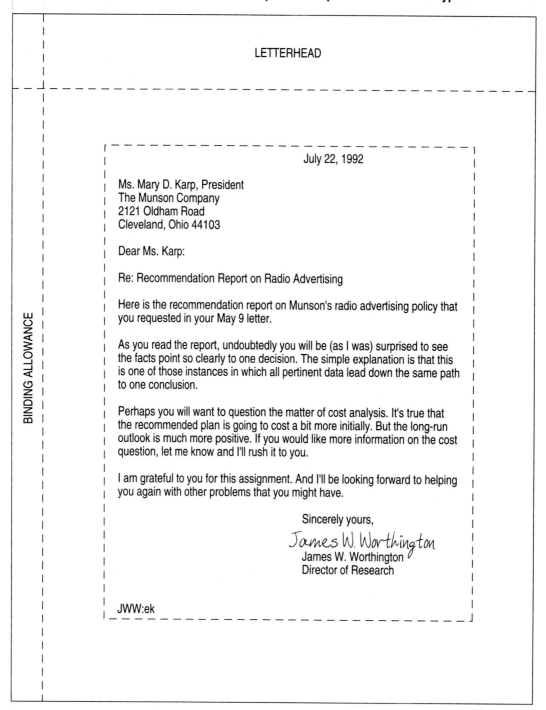

event that you need to make numerous acknowledgments, you may construct a special section for this purpose. This section, bearing the simple title "Acknowledgments," has the same layout as any other text page in which a title is displayed.

* The table of contents displays the outline with page numbers.

Table of Contents. The table of contents is the report outline in its polished, finished form. It lists the major report headings with the page numbers on which those headings appear. Although not all reports require a table of contents, one should be a part of any report long enough to make such a guide helpful to the readers.

FIGURE 21-17   Good Layout and Mechanics in the First Page of the Table of Contents

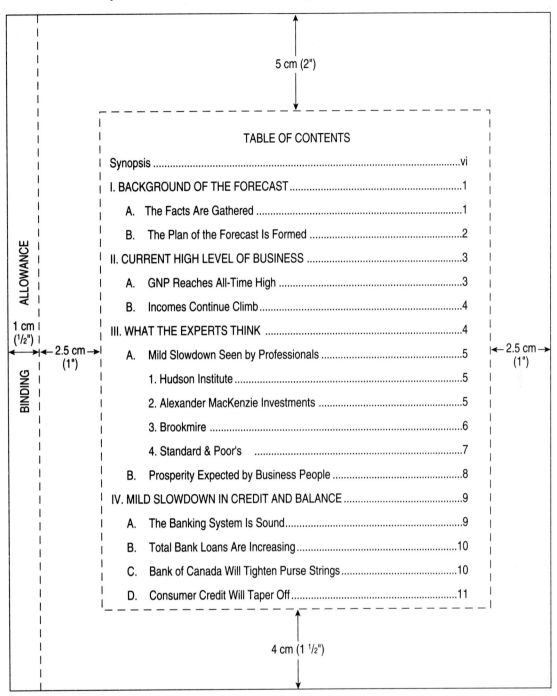

5 cm (2")

TABLE OF CONTENTS

Synopsis vi

I. BACKGROUND OF THE FORECAST 1

    A.   The Facts Are Gathered 1

    B.   The Plan of the Forecast Is Formed 2

II. CURRENT HIGH LEVEL OF BUSINESS 3

    A.   GNP Reaches All-Time High 3

    B.   Incomes Continue Climb...4

III. WHAT THE EXPERTS THINK 4

    A.   Mild Slowdown Seen by Professionals 5

         1. Hudson Institute 5

         2. Alexander MacKenzie Investments 5

         3. Brookmire 6

         4. Standard & Poor's 7

    B.   Prosperity Expected by Business People 8

IV. MILD SLOWDOWN IN CREDIT AND BALANCE 9

    A.   The Banking System Is Sound...9

    B.   Total Bank Loans Are Increasing..10

    C.   Bank of Canada Will Tighten Purse Strings..................................10

    D.   Consumer Credit Will Taper Off..11

ALLOWANCE

BINDING

1 cm (½")

2.5 cm (1")

2.5 cm (1")

4 cm (1 ½")

The table of contents is appropriately titled "Contents" or "Table of Contents" as shown in Figure 21–17. The layout of the table of contents is the same as that used for any other report page with a title display. Below the title, set up two columns. One contains the outline headings, generally beginning with the first page after the table of contents. You have the option of including or leaving out the outline letters and numbers. If you use numbers, arrange them so that their last digits are aligned. In the other column, at the right margin and headed by the word *Page,* place the page numbers on which the outline headings may be found. Align these numbers on their right-hand digits. Connect the two columns by leader lines of periods, preferably with spaces between them.

• Set up the outline headings in a column to the left and the page numbers in a column to the right. See Figure 21–17.

A good rule to follow is to place line spaces above and below all headings of the highest level of division. You should uniformly single-space or double-space headings below this level, depending on their overall lengths. If the headings are long, covering most of the line or extending to a second line, single-spacing within the heading and double-spacing between headings gives clarity. Another option is to double-space all the content entries when double-spacing is used in the text.

You may vary the type to distinguish different heading levels, but the type variation of the table of contents need not be the same as those used in the text of the report. The highest level of headings is usually distinguished from the other levels, and sometimes type differences are used to distinguish second-level headings from lower-level headings. However, it is not wrong to use plain capitals and lowercase for all levels of headings in the table of contents.

- A table of illustrations may be a part of the table of contents.

Table of Illustrations. The table of illustrations lists the graphic aids presented in the reports in much the same way as the table of contents lists the report parts. Such a table may be either a continuation of the table of contents, as shown in Figure 21–18, or a separate table.

In constructing this table, head it with an appropriately descriptive title, such as "Table of Charts and Illustrations," or "List of Tables and Charts," or "Table of Figures." If you place the table of illustrations as a continued part of the table of contents, you should begin it after spacing four or more lines from the last contents entry. And if you place it on a separate page, the layout for this page is the same as that for any other text page with a displayed title.

The table consists of two columns—the first for the graphic-aids titles and the second for the pages on which the graphic aids appear. Line spacing in the table of illustrations is optional, again depending on the line lengths of the entries. Before the title, give the number of each graphic aid, for example Figure 1, Table 6, etc. If your report contains two or more illustration types (tables, charts, maps, and the like) and you have given each type its own numbering sequence, you may list each type separately.

- When using secondary data, note the sources in a bibliography.

References or Bibliography. Anytime you use another's idea, you need to give credit to the source. Sometimes business writers interweave this credit into the narrative of their text. But often these sources are listed in a reference or bibliography section at the end of the report. Typically, these sections are organized alphabetically, but they can also be organized by date, subject, or type or source. The format and content of references vary by style used. Among the widely used formats are *The Chicago Manual of Style, The MLA Style Sheet,* and the *Publication Manual of the American Psychological Association.* A full discussion of footnotes, references, and bibliographies appears in Appendix B.

Need to Improvise

- For form matters not covered in this review, base your decision on clarity and attractiveness.

The foregoing review covers most of the questions of form you will encounter in preparing reports. But if there are others, simply improvise an arrangement that appears right to the eye and helps the reader understand your message. After all, what appears right to the eye is the basis of conventional report form.

FIGURE 21-18   The Last Page of a Table of Contents with an Attached Table of Illustrations

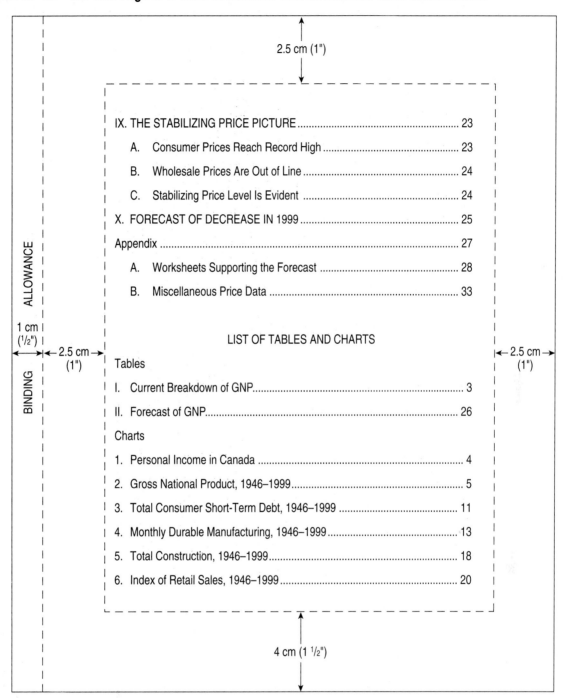

2.5 cm (1")

ALLOWANCE

1 cm
(1/2")

BINDING

2.5 cm
(1")

2.5 cm
(1")

LIST OF TABLES AND CHARTS

4 cm (1 1/2")

QUESTIONS FOR DISCUSSION

1. "Business people don't care about the medium for transmission. It's the information not how it gets there that counts." Comment on this opinion.

2. Identify and describe the presentation decisions common to letters, memos, and reports.

3. "The appearance of a letter or a report plays a significant role in communicating the message." Explain this statement.

4. Describe the requirements of these standard parts of a letter:

   a. Dateline
   b. Inside address
   c. Salutation
   d. Subject line
   e. Second-page heading
   f. Complimentary close
   g. Signature block
   h. Information notations

5. Demonstrate the proper folding of a letter for long and short envelopes.

6. Describe the form for addressing envelopes required by Canada Post.

7. Identify the elements of the headings in memos and what information each contains.

8. Describe the layout of a conventional page of text in a report.

9. Describe the page-numbering procedure of a formal report, beginning with the title fly and ending with the last page of the appended parts.

10. Give examples of headings in a report using the two basic ways of giving emphasis.

11. Discuss the content and layout considerations of the title page.

12. Describe the form of the letter of transmittal.

13. In what ways may acknowledgments be handled?

14. Summarize the layout and mechanics of the table of contents.

A TEST OF SPELLING, PUNCTUATION, AND GRAMMAR

The following test is designed to give you a quick measure of your ability to handle some of the most troublesome punctuation and grammar situations. The underlined portions of each sentence may contain an error. There are three ways to complete the test. You can identify the error by selecting the *a, b, c,* or *d* option, rewrite the sentence in the space provided making the correction, or do both. The recommended corrections are found at the end of this appendix.

If your score is less than 75 to 80 percent on this diagnostic test, you are strongly encouraged to do some remedial work in grammar, punctuation, and spelling. The student workbook prepared to accompany this text is one source of additional help.

1. An important fact about this electronic piano <u>is,</u> that <u>it</u> has the full <u>88</u> keys.

a) is,

b) it

c) 88

d) There is no error.

_____

_____

2. <u>Goods</u> received on Invoice 2741 are as <u>follows;</u> three dozen white shirts, size 15-33; four <u>men's</u> felt hats, brown, size 7; and five <u>dozen</u> assorted ties.

a) Goods

b) follows;

c) men's

d) dozen

_____

_____

3. Rob <u>Wiersma</u> president of the new <u>union,</u> started the <u>campaign</u> for the retirement fund.

a) Wiersma

b) union,

c) campaign

d) There is no error.

_____

_____

4. We do not <u>expect</u> to act on this <u>matter,</u> <u>however;</u> until we <u>hear</u> from you.

a) expect

b) matter,

c) however;

d) hear

_____

_____

5. Shipments through <u>September 20, 1998,</u> totalled 69,485 kilograms. The increase is <u>seventeen</u> percent over last <u>year's</u> total.

a) September 20, 1998,

b) seventeen

c) year's

d) There is no error.

_____

_____

6. Brick is <u>reccommended</u> as the building <u>material,</u> but the <u>board</u> is giving serious consideration to a substitute.

a) reccommended

b) material

c) board

d) There is no error.

_____

_____

7. Sales for the <u>month</u> total <u>$534,000,</u> never before has the store done so much <u>business</u> in just <u>30</u> days.

a) month

b) $534,000,

c) business

d) 30

_____

_____

8. <u>It was only</u> after long <u>experimentation,</u> that <u>manufacturers</u> perfected <u>run-resistant,</u> sheer pantihose.

a) It was only

b) experimentation,

c) manufacturers

d) run-resistant,

_____

_____

9. Available in <u>white,</u> green, and <u>blue,</u> this paint <u>will sell</u> by dealers all over the country.

a) white,

b) blue,

c) will sell

d) There is no error.

_____

_____

10. Tony <u>Ferraro who</u> won the <u>trip,</u> is our <u>most</u> energetic <u>salesperson.</u>

a) Ferraro who

b) trip,

c) most

d) salesperson.

_____

_____

11. <u>"Good"</u> he <u>replied.</u> "Sales are sure to <u>increase."</u>

a) "Good"

b) replied.

c) increase."

d) There is no error.

_____

_____

12. Frank <u>Hogan's</u> <u>article,</u> <u>Worker Security,</u> is printed in the current issue of *Management Review.*

a) Hogan's

b) article,

c) Worker Security,

d) There is no error.

_____

_____

13. Formal <u>announcement</u> of our pre-inventory <u>sale</u> will be made in <u>thirty</u> days.

a) announcement

b) sale

c) thirty

d) There is no error.

_____

_____

14. Although easily <u>solved,</u> <u>we</u> find new problems almost <u>every day.</u>

a) solved,

b) we

c) every day

d) There is no error.

_____

_____

15. A list of <u>models,</u> sizes, and <u>prices</u> of both competing <u>lines</u> <u>are</u> being sent to you.

a) models,

b) prices

c) lines

d) are

_____

_____

16. The <u>manager</u> could not tolerate any <u>employee's</u> <u>failing</u> to do <u>their</u> best.

a) manager

b) employee's

c) failing

d) their

_____

_____

17. A <u>series</u> of tests <u>were</u> completed <u>only</u> yesterday.

a) series

b) were

c) only

d) There is no error.

_____

_____

18. <u>There</u> should be no <u>misunderstanding</u> between you and <u>I.</u>

a) There

b) misunderstanding

c) I.

d) There is no error.

_____

_____

19. He <u>runs</u> the accounting department very <u>well</u> for the last <u>five</u> years.

a) runs

b) well

c) five

d) There is no error.

_____

_____

20. The inside <u>address</u> on these <u>letters</u> <u>is</u> typed <u>incorrect.</u>

a) address

b) letters

c) is

d) incorrect.

_____

_____

21. <u>Who</u> did you <u>interview</u> yesterday for the position of <u>Communication Assistant</u>?

a) Who

b) interview

c) Communication Assistant

d) There is no error.

_____

_____

22. The report <u>concluded</u> that the natural resources of the <u>Southwest are</u> ideal for the chemical industry.

a) concluded

b) Southwest

c) are

d) There is no error.

_____

_____

23. This applicant is <u>six</u> feet <u>tall, 75 kilograms,</u> and is <u>28 years</u> old.

a) six

b) tall, 75 kilograms,

c) 28

d) years

_____

_____

24. <u>While reading the report,</u> a gust of wind came <u>through</u> the <u>window,</u> blowing papers all over the room.

a) While reading the report,

b) through

c) window,

d) There is no error.

_____

_____

25. The <u>company's</u> sprinkler system <u>has been checked</u> for the summer on <u>June 1.</u>

a) company's

b) has been checked

c) June 1

d) There is no error.

_____

_____

1.*a* An important fact about this electronic piano is that it has the full 88 keys. (Comma)

2.*b* Goods received on Invoice 2741 are as follows: three dozen white shirts, size 15-33; four men's felt hats, brown, size 7; and five dozen assorted ties. (Semicolon/Colon Error)

3.*a* Rob Wiersma, president of the new union, started the campaign for the retirement fund. (Comma)

4.*c* We do not expect to act on this matter, however, until we hear from you. (Semicolon/Comma Error)

5.*c* Shipments through September 20, 1998, totalled 69,485 kilograms. The increase is 17 percent over last year's total. (Number Form)

6.*a* Brick is recommended as the building material, but the board is giving serious consideration to a substitute. (Spelling)

7.*b* Sales for the month total $534,000; never before has the store done so much business in just 30 days. (Comma/Semicolon Error)

   Or Sales for the month total $534,000. Never before has the store done so much business in just 30 days. (Comma Splice)

8.*b* It was only after long experimentation that manufacturers perfected run-resistant, sheer pantihose. (Comma)

9.*c* Available in white, green, and blue, this paint will be sold by dealers all over the country. (Verb Tense)

10.*a* Tony Ferraro, who won the trip, is our most energetic salesperson. (Comma)

11.*a* "Good," he replied. "Sales are sure to increase." (Comma)

12.*c* Frank Hogan's article, "Worker Security," is printed in the current issue of *Management Review.* (Quotation Marks)

13.*c* Formal announcement of our pre-inventory sale will be made in 30 days. (Number Format)

14.*b* Although easily solved, new problems are found almost every day. (Dangling Modifier)

15.*d* A list of models, sizes, and prices of both competing lines is being sent to you. (Subject-Verb Agreement)

16.*d* The manager could not tolerate any employee's failing to do his or her best. (Pronoun Agreement)

17.*b* A series of tests was completed only yesterday. (Subject-Verb Agreement)

18.*c* There should be no misunderstanding between you and me. (Pronoun Case)

19.*a* He ran the accounting department very well for the last five years.

   Or He has run the accounting department very well for the last five years. (Verb Tense)

20.*d* The inside address on these letters is typed incorrectly. (Verb-Adverb Agreement)

21.*a* Whom did you interview yesterday for the position of Communication Assistant? (Pronoun Case)

22.*d* The report concluded that the natural resources of the Southwest are ideal for the chemical industry. (No Error)

23.*b* This applicant is six feet tall, weighs 75 kilograms, and is 28 years old. (Parallelism)

24.*a* While she was reading the report, a gust of wind came through the window, blowing papers all over the room. (Dangling Modifier)

25.*b* The sprinkler system was checked on June 1. (Verb Tense)

B

Documentation and the Bibliography

In writing reports, you will frequently use information from other sources. As this material is not your own, you need to acknowledge it. Acknowledging your sources protects you against charges of plagiarism and is the first step in complying with copyright regulations. A brief overview follows, but for more details, refer to guides such as the *MLA (Modern Languages Association) Handbook for Writers of Research Papers,*[1] *The Chicago Manual of Style,*[2] or *The Canadian Style: A Guide to Writing and Editing.*[3]

WHEN TO ACKNOWLEDGE

Your decision to acknowledge or not acknowledge a source should be determined mainly on the basis of giving credit where credit is due. Direct quotations are a clear case. If you are quoting the words of another, you must give credit. The case may seem less clear if you are paraphrasing (using someone else's ideas in your own words). However, you must give credit to the original source of an idea even though the exact words are your own. Only if the material is considered general knowledge are you free to use it without acknowledgment because no one (including you) can rightfully claim credit.

PLACEMENT OF QUOTED AND PARAPHRASED INFORMATION

If you use data obtained from secondary sources, first decide if you are going to quote it verbatim (exactly as the original author worded it) or paraphrase the information (express it in your own words). Paraphrased material is acknowledged, but it is not distinguished from the remainder of the report text by punctuation or layout. A direct quote is acknowledged and clearly distinguished in one of two ways.

If the quoted passage is four lines or less in length, it is typed within the report text and distinguished by quotation marks. If a longer quotation (five lines or more) is used, the conventional practice is to set it in about five spaces from both the left and right margins. No quotation marks are used. If the text is double-spaced, the quoted passage may be further distinguished with single-spacing.

Frequently, you will find it best to use only fragments of the quoted author's work. Because omissions may distort the meaning of a passage, you must clearly indicate them using an ellipsis (a series of three periods). If an omission begins after the end of a sentence, you use four periods—one for final punctuation plus the ellipsis points.

---

[1] Joseph M. Gibaldi and Walter S. Achtert. *Modern Language Association Handbook for Writers of Research Papers.* 3rd ed. (New York: MLA, 1988).

[2] *Chicago Manual of Style.* 14th ed. (Chicago: University of Chicago Press, 1993).

[3] Department of the Secretary of State. *The Canadian Style: A Guide to Writing and Editing.* (Toronto: Dundurn, 1985).

of those opposing the issue, Rob Haraga makes this observation:

> It is a curious paradox that academics display a scientific attitude toward every universe of inquiry except their own profession. . . . Lacking precise qualitative criteria for measuring good teaching, administrators substitute rather crude quantitative measures. (328)

These logical, straightforward arguments for teacher evaluation are difficult to refute.

HOW TO ACKNOWLEDGE

Two methods are commonly used in business to acknowledge sources: (1) parenthetic references within the text and (2) footnote references.[4]

THE PARENTHETIC METHOD

Clarity and simplicity for both writer and reader make parenthetical references increasingly popular. In this method, the author's last name and the page reference are placed in parentheses in the text immediately following the material cited. The books and articles referred to must also appear in the Works Cited, a list at the end of the report giving the full bibliographic description of your sources.[5] To find the complete description of the work in the parenthetical reference (Sanders 19), for example, the reader would find Sanders in its alphabetical place in Works Cited. Here is an example of a reference to a book.

Although theft of goods by employees increased 6.5 percent over those five years, more recent years have shown a moderate decline. (Callahan 117–118)

If you use the author's name in your sentence, only the page reference appears in the parentheses.

As Callahan points out, although theft of goods by employees increased 6.5 percent over those five years, more recent years have shown a moderate decline. (117–118)

If there are two or three authors, all their last names are listed. For works with more than three authors, *et al.*, meaning *and others* is used:

(Smith, Corley, and Doran 31)

(Clovis et al. 154)

If more than one publication by the same author is used, the works would be distinguished by the first word or two of the title. The format would also show whether the work was an article (in quotation marks) or a book (in italics).

(Sanders "Popular" 3)

(Sanders *Basic* 321)

When no author is listed, as in unsigned publications issued by a company, government agency, or organization, use the corporate name. For short brochures, there may be no paging.

(Transport Canada)

(Canadian Automobile Association 31)

For short magazine or newspaper articles with no listed author, use the word by which the article is alphabetized in your list of Works Cited. Normally, this would be the first word of the title or headline. Note that again the quotation marks indicate that this work is an article contained in a larger publication.

The growth in the economy has slowed because of rising interest rates in the United States. ("Forecast" B6)

---

[4]Endnote references follow the same rules as footnotes, but endnotes are gathered together at the end of the report while footnotes appear at the foot of the page as needed. Endnotes are less common than footnotes primarily because readers prefer to have the source information readily available on the page. Also, the typing advantage of gathering all the notes at the end of a document has been eliminated by word processing systems that automatically number and place the footnotes.

[5]For the format of the Works Cited list, see the section on creating a bibliography.

THE FOOTNOTE METHOD (MLA OLD STYLE)

The traditional method of acknowledging sources is by footnotes. A footnote is a reference placed at the bottom of the page and keyed to the text material by a superscript (raised Arabic number). The numbering sequence of the footnotes is consecutive through the whole work if it is short or through each chapter. Footnotes are placed inside the page layout and single-spaced. As previously noted, footnotes are more cumbersome and therefore losing popularity in favour of parenthetic references. For formal works, however, the footnote method is still preferred.

Footnote for a Book

A footnote has many similarities with the entry in a bibliography, but there are also some significant differences in order, format, and punctuation. In the following list, all the items that *could* be placed in each footnote are named in the order of arrangement. Depending upon the circumstances, some items may be optional.

1. *Superscript.* Arabic numeral keyed to the text reference.

2. *Name of the author, in normal order.* If a source has two or three authors, all are named. If a source has more than three authors, the name of the first author is followed by the Latin "et al." or its English equivalent, "and others."

3. *Capacity of the author.* Needed only when the person named is actually not the author of the book but an editor, compiler, or translator. The author section is closed with a period.

4. *Book title.* Book titles are placed in italics or underlined. Volume numbers for multi-volume works are included. The title section is closed with a period.

5. *Edition.* Examples are Rev. ed., 2nd Canadian ed., 6th ed.

6. *Location of publisher.* The publishing information is placed in parentheses. If more than one city is listed on the title page, the one listed first should be used. If the city is a major centre, the name of the city is sufficient; otherwise, the city and state (or province) are given. Compare New York; Toronto; but, Homewood, Illinois; Kingston, Ontario. Use a colon after the city and before the publisher.

7. *Publishing company.* Omit words such as "Co., Ltd." but include "& Sons." Use a comma to separate the company from the year.

8. *Date.* Year of publication. If revised, year of latest revision (usually the latest copyright date). Close the parentheses after the date.

9. *Page or pages.* Specific page or inclusive pages on which the cited material is found—not the total number of pages in the work. Close the entry with a period.

The following are examples of FOOTNOTE entries for books.
Footnote for a typical book:

[1]Cindy Burford, Aline Marie Hebert, and Peter R. Jutra. *Writing for Results.* 4th ed. (New York: Charles Storm Publishing, 1990) 17–18.

Footnote for a book written under the direction of editors:

[2]W.C. Butte and Ann Buchanan, eds. *An Encyclopedia of Advertising.* (New York: Binton Publishing, 1991) 99.

Footnote for a book written by more than three co-authors:

[3]E.L. Franck, et al. *Anthology of Public Relations.* (New York: Warner-Bragg, 1990) 137.

Footnote for an Article in a Periodical or Encyclopedia

The footnote for an article differs in format from the footnote for a book. It is also different from the listing in the bibliography.

1. *Superscript.* The same as a footnote for a book.

2. *Author's name.* The author section is the same as for the author of a book except that you end the section with a comma. If no author is given, go directly to the article's title.

3. *Article title.* The title is enclosed in quotation marks with the key words capitalized. A comma inside the quotation marks closes the title section.

4. *Periodical title.* The title of the magazine or periodical is set in italics or underlined to distinguish it from the title of the article. No punctuation is used after the periodical title.

5. *Publication identification.* No place or publisher is listed for a periodical. The date of publication (month and year; season and year; or day, month, and year) is all that is required. In some cases, the volume number is included. Close the date section with a colon.

6. *Page or pages.* Again, these pages are the pages for the material used, not the pages for the entire article.

Examples of FOOTNOTES using periodical articles are shown below:

[1]Mildred C. Kinnig, "A New Look at Retirement," *Modern Business* 31 July 1993: 31–32.
[2]William O. Schultz, "How One Company Adopted TQM," *Business Is Business* Spring 1991: 17.
[3]Mary Mitchell, "Report Writing Aids," *ABCA Bulletin* October 1994: 13.

Footnote for a Newspaper Article

1. *Superscript.* Follow the instructions for books and periodical articles.

2. *Source description.* If the article is signed, give author's name. If no author is indicated, begin with the headline.

3. *Main headline of article.* Use the headline as a title placing it in quotation marks with the key words capitalized. Subheads not usually included. For clarity, you may give a description of the article, such as "United Press dispatch" or "Editorial" after the headline title if an author has not been given.

4. *Newspaper title.* The name of the newspaper is italicized or underlined. If the title does not include the city of publication, include the city and province (state, or country) names in square brackets at the appropriate point in the name. Province or state names may be omitted in the case of very large cities, such as New York, Toronto, and Los Angeles.

5. *Date of publication.* Include the date, month (abbreviated or in full), and year. The day of the week is not used.

6. *Page numbering.* Newspapers vary in the way they number their pages. Give the page number as found in the newspaper you are using. A column (col.) indication may be used but is usually unnecessary.

The following are FOOTNOTES for typical newspaper article entries:

[1]Jim McCoy, "Rival Unions Sign Pact," *Toronto Star,* 3 September 1990: B1, B3.
[2]"The North Moves South [Editorial]," *London [Ontario] Free Press,* 3 February 1989: 2.
[3]James Moore, "Soil Erosion Worries Farmers in Southwestern Ontario," *The Reporter,* [Cambridge, Ontario], 6 March 1990: C7.

Footnote for Letters or Documents

Because documents vary widely, the appearance of the footnote will also vary. However, the goal of identifying the source and of giving credit for the use of another person's ideas or words will be achieved. The following list identifies the elements to be described in a footnote for documents.

1. *Nature of the communication.* Try to assign a specific name to identify the type of document such as letter, memo, will, news release, and so on.

2. *Name of the writer.* For clarification, consider including the person's title or position and the organization concerned.

3. *Name of the recipient.* Again, for clarification, include additional information such as the person's title and the company name.

4. *Date of writing.* Include the date, month, and year, but not the day.

5. *Location of a copy.* The document may be filed in a library, in a personal collection, or in company records, for example.

An example of an entry citing a letter is given below:

[1]Letter from J.W. Wells, President, Wells Equipment Co., to James Mattoch, Secretary-Treasurer, Northern Mining Association, June 10, 1988, filed among Mr. Mattoch's personal records.

Footnotes for Interviews

To support a quotation from an interview you have conducted with a resource person, use the name of the person interviewed, an explanation (Personal interview), and the date.

Tom Achtymichuk. Personal interview. 16 October 1996.

For an interview conducted on television or radio, give the name of the person interviewed, an explanation (Interview), the name of the program in italics, the station name and place, and the date.

Kim Campbell. Interview. *Saskatchewan Sunrise.* CSRG-AM. Regina, SK. 30 October 1995.

Footnotes for Electronic Sources

As research using electronic media is recent, standards for referencing it are in the developmental stage. Guidelines for citing some electronic sources are included in the MLA style guide, while other guidelines have been developed since the guide was published. A useful source to watch for current information is Janice Walker's site on the world wide web.[6]

A distinction is made between changeable and unchangeable sources. If a work is printed, it is considered unchangeable. The page numbers, for example, will be the same in the future as they are today. Even if a new edition is printed, the reference to the old edition will be correct. An example of a changeable source is a web site. The URL (Uniform Resource Locator, i.e., address) may be the same, but the document could look quite different in the future. With changeable sources, the date on which the source was last checked is included in the reference.

A periodical on CD-ROM:

Annette Worthy, "Electronic meeting systems and the quality of decisions made," *Journal of Business* March 1997: 27–40. CD-ROM.

Nonperiodical source on CD-ROM:

"The Charter of Rights," *The Canadian Encyclopedia Plus* 2nd ed. CD-ROM (Toronto: McClelland & Stewart, 1996).

E-mail:

Gord Moore. "Interesting WWW site." E-mail to Agnes Janz. 20 October 1997.

World Wide Web:

Canada Employment Centres, Metro Toronto Labour Market Analysis Group. *Towards 2000: Occupational Trends.* http://www.the-wire.com/hrdc/trend96.html (6 June 1996).

The types of entries discussed in the preceding paragraphs are those most likely to be used. Yet, many unusual types of publications (not books or periodicals) are likely to come up. When they do, you should classify the source by modifying the form it most closely resembles—a book or a periodical. Frequently, you will need to improvise as you strive for clarity, completeness, and consistency.

---

[6]Janice Walker. "MLA-Style Citations of Electronic Sources." http://www.cas.usf.edu/english/walker/mla.html (15 October 1996).

STANDARD ABBREVIATIONS

Depending upon the style guide you use, some abbreviations may be found in footnote entries. The more common ones are as follows:

ABBREVIATION	MEANING
cf.	Compare (directs reader's attention to another passage)
col.	Column
ed.	Edition, Editor
e.g.	For example
et al.	And others
f., ff.	Following page, following pages
ibid.	In the same place
i.e.	That is
l., ll.	Line, lines
MS, MSS	Manuscript, manuscripts
n.d.	No date
n.n.	No name
n.p.	No place
p., pp.	Page, pages
vol., vols.	Volume, volumes

DISCUSSION FOOTNOTES

Through discussion or content footnotes the writer strives to explain a part of the text, to amplify discussion on a phase of the presentation, or to make cross-references to other parts of the report. The following examples illustrate some possibilities of this footnote type.

Cross-Reference:

[1] See the principle of focal points on page 72.

Amplification:

[2] Lyman Bryson says the same thing: "Every communication is different for every receiver even in the same context. No one can estimate the variation of understanding that there may be among receivers of the same message conveyed in the same vehicle when the receivers are separated in either space or time." See *Communication of Ideas*, 5.

Comparison:

[3] Compare with the principle of the objective: Before starting any activity, one should make a clear, complete statement of the objective in view.

THE BIBLIOGRAPHY AND WORKS CITED

A bibliography is an orderly list of material on a particular subject. In a formal report the list covers references on the subject of the report. The entries in this list closely resemble footnotes, but the two must not be confused. The bibliography normally appears as an appended part of a formal report and is placed after the appendix. It may be preceded by a fly page containing the one word "Bibliography." In any case, the page that begins the list bears the main heading "Bibliography," usually typed in capital letters. Below this title the references are listed in alphabetical order. If the bibliography is very long, the references may be divided into broad categories and alphabetized within the categories. As with footnotes, variations in bibliographic style are numerous.

Works Cited is also a list of the sources used. It appears when the parenthetic method of documentation is used. Although very similar to a bibliography, a works cited list, as the name says, includes only the works directly quoted or paraphrased in the report. In other words, all the works listed here have parenthetical references in the report. If other sources were read but not quoted, they do not appear in this list. It is possible, therefore, to have both a Works Cited and a Bibliography.

The procedure for creating a bibliography or works cited list is very similar to the one described above for footnotes, with five major exceptions:

1. The author's name is listed in reverse order with the surname first for alphabetizing. If an entry has more than one author, only the name of the first author is reversed. Entries are not numbered.

2. The entry is generally typed in hanging-indentation form. That is, the second and subsequent lines of an entry begin some uniform distance (usually about five spaces) in from the left margin. The purpose of this indented pattern is to make the alphabetized first line stand out.

3. The entry gives the inclusive pages for articles, but not for books, and does not refer to any one page or passage.

4. Second and subsequent references to publications of the same author may be indicated by a uniform line (see bibliography illustration). This line may be used only if the entire authorship is the same in the consecutive publications. For example, the line could not be used if consecutive entries have one common author but different co-authors.

5. The punctuation is different.

A pattern to follow for the more common examples is outlined here. To use it, substitute the specific details from the work you are trying to list.

Books with single author:

Surname, First Name. *Short Title: Subtitle.* City, Province: Publisher, Date.

Books with more than one author:

Surname, First Name, First Name Surname, and First Name Surname. *Short Title: Subtitle.* City, Province: Publisher, Date.

Books with many authors:

Surname, First Name, and others. *Short Title: Subtitle.* City, Province: Publisher, Date.

Periodical articles with one or more authors:

Surname, First Name, and First Name Surname. "Article Title." *Periodical Title,* Optional Volume Number, (Date of Issue): inclusive pages.

Periodical articles with no clear author:

"Article Title." *Periodical Title.* Optional Volume Number, (Date of Issue): inclusive pages.

Newspaper articles:

"Title of Article," *Title of Newspaper,* [City, Province], full date: pages.

Government publications:

Government and Department. *Short Title: Subtitle.* City: Publisher, Date.

Following is an example of a bibliography. Because it is short, all types of materials are listed in one alphabetical sequence.

BIBLIOGRAPHY

Access Canada: Micromedia's Directory of Canadian Information Sources. Toronto: Micromedia, 1990.

Canada Human Rights Commission. *A Guide to Screening and Selection in Employment.* Ottawa: Minister of Supply and Services Canada, 1985.

The Canadian Encyclopedia. 2nd ed., 4 vol. Edmonton: Hurtig Publishers, 1988.

The Canadian Encyclopedia Plus. 2nd ed. CD-ROM. Toronto: McClelland & Stewart, 1996.

Canadian Parliamentary Guide/Guide Parlementaire Canadien. Toronto: InfoGlobe, 1990.

Gage Canadian Dictionary. Toronto: Gage Educational Publishing, 1983.

Lovelock, Christopher M., and John A. Quelch. "Consumer Promotions in Service Marketing." *Business Horizons.* (May/June 1983): 66–75.

Norton, Sarah, and Brian Green. *The Bare Essentials.* Toronto: Holt, Rinehart and Winston of Canada, 1988.

Shapiro, Benson P. "Marketing for Nonprofit Organizations." *Harvard Business Review.* 51 (September/October 1973): 123–132.

Shea, Gordon F. "A Case for Clear Writing." *Training and Development.* (January 1992): 63–66.

U.S. Department of Commerce. *Business Statistics: 1990.* Washington, D.C.: U.S. Government Printing Office, 1991.

_____. *Survey of Current Business: 1988 Supplement.* Washington, D.C.: U.S. Government Printing Office, 1989.

Wasserman, Paul, ed., and others. *Encyclopedia of Business Information Sources.* 5th ed. Detroit: Gale Research, 1983.

THE ANNOTATED BIBLIOGRAPHY

Frequently, in scholarly writing each bibliography entry is followed by a brief comment on its value and content. That is, the bibliography is annotated. The form and content of annotated bibliographies are illustrated in these entries:

ANNOTATED BIBLIOGRAPHY

Donald, W.T., ed. *Handbook of Business Administration.* New York: Shannon-Dale, 1990.

Contains a summary of the activities in each major area of business. Written by foremost authorities in each field. Particularly useful to the business specialist who wants a quick review of the whole of business.

Braden, Shelby M., and Lillian Como, eds. *Business Leader's Handbook.* 4th ed. New York: Mercer and Sons, 1989.

Provides answer to most routine problems of executives in explicit manner and with good examples. Contains good material on correspondence and sales letters.

C

Logical Fallacies

A logical fallacy is an error in thinking. It is a flaw in reasoning that will lead to a faulty conclusion. Despite their illogical nature, logical fallacies seem plausible on the surface. This quality makes them effective, and therefore dangerous, in persuading a listener or reader. The unsuspecting receiver can be fooled by a skillful user of these faulty arguments. The fact that logical fallacies sound reasonable is also the reason they are used accidentally. The sender may use a faulty argument to draw a conclusion without ever realizing that fault.

To avoid being caught by logical fallacies, you should study the following list of common logical fallacies. As well as becoming familiar with these examples, you can examine underlying assumptions critically, build conclusions on ample, relevant evidence, and use words that are clear and unambiguous.

The Circular Argument

Also known as *begging the question,* this argument restates a claim in different ways. The repetition using new words appears like new evidence, but it is not.

Example:

This is a good price because this desk is on sale. The full price is much higher than this excellent sale price.

Post Hoc Ergo Propter Hoc

This Latin phrase means *after this, therefore because of this.* The relationship between the timing of two events may or may not be a causal relationship. The events may be unrelated. Superstitions are usually based on this type of argument.

Example:

The steady fall in the unemployment rate since our election three months ago shows that our economic policies are working for the good of all Canadians.

Either/or Reasoning

Assuming yourself or telling someone else that there are only two options available—yours and the wrong one. Or forcing a simple choice when the situation is more complex.

Examples:

Wear your hat or you'll freeze to death.
A vote for the XYZ party is a vote for economic chaos; a vote for me is a step toward prosperity.

Wide Generalization

Words such as *never, always,* and *all* are clues to the wide generalization. The statement has some truth in it perhaps, but that truth is stretched beyond a reasonable limit.

Examples:

You will never find a detergent that will wash your clothes as clean as XYZ.
Canadians are conservative and always wait too long before taking a risk.

Red Herring

A red herring is an attempt to take the discussion off course by introducing an unrelated or irrelevant issue. The term comes from hunting when fish were dragged across the trail to try to trick the dogs and put them off the scent of their prey. A red herring may involve an appeal to some emotional point meant to upset and distract the other person. The second example also contains faulty either/or reasoning.

Examples:

I would be the last one to suggest that women should be at home with children.
What's wrong with a strong central government? Is anarchy and chaos what you want?

The Band Wagon

This fallacy is based on the belief that people want to be part of the group. Children will often use this type of argument with their parents.

Examples:

Get your membership card today! After all, three million Canadians can't be wrong.
I'm the only kid in school without access to the Internet from home! We just have to get a new computer.

Faulty Appeal to Authority

The use of an authority to support a position is valid as long as that person is an authority in the correct field. Using an Olympic skier to endorse ski equipment is appropriate. Quoting the same athlete about investment services is unreliable.

Oversimplification

Oversimplification is related to several other logical fallacies. It is dangerous because it hinders careful consideration of the topic from all sides.

Examples:

If everyone just gave one dollar, we could end world hunger.
Milk is an excellent source of calcium. Everyone should drink several glasses a day.

False Analogy

The false analogy tries to explain by drawing a parallel. Comparisons are often helpful in understanding new concepts, especially if they are abstract. However, if the parallel is invalid, or even just weak, the result is misleading.

Example:

Overeating is just like drug abuse. They are both the result of lack of self control. [Note the oversimplification in this example as well.]

Index